FROM THE BOWERY TO BROADWAY

From the Bowery

To Broadway

*Lew Fields
and the Roots of
American Popular Theater*

Armond Fields and L. Marc Fields

New York   Oxford
OXFORD UNIVERSITY PRESS
1993

Oxford University Press

Oxford   New York   Toronto
Delhi   Bombay   Calcutta   Madras   Karachi
Kuala Lumpur   Singapore   Hong Kong   Tokyo
Nairobi   Dar es Salaam   Cape Town
Melbourne   Auckland   Madrid

and associated companies in
Berlin   Ibadan

Published by Oxford University Press, Inc.,
200 Madison Avenue, New York, New York 10016

Oxford is a registered trademark of Oxford University Press

Library of Congress Cataloging-in-Publication Data
Fields, Armond, 1930–   . L. Marc Fields, 1955–
From the Bowery to Broadway :
Lew Fields and the roots of American popular theater /
Armond Fields and L. Marc Fields.
p.   cm.   Includes bibliographical references and index.
ISBN 0-19-505381-8
1. Fields, Lew, 1867–1941.   2. Theater—United States—History—20th century.
3. Comedians—United States—Biography.
I. Fields, L. Marc.   II. Title.
PN2287.F44F54   1993   792'.0232'092—dc20
[B]   92-34456

Frontispiece: Publicity photo for the Weber & Fields' Jubilee Company, 1912.
From left: Fay Templeton, Joe Weber, Lew Fields, and Lillian Russell
(Billy Rose Theater Collection, New York Public Library)

9 8 7 6 5 4 3 2 1

Printed in the United States of America
on acid-free paper

Lew Fields and the Roots of American Popular Theater

FOREWORD BY HELEN HAYES

Nine-year-old Helen Hayes in her
first Broadway role,
in the Lew Fields production of
Old Dutch (1909).
(Museum of the City of New York)

I was six years old when Lew Fields "discovered" me. Miss Minnie Hawke's Dance Studio was presenting its annual charity matinee presentation at the Belasco in Washington, D.C., and I performed a song and impersonated a Gibson girl. The fact that Fields was even in the audience that day was typical of his generosity. He had loaned Minnie Hawke some scenery—an arbor covered with flowering vines, I think—and she had invited him to our little show. At the time, Fields was the producer and star of the largest Broadway touring company, but he came to our performance anyway. Afterwards, he sent the manager a note saying that if my parents were interested, he wanted to be the first in line to offer me a stage career.

Three years later, in the summer of 1909, my mother brought me to New York to make the rounds of Broadway producers. We were barred by office boys from seeing any of the producers of serious, high-minded dramas. My mother avoided Lew Fields because she associated him with musicals, which she considered to be a less respectable form of entertainment. Finally, a stage director we knew persuaded her to go and see Fields. Fields, the director informed us, was a partner of the Shuberts, and "could get them to do anything."

We waited nervously for several hours outside Fields' busy office at the Broadway Theatre. Fields emerged in the company of a dark-haired beauty, Lotta Faust (a musical star), and escorted her to the elevator. When he returned, my mother pushed a photo of me as the Gibson girl into his hands and asked, "Do you remember this child, Mr. Fields?" He looked me over with his sad brown eyes, and then he smiled at me with his great warm smile, and an instant bond was formed.

He signed me immediately, and created a small part for me in his next production, *Old Dutch*, an operetta by Victor Herbert. In that same company was another of his discoveries, a lanky young Englishman named Vernon Castle, whom he had also taken in hand. From my innocent perspective, my four seasons with Lew Fields were like a journey through a fairy-tale kingdom. He protected me from the ugliness and the disillusionment that soured so many other young players, perhaps because he had been a child actor himself and had seen it firsthand. He was unusually genteel and straitlaced, much to my mother's relief; he would dock the pay of any company member overheard using foul language around me.

At the same time, I learned a great deal. He was an indefatigable worker. He had been a performer for over thirty years, but he still played every performance as if it were a first night, and he expected his performers to do the same. The only thing that roiled his eternally good nature was a lazy or insincere actor, or a ham. There was one like that in our company, and Fields made his life miserable.

Now almost completely forgotten, Lew Fields was one of our greatest comedians (his few sound film appearances occurred late in his life and do not begin to do him justice). Next to Chaplin's, Fields had the most perfect comic mask I have ever seen. It was Fields who first revealed to me the power of creating laughter in an audience. He applied more craft to the creation of a comedy routine than most serious actors did for a dramatic role. Anything I possess in the way of precision or accuracy in the timing of comedy I learned from him. I remember, too, his expressive hands; I learned from him the importance of hands onstage. Most important of all, he taught me the terrible responsibility of a star, both onstage and off.

He was more than a gifted comedian. For over a decade, he was Broadway's most inventive, extravagant, and prolific musical producer. If he had any weakness as a showman, it was that he was not very good at self-promotion. Though his shows were lavish indeed, he was not by nature a flamboyant man. He was too busy producing shows to produce myths, which may explain why he is not as well known today as George M. Cohan or Flo Ziegfeld. As much as either of his more famous colleagues, Lew Fields shaped the American musical in its early stages of development.

I am delighted to see that this gentle, unsung pioneer is finally receiving the recognition he so richly deserves.

H. H.

Acknowledgments

In creating this biographical and theatrical history, we relied upon the interest, expertise, and cooperation of many people. To them, we are deeply grateful.

The experts who assisted us, and the institutions they represent, are:

Miles Kreuger of the Institute of the American Musical

Maryanne Chach, Reagan Fletcher, and Brooks MacNamara of the Shubert Archive

Ned Comstock and Michael Cropper, University of Southern California Special Collections Library

Sam Gill, Academy of Motion Picture Arts and Sciences

Kathryn Mets of the Museum of the City of New York

Susan Dalton of the American Film Institute

Milt Larsen and the staff of the Variety Arts Theater Library

Melissa Miller-Quinlan, University of Texas Albert Davis Collection

Randy Gitsch, RKO Radio Corporate Archives

Ron Magliozzi, Museum of Modern Art

Jason Rubin, New York University, Ph.D diss., "Lew Fields and the Development of the Broadway Musical", 1990

In addition, we relied heavily on the resources of the following institutions:

New York Public Library at Lincoln Center–Billy Rose Theater Collection
The Museum of the City of New York
The Library of Congress
University of California at Los Angeles Film Archives
Culver Pictures

The following people shared with us their enthusiasm and knowledge about Lew Fields and popular theater: David Lahm, Ray Marcus, Anthony Slide, Robert Snyder, Jimmy McHugh, Jr., Marjorie Downey, Gladys Marcus, Marion Fields, Lucille Weill, Maxine Mosely, Marshall Robbins, Lucille Myers, and Susan French.

Our sincere thanks to Helen Hayes for contributing the foreword to this book along with her fond memories of Lew Fields. We are also grateful to Sheldon Meyer, Senior Editor of Oxford University Press, for his support and guidance.

The dedicated researchers who helped us collect and verify the information were Janet Pyle, Elise Davis, Amy Spencer, Ann Trotter, and Carol Jennings.

The photographic skills of Bruce Howell made it possible to reproduce pictures in this book, many of which were rare and timeworn.

Bernie Polansky and Jack Silver generously contributed reprographic services free of charge. Thanks to Mara Purl for guiding the manuscript through the labyrinth of copy editing and typing.

Finally, we offer loving gratitude to our wives, Sara Fields and Nancy Spencer, who lived with our total immersion in theater history and theatrical personalities, who always listened to our discoveries, thoughts and ideas, and who supported our efforts in making this book a reality.

Armond Fields   L. Marc Fields

Contents

Introduction

The career of actor-producer Lew Fields began in the Bowery dives in the late 1870's and ended on Broadway in the early 1930's. In the half-century between his stage debut—a bumbling youngster in a neighborhood amateur show—and his farewell appearance on the opening night bill at Radio City Music Hall, Fields was involved in almost every form of popular entertainment: dime museum, minstrel show, circus, variety, vaudeville, burlesque, operetta, revue, and "book" musical, as well as records, silent films, radio, and talkies.

A listing of his collaborators, performers, and business partners is a "Who's Who" in American theater for the period: Lillian Russell, Fay Templeton, David Warfield, William Collier, Julian Mitchell, Victor Herbert, Oscar Hammerstein I, the Shuberts, Blanche Ring, Ned Wayburn, Helen Hayes, Vernon and Irene Castle, Nora Bayes, Marcus Loew, Marie Dressler, David Belasco, Richard Rodgers and Lorenz Hart, Busby Berkeley, William Gaxton. . . . Fields' long and varied career is a panoramic window through which we can see the emergence of "show biz" as a totality: the development of the entertainment industry in conjunction with its most characteristic aesthetic forms.

The man himself can only be understood through his work. From his early youth, the stage was his passion and his meal ticket. Growing up in the Bowery slums in the 1870's, the fourth of eight children in a family of Polish-Jewish immigrants, the young Lew Fields embraced acting as an alternative to working in a sweatshop like his father and brothers, or running with a gang like some of his neighbors. His first audiences were his classmates at Public School Number 42, on Allen Street; their laughter encouraged his acrobatic antics while the teacher's back was turned. From the very beginning, Fields' philosophy was simply, in his own words, "to give the public what they want."

Applause meant approval and recognition; success at the box office provided the means to achieve social legitimacy. This desire for "respectability"—meaning material comfort *and* acceptance by genteel (Gentile) society—was a driving force in both his personal life and his career. Once, at a Friars' Club dinner, he was jokingly accused of not being a "true" actor because he was still married to his first wife. Fields found the joke doubly satisfying: at the same time it ridiculed the stereotype of the loose-living actor, it acknowledged that Fields had managed to transcend the stereotype.

At first glance, Fields' story resembles those of other, more familiar entertainment figures whose families came from Eastern Europe by way of New York's Lower East Side or a similar urban ghetto: Irving Berlin, Eddie Cantor, Fanny Brice, Al Jolson, and the movie moguls Marcus Loew, Adolph Zukor, William Fox, and Sam Goldwyn. The difference is that Fields did it a generation earlier. The Schoenfeld family arrived in New York in 1872, a decade or more before the first wave of Eastern European Jewish immigration began. Lew Fields and his vaudeville partner, Joe Weber (who had the same background) were quite possibly the first Jewish performers outside of the legitimate stage to succeed with an American mass audience.

Fields came of age at a time when the popular stage performer was relegated to the margins of respectable society. The minstrel man or music hall comedian was a social outcast, occupying a social stratum somewhere between that of a vagrant and a gambler. Having overcome his father's strong disapproval, Fields still had to overcome the prejudices of the social class he aspired to. As an actor and producer, he succeeded in "cleaning up" the popular stage and attracting a middle-class audience. For Fields, this was not only a commercial breakthrough, but a personal validation. His repeated attempts to cross over and become a "serious" actor on the "legit" stage were similarly motivated. Fields saw that the great tragedians elicited more respect than the great clowns; he chafed at the notion that it was only the stage of Booth and the Barrymores that was designated "legitimate."

His lifelong concern for the status of the actor also put him in the middle of many of the key events that shaped the emerging entertainment industry. With Joe Weber, he led the opposition to the Theatrical Trust (a.k.a. "the Syndicate"), the industry's first monopoly. At the same time, they provided substantial financial support for the first actors' union, the White Rats, which was organized to counter the extortionate booking practices of the vaudeville circuits dominated by the Keith-Orpheum organization. In 1906, Fields became an important early partner of the young Shubert brothers as they began to challenge the Syndicate's supremacy. In the course of their long and stormy partnership with Fields, the Shuberts surpassed the Syndicate in the scale and, some would say, the ruthlessness of their theatrical empire. Fields found himself increasingly at odds with the Shuberts over his expensive productions, which included generous salaries for his performers.

During the Actors' Equity strike of 1919, Fields was the only Broadway producer to support the actors, even though it was against his best interests as a producer. Here he came into direct conflict with several of his ex-partners, as well as his colleague George M. Cohan, another actor-turned-producer. Fields, like Cohan, knew firsthand the grueling life of the vaudevillian; the crooked booking agents, the long separations from loved ones, the low regard in which actors were held by respectable society. In his business practices as well as his art, Fields was not one to forget where he came from.

For twenty-five years, until 1904, Lew Fields' name was inseparable from that of his boyhood friend and vaudeville partner, Joe Weber. At the turn of the century,

Weber & Fields were the most beloved and ambitious of comedy teams. Their style, Dutch knockabout ("dutch" from *deutsch*, or "German"; and "knockabout," the predecessor of slapstick), was a seamless blend of verbal and physical mayhem. "Don't poosh me, Meyer!" a piping voice would protest from offstage, but the round little immigrant would enter backward, unceremoniously shoved by his lanky buddy. Fields played Meyer, the tall and scheming one, who constantly tried to bully his trusting pal Mike into submission. They delivered their patter in a exaggerated German dialect loaded with malapropisms, a parody of immigrants learning English. The violence they did to the language was exceeded only by the violence they inflicted on each other. Meyer's protestations of eternal friendship were delivered while choking Mike: "When you are away from me, I can't keep my mind off you. When you are with me, I can't keep my hands off you!" At times the expressions of their love-you, hate-you relationship became a kind of cock-eyed poetry—or "poultry," as they called it: "if you luffed me like I luf me, no knife could cut us togedder."

The stage personas of Mike and Meyer were the prototypes for generations of two-acts to come: Smith & Dale, Laurel & Hardy, Abbott & Costello, Gleason and Carney. Their spirit and methods were also carried forward in some of the most inventive early comic strips such as "Mutt and Jeff" and "Krazy Kat," two series that began during periods when Weber & Fields were at the peak of their popularity. And the shades of Weber & Fields yet survive in two standard gags of American comedy they deserve credit for—the custard pie in the face, and the joke that begins, "Who was that lady I seen you with last night?"

Weber & Fields' other achievements, as we shall see, also warrant more than a cultural footnote. In 1896, after six years at the head of their own touring companies, they realized their dream of having their own Broadway theater. They were not yet thirty years old. During the next eight years, an evening at the Weber & Fields Music Hall (Broadway and Twenty-ninth Street) became the hottest ticket in town. First-night tickets were auctioned off, with some box seats going for $1,000 and orchestra seats for $100 each. First-nighters included many of New York's social elite: William Randolph Hearst, Hamilton Fish, Stanford White, "Diamond" Jim Brady, Richard "Boss" Croker, Richard Mansfield, and others. On subsequent nights, the audience was probably the most heterogeneous of any New York theater's, from the shopgirls and clerks in the galleries to the "smart set" in the front rows.

The "Weberfields" (as the troupe were affectionately known) were the undisputed masters of burlesque. This was not the "burlesque" of bump-and-grind and dirty jokes, but "burlesque" in its original sense: a satire or lampoon using grotesque exaggeration and comic imitation. Their ostensible targets were current Broadway plays and topical events, but their real subjects were their affluent, upwardly mobile patrons—the proverbial "tired businessman" and his wife. Only people who coveted respectability for themselves could ridicule that desire in others with such lethal accuracy and such compassion.

It became a mark of distinction to be lampooned at the Music Hall. Weber & Fields sugarcoated their satire with their own endearing buffoonery, surrounding themselves with an all-star cast of comedians, dancers, and the biggest and most beautiful chorus line Broadway had ever seen. Their innovative burlesques were a wellspring for future musical comedies and revues. In the age of television, their burlesque methods are still thriving; *Your Show of Shows* and *Saturday Night Live* are two good examples of the enduring vitality of the Weber & Fields Music Hall tradition.

With Weber, Fields had been a major force in the growth of vaudeville, but his most lasting—and most overlooked—contributions helped transform the look, themes, and tone of nineteenth-century popular entertainments into the distinctly modern genre of the Broadway musical. After his highly publicized split with Weber in 1904, Fields blossomed into the most prolific and versatile showman of the pre-war period. Between 1904 and 1916, he produced or starred in over forty stage entertainments, covering the entire spectrum from vaudeville and burlesque, through musical comedies and revues, to straight comedies and Victor Herbert operettas. In the 1909–1910 season, for example, Fields produced eight of the thirty-seven musicals on Broadway (starring in two of them). He also sent two companies from his previous seasons' hits on extended tours. His payroll was Broadway's largest, with almost two thousand people listed for the season.

At a time when most producers were slavishly imitating Viennese operettas and English musicals, Fields announced his intention to develop a new form of musical theater that would be "typically American," with coherent plots and characters, and production numbers integrated into the story. "Musical comedy," "revue," ("review," as it was then called) and "vaudeville" were more likely to be labels applied at the whim of a promoter than designations of distinct stage formats. Fields' wide-ranging activities during this period reflected his desire to find a happy medium between the oral, improvisatory tradition of vaudeville and the scripted, highly structured practices of operetta; in essence, to reconcile the popular theatrical forms of the Old World with those of the New.

If his intentions at times seemed to outstrip his achievements, then we should keep in mind that he was first and foremost a popular artist, subject to the absolute power of box office receipts and the volume of the applause. He was an astute judge of audience tastes, a talent that saved his career at several crucial junctures. His stated philosophy was still "to give the public what they want," but with an added clause: "at all costs." The added clause was what distinguished him from most other popular artists and producers, and it implied that there was more at stake for Fields than mere box office success.

His belief in the first part of this dictum was what had made him a star, and it was also what kept him from being a better artist. "Giving the public what they want" could be used as a justification for trying something new or a cynical excuse for trotting out the same old *shtick;* Fields used it both ways at different points in his career. "Sometimes these big ambitions have to be put up in alcohol and preserved on the shelf," he admitted in 1911. "They won't always do for the box office."

He was never, however, as commercially driven as he pretended to be, or should have been, if wealth had been his only goal. He had to be on the brink of financial ruin before he would produce or act in a show that simply capitalized on his past success. He would not have disagreed with the vaudeville hoofer who said, "My job is to dance 'til they applaud. The art's thrown in extra." But in most of Fields' productions, the art was not an afterthought. Fields' innovations in stagecraft, chorus routines, subject matter, and acting styles became the foundation for the theatrical innovators of the next generation: George and Ira Gershwin, George S. Kaufman, Oscar Hammerstein II, George Abbott, Cole Porter, and others.

His phrase "at all costs" was not just show biz ballyhoo. Fields' shows were consistently the most lavish and expensive until Ziegfeld's Follies in the mid-teens. In the slang of the day, Fields was a "plunger," a prodigal spender and risk-taker when it came to placing bets at the track or staking his money and reputation on his next Broadway venture. Once, while enjoying a typically high-rolling vacation at Saratoga, Fields had a losing day at the track, and an even worse evening at the roulette table at Canfield's chic casino. His betting losses had reached the house limit. Unchastened, he prevailed upon his friend Richard Canfield to raise the limit for one more bet. Fields piled his chips on one number, then surrounded that number with the remaining chips in the form of a Maltese cross. With the next spin, he won enough to cover his entire week's losses. It was the same risk-taking mentality that allowed him to gamble on new staging techniques, or on young unknowns such as Pauline Fredericks, Helen Hayes, Vernon Castle, Richard Rodgers and Lorenz Hart, Frederic March, William Gaxton, and Busby Berkeley.

To the generation responsible for the Golden Age of the Broadway musical, "Pop" Fields, as his employees referred to him in the 1920's, was a benevolent but demanding father figure. As a father, he provided considerably less encouragement. Nowhere was his ambivalence about the social legitimacy of the theater profession more apparent than in his relationship with his children. Because of his penchant for risk-taking both on- and offstage, his family's upper-middle-class lifestyle was often more precarious than any of them knew at the time. Nevertheless, Lew and his wife, Rose, were determined that their children would grow up to pursue respectable occupations. They actively discouraged their four children from careers in theater.

Fortunately for the American stage, three of the Fields children disobeyed. Joseph, after an unhappy stint as a screenwriter in Hollywood, became a successful Broadway playwright, co-author of *My Sister Eileen, Anniversary Waltz, Wonderful Town, Gentlemen Prefer Blondes,* and *Flower Drum Song.* Herbert wrote the librettos for eight Rodgers & Hart shows (including *Peggy Ann* and *A Connecticut Yankee*) and six for Cole Porter. His collaborations with his younger sister Dorothy included the books for *Mexican Hayride, Up in Central Park,* and *Annie Get Your Gun.* Dorothy, who was once thrown out of a music publisher's office on the orders of her father, became one of the premiere lyricists in musical theater and films. Working with composers such as Jimmy McHugh, Jerome Kern, Sigmund Romberg, Arthur Schwartz, and Cy Coleman, she wrote the words for some of the enduring hits of American popular song: "I Can't Give You Anything But Love," "On the Sunny Side of the Street," "Don't Blame Me," "I'm in the Mood for Love," "A Fine Romance," "The Way You Look Tonight," "Big Spender," "If My Friends Could See Me Now," to name but a few. Considered together, Lew Fields and his children represent a tradition of the American musical theater that spans a century. For reasons of length, this book can only tell the first half of the story.

One measure of the distance between Lew Fields' time and our own is the confusion that surrounds the terms used to label certain types of popular entertainments. Who today, other than a specialist in popular culture, knows what a dime museum was? What was the difference between "variety" and "vaudeville"? What were olios and afterpieces? It is safe to assume that few readers have firsthand memories of dime museums, minstrel shows, or even vaudeville; we have gamely attempted to re-create in prose the experience of these lost entertainments.

For similar reasons, we have elected to describe in detail a wide range of Fields' productions, drawing on extensive newspaper and magazine accounts, photos, published and unpublished interviews, and rehearsal scripts. The "Fieldsian" style—the topicality of his material and his insistence on real-life models for his comedy—makes it essential to try to re-create the immediate social context of his work. Caricatures, as Emerson observed, are often the truest history of their times; Fields trafficked in well-wrought caricatures, so his comedy cannot be properly appreciated out of context. Everything within the limits of propriety was potential material for his comedy. "A comedian talks to everyone without discrimination," he once said, for "a good joke might appear anywhere." The situations and settings for most of Fields' productions were meticulously observed re-creations from everyday life: a pool room, a shooting gallery, a department store, a barbershop, a late-night cabaret—the public sites most familiar to him and his audience. From his early days onward, his stage characters were modelled on his neighbors and family—parents, siblings, and later children. He took great pride in the mimetic basis of his work, once claiming that "every gesture, every intonation" he employed was copied from life. Fields' working methods thus encouraged us to seek parallels between his personal life and work. Of course, not all the parallels he created were deliberate, and it is these unintended reflections that are often the most revealing.

The limited family lore we had access to had the embroidered texture of twice- and thrice-told tales, more useful as indications of a sensibility than as verifiable proof of specific personal facts. From all indications, Lew Fields had no interests apart from his work and his family, except for gambling. It is likely that those who worked with him closely over the years knew him better than his immediate family, at least until his children became his collaborators. Unfortunately, none of these people were still alive to be interviewed for this book. He left no diaries and only a few personal letters. This will no doubt disappoint those who think that "biography" is a synonym for "gossip." He was, however, a favorite subject of interviews, equally good for a funny anecdote or a quote about the state of the theater. While many of his theater colleagues treated the press with suspicion, Fields was unusually accessible and candid about his work.

Whether he was performing in a dime museum or producing a Broadway musical, the crucial ingredient in Fields' success was comedy. Comedy, however, is a highly perishable commodity. Fields knew it; he compared styles of comedy to ladies' fashions and newspapers. Styles of comedy are in fact revealing cultural artifacts that can tell us much about the people who used them and the context in which they were used. The problem is that many of these popular entertainments came from a performance tradition that predated films and records and eluded the printed page, so what can we really know about them? We know that people laughed, but what were they laughing at?

Today, when American musicals such as *Show Boat* and *Porgy and Bess* have become a part of the grand opera repertory, and songwriters, dancers, and actors get medals from the President, it is too easy and convenient to forget that the American popular theater had its origins in the minstrel shows, freak shows, and saloons of the late nineteenth century. The Broadway musical—that slick, all-American, over-domesticated entertainment—was initially a hybrid creation, the theatrical equivalent of "carpenter's gothic," a ramshackle structure scavenged and patched together by immigrants and minorities hustling to make a buck. Through the career of Lew Fields, we can rediscover the bumptious, street-carnival spirit of the Bowery that once animated the Broadway musical.

In the end, our journey from the Bowery to Broadway has a threefold purpose: to tell the story of an ambitious immigrant kid named Lew Fields, seeking his fortune in "show biz;" to examine the history of the American popular theater in its most crucial stages of development; and to provide an account of the changing tastes of the American public over a fifty-year period.

FROM THE BOWERY TO BROADWAY

Actors are indeed the abstracts and brief chronicles of their time.

Brooks Atkinson

Burlesque itself should not be deprived of all claims to seriousness simply because, in its fidelity to nature, it chooses more often to laugh with the world than to weep.

Lew Fields

CHAPTER I
From the Bowery to Broadway

E VEN before it became the theater center, the mere mention of the name "Broadway" evoked images of glamor and success. In the early 1880's, Broadway between Eighth Street and Madison Square (whose northern edge was Twenty-sixth Street) was famous for its first-class hotels, restaurants, and shops. Elegant hotels such as the St. Denis, the Clarendon, the Fifth Avenue, and the white marble Hoffman House were oases of luxury in a chaotic city, offering travellers the latest in mechanical conveniences: running water, electric lights, steam heat, speaker-tubes, and call-buzzers. Broadway was the spine of the main shopping district, otherwise known as the Ladies' Mile. A. T. Stewart, James McCreery, Lord & Taylor, W. & J. Sloane, Brooks Brothers, and B. Altman built sprawling retail palaces with ornate cast-iron façades, grand staircases, and wide, arched windows. This concentration of retailers attracted the affluent carriage trade, and with it, all sorts of people—rich women, local politicos, salesmen, pickpockets—who wanted to take advantage of the city's most fashionable commercial neighborhood. The Broadway crowd was unique, as a writer for *Harper's New Monthly Magazine* noted: "There is a cheeriness, impetuosity, vehemence, and brilliancy in a Broadway crowd. . . . It has a Champagne sparkle even in the parts where business is supreme; its tread is elastic, buoyant, and almost rhythmic, as it follows the rattle and roar of vehicles. . . ."

In short, Broadway was already a symbol of success before it became a synonym for theatrical entertainment. "Failure has no place in [this] street," wrote journalist John McCabe in his 1882 guidebook, *New York by Sunlight and Gas Light.* "Successful men alone deal here, no matter what methods the success was won. . . . Broadway glitters in the sunshine of prosperity." Though McCabe was commenting on the social prestige conferred by commercial success, his comments would still be appropriate thirty or forty years later.

Prestige, glitter, the aura of success—Broadway embodied the uptown aspirations of merchants and shoppers alike. This was the Broadway that inspired the entertainers and entrepreneurs who shaped the popular theater at the turn of the century. Show business pioneers like Oscar Hammerstein I, Lew Fields, George M. Cohan, the Shuberts, and Florenz Ziegfeld created an artistic and economic institution that perpetuated and enlarged upon this pre-existing notion of "Broad-

3

way." Given this model, it should not be surprising that these early showmen tried to attract the same class of customers, as typified by the turn-of-the-century theater advertisements promising diversion "for the family and its tired business-man." In their values and work habits, most of the early showmen qualified as tired businessmen themselves.

The emergence of show business and the art of the popular stage were com-plementary developments; "Broadway" was the label that was eventually applied to their sum total. In the 1880's, Broadway's most characteristic entertainment—the musical comedy—existed only in its most rudimentary forms; in weak imita-tions of Gilbert & Sullivan, in revivals of *The Black Crook* and other musical extravaganzas, in minstrel shows, and more promisingly, in the farces of Harrigan & Hart. Most of the reputable theaters were clustered around Union Square (Fourteenth Street). A few theatrical agents had opened offices in the vicinity, but they conducted their business in the street or on park benches, or in the barrooms of nearby hotels. Broken contracts were the rule. There were few or-ganized theater chains or circuits, no theatrical unions, no music publishers. The only songs heard on Twenty-eighth Street between Broadway and Sixth Avenue—future headquarters of Tin Pan Alley—were probably emanating from the parlors of the many "temples of love" located in the neighborhood. At the corner of Sixth Avenue and Twenty-third Street stood Edwin Booth's Theater, a florid granite structure that was intended as "a great national temple" to dramatic art; but the venture was unsuccessful, and in 1883 the theater was converted into stores. North of Twenty-third Street, there were no theaters except for the exotic-looking Casino Theatre, which opened as a concert hall in 1882. "The Rialto" and "the Great White Way" did not exist.

If the art and business of modern Broadway could be said to have a specific birthplace, it was in the Bowery, in its dime museums, dance halls, and beer gardens, and its date of birth was in the early 1880's. The Bowery was Broadway's antithesis; they were opposite sides of the same coin. "Next to Broadway," John McCabe wrote, "the Bowery is the most characteristic street in New York." Like Broadway some forty years later, the Bowery underwent a transformation after dark:

> To see the Bowery in its glory, one must visit it at night. It is a blaze of light from one end to the other. . . .
>
> There is nothing in this glare of light, nothing in this swarming pavement, to indicate that midnight is passed. The windows gleam, the saloons are all aglare, a half-score pianos and violins send as many airs floating into the night to blend into . . . the roysterer's song, the brawler's oath and the hundred strange voices of the night.[1]

The Bowery in the early 1880's was already the most notorious thoroughfare in New York. The adjoining wards contained over 200,000 people per square mile, and the biggest waves of immigration were yet to come. In the evening, the dili-gent sweatshop girls, the pickpockets, the society men out for a good time, the child beggars, the bellowing pushcart peddlers, the streetwalkers, the greenhorns on their way to night school all jostled their way along the same sidewalks. Innocence and corruption, extravagance and deprivation, hope and despair; nowhere else in the country were the extremes of the human condition more apparent or more cruelly juxtaposed. It was the first stop on the way up and the last stop on the way down.

As a place name, "the Bowery" was a catch-all term for the teeming Lower East Side neighborhoods where the immigrant hordes lived. West of the Bowery, the Irish were firmly entrenched; to the east were the Germans and a sprinkling of German and Polish Jews, with Chinatown wedged between the Irish and German territories. "Little Africa" grew up around the swampy edges of Lower Thompson Street (later called SoHo). Later in the 1880's, as the Irish and Germans moved uptown or to other boroughs, Eastern European Jews took over the German sections, and the Italians began to supplant the African-Americans in southern Greenwich Village. This only begins to hint at its human variety; according to McCabe, there were also "the piratical-looking Spaniard and Portuguese," "the chattering Frenchmen," and "the brutish-looking Mexican."

More than just a place name, "the Bowery" represented a cultural milieu: it had its own characteristic denizens (the lower-class immigrant), dwellings (the tenement), commerce (cheap retail stores, street vendors), and most important of all, its own entertainments. What impressed McCabe was the Bowery's dazzling array of disreputable diversions:

> The street is the paradise of beer saloons, bar-rooms, concert and dance halls, cheap theatres, and low-class shows. . . . Wretched transparencies mark the entrances to the low dives, in and out of which a steady throng pours. The pavements are full of abandoned women, boldly plying their trade, regardless of the police. . . .
>
> The theatres are well-filled with pleasure-seekers. The admission is cheap, and the performances adapted to the tastes of their patrons. . . . Vice offers every inducement to its votaries, and the devil's work is done nightly upon a grand scale in the Bowery.

In the popular imagination—in songs, plays, newspaper articles, and political campaigns—the Bowery evoked images of poverty, coarseness, and shame, enhanced perhaps by the curious fact that it was the only major New York thoroughfare not to be the site of a church. As McCabe's description indicates, the essence of what the Bowery stood for could be found in its entertainments.

Chatham Square was the geographical starting point for the Bowery, and its drain sink; a place where every type of citydweller was bound to pass through sooner or later. Here was the junction of the recently completed Second and Third Avenue elevated railways. With the completion of the Third Avenue El in 1878, the Bowery had entered the age of rapid transit. From South Ferry, the El snaked its way up to Chatham Square and then continued up the Bowery, crossing over to Third Avenue above Fourteenth Street and terminating at Forty-second Street. The steam locomotives burned soft coal and spewed thick smoke and hot cinders on the pedestrians below; a woman wearing a veil would arrive at her destination with the pattern of her veil tattooed in soot on her face. No matter—commuters now could get from Fifty-ninth Street to the downtown area in thirty minutes or less. Few people objected that the thundering trains added to the already painful din of the horsecars and carriages on the cobblestone streets below, or that the El relegated the street to permanent shadows and turned second- and third-storey windows into a fleeting series of *tableaux vivants* through which passengers could glimpse the humblest and most intimate of domestic scenes.

The sidewalks and streets around Chatham Square were crowded day and night with a motley throng of laborers, beggars, shoppers, and newsboys. Above the din, one could hear snatches of conversation, mostly in German with the odd English word thrown in, or the cries of pushcart peddlers hawking their wares: "Gutes frucht! Drei pennies die whole lot!" The neighborhood was the headquarters for every cheap retail enterprise imaginable, with secondhand clothing and pawn shops predominating. The shopkeepers' aggressive *spiels* and their attention-getting stunts added to the carnival atmosphere.

The buildings around Chatham Square were unprepossessing—squat tenements and a few wood-frame houses—except for the stately Thalia Theatre up the block, with its imposing Greek columns obscured by the El tracks. Interspersed among the cheap retail stores were saloons, shooting galleries, gaming and assignation houses, and other low-class entertainments, any combination of which could be jammed under the same roof. Providing diversions for the working man on his night out, or for the young swells "slumming it," was serious business, brutally competitive but profitable for the lucky few even when other businesses were failing. Depending on his budget and tastes, the fun-seeker in Chatham Square in the early 1880's could choose from a broad spectrum of popular entertainments, ranging from "abandoned" women to a burlesque of *H.M.S. Pinafore* or the blood-and-thunder melodrama of *Robert Macaire*. Families frequented the German beer gardens—the Atlantic Garden, and across the street, the German Winter Garden—where for a small admission fee they could enjoy beer, radishes, cheese, and Strauss waltzes. Since Sunday was the working man's day off, the beer gardens found it profitable to circumvent Sunday blue laws by presenting Sabbath "Sacred Concerts."

Of all the popular entertainments current in the 'Seventies, it is the dime museum that best demonstrates the moral ambivalence that lay at the heart of American culture. The term "museum" was itself a euphemism, a clever stratagem developed by showmen in the early nineteenth century to deflect the strong puritanical bias against frivolous entertainment. The museum's activities were cloaked in high-minded rhetoric: the exhibits were "wonders" of science, nature, and history; the auditorium where they were displayed was called a "lecture room"; the variety acts and playlets were called "moral" or "edifying" dramas. The live performers included singers, acrobats, trained animals, and Punch and Judy Acts, as well as theatrical favorites such as *The Drunkard* and *Uncle Tom's Cabin*. In reality, the successful museum at mid-century featured human freaks, bizarre curios (often faked), bloodcurdling waxworks and dioramas, and a stage show. P. T. Barnum opened his American Museum at Broadway and Ann Street in 1841, and it quickly became the prototype for the cheap amusements of the next half-century.[2]

The first- and second-generation immigrants flocked to the dime museums for entertainment that was inexpensive and easy to comprehend. The freaks, curios, and variety acts demanded only the most rudimentary knowledge of English, and they satisfied the Bowery audience's craving for novelty and brutality. While the museum bill was never without its grotesque or sensational attractions—an animal monstrosity, or a gory waxwork—outright obscenity was rare, though there were a few isolated exceptions. For the most part, museum managers had learned the value of a mixed audience (including children) well before it occurred to their counterparts in variety. South of Fourteenth Street, the dime museum was the most popular form of family entertainment.

On the Bowery, garish banners and transparencies depicted the main attractions, usually the freaks—the living skeleton, the fat woman, Siamese twins, etc.—and sensational curios, such as the hands of a famous murderer, preserved in a jar, or the mummy of a little mermaid. "Outside talkers" worked the sidewalk in front of the museum with a prepared pitch to entice customers into parting with the dime required for admission. The "inside talker" was usually the museum lecturer, often referred to as "Professor." In his extravagant rhetorical style, he described each of the platform shows, and then directed his patrons to the "theatorium": "Now you've seen our wondrous wares / Next is the big show given downstairs / You'll see a drammer most intense / The stars they'll cost you but five cents." Downstairs, a barker at the entrance to the theatorium beckoned to the patron.

In the demimonde of the dime museum, there were two classes of performers: the freaks and the variety acts. The variety acts, or "artists," as they preferred to call themselves, were second-class citizens. Despite the fact that the variety acts were often quite strenuous, artists were required to perform anywhere from ten to twenty turns a day, and their pay was a fraction of what the freaks received. To the manager's way of thinking, the artists—mostly Bowery kids, or down-and-out actors—were easy enough to come by, and frequently undependable, but a true natural freak was a worthwhile investment.[3]

Morris and Hickman's East Side Museum was known around Chatham Square as a "clean" house, meaning that there was no gambling or prostitution on the premises, or any of the lewd "medical" exhibits found in the the sleazier museums. Working-class women could watch the Morris and Hickman variety acts without fearing for their reputations, though they had reason to fear for their purses. The big money-maker was the phrenologist, whose hidden talent as a pickpocket was eventually discovered and resulted in the museum's closing.

Like its competitors, Morris and Hickman's was open from noon till midnight, and it did its heaviest trade in the evenings. A dime spent here entitled patrons to two full floors of attractions. The ground floor featured the natural freaks—the Chinese Giant, the Turtle Boy—and the self-made wonders, such as the tattooed man and the glass-eater, who often supplemented their salaries by selling autographed pictures of themselves. Upstairs in the curio hall, there were exotic animals and would-be religious relics and historic artifacts: arrows from Custer's Last Stand, or a stuffed rat, supposedly the one trained in prison by Charles Guiteau, assassin of President Garfield.

For an additional nickel, the Professor—a kind of low-rent *compère*—invited

the patrons to the theatorium to see "a musical genius on fourteen different instruments, and the skatorial phenomenon in his fine parlor skating and amusing
imitations, and the hilarious pair of Hibernian hellions in their skull-cracking specialty act, to be followed by a laughable farce sure to please young and old."

In the basement of Morris and Hickman's was a long room with a makeshift
stage, a narrow wooden platform at one end. The ceiling was low, and the cement
floor was covered with sawdust to sop up the spilled beer and tobacco juice. Day
or night, small gas jets spaced along the side walls provided the only illumination.
The meager lighting was further diminished by the dense clouds of cigar and
cigarette smoke that lingered in the unventilated room from one day to the next.
The audience—mostly male, mostly recent immigrants—arranged the wooden
benches and folding chairs in small groups, and settled in with their drinks. If the
performers were mediocre, no matter. The dime museum audience enjoyed heckling the bad acts almost as much as they enjoyed laughing at the good acts.

A string of gas jets offset the front of the stage from the ambient darkness
of the room. The museum manager stood off to one side, chatting with his customers. He would note the crowd's response in the previous act, and in a voice
hoarse from long hours of high-volume hype, he would introduce the next act. If
necessary, performers could be accompanied by the standard "three-piece orchestra"—a piano, its stool, and its cover.

Most museums in the 1880's made it a point to have a "kid act" on the bill.
At Morris and Hickman's, the kid act followed the animal act and the magician:
"Now hold onto your buttons or they'll be fit to burst. It's those hilarious Hibernian lads, Fields and Weber. . . ." In the first weeks of their professional careers,
Lew Fields and Joe Weber had been arguing about first billing, so they agreed to
take turns. Starting the following week—and for the next half century—their
partnership would be known as "Weber & Fields."

For two years, they had been preparing for their first professional appearance by doing benefit performances, amateur nights, and tumbling acts on Bowery street corners. At Morris and Hickman's, the two twelve-year-old boys entered
single file, with Fields' hand on Weber's shoulder, carrying canes and singing:
"Here we are, an Irish pair / Without any troubles or care / We're here once more
to make the people roar . . ." as they performed a clog dance of two or three
trick steps that they had bribed an older boy to teach them. Their costumes
included green vests and kneepants, derbies, and canes. With their Semitic profiles and dark eyes, they didn't look any more "Hibernian" than the blackface
performer looked "Ethiopian."

Fields wore lifts in his dancing clogs so that he would appear taller than
Weber. Weber wore a huge stuffed pillow under his vest. As he danced, the padding would slip from his vest into his trousers, and his exaggerated efforts to
readjust it delighted the audience. A few weeks earlier, the slippage had provoked
unintended laughs, so the boys elaborated on it and incorporated it into their act.

As they finished their clog dance, Fields would glare at his partner with
mock disapproval and, in heavy Irish brogue, reprimand him for being such a
clumsy dancer. Weber would protest and try to prove that he was actually the
better dancer, encouraging the audience to indicate its preference. Upset at being

upstaged, Fields would unleash a torrent of clever insults. As Weber finished his demonstration, Fields—now quite frustrated—would wind up and give Weber a kick to the belly, followed by a whack to the backside with his cane. Weber would retaliate by using the crook of his cane to snag Fields by the neck and drag him across the stage. This was what the act was building towards, and the audience responded with hoots of laughter and encouragement. The ensuing free-for-all was actually a carefully choreographed tumbling sequence, consisting of back flips, cartwheels, and "alley-ups"—Weber would hold his fingers locked as Fields stepped into his hands and was somersaulted into the air. Fields would land on his feet, and together with Weber, reprise their song and clog-dance off the stage.

The museum manager had to notice the vigorous applause and the audience's enthusiastic comments: "Whoozis act?" "Fields and Weber?" "Dey're a panic! Dem two jays're deh funnies' t'ing I ever saw!"

For ten or more turns a day, every day, Joe Weber and Lew Fields each earned three dollars a week.

Forty-five years later and a few miles uptown, Rodgers' and Hart's *Peggy-Ann* opened at the Vanderbilt Theater. "The entire production," according to the program, "is under the supervision of Lew Fields." Working in a similar capacity for five of the early Rodgers and Hart shows, Fields demonstrated his faith in the young team's innovative approach at a time when no other producers would take the gamble. As a well-respected stage veteran, Fields' involvement assured backers and audiences of a quality entertainment. Rounding out the team was his son Herbert, who had joined forces with Rodgers and Hart in 1921 and wrote the books for most of their shows in the 1920's, including *Dearest Enemy, The Girl Friend,* and *Connecticut Yankee.*

Peggy-Ann was a well-crafted combination of old and new. Herb Fields' libretto was a reworking of his father's 1910 hit, *Tillie's Nightmare,* which had starred the formidable comedienne Marie Dressler. In the new version, the title role was played by the petite, vivacious Helen Ford, and the other cast members were drawn from the ranks of vaudeville and the legit stage: Lulu McConnell, Lester Cole, Betty Starbuck, and Edith Meiser. Herb's adaptation took what had been a rather broad comedy about a boardinghouse drudge who dreams of unattainable pleasures and turned it into a sophisticated Cinderella tale, with dream imagery courtesy of Sigmund Freud.

Although the premise of *Peggy-Ann* was not anything new, its tone, staging, and musical numbers were innovative indeed. To emphasize the bleak reality of Peggy-Ann's daily existence, there were no songs or dancing in the first fifteen minutes of the play. And instead of the usual raucous finale, Fields and his choreographer, Seymour Felix, devised a closing number that was played as a quiet, romantic dance on the darkened stage. In between, the dream-time adventures of Peggy-Ann displayed the characteristics that distinguished a Lew Fields production: a blend of slapstick, satire, and pathos, clever and fanciful stage effects, novel chorus routines, and brisk pacing.

One of the evening's biggest laughs occurred when Peggy-Ann, dreaming that she has escaped to Manhattan, wanders into an elegant Fifth Avenue department store. There she discovers Mrs. Astor, Mrs. Biddle, and Mrs. Gould shooting craps on the floor. It was essentially a sight gag of little consequence, but it typified the kind of burlesque that Fields' audiences had come to expect ever since the days of the Weber & Fields Music Hall.

Another typically "Fieldsian" touch was displayed in the interlude between two scenes, as the forlorn Peggy-Ann falls asleep in the dreary boardinghouse and her imaginary escapades begin. The scene change is played in front of a drop curtain while the stage is being reset. The scrim depicts the intersection of Forty-second Street and Fifth Avenue. To suggest the transition from the country to city, twelve chorus girls appear dressed as hicks, singing:

> We're not dressed in sable
> Our clothes bear the label
> Of barnyard and stable and hay;
> [. . .]
> We're gonna go down where
> Ladies' backs are bare
> And the farm girls all go astray;
> Our old clothes are dowdy,
> We want to be rowdy,
> And so we'll say Howdy to Broadway.[4]

As they sang and danced, their costumes changed from gingham frocks to flapper outfits in full view of the audience. To convey Peggy-Ann's bewilderment as she began her dream journey, the Forty-second Street backdrop was highly stylized, with distorted, surrealistic lines and colors, including a policeman in a pink uniform and an uncooperative traffic signal. The otherworldliness was reminiscent of operettas; the chorus recalled similar routines Fields had used in his summer musicals dating back almost twenty years; and the sly, playful tone was pure Jazz Age hipness.

Equally characteristic was Fields' ability to get the best out of the young talent he collaborated with. Herb's book, in addition to having fun with the heroine's subconscious fears and fantasies, had its share of quips, such as "there's lots of things in this world better 'n money, but it takes money to buy them." There were also a few wheezes borrowed from Pop's joke book to replace lines that did not work in rehearsals or previews. The old line "he's so fast he can turn off the light and jump in bed before the room gets dark," was given a new twist when it was used to describe the sexual aggressiveness of the men in New York. This sets up one of the show's most delightful numbers, "A Little Birdie Told Me So," sung by Helen Ford. Hart's lyrics were daring for the time, but Rodgers' fluid, graceful melody made them seem less risqué:

> . . . He'll say his love is mental
> And very transcendental.
> His talk will soon get boorish,
> And very ostermoorish.

He'll use poetic words that no one understands,
And illustrate the meaning with his hands.[5]

A long way indeed from the dime museum where two immigrant boys sang,
"Here we are, an Irish pair . . ." and battered each other over the head with
canes.

At first glance, the contrasts between the primitive Bowery entertainments
and sophisticated Broadway musicals may seem extreme. In the case of Lew
Fields, they simply represent two different stages in the career of a pioneering
showman.

CHAPTER II

Adventures in Human Nature

MIKE: I am delightfulness to meet you.
MEYER: Der disgust ist all mine.
from Weber & Fields' "Choking Scene"

To many of these people, articulate as they were, the great loss was of language—that they could not say what was in them to say. You have some subtle thought and it comes out like a piece of broken glass.
Bernard Malamud

HAD he been less eager to conceal his immigrant origins, Lew Fields would have appreciated the fact that the first American building he set foot in—the State Emigration Depot at Castle Garden—was a converted theater. To mention this rather pleasant irony, however, would have compromised Fields' claim to being American-born, a fiction that was expedient early in his career and one that he chose to maintain for the rest of his life.

Neither Weber nor Fields was ever reluctant to discuss what it was like to grow up as the son of immigrants in the Bowery; it was, after all, the source of their material, and for their rapport with their audience. In later years, in celebrity interviews, or meeting for lunch at the Brown Derby near their homes in Beverly Hills, they would wax nostalgic on the subject of their Bowery days. But on the question of their national origins they were curiously misleading. According to U.S. immigration and census records, the Schoenfeld family, including five-year-old Lew (then known as Moses), landed at Castle Garden, New York, in the fall of 1872. Lew Fields was, in fact, not only the son of an immigrant, but an immigrant himself.

Castle Garden, an island annexed to the southern tip of Manhattan by landfill, was originally constructed in the early 1800's as a a fortress to defend against British invaders. Known then as Castle Clinton, it was sold to the City of New York in 1823 when the ramparts were found to be too weak to bear the weight of heavy artillery. The following year, the city roofed over the fort to convert it into a "summer-garden," with a fountain and a promenade, and leased it as a civic hall for public entertainments. Castle Garden quickly became a popular site for many types of public events—concerts, melodramas, political rallies, firework displays, balloon ascensions. It was at Castle Garden, in 1842, that inventor Samuel F. B. Morse demonstrated his electric telegraph. Eight years later, showman

P. T. Barnum presented Jenny Lind, the "Swedish Nightingale," in her American concert debut to a sellout crowd of six thousand exuberant Manhattanites. And in 1852, Lola Montes scandalized the Castle Garden audience with her sensuous dancing and revealing costumes.

By the mid-1850's, however, the rising tide of immigration had overwhelmed the existing facilities, and Castle Garden was hastily converted into an immigration depot with minimal alterations to the interior. Between 1855 and its closing in 1890, over 7.6 million newcomers crossed its threshold. Among them were Solomon and Sarah Schoenfeld and their four sons: Max (age eleven), Abel (eight), Moses (five), and Henry (one).

Solomon Schoenfeld and Sarah Frank were married by arrangement at the age of seventeen, and settled in a *shtetl* west of Warsaw in 1858. Solomon's future looked promising: he was clever and industrious, he had apprenticed as a tailor, and he could read and write. With his wife's help, he opened his own shop and began to build a steady clientele. Yiddish was the Schoenfelds' first language, but it was a dialect closer to the standard German than the brand of Yiddish spoken by the Polish and Russian Jews who came later. In cultural matters as well, the Jews from the Posen and Great Poland regions looked more towards the adjacent German empire than to czarist Russia. This German identity came to matter greatly to the Jewish immigrants of the 1870's; with the onslaught of Russian-Jewish immigration after 1885, the distinction between German and Eastern European Jews became a crucial indicator of social status. Naturally, those caught in the middle preferred to identify with the affluent, sophisticated German Jews rather than the poor, semiliterate Russian Jews. The younger generation of Schoenfelds continued to insist on their German origins until World War I made it awkward, and then their parents were said to be Polish or Russian.

In the early 1870's, the Jews of Poland were experiencing a period of relative tolerance under the rule of Czar Alexander II. Forced assimilation and most anti-Jewish taxes and business restrictions had been abolished, and the compulsory conscription period for Jews was limited to five years. Nevertheless, the news of the Easter 1871 pogrom in Odessa (hitherto the most cosmopolitan and liberal city for Jews) raised fears for the future. It was still not uncommon in Poland in the 1870's for Jewish boys as young as thirteen to be pressed into service in the Czar's army, where the conditions were particularly brutal for the Jewish recruits. The Schoenfelds' eldest son, Max, was eleven, and there were three more boys behind him. In the years to come, Solomon was counting on them to help run his tailor shop. Family lore has it that it was the threat of forced conscription that prompted the Schoenfelds' decision to emigrate. It is equally likely that there was word from Sarah's brother David in America about the money to be made in the needle trades.

In the autumn of 1872, the Schoenfeld family made the illegal crossing from Poland into Germany, paid off the necessary customs officials and ticket agents in Bremen (or Hamburg), and embarked on a German steamer bound for New York. The Schoenfelds' experiences in steerage were no better than those of the many memoirists who wrote about the trip. In other words, it was an unforgettable ordeal: people huddled together like cattle belowdecks, their cries and moans uttered in a babel of tongues; families of four crammed into wooden berths, stupefied by seasickness and the inadequate ventilation that trapped the stench of vomit, open toilets, tobacco, and rotting fruit. The food, ladled out of huge kettles into tin pails provided by the steamship company, was usually inedible. Orthodox Jews like the Schoenfelds were usually better off trying to uphold their kosher dietary laws, eating what bread and such that they could manage to bring.

Yet, for a healthy, inquisitive five-year-old boy, the voyage was also an adventure. Comforted by stalwart parents and protected by his older brothers, little Moses Schoenfeld found no shortage of novel sensations. First, there was the ship itself, a throbbing, smoke-snorting mechanical Leviathan, and the burly sailors who ran it. There was cardplaying and endless talk about where they came from and speculation about what lay in store. Though steerage reduced its passengers to a common misery, a few hardy and high-spirited souls managed to find ways to amuse themselves and their fellow sufferers with music and even some dancing. In retrospect, such memories sometimes redeemed the voyage, or at least made recollection less painful. As an adult, Lew Fields took pleasure in transatlantic cruises—traveling first class, of course—sometimes spending less than a week at his destination before returning. Perhaps it was this early experience at sea that accounts for his odd affection for Joseph Conrad's sea stories; that and the fact that Fields admired the Polish-born Conrad's mastery of English.

Compared to their fellow passengers in steerage, the Schoenfelds were fortunate. The cost of getting to the port, along with the expense of steerage tickets for a family of six, was the equivalent of a small fortune. Solomon's sale of his tailor shop allowed him to emigrate with his family intact, rather than having to come over alone to earn enough to pay their way at a later date. Nevertheless, it is likely that they arrived in New York nearly penniless. His four boys and his pregnant wife, Sarah, survived the squalid conditions of their passage in reasonably good health. A few years earlier, the family of Fields' future partner had not been so lucky. The Webers' youngest child, an infant, died at sea, with two days left before landfall. Determined to give her child a proper Jewish burial in the New World, Mrs. Weber pretended to nurse and care for the baby's corpse until the family made it to Customs at Castle Garden.

The German steamers dropped anchor in the Hudson at Quarantine Point, near Staten Island, while a squad of health officers examined the steerage passengers for signs of smallpox, typhus, yellow fever, and cholera. In the nearby bay was moored a battered hull with no masts or above-deck cabins: a floating hospital for those found to be infected. The healthy immigrants boarded a barge with their luggage. In their slow approach across the Hudson to the Castle Garden depot, they saw a huge, circular structure loom into view. With its red sandstone walls and its sloping roof topped by an arched cupola, the building looked somewhat like a prison. As the barge came closer, they could see that the land side was completely enclosed by a high wooden fence, with one guarded gate. Despite its imposing appearance, the sounds reaching them over the water were inviting, almost festive, like the din of a huge marketplace. The docks alongside the depot bustled with activity: dazed steerage passengers clinging to their loved ones, customs inspectors bellowing instructions, stevedores unloading baggage, and porters pulling overloaded hand carts.

When the Schoenfelds arrived in 1872, Castle Garden had long since ceased to be an official site for public entertainment, but to new arrivals who had just spent the last four weeks at sea, the emigration depot still presented a dizzying assortment of dramas and spectacles. Through the eyes of five-year-old Moses Schoenfeld, Castle Garden was theater of the highest order. ("A perfect farce," was how one New York State commissioner described it, though he was probably referring to the rampant corruption and mismanagement.)

As the immigrants waited outside the main rotunda to be registered, little Moses Schoenfeld watched the parade of familiar and unfamiliar costumes. There were more different kinds of hats than he could imagine—peasant caps with stiff black visors, flat derbies like fried eggs, bushy fur hats, bowlers worn at a jaunty angle, top hats with tiny brims, wide-brimmed felt hats, and the women in straw hats, bonnets, and scarves. Most fascinating of all to the five-year-old were some of the men who pulled the hand carts loaded with baggage: their skin was black, and they made his father look small by comparison.

Structurally, the inside of the rotunda had changed surprisingly little from its days as a theater. Renovators had presumably removed the stage platform, but the galleries and much of the permanent seating were still intact. Center-stage was the simple desk where the customs inspector entered in his ledger the name (or an approximation thereof), age, nationality, and destination of each new arrival. To the right and left of the main entrance, the refreshment stands had been replaced by a series of enclosures containing a railroad ticket office, post office, money exchange, restaurant, and police office—the kinds of essential everyday transactions that became the basis of many early variety routines, including those of Weber & Fields.

Those not fortunate enough to be met by a kinsman or *landsman* (a friend from the same town in the old country) found themselves spending their first night in America sleeping on the hard floor of Castle Garden, waiting for the arrival of the moneychangers at dawn so that they could pay another official to "locate" their baggage. The Schoenfelds were met by Sarah's older brother David Frank. Uncle David was a bit of a *makher* (operator) himself, and therefore the perfect guardian to guide them through the snares and chaos of Castle Garden.

Because so many of the newcomers spoke only German, many of the depot signs were in German; for those arriving with enough money to take them to the West immediately, the ferry from "Castle Garden nach der Erie Eisenbahn" took them to the Jersey City terminal for trains to Cleveland, Cincinnati, Louisville, Detroit, St. Louis, Chicago, and San Francisco. Twenty years later, these same cities became the mainstays of the Weber & Fields tours, and the basis for the vaudeville circuits.

At the time of their arrival in 1872, the United States was riding the crest of the post–Civil War boom that would transform it from a rural, agricultural society into an urban, industrial society. Just the previous year, the population of the City of New York had topped the one-million mark. In lower Manhattan, the mansions and wood-frame houses vacated by the well-to-do were quickly taken over for use as boardinghouses and tenements for the burgeoning immigrant population. Backyard houses were built with no direct access to the street, no toilets or water supply, no consideration for ventilation and light, no fire escapes, and walk-ups of as many as seven floors. The epitome of slum living—the "dumb-bell" or "double-decker" tenements—had not yet been designed. The dumb-bell design was the winner of an 1878 contest sponsored by a trade journal for sanitary engineers. Incredible as it may seem, the implementation of the dumb-bell design after 1879 was an improvement over the types of dwellings that the Schoenfelds lived in during their first few years in New York.

By 1872, a handful of reform-minded journalists had brought to the public's attention the unprecedented corruption and mismanagement practiced by "Boss" William Marcy Tweed and his Tammany Hall cronies. Conservative estimates indicated that the Tweed Ring embezzled $75 million of city revenues, of which just over one million was ever recovered. Although Tweed clearly had the support of the city's most influential citizens, it was the Irish, and to a lesser extent, German, immigrants who were the source of Tweed's power at the polls. Tweed's lieutenants effectively organized the new arrivals at the ward level, manipulating city services like sanitation, police protection, and construction and business permits.

Nowhere were the effects of municipal corruption more obvious than in the Bowery. The five square blocks off of the Bowery between East Broadway and Grand Street were home to over 120,000 people, making it the most densely populated area in the city, comparable to Calcutta. The construction activity that was transforming Manhattan north of Fourteenth Street did little for the Bowery except drive up the rents. With the growing population and official neglect came related problems: primitive and inadequate sewage facilities, no citywide potable water system, erratic garbage removal. Without a dependable water supply, firefighting was often limited; urban fires were frequent and devastating (the Chicago Fire of 1871, which burned 2,124 acres, being the latest, and most disastrous, example). Bowery tenements in the 1870's, overcrowded wood frame structures, many without fire escapes, were often inaccessible to the Fire Department's horse-drawn steam fire engines, and therefore were firetraps of the worst kind.

The only structures more hazardous than the tenements were the theaters. The few existing fire laws were widely ignored and unenforced. Gas-jet illumination, flammable curtains and sets, narrow aisles, and packed seating made theater fires a terrifying and all-too-frequent occurrence. In December, 1872, Barnum's new Hippodrome on Fourteenth Street was completely razed, killing all of the animals except for two elephants and a camel. It was the third such fire in a Barnum house in eight years. On the evening of December 5, 1876, near the end of a performance of *The Two Orphans* at the Brooklyn Theatre, a kerosene lamp set fire to a piece of scenery. Spectators panicked and jammed the one narrow staircase to the main floor. Within minutes, the roof and walls collapsed. It was never known exactly how many died in the blaze, with estimates ranging between two hundred and three hundred. One out of four theaters built between 1872 and 1882 burned down.

"Little Germany," or "Dutchtown," centered at the intersections of Canal, Essex, and East Broadway in the heart of the Lower East Side, was the first distinctly Jewish neighborhood in New York. The Schoenfelds' first lodgings on Division Street were a block away. Two blocks north, in the thriving shopping district along Grand Street, the German Jews had established themselves as clothiers, milliners, and jewelers. East Broadway, Broome, and Chatham Streets were crowded with pawnshops and secondhand clothing stores. Enterprising retailers advertised "Broadway goods at Bowery prices." Shopping here was a war of wits. Virtuoso performances by the pawnbroker or salesman—haggling, cajoling, or deceiving customers—were daily occurrences, a matter of survival for the shopkeepers. Trying on a dress coat, the shopper was told, "it fits like der paper on der vall," not realizing that the salesman's friendly hand on his back was actually taking up the slack in the garment, or that the velvet cuffs were really wool treated with black shoe polish.

The Polish Jews of the "tailor's migration" in the 1870's had sound economic reasons for settling near the clothing establishments of the Dutchtown merchants. Garment manufacture was a cottage industry; the people who cut and sewed the clothes worked out of their own dwellings, picking up raw materials and delivering the finished goods on foot.[1] Large families such as the Schoenfelds were the ideal business unit. Every member of the family over twelve had a task: the father and older brother were cutters, bundlers, and machine operators; the mother (in addition to doing housework and caring for young children) did the sewing and finishing work with the older daughters, though women later became machine operators as well; the younger boys did basting and pressing, as well as pickups and deliveries. The father/boss would contract with a Grand Street merchant to convert bundles of cloth into ready-made clothing—knee pants, for example—for a set price. With luck and hard work, the tailor would become a contractor who hired other immigrants to work for him.

At the time of the Schoenfelds' arrival in 1872, various German dialects had begun to overwhelm the Irish brogue in the neighborhoods east of the Bowery. Over half of the storefronts in the area displayed signs in German or German and English. By the end of the decade, German expressions—gabfest, plunderbund, it listens well, bum, dumb (as in "stupid")—began to show up in everyday American usage. The Jewish quarter was expanding along East Broadway as far as Clinton Street to the east, Delancey to the north, and Madison to the south. The rest of the Bowery was still firmly in the grips of the Irish and German Gentiles.

Solomon Schoenfeld set up his sweatshop in the family's three-room apartment on Division Street. His specialty was known in the trade as *bigelling* ("altering") pants. The kitchen and living room were used as workrooms, with a gasoline stove to keep the pressing irons hot and ready for use. The gasoline fumes mingled with the odors wafting up the stairwell from the basement privies and uncollected garbage below. Even in the most sweltering days of summer, the windows stayed closed because the stench was considered to be less tolerable than the heat. Window space was reserved for the sewing machines. Piles of finished and half-sewn garments covered the floor, the chairs, and the table. By midday, the faces and hands of everyone in the apartment would be black from working with the cloth.

The Schoenfeld boys were immediately enrolled in public school. When they were not in school, the eldest sons, Max and Abel, were expected to help with the business. Sarah had her hands full supervising little Henry and caring for the newest family member, Charles, who was born shortly after their arrival in New York. Six-year-old Moses attended the Henry Street School, where a teacher (always a woman) was customarily put in charge of a class of fifty to a hundred children, many of them unable to speak English. A born mimic, eager to impress his new classmates, Moses picked up English quickly, and was equally quick to learn to imitate the various dialects and street argot of the different ethnic groups that settled in the Bowery: each with their own vernacular, their own version of English. On any given day in the Bowery—at school or in the streets—Moses could witness the miscommunications and frayed tempers of people whose only common denominator was their idiosyncratic grasp of English.

To discover the source of Lew Fields' comedy style—his knack for cultural and ethnic pastiche—one must begin with the language of his early childhood. The Yiddish he spoke as a boy in New York was a hybrid of German, Hebrew, Polish, Russian, and Bowery English, a street tongue with a special capacity for self-mockery and contentiousness. His Bowery childhood was living proof that pastiche is a gift of peoples who live in culturally ambivalent situations.[2] He did not have to leave the apartment to hear the kind of hashed grammar and unintended word-play that became a comic device for the Mike and Meyer routines. Dinner at the Schoenfelds' provided examples in abundance, particularly when the children tried to explain to their parents an unfamiliar activity: baseball, or chewing gum, or a new bit of American slang. The hidden values of language—how it was used and abused, and by whom—were lessons that young Moses Schoenfeld learned early and never forgot. Moses never did complete grammar school, but the adult Lew Fields surprised and impressed interviewers with the genteel, unaccented English he used offstage.

The schools of the era took immediate steps to hasten the Americanization of foreign-born students. When the teachers or administrators recorded the children's names, the spelling and often the pronunciation were "simplified" to suit American ears. Children were assigned, or allowed to choose, "Christian" names, whether or not they were Christians. In the Schoenfeld family, Marx became Max, Abel became Sol, and Moses, for reasons unknown, assumed the name Lewis Maurice. As the children became accustomed to their new names, it was not unusual for their parents to start using the children's new last name. Thus, Schoenfeld became Schanfield or Shanfield; all three variants of the family name were used by family members and appeared in the New York directories between 1878 and 1890. Father used a different spelling than son, who spelled it differently from his brothers. As another Lower East Sider explained it, "We honor our fathers just as much, even if we drop their names. Nothing good ever came to us while we bore them; possibly we'll have more luck with the new names."

Shortly after the Schoenfelds' arrival, in September, 1873, a series of bank failures caused by the collapse of the bank of Jay Cooke and Company led to a panic on Wall Street (known thenceforth as the Panic of '73). The underlying causes—overspeculation in railroad securities, the widespread practice of selling watered-down stocks for public service companies—guaranteed a depression following the panic. The country would not fully recover for six years, during which time a half-million workers were unemployed, and immigration slowed to its lowest point since 1862. The depression brought out latent anti-Semitism, as populist politicians and preachers fulminated against the "gold conspiracy" and the "usurers" and the Wall Street Jews who were supposedly behind it. Affluent Jews discovered that wealth and sophistication were not enough to entitle them to a place in fashionable New York society.

In the Bowery, hundreds of retail shops and small businesses closed, to be replaced by all manner of cheap diversions: saloons specializing in five-cent whiskey, faro houses, shooting galleries, and dance halls. Almost daily, Lew or his brothers would return home with news of another neighborhood business or shop closing down: in the Bowery argot, "Peter Funk's takin' over Mr. So-and-so's." "Peter Funk" was a generic term for a kind of bankruptcy auction, organized by opportunistic bands of hustlers to sell off a store's stock or a pawnbroker's unredeemed pledges. The auctions were crowded, raucous affairs, a combination of scam and sideshow. The relationship between seller and buyer echoed the interplay between the slicker and dupe (straight man and comic) on the variety stage. The Peter Funk auctions were an irresistible attraction to the local children, especially since they did not charge an admission fee.

The fact that Solomon Schanfield had no shop of his own, and no employees except his sons, may have actually helped his business survive the six years of depression following the Panic of '73. By the mid-'70's, Lew's older brothers, Max and Solly, worked full-time with their father, and Lew (not yet ten years old) was expected to help when he was not at school. Lew preferred tasks that took him out of the sweatshop and allowed him to observe the tumult of the streets: running errands, picking up and delivering bundles of finished clothing. Once on the street, Lew would inevitably get distracted from his original purpose. Undependable as an errand boy and too young to be much help in the sweatshop, Lew earned small change working for street vendors.

Like many immigrant families, they moved frequently, sometimes two or more times in a year, to better quarters when business improved—a front apartment, or a cleaner building. When business was bad, they would take in boarders. It was not unusual for landlords to find some desperate souls willing to pay a higher rent than the current tenants, so the current tenants were turned out if they were not willing to match the higher rent. ("You've been trown' out in the street so much," an old Weber & Fields joke began, "dat your mother's made curtains vot match the sidewalk.")

As a result of one of these moves, Lew transferred to Public School Number 42, on Allen Street, a noisy and narrow thoroughfare in the heart of Little Germany, with three or more saloons on every block and a reputation as one of the city's most notorious red-light districts. Lew's best friend, Morris ("Joe") Weber, lived several blocks away, on Essex Street, in an apartment beneath a saloon. Joe also came from a large family—he was the youngest of thirteen children—and being only six months older than Lew, he also still enjoyed relative freedom from the responsibilities imposed on the older siblings. The fact that the Webers were *landsmen* strengthened the bond.

Joe's father was a kosher butcher—a *schechter*—paid by the head for the chickens he slaughtered and prepared. This messy task was performed in the Webers' apartment, making it even less habitable as living quarters than the Shanfields'. The *schechter* was a lay-officer of the synagogue, addressed as "Rabbi." Joe's father took his position, and life in general, very seriously; he had the habit of preaching to his family as if they were his congregation. Rabbi Weber did not approve of a son who wanted to make his livelihood "making foolish people laugh." Fortunately, Joe was able to win over his mother with the help of his older brother. Max, or "Muck," as he was affectionately called, was Joe's protector, much respected in the neighborhood for his skill as a boxer. Muck taught Joe how to throw a punch, and he stepped in whenever Joe's smart remarks led to physical confrontations. Muck bought Joe his first pair of dancing clogs. In the years to come, he would be Joe's closest advisor.

It was as would-be performers that Lew Schanfield and Joe Weber first met, watching a clog-dancing match between classmates on the playground of the Henry Street School. The eight-year-old Lew admired Joe from the first time he saw him. Though only six months older, Joe was almost six inches taller, with sparkling blue eyes, a sharp tongue, and the kind of street smarts that city kids respect. At their first encounter, Joe was smoking a cigarette with adult ease. Lew tried to imitate him but it made him sick. This made him admire Joe even more.

To impress Joe, Lew knocked the clog dancers and bragged that he could do better: he could dance on a plate without breaking it. The rest of the boys scoffed at this, and Weber likewise ignored it. Fields repeated his preposterous claim whenever a group of his clog-fancying classmates got together. Eventually he had made the boast so often that he believed it himself. Finally, Weber took him up on it. In the hallway of his tenement, Lew was put to the test. He broke the first plate he stepped on; then four more in identical fashion. Hearing his comings and goings, his mother became suspicious. Upon seeing the fate of the family china, she burst into tears and led Lew away. Joe stayed long enough to hear Lew get a licking.

"I thought Lew was young, and I patronized him," explained Weber regarding their first encounter. "I always thought he was a good-looking fellow. He had fine eyes and teeth, and a warming kind of smile, a regular heart breaker."[3]

"Child's play" on the Lower East Side was something that occurred behind the local cop's back, amid piles of garbage, on rotted wood sidewalks and unpaved streets clogged with traffic. Hawkers sold all kinds of eatables: ginger cakes; hot corn on the cob slathered with rancid butter or oleo from a rag-wrapped stick; raw oysters, a penny apiece, sprinkled with hot pepper sauce. The discarded corncobs, oyster shells, and pigs' knuckles were handy missiles for the youth gangs. Other favorite pastimes included shooting craps, filching vendors' goods, and running errands for shady characters—gamblers, fences, and prostitutes.

Every neighborhood had its gangs, some relatively benign (younger boys protecting their patch of sidewalk), and a few positively lethal (the Whyos, for example, who specialized in burglary and murder for hire). Jews who ventured out of Dutchtown were favorite targets of gangs of Irish and German youths. A trip to the bathhouse or a favorite amusement spot was like running the gauntlet.

Even if the gang's primary purpose was not criminal, the opportunities and incentives to mischief were often overwhelming. The neighborhood kids who chose not to run with the pack—or whose parents were strong enough to forbid it— still had to make arrangements to stay in the gang's good graces. If you were not quick with your fists, or inclined to criminal activities, you needed something else of value to ransom for your safety. To be able to clown, to deliver a barbed insult at the right target, to perform daredevil stunts, were valuable talents that might make you somebody worth protecting. If you were good enough, your street skills could become a marketable commodity, an alternative to the sweatshop or manual labor or crime. The wisecrack, the impertinent retort, the pratfall, and the mischievous prank were the Bowery's version of witty repartee and refined humor. Do the same thing on stage, in costume and dialect, learn a few dance steps, and these crude street skills become the basis of vaudeville: knockabout comedy, the sidewalk dialogue, the one-liner, the topical jest.

The everyday experiences of life on the Bowery provided Lew Fields with his earliest comic inspirations. The Bowery in the 1870's and '80's was a fertile ground for observing humanity at its best and its worst, provided that the observer was resilient enough to withstand its pervasive despair and corruption. For its beleaguered denizens, bullying, exploitation, and physical cruelty were an inescapable part of their daily lives, whether it was the neighborhood gang beating up an outsider or news of Gould and Vanderbilt crushing a competitor; a prostitute drugging a john with knockout drops, Boss Tweed's cronies collecting protection money, a cabbie abusing his horse, or a sweatshop contractor exploiting child labor.

"In New York," wrote William Dean Howells in *A Hazard of New Fortunes*, "one gets life in curious slices." In the Bowery, the "curious slices" were especially cruel and raw, and the Bowery dwellers' diversions reflected their harsh circumstances. Faced with a semiliterate audience with no common cultural heritage, often lacking even a common language, Bowery entertainers took their sordid realities and gave them a comic or sensational twist. The audience's limited comprehension of English, as well as their generally intoxicated condition, meant that the jokes and stories had to be sledgehammered home. News stories from the tabloid *The New York Weekly* were dramatized on stage, museums displayed re-creations of bloody crimes. Showman Tony Pastor made a name for himself singing satirical songs. An early Harrigan & Hart sketch, "The Donovans," was based on a famous kidnapping. Harrigan, a native son of the Bowery, developed comedy sketches set against a background of New York immigrant culture and machine politics.

Not surprisingly, the entertainments usually included a dose of wishful thinking to vitiate the harsh actualities. The Old Bowery Theatre, for example, presented a life of General Custer, in which the villain Sitting Bull was killed in a knife fight with an apocryphal character named Daring Bill. The appetite for stage melodramas and dime novels revealed the desperate need for a few fleeting moments of an orderly moral universe where virtue was always rewarded and evil punished. A desire to see justice served right away—a more corrosive and merciless brand of justice—was behind the Bowery's favorite humor as well. The same cruel and curious slices of Broadway life that inspired Harrigan, Pastor, and teams of Irish knockabout comedians also shaped the comedy methods of Weber & Fields. In a 1912 article called "Adventures in Human Nature," they explained the impulse behind their humor:

> Human nature . . . is such a curious thing that it will invariably find cause for extreme mirth in seeing some other fellow being made a fool of, no matter who that fellow may be. . . . We figured it out, in the first place, that nothing pleased a man much more than when he saw another man being made to look silly in the eyes of others. . . .
>
> As for the quirk of human nature that shows great gratification at the sight of a man betting something when he is bound to be a loser: in inelegant language, this relates simple to the universal impulse to laugh at a "sucker." It is just like standing in front of a sideshow tent after you have paid your good money, gone in, and been "stung," and laughing at everyone else who pays his good money, comes out, and has been equally stung.[4]

Those who laugh loudest at the sucker are the ones who have been duped themselves. Fear of being duped and scorn for those who were—Bowery audiences experienced both sides on an almost daily basis.

The two primary components of Weber & Fields' comedy—slapstick and satire—appealed to the audience's desire to see differences ridiculed and pretensions deflated. The difference between the outright violence of the poke in the eye or boot to the rear (early Weber & Fields knockabout) and the spoofs of David Belasco, Clyde Fitch, and topical issues (from the Weber & Fields Music Hall) was only a matter of degree. As seen through immigrants' eyes, slapstick redressed the cruelties of city life, and satire demystified its pleasures.

Ridicule was inevitable when the very act of speaking made one sound foolish. Dialect humor was the collision of slapstick and satire in the realm of spoken language. At any moment, the speaker's clumsiness might result in an embarrassing slip, an unintended insult, or gross gestures of frustration. An early Weber & Fields routine (circa 1884) capitalized on the immigrant's simultaneous struggle with an intractable new language and an unfamiliar metropolis where even the street names are a source of frustration. Quite possibly, the street in question—Watt Street—initially caused some confusion for the comedians themselves.

WEBER: *(in dialect)* . . . So you tell me where you work, I'll come and pick you up and we'll go have lunch together.

FIELDS: *(in dialect)* That would be wonderful.

WEBER: So tell me the street you work on, I'll come and pick you up.

FIELDS: Watt Street.

WEBER: The street you work on. So I come pick you up, we go have lunch.

FIELDS: Watt Street.

WEBER: The street you're working on.

FIELDS: Watt Street.

WEBER: *(nervously)* Why don't you tell me what street you're working on?

FIELDS: I'm telling you.

WEBER: You're not telling me, you're asking me!

FIELDS: Oh, I see. Look, when I say "Watt Street," I don't mean "What street?" I mean "Watt Street."

WEBER: Ohh-h-h—Look, when I say you're crazy, I don't mean you're insane, I mean you're nuts!—that's what you are.

FIELDS: Now take it easy. Be calm. . . .

The best intentions of the two pals are undone by the booby traps in their adoptive language. Instead of a friendly lunch, they have a fight. Over half a century separates "Watt Street" from Abbott and Costello's famous "Who's on First?" routine, but the basic comic device and progression are the same. The only difference is that the comic misunderstanding in "Watt Street" is predicated on the characters' limited command of English.

Another Weber & Fields routine, from the same era, was built around the confusion over the homonyms *die/dye:*

WEBER: You got a good job?

FIELDS: Pretty good.

WEBER: What are you doing?

FIELDS: I'm dyeing.

WEBER: *(slow, blinking take)* You look good. . . .

Which develops into:

WEBER: *(incredulous)* You mean I gotta belong to the union to die?

FIELDS: Sure. You want to dye a scab?

WEBER: I'll die any way I want to!

FIELDS: You may dye, but we won't recognize you. . . .[5]

The emphasis here is on a comic exaggeration of everyday life, not on snappy one-liners or physical buffoonery. The topical references to unions were also of immediate interest to their audience.

In addition to his clog-dancing abilities, Joe Weber demonstrated an early talent for business. One Sunday he asked his mother to bake some gingersnaps, which he and Lew, dressed like street urchins, took uptown to sell. Weber imitated a stutterer—"P-please b-buy my gingers-n-naps"—while little Lew, with his big, sad, brown eyes, would silently hold out a dirty hand. The charade proved to be particularly effective with the ladies. Unofficially, it was their first paid performance as a team. After a few of these Sunday performances, the part-time jobs in the tailor shop and the cigarette factory (where Joe worked) began to seem like intolerable drudgery.

Lew used his spare pennies to bribe older boys to teach him dance steps and tumbling tricks, which he would practice with Joe on the family's mattresses, on wooden plank sidewalks, and at school. That last habit made them popular with their classmates at the Allen Street School, but did not endear them to their teachers. Lew demonstrated his new tricks while the teacher's back was turned. One day—when he was doing back flips—he was caught in mid-air. For a similar stunt, Joe's teacher demanded that his mother accompany him to class the next day. The following morning, when the teacher asked after Mrs. Weber, Joe replied, "She is sick in bed, teacher, but she sent her picture," whereupon he produced her photo.

"We were comedians at recess, and couldn't stop when we got in line," explained Weber. "The children would keep on laughing," said Fields. As for the corporal punishment that invariably followed such stunts, the boys had already learned a basic slapstick technique to minimize the damage: "Their [the teachers'] touch was light. We backed up to it." For diligently practicing their future occupation, Joe and Lew were expelled from the fourth grade at the Allen Street School.

Joe and Lew now had the run of the streets, and their real education began in earnest. Their usual activities fell into either of two complementary categories: first choice was going to dime museums, minstrel shows, or melodramas (sneaking in whenever possible); and their next choice was dreaming up ways to make money to indulge their first-choice activity. Lew got a job tending a sidewalk soda-water fountain for a man named Gump; combined with the money from their ginger enterprise, they saved the four dollars they needed to buy their own clogs. And when the boys were desperate for the price of admission to see a local favorite (known for his impressions of Pat Rooney and other celebrities), Joe masterminded a scam that took advantage of Lew's position to raise the necessary funds. Gump's fountain sold a half glass of soda for one cent, a whole glass for two, and with milk, three cents. Joe, over the course of a morning, repeatedly patronized Lew's fountain, ordering a half glass each time; Lew went through the motions of making change and returned to Joe two cents. When Joe could stomach no more, Lew made up an excuse to leave and appointed Joe as his stand-in. After a decent interval, Lew returned—this time as a customer—and the operation was repeated, with Joe as the vendor. By the end of the day, they had enough for two gallery admissions to the National Theatre, and a bad case of nausea.

The price of admission included a comedy sketch, a melodrama, and three or four specialty acts. The curtain went up promptly at eight, and the show lasted until half-past midnight. Boys and young men would cluster around the gallery door for a half hour before it opened. The gallery usually filled in less than ten minutes, and the youths were demonstrative about their likes and dislikes: hissing, jeering, commenting, whistling at the actors as well as other members of the audience.

For two boys as stagestruck as Weber and Fields, it is reasonable to assume that they saw or heard about every theatrical event below Fourteenth Street from the early 1870's until they began touring extensively in the late 1880's. They searched out the saloons and boardinghouses frequented by actors, and waited outside, hoping to catch a glimpse of one of the local favorites. Once, they persuaded a bootblack to let them work at his shoeshine stand because a famous song-and-dance man was rumored to stop there, and they fought over who would have the privilege of shining his shoes. Fifteen years later, Fields dismissed the same song-and-dance man from his company—proof that you meet the same people on the way up as you do on the way down, and that the kid who fetches your coffee (or shines your shoes) today could be your boss tomorrow.

Despite their limited education and means, the young Weber and Fields' theatrical fare was not exclusively third-rate. In the mid-1870's, Edwin Booth performed Shakespeare at the Lyceum; the Kiralfys' staged *Around the World in Eighty Days* at the Academy of Music (on Fourteenth Street); J. K. Emmet portrayed a German immigrant in *Fritz, Our German Cousin*, a play-with-songs at Wallack's (Broadway and Thirteenth Street). Somehow, Joe and Lew managed to get a healthy dose of "legitimate" theater, though what impact it had on their future work is difficult to say. "We worked hard," recalled Weber, "determined all the time that we would both be great tragedians. Whenever we could save a few pennies we went to see Booth and Barrett and Salvini and the other great actors of those days. The fact that we appeared on the same bill as Jo-Jo the Dog-faced Boy did not prevent our hoping to play *Hamlet* some day."

By 1880, the theatrical center of New York had begun to move north of Fourteenth Street. Within a few blocks of Fourteenth Street, one could see opera, extravaganzas, Shakespeare, melodrama, minstrel shows, variety, and dime museums. It is in this crazy quilt of theatrical genres in the 1870's that we can begin to perceive the American popular theater of the next fifty years—vaudeville, musicals, and revues—taking shape. Here, too, we can glimpse the range of Lew Fields' earliest theatrical influences.

Looking back at his pre-professional days, Fields' most vivid memories were of the musical extravaganzas. *The Black Crook* premiered at Niblo's in 1866, and enjoyed numerous revivals throughout the next two decades. It was a hybrid creation that combined a second-rate adaptation of Carl Maria von Weber's romantic opera *Der Freishutz* with dancing by the Great Parisian Ballet Troupe. What is often considered to be a breakthrough in the development of the American musical was actually the result of a theater fire: the ballet troupe had been booked into the Academy of Music, but the theater's destruction forced the desperate managers to seek alternatives. They persuaded the manager of Niblo's Garden to absorb the ballet troupe into the melodrama that was being staged there. The resulting spectacle was over five hours long; the story was humorless, the characterizations wooden, and the songs undistinguished. And for immigrant boys just a few years off the boat, the spectacle's overblown Victorian dialogue could not have been too easy to follow. None of that seemed to matter to Joe and Lew, nor did it lessen the general public's enthusiasm. *The Black Crook's* ballet was the thing, with its buxom girls in flesh-colored tights and its romantic choreography, interspersed with as many as one hundred pretty chorus girls marching in precise drills known as "Amazon marches." Male theatergoers could savor the undraped, uncrinolined female form without having to go to a disreputable Bowery variety house or a concert saloon. Religious and civic leaders sounded dire warnings, proclaiming that to see *The Black Crook* was to risk spiritual and social damnation. *The Black Crook* was revived almost annually throughout the 1870's and 1880's.

More daring than *The Black Crook* and more pointedly satiric, the Lydia Thompson Burlesque Company featured four English beauties in songs, dances, skits, and tights. In a city of brunettes, Thompson's troupe were all radiant blondes. They not only looked good in tight trousers, they could also clown and sing. *Ixion; or, The Man at the Wheel* was a tongue-in-cheek retelling of a recent play about a man tied for eternity to a revolving wheel as punishment for pursuing a goddess. Filled with irreverent asides and satirical references to recent plays and topical events, *Ixion* and its successors *The Forty Thieves* and *Sinbad* fit the traditional definition of "burlesque." But the genre's inherent playfulness and the implied intimacy of the audience only served to amplify the moral objections to its "promiscuous" display of the female form. In 1868, an outraged theatergoer wrote *The New York Times:* "Look at the glaring and flaunting spectacular shows! Look at the sensual exhibitions of the feminine form! Listen to the salacious music! See the appeals to the sensational and the pandering to the base and vulgar elements of human nature! . . . Who will deny that these things are immensely damaging to the public taste and terribly ruinous to the public morals? Who will estimate all the baneful influences they exert upon the life and character of the people?"[6] Thus the fortunes of Thompson and her players were guaranteed. The vilification of the entertainment helped assure a record-breaking run.

More significantly, the moral flavor surrounding the British Blondes forever changed the connotations of "burlesque" as a label for popular entertainment. Combining beauty, comic talent, and personal charm, Thompson's blonde burlesquers were the prototypical "show girls" of the sort who would be celebrated twenty-five year later in the chorus line at Weber & Fields' Music Hall.

Together or individually, the members of Lydia Thompson's quartet were popular attractions throughout the 1870's. Of course, it is doubtful that as nine-year-olds Joe and Lew appreciated the displays of feminine pulchritude, but the publicity it generated and its immediate influence on popular stage styles were inescapable. Frowzier imitations of the Lydia Thompson formula became mainstays of the dime museum and variety stages. One of these imitators, the Adah Richmond Burlesque Company provided Weber & Fields with one of their earliest gigs.

The depression that followed the Panic of '73 took its toll of the New York theatrical scene as well. Hardest hit were the minstrel shows. Once the most popular form of entertainment, it had dwindled by 1875 to one permanent company, the San Francisco Minstrels. Some commentators have tried to explain this with the observation that plantation life and slavery, which minstrelsy was based on, had become too remote for city audiences to serve as a source of humor. Yet many elements of the minstrel show survived in variety virtually intact: blackface teams such as McIntyre & Heath and Montgomery & Stone were among vaudeville's most enduring acts; clog dancing, the "cake walk," the banter between straight man and comic; the afterpiece at the end of the program became essential ingredients for variety shows. Whether or not it existed as an independent economic entity, minstrelsy survived in the heart of vaudeville and musical comedy, just as the blues form survives in the heart of jazz and rock 'n' roll.

To New York audiences in the 1870's and '80's, the blackface comedian was just another dialect act along with the Irish and Dutch acts. The most successful stage comedians of the day, Harrigan & Hart, were proficient in all three; others attempted to follow suit. As Weber & Fields' early performances demonstrate, much of the same material could be used in all three dialects. Outside of New York, minstrel shows continued to be popular, even in cities (Philadelphia, St. Louis, and San Francisco, for example). The touring minstrel troupes became a valuable training ground for the next generation of vaudeville and musical performers, including Harrigan & Hart, Weber & Fields, Francis Wilson, Eddie Foy, and Eddie Leonard.

Variety halls of the period were decidedly unsavory places—little more than saloons with live entertainment. "Dumps, slabs and honky-tonks" was how Douglas Gilbert, in *American Vaudeville*, referred to them, places where "roughhouse turns and afterpieces were smuttily 'blued' to amuse the tosspots, strumpets, dark-alley lads, and slummers who in those years made up variety audiences from Boston to San Francisco." Not every act, however, used risqué dialogue or songs, and not all the afterpieces were obscene. To some extent, variety's sinister reputation was based on prejudicial assumptions about its audience by "proper" New Yorkers. Newspapers warned that unaccompanied women daring to venture into a variety house were easy targets for pickpockets, "mashers," and "white slavers." Gentlemen were warned about gold-digging actresses who invited the amorous attentions of an affluent male and then blackmailed him with the threat of a "breach of promise" suit and public exposure.

Tony Pastor, a devout Catholic and a family man, was not proud of variety's low reputation. Born in New York City in 1832, Antonio Pastor made his debut as a singer at age fourteen at Barnum's Museum. After spending his early years in minstrel shows and circuses as a singer, acrobat, and ringmaster, Tony Pastor opened his first music hall, at 444 Broadway, around 1861. Regulars called it the "444," and Pastor's reluctance to discuss it later in his life suggests that he was ashamed of its notoriety. In 1865, he took over Volk's Garden at 201 Bowery, renamed it "Tony Pastor's Opera House," and presented the best of the new variety artists: Harrigan & Hart, Gus Williams, Jefferson DeAngelis, Nat Goodwin. Pastor appeared on the bill singing original songs about patriotism, home, and the virtues of the simple life, as well as topical numbers culled from newspaper headlines and the latest fads: "The Great Atlantic Cable," for example, or the "Waterfall" hairstyle. (At least one of these songs—"Down in a Coal Mine"— became a barroom standard.) He claimed to know fifteen hundred songs, singable on request, and at the appropriate moment he'd say, "Now, folks, join in the chorus." Although his Opera House at 201 Bowery included a bar, he forbade rowdy and bawdy behavior. He also made a policy of booking the best young talent available. In 1872, this had included the minstrel show headed by Edward Harrigan and Tony Hart. The emphasis at Pastor's was on comedy, dancing, songs, and sketches—no bare-knuckle prize fights, human oddities, or lewd women. It was at Tony Pastor's that young hopefuls like Joe Weber and Lew Fields could see the pros at work: Gus Williams, one of the first "Dutch" comedians, doing his nutty German dialect act; Georgina Smithson, "The Gainsborough Girl"; Johnny Wild, a blackface performer known as "the coon dandy"; and other prominent minstrel men. In the mid-'seventies, Pastor also presented the Kernell brothers (Harry and John) in their sidewalk conversations, and the first "Hebrew" comedian, Frank Bush. It is safe to assume that Joe and Lew did not dare to think that they would one day employ some of the stars that wowed 'em at Pastor's.

Even before he opened his New Fourteenth Street Theatre in 1881, Pastor was one of the most popular showmen since Barnum. A bouncy, jovial man with a fireplug build and sparkling black eyes, Pastor would greet his patrons at the door, calling the regulars by name and asking about their children. With his waxed black mustache, tall boots, silk top hat and black overcoat, he was an immediately recognizable figure to two generations of theatergoers. Because he considered himself a performer first and then a manager, he was extremely sympathetic to actors. Actors loved Pastor, despite his reputation for paying cut-rate salaries. He was a notoriously soft touch for actors who were ailing or otherwise down on their luck, and he never closed an act before the end of its contracted run. To get acts for a pittance, he encouraged promising youngsters and unknowns. With the experience and exposure of playing at Pastor's, many of them went on to become famous on their own: Harrigan & Hart, Jennie Yeamans, Lillian Russell, Weber & Fields, the Four Cohans, and Montgomery & Stone, to name but a few.

"Now, folks, don't be nervous about the place and don't overwork," was Pastor's advice to young performers. "Why, jiminetty, the audience out there are just people same as every place else. I know you're all right and I'm glad to have you here."[7] It is difficult to imagine a similar sentiment coming from B. F. Keith, Ed Albee, or Abe Erlanger—the moguls who made millions on Pastor's invention.

If any single theatrical figure could be said to embody the qualities that the young Weber and Fields admired, it was Pastor. Pastor's progress—from the bawdy nights at the "444" to the Ladies' Matinees at the New Fourteenth Street Theatre—was a moral lesson to the aspiring performers and managers of the 'seventies and 'eighties. Pastor proved that a straight, clean variety show could turn a profit. His move was actually a calculated bid to double his profits by attracting respectable men *and* women: what was referred to as the "carriage trade." The wholesomeness of the entertainment also appealed to immigrant families offended by the typical variety and dime museum fare. The quality of the comedy, singing, and dancing was good enough to keep the "swells" and "sports" happy, even without the blue material. After Pastor shut down the barroom and banned smoking and obscenities in 1881, the audience that Joe and Lew saw at Pastor's represented the widest cross-section of New Yorkers that they would be likely to see at any theatrical event until the heyday of their own Music Hall at the turn of the century.

Though he risked losing the cruder and more customary members of his audience, Pastor made a deliberate choice to promote respectability and decency in popular theater. By making the theater environment safe and attractive, and the stage material decent within the standards of middle-class propriety, Pastor also improved the moral complexion of those who performed there. His was an early and sincere effort to establish the professional and social legitimacy of the popular entertainer: he insisted on calling them "artists." Pastor's crusade raised essential issues of respectability, decency, and the nature of the audience that would preoccupy Lew Fields for most of his career.

Of course, most of the variety houses in the late 'seventies found it easier to turn a profit without Pastor's pretensions to quality and decency. Variety-style entertainments were becoming "smart"; throughout the country, empty store-fronts, barns, even churches, were hastily converted into variety halls (with bars), concert saloons (with entertainment) and dime museums. North of Chatham Square, the Bowery was now densely lined with un-Pastorized fun spots. The years between 1875 and 1881 witnessed the opening of many of the music halls and museums frequented by Weber & Fields: Harry Miner's Bowery Theater, the London, the Globe Museum, Bunnell's Museum, Koster and Bial's (at Twenty-third and Sixth Avenue), and Hyde and Behman's (on Adams Street, in Brooklyn).

One of the most remarkable of these low-class variety houses was the Grand Duke's Concert Hall, located in a basement beneath a beer dive at 21 Baxter Street. The neighborhood, only a few blocks west of Chatham Square, was known as Five Points, and it contained what were considered to be the most wretched slums in the New World: streets nicknamed "Ragpickers' Row" and "Bottle Alley," rookeries where the people were packed together in filthy, decrepit buildings. Here even the police feared to go. In the midst of this hellhole was "The Grand Dook," as it was called by its patrons, a Dickensian haven for the tough young would-be performers of the Bowery. A visitor described it as follows:

> The establishment is managed and controlled by boys, and the audiences consist chiefly of bootblacks, newsboys, and the juvenile denizens of the east side of the city, ranging in age from three to 20 years. The company is composed of youths yet in their teens, and the performances are of the blood-and-thunder order, interspersed with "variety acts" of a startling description. The house and its appointments are primitive, and the stage and scenery equally so. . . . The manager acts as his own policeman, and enforces order by punching heads of disorderly spectators, or by summarily ejecting them. The performances are crude, but they satisfy the audience. . . .[8]

The Grand Duke was the pride and joy of an infamous juvenile gang, the Baxter Street Dudes, led by an angelic-looking tough known as Baby-Face Willie. The Dudes produced on the cheap, stealing whatever they needed from Bowery theaters and merchants. Admission was ten cents, or "swag" of greater value, and the theater was a favorite resort of street boys from all parts of the city.[9]

Joe and Lew were occasionally a part of the audience, and it provided them with a convenient way to measure themselves against the local competition, to see what "went over" and perhaps even find out how it was done. One of the

performers was an English boy named Sam Bernard, who at the time was performing in an Irish or German act with his brother Dick. Bernard was born Barnett, but a printer mangled his name on a program, and the young performer
decided to keep it. While many Irish, Jewish, and Italian immigrants Anglicized
their names to go on the stage, Bernard was perhaps the sole example of an actor
who changed his name to something more ethnic-sounding. Sam Bernard's career
paralleled Weber's and Fields' through dime museums and vaudeville into musicals and movies. He became their lifelong friend and occasional collaborator.

Other juvenile gangs were jealous of the Grand Duke's success, and bombarded the theater with stones at performance time. Scarcely a night passed without a fight. One of these gangs recruited Weber & Fields as rivals to Sam and
Dick Bernard to be featured in a makeshift playhouse in a cellar in their own
neighborhood.

The museums that sprang up along the Bowery in the 1870's and 1880's were
neither as grand as Barnum's nor as constrained by their audience to provide
moral justifications for amusement. George Bunnell's Museum, at 103–105 Bowery, was one of the most successful of the Bowery museums, and a favorite of
Joe and Lew's. In the fall of 1876, Bunnell's Museum opened its doors with an
innovative policy of reduced admission and a complete variety bill for an additional nickel. The opening attractions included "A Grand Poultry Show," a tattooed man, and "the Double-Brained Child" (the only evidence of this being the
boy's abnormally large head). A subsequent attraction, recalled by Weber and
Fields, was "Old Zip," who was introduced by the lecturer, Professor Hutchings,
as "the connecting link between human and ape creation." (Old Zip, incidentally,
continued to be a popular freak-show attraction into the 1920's.) The featured
exhibit at Bunnell's was Dante's Inferno, a garishly lit waxwork assembly of sinners that included models of Boss Tweed, Jay Gould, an infamous ax murderer,
and a rival museum owner. But it was the variety bill accompanying the curiosities that ultimately proved to be the most popular.

Bunnell's stage was too cramped and primitive to present some of the big
circus-style acts and spectacles that played at Barnum's. Wisely, Bunnell used the
forced intimacy of his theatorium for "artists" and acrobats. The typical bill consisted of anywhere from four to seven acts, with some performers doubling up
in comedy sketches or, on occasion, changing costumes and appearing under a
different name. The program ended with an afterpiece, a convention borrowed
from the minstrel show and usually done in blackface. In just over three years,
Bunnell's hybrid of freak show, curios, and variety bill had become profitable
enough to justify moving the museum to a larger building on Broadway at Ninth
Street. There, he was able to attract a classier audience.

By the end of the 1870's, the Schanfield family could occasionally afford to
spend a few cents on something besides the bare necessities—a trip to a beer
garden perhaps, or one of the shooting galleries that lined the Bowery. With the
help of Max, Solly, and sometimes Lew, Papa Schanfield's tailoring business would
bring in as much as twenty-five dollars a week in a good week. In the Bowery,
this would have been considered affluence had there not been so many mouths
to feed. There were now six children, and Sarah was pregnant with their seventh.

The Bowery in 1879, looking south from the "El" station at Canal Street. The entertainment at the Thalia (the old Bowery Theater) and the Atlantic Garden reflected the recent influx of German immigrants to the Lower East Side. *(Museum of the City of New York)*

The Allen or Chrystie Street Public School in the late 1880's. Weber & Fields' first audience, when the teacher's back was turned, Joe and Lew did backflips to amuse their classmates. *(Museum of the City of New York)*

The young entrepreneurs (age 11 or 12) in their earliest known photo (around 1879), emulating established entertainers like Harrigan & Hart and McIntyre & Heath. *(Special Collections Library, University of Southern California)*

"Night Scene in the Bowery in New York," from *Harper's Weekly*, 1881. At the entrance to a dime museum, the "outside talker" describes the wonders that lie within. *(Author's collection)*

"The Merry Partners," Edward Harrigan and Tony Hart. Their musical farces used broad ethnic comedy and catchy tunes to depict the scullery side of New York life. *(Albert Davis Collection, University of Texas)*

James McIntyre and Thomas Heath, the "Georgia Minstrels." A blackface team that was an important early influence on Weber & Fields and later toured in one of their vaudeville companies. *(Variety Arts Theater Library)*

Ethnic humor—blackface, Irish, German, Italian, and French—dominates an 1880 playbill from Tony Pastor's theater. As youngsters, Weber & Fields stayed in demand by using the same physical routines with different ethnic characterizations. *(Special Collections Library, University of Southern California)*

Tony Pastor, the beloved father of variety. He greeted his patrons by name, treated his performers with unprecedented respect, and transformed variety into clean, high-quality entertainment. *(Special Collections Library, University of Southern California)*

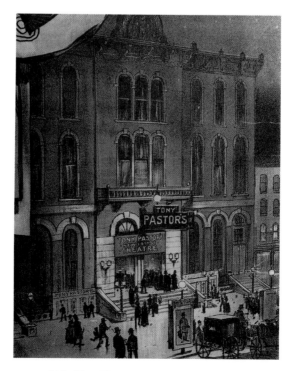

In 1881, Tony Pastor opened his New Fourteenth Street Theater in the Tammany Hall building in the heart of the shopping district. Pastor presented the best young talent of the day: Harrigan & Hart, Lillian Russell, May Irwin, John W. Kelly, and Weber & Fields. *(Special Collections Library, University of Southern California)*

John Carncross, proprietor of Carncross' Minstrels, in Philadelphia. When Weber & Fields' rough-and-tumble act flopped on his stage, he advised them to buy dress suits and shake hands at the end to reassure the audience they were friends. *(Albert Davis Collection, University of Texas)*

Gus Hill, champion club swinger and owner of Gus Hill's World of Novelties. As teen-agers, Weber & Fields toured in his company for two seasons, sometimes performing three different acts on the same bill. *(Albert Davis Collection, University of Texas)*

Weber & Fields' first company, 1889. Personnel included: James F. Hoey ("nut" comedian); Billy Emerson (blackface song-and-dance); Lottie Gilson (soubrette); the Garnella Family (acrobats); Staley and Burbeck (scenic quick changes); the Great Ronelles (trained birds). *(Albert Davis Collection, University of Texas)*

Benjamin Franklin Keith, vaudeville's overlord. With his partner E. F. Albee, he popularized "continuous vaudeville" and palatial theaters. Their United Booking Office was a monopoly that few performers could afford to defy. *(Special Collections Library, University of Southern California)*

When Keith's Colonial Theater opened in Boston in 1893, its architectural splendor and engineering sophistication surpassed most legit houses. Such settings made the entertainment presented within seem respectable and refined. *(Billy Rose Theater Collection, New York Public Library)*

Six-year-old Henry, unlike his three older brothers, showed little interest in theater, either as a performer or a spectator. The first American-born Schanfield, Charles, was now a chubby five-year-old; a daughter, Anna, was born in 1874.

It had now been almost two years since the clog-dancing contest in the schoolyard. In the September following their expulsion from fourth grade, after making sober promises to mend their ways, the boys were readmitted to school. Forbidden to perform for their classmates, they took advantage of lax truancy regulations to seek out new audiences whenever they needed to try out new material—on street corners, at the East River wharves, in livery stables, and in empty lots. Parental pressure dictated that Lew continue his part-time job at the soda stand, while Joe still had his job in the cigarette factory; neither the Webers nor the Schanfields could afford to be without the few dollars a week that the boys earned. Thus, the only way for Joe and Lew to further their theater education was to cut afternoon classes once or twice a week.

After watching a variety bill from the gallery of the London or the Bowery Theatre, Joe and Lew would rush over to the Webers' basement apartment on Essex to try to imitate what they had just seen. Using feather pillows as padding and mattresses to cushion the falls, Joe and Lew would re-create the Irish knockabout routines—the whacks with a shillelagh, the pugilistic bouts, the somersaults and flops—until soreness or Mrs. Weber stopped them. When they were ejected from the apartment, they rehearsed in the hayloft of a nearby livery stable. As they grew more confident, they moved on to more solid ground—dirt, and finally, cement. To practice their clog dancing, they used cellar doors, until the annoyed owners hammered nails across the doors, leaving the nailheads protruding by an inch or so. To practice their limited repertoire of songs, they made up lyrics to fit the tunes that they could remember.

Joe and Lew naturally picked the models that were closest at hand. In the mid-'seventies, comedy in the popular theater was almost exclusively ethnic. Blackface acts predominated, with Irish teams a close second. "Dutch" dialect acts were a recent and growing trend. Joe Laurie, Jr., the "Homer of vaudeville," summarized the historical development of ethnic comedy as follows, using the two-act (duo) as an example:

> The original two-man acts were in blackface, and really tried to portray the Negro in looks and dialect. They later worked as blackface comic and straight man. The next teams to win favor were the double Irish, with exaggerated make-ups; later they too began working as straight man and Irish comic. Then came the double Dutch acts; . . . they too followed the trend. . . . You will notice that the comic characters followed the pattern of our immigration. The last character two-man acts were Italian. . . .[10]

Despite the fact that Jews now made up almost ten percent of New York's population, the Jews—still overwhelmingly German in origin—were almost entirely absent from popular stage, and remained so until the 1890's, after the great influx of Eastern European Jews had already begun to reshape Jewish identity. It may be difficult for us to imagine American show business minus the participation of Jews—long before Irving Berlin, Jerome Kern, and Gershwin, the Shuberts, Goldwyn, Al Jolson, or Fanny Brice—but that was the social reality would-be actors Joe Weber and Lew Schanfield found themselves in. In the late 'seventies, the only "Hebe" comedians, as they were called, were Frank Bush, a monologist who appeared at Tony Pastor's wearing a plug hat, a gabardine, and a long pointed beard; Sam Curtis; and Howard & Thompson, none of whom was Jewish. It is important to note that despite similarities in the sound of the dialect, "Hebrew" referred to a comedy style whose characterizations (stereotypes, if you will) were distinct from the Dutch acts. Sheridan & Mack, for example, were the earliest "double-Dutch" act; they performed a sketch called "The Emigrants," which predates the Hebrew acts by more than a decade. Gus Williams, with his malapropisms and mangled German-English, was considered to be the best of the Dutch single acts; by 1880, he was appearing in full-length plays. In general, the vast majority of the Dutch acts (including Watson & Ellis, Murphy & Shannon, and Weber & Fields) did not hit the boards until the early 'eighties. Before 1890, a "Hebrew" act could not have survived on the road: the audience would not have been familiar with the stereotype. A change in slang usage to describe Weber and Fields' neighborhood was evidence that New Yorkers noticed the growing Jewish presence: before 1890, uptowners called it "Dutchtown"; after 1890, they called it "Jewtown."

Of the many blackface acts performing in the 1870's and 1880's, the most accomplished and enduring was McIntyre & Heath, who came together in a dialect two-act in 1874 and continued together as big-time draws for almost fifty years. Their skit, "The Ham Tree," featured Heath as Hennery, a big-mouthed know-it-all with a padded belly and threadbare dress clothes, and McIntyre as Alexander, a wiry stableboy with a reedy voice and a pessimistic demeanor. "The Ham Tree's" story line has Hennery luring Alexander away from his job at the livery stable to join a fly-by-night minstrel show. Unlike most of the Irish acts, their humor was primarily verbal, rather than physical, derived from the personality traits of the characters themselves.

By contrast, the Irish acts in the 'seventies were positively bruising. Even their songs were tough. Not for them the minstrel singer's romantic idylls 'neath the Southern moon; the Irish teams sang about manual labor, strikes, and payday. In the words of Douglas Gilbert, "these rough humors and characterizations conveyed nation-wide the scullery side of metropolitan life." The toughest (and it often followed, most popular) of the early Irish teams was Needham & Kelly, who did a song-and-clog-dance act. Their costumes consisted of Prince Albert coats, multicolored pants, bear-up plug hats, short side whiskers, and wooden shoes. Their song "The Roving Irish Gents" was a favorite with variety audiences in the 'seventies:

> Oh we are two rollicking roving Irish gentlemen, in the Pennsylvania
> quarries we belong,
> For a month or so we're working out in Idaho,
> For a month or so we're strikin' rather strong. . . .

After a verse and chorus of this, Needham & Kelly would break into a waltz clog or a hugely exaggerated and brutal sparring match that ended in "bumps"—insider's jargon for a series of hard falls on the head, neck, and shoulders. Not all of the Irish comedians played tough louts; Pat Rooney, Sr., began to make a reputation with his witty monologues, and John and Harry Kernell popularized crossfire dialogues and sidewalk conversations. Basically, they applied the comic devices of minstrelsy to Irish characters.

In 1877, Weber & Fields were busy ten-year-olds, diligently cribbing from the Irish and blackface acts that played at Bowery theaters. More important, they were also getting to know the Bowery audiences—what made them laugh, which acts were popular, and why. Even at this early stage, many of their decisions appear to have been based on their intuitive understanding of the Bowery audience.

The boys argued about the name for their act, and their billing. It was agreed that Joe, being the oldest, should have his name first. But a two-act called "Weber & Schanfield"? It sounded too foreign; it contained an ethnic label that would limit their appeal. The boys knew of several big-time and local actors named Fields. Perhaps Lew decided on "Fields" for the same reason that hundreds of other immigrants did: it was neutral and nonspecific, an all-purpose Americanization that worked equally well to domesticate the oddball names of Irish, Germans, and Eastern European Jews. It may have occurred to Lew that circumstances had tampered with his family name once already. Besides, it was customary for actors to change their names out of respect for their families.

In the 'seventies, it was not uncommon for private groups—political clubs, store employees, churches—to stage entertainments to raise money. The residents of "Dutchtown" were particularly fond of social clubs; the Saengerbunds, Maennerchors, Turnvereins, and Harmonie Bunds all sponsored weekend shows. Anybody who could afford the cost of printing handbills and renting a hall could stage a benefit. Two assembly halls had been built in the area expressly for the purpose of benefit entertainments and balls: Walhalla Hall, at Orchard and Grand Streets, built in 1868; and Turn Hall (short for *Turnverein*, "gymnastic club"), on East Fourth Street, built in 1871. (A decade later, Turn Hall was the site of the first performance of a Yiddish play in the United States). Admission was charged, but the beer and wine concessions generated most of the revenues. The stage, scenic equipment, and seating were often better than those of the local variety houses. It was at entertainments like these that many beginners and amateurs were given the chance to perform.

Weber & Fields' big break came when five young men from the neighborhood, calling themselves the Elks Serenaders, decided to stage a benefit for their social club. As luck would have it, one of Joe Weber's older sisters was being courted by a member of the Elks Serenaders' Social Club. Hearing that the club was sponsoring a benefit, Joe's sister convinced the club's entertainment chairman that Joe and Lew were a promising song-and-dance team. Their act was added to the "Host of Volunteers." Their pay was to be a quarter each and two complimentary tickets. With only a few days to perfect their routine, Joe and Lew still had to make a fundamental decision about their act. They knew how to do simple dance steps and some acrobatic rough-housing, but in what style? Should it be Irish, or blackface, or the new style, Dutch? Most accounts agree that the first stage appearance of Weber & Fields was at Turn Hall in 1877, but there is contradictory information—much of it from the performers themselves—regarding the type of act they presented. An interview in 1893 mentioned the Turn Hall engagement as being in blackface; interviews in 1904 and 1907 said their first performance was an Irish act; at the time of their 1912 reunion, they referred to their first act as a "pickaninny act."

Gallery denizens as sharp as young Joe and Lew could not help but notice that about half of the variety headliners in 1877 were blackface acts. Moreover, the Irish knockabout acts required timing, physical coordination, and experience—all of which, understandably, the boys had in short supply. The blackface act could showcase their clog dancing, vaults, and somersaults; the plantation dialect was much easier to fake, given the number of true Irish accents the audience heard every day. Interestingly, there is no evidence at this early stage in their careers that they considered doing a Dutch act.

For their debut, Lew's brother Max made little white linen suits for the boys, with knee-britches and vests. Mrs. Weber and Mrs. Schanfield were the recipients of the complimentary tickets. At six o'clock of the momentous night, they arrived at Turn Hall with their sons, a full two hours before curtain. The would-be stage mothers chose the front-row seats nearest the stage door. Mrs. Weber was carrying an old-fashioned bouquet with a tinfoil handle and trimmed with white paper scallops. The plan, as the boys explained it to their mothers, was for the bouquet to be handed up to them onstage when they came out to take their bows.

Backstage, the boys were nervously preparing. Unable to afford proper blackface make-up (and just savvy enough to refuse the lampblack offered by a backstage joker), they pilfered lumps of coal, which they crushed into powder to apply as blackface. Unable to reproduce the desired effect, they added water, and succeeded only in making themselves look deathly ill. An hour went by, and they managed to make their faces look extremely dirty, but not at all black. They could hear the orchestra warming up, and people arriving. Verging on panic, they ran through their act, repeating the lyrics to their song and rehearsing their dance steps. Trickling sweat made stripes on their sooty faces. At the last moment, they decided to make their entrance backwards. Whether this was to mock the conventional single-file, hand-on-the-partner's-shoulder entrance, or to avoid looking at the audience, is unknown.

A stagehand yelled, "You kids are next!" and they backed their way on stage. The orchestra leader, confused, waited in vain for their cue. The boys launched into their song before turning around, and in different keys. The orchestra hurried to catch up, but never quite did. Their clog dance ended, but the music continued, burying their voices as they rushed through their few lines of dialogue. The music finally stopped as they began their acrobatic routine, leaving them to do their tumbling to the accompaniment of the audience's nervous giggles. After what must have seemed like an eternity, they heard their exit tune and danced off stage. The audience, composed mainly of friends and family of the performers and club members, applauded graciously. Encouraged by the applause, Joe and Lew quickly returned, and their plan was to reprise their best trick before taking their bows. Joe locked his fingers with his hands palm-side up. Lew took a couple of running strides and stepped lightly into Joe's hands, to be catapulted in the air, turn a somersault and land on his feet. In the excitement, they mistimed the catapulting motion. Lew did not have enough momentum to turn a complete flip: he hit the boards head first, with a resounding thud. Needless to say, they had not planned on ending their turn with the "bumps." As Joe tried to help his dazed partner to his feet, the stage manager brought down the curtain.

Backstage, Joe demanded to know why the quick curtain. The stagehand kindly explained that the curtain man had accidentally let the curtain rope slide through his hands. "You boys have a great act," he added (not content with his first lie); "you oughta take it over to Tony Pastor's and show it to him." When their mothers finally found them backstage, the boys were bursting with pride. Lew, his head still throbbing, announced that he and Joe had an appointment the next morning to see the great Tony Pastor. Sitting in the horsecar that carried them down the Bowery to Chatham Square, Joe and Lew bickered over who should keep the bouquet.

At seven o'clock the next morning, Joe and Lew had stationed themselves in the lobby of Tony Pastor's New Theatre, at 587 Broadway. For the next four hours, they watched for the legendary figure with the hussar's mustache and high boots. Seeing him approaching, the boys yelled, "Good morning, Mr. Pastor!" and frantically started doing flip-flops and dance steps from their act. "Good morning," Pastor replied as he strode into his office without looking up.

It would take another ten years before Pastor would even give them a look.

CHAPTER III
The Emigrant Train

It's Ireland and Italy, Jerusalem and Germany,
Oh, Chinamen and naygers, and a paradise for rats.
All jumbled together in the snow or rainy weather. . . .
McSorley's Inflation, Edward Harrigan, 1882

THE earliest known photos of Lew Fields were not with his parents or siblings, but with his friend and partner, Joe Weber. A photo of Weber & Fields from 1878 or '79, when the boys were eleven or twelve, shows Joe seated and Lew standing to his right. The boys are wearing adult street clothes: starched collars, cravats, and frock coats. With his right arm bent at the elbow, Lew holds a derby hat by its brim, affecting the stereotypical pose of a gentleman. Lew's expression is serious, even slightly sad, and his gaze is directed off-camera. His left hand rests deferentially on his partner's shoulder. It was customary in those days for the taller subject to be seated: at age twelve, Joe Weber was still several inches taller. (Married couples were posed in a similar fashion.) With a hint of a sly smile, Joe looks directly at the camera, showing a quiet confidence that belies his youth. From the start, he was the partnership's spokesman in business matters. While Joe haggled with wily museum managers, it was Lew who would often take charge in rehearsals. "No, Web," he would interrupt, "let's try it like *this*," and he would demonstrate his idea. When Joe would bring in a new bit of stage business—borrowed from an act appearing at Pastor's, the London, or the National—Lew would figure out how to work it into their routine.

In the days before the snapshot, a studio photo such as this would not have been wasted on school chums or their childish whims. This is a portrait of business partners: two young entrepreneurs whose profession was making people laugh. The leading variety acts of the time posed in a similar way for promotional photos that appeared on sheet music, posters, souvenir cards, and in newspaper ads (as engravings).

The sheet music and programs for minstrel shows were especially elaborate, with pictures of the performers in blackface and antic poses next to pictures of the same performers looking serious and upstanding in their street clothes. Initially, the purpose of this display was to reassure naïve audiences that the minstrels were indeed white men. But these before-and-after illustrations may have also had a special significance to the actors themselves, for they proclaimed the distance between the human being and the caricature, between the serious actor and the performing clown. The representation of this contrast lent a craftsman's dignity to an otherwise suspect profession.

This distinction was of lasting significance to Fields. Later in his career, he admitted to being occasionally vexed when introduced to people who seemed amazed that he did not actually speak with the same heavy dialect that he used on stage. "Evidently these people did not consider that I was an actor at all," he complained. This slight to his craft (and, implicitly, his social status) he described as "crushing."[1]

Weber & Fields' earliest turns in the Bowery dime museums probably paid for their first professional portrait. The boys had modelled themselves on the minstrel men and Irish acts; by 1879, they were equally comfortable in blackface or in green knee-pants. To be sure, their first photo was probably more useful as a personal talisman or statement of intent than as a promotional piece. But what makes their photo especially endearing is its pretense: it is a portrait of children emulating adults who were, in turn, actors emulating respectable businessmen.

In 1879, Papa Schanfield was no longer simply *bigelling* pants; he had upgraded his listing in the New York City Directory from "tailor" to "clothier." Lew's elder brothers, Max and Solly, were helping Papa service a better class of clientele. In the U.S. Census of 1880, Lew is listed as a tailor along with Max and Solly, but it is questionable how much tailoring Lew actually did. Younger brothers Henry (eight) and Charles (seven) were, according to the census, "at school," leaving Sarah to care for the five-year-old Annie and the toddler Nathan. Later that year, Sarah gave birth to Rene (called Ray), the eighth and final Schanfield child.

During that same year, the family moved from the Henry Street apartment to 120 Broome, near Willet Street. A Jewish congregation from Bialystok, Poland, had recently moved into the neighborhood, leading Papa Schanfield to hope that he had found a safe haven from the corrupting influences of the Bowery. The polyglot character of the Bowery was repeated on a small scale in their building: immigrants from Ireland, Scotland, England, Germany, and Russia, as well as Poland.

Less than a year later, the Schanfields moved down the block to 224 Broome. Living within sight of the Essex Street Police Court and the Ludlow Street Jail, Lew could watch the motley parade of drunks, petty thieves, and prostitutes arriving in the Black Marias or in the custody of burly patrolmen. At night, he could see the vagrants straggle into the police station, where a few would be allowed to sleep in the basement. For young Lew Fields, these were vivid moral lessons, a series of cautionary tales dramatized daily on the sidewalks of his neighborhood. The spectacle would continue long into the night, especially in the summer, when the heat made it impossible to sleep in the unventilated apartments, and entire families would take to the roof, or sit in front of their building, since the pre-1880 tenements had no fire escapes.

The family business was looking up, but their home was still a sweatshop, one of the half-dozen or so in their building. The dimly lit apartment, with the reek of cooking and gasoline and decaying garbage, the constant whirring of the sewing machine, and bundles of half-sewn garments occupying every horizontal surface, must have seemed especially oppressive to a boy used to having the freedom of the streets. On the street, the sweatshop worker was easy to spot: pale, stooped, and coughing thickly, the telltale sign of tuberculosis—"the tailor's disease," "the Jewish plague." The sight of his father and brothers hunched over the sewing machine and cutting tables for twelve hours a day, six days a week, was a grim reminder of what Lew could look forward to if he failed as an actor. Despite the dreariness of their daily lives, their diligence and stamina set an example he would not forget.

Meanwhile, Joe was working in another type of sweatshop—a cigarette factory—and he and Lew would improvise wishful dialogues around what to say to Joe's boss when they finally hit it big. Joe's plan was to light up a cigarette (strictly forbidden!) and, after exhaling the smoke in his boss's face, tell him to send his last day's wages to the theater where Weber & Fields were appearing.

The boys used school as a cover, attending in the morning and cutting classes in the afternoon to rehearse and attend the variety halls and museums. They avoided the Schanfields' block; working on their routines in the Webers' basement apartment, or on the East River wharves around Rutgers and Clinton Streets. In the two years following their inauspicious debut at Turn Hall in 1877, the only takers for the Weber and Fields "pickaninny" act had been the organizers of three or four similar benefit programs. At one of these performances, Lew showed a decided improvement in poise, if not in technique: when the whistles and catcalls of the kids at the back of the house made him forget a line, he turned to a couple sitting in the front row and said, as if they were the most important people in the house, "Ladies and gentlemen, please excuse the interruption. We'll start all over again." So Weber & Fields entered again, singing.

The boys were quick to spot the new gimmicks and trends in the Bowery variety acts. As New York's resident minstrel companies were reduced from five to one, enterprising managers added the blackface acts to the ethnic smorgasbord of the variety bills. In 1879, MacIntyre & Heath appeared for the first time in New York at Tony Pastor's, as did future minstrel star Lew Dockstader (then performing with his brother Charles).

Ever mindful of the changing local tastes, Joe and Lew began working up an Irish song-and-dance routine. Irish acts had lately become all the rage, assimilating knockabout, sidewalk dialogues, monologues, female impersonators, and more extended sketches. The boys stole from the best, borrowing bits from their favorite performers: the brutal knockabout of Needham & Kelly, the sidewalk patter of Harry and John Kernell, the singing and clog dancing of the American Four.

In the earliest days of the Weber & Fields partnership, Lew did not tell his parents that he was working (or trying to work) as an actor. He had to prove that he was no slacker or ne'er-do-well. His plan was to reveal his secret after his first big theatrical payday, perhaps hoping that this demonstration of his earning power as an actor would soften his father's disapproval. In his childish optimism, Lew had not figured on how long it would be before the team of Weber & Fields earned anything besides a sandwich and a pair of comp tickets. Fortunately, brothers Max, Solly, and Charlie sympathized with Lew's aspirations. Quietly delighted by the prospect of a celebrity in the family, they conspired with Lew to conceal his activities from their parents. Max and Solly covered for Lew in the sweatshop, and their mother may have also indulged Lew's extended absences and late evenings. In the years to come, Lew would reward his siblings for their support: Max, Solly, Charles, and Nat worked in the Weber & Fields' touring companies and the Music Hall as actors, advance men, and stage or business managers.

The revelation of Lew's secret career did not meet with the kind of paternal enthusiasm that Lew and his brothers had hoped for. In his earnestness to prove himself, Lew misunderstood the nature of his father's opposition to the acting profession. For their first two-week engagement at Morris and Hickman's East Side Museum, twelve-year-olds Joe and Lew netted six dollars apiece. At that time, the average adult laborer was paid two dollars a day, and a nimble worker with a sewing machine earned around a nickel per pair of knee-pants. At three dollars a week, Joe and Lew were already making as much as most women and children sweatshop workers. By the end of 1880, the boys were receiving anywhere from twelve to twenty-five dollars a week for their blackface and Irish acts—not too much less than what Papa himself was probably earning.

None of this swayed Papa in the least. To him, the Bowery provided daily proof that the Devil's work is well paid. A demanding, Old Testament–style patriarch, loving but severe, Papa Schanfield fought a losing battle to force his family to practice Orthodox Judaism. His zeal was such that some of his descendants were under the mistaken impression that he was a rabbi. At his funeral, he was eulogized (by Lew's press agent, William Raymond Sill) as "stern and rigid in his unbending adherence to the laws of his church," and "an earnest talker [who] delved deep into the heart of things." In other words, he resisted Americanization when it clashed with Orthodox Jewish tenets, and he did not hesitate to argue the point with anyone who challenged him.

Like many of his generation, Papa Schanfield believed that play was pointless, even corrupting. The insidious lure of the street—stickball, marbles, gambling, stage shows, saloons—all conspired to incite Jewish children to stray from the ways of their fathers. Education was the only legitimate excuse for a healthy twelve-year-old not to be working, and Lew had used this excuse to deceive his father. And for what? To mix with drunkards and bawds, to make a fool of himself making Gentiles laugh!

Lew's choice of the popular stage as a profession created a rift between father and son that would not be healed until after the turn of the century, when Papa had retired and Lew was the toast of Broadway. While Lew's mother, Sarah, saw his first appearance at Turn Hall, and continued to attend her son's New York performances until a few years before her death in 1926, Papa Schanfield did not attend a single one of his son's performances until the heyday of the Weber & Fields Music Hall. By then, all of Lew's siblings had adopted his stage name as their own last name; all of the brothers (except for Henry) were working for Lew; and Ray's husband, Leo Teller, was the Music Hall's business manager.

In part, it may have been his father's disapproval of the acting profession that motivated Fields' lifelong effort to make popular theater into a "respectable" middle-class entertainment.

Given the hard realities of sweatshop life and paternal disapproval, it is not surprising that there are few accounts of Lew Fields' childhood that reveal anything about his personal relationships or activities outside of the theater. For those who have lived it, poverty is a very private thing. In the many interviews he gave and the nostalgic anecdotes he told in the course of his long career, there are no fond remembrances of family outings, no affectionate descriptions of family members (with the exception of his mother and his eldest brother), no sympathetic portraits of domestic life, and no mention of bar mitzvahs or of any holiday observances that might identify him as a Jew.

From Lew's vantage point, it was Papa Schanfield's religious beliefs that led to the harsh moral judgements. This, as much as the prevailing social pressures to assimilate, may explain Fields' ambivalence about his ethnic and religious background, as well as his reticence about his childhood. When it was Lew's turn to be a father, he raised his own children with little or no religious instruction whatsoever. To a great extent, the contradictions and omissions in Fields' answers to questions about his childhood, his nationality, and his ethnic origins can be linked to his reluctance to discuss anything that would touch on his troubled relationship with his father. Had he gone on to become a tailor or a banker, these questions of identity would be of no further interest. But in the context of the coming of age of an ethnic comedian, these personal conflicts have an intriguing resonance.

New Year's Day, 1879—Lew Fields celebrated his twelfth birthday while the rest of the Bowery celebrated its own rowdy adolescence. The months immediately before and after this benchmark were bursting with promising new developments. Physically and culturally, the Bowery was in the throes of a radical transformation: electric lights, the construction of the first "dumbbell" tenements, the opening of the Third Avenue Elevated and Miner's Bowery Theater, and during the same week, the New York premieres of *H.M.S. Pinafore* and *The Mulligan Guards' Ball*. And in the midst of all this tumult, an event that went unnoticed: the first professional appearances of Weber & Fields.

By 1879, the Bowery between Chatham Square and Houston Street was a mile crammed with cheap thrills. In the wake of the depression that followed the Panic of '73, the dime museums, concert saloons, shooting galleries, beer dives, and other entertainment "resorts" gradually supplanted the retail shops and the once-fashionable hotels and residences. To aspiring entertainers and impresarios, the Bowery must have seemed rich with opportunities, provided one was not too choosy about the moral character of the audiences of the places doing the hiring. Here was the city's—the entire country's—entertainment center, comparable in its economic and social impact to other urban neighborhoods devoted to a single industry or business such as meatpacking, banking, or printing.

With the El rumbling overhead and a nonstop carnival in progress, the young Weber & Fields made the rounds of the Bowery resorts, hoping to impress the manager of a dime museum or music hall with an impromptu audition. Their weekly quest for employment would begin at Chatham Square, and it took them past the best and worst that the Bowery businessmen had to offer.

The beer dives, faro banks, and brothels were as much a part of the landscape Weber & Fields grew up in as the dime museums and variety houses. On the east side of Chatham Square—Number Nine—was Paddy Martin's basement saloon, with a backroom opium den frequented by Chinese laborers. Continuing uptown, the block between Catherine and Bayard Streets was known as Panhandler's Paradise. Here, beggars and cripples played upon soft hearts with crutches, bandages, and wheelchairs supplied by the nearby saloon keepers and lodging-house owners. Their business arrangement was straight out of *The Beggar's Opera:* the proceeds of each day's beggary had to be spent on the whiskey, food, and lodging sold on the block. Violators lost the privilege of hiring their crutches and bandages there and were told to panhandle elsewhere.

On the northwest corner of Pell Street stood Barney Flynn's saloon, a meeting place for neighborhood racketeers and politicos. Upstairs was reputed to be a panel house—private rooms rented to hookers and their clients. During the rendezvous, an accomplice would sneak into the room via a sliding wall panel and empty the man's wallet. Having paid in advance, the man (usually inebriated) would not discover the theft until much later.

Some legitimate businesses remained; a few even prospered. At 28 Bowery, A. C. Benedict's jewelry store supplied the local high-rollers with diamonds rings and studs, watches, and pearl necklaces. Diamonds could be purchased on time; customers who could not keep up their payments had to return the ring so that the same diamond would temporarily adorn several people's hands before finding a solvent buyer. To sport diamond shirt studs with a heavy gold watch chain across your vest was an announcement that you were "in the money," even if these pricey props were in hock by the end of the week. As young managers struggling to reassure their backers and employees, Joe and Lew learned the value of a judicious display of diamonds.

Continuing north on the Bowery, the boys passed a familiar landmark near Canal Street: the Bowery Theatre, its massive pillars and neoclassical façade now obscured by the El tracks. During the 1870's, Lew Fields went there to watch blood-and-thunder melodramas such as *Robert Macaire*, and racy spectacles such as *Mazeppa; or, the Wild Steed of Tartary*, starring Fanny Herring. In 1879, in another indication of the changing ethnic character of the area, the Bowery Theatre "went German." Renamed the Thalia, it presented German opera and melodrama. The change in name did nothing to improve the basic behavior of the Bowery audience: foreign actors were outraged by the gallery patrons stomping in time to the music and the loud smacking noises that they made when, say, Othello kissed Desdemona. Next door to the Thalia was Theodore Kramer's Atlantic Garden Music Hall—family entertainment in the style of a German beer garden.

The block above Hester Street contained the best and worst of the era's most popular diversions. Worth's Museum, at 99 Bowery, prided itself on its menagerie of exotic animals. Once a week, the first five children to arrive with a live mouse were admitted free. The mice were fed to the rattlesnakes—one of the museum's more popular attractions. Worth's also offered a variety bill for an additional dime. Its primary competition was, for a time, right next door. George Bunnell's Museum, upstairs at 103–105 Bowery, first opened its doors in the fall of 1876. His curiosities and displays, including the Dante's Inferno waxworks, occupied three stories. Early in 1879, Bunnell moved up the block to 298 Bowery and opened the Great American Museum, which he sold to George Middleton, who renamed it the Globe Museum. Bunnell then opened an even larger museum on Broadway and Ninth, with six rooms of curiosities and a variety stage. His was considered to be a high-class house; to appear at Bunnell's was the great ambition of many aspiring Bowery performers, including the young Weber & Fields.

Underneath Bunnell's Museum at 103 Bowery was the notorious saloon of Owney Geoghagen (pronounced Gay-gun). Owney featured a "free-'n-easy"—an amateur boxing bout—every night, in a small ring surrounded by tables for drinking and betting. Owney's waiters were expected to be able to sing and dance on request, and on occasion, participate in the free-'n-easy to fill in for an absent sparring partner. By 1879, variety was no longer only an adjunct of the dime museum. Across from Bunnell's Museum and Geoghagen's saloon was the National Theater, where variety bills alternated with pulp adventures and melodrama like *The Boy Detective*. For a time, the National also offered "Female Minstrels."

In contrast to Bunnell's and Worth's, the Grand Museum (just off the Bowery on Grand Street) was sordid proof of how low museum entertainment could be. Besides the usual freaks, the Grand Museum featured graphic waxworks of people with exotic diseases, the object being to frighten the patrons into paying for a "consultation" with a quack who would them sell his patent medicine. It was managed by a well-known local thug by the name of "Broken-Nose" Burke, and was a popular hangout for newsboys.

The Bowery's most famous clothier—Nicoll the Tailor—had his shop at 147 Bowery, between Grand and Broome. Nicoll's shop was three storerooms wide; here the Bowery sports could purchase suits that were unrivalled in the loudness of their material and the swagger of their cut. To a generation of German tradesmen, Irish laborers, and ward politicos, a suit from Nicoll's represented the apogee of Bowery style. Up the block, at Miner's Bowery Theater, or at the London, Nicoll was one of the local celebrities lampooned by the variety show comedians. The outrageous plaids, tight jackets, and oversized pants that so appealed to Nicoll's immigrant patrons may have been the inspiration for many a vaudeville act's costumes, including that of Weber & Fields' feuding Dutchmen.

North of Broome Street, at 165–167, was Miner's Bowery Theater. If any single institution could be said to epitomize the spirit of the Bowery, it was Miner's. Many of the most prominent variety and vaudeville artists were alumni of Harry Miner's informal academy: Pat Rooney (who coined his famous line, "Are yez all looking'?" here while dancing a jig), McIntyre & Heath, the Cohans, Ross and Fenton, Kitty O'Neil (champion jig-dancer), Gus Williams, Jennie Yeamans, Sam Bernard—a generation of performers up to and including Eddie Cantor. For

Weber & Fields, Miner's audience was the hometown crowd; Miner's was the place where Joe and Lew would test a new gag or look for new talent to add to their stock company. Throughout the 'eighties and until they opened their own theater, Weber & Fields appeared here (and at Miner's other theaters) several times each season.

A shrewd, outgoing ex-cop and a native son of the Bowery, Harry Miner first opened his variety hall in late 1878. By the 1890's, he owned a chain of New York theaters and had been elected to Congress. Miner perfected the policy (begun by Tony Pastor) that became the model for variety and vaudeville: a two-part program consisting of a series of specialty acts followed by a short melodrama or burlesque, in which the best of the specialty performers reappeared in new makeup and costumes. In December of 1879, A. H. Sheldon, Miner's resident playwright, stage manager, and leading man, staged what was reported to be a brilliant burlesque of *H.M.S. Pinafore*—short for "Harry Miner's Pinafore"—with a cast including Sheldon, Louise Montague, Bobby Newcomb, Daisy Remington, and Tillie Malvern. Sheldon left the music intact, but adapted the book and lyrics to suit the comic tastes of the Bowery audience. Unfortunately, as is true with the vast majority of variety afterpieces, no printed text survives. Sheldon's sketches, like most afterpieces, were hurriedly written and barely rehearsed, relying on the richness of the premise and the inventiveness and poise of the performers. The success of Sheldon's burlesque was the birth of a Miner's tradition: the burlesquing of current musical shows. While the *Pinafore* craze spawned numerous spoofs—Tony Pastor, for example, presented "T.P.S. Canal Boat Pinafore," and a minstrel group put on "Her Mud Scow Pinafore"—Sheldon's burlesque was superior in the cleverness of its gags and repartée, and the comedic talents of its cast.

This early lesson in burlesque staging was not lost on the young Weber and Fields. Joe and Lew were among the impatient throng of boys who lined up at Miner's gallery door, where a dime would entitle them to a hard wooden seat. For seventy-five cents, patrons hoping to make an impression could buy a box seat and be seen by everybody. The parquet cost fifty cents; the balcony, a quarter.

The gallery filled up quickly, and the vocal outbursts the gallery was famous for soon began: "Aw, g'wan! H'is the rag! You got our money, give us de show!" A house policeman patrolled each tier. The one at floor level was a stocky man with a drooping mustache, a derby hat, and a cane, who would stride down the center aisle and stand back-to-back with the orchestra conductor, surveying the audience like a schoolmaster. The enforcer in the gallery was known as the "Post": a tall, gaunt, spoil-sport who patrolled the aisles with a braided rattan cane. His mission was to make sure that the rowdies in the gallery did not annoy the patrons in the more expensive seats below. Boisterous laughter, wisecracks, foot-stomping were tolerated; tobacco-spitting, throwing paper wads, fisticuffs, and mashing were punishable offenses. After the last bars of the overture, when the curtain bell rang backstage, the Post would slap the wall with his cane and demand, "Hats off, youse! Hats off, all o' youse!" When the noise would become too boisterous, he would stride down the aisle and rap his cane against the side of the bench, or tap the offender with his cane and say, "Cheese it!" Repeat offenders were grabbed by the shirt and, depending on their age, evicted from the premises with a blow from the cane or brass knuckles.

The audience at Miner's never left feeling shortchanged. An evening's entertainment usually lasted over three hours and featured the best of the variety acts. To offset the cost of his bountiful variety bills, Miner ran a bar in the northeast corner of the building, with a saloon and poolroom adjoining the theater. Waiters worked during the performances; patrons who raised a finger and passed a nickel down the row would be served a thick glass *seidel* of beer. George Odell, describing Miner's in *Annals of the New York Stage*, commented: "The question again gaspingly arises as to how much [entertainment] could be offered for so slight an admission fee; surely much beer and liquid refreshment must be sold to make up the expenditure!"[2]

Miner's saloon and poolroom were also an unofficial club for variety actors, a place to pick up mail, make bets, and a general loafing place between gigs. Dues were paid over the bar by the glass, with a charge for billiards by the hour and rotation pool at two and a half cents a cue. Since Joe and Lew did not drink, they developed a peculiar variation on rotation pool that would draw out the game indefinitely. They became the youngest of the regulars, their ears open for scraps of gossip, news of auditions, and tricks of the trade.

Continuing up the Bowery, across Delancey Street, Joe and Lew were in variety heaven. In 1883, Harry Miner bought the building at 201 Bowery, renovated it, and renamed it Miner's People's Theatre. The People's Theatre paralleled the pluralistic booking practices of the Windsor and the National, with longer melodramas and musical farces interspersed with variety acts. The object was to present a menu that would appeal to all tastes. It presented a daunting challenge for the era's variety artists: they would have to go on stage and elicit laughs from a weepy audience immediately after Uncle Tom had been sold to Simon Legree, or after Camille's dying scene.

The entertainment at No. 210 Bowery was less high-falutin'. Besides the usual freaks and curios, the New York Museum presented the Ford Brothers—the killers of Jesse James—in lectures and re-enactments. Up the block at the London Theatre, Jim Donaldson presented a generous bill of fare to rival that of his former partner, Harry Miner. The London featured the comic talents of Murphy & Mack, whose series of ethnic farces—"Murphy's Wedding," "Murphy's Divorce," "Murphy's Campaign," and so on—were patterned after Harrigan's Mulligan plays. It was at the London in 1890 that Weber & Fields' Own Company made its first New York appearance.

The boys' circuit of Bowery resorts ended just north of Houston Street, at the Globe Museum. The proprietor, George Middleton, went on to become half of the firm Kohl & Middleton, an important force in the growth of vaudeville in the West. In 1879, Middleton was known for his chinchilla overcoat and his willingness to take on new talent. His roster of freaks included George the Turtle Boy, Chang the Chinese Giant, and Laloo, called the East Indian Enigma by virtue of the small girl's head that grew out of his body.

One of the most popular teams appearing in the Bowery theaters in the late

1870's was an Irish song-and-dance act called the American Four. The American Four sang a song called "The Land of the Shamrock Green," and were pretentious enough to claim it as their own. Copyright protection for popular songs, routines, and sketches was virtually unknown. To claim exclusive rights to a song or a routine seemed ludicrous, as if only one vendor in town had the exclusive rights to sell oysters or corn on the cob. There were many vendors: what mattered was the quality of the goods they offered for sale. Weber & Fields needed an entrance song, so they borrowed the melody of "The Land of the Shamrock Green" and made up their own lyrics. They kept the clog dancing and tumbling from their blackface routine, polished it, and repackaged it with an Irish dialect and their pirated entrance song.

Whether it was foresight or luck, the lyrics that Joe and Lew devised for their entrance song were easily adapted to whatever ethnic routine they were hired to perform:

> Here we are, an Irish pair,
> With no troubles or care,
> We are here once more,
> To make the people roar,
> Before we go to the ball.
>
> When first we landed over here
> The people said we looked so queer;
> But we leave that to you;
> It's the best thing we can do.
> We're going down to the fancy ball.

Substitute "colored" or "German" for "Irish," use the appropriate costumes and dialect, and Weber & Fields had the quintessential, all-purpose ethnic act by the time they made their first professional appearances in the dime museums. The ethnic characterizations were all variations on the same theme: the struggle to learn American ways and to succeed, either by guile or by force. To the Bowery audiences, it did not matter that Joe and Lew—both of whom had decidedly Semitic profiles—did not look Irish. The boys turned this to their advantage: when their Irish act needed a big laugh right away, they would enter singing "Here we are, an Irish pair," with their hands covering their noses. The gesture never failed to delight the Bowery audience.

In the spring of 1879, a new dime museum opened up on Chatham Square in a building vacated by a secondhand clothing shop that had recently been cleaned out by a Peter Funk auction. Weber & Fields won over the inexperienced manager, a Mr. Morris, with a flurry of clog steps and cartwheels. Their debut engagement at Morris & Hickman's East Side Museum lasted only two weeks, prematurely ended by a police raid that closed down the museum. The boys made the most of their brief engagement: they appeared in ten to twelve turns a day, and between turns, they worked on new gags and gymnastics.

Proud as they were, they were savvy enough to realize that their act was too limited to please the novelty-loving Bowery audience for more than the occasional two-week stint. Only a handful of dime museums were hiring variety acts, and no manager wanted to pay for the same act that had played down the street within the last eight weeks. After Weber & Fields' debut at the East Side Museum, they found it relatively easy to secure their next engagement at the New York Museum as a blackface duo. With their first two weeks guaranteed, the boys spent their offstage time trying to come up with a new routine. Appearing on the bill with them was a veteran performer known as the Paper King, who made his living by tearing folded pieces of tissue paper into intricate patterns and the likenesses of famous people. While tearing what seemed to be random pieces out of the fold, he would dance a few steps and deliver a pleasing line of patter. At the end of his act, he would present the "tidies," as they were called, to women and children in the audience for souvenirs.

Joe and Lew made no secret of their admiration for the Paper King's handi-work. The Paper King quickly recognized the boys as "brother artists" and of-fered to help them elaborate their act. For their second fortnight, Joe and Lew did a "neat" act. They put aside the burnt cork and donned Little Lord Fauntleroy suits of velvet made by Lew's brother Max. Their routine consisted of dancing and tearing tidies. As Weber later described it, "That brought the women, who hadn't cared much for our song and dance, over to our side. We played at the New York for nine weeks, and our salary, increasing with our popularity, was twelve dollars and fifty cents the last week." "By that time," added Fields, "noth-ing could drive us away from our set purpose of continuing on the stage. We left school and let our parents in on our game."

Next, Joe and Lew returned to the familiar lobby of the Globe Museum to present their new credentials to George Middleton. After watching their blackface and Irish neat routines, Middleton's stage manager informed them, "I can't pay you much."

"How much?" they shouted in unison.

"All I can pay you boys is twenty-five dollars a week for the act."

Tears welled up in Lew's eyes. Joe, thinking fast, pretended to comfort his partner, thereby saving Lew from the overwhelming urge to fall to his knees and utter profuse thanks.

Four weeks into their lucrative engagement at the Globe, Weber & Fields heard a rumor that Middleton was looking for a German act, and had agreed to audition two of the boys' schoolmates. Joe and Lew were worried; a new juvenile act with the added novelty of being Dutch would certainly mean that their ser-vices would no longer be required. Before the interlopers' sketch was over, Joe and Lew were already telling the stage manager that they could "do a better Dutch act than that." When the new act flopped, the stage manager expressed an interest in seeing the Dutch act that Joe and Lew had been holding back. He asked the boys if they would be ready to go on with it tomorrow. Sure, they shrugged, they would be ready. In truth, until that day, they had not seriously considered doing a Dutch act. "But we yessed 'em all in those days," explained Weber. "Had we been asked if we could do Antony and Cleopatra or Uncle Tom and Little Eva, our answer would have been the same. 'Yes' took no more breath than 'no' and had a lot more possibilities.

Their Dutch dialect was not difficult for them to come by, but they knew that Bowery audiences could distinguish between the dialect of the Dutchman (the German laborer or shopkeeper) and the Jew comic. While rehearsing their routines in the Weber's basement at No. 10 Essex Street, they eavesdropped on the goings-on at Simon's saloon directly above them. Overhearing the conversations of German laborers and merchants enjoying *seidel* after *seidel* of beer, the boys had a splendid opportunity to study the peculiar brand of English used by Bowery Dutchmen in their most unguarded moments.

Lew hit upon the winning formula: they would use an Irish knockabout routine but deliver their lines in the kind of mangled English they heard at Simon's saloon. For costumes, they borrowed pieces of men's suits, the more mismatched the better. Since Joe would bear the brunt of the physical punishment, he stuffed his oversized clothes with pillows. A neighborhood pal—a boy named Harry Seamon, who went on to become a successful burlesque producer—borrowed his father's housepainting equipment for props. In a caricature of the current fashion among German immigrants, the boys whitened their faces with paint and glued bristly goatees to their chins. Overnight, they developed the prototype of the act that they would use with increasing success for the next twenty-five years. What they presented the next day at the Globe was crude, but the novel mixture of breakneck antics and Dutch dialect was enough to win over the none-too-critical audience.

By the middle of June, most of the dime museums and variety houses had closed down for the summer. Faced with the grim possibility of having to return to the sweatshops to earn their keep, Joe and Lew could not afford to be choosy about where they worked. Harry Hill's Dance Hall, on the corner of Houston and Mulberry, was then known as the "only reputable vile house" in the city.[3] The male clientele represented all classes of society; the women were almost exclusively streetwalkers. Harry Hill made sure that only the most attractive and best-dressed were admitted, and saw to it that no crime was ever committed on his premises. (Harry Hill's was the model for the dance hall in which Stephen Crane's heroine began her precipitous decline in *Maggie, a Girl of the Streets.*) It was the kind of place that Rabbi Weber and Papa Schanfield had warned their sons about.

A former trainer for the barefisted boxer John L. Sullivan, Harry Hill favored sparring and wrestling matches as entertainment for his patrons. In a concession to the growing popularity of variety shows, he also began booking simple variety acts—pretty female singers and skirt-dancers (one flyer promised "seven distinct changes of dress in the presence of the audience"), acrobats, knockabout comedy teams. The idea of two twelve-year-old boys engaged in mock fisticuffs would undoubtedly have appealed to him. Weber & Field's performances at Hill's began with the Irish song-and-dance number, then segued into a parody of a wrestling match, and climaxed with a parody of two free-swinging boxers. The boys were used to wreaking havoc on one another with various props, but had not yet mastered the art of pulling and slipping punches. Weber, in particular, took a considerable beating during each show. A concerned waitress asked him, "Why don't you stop some of those blows?" Joe pondered this for a moment, then replied, "None of 'em's passed me so far."

Unintentionally, Weber & Fields had developed the routine that would guarantee them employment during the summer off-season. The free-'n'-easy's in the summer resort areas—Coney Island, Rockaway Beach, Atlantic City—were patterned after Harry Hill's. Coney Island in 1879 was just emerging as the people's resort, a rowdier and less exclusive version of Brighton Beach and Manhattan Beach to the west. To cater to the thousands of day-trippers who came out to Coney Island to beat the city heat, there were seafood restaurants, bathing pavilions, band concerts on the pier, variety shows, and shooting galleries. In terms of its patrons and the entertainment it offered, Coney Island was Bowery Beach.

Duffy's Music Hall and Pavilion was a seaside saloon constructed on stilts over the beach. Duffy agreed to pay Weber & Fields two dollars a day plus five beer checks each; at the end of the week, after the boys cashed in their beer checks, their joint weekly income came to thirty dollars. To save transportation costs, Joe and Lew stayed at the shore, returning to their families once a week to drop off their laundry and their wages. In return, Duffy insisted on the exclusive rights to Weber & Fields' services from 10:00 a.m. to midnight. In addition to performing their Irish song-and-dance routine fifteen times a day, they were expected to help promote Duffy's establishment by passing out handbills, dancing on crates in front of the saloon, or carrying signboards.

Joe and Lew quickly lost interest in these mundane activities and invented their own promotions to attract customers to Duffy's. On the boardwalk, they staged an argument that quickly attracted the attention of a crowd. Blows were struck, and the battling boys fought their way down to Duffy's, through the door, and right up onto the stage, with an enthusiastic crowd right behind them. A different strategy for luring customers was less successful: at Duffy's beach, Lew swam out in the surf and started yelling and waving his arms frantically as if he was drowning. A large crowd gathered, and Joe rushed in to "save" his buddy. Unfortunately, by the time Joe got to him, Lew was in a genuine panic, and Joe could not subdue him. Finally, a beefy lifeguard swam out, and following the standard practice of the day for rescuing hysterical victims, punched Lew unconscious and carried him back in. There was a bigger-than-average crowd slaking its thirst at Duffy's that day, but the boys were docked a day's pay because Lew could not perform.

Appearing in a Coney Island variety hall during this same period was a familiar face from the Bowery: Sam Bernard, late of the Grand Duke Concert Hall, and future Weber & Fields collaborator. What used to rankle Joe and Lew was the way their peer Bernard would, in their words, "high-hat" them. As Bernard described it, "they were singing in a beer hall, and I used to feel way above them, because people had to pay to hear me and their show was thrown in with a glass of beer." He also recalled that Weber & Fields' costumes included tight knee-pants with no pockets. It was considered foolhardy to leave valuables at the boardinghouse, so the boys developed the habit of hiding their daily wages in the sand beneath Duffy's and marking the spot discreetly. One evening, however, an unusually high tide washed away their marker, and they spent the night fruitlessly digging in the sand for their stash.

As a result of their experience at Duffy's, Weber & Fields returned to the

Bowery with an Irish turn that was becoming more knockabout than song-and-dance. At the same time, they still had their "neat" paper-tearing routine and their blackface and Dutch variations on "Here we are, a jolly pair." The stage manager at Worth's Museum appreciated this kind of versatility, so he hired the boys at twenty-five dollars a week. During an appearance at Worth's, they attracted the attention of the Gerry Society, a.k.a. the Society for the Prevention of Cruelty to Children. Led by socialite Elbridge T. Gerry, this private organization was entrusted with enforcing the laws concerning the appearance of children under sixteen on the stage. In practice, the law was enforced selectively, subject to the same favoritism, payoffs, and arbitrary judgements as the rest of the municipal legal code. Reflecting the uptown social prejudice against variety as a "low" form of entertainment, the Gerry Society targeted the children in the variety shows and dime museums. Children playing in "legitimate" dramas, spectacles, or operettas—no matter how sexy or sordid the shows were—were routinely granted permits. As Joe Keaton observed (when the Gerryites came after his son Buster), there were thousands of homeless and hungry abandoned children wandering the streets of New York, selling newspapers, shining shoes, working in sweatshops, or engaged in petty crime. Why didn't the Gerryites direct their energies to where they were needed most?[4]

The Gerryites were particularly concerned for Joe's welfare. On stage, Lew wore lifts in his shoes and tight-fitting clothes to create the illusion of height while Joe's baggy clothes, exaggerated girth, and much-abused stage persona evoked real sympathy. In real life, Lew was still the shorter (and less aggressive) of the two. What alarmed the Gerryites was the amount of physical punishment that Joe absorbed while performing the Irish knockabout act nine or ten times a day. Lew's mother enlisted the help of a distant relative who was a lawyer to plead their case at City Hall. By greasing the right palms and by agreeing to perform only three turns a day, Weber & Fields were allowed to continue on the stage.

At Worth's, their repertoire ran the gamut of the ethnic styles currently appearing on the popular stage. Weber & Fields' most basic question—which ethnic characterization to use, blackface, Irish, or Dutch?—was still unresolved, and would remain so until the mid-1880's. Weber & Fields' sampler of ethnic comedy styles reveals much about the preoccupations of the variety audience and the changing role of the popular stage in urban America. Ethnic humor was the lifeblood of variety. Its subject matter was of immediate consequence to the variety audience, unlike the fairy-tale stories of comic operas and extravaganzas. It is in the variety acts and sketches of the 1880's—the vast majority of which had ethnic targets—that we can detect the first stirrings of an indigenous theatrical form.

As successive waves of immigrants poured into Castle Garden, ethnic tensions became as much a part of everyday life in the Bowery as the saloon and the El. Close scrutiny of the era reveals that the familiar metaphor of the melting pot does not accurately describe the relations between ethnic groups in the Bowery; it was probably more like tomcats tied in a sack, trying to claw their way out. Not surprisingly, the encounters between ethnic groups trying to succeed in their strange new homeland quickly became the favorite subjects for the popular stage. The ethnic comics naturally seized upon the peculiarities in the appearance and behavior of different immigrant groups as potentially rich comic material. The brutal knockabout was the physical corollary of the crude ethnic caricatures.

Variety's shifting gallery of stereotypes—the loutish Irishman, the slow-thinking German, the lazy black, the conniving Jew—all shared their audience's interest in the pursuit of material success, and, implicitly, assimilation. If ethnic humor inspired any sense of common humanity among its heterogenous audience, then it was in this generalized aspiration. It was not the complicity of "we're all in this together"; rather, it was the momentary bond formed by their aggressive laughter at the plight of a harassed minority. No matter what your background was, variety gave you a target to laugh at.

While the variety program fulfilled the aggressive impulses of its audience, the variety theater itself was a neutral ground—a demilitarized zone—where the competing ethnic groups sat side by side in an uneasy truce. Outside the theater, the prejudice and exploitation experienced by the immigrants meant suffering and despair. Inside, the clever and outrageous exaggerations by variety artists transformed the prejudice and suffering into popular entertainment—ethnic humor, knockabout comedy, topical songs, and burlesques. At heart, the ethnic humor of this era was a coping strategy, best summarized in modern terms by comedian and activist Dick Gregory: "If you can laugh at me, you don't have to kill me. If I can laugh at you, I don't have to kill you."

Nowhere was the ethnic conflict more apparent than in the plays of Edward Harrigan. The knockdown and slapbang of Harrigan's farces about the Mulligan family elevated the dialect act from a crude caricature into a disarmingly effective tool for social commentary. His objective was stated on his programs: "to catch the living manners as they rise."

South of Fourteenth Street, most of the "living manners" were seen through the distorting lens of ethnic conflict. Between 1878 and 1881, the colliding fates of the families Mulligan and Lochmuller had figured in seven Harrigan works, supported by an assortment of black, Italian, Chinese, and Jewish characters. Ethnic conflict permeated every aspect of Harrigan's work, from major plot turns to sheet music. The litho ad for *McSorley's Inflation*, for example, showed a gesticulating German butcher arguing with an Irish dandy; behind them, a Chinese holding a trombone is being tossed from a second-storey window onto the head of an unsuspecting black, who is carrying a bundle of laundry.

Harrigan's *The Mulligan Guard's Ball* (1879) was more than a musical sketch but still not quite a full-length play, and it was presented with a variety-style olio that changed weekly. The playlet begins with dinner at the Mulligans: Dan (Harrigan), his wife Cordelia (Annie Yeamans), and his son Tommy (Tony Hart) are discussing the upcoming Mulligan Guards' Ball. The harmony is shattered when Dan hears of Tommy's love for Katy Lochmuller, the butcher's daughter. Although she is only half-German (her mother is Irish), Dan swears, "The devil a Dutch drop of blood will enter this family." Furthermore, Cordelia detests Bridget Lochmuller (Annie Mack). Gus Lochmuller (Harry Fisher), about to pay a visit to the Mulligans, overhears the insults and plots revenge.

On a city street, Tommy and Katy meet and devise a plan to elope during the ball. Elsewhere on the street, the black minister Palestine Puter (Billy Gray) tells his friend Simpson Primrose, a barber (John Wild), about the problems he is having booking a hall for their black marching corps, the Skidmore Guards. Puter reveals that he finally managed to reserve an Irish club, the Harp and Shamrock. Naturally, it is the same place Dan rented for the Mulligan Guards. As the blacks exit the stage on one side, Dan and a friend enter on the other, staggering drunk, vowing revenge on Lochmuller and reminiscing about the old days. The bout of nostalgia is a ready excuse to launch into David Braham's hit from seven years earlier, "The Mulligan Guards":

> We shouldered arms and marched and marched away,
> From Baxter Street we marched to Avenue A.
> With drums and fifes how sweetly they did play,
> As we marched, marched, marched in the Mulligan Guards.

On the night of the ball, the Mulligan Guards assemble at the Harp and Shamrock, where Dan serenades them with "The Babies on Our Block," a song that quickly became part of the growing canon of Harrigan and Braham show-stoppers.

When the Skidmores arrive, the hall manager persuades them to move to an upstairs room. But the blacks' stomping and dancing makes the floor collapse, and, in one of Harrigan's most memorable scenes, the Skidmores come crashing down into the Mulligans' celebration. Tommy and Katy exploit the confusion to steal away together to elope.

The free-for-alls that Harrigan called for at the climax of his plays (usually called "Tumult with all") were not simply dramatic contrivances, or excuses for knockabout. Violent confrontations sparked by racial prejudice were daily occurrences. Critic Richard Harding Davis pointed out that the humorous confrontations involving the Mulligans, the Lochmullers, the black Skidmore Guards, et al., were no more outlandish than many real-life incidents. He cited as an example the case of an enraged Irish laborer who tried to kill his foreman because the foreman had mistakenly listed the laborer on the payroll as Italian. Another instance involved two Irish boys who tried to dynamite the statue of Garibaldi in Washington Square because "no Dago on earth" deserved such a monument.[5]

More often than not, the most ludicrous ethnic comedy routines had their origins in the careful observation of New York street life. Fields, like Harrigan, used the close observation of street life to develop his ethnic characterizations, and the process remained the basis of his acting technique long after he stopped appearing in variety. To create a character for one of his musical comedies, Fields would take to the streets to find living models of the character he wanted to play: a barber, a soda jerk, a henpecked husband, a floorwalker in a department store; sometimes following his chosen subject for days, occasionally even buying a piece of the man's clothing. This was what Harrigan meant by comedy that was "planted in the truth." Fields explained: "One must live his part as it is lived in real life.

Of course, in the pieces such as I give, which are mostly of a burlesque order, everything is overdone, and exaggerated, but this is all the more reason why those little life-like touches should be given."[6]

Early in 1880, Tony Pastor presented a playlet by William Carleton (author of "Fritz in Ireland") in which the uneasy intermingling of the city's ethnic groups was the work's central gimmick. It was typical for its day. Entitled "The Emigrant Train; or, Go West," it included almost every type of dialect comedian then current on the variety stage. Sheehan and Jones appeared as the Irish immigrants; Lena Tettenborn as the Dutch immigrant; Bonnie Runnells as Hans Munchausen and the Dutch conductor; Billy Courtright as the tramp; the Sparks Brothers as the Italian immigrants; Mose W. Fiske as the policeman; Nellie Hadfield as the Italian violin girl; and the Four Eccentrics (Perry, Hughes, Curdy, and Magrew) as the Negro Exodus. The formula for ethnic humor was simple and dependable: put as many volatile elements as you can find into a closed container, and shake. For the variety audience, it was the perfect expression of their own predicament.

For the variety artist in the 1870's and 1880's, the ability to play several ethnic different types meant survival. Many in the first generation of vaudevillians—Weber & Fields, Sam Bernard, the Russell Brothers—spent their early days in variety playing several different ethnic types. But even when a real Irishman played a stage Irishman, the ethnic characterizations were treated as comic masks donned by the performer.

There was one mask, however, that Weber & Fields would never wear willingly. In many ways, it would have been the most obvious choice: the stereotype known as "Hebrew" or the Jew act. It would be easy (and misleading) to see their Dutch act as another name for a Yiddish act (*à la* Brice or Jolson) that was ahead of its time. This is simply not the case: the models for their Dutch act were the gentile Germans of the Bowery. Mike and Meyer's characteristic makeup, costumes, and behavior remained true to their sources even after the models had blended into the American mainstream or had been supplanted in the public eye by stranger newcomers. Later in their careers, on the strength of the personalities they had created for Mike and Meyer, they enjoyed renewed popularity as dialect comedians who represented the quintessential immigrants, the emblematic foreigners.

The reasons Joe and Lew did not do a "Hebrew" act may have had more to do with personal convictions than a precocious pragmatism about what the variety audience would or would not applaud. Perhaps the young Weber & Fields feared that the Hebrew mask was one they would not be able to detach themselves from. Already faced with the disapproval of Rabbi Weber and Papa Schanfield, the boys may have wanted to avoid what would have been perceived as an added insult to their fathers' religious convictions. To Joe and Lew, doing a Hebrew act may have elicited the same kind of discomfort that black vaudevillians felt when they had to wear blackface makeup to be allowed to perform.

Growing up in a world of sharply defined ethnic categories, Lew Fields attempted to blur or conceal the distinguishing characteristics of his own background: his nationality, his religion, even his name. It is as if this pioneer of ethnic humor had to purge himself of his own ethnic identity to create the characters that would make him famous. Offstage, he made himself ethnically "neutral," a living *tabula rasa*, awaiting the character delineation that came with blacking up, donning green knee-pants or the Dutchman's chin whiskers and flat derby. He became the primed canvas on which the Bowery audiences would paint their grotesque self-portraits.

CHAPTER IV
Tambo & Bones in Whiteface

> When we bled, our audiences liked us all the more.
> from an interview with Lew Fields, 1904

FOR four years, Weber & Fields played the dime museums up and down the Bowery, but there was one museum manager who still refused to hire them. George H. Bunnell had moved his Bowery museum to the corner of Broadway and Ninth Street; being off the Bowery, it appealed to a higher class of patron. Every week, the boys would write to Bunnell to ask him for an engagement. Every week they received a postcard stamped with the words "All time filled."[1]

Weber & Fields' recent debut on a variety stage had redoubled their determination to play at Bunnell's. In October, 1882, they joined the inner circle of professionals at their hangout, Miner's, when they appeared on the bill doing "Dutch breakneck songs and dances." Joe and Lew were convinced that once Bunnell saw how well their act went over in front of an audience, he would want to hire them. The boys devised a plan: they knew that the dime museum managers were always on the lookout for new freaks, particularly if they came from exotic places. If the performers were blacks or Chinese, all the manager needed to do was to give them exotic props and costumes to pass them off as freaks. At Bunnell's and other dime museums in the 1880's, the preoccupation with ethnic differences extended beyond the variety acts to include the freaks. Ethnicity was in itself a type of freakishness; thus, the ideal attraction was an ethnic performer with a physical oddity. Middleton's had featured Chang, "the mighty Chinese giant," and a group of "genuine Chinese musicians." Bunnell, who consciously emulated P. T. Barnum in personal appearance as well as business practices, lured Chang away from his competitor and teamed the giant with Che-Mah, the Chinese dwarf. For his patrons' edification and amazement, Bunnell also procured a Chinese lady with small feet, the Wild Men of Borneo, the Giant Zulu Chief (along with Zulu princess and baby), and Princess Nenemoosha and her troupe of war chiefs and papooses.

With this trend in mind, Joe and Lew called on Bunnell at his office, and told his doorkeeper that they had found a new "curiosity" for the museum: a Chinaman with an eye in the middle of his forehead. Suddenly, Bunnell had the time to talk with the boys.

His interest piqued, Bunnell asked where he could find this remarkable Chinaman. Lew said that he and Joe had seen the freak on Mott Street, in Chinatown, and that they knew which house he lived in. But before taking him there, the boys wanted to know what their reward would be for telling him about this curiosity. Bunnell asked them what they wanted, and the boys sprang their trap: they wanted to perform at his museum starting the following day.

In November, 1882, Weber & Fields—billed as "juvenile comedians"—began a two-week engagement at Bunnell's New Museum on Broadway, followed by an additional week at his Brooklyn museum. Their turn probably combined Dutch, Irish, and blackface routines in a kind of ethnic quick-change act. Later in the month, they played a week at the National, performing "specialties, changing from black to white, the 'Cream de la Cream' of Comedy."

Joe and Lew managed to string Bunnell along for three weeks, until the day when he sent word backstage to the boys to hustle into their street clothes. They drove downtown in Bunnell's carriage, and after hemming and hawing for as long as possible, one of the boys pointed to a house on Mott Street. Bunnell rapped on the door with his cane. An elderly Chinese man peered through the slot and, instantly suspicious of the *low faan* ("outsiders"), refused to open up. Enraged at being denied entrance, Bunnell went to the office of the Chinese consul.[2]

Bunnell demanded that the consul help him find the freak, and that he was going to have him no matter what the cost. The consul, gentlemanly and calm, insisted that he had never heard of such a man. Perhaps someone was pulling Mr. Bunnell's leg?

"He never said a word to us all the way back to the museum," recalled Fields. "He realized that he had been duped by a couple of youngsters. . . . When he got back to his place he took us off into a corner and said to us, 'By Jimminy, if you two weren't a couple of little Jews you wouldn't be so smart. Go back to work.' We stayed there four weeks longer and Mr. Bunnell always called us his boys after that."[3]

It is unlikely that Bunnell would have been such a good sport if Weber & Fields had not been a good act. As proof of his appreciation for their talents, Bunnell paid them twenty dollars a week—the same fee he would pay to the Zulus or the India Rubber Man or any of the top freak acts.

The long engagement at Bunnell's opened the doors of the Bowery variety houses for Weber & Fields. Using a variation of the ethnic quick-change act they had featured at the National, they performed at the London Theatre in January, 1883, where they were described as "the smallest Dutch team in the world, making a complete change from white to black in fifteen seconds." Their billing made them sound as much like museum freaks as variety performers.

Inspired by the surging popularity of Gilbert & Sullivan parodies and Harrigan's plays, the London's Jim Donaldson decided to emphasize sketches rather than specialties. At the London, Weber & Fields appeared in their first sketch, "The German Fancy Ball"; one of several sketches on a program that also included "Fritz and Lena at Home," "Scenes at a Boxing School," and "A Subject for Dissection."

This potpourri of popular stage formats, mixing variety, minstrel shows, melodramas, musical farces, and burlesque, was already proving to be a money-maker at Pastor's, Miner's People's Theater, the Windsor, and the National. Theaters like these were referred to as "combination houses." The combination house policy also caught on in smaller cities, for it gave variety managers the flexibility to book whatever companies or miscellaneous performers happened to be passing through. This in turn further encouraged the cross-pollination between popular stage formats.

Two months later, Bunnell had "his boys" back at his Broadway and Brooklyn museums, where they presented their "German and Negro impersonations." Museum and variety managers from out of town would sometimes visit Bunnell's and the other Bowery museums to scout young talent for their own establishments; more often, talent was procured at a distance, by referrals, through the mail, or by telegram. The mere mention of having played at Bunnell's, Middleton's, or Worth's was enough to secure an out-of-town engagement.

Since Joe and Lew could not count on more than two engagements a season from each of the New York museums, they knew they had to attract the attention of managers from outside of New York. To this end, they purloined a supply of stationery from the Gilsey House and the Fifth Avenue Hotel, and spent their afternoons in Miner's saloon, writing to out-of-town managers.

In the days before agents, syndicates, unions, and circuits, booking and touring practices were quite simple. Most museum and variety performers handled their own bookings; the more successful ones signed with a troupe specially assembled for one tour, headed by a veteran showman such as M. B. Leavitt or Tony Pastor. Travel was by train, and relatively expensive, unless one happened to be touring as part of a troupe. Road engagements were confined to a geographical region, depending on the performer's base of operations—the Far West (San Francisco, Portland, Denver), the Midwest (Minneapolis, Milwaukee, Chicago, St. Louis), and the East (Boston, New York, Philadelphia, Baltimore). Performers tried to avoid making long jumps between cities, preferring instead to play at all the available theaters in a given city before moving on to the next-closest city on the railroad line.

With Bunnell and Middleton as references, Weber & Fields' letter-writing campaign began to produce results. The word around Miner's was that Weber & Fields were going "out West" for a museum engagement. The Weber and Fields families put their nickels together to buy Joe and Lew a trunk—papier-mâché, with straps painted on—in which to carry their costumes, makeup, and a change of clothes. Several older siblings accompanied the boys to Hoboken, New Jersey, where west-bound trains originated. After a round of emotional goodbyes, the boys boarded the train and settled in for the journey to their destination: Paterson, in the wilds of New Jersey, a half hour down the line.

If it was cowboys and Indians that the boys were expecting, they were not disappointed. Their first out-of-town engagement coincided with the first East Coast tour of Buffalo Bill's Wild West Show, and it was in Paterson that their paths crossed. Several of the museum performers were bumped from their accommodations to make room for members of the Wild West Show. After performing eight knockabout turns a day, Joe and Lew slept on the floor of the lobby, huddled around the stove with the Living Skeleton, the Armless Wonder, and the other freaks. This arrangement was preferable to the alternative offered by the manager: the boys could share a room with the Indians, though the manager expressed concern for the safety of the boys' scalps during the long night.

From their first out-of-town engagement, Joe and Lew quickly discovered that the only thing more grueling than performing in a museum was to perform in one on the road. For the two fifteen-year-olds—already so sly in the ways of the theater but still so naïve about the world at large—the excitement of travelling and the promises of advancement more than compensated for the hardships.

In the early 1880's, when Weber & Fields began to get a taste of life on the road, dime museums were opening up in almost every urban center. Not surprisingly, it was the cities with the greatest number of recent immigrants that became the main stops on this primitive touring circuit: Buffalo, Rochester, Boston, Providence, New Haven, New York, Brooklyn, Jersey City, Philadelphia, Wilmington, Baltimore, Pittsburgh, Cincinnati, Chicago, and St. Louis—all of them had thriving museums.

During 1883 and 1884, Joe and Lew spent more time on the road than in their familiar Bowery haunts. From what can be pieced together from the sketchy records for the dime museums outside New York, it appears that Weber & Fields travelled throughout the East in a piecemeal fashion. Their growing versatility as performers meant that managers could book them for return appearances every three or four months without sacrificing novelty. Using various combinations of Dutch and Irish dialects, and their knockabout and neat song-and-dance routines, they made the rounds of the museums in Baltimore (Herzog's), Philadelphia (Gilmore's), Providence (Drew's), Boston (Austin & Stone's and Keith & Batchelder's), and New Haven (Bunnell's). Their engagements generally lasted two to four weeks, and the salaries were often double what the variety houses in New York were paying. The dime museums paid forty (or fifty) dollars a week, not including board, which usually came to an additional four to eight dollars.

To save on travel costs, Joe and Lew pretended to be under twelve and purchased half-fare railroad tickets. Despite their scrawny, undersized physiques and their best acting efforts, they did not look to be less than their actual age of fifteen. In fact, when they were not engaged in laugh-making activities, they gave the impression of being old beyond their years. As they crisscrossed the Eastern circuit, their faces became familiar to the railroad conductors, and their attempts to fool the authorities became a battle of wits. During one trip, Joe and Lew decided to travel in separate cars, hoping to avoid suspicion when the conductor came by to collect their half-fare tickets. The conductor, however, recognized the boys as the ones who had gotten the laugh on him once before; he put Joe off the train at the next station but did not inform Lew when and where his partner had disembarked. Fortunately, Joe managed to sneak onto the open platform of the last car as the train pulled out, and he hid himself next to a large, slumbering passenger until they reached Baltimore.[4]

If they were fortunate enough to encounter other teams of kid performers, the seats were turned face to face; a large suitcase was laid across their knees; somebody would hand out cigars, and somebody else would produce a deck of cards. Out of a dense cloud of cigar smoke, the poker players would pause in their poker game to hand over their half-fare tickets to the dumbfounded conductor.

On their first trip to Boston, Weber & Fields reported to the recently opened museum at 585 Washington Street and found its three-storey façade swathed in the biggest, most garish banners and signs they had ever seen. Here, in the heart of downtown, next to the old Adams House, two former circus men—Benjamin Franklin Keith and George Batchelder—had converted a hatter's store into a Barnum-style museum. Keith's first exhibit was a good indication of his delicate sensibilities and those of his patrons. The man who would someday be the figurehead of vaudeville's most powerful trust began his career exhibiting "Baby Alice," a premature black infant weighing a pound and a half. Keith hyped "Baby Alice" as being so small that she could fit inside a milk bottle. Baby Alice grew fast, however, and he soon had to find other oddities to edify his patrons, such as knickknacks from the Greeley Expedition to the Arctic.[5]

"The greatest, most astounding aggregation of marvels and monstrosities ever gathered in one edifice. Looted from the ends of the earth . . ." proclaimed Keith's outside talker, a wiry young man with steely blue eyes and an insistent manner. Edward F. "Ned" Albee was the "mouth" of the partnership; in a few years, he would also become its brains. A cold, tightfisted little man, Keith paid Weber & Fields the going rate of forty dollars a week for eight turns a day, but then charged them six dollars a week each for room and meals at the boardinghouse run by his wife, Mary Catherine. The Keith boardinghouse was actually the attic of the museum building, which was partitioned into eight-by-ten cubicles where the freaks and performers slept and dressed. In the center of the attic was the dining-room table, at which ten-year-old Paul Keith helped serve up the meals. A devout Catholic, Mrs. Keith took a personal interest in seeing that there was no moral stigma attached to her husband's enterprise. With the growth of the Keith-Albee circuit in the late 1880's, she let her preferences be known with a "Notice to Performers" that appeared on the backstage bulletin board of every Keith house:

> Don't say "slob" or "son of a gun" or "Holy gee" on the stage unless you want to be canceled peremptorily. Do not address anyone in the audience in any manner. If you have not the ability to entertain Mr. Keith's audience without risk of offending them, do the best you can. Lack of talent will be less open to censure than would be an insult to a patron. If you are in doubt as to the character of your act, consult the local manager before you go on stage, for if you are guilty of uttering anything sacrilegious or even suggestive, you will be immediately closed and will never again be allowed in a theater where Mr. Keith is in authority.[6]

Weber & Fields were working in Boston for Keith's competitors, Austin & Stone, when an urgent telegram arrived for Joe, informing him that his father had died. Joe, the youngest child, was now the primary breadwinner for his mother and the four or five siblings still living at home.

Of all the Eastern cities visited by variety artists in the early 1880's, Philadelphia was the one most likely to inspire trepidation. In contrast to the social extremes that characterized New York and Boston, where immigration and urban growth produced cultural turmoil, Philadelphia maintained an Old World self-restraint and gentility. Here, the Puritan tradition condemning the theater as the Devil's pastime still lingered, as it did in much of the American heartland. The moral strictures that stifled the legitimate stage had the paradoxical effect of encouraging various popular forms, including the dime museum, variety, and the minstrel show. In the early 1880's, Philadelphia reportedly had more than twenty variety houses—a surprising number of them built in former churches.

It was no coincidence that the specialties that went over best in Philadelphia—song-and-dance teams, monologists, ballad singers, musicians, and acrobats—were the ones most characteristic of minstrel shows. Like many native-born and rural Americans, Philadelphians made a curious distinction between the sinful indulgences of theater and the "innocent" diversions provided by the minstrel show. As minstrel authority Robert C. Toll explained it, "The blackface mask allowed performers, and perhaps also their patrons, to cast off their inhibitions and to play out their fantasies of themselves in their stereotypes of blacks."[7]

In the spring of 1883, Weber & Fields survived a week's engagement at Philadelphia's most successful variety house, Gilmore's Grand Central Theater. Among variety artists, William Gilmore was known as a crusty, temperamental character, who frequently fired acts that displeased him after their first performance. It was because of managers like Gilmore that vaudevillians used to say, "Don't send out your laundry until after the first show." When the boardinghouse owner heard where Joe and Lew were working, she suggested that they find other lodgings; Gilmore's whims had cost her too many defaulted bills.

Appearing on the bill with Weber & Fields was a mild-mannered young song-and-dance man, Eddie Foy, loaned to Gilmore for the week by minstrel manager John L. Carncross. Foy's act was unique in its day for its quiet charm and restraint; he forswore the violent physicality and aggressive delivery of his contemporaries. In this, Foy's style was ideally suited for the Philadelphia audience, and the exact opposite of the kind of act that Weber & Fields were performing. Yet Foy recognized that theirs was no ordinary knockabout act, and he mentioned them to Frank Dumont, Carncross' stage manager. Shortly after Weber & Fields' return to New York, they received a letter from Carncross asking their terms.

Miner's saloon was abuzz. Carncross advertised his minstrels as "The Star Troupe of the World"; with Lew Dockstader and Eddie Foy as the end men, Chauncey Olcott singing sentimental ballads, and John Philip Sousa in the orchestra, the claim was only the slightest hyperbole. Between 1878 and 1896, every major minstrel performer who came to Philadelphia appeared at Carncross' Eleventh Street Opera House. After consulting with a few of their more experienced colleagues at Miner's, Joe and Lew decided to ask Carncross for the princely sum of seventy dollars a week.

What puzzled the regulars at Miner's was that Carncross had never before hired a whiteface act. In retrospect, it would seem that Carncross was responding to the same pressures—the increasing competition from variety, dime museums, and burlesque—that had all but eliminated the resident minstrel companies of

New York. If minstrelsy were to survive, it had to cater to the public's tastes for spectacle and novelty. Weber & Fields' Dutch knockabout act at least promised to satisfy the latter objective.

Although Weber & Fields had never actually appeared in a minstrel show, the structure was familiar to them, and not simply because they had been enthusiastic members of the audience for Kelly and Leon's Minstrels, the San Francisco Minstrels, and the many ad hoc troupes that passed through New York. Performing within variety's flexible format led to an implicit grasp of the minstrel form.

Historically, minstrelsy began as a specialty act within a primitive variety show in the 1820's; by 1900, the minstrel show had been reabsorbed by variety and vaudeville. In the intervening years, however, the overlap in material, performers, and audiences was considerable.[8] The characteristic three-part form of the minstrel show emerged in the 1840's and 1850's, due largely to the innovations of the Christie Minstrels.

The first part of the standard minstrel show was by far the most rigidly structured. Singing and strutting and waving their arms, the minstrels positioned themselves on stage in a semicircle. In the middle of the blackface clowns stood the interlocutor, a pompous-looking man in a full-dress suit, the only performer not in blackface. "Gentlemen, be seated!" he would order, and the show would begin. With his self-important manner and overblown rhetorical style, the interlocutor acted as the master of ceremonies, introducing the acts and engaging in a running dialogue with the two end men. Called "Tambo and Bones" for the tambourine and bone clackers they used to underscore a joke or a trick, the end men dressed in gaudy clothes and kinky fright wigs, and spoke in a heavy plantation dialect replete with malapropisms and puns. The interlocutor was the quintessential straight man or foil for the comic end men, feeding Tambo and Bones the set-up lines, yet always maintaining the dignity of a man too full of himself to realize that the halfwits around him are getting the best of him. The give-and-take, "crossfire" banter between the interlocutor and the end men was the pretext for introducing the set numbers: tenors singing sentimental ballads and love songs, satiric lectures on topics like women's rights, hit songs like Stephen Foster's "Oh, Susanna!" or "Old Folks at Home," and dances that ranged from the forerunner of the soft shoe to fast-tapping jigs.[9] The first part ended with another up-tempo song and dance by the ensemble—the cakewalk or "walk-around."

The second part of the show was performed in front of a drop curtain, primarily to allow time for simple scenery to be shifted on stage. The "olio"—so named because of the kitchen product that was commonly advertised on the theater curtains—most closely resembled a variety bill, since it was performed without the interlocutors and end men as intermediaries. The emphasis here was on individuals whose specialties were short, self-contained turns of particular merit: banjoists, performing dogs, comedy teams, and, most notably, "he-she's" (female impersonators) and "stump speakers" (monologists).

The female impersonator was another mainstay of vaudeville and the revue that had its origins in the minstrel show olio. As far back as the 1840's, George Christie donned women's clothing to sing the sentimental ballads that the audience would have otherwise considered to be unmanly. More often, however, the female impersonator performed satire, playing the doting mammy or the cantankerous old lady.[10] On the variety stage, Tony Hart's cross-dressing in Harrigan's plays was a dependable crowd-pleaser; whether he was playing a female in blackface or Irish makeup, he was widely considered to be the era's finest "wench." The Russell Brothers, in their wickedly hilarious portrayals of two Irish maids or "biddies," were a big vaudeville draw for almost twenty years, eventually headlining for one of Weber & Fields' touring companies in the 1890's. By the 1880's, the female impersonator's primary objective became mimetic rather than satiric: to amaze the audience with a convincing illusion of femininity. Francis Leon, of Kelly and Leon's Minstrels, attired himself in fashionable women's clothes instead of plantation glad rags. His feminine grace and fragility were uncanny, especially when he danced in the classical ballet style.

The monologist's "stump speech" was delivered in a heavy black dialect, a parody of preachers and politicians. The art of the stump speaker lay in his ability to take outrageous puns and malapropisms, pregnant pauses, twisted logic and double talk, and bizarre imagery and string them together in a seamless whole. Variety artists and circus clowns were quick to adapt the stump speech format, performing it in Irish, Dutch, rube, and, eventually, Jewish dialects.

The third part of the standard minstrel show was an extended sketch called the "afterpiece," a broad burlesque of a topical event or a stage play, with songs and dances. This blending of comedy, music, and dancing, tied together by the thinnest of plots, was the inspiration for Harrigan's musical farces, and, arguably, the most direct formal antecedent of the American musical. The charm of the minstrel afterpiece, however, derived from its spontaneity. Whether the story was a stock situation (e.g., a railroad station, a mock trial, a schoolroom) or a burlesque (of Uncle Tom's Cabin, a Shakespeare excerpt, or a current stage hit), much of the material was put together—"worked up"—in rehearsals and actual performances, and adapted to local tastes and news of the day.[11] These afterpieces put a premium on the actor's resourcefulness and command of his craft: cues and blocking were established in the last rehearsal before the show; deletions and additions continued right through the last performance. The minstrel tradition of the afterpiece, with an ensemble of experienced comedians improvising around a familiar storyline, had a lasting influence on the working methods of Weber & Fields. Fifteen years after their minstrel show experience, they kept the spirit of the afterpiece alive in the travesties they presented at their Music Hall.

The Carncross Minstrels' show stuck to the conventional three-part format, without the latest gimmicks—no big casts, lavish sets, or serious female impersonators. Presumably, what made Weber & Fields attractive to John Carncross was their versatility. Eddie Foy would almost certainly have mentioned their "complete change from white to black," as well as their Dutch knockabout. This meant that the duo could do their specialty in the olio, and play supporting roles in the first part and the afterpiece.

Weber & Fields opened in the olio at the Eleventh Street Opera House on a Monday night, doing their Dutch knockabout turn. Carncross' audience did not know what to make of the act. Silence reigned from the duo's entrance to their exit. In the jargon of vaudeville, Weber & Fields died standing up. After the show, Joe and Lew waited in the dressing room for word of their dismissal.

Streetwise though they were, they had little experience coping with the pain of an audience's rejection. When Carncross arrived, the boys did their best to hide the fact that they had been crying. Instead of firing them, however, the veteran manager gave them some advice. Carncross admitted that his was a peculiar audience, very conservative, and slow to accept an unfamiliar joke or piece of stage business. "They seem to think that your stage fight is real," observed Carncross, "and they're uneasy." (How unlike the Bowery audiences that Joe and Lew were accustomed to!) Carncross suggested that at the end of their argument, the boys should shake hands and smile at the audience "to show them it was all in fun." He also recommended that they replace their usual costumes—the loud checked suits—with full-dress suits, similar to the kind the interlocutor wore. Relieved and grateful for one more chance, the boys went to a nearby second-hand store the next morning and purchased two dress suits with money advanced by their kindly employer. Fields later claimed that this was the first use of formal evening dress by a variety act on the American stage.[12]

Carncross had read his audience perfectly. By the end of the first week, the minstrel show patrons were warming to Weber & Fields' revised turn. A week more, and the boys were getting curtain calls. It was, in Fields' words, "our first experience in educating an audience." Carncross asked them to stay for the rest of the season, providing they were willing to take a cut in their seventy-dollar-a-week salary. Joe and Lew agreed, figuring that a lower salary and a long run with a prestige outfit was worth it. The minstrel manager named his price: he would pay the boys sixty-nine dollars a week, in accordance with the superstition that it was bad luck to pay out an even sum.

Weber & Fields' eight-month stint with the Carncross Minstrels exerted a lasting influence on their material, their work methods, and their future managerial style. Their new outfits accentuated the differences between the straight man (Lew) and the comic (Joe): the dress suits made Lew look slicker and more dignified, while Joe, with his exaggerated padding and oversized clothes, looked more than ever like a buffoon. Undoubtedly, the experience of playing Tambo and Bones and engaging the interlocutor in crossfire dialogues helped sharpen their own comic–straight man exchanges. Some commentators even maintain that Weber & Fields were the first real straight man–comic team in variety. While such assertions are impossible to prove with any certainty, it is safe to say that Weber & Fields popularized the classic straight man–comic relationship, and thus became the models that most future vaudeville duos were based on.

Similarly, Weber & Fields are widely credited with the oldest wheeze in show biz—"Who vas dot lady I saw you vit last night?"—which probably dates from about this time (1883–1885). But it is equally likely that the boys first heard the joke delivered with a plantation accent, in the banter between the interlocutor and the end men. Adapting the joke to their Dutch knockabout act and presenting it in variety houses and dime museums all over the East, Weber & Fields made it their own.

Olio performers were also expected to play in the afterpiece. Typically, on a

Monday morning, the stage manager gave each player a list with his character's cues. Players were expected to be familiar with the storyline and their characters' traits. On Monday evening, it was usually a case of every man for himself, with the victor being the one who got the most laughs. In the minstrel show and variety afterpieces, it was not uncommon for certain veteran actors to haze the novice, to humiliate (with the audience's gleeful participation) the inexperienced or slow-witted performer who could not respond to an ad-libbed comment or bit of slapstick. Undaunted, Joe and Lew learned to hold their own, countering the veterans' intimidation techniques with antics of their own.

In an interview in 1914, Fields discussed the valuable training provided by the afterpiece:

> The older low comedians had a different training from that of the youngsters who are now coming to the forefront. . . . That training [afterpieces] developed any latent resourcefulness we might have had. . . . It was a splendid schooling for our later activities. Every one who later associated with us in our music hall had that same training, and that was why there was always an indescribable spontaneity and sparkle in the performances given there. . . .
>
> I know of half a dozen successful young comedians of the present day whose names are on the billboards and on the electric signs, who would have about as much chance as the proverbial snowball in the nether regions if they were put on the stage with that group of comedians surrounding us a few years ago. They would be backed into a corner and kept there simply because they have not learned how to give and take.[13]

It is this "give and take," Fields pointed out, that is at the basis of light comedy acting. Unwittingly, Fields also pointed out a stylistic link between the minstrel show afterpiece and its modern-day counterparts, the television variety sketch and the situation comedy.

Every week for their eight months with Carncross, Joe and Lew had respectable paychecks to send to their families in the Bowery. The boys held out only the six dollars a week for room and board, and money for incidental expenses such as costume and prop replacements, or for an occasional ad in the trade papers. Given the straitened circumstances of the Weber family, Joe's contributions must have seemed heroic. Lew's weekly checks were handled by his older brother Max; Papa Schanfield apparently was still unwilling to accept his prodigal son's success.

Coincidentally, Weber & Fields' homecoming in December of 1883 corresponded to the closing of New York's last resident minstrel troupe, the San Francisco Minstrels, which was absorbed by Haverly's burgeoning company. A. H. Sheldon, the stage manager and sketch-writer for Miner's Bowery Theatre, welcomed the boys home by hiring them for back-to-back engagements at Miner's Bowery and the Eighth Avenue Theaters beginning the week after Christmas. With their minstrel show experience and their growing local reputation, Weber & Fields were no longer merely an opening or "filler" act on the variety bill, but neither were they featured performers.

By the mid-1880's, variety managers had begun to develop a set of conven-

tions governing the types of acts and their optimum placement in the program.
The typical bill had between nine and twelve acts; with each slot possessing more
or less status according to where it fell in relation to the intermission and the
end of the program. There were usually two headliners (more at Miner's and
Pastor's), one for each half of the bill. The last act before the intermission was a
status slot, where the manager put a big-name act to give the audience something
to rave about during the intermission. The top headliner—the act they had all
been waiting for—appeared second from the last ("next to closing") on the bill,
followed only by the afterpiece (in the slot that later came to be known as the
"chaser"). Of course, every comedy act aspired to appear next to closing. Thus,
one can chart the rise and fall of vaudeville stars by where they appeared on the
bill, and what kind of act preceded or followed them.

At Miner's theaters in early 1884, Weber & Fields performed their Dutch act
immediately after the intermission. The first act after the intermission was considered to be a difficult position to fill because the performers had to regain the
patrons' interest and renew the momentum of the show as it headed towards its
"wow" finish. For this reason, the manager or booker (often the same person, in
those days) preferred a strong comedy act, but one that would not diminish the
impact of the full-stage act or sketch that usually followed. Appearing in the
opening slot after intermission, Weber & Fields performed their new routine, "The
Deutscher's Picnic," inspired by the revival of Harrigan's *The Mulligan Guards'
Picnic* a few months earlier.

For reasons that remain unclear, this was Weber & Fields' last appearance
as a German dialect act until December 1885. Conceivably, they were responding
to the fact the biggest variety draws were the Irish acts, such as the witty song-
and-dance specialist, Pat Rooney. For the next two years, Weber & Fields performed their neat Irish song-and-dance, and sometimes their tidy-tearing, at Miner's theaters, the Windsor, the National, the Globe, and the New York Museum.
In addition to their specialty, they appeared in simple sketches built around their
Irish characterizations: "The Happy Irish Pair," "Land of the Shamrock Green,"
"Strolling through the Clover," "Success to the Shamrock." The last number was
a Bowery crowd-pleaser that appealed to the same sort of righteous sentimentality as George M. Cohan's jingoistic hits some twenty years later:

> Success to the shamrock, and soon may it be
> Entwined with the violet, and the emblem of the free.
> Ireland for the Irish.
> May God give freedom to their isle,
> Acushla Gall Machree.[14]

What the last line meant, neither Joe nor Lew could say, but the enthusiastic
outbursts it provoked were gratifying. The audience laughed at the gentle parody
(the two Jewish boys with their hands over their noses, claiming to be "a happy
Irish pair"), and applauded the clog dances and paper-tearing. Imperceptibly,
however, the basis of Weber & Fields' appeal had shifted from their earlier brash-
ness and inventiveness to a slick reworking of familiar material. Having tasted

success, they feared failure all the more. To flop at a New York house in the way they did when they started with Carncross' Minstrels would have been a serious setback. Their routine "The Happy Irish Pair," for example, was most likely cribbed from a routine of the same name by the Parker Twins, who had performed it two years earlier. Weber & Fields and the Parker Twins were travelling companions on the museum circuit, sharing the train rides, filling the time with poker, trade gossip—and rehearsals.

Simply put, Weber & Fields' act was getting stale. At age eighteen, they could no longer be considered a kid act, and they could no longer count on precocious charm to smooth over the weak spots in their act. Certainly their presentation was more polished, their costumes more professional, and they had incorporated new bits of business along the way, but except for an occasional Dutch knockabout turn, they had been doing essentially the same old song and dance for almost six years.

They were still using the entrance song—"Here we are, an [ethnic] pair"—that had been a part of their professional debut at the Chatham Square Theatre in 1877. At that time, the boys (like many variety performers) had "borrowed" a popular tune from a better-known act and refitted it with their own lyrics. For the week of February 23, 1885, however, they found themselves sharing the bill at Miner's Bowery with the originators of their entrance song. It was Monday morning, and Weber & Fields were giving the orchestra its cues, when Charles Pettingell of the American Four interrupted. In a voice dripping with sarcasm, he asked Joe and Lew how they had come up with the melody for their entrance song. What a coincidence that their entrance song sounded just like one that the American Four had been singing for almost ten years. Pettingell then pointed out that the management would not take kindly to small-timers' stealing from the featured act on the same bill.

Joe and Lew knew better than to challenge the veteran, and they may even have been secretly grateful for the warning. They had only a few hours to rehearse a new entrance, but their minstrel show experience had given them confidence in their ability to vamp (improvise) as they went along. They decided to enter arguing, with Weber emerging from the wings backwards, propelled by Fields' physical and verbal sallies. At center stage, they would notice the audience with a double-take and then break into their familiar clog dance. Although they intended it as a stopgap solution, they would eventually develop it into a classic bit of stage business. But in the remaining months of 1885, the new entrance seemed to have little effect on the team's declining fortunes.

With unaccustomed time on their hands, Joe and Lew perfected their pool shooting in the saloon behind Miner's Bowery while trying to come up with the new bit that would save their careers. The prodigies of 1880 were in danger of becoming the has-beens of 1885. As if to postpone this unhappy future for as long as possible, they managed to keep their games of rotation pool going indefinitely. If one of them happened to pocket a ball, the other would call "Scratch!" and return the ball to the table. The saloon's billiard marker would usually end the game by decree before the final ball would ever fall.

One Friday night during one of these marathons, stage manager A. H. Sheldon walked through the saloon to take inventory of the roomful of variety actors currently "at liberty." The Adah Richmond Burlesque Company was to open on Monday, and they needed a Dutch act to fill in the specialty portion of the program. Sheldon recalled that Weber & Fields used to do a Dutch knockabout routine; would the boys be interested in dusting off their old routines? Their eagerness made it easy for Sheldon to tell them that the pay was twenty dollars, which was considered low for a two-act. Miner's had previously paid them (and other secondary acts) thirty for the week; an established team received fifty.

For Joe and Lew, it was back to the featherbeds in the Weber's basement apartment for two days of bruising rehearsals. Choreographing the violent blows and falls was easier for them than before, since they were better coordinated and more experienced. But if they put aside their song-and-dance material, where was their patter to come from? Lew suggested that they take some of the minstrel show gags, talk them up in the fractured English of the German laborers upstairs in Simon's saloon, and wind up with the knockabout. They were already using a variation on the minstrel show crossfire dialogue style for their entrance; why not just expand it and punctuate it with knockabout, and make it an extremely animated sidewalk conversation?

The East Coast tour by the Adah Richmond Burlesque Combination in the fall of 1885 was one of the first by an American burlesque troupe. In contrast to the tradition of burlesque (travesty) exemplified by *Evangeline* and *Adonis*, Adah Richmond performed burlesque in the risqué style of Lydia Thompson and Pauline Markham. As presented by Richmond, *The Sleeping Beauty* consisted of three parts: the first and third parts burlesque, with an olio of four specialty acts in between. Miss Richmond played Princess Is-a-Belle; her ladies-in-waiting provided the requisite displays of feminine pulchritude and sensuous dancing, while Ed Connelly (the company's stage manager) supplied some degree of vocal and comic talent. His wife, Virginia Ross, housed an impressive coloratura voice in what was, apparently, a formidable physique. In the usual stage blocking of the day, the chorus would stand in groups behind the featured singers, listening respectfully.

The specialty performers were also expected to augment the ranks of the burlesque chorus. Weber & Fields, however, found it next to impossible to be onstage and not move or speak. They were sure that something more was expected of them. Perhaps, as the voices of Mr. Connelly and Miss Ross mingled in a romantic duet, Weber & Fields were seized with the same kind of mischievous impulse that inspired the Marx Brothers whenever they were around Margaret Dumont. Behind the singers, Joe and Lew launched into a broad pantomime. Sniggers turned to guffaws as the audience began to catch on. The stately Miss Ross looked distressed, and her partner tried to whisper a discreet warning over his shoulder. Encouraged by the audience's laughter, Weber & Fields misunderstood Connelly's intent. Their clowning escalated to slapstick kicks and a climactic fall. The curtain came down with the audience roaring; Miss Ross began ranting hysterically, and Connelly threatened to fire the scene-stealers on the spot.

Being the cheapest act on the bill had one advantage: it meant that they opened the olio. Connelly could not scrub their act without a replacement, so

Weber & Fields were allowed to go on. Backstage, Sheldon tried to persuade Connelly that the boys' efforts were not malicious.

Having billed themselves as "The Skull Crackers," Weber & Fields planned to make good on this promise from the moment they appeared on stage. They entered arguing and gesticulating, sputtering malapropisms and mangled English in an exaggerated German accent. Previous Dutch comedians had used twisted speech, but never to this extreme, and never in combination with knockabout. Moreover, thanks to the lessons of Mr. Interlocutor, Tambo, and Bones in the minstrel show, Weber & Fields were now projecting distinct stage personalities; the straight man (the scheming bully) and the comic (the harassed moron). And keeping in mind Carncross' advice, in the midst of trading blows and insults, the two feuding Dutchmen made it clear that they were actually the best of friends. The audience was delighted, insisting on several encores before they would allow the program to continue.

The Tuesday afternoon show at Miner's Bowery was the actor's matinee, free to managers and actors, and a critical house if ever there was one. Once again, Fields kicked Weber's padded stomach, Weber whacked Fields over the head with his cane, and Fields hooked his cane around Weber's neck and dragged him across the stage. Their colleagues' responses were gratifying indeed: a dozen encores, and an invitation from Sheldon to play Miner's Eighth Avenue Theater the following week. Joe took advantage of their new-found popularity and persuaded Sheldon to pay them at the premium rate—fifty dollars for the week. Sheldon squawked but ultimately gave in, confident that the boys' new act was a money-maker.

As he predicted, Weber & Fields' skull-cracking specialty was a hit. One of those applauding it at Miner's Eighth Avenue was Colonel Hopkins, owner of the Theatre Comique in Providence, in town looking for new acts for his house. Eddie Talbot, a fellow actor on the bill (and another occasional travelling companion) had been booked for Hopkins' theater, but was unable to keep the engagement. He suggested Weber & Fields as a replacement. When Hopkins asked for their rate, Talbot suggested that they ask for "a yard and a quarter"—one hundred and twenty-five dollars—an outrageous sum.

To their surprise, Hopkins agreed without further negotiation. Joe and Lew were immediately suspicious. "That man will skin us sure," predicted Lew. "Why, there's no money in all the world like one hundred and twenty-five dollars." They spent the next week trying to line up another engagement, figuring that Hopkins' offer was too good to be true. When they failed to turn up anything else, they decided to take the chance on Hopkins. Lew reasoned, "At least we'll get our board out of it."[15]

There were two ways of getting to Providence: by train via New Haven, or by steamer to Fall River and from there, by rail. Joe and Lew opted for the steamer since it was cheapest. The morning of their departure, they bought passage on the *Pilgrim* and checked the trunk containing their props and costumes. The ticket agent, however, failed to mention that the schedule had just been changed, so that all departures had been moved up by ten minutes. After strolling around the neighborhood for several hours, Joe and Lew returned to the wharf just in time to see the *Pilgrim*—with their trunk on board—pulling out. In desperation, they hurried to the old Grand Central Station and started begging for enough change for two train tickets. A team of acrobats, also heading for Providence, sympathized with Weber & Fields' hard-luck story and lent them some money, then kept them up all night with trade gossip and stories.

Besides their costumes, bamboo canes, and make-up, the trunk contained the specially designed padding that protected them from the violent blows and falls that were the Skull Crackers' main appeal. Because of the unusual violence of their act, and the importance of differentiating between their comic roles, the usual body pads, skullcap, and heavy makeup were inadequate.

What little makeup they needed they borrowed from the acrobats. The only canes they could find, however, were blackthorns, made of unforgivingly hard, knotty wood. They sneaked pillows from their hotel, knowing that the down in the pillows was not as dense as their usual padding. A member of the Zanfretta family (mimes and sketch artists) lent Joe a skullcap. Joe stuffed a handkerchief underneath it for extra protection—a poor substitute for the steel-reinforced wig sitting in an unclaimed trunk in Fall River. Lew's aim with the blackthorn would be critical, and Joe rehearsed him on the exact location of the handkerchief.

The first part of the program at Hopkins' Theatre Comique was an odd mix of burlesque and minstrel show, with young women wearing tights and short skirts sitting in swings on either side of the end men, Tambo and Bones. After the crossfire dialogue and plantation songs, the young women abandoned their swings and performed a dance.

Given their salary, it may be assumed that Weber & Fields were one of the featured acts in the second part. On opening night, they came on in their street clothes, with their makeshift padding—all that they could fit—underneath. The audience at Hopkins' was as demonstrative and as bloodthirsty as any from the Bowery. As Weber & Fields launched into their knockabout, the audience exhorted the boys to further mayhem. During the vigorous give-and-take, Joe's improvised skull protector slipped out of place. The clout from Lew's blackthorn was on target—right where the thickest padding was supposed to be, but wasn't. Blood streamed from Joe's head, and the audience stamped their feet with delight.

Terrified, Lew kneeled to help his wounded partner, but Joe shook him off, unaware of the blood. Still in character, Joe continued with the performance, dazed but feeling no pain, buoyed by the applause and the adrenalin, accustomed to the feel of perspiration pouring down his face and neck. Lew tried to hurry along the rest of the act, but there was no way to hasten the curtain calls. The house was in an uproar; Joe, now quite lightheaded, was savoring the moment. He wiped his forehead with his hand, stared in horror at the blood, and collapsed in a faint. This final embellishment at the end of a successful act was known in the business as "a wow finish."

Lew dragged his partner into the wings, put him in a chair, and pressed a cold, wet sponge to Joe's wound. Drawn from the box office by the sound of his patrons' cheering, Colonel Hopkins saw the end of Weber & Fields' act and rushed backstage to congratulate them. He was most impressed by the bleeding gag; how did they do it? It was not in the act he saw at Miner's, but he advised them to keep it in for the future. The following night, despite Lew's best efforts, his blows reopened Joe's scalp, and Joe took advantage of the opportunity to improve upon his fainting bit.

Weber & Fields' trunk arrived by mid-week, and Lew's blows resumed their former intensity without the bloody consequences. Colonel Hopkins was disappointed, and did not rehire them after their week's commitment was fulfilled. Recalled Fields: "Providence liked our murder act. It was rough work. . . . When we bled our audiences seemed to like us all the better." The Providence gig marked the beginning of the curious blend of sympathy and sadism with which audiences regarded Weber & Fields for the next forty years. Looking back on their popularity, Weber indulged in uncharacteristic self-pity as he complained about a career spent absorbing his partner's blows, kicks, and eye-gouging: "All the public wanted to see was Fields knock the hell out of me."[16] This was only partly true at best, unfair to the talents of Weber & Fields and the sensibilities of their audience. Rarely did the scheming and bullying of Fields' character carry the day; the Weber character usually managed to extricate himself, whether through Fields' incompetence and pomposity, or sheer bad luck. And physically, at least in their pre–Music Hall days, Weber gave as good as he got: during another performance, for example, he meant to club Lew in the chest, but he caught him across the lips.

Immediately upon returning to New York City, Weber & Fields were hired to bring their "Rough songs, dances and eccentricities" back to Miner's Bowery (at fifty dollars for the week). Word was out that their new Dutch knockabout style was a panic; there was even a favorable mention of their act in the *New York Clipper*, the weekly trade journal for sports and popular stage news.

Gus Hill, co-owner of a touring variety company, heard the rumors and came to see Weber & Fields' act. Hill was familiar with the team, having played in many of the same houses over the past four years, once or twice on the same bill. He had a keen eye for young talent, and he was quick to spot the ones who had promise but did not yet know what it was worth. Now in the midst of a lackluster tour, he was scouting for replacements for several featured acts who had left the company. This was a common problem, given the harsh touring conditions and primitive booking practices. Illness or injury, better engagements, and personal differences all contributed to the high attrition rate among travelling companies.

Hill was impressed with Weber & Fields' Dutch knockabout, and he also remembered their Irish song-and-dance and paper-tearing routines. These versatile young men could fill several of the gaps in his program, all for the price of one act. He offered to take the boys on for the rest of the tour—fifteen weeks, at thirty dollars, with room, board, and transportation included—and if they worked out, he would include them in the next year's tour.

Notwithstanding the taste of wealth provided by the Providence engagement, the promise of steady work, even at a relatively low salary, appealed to Joe and Lew. After all, less than one month earlier, they had been loafing around Miner's pool table, wondering if they were indeed just another overgrown kid act with a great future behind them.

Physically as well as artistically, Joe and Lew were growing into their stage personas. Lew no longer needed lifts and undersized suits to accentuate his tallness. At five feet eleven inches, he towered over Joe, who had reached his full height—five feet four inches—when he was fifteen. Their offstage personalities seemed to be almost the complete opposite of their stage personas: offstage, Weber was the schemer and the wisecracking wheeler-dealer, Fields was the plunger, the ever-hopeful dreamer.

Their new boss and mentor, Gus Hill, was born in the Bowery in 1858. He began his career as an Indian-club swinger, wrestler, and boxer in the circus, eventually making the transition to variety in the early 1880's after he had established his reputation as a "champion" club swinger and exhibition wrestler. To modern sensibilities, watching a hulk of a man lift, twirl, and occasionally juggle heavy Indian clubs may seem like one of the more uninspiring demonstrations of physical prowess, but Gus Hill was a consummate showman.

He was also a charlatan, a hustler, a skinflint, a resourceful manager, and, by the turn of the century, one of the wealthiest men in show business. As a club swinger, he would display his clubs in the lobby before the show and invite the men in the audience to try to lift them. Few could, much less perform the feats of strength and dexterity that Gus Hill did so effortlessly on stage. Before coming on stage, he opened the clubs' false bottoms and removed the lead weights that made them so unwieldy.

The road was Hill's home and his fortune. He was one of the first variety managers to take advantage of the fact that the entertainment tastes in America's heartland did not necessarily parallel those of the audiences in the big Eastern urban centers. Building on his experiences in variety, he later produced and toured popular-priced musical comedies—*Bringing Up Father*, for example—that were never intended for Broadway. They were called trunk shows, so called because the scenery folded into specially designed trunks, making an extra baggage car unnecessary.

During their three seasons with Gus Hill, Weber & Fields learned much about the business aspect of road shows: booking, assembling programs, gauging different audiences, and managing and evaluating talent. These lessons would serve them well, for it was their touring companies that kept them solvent during the heyday of the Weber & Fields Music Hall. And later, during Fields' partnership with the Shuberts, there were several seasons when his touring companies were the only ones making money for the Shubert organization.

Compared to the murderous performance schedule and unpredictable touring practices in the dime museum circuit, Weber & Fields found life on the road with a variety company to be relatively pleasant. To their great relief, their travel arrangements were handled by the manager. If the bookings were properly arranged, the longest train ride was half a day, usually on a Monday morning. At their destination, the performers were taken to a hotel or boardinghouse that catered to theater people. (In every city, there were still a few hotels and boardinghouses that refused to rent to actors, with signs that read "No dogs or actors allowed.")

To save on lodging expenses, the owner of a travelling company would sometimes buy boardinghouses in several cities along the tour route. Performers slept two to a room, or in dormitory-style sleeping accommodations. The boardinghouses provided meals; if the troupe was staying at a hotel, veteran members of the company would usually be able to recommend an affordable restaurant nearby.

Upon arrival at the boardinghouse, the company manager gave each performer several dollars' worth of checks, worth five cents apiece, good for drinks at the bar. At the end of the week the checks were tallied and charged against the performer's salary. This was supposedly done out of concern for the typically spendthrift, hard-drinking actor, but it also generated additional revenue for the managers, who probably figured that they might as well benefit from something that the performers would do anyway. Unlike most of their colleagues, Weber & Fields had not cultivated a taste for "a dhrop o' th' cratur." They used their bar checks as poker stakes, or else redeemed them at the end of the week for a little extra cash, much to the manager's chagrin.

Gus Hill countered this by charging interest on any money he advanced to his actors. Salaries were paid on Wednesday nights for the previous week ending on Saturday. Since Joe and Lew sent most of their wages back to their families, they sometimes came up short by Sunday or Monday. Hill always obliged, but he deducted the interest in advance.

Joe and Lew quickly adjusted to the daily routine. Typically, actors slept late, and then ate a large breakfast to fortify themselves for a long morning of rehearsals. Rehearsals were held at the theater if it was nearby; otherwise, the actors practiced their routines in the banquet room of the hotel, or the dining room of the boardinghouse. Knockabout acts and acrobats were understandably unpopular with the management when they rehearsed on the premises.

After a light lunch, the performers had the afternoon off to take care of personal business—haircut, laundry, correspondence—or to relax. If it was an unfamiliar town, Joe and Lew enjoyed walking around and seeing the sights. Whenever possible, they tried to strike up conversations with the natives, but it was often difficult to find any respectable folks to talk to. Travelling variety performers were generally regarded with suspicion and distaste. When personal interactions were impossible, Lew would spend afternoons observing the tradespeople and the pedestrians. If the town was too familiar, or the weather inclement, Joe and Lew would hang out at the boardinghouse, where there was always a poker game, or a group of actors swapping stories in the bar.

Boredom was a problem for certain veterans of the circuit, a further inducement to boozing or gambling. Often, the boardinghouses were in the city's Tenderloin district, where faro games and female companionship (for a fee) were readily available. There were occasional brawls between performers, or run-ins with the local police, who could insist on command performances at the station for their night shift (after the regular performance) in return for not enforcing certain laws. For Joe and Lew, however, there was little that the road could offer that they had not already seen in the Bowery.

Dinner was at six; by seven, the performers were at the theater preparing for their acts. The dressing rooms were few, and cramped at that. Headliners, of course, had the first choice of dressing rooms; only the stars' room contained a washbasin. The other actors washed up at long troughs, one for the men, another for the women. In the older theaters, the dressing rooms were usually located in the basement, an afterthought built next to the boiler-room or in an unheated, unventilated corner. And always, there were the rats.

Weber & Fields recalled that the rats were particularly numerous at the Academy of Music in Pittsburgh, because the owner, Harry Williams, refused to allow cats in his building. He may have also been responsible for perpetuating the superstition among vaudevillians that no rat would visit the dressing room of an act that had flopped: having a nest of rats in your cubicle became as important as a good press notice. The Academy rats had a particular predilection for grease-paints, and the more experienced performers left open tins on the floor to protect their own supply. Few sights in backstage life could have been more unnerving than to return to the dressing room after an exhausting performance (and a for-tifying drink or two) to find these fat, arrogant rats with their noses and whiskers smeared white, yellow, and red.

In their first tour with Gus Hill (a half season), Weber & Fields called their act "Teutonic Eccentricities," possibly reintroducing some song-and-dance ele-ments into their knockabout. They also appeared in the afterpiece, helped shift scenery, and ran errands on Hill's command. There was little time to work on new routines, but daily performing gave them the opportunity to revise and polish in front of a live audience. Hill expected them to be at his beck and call, but in the process, they were getting an education in the kinds of administrative and managerial problems that a variety manager had to confront.

The season ended in April in Chicago. The train ride back to New York began on an upbeat note: Hill asked Joe and Lew to join the new company he was forming for the coming season beginning in September.

CHAPTER V

A Company of Their Own

I go to the theater to laugh. Shall I go there and be tormented when life itself is a plague? No, give me rather a mad jester or the antics of a spry wench.

Henry Roth, *Call It Sleep*

Yet New York was a city of contradictions, reminding one visitor of "a lady in ball costume, with diamonds in her ears, and her toe, out at her boots."

Arthur Meier Schlesinger, *The Rise of the City*

I made Weber & Fields," claimed Gus Hill, with less grace than he employed juggling his Indian clubs. "When they came to my show, Fields wasn't hitting Weber hard enough. I told him to give it to Weber. He did. Right on the top of the head. . . ."[1] Of course, Hill did not "make" Weber & Fields by himself, any more than Carncross had three years earlier when he advised the boys to shake hands and smile at the audience "to show them that it was all in fun." Taken together, however, the suggestions of Carncross and Hill helped Weber & Fields exploit the comic contradictions of their stage relationship. The juxtaposition of an act of aggression with an act of affection was fertile and relatively unexplored territory, at least on the museum and variety stages. The immigrant audiences who supported variety responded enthusiastically to comedy built around the "I-hurt-you-because-I-love-you" premise. Weber & Fields' two-act lent itself quite naturally to the expression of the dynamic tension inherent in this premise, and the premise added some emotional depth to the relationship between the two characters.

As Weber & Fields tried to reconcile Hill's blows with Carncross' handshake, the comic personas of Mike and Meyer began to take shape. One of the earliest and most beloved Mike and Meyer routines, the "Choking Scene," spelled out their brutally affectionate relationship, excerpted here without the dialect:

FIELDS: You look like a furnished room.

WEBER: Why do you go with me, then?

FIELDS: Why? Why? Because I *like* you! Mike when I look at you—I have such a— a—feeling—that oh, I can't express myself! Such a—oo-oo-oo-oo! *(Chokes Weber, then turns to audience)* Why do I go with him? *(Pointing at Weber)* When I look at him my heart goes out to him. *(To Weber)* When you are

73

away from me, I can't keep my mind off you. When you are with me I can't keep my hands off you! *(Chokes him)* But sometimes I feel you do not return my affection. You do not feel that—something that—oo-oo-oo-oo! *(Chokes him again, etc.)* [2]

During the summer of 1886, Weber & Fields stayed sharp by playing at Miner's Bowery or Miner's Eighth Avenue for one week out of each month. In August, they were the headliners with Thomas & Watson's Comedy Company at a popular summer resort, the Harlem Pavilion, and were featured in the afterpiece.

With work guaranteed for the fall, Lew could afford to spend more time at home with his family. His brother Max was trying to make a go of his own tailor shop at 195 Henry Street, across the street from the tenement where the family had lived eight years earlier. Lew's steady contributions made it possible for the Schanfields to move to what they hoped would be more comfortable quarters, a front apartment at 181 Clinton.

In September, Gus Hill called for his World of Novelties Company to assemble at the London Theater for the start of the 1886–1887 season. The new lineup consisted of the Five Japanese Ambassadors (acrobats), Mlle. Anna ("feats of jaw strength"), Dollie Foster (soubrette), Webber *[sic]* & Fields ("Two Skull Crackers"), Lottie Gilson ("descriptive vocalist"—and a future member of Weber & Fields' Own Company), Gus Hill (club swinging), Nat Haines & Will Vidocq (song-and-dance), Mlle. Alberta (on the high wire), and John and Edna Vidocq (sketch artists). The afterpiece, "Two Old Sports"by William Carroll, featured Sheridan & Flynn (Irish song-and-dance) and the Vidocqs, supported by the rest of the company.

Once clear of the New York area, Hill revised his program to suit local tastes. In general, this meant a greater emphasis on circus-style specialties. By January, when he was in the Midwest, he had added a female trapeze duo, and combined three of his specialty acts in "a grand triple performance" to open the second half of the program. Mademoiselle Anna clenched her iron jaw around a rubber strap and hung from a perilous height, while Mademoiselle Barretta contorted herself wondrously, and "The Paper Kings"—Matt Smith and Charles Way—danced a clog dance and tore tidies at the same time. "Smith & Way" were, of course, Weber and Fields, appearing as a neat act without their German dialects. Hill rechristened them with the names of the company's advance man and "angel" (backer). In addition to their backstage duties, Joe and Lew performed three times on each bill: as Webber *[sic]* & Fields, Smith and Way, and, in supporting roles, in the afterpiece. Hill did not hesitate to take full advantage of Weber & Fields' versatility and their youthful enthusiasm.

Some of the most valuable lessons that Joe and Lew learned from Hill were examples of what *not* to do. When Gus Hill's Company finally returned to New York to play the London in April, 1887, Weber & Fields and the Vidocqs were the only acts remaining from the opening of the tour. The constant turnover of acts and the difficulty in securing performers for an entire season plagued the early touring companies. Hill's tightfistedness contributed to the problem: acts would jump the tour whenever a rival manager held out the promise of a larger salary.

On the other hand, contracts were renewable with each new engagement, so Hill could terminate an act without warning or further compensation. Hill's top salary was thirty dollars a week for a team, low by the standards of the day. He paid his top dollar to Weber & Fields and, presumably, the Vidocqs (who were talented writers as well as comedians) because they were willing to do double (or triple) duty.

For Joe and Lew, the high point of the season was saved for the last. On May 2, 1887, Gus Hill's World of Novelties opened in New York at Tony Pastor's Fourteenth Street Theatre. Pastor's was now a combination house, alternating variety, melodramas, comedy plays with and without music, and an occasional minstrel company. During the summer months, Pastor assembled a variety company for a brief (and lucrative) tour of the Eastern circuit. Of late, however, the quality of his programs had been hurt by the defection of several of his regular stars—Nat Goodwin, Francis Wilson, May Irwin, Lillian Russell, J. K. Emmett—from the variety stage to musical farce and comic opera. To revive flagging attendance, he promoted his matinees with giveaways to appeal to female patrons—dresses, sacks of flour, or dolls.

Ten years earlier—half a lifetime for Weber & Fields—a Turn Hall stagehand had enjoyed a good laugh at their expense when he advised them to go immediately and introduce themselves to the great Tony Pastor. The next day, in the lobby of his theater at 585 Broadway, Tony Pastor had brushed by two scrawny boys who tried frantically to attract his attention with somersaults and pratfalls. In May, 1887, Weber & Fields finally got the last laugh on that stagehand. Now Pastor was pleased to have them performing on his stage, and he would have them back every year until they opened their own Broadway theater.

During their engagement at Chicago's Lyceum Theater in the spring, a circus owner named Tom Grenier approached the boys about going out with his circus for the coming summer. Grenier had recently purchased the Burr-Robins Circus; he was looking for clowns to perform in the big ring and for acts to round out the concert portions of his show. The ongoing crossover of talent and material between the dime museum, variety, and the minstrel show extended to the circus as well. During the warmer months, comics and acrobats from variety halls often worked in circuses. During the winter, the circus' freaks and exotic animal acts found their way into dime museums and variety halls.

Grenier offered Joe and Lew forty dollars a week and expenses, as well as ten percent of whatever they netted from selling songbooks. Joe and Lew knew that reliable summer gigs were difficult to come by, since variety houses and dime museums in the New York area closed down for July and August. After working for Gus Hill, Grenier's offer seemed generous. And, all practical considerations aside, the boys were not immune to the romance of the big top.

For rural Americans in the last two decades of the nineteenth century, the circus was the principal source of entertainment. In 1881, P. T. Barnum dissolved his partnership with W. C. Coup and joined forces with his chief competitor, James A. Bailey. The Barnum and Bailey Circus—the original "Greatest Show on Earth"—made its New York debut in March, 1881. Speculators sold tickets for window space along Broadway to watch the circus parade, which, as one newspaper reported, included "four brass bands (one composed of genuine Indians), a calliope, a fine chime of bells, a steam organ, a squad of Scotch bag-pipers, and a company of genuine plantation Negro jubilee singers."[3] The following year, Barnum bought the world-famous elephant, Jumbo, from the London Zoo. He also made a temporary agreement with his biggest remaining rival, Adam Forepaugh, to divide up the touring circuit.

For rural Americans, the news that the circus was coming to town inspired a strange combination of fear and delight, as expressed in a half-serious prayer: "God save us from war, pestilence, famine and the circus." It was widely believed that wherever the circus went, a crime wave followed in its wake: fights, burglaries, gambling, and dishonored daughters. "The entrance of the theatre is the gateway to hell," insisted one preacher, "and the ring of the circus is the bottomless pit." With the clowns, acrobats, and exotic animals traveled a sleazy crew of pickpockets, burglars, gamblers, con men, and short-changers. Yet the circus prospered, its promises of dazzling entertainment and death-defying feats overcoming its sinister reputation. The arrival of the circus was an excuse to celebrate, a holiday for the normally sober and hardworking farmers and tradesmen and their families.

Liquor was an important part of their celebrations. The drunker the customers became, the easier it was for the circus hustlers to scam them—and the more likely it became that a resentful local would resort to violence to settle his claim. The resulting confrontation was known as a "clem," and they occurred with enough frequency that the circus crews, by necessity, became highly disciplined corps for fighting the mobs of angry and drunken locals. "Hey, Rube!" was the circus man's call to arms, a signal to rally 'round the tent poles with every available weapon. Weber and Fields knew the circus by reputation, but probably figured that a rowdy drunk from Keokuk was not much different from his counterpart in the Bowery.

Grenier's circus was a two-ring railroad show based in the Midwest and patterned after the highly mobile, large-scale presentations of W. C. Coup. Weber & Fields caught up with their new employer in Chicago in late May. Upon arrival, they were hustled into clown makeup and told to ride on top of the animal wagons and be funny during the parade. In the rigidly stratified circus subculture, this was a low-status (and high-risk) post. Much of the clowns' funny business on top of the wagons involved dodging rocks and rotten fruit hurled by witty spectators.

Grenier's circus played for a month in the Chicago area before heading into the boondocks, moving on a daily basis from one vacant lot to another. For their parade clowning, the boys devised a burlesque crap game. In a few days, they were joined on the wagon tops by other more senior clowns, who overlooked the compromise in status to get in on the action, for amidst the pantomime and slapstick, the stakes were real.

Sketchy and contradictory records make it impossible to determine the exact route followed by Grenier's circus after leaving Chicago. Since it was a railway show, however, we can extrapolate a rough itinerary based on the existing railroad lines and a few anecdotal references. The circus headed west from Chicago, across Iowa, probably through Iowa City and Des Moines. In a little town named What Cheer (on the North Skunk River), the main tent was flattened by a tornado, and the grounds flooded by a torrential rain. From Sioux City, the circus went south along the Missouri River as far as Omaha. Trouping westward across Nebraska, their route paralleled the Platte River, terminating in Denver.

Joe and Lew quickly discovered that daily life in the circus made the ten shows a day in the dime museums seem like a picnic by comparison. Performers and crew slept in bunk cars, two or three to a berth. The day began at eight o'clock. Everybody in the troupe, except for the cat tamers, equestrians, and acrobats, was expected to help load and unload, set up and strike. After breakfast, the performers assembled for the parade through town, while the canvas men began erecting the tents. The procession moved slowly through town to attract the maximum amount of attention. Once the parade arrived at the tent site, there was rarely enough time to change into street clothes before the afternoon show, or between the afternoon and evening show. Tearing down began before the evening performance was over. The last of the equipment was loaded onto the train by two a.m., and the train headed to its next destination while the circus members slept.

Unloading, performing, helping feed and water the animals, and tearing down— Weber & Fields probably did not have the time to worry about whether they were using their full talents. Being young and new to the ring, they were subjected to practical jokes—left to hold up a tent pole, or seated with the freaks at the far end of dinner table next to the Armless Wonder, so that they had to ask him to pass the food (which he did with gusto, pleased to show off his remarkably prehensile feet). Weber & Fields took it so good-naturedly that their tormentors soon tired of trying to tease them.

As the novelty and sense of adventure settled into a grinding routine, their good-natured acceptance of the hardships of circus life gradually faded. For the first time in their four years of touring, they felt homesick. Until now, they had played on variety stages to predominantly immigrant audiences in an urban setting. Implicit in their humor was the assumption that the only thing that separated them from their audience was the extent of their exaggeration. Offstage and in street clothes, Joe and Lew were a part of the ebb and flow of city life. The hinterlands of Iowa and Nebraska felt like a foreign country to them, where the natives treated the circus like an invading army, sometimes cheering and sometimes attacking. Moving through a potentially hostile countryside, life in the circus became insular and all-encompassing.

Two events contributed to the boys' growing disenchantment. Among the acts that they burlesqued were the trapeze artists. Joe, being the smaller of the pair and the most agile, had to leap from a platform and miss Lew on the swinging trapeze, who pretended to be momentarily distracted. As he fell into the net below, Joe did a comic pantomime of a falling man. During an afternoon performance, as Joe and Lew and the rest of the audience watched in horror, one of the trapeze artists slipped and plummeted to his death. Joe was so shaken that he could not do his trick in the evening show, and Lew told Grenier that Joe was too ill to perform.

But it was a "clem"—a violent skirmish with the locals—that finally put an end to Weber & Fields' circus days. The site was a few miles south of the Platte River, near David City, a county seat in eastern Nebraska. The trouble started in the usual way—a local lost his week's pay in a three-card monte game and then assaulted the dealer. Always on the alert for disgruntled clients, the monte dealer's circus colleagues came to his aid and forcibly ejected the troublemaker from the grounds. Word quickly circulated to listen for "Hey, Rube!" during the evening performance.

A veteran clown gave Joe and Lew some solemn advice. Put your costumes on over your street clothes, he said, and don't wear any makeup for your final appearance in the concert. At the first sign of trouble, ditch the costumes and follow the railroad tracks back to the circus cars instead of cutting through town. The show's cars were on a siding about a mile away, on the other side of town.

As the old clown had predicted, the mob waited until the end of the evening performance to attack. During the concert, Joe and Lew were motioned to the tent flaps and, along with several other noncombatants, they sneaked away from the grounds and headed for the railroad embankment. Only then did they hear the infamous cry, "Hey, Rube!" Pandemonium followed: the mob (many of them planted in the audience) attacked the main tent, armed with knives and clubs. The canvas men and razorbacks (teamsters) were ready for them. Over their shoulders, Joe and Lew saw flames consume the main tent. Human cries mingled with the sounds of panicked animals. The boys did not linger to see the outcome, and ran the rest of the way to the safety of the circus cars.

Four men died during this particular clem, but by morning, the circus was on its way again. They missed their next performance waiting for a new tent to come from Omaha. Grenier was too preoccupied with repairs and legal matters to argue with Joe and Lew when they announced their resignation. He paid them off and commented, "Now you've got something to tell them on the Bowery." The all-girl brass band played as the other members of the troupe accompanied Weber & Fields to the station. The boys boarded a Chicago train and said goodbye to the circus, never to return, even as spectators.

Returning to the Bowery to spend a few weeks with their families, Joe and Lew found their familiar variety stages showing the influence of comic opera's growing popularity. Pastor's, the London, and Koster & Bial's now dispensed with olios for several weeks a season and filled the time with musical farces and burlesques of Gilbert & Sullivan plays. Even before D'Oyly Carte's production of *The Mikado* began its run of 250 performances at the Fifth Avenue Theater in August, 1885, Henry Miner staged a pirated version at his People's Theater. At Niblo's, the minstrel company of Thatcher, Primrose, and West presented blackface burlesques of *Adonis* and *The Mikado*: "Black Adonis" and "The Mick-ah-do," although the format owed more to variety than to traditional minstrelsy. The Fourteenth Street Theater revived *Evangeline*, with Fay Templeton as Gabriel, for that play's longest continuous run in New York (201 performances).[4]

The efforts of Pastor, Miner, *et al.* to attract a middle-class audience were reflected not only in their upgraded theatrical fare, but in the decor of their theaters. Variety—or, as it was being called with increasing frequency, "vaudeville"—was becoming "smart." Of late, the only difference between the entertainment at Koster & Bial's, with its plush and gilded interior, and the more humbly appointed Miner's Bowery was the price. During the summer of 1887, Miner made good on his promise that his Eighth Avenue Theater would be "elegantly" redecorated. When it reopened, a program note boasted: "Smoking not permitted. A First Class Family Theatre, where Ladies and Children can enjoy with perfect comfort a Pure, Wholesome and Delightful Entertainment."[5]

Most emblematic of the middle-class New Yorker's growing appetite for musicals was the Casino Theater, at the southeast corner of Broadway and Thirty-ninth Street. Built by producer John McCaull and his partner, Rudolph Aronson, the Casino opened its doors in October, 1882, with a production of Johann Strauss' *The Queen's Lace Handkerchief*. The Casino's Moorish-inspired exterior (which included a fully detailed roof garden) was the ideal architectural corollary to the entertainment offered within: lavish and trendy comic operas from abroad, with a harem of statuesque chorus girls. The "Casino girls" were as important to attendance as the Strauss and Offenbach music and the exotic storylines.

It was within this Victorian daydream of Arabian nights that a golden-haired, silvery-voiced, curvaceous beauty came into her own. Helen Leonard attracted attention from her earliest appearances in Tony Pastor's variety company in 1880, when she was nineteen. Pastor thought that she needed a stage name more befitting her charms. As Lillian Russell, she performed in a burlesque of *Patience* and then played the leading role of the straight version. After several light opera appearances, she starred in the Casino production of Strauss' *Prince Methusalem* in 1883. Rather than playing the female lead, Russell played the Prince. It was her second trouser role in succession, this being the only respectable way for a lady to display her shapely legs on stage.[6] The basis of Russell's appeal to male theatergoers is obvious, but she was equally popular with women in the audience. Whether wearing trousers or the spectacular gowns she became known for, Russell commanded center stage with humor and grace. Her well-publicized private life (four marriages and several liaisons) and her outspoken views on women's rights enhanced the image of the modern, self-reliant woman that she projected on stage.

As adolescent performers in the 1880's, Weber & Fields appreciated the legendary Lillian on several levels. She was not the only Casino star to make a lasting impression on the future Music Hall producers. Over the next decade, Fay Templeton, DeWolf Hopper, and David Warfield established their reputations on the Casino stage before joining Weber & Fields' Music Hall Company. In terms of performers and staging techniques, the Casino was to be as significant an influence on the Weber & Fields' Music Hall as the pair's long years of variety appearances. Over the next ten years, Weber & Fields tried to create an entertainment that would appeal to the kind of audience they saw attending the comic operas at the Casino.

The Bowery in the late 1880's was reeling under the impact of a new wave of immigrants, refugees from Eastern and Southern Europe who were generally poorer, less educated, and more clannish than their predecessors. The Bowery's Germans and Irish residents were moving north to Harlem or to Brooklyn. Newly arrived Italians crowded into the old Irish neighborhoods west of the Bowery. Russian and Polish Jews flocked to the former German district to the east.

The huge influx of immigrants and the continuing municipal neglect combined to make the tenuous living conditions even worse. By 1888, Manhattan was the site of 32,000 tenement buildings. The lack of adequate sewage, garbage disposal, and a reliable potable water supply created conditions in which typhus ran rampant. Tuberculosis cases soared, particularly among those who, like the Schanfield family, lived and worked in sweatshops.

Around the corner from the Schanfields' Clinton Street apartment was Hester Street, now the principal shopping area for the city's most densely populated slum, and the heart of the Tenth Ward. Hester Street between Clinton and Bowery was referred to as "the Pig-Market": eight blocks of cluttered sidewalks and unpaved streets, pushcarts and piles of rotting food. The corner of Clinton and Ludlow was the site of the daily "shape-up," where unemployed garment makers gathered in the hopes of being hired for piecework. Under the protection of Tammany Hall, prostitution was flourishing on Allen Street (where Fields had attended grade school), Rivington, and Stanton Streets. Young boys peddled *cartes de visites* for the brothels, and the whores called to the Jews passing by on their way to synagogue. The area between Clinton and Essex Streets became such a hopeless slum that it was finally razed in 1898 and replaced by Seward Park, much as the notorious Mulberry Street Bend was levelled to create Columbus Park a decade earlier.

In the late 1880's, the Tenth Ward averaged over five hundred people per acre, as opposed to sixty per acre for the entire city. (By 1894, the average swelled to 986 people per acre.) Health officers called the Tenth Ward the "typhus ward"; according to the Bureau of Vital Statistics, it was the "suicide ward."[7] Small wonder that Lew Fields spent so little time at home during this period. There is no indication that Papa Schanfield's disapproval of his son's choice of career had softened, despite Lew's proven dependability as a breadwinner. With Lew on the road and Max in business for himself as a dressmaker, Papa Schanfield still had a family of seven to support. Sol, Charlie, and Henry worked alongside their father. It had become decidedly more difficult of late for Papa Schanfield to maintain the family's standard of living. Over half of the arriving hordes of Polish and Russian Jews went to work in the needle trades. The availability of cheap labor slashed garment workers' wages in half, from an average of fifteen dollars to seven dollars a week. Contractors had to become ruthlessly exploitative to remain competitive. In this environment, Lew's contributions probably made the difference between subsistence and comfort, at least by the reduced standards of the Bowery. Lew's total earnings for the 1886–1887 season were approximately $700, most of which he sent to his family. Any hopes he had of seeing his family move out of the Bowery depended on his continued touring.

On September 5, 1887, three weeks after returning from their adventures with the Grenier circus, Weber & Fields reported to the London Theater to begin their third season with Gus Hill's World of Novelties. Weber & Fields unveiled a new routine entitled "Crazy Dutchmen," which received an enthusiastic review from the *New York Clipper:* "[they] did not quite break their necks, but at times it looked as if they would do so. Their rough song and dance turn, though boisterous, is highly acceptable." Later in the month, at Tony Pastor's, they once again did not quite break their necks. Gus Hill's troupe toured the East Coast variety and combination houses during the fall, returning to New York in November to play at Miner's Eighth Avenue and at the London, where Weber & Fields were being touted as the "greatest of all versatile comedians-knockabout artists."

True to character, Hill refused to pay the duo any more than he had for the previous two seasons (thirty dollars a week plus board), no matter how good their press was. Joe and Lew decided to look for a better situation, but to do so without alerting Hill to their intentions. At the end of January, 1888, Gus Hill's company played a week at Hyde & Behman's Theatre, Brooklyn's leading variety house. Weber & Fields' "Crazy Dutchmen" routine impressed manager James Hyde, and he quietly offered them a featured spot in his touring company when they returned to the East. In March, Weber & Fields appeared with Gus Hill in Baltimore, Washington, and Alexandria, while most of the Eastern and Midwestern theaters were closed by a deadly snowstorm.

By April 9, Weber & Fields were knocking each other about on the London's familiar stage as members of Hyde's Comedians for an additional twenty dollars a week. Besides Weber & Fields, the company included Fred and Jennie Mackley, Imro Fox (magician), Leopold and Bunnell, Kitty O'Neill, and Sam Devere (who was reputed to have killed a man with his banjo during a brawl in Texas). According to theater chronicler George Odell, it was "the finest aggregation seen that season at the London."

There is no record of any other stage appearances for the remainder of the summer. In July, Weber & Fields joined the touring roster of Austin's Australian Novelty Company for their 1888–1889 season. Austin's manager, Charles F. Cromwell, surprised Joe and Lew by immediately agreeing to their asking price—seventy dollars a week. It was the start of a rewarding relationship.

Charles Cromwell's managerial career began in 1880, when he was the manager and lecturer for a small medicine show that toured the East. The following season, and for the next three seasons, he was business manager for the Acme Dime Comedy Company, one of the few variety troupes to turn a profit playing the smaller towns of the West. Shortly after the close of the 1884–1885 season, R. G. Austin, Cromwell's neighbor at his summer home in Bath Beach, Long Island, hired him to manage his Australian Novelty Company. With Austin's backing, Cromwell was able to secure first-rate variety and circus acts. Better bookings followed, and within two years, the Austin troupe was considered to be one of the leading touring companies.

A native of Australia, former circus man R. G. Austin built his company around the talents of his wife, known as "Mademoiselle Aimee," and her sister Rose. The Austin Sisters were gymnasts who performed on the flying trapeze. In the finale of their act, Mlle. Aimee swung herself upward by trapeze until she could plant both feet simultaneously on a polished platform suspended from the theater ceiling. Attached to her shoes were powerful rubber suction cups devised by her husband. With the cups gripping the platform, she released the trapeze and stood upside down on the platform, forty feet above the orchestra seats. Then, as the audience gasped, she would slowly slide one foot and then the other to the end of the platform, pivot, and then return to her starting point. The secret of these amazing suction cups went to the grave with their inventor.

Austin's season began September 10, at H. R. Jacob's Third Avenue Theatre. Weber and Fields appeared in the fourth slot, billed as "the autocratic representatives of all knockabout artists," in a revised version of their "Crazy Dutchmen" routine. Their turns now began with Meyer (Fields) pushing Mike (Weber) on stage, with Mike protesting, "Don't *poosh* me, Meyer!" Upon reaching center stage, Mike and Meyer would shake hands:

> MIKE: I am delightfulness to met you.
>
> MEYER: Der disgust is all mine.
>
> MIKE: I receivedidid a letter from mein goil, but I don't know how to writteninin her back.
>
> MEYER: Writtenin her back! Such an edumuncation you got it? Writteninin her back! You mean rotteninin her back. How can you answer her ven you don't know how to write?
>
> MIKE: Dot makes no nefer mind. She don't know how to read.
>
> MEYER: If you love her, vy don't you send her some poultry?
>
> MIKE: She don't need no poultry, her father is a butcher.
>
> MEYER: I mean luf voids like Romeo und Chuliet talks: "If you luf you like I luf me / No knife can cut us togedder."
>
> MIKE: I don't like dot. . . .

What is not immediately apparent in a transcript of their act is the physicality of their performance. This was, after all, knockabout. But unlike most knockabout, the dialogue was not merely a pretext for physical mayhem. In the Mike and Meyer routines, the patter provided a necessary counterpoint to the slapstick, creating characters whose tenderest feelings could only find expression in the most brutal behavior. The dialect distortions emphasized the frustration of all immigrants trying to communicate their humanity through the coarse filter of an unfamiliar language. The violence did not arise out of antagonism or hostility, although it was often provoked by a competitive urge run amok. It was in the name of friendship and mutual understanding that the two "Dutchmen" strangled, gouged, punched, and kicked each other around the stage.

> MIKE: In two days I vill be a murdered man.
>
> MEYER: A vot?
>
> MIKE: I mean a married man.
>
> MEYER: I hope you vill always look back upon der presendt moment as der habbiest moment uff your life.
>
> MIKE: But I aind't married yet.
>
> MEYER: I know it, und furdermore, upon dis suspicious occasion, I also vish to express to you—charges collect—my uppermost depreciation of der dishonor you haf informed upon me in making me your bridesmaid.
>
> MIKE: Der insult is all mein.

MEYER: As you standt before me now, so-o-o young, so-o-o innocent, so-o-o obnoxious, there is only one void dat can express mein pleasure, mein dissatisfaction—

MIKE: Yes, yes?

MEYER: Und I can't tink of der void.

MIKE: I know I vill be happy.

MEYER: I know you vill be. *(He shakes Mike's hand feelingly.)* Und later on, ven you lose your money, und your vife goes back on you, und your house burns down, and your children get run over, then I, your best friendt, vill take you by der hand—

MIKE: *(wiping a furtive tear away):* Yes, yes!

MEYER: Und say—

MIKE: Yes, yes!

MEYER: Und say, "I told you so!"[8]

As their dialogues became more elaborate, it became necessary to augment their repertoire of brutalities. They discovered the mirth-provoking possibilities of eye-gouging by accident during a performance, when Weber got something in his eye, and his partner tried to remove it. Likewise, the spit-in-the-eye gag was worked up from one's natural response to an exploding consonant.

Greater brutality required greater planning. During the season with Austin, Weber wore a long nail in the toe of one shoe, and Fields concealed a block of cork; when Weber kicked Fields in the shin, the nail sank in and held fast, prompting a three-legged jig. As a variation, Fields kept an explosive cap in the toe of his shoe, which detonated when he kicked his partner. For an encore, they borrowed a bit of business from a rough Irish act that was popular in at Tony Pastor's around 1880. After a routine of hard falls and "bumps," Ferguson and Mack finished their act with the latter sinking a hatchet into the former's skull. The hatchet stuck there as they made their exit.[9] Weber added a cork cushion to the top of his steel-plated wig, and took his bows with hatchet in head.

In Austin's afterpiece, Weber & Fields took the opportunity to write and perform a more extended sketch. "The Dutchman's Day Off" featured Lew as Hans Liederkranz, and Joe as Denis Mulcahy. No description of its storyline or gags survives, but it is likely that the German and Dutch characters squared off in much the same way that Harrigan's Mulligan feuded with Lochmuller. Worth noting, too, is the choice of subject matter, familiar to the audience from everyday life: how the city dweller spends his free time. The burlesque of the era's leisure-time activities—pool, sharpshooting, bicycling, baseball, ballooning—became the basis for Weber & Fields' most successful routines in the coming decade.

Between September and mid-December, Austin's Australian Novelties Company played one-week stands in twelve cities besides New York: Boston, Philadelphia, Pittsburgh, Washington, D.C., Hoboken, Brooklyn, Syracuse, Rochester, Troy, Montreal, Buffalo, and Chicago. In Chicago, Cromwell "let go" the entire troupe, with the exception of Weber & Fields and the Austin Sisters. When the company finally reassembled in St. Louis on January 21, 1889, Weber & Fields were the only straight comedians on the bill. The balance of the program was now composed of circus and museum acts: sharpshooters, a ventriloquist, a magician, and so on. It is was not long before Weber & Fields realized that the non-comic acts provided rich material for burlesque. Circus clowns knew that burlesquing the preceding act was a surefire belly laugh. During the second half of the season, Weber & Fields performed a burlesque of the magic act. Exaggerating the hocus-pocus gestures of the magician, they placed a bottomless bottle over a hole in the stage. Then, with a ripple of Weber's loud plaid handkerchief, they would begin to pull an increasingly absurd assortment of objects out of the bottle until their bickering caused them to reveal the mechanics of the hoax.[10]

The company worked its way back to the East Coast; in Louisville, the *New York Clipper* reported "immense business," and their show at Miner's Bowery was "much improved." Cromwell's daring move had turned a middling tour into highly profitable one. Nevertheless, Austin's tour was cut short in early March during the company's swing through the Northeast. A young giant flexed his muscles and demonstrated his growing power. For reasons unknown, B. F. Keith cancelled Austin's bookings in the Keith & Albee theaters in Boston and Providence. Perhaps Cromwell had had the audacity to protest Keith's typically high percentage of the gross.

Weber & Fields had no trouble making up the engagements. By mid-March, they were appearing at Koster & Bial's, part of a specialty bill supplementing the musical farce, *A Night in Pekin*. They remained there for three weeks, then picked up another two weeks at their old standby, the London. During their first week at the London, they appeared with Harry Kernell's Company. Harry Kernell, along with his brother John, were veteran song-and-dance men who had recently reunited to form their own touring company. The Kernells were looking for headliners for the 1889–1890 season. Having seen the latest edition of Weber & Fields' act at the London, they signed the Dutch team for the tour at a salary of one hundred dollars a week.

Nevertheless, Weber & Fields viewed the possibility of another summer of turkey shows and hanging out at Miner's with little enthusiasm. In their five years on the road, they had learned as much about managing as they had about performing. Joe understood the basic principles of bookkeeping and cash flow, and had already demonstrated a knack for negotiating contracts. Fields had developed a good eye for talent, and his quiet, easygoing manner gave him a ready rapport with other actors. Together, they had an intuitive understanding of what audiences wanted to see.

Still, one cannot blame the crew at Miner's for snickering when Joe and Lew mentioned that they were thinking of putting together their own company. After all, Joe and Lew were only twenty-two years old, younger than most of the regulars at Miner's. To the men in Miner's poolroom, Joe and Lew were a couple of neighborhood kids with a clever two-act. But Weber & Fields as producers? Where was their capital coming from? What did they know about booking? Was this the set-up for a new Mike and Meyer routine?

James Donaldson, the London's owner and manager, had known Joe and Lew since the days when they performed blackface routines, and he took a paternal interest in their careers. During their pickup engagement at the London in early May, they spoke with him about putting together a vaudeville company, and he didn't laugh. Instead, he promised them a week in June if they could put together a bill that met with his approval.

The guarantee of a week's engagement at the London gave Weber & Fields some credibility with their skeptical colleagues. The two novice producers began to sign up the acts, and as the program came together, they realized that they should take advantage of the opportunity to arrange additional bookings. They approached Charles Cromwell, who responded with characteristic enthusiasm. He secured additional bookings in Philadelphia and New York.

The first vaudeville company to bear the name of Weber & Fields appeared at the London Theater for the week of June 3, 1889. It consisted of ten acts: the Tally Ho Trio (singers), the Rogers Brothers (Dutch neat song-and-dance), Murphy and Murphy, Weber & Fields, Rosina (male impersonator), Swift and Chase, Kelly and Murphy, Florence Miller (soubrette), Baldwin and Daly, and Charles Hunn, followed by Weber & Fields' sketch, "A Dutchman's Day Off."

In the companies of Gus Hill and R. G. Austin, the emphasis had been on circus and sideshow acts, but in Weber & Fields' company, the overall character of the bill was comedy. All of the acts, whether they sang, danced, juggled, balanced, or knocked each other about, contributed to an atmosphere of hilarity rather than amazement, culminating in Weber & Fields' popular sketch. There was no intermission to interrupt the show's momentum.

The *New York Clipper* reported "medium receipts" for the week at the London and for the following week at the Central Theater in Philadelphia. Returning to New York, Weber & Fields' Company closed out the season at the Windsor before going their separate ways. Despite the unremarkable response (which may have had as much to do with the weather as with the talent), Weber & Fields felt encouraged, just as they had twelve years earlier by the polite applause of the Turn Hall audience. After their botched debut at Turn Hall, they had insisted that they would soon become actors; likewise, after their June 1889 bookings, they were certain that they would soon be managers of their own company.

Harry and John Kernell were among the most enduring Irish two-acts in the business, a mismatched set of brothers whose song-and-dance and crossfire conversations delighted a generation of variety audiences. Gifted comedians, and a soft touch for their colleagues, the Kernells were mediocre managers. Their partnership was suspended on several occasions because of "temporary inharmony" (as the trade papers tactfully put it). When Weber & Fields joined the company in late 1889, Harry Kernell was already showing signs of the erratic behavior that were symptomatic of the disease that led to his confinement in the Bloomingdale Insane Asylum, and his death in 1893 at age forty-five.

It was a popular myth of the age that the incidence of insanity (from the advanced stages of alcoholism and syphilis) and suicide among actors was at near-epidemic proportions. In fact, it was no higher among actors than in the working-class population at large, but the guardians of Victorian morality found it useful to portray these sordid ends as the direct consequences of life in the theater. Newspapers of the day were too discreet to mention syphilis, except when in its advanced stages—called "paresis"—it afflicted a member of the theatrical profession. The most famous case hit the press the year before Weber & Fields joined the Kernells, when Harrigan's much-beloved partner, Tony Hart, was celebrated in a Grand Testimonial Benefit before being confined to the Worcester asylum. And in 1892, a New York newspaperman amused himself and his public with the yarn that there would be a joint tour of two popular Irish comedians, Harry Kernell and William J. Scanlan, under the management of Max Clayton. The clever reporter suggested that this was appropriate because they had so much in common: all three were patients at the Bloomingdale Asylum, and all three were suffering from paresis.

Harry and John Kernell were in the midst of one of their "inharmonious" periods when their company (temporarily renamed Harry Kernell's Big Company) opened its season in late September at Tony Pastor's Fourteenth Street Theater. It was an all-star cast: Harry Kernell, the Braatz Brothers (comic acrobats), Fred Huber & Kitty Allyne, the Inman Sisters ("best general dancers in the world"), Ward & Vokes ("Ethiopian," later to become famous as Percy & Harold, tramp comedians), Queenie Vassar & Emily Vivian (soubrettes, and the wives of Harry and John, respectively), Charles Harding & Little Ah Sid (character comedians), and "the great German team, Webber [sic] and Fields, the only real knockabout German dudes in their funny songs and dances." "Only real knockabout" was a precautionary designation to distinguish them from the growing number of imitators that their success had spawned.

The Kernell troupe played to "very large business" and "immense audiences" in New York–area variety houses during October and early November, and then departed for other stages of the Eastern vaudeville circuit. Weber & Fields were singled out for praise, having "caught the house emphatically with their Teutonic effusions." They did not unveil any new routines. Rather than working up new gags, they spent their free time in the afternoons consulting with Charles Cromwell. While headlining what was arguably the season's most talented touring group, Weber & Fields were planning their own company.

In December, 1889, a short notice in the *Clipper* announced: "Weber & Fields, now with Harry Kernell's Company, inform us that they have secured some excellent attractions for next season. Their paper, they say, will be as fine as any company on the road. They will also carry two advance agents." It was not unusual for top performers to announce their next year's plans, but Harry Kernell was convinced that Joe and Lew were plotting behind his back. His suspicions were not entirely unfounded.

Two weeks later, another article mentioned that manager Charles Cromwell had signed the team of Fred Huber & Kitty Allyne for the Weber & Fields Company, and that nearly half the season was already booked. Kernell took this as proof that Weber & Fields intended to steal his company out from under his nose. January 1890 playbills reveal that Huber & Allyne were no longer part of Kernell's Company, having been replaced by Harry Watson & Alice Hutchings. At about the same time, still another *Clipper* article announced that Weber & Fields had "engaged" the best-known Jewish comedian, Frank Bush, and his wife, Isabella Ward, along with Rosina the male impersonator, and Collins & Welch.

Cromwell's publicity efforts succeeded in establishing Weber & Fields' credibility as producers, but at a high cost. Harry Kernell would probably have fired
them outright, had he not reconciled with his brother John, who may have pointed
out that such a move could have a disastrous effect on the company's receipts.
On stage, the Kernells resumed their sidewalk conversation sketch; backstage,
they plotted their revenge. They paid Weber & Fields' hundred-dollar-a-week salary in pennies, nickels, and dimes, and spoke of replacing them with another
Dutch team.

The Kernells' tour collapsed in March, and the company was left stranded—
"busted up"—in Rochester. The next booking was not until April 21, at Tony
Pastor's. Weber & Fields had been setting aside a large portion of their salaries
to bankroll their new venture. The gap in the bookings did more to damage
Weber & Fields' plans than all of the Kernells' deliberate harassment. Cromwell
busied himself with lining up summer engagements.

On the Monday morning of their opening at Pastor's, Weber & Fields noted
in passing the changes in the Kernells' lineup: the addition of Charles & Lottie
Fremont (dancers), and the Rogers Brothers. The latter duo had been part of the
company that Weber & Fields had assembled at the end of the previous season.
Joe and Lew remembered their act as a neat German song-and-dance, and the
brothers Max and Gus as inexperienced Bowery kids. Other members of the tour
group had subjected the Rogers Brothers to the ritual hazing of newcomers, so
Joe and Lew had invited them to share their dressing room. On reflection, it
seemed strange to Joe and Lew that Harry Kernell would hire two such novices
to play at Pastor's. But the afternoon rehearsals made Kernell's intent clear. As
the Rogers Brothers rehearsed, Weber & Fields realized that they were watching
a letter-perfect imitation of their own act—gag for gag, sputter for sputter, and
identical makeup and costumes, down to the same protective padding. The Rogers had been well coached. Harry Kernell grinned smugly at Weber & Fields, and
reminded them that the Rogers Brothers would precede them on the bill. If Kernell's scheme were successful, New York audiences would no longer believe that
Weber & Fields were "the only real knockabout German Dudes."

By the time of the Tuesday matinee, Weber & Fields succeeded in coming
up with enough new lines and business to differentiate their act from the Rogers'.
Harry Kernell stood in the wings and took notes, and by the evening performance,
the Rogers' turn once again anticipated that of the older team. The duel continued throughout the week at Pastor's, and for the following week at Gilmore's in
Philadelphia. When the Rogers had difficulty incorporating so many new gags in
their act every night, Kernell would stand in the wings and prompt them.[11] In the
hour or so between the Rogers Brothers' turn and Weber & Fields', the latter
team would reconstruct their act to avoid the gags the audience had already seen.
But there were characteristic stylings—the kicks and blows, the mangled English,
the relationship between Mike and Meyer—Weber & Fields could find no substitutes for.

Ironically, the two weeks that the Rogers Brothers spent aping Weber &
Fields launched the younger team's career. Ten years later, after Weber & Fields
had refused to cooperate with the Syndicate's monopolistic booking practices,

the Syndicate backed the Rogers Brothers in a revue that was supposed to compete with the burlesques at Weber & Fields' Music Hall, and finally installed the Rogers in their own theater.

From Cromwell came news that made it easier to forget Harry Kernell's bizarre vendetta. Capitalizing on his earlier experiences touring the Western circuit, Cromwell had arranged for Weber & Fields to headline at the Orpheum Theater in San Francisco for the handsome salary of $175 a week, and then tour the West Coast for ten to twelve weeks.

While working in San Francisco with the Acme Dime Comedy Company in 1884 and 1885, Cromwell made the acquaintance of a cheerful three-hundred-pound German named Gustav Walter, then manager of the Wigwam Theater. Walter, almost singlehandedly, had been responsible for bringing variety to San Francisco. In 1887, he opened the Orpheum, on the south side of O'Farrell Street, between Stockton and Powell. Unlike the other variety houses in town, which were actually glorified saloons, the Orpheum was built as a theater with an adjoining bar. Drinking and smoking were allowed, even encouraged, with aggressive waiters in the aisles and little shelves on the backs of the seats to hold steins, snacks, and ashtrays. The women of San Francisco, unlike their Eastern counterparts, attended variety shows without hesitation.

To San Franciscans, theatergoing was a badge of status. The Nob Hill *nouveaux riches* went to see tragedies and opera companies imported at great expense from the East. The shopkeepers, clerks, and laborers patronized the variety halls—the Orpheum, the Bella Union, the Wigwam, and the Cremorne. Arias and olios were received with equal enthusiasm; managers were able to offer high salaries to make the transcontinental train ride more attractive to New York–based stars such as Lillian Russell and Tony Pastor's Company. The inadequacy of the local talent pool in satisfying the public's appetite for vaudeville was further incentive for theater managers to book performers from "back East." On any given evening, the phrase "Direct from New York City" or "Chicago's favorites" was enough to pack the house.

In early May, Weber & Fields stopped by the Southern Pacific office to pick up their tickets to San Francisco—second class, and only one way, but paid for by Gustav Walter. Cromwell could not accompany them; he had to remain in New York to finish signing up acts and booking theaters for Weber & Fields' debut season. Lew's eldest brother, Max, was listed as the proprietor of this edition of Weber & Fields' Own Specialty Company—actually, an aggregation of locally recruited talent to whom Weber & Fields rather graciously lent their name.

Although Max Schanfield had his own tailor shop, he was continuing to assist the duo in an informal capacity as an advance man, business manager, and financial advisor. It was to Max that Lew sent his earnings during the previous five years on the road, and Max had disbursed the money to the Schanfields. During the 1889–1890 season, he set aside the money for the new company in a savings account. In November, 1889, when Weber & Fields gave a benefit at Turn Hall, the program listed Max Schanfield as manager. For Weber & Fields' West Coast fund-raising drive, Max went out ahead as a combination talent scout and advance man, to line up the other acts that were to appear on the bill as part of Weber & Fields' company, and to arrange additional West Coast bookings.

It took eight days to cross the country by rail. At the end of eight days in day-coach, their twenty-dollar food allowance long gone save for some small change, Joe and Lew disembarked at the Oakland terminal, and transferred to a ferryboat for a four-hour ride to San Francisco. Tired, rumpled, and unshaven, they did not look anything like the sensations touted by the billboards and posters plastered all over town: "Weber & Fields—the Funniest Men in the East," "The Great Eastern Stars," "The Greatest Dutch Comedians."

When Max had inquired about accommodations, he was told that the East's greatest comedians would undoubtedly want to stay at the Palace. When the dishevelled duo arrived at the swank hotel and tried to check in without luggage (the stage trunk containing their street clothes having been sent directly to the theater), the desk clerk demanded cash in advance. Weber & Fields persuaded him that they were the famous Dutch team that was going to open at the Orpheum on Monday night, and that they would be seeing Gustave Walter to get an advance.

The clerk proved to be easier to convince than Walter. The next day, when Joe and Lew presented themselves at the theater, Walter reacted with dismay. They looked barely eighteen years old (though they were actually twenty-three), and their dishevelled appearance made them look more like newsboys than successful actors. These were supposed to be "the Funniest Men in the East," worth $175 dollars a week and train fare, the big draw that would stave off the Orpheum's creditors? Walter shook his head at being duped—funny men indeed, only the joke was on him. "Vell, if you are zo funny," Walter sputtered, "make me laugh." Neither Joe nor Lew had any intention of launching into their Dutch act in response to this challenge, particularly since Walter looked and sounded like a jumbo version of Weber's character, Mike. Instead, Weber asked for a fifty-dollar advance. Walter muttered a curse in German, and told them that when they earned fifty dollars, they would get fifty dollars.

San Francisco had no closing or blue laws, so the variety shows began at eight o'clock and rarely ended before four in the morning. The Orpheum filled up after the legitimate theaters had closed for the evening—around one a.m. When Weber & Fields first learned that they were scheduled to appear at 1:30 a.m. they were convinced that Walter was setting them up for a "Brodie" (vaudeville-ese for a "flop"). They sent word to the theater that they would refuse to perform unless Walter gave them the ten o'clock slot, and then returned to their hotel room to await his reply. All afternoon they waited in their room, afraid that by going out they risked missing Walter's messenger. It was a desperate (and misguided) bluff; they were flat broke, with not even a return ticket, and their reputation as performers and their future as managers were on the line. At seven o'clock, a messenger arrived saying that Walter had agreed to put the turn on at ten o'clock. Apparently, Walter could not afford to call their bluff.

Walter's extensive advertising succeeded in drawing a packed house, even at that early hour. The local audience was unaccustomed to Weber & Fields' "cold" entrance (without music or singing), and their twisted "Dutch" dialect, but they chuckled at Mike and Meyer's makeup and costumes. During one particularly heated exchange of twisted English, Weber's mispronunciation was punctuated with a spray of saliva. Fields responded by covering his eye with one hand, and then, with each new assault, cleaning it out with increasing exasperation and disgust. The spit-in-the-eye routine was something the locals had never seen before, and it won them over.

So did a topical joke about the Harrison-Cleveland presidential election of 1888, now two years old. Fields claimed to have known all along that Harrison would beat Cleveland. Weber doubted it, but Fields pointed to the number of Harrison banners he had seen. "But panners don't vote," pointed out Weber.

"Shure, panners don' vote," explained Fields. "But dey show vich vay der windt blows."

After the show, Walter gave Joe and Lew a fifty-dollar advance, and the duo agreed to push back their turn until 1:30 a.m. Despite an undistinguished bill of supporting acts—Alvan Dashington the Boneless Wonder and Ouda the Marvel, among others—Weber & Fields drew record crowds at the Orpheum for four weeks. Their popularity carried over to the stages of the Orpheum's competitors down the street: engagements at the Wigwam and the Bella Union, at two hundred and fifty dollars per week.

As word of Weber & Fields' success in San Francisco filtered back to Miner's, the skeptics at the bar stopped snickering at the team's ambitious plans. In July, as Weber & Fields headed for three weeks of performing in Portland, Cromwell announced in the *Clipper* that he had signed a California blackface pair, Wilson and Cameron, for Weber & Fields' fall company. Cromwell boasted that to get the team, he had to outbid Messieurs Hyde, Reilly, Hill, and H. W. Williams, adding that "Nothing is too good for the big show next season." Admittedly, Cromwell's statement was show-biz hype, but in the coming decade, it expressed an attitude that Weber & Fields would transform into the guiding principle of their touring companies and music hall.

On August 16, 1890, Minneapolis' outpost of refined entertainment, the Pence Opera House, opened its season with Weber & Fields' Big Specialty Show. As with the Orpheum engagements, the Company was an uneven assortment of local talent drawn from the Midwestern circuit and presented under the Weber & Fields label. The *Clipper* reported that people were turned away for lack of space, and that advance sales were large.

Having cleared around $2,000 from their summer tour, Weber & Fields returned to New York to launch the first full season of their own vaudeville company. Flash equaled cash in the eyes of variety artists. To prove that they were owner-managers capable of meeting a payroll, Joe and Lew had to dress the part. They made a point of being seen around the Bowery wearing their new finery: Prince Albert coats, patent-leather shoes, derby hats, black silk shirts, and black bow ties. To complete the outfit, they each wore a three-carat diamond stud, bought from a Chatham Street pawnshop for twenty-five dollars down and ten dollars a week, and a gold watch and chain. These props came in handy when negotiating with actors, booking agents, and prospective backers.

Weber & Fields' timing as performers and aspiring showmen could not have been better. By 1890, theatergoing had become the country's principal leisure-time activity. While serious drama and operas were attracting a loyal American audience, the vast majority of patrons craved the escapism and laughter provided by musicals and vaudeville. Vaudeville by itself now drew half of all theatergoers. It was theater for the new Americans who would otherwise have had little chance or desire to attend.

Evidence of the rapid growth of the popular theater covered the tenement walls, billboards, and street lamps. In every major city, playbills proliferated layer by layer over every available vertical surface, like tree bark in a thriving forest. New theaters opened in every metropolis, presenting a miscellany of programs to appeal to all tastes, from Uncle Tom shows to comic opera. When Weber & Fields began their apprenticeship with Gus Hill in 1885, there were fewer than twenty variety companies touring the East; by spring of 1889, there were thirty; and one year later, that figure had been doubled. The demand for actors, stimulated by the growing number of theaters and touring companies, far outstripped the supply. Vaudeville managers advertised heavily in the *Clipper* for "quality" acts to fill out their program, and offered better pay than legit managers. In 1880, the United States Census listed 5,000 professional actors (legit and musicals); by the turn of the century, there were nearly fifteen thousand.[12] Had vaudevillians been included, those numbers would have been doubled; but significantly, vaudevillians were not officially recognized as professionals.

Weber & Fields started their company in a seller's market, at a time when the business of entertainment was an unclaimed and unexplored frontier. The actor-manager was the rugged individualist who wrested a precarious livelihood from the isolated outposts of popular entertainment that were opening up across the country. In 1890, it was still possible for a successful actor to become a successful owner and manager based on his own reputation and talent—the commodity he produced by himself. Weber & Fields' chief commodity—their Dutch act—became the cornerstone of their vaudeville program. In subsequent years, their name on the masthead of a vaudeville company became a guarantee of quality entertainment.

The basis of the dialect act's appeal can only be understood within a broader cultural context. Weber & Fields' use of puns, malapropisms, and twisted syntax reflected their audience's fascination with the spoken word. At a time when public education and newspapers were encouraging the standardization of American speech, Americans delighted in humor based on dialect differences. The interest was not confined to the working-class audience of popular theater. The renaissance of American letters—the work of Mark Twain, Bret Harte, Stephen Crane, and William Dean Howells, among others—was preoccupied with vernacular speech and subject matter. In the 1880's, the Uncle Remus tales of Joel Chandler Harris won a wide readership by putting on paper the same dialect, imagery, and narrative structure that were usually found only in the monologues of minstrel-show stump speakers. Twain's *The Adventures of Huckleberry Finn* (1884), with its first-person vernacular narration and irreverent humor, may have owed less to contemporary literary forms than to the "hick" or "rube" monologists who were becoming increasingly popular on variety stages.

The hayseed and the Dutchman were variations on the same theme—foreigners to the big city and its ways. In 1890's usage, "Dutch" referred to any immigrant who was slow-witted or old-fashioned; it was not uncommon for children to refer to their immigrant parents as "Dutch." Gradually, Weber & Fields' Dutch act lost the specificity of its original inspiration (the German immigrant) and became increasingly emblematic of urban newcomers in general. To emphasize the distinction between their Dutch act and a caricature of Jewish immigrants, Weber & Fields almost always included a "Hebrew" comic (e.g., Frank Bush, Joe Welch, or later, David Warfield), as part of the balanced mix of Irish, Dutch, blackface, and hicks in their program. Audiences were not likely to confuse the two characterizations until Jewish comedians came to the fore in the 1900's; by then, Weber and Fields' act was considered *sui generis*.

In 1888, Lew's brother Max filed his naturalization papers and took the oath of citizenship; Lew simply made himself an American by claiming to be. As an entertainer and businessman, he could not afford to ignore the wave of nationalism that was sweeping the country. To present a truly American entertainment, one had to be an American.

In a notice in the *New York Clipper*, Joe and Lew called for the first rehearsal of Weber & Fields' Own Company for September 24, 1890, at 9:30 a.m., at Miner's Eighth Avenue Theater. Their announcement was a revealing mixture of jingoism and entrepreneurial calculation: "The roster . . . gives promise of an admirable show, and its American makeup ought to thrill the patriotic lovers of vaudeville entertainment." What would be more American than a program of Dutch, Irish, Jewish, blackface, and tramp comedians, with sexy soubrettes, acrobats, and trained animals thrown in for good measure?

CHAPTER VI

In-and-Outers

Der one dot gets der money is der vinner. . . .
from Weber & Fields' "The Pool Room," 1892

WHEN Weber & Fields first began touring in the middle 1880's, the variety business was a free-wheeling, shoot-from-the-hip affair, and the legitimate stage only slightly less so. Booking was generally arranged by correspondence or by summer visits to New York by out-of-town managers. Union Square was the theatrical center of the city; permanent offices were rare, and the business was conducted on park benches and in the lobbies or barrooms of nearby hotels. Hopeful actors congregated around the equestrian statue of George Washington, and the area became known as "The Slave Market." Managers of theaters played hide-and-seek with managers of attractions, searching out the best-drawing companies and avoiding those with lesser reputations until forced to consider them for lack of anything better.[1]

Written contracts were the exception rather than the rule. As the theaters became increasingly dependent on travelling companies for their programs, and the travelling companies tried to avoid long jumps and smaller cities, the deliberate disregard of contractual obligations became a convenient weapon used by theater managers, company managers, and actors alike. Broken dates, conflicting engagements, and last-minute changes in the program caused by theater managers or company managers or actors who had found a better gig, all pointed to the need for a more efficient business structure. For all concerned, centralization appeared to be a logical—and desirable—step.

In the early 1880's, Michael B. Leavitt, manager of a variety theater in San Francisco, found that he could not secure acts from the East Coast because the acts could not be guaranteed any engagements between Omaha and San Francisco—a long and costly "jump." Leavitt began organizing Western theaters into a circuit for which he booked "leading attractions of every branch [type of theater] in rapid succession." In return for this service, Leavitt received a certain percentage of the theater managers' receipts. A decade later, one of Leavitt's former managers, Al Hayman, applied the same principle to create the Theatrical Syndicate, the dominant financial force in turn-of-the-century American theater.

By the late 1880's, a handful of ambitious managers controlled most of the circuits. In the Northeast and Midwest, there was H. R. Jacobs' Own Imperial

Circuit, which consisted of theaters in the major cities of New York, New Jersey, Pennsylvania, Ohio, Canada (Montreal and Toronto), and as far west as Chicago. His former partner, F. F. Proctor, had a prosperous circuit of twelve theaters in New York and New England.

In May, 1887, the managers of most of the theaters Weber & Fields played in (or hoped to play in) met in Philadelphia at the Grand Central Theatre to form the Board of Managers of Vaudeville Theaters. Charter members included William Harris, Henry Miner, W. J. Gilmore, H. W. Williams, and James Kernan. Their purpose was to standardize the booking practices in the Eastern vaudeville circuit, and to set up a central booking office in New York City.

The development of controlling interests within circuits and the manipulation of the booking process marked the beginning of the movement towards trusts. The circuits provided the organized entities from which a "super-circuit" would emerge, in much the same way that U. S. Steel and American Telephone & Telegraph organized already-existing companies into single business units. Once this organizational process began, the business side of popular theater developed with startling rapidity, becoming a fully rationalized industry comparable to the railroads or the oil companies by the turn of the century.

By 1890, with the control of theater business firmly concentrated in the circuits, the next step in the centralization process—the rise of the booking offices, and with it, the middleman—would produce yet more dramatic changes. It was at this stage that popular theater was transformed from a pushcart-type enterprise into a big business, and it was in this environment that Weber & Fields tried to make good as managers.

Known variously in its first full season as Weber & Fields' "Own" Company, Weber & Fields' "American," "Thoroughly American," "Novelty," and "Specialty" Company, the Weber & Fields touring company of 1890–1891 was most consistent where it counted—at the box office. From the start, the size of their payroll (between $900 and $1,000 a week, excluding Weber & Fields) left no room for failure. Two weeks in a row of light attendance and the company would have to fold. To realize a profit, the company had to play to capacity houses week after week. Experienced managers like Gus Hill predicted that Weber & Fields' company would not last out the season—or so they hoped, afraid that Weber & Fields' generous salaries would raise the ante for procuring performers. Some may have wondered if Lew Fields' deadpan defiance of the odds at the poker table and racetrack had been embraced by his partner Weber as a way of doing business.

Privately, Joe and Lew were considerably less sanguine. With their season set to begin at Kernan's Monumental Theater in Baltimore, Joe mentioned that their start-up capital was nearly exhausted. Incredulous that the vast sum of $2,000 could disappear so quickly, Lew reviewed the expenditures. One thousand dollars went to the printer who produced the show posters and window cards. The printer—the job plant of a New York newspaper—had a monopoly on the theatrical lithography business, and he did not extend credit to theater companies. As was the case with other theatrical troupes, Weber & Fields' Company's "paper" would be printed on a weekly basis and charged against the deposit (hence the insider's term "good paper" to indicate the solvency of a touring company).

Advances to company members had eaten up much of the remaining money, thanks to Lew's soft heart and Joe's desire to inspire confidence in his new employees. Fifteen tickets to Baltimore accounted for another two hundred dollars, and there would be additional expenses for the boardinghouse, backstage supplies, and tips for the prop men and musicians (woe to the vaudevillians who didn't tip the prop men and musicians!). Weber & Fields had to clear no less than $1,200 from the first week's engagement to meet their payroll and buy return tickets to New York.

A few quick calculations reveal the precariousness of their position. The Weber & Fields companies of the early 1890's appeared in theaters belonging either to H. R. Jacobs or F. F. Proctor, or those of big-city independents such as Miner, Kernan, Gilmore, and Williams. Both the Jacobs and the Proctor circuits charged "popular" prices: Jacobs' theaters had a 20-30-50–cent scale, with box seats at 75 cents and, in the New York area, one dollar, while Proctor initiated the 10-20-30–cent scale, and generally had larger-capacity houses.

Based on information pieced together from newspapers and programs, we can estimate that the largest seating capacity of the theaters visited by Weber & Fields' 1890 company was approximately 1,200. For popular shows, it was usually possible to jam in an additional two to three hundred standees, since local fire laws, if any, were not enforced. The cheapest seats (the gallery) were always the most plentiful; although accurate figures for the exact number of seats at each price level are not available, one could hazard a guess that the paid admission averaged out to the medium-priced ticket. Theater managers of the big-time circuit customarily took anywhere from thirty to fifty percent of the gross. In the days before continuous vaudeville took hold, a vaudeville company in a big-time house performed six evening shows a week, plus two matinees, usually on Wednesdays and Saturdays.

With these approximate figures in mind, one can begin to appreciate Weber & Fields' gamble. Playing at a Proctor theater to a standing-room-only audience of fifteen hundred, and assuming a forty percent share for the house, the company would clear $1,440 for the week—enough for Weber & Fields to meet their payroll, pay themselves, and still have roughly $200 to use for transportation or other expenses. The rest, if any, was profit.

If, however, turnout for the week was only moderately good by the standards of other road companies—say, one thousand customers per show—Weber & Fields would not clear a thousand dollars for the week, and thus would not be able to pay all their performers in full, or cover the costs of transportation to their next engagement. A heat wave in September or a blizzard in March (such as the one in 1888 that shut down much of the Northeast) reduced theater attendance no matter how good the program promised to be. On occasions when the week's earnings fell short, Lew would send his brother Max, who was travelling with the company as its business agent, to the local pawnbroker to pawn the partners' diamond studs. A week or so later, Max would return to the pawnshop with money from the current week's receipts to get the diamonds out of hock. If any members of the company happened to ask, they were told that the diamonds had been sent back to New York for safekeeping.

The firm of Weber & Fields opened its season in Baltimore with a zero balance, and had to earn its way back to New York. The engagement at Kernan's Monumental Theater would be the first test of Weber & Fields' all-star approach to programming. Opening night—September 29, 1890—was unusually hot and humid. As Joe and Lew put on their makeup in their dressing room, it was more than the weather that was making them sweat. Once before they had been this nervous: thirteen years earlier, on the afternoon of their first performance at Turn Hall.

According to the *New York Clipper*, Weber & Fields' Own Company inaugurated the season at the Monumental "to the capacity of the house. Hundreds were unable to gain admission. Every act scored a pronounced success. . . ." The anonymous reporter ended by sounding the crowd-pleasing notes of patriotism and financial optimism: "the performance was as good as a U.S. bond."

The company's first New York engagement was not in the hurly-burly of the Bowery but in the up-and-coming middle-class community of Harlem. The sedate and respectable residents of Harlem did not need to go downtown for diversion; they had their own beer gardens, billiard rooms, restaurants, and theaters. On October 6, Weber & Fields began a week's engagement at a favorite Harlem resort, the Olympic Theater, "to a tip top house," offering the right balance of knockabout ethnic humor, pretty singers and dancers, and farcical sketches for the conservative, pinochle-playing audiences of Harlem.

The following week at Brooklyn's Grand Theater provided the company with its final dress rehearsal before its downtown debut. The packed houses in Harlem and Brooklyn boosted the advance sales at Jim Donaldson's London Theater, and manager Cromwell's poster campaign made it impossible to cross lower Manhattan without being reminded of the imminent arrival of Weber & Fields' Thoroughly American Company to the Bowery.

In the early years of vaudeville, before the Association of Vaudeville Managers gave Keith and Albee a stranglehold on the industry, the New York downtown theaters—Pastor's, Miner's, the London—were still the bellwethers for the touring circuits. New York City vaudeville audiences were demanding, savvy, and demonstrative. Inasmuch as many of their favorite stars were local products, they treated the performers like talented offspring, expecting nothing less than the freshest jokes and novelties, perfectly executed. Those who were able to live up to these expectations were welcomed with open arms and open wallets. If an act made good at these houses, out-of-town managers would be eager to book it.

Weber & Fields arrived at the London as the Bowery's favorite sons, the local boys who had made good. With its greater seating capacity, higher price scale, and extra matinees, a week of full houses at the London could be very profitable. Equally important to Joe and Lew was their desire to show Jim Donaldson that his long-standing confidence in them was justified. He had not only helped arrange their trial run the previous spring, but there is also some evidence that he made spot loans to Weber & Fields during their first season.

Donaldson's investment paid off. The *Clipper*'s account of Weber & Fields at the London is noteworthy not only for its account of the new managers' success, but for its detailed description of a first-rate vaudeville program before the continuous vaudeville format took hold:

> The Weber and Fields Thoroughly American Company made their first appearance this season at a downtown theater at the above house [the London] October 20 and drew two crowded audiences. The Fremonts, Charles and Lottie, opened the bill in good shape, Miss Fremont's dancing calling forth rounds of applause. Isabella Ward, in her musical act, gave a clever and pleasing performance. Miss Ward's well molded figure is set forth to excellent advantage in full evening dress. Her reception was hearty. Wilson and Cameron, in black face, tickled the boys, their flip flops going well. Lottie Gilson, that clever little song and dance performer, evidently has a stronghold on the London patronage, for she was royally welcomed and had to respond to several encores.

> Next came the heads of the show, those funny German dialect comedians, Weber and Fields. Their broken English caused loud bursts of laughter, while their kicking and jumping on each other were of the roughest kind, and caught on heavily. . . .

The kicking and jumping occurred at the climax of Weber & Fields' act. Weber, in evening clothes and top hat, sat down in a chair while delivering some patter to the audience. Standing off to one side, Fields smiled mischievously at the audience, dismissed the devilish idea he clearly had in mind, and finally gave in to it. He then ran full-tilt at his seated buddy. Before Weber could react, Fields leaped feet-first, planting both feet squarely on Weber's well-padded chest. As Weber tumbled backwards, Fields used Weber's chest as a springboard for a forward roll, landing on his feet. After he calmly smoothed the creases in his own evening suit, Fields strolled over to where Weber was floundering like a beached whale and helped him up.

The rest of the bill included Drawee (juggler and equilibrist), Richmond & Glenroy, Ramza & Arno (grotesque bar act), and Frank Bush, the well-known Hebrew comedian. The afterpiece was appropriately called "Crazy Quilt," and according to the *Clipper*, it "sent the audience home in excellent humor."

From New York, the company travelled to Paterson, Newark, Philadelphia, Providence, Montreal, Toronto, and Buffalo. In late December, they arrived at the western terminus of their tour, the Lyceum Theater, Chicago (managed by Tom Grenier, Weber & Fields' former circus boss), and then played a week in Milwaukee. An article in the *Clipper* noted that the Weber & Fields Company was doing "excellent business." In the same piece, business manager Cromwell boasted that "the company contains the same people now as it did when they started in September."

To understand why this information was considered newsworthy, one need only recall the turnover of performers that characterized other touring companies, including those Weber & Fields had served with. Signing their attractions to season-long contracts put an additional strain on their payroll, but it also increased their box-office appeal when they made their return engagements in the second half of the season. The generous salaries also made it less likely that a rival manager or theater owner would be able to lure away a performer in mid-

season. Actors particularly appreciated the fact that by signing with Weber &
Fields, they could count on twenty to thirty weeks of bookings without further
hassle. It would be another five years before vaudeville booking agents could put
together an entire season of big-time bookings like the ones that Weber & Fields
arranged for their own company.

The year 1891 began with Weber & Fields' Own Company retracing its steps
among the East Coast theaters, followed by a brief excursion to the Midwest. A
return engagement at the London at the end of February broke house records:
"long before the curtain rose on the afternoon and evening performances, standing room was being sold." The same proved to be true at the Howard Atheneum
in Boston and in two Philadelphia theaters.

Weber & Fields had intended to close their season after the Philadelphia
engagements ended in early April, but Cromwell had arranged for an additional
six weeks of "gilt-edged" dates (or so they were called by the *Clipper*). Two
weeks into their extended season, Weber & Fields left their company in Cincinnati to honor a long-standing commitment to headline for Tony Pastor's semian-
nual tour. Rather than cancel the rest of their own company's dates, Weber &
Fields elected to send them out, bolstered by the addition of several veteran
performers: James McAvoy, Bessie Gilbert, and the song and dance team of Ryan
& Richfield. It was another calculated gamble. Weber & Fields were counting on
the fact that most of their performers were stars in their own right, and that most
of the other road companies had closed for the season, so they stood a good
chance of breaking even or better. Besides, Pastor would pay $250 a week for
their Dutch act, which could be set aside as working capital for next season's
tour. Weber & Fields' Specialty Company finally closed out its "long and prosperous season" in Cleveland on May 2, 1891, without its eponymous proprietors.

Weber & Fields, meanwhile, appeared with Pastor's troupe of stars, which
included Maggie Cline and the Russell Brothers, all of whom were to become
members of Weber & Fields' companies in the near future. Pastor's combo trekked
through Brooklyn, Albany, Syracuse, Buffalo, Detroit, Toledo, and Chicago for
two weeks, and then returned to New York to finish the season with two weeks
at his Fourteenth Street Theater.

Among the enthusiastic fans at Tony Pastor's were Lew's sister Annie, now
seventeen, and her friend from Brooklyn, a poised and stylish sixteen-year-old
named Rose Harris. Because Pastor's theater had earned a reputation for genteel
entertainment (with its top ticket, at $1.50, the same price as the legitimate the-
aters), the Schanfields and Harrises had no qualms about letting their daughters
attend. Annie had introduced Rose to Lew a year earlier, after his triumphant
return from the West Coast. As a rather plain fifteen-year-old, Rose Harris apparently had made little impression on Lew at the time. One can imagine her tenta-
tiveness in meeting an actor whom she assumed to be accustomed to the company of actresses, beautiful and talented women like Lottie Fremont and Isabella
Ward. Since that first meeting, Rose had confessed to having a crush on Annie's
famous brother. When Annie re-introduced them a year later in the lobby of Tony
Pastor's, it was Lew's turn to take notice.

To the Lower East Side *shadchens* (the matchmakers, or "Cupids of the

Ghetto"), Lew's good looks and local notoriety made him a very eligible bachelor: vaudeville performer and manager with bright prospects, early twenties, slender, above-average height, wavy black hair, big brown eyes, and a heart-warming smile. Did not drink, played pinochle and gin (and high-stakes poker, but they would keep that quiet). Aside from the diamond stud in his shirt front, he dressed conservatively, emulating the look of a businessman rather than that of the "hot sports" who set the style for rest of the Bowery's young men. Indeed, Lew's street clothes reflected the style of the clientele he hoped to do business with. The *shadchens* could only shake their heads wistfully, because Lew Fields was not in the market for a wife; anyway, he was too Americanized to agree to an arranged marriage.

There were other obstacles to consider. A successful vaudevillian could expect to be on the road for anywhere from twenty to thirty weeks a year, and the road took a predictably heavy toll of relationships. Including the stint with Tony Pastor, Weber & Fields in their first full season as managers had been on tour for thirty-seven weeks without a break. Eleven weeks of that time was spent playing in theaters in New York City or its environs (Harlem, Brooklyn, Newark, Patterson), which presumably allowed them to sleep at home. Their responsibilities as managers and performers left little time for visiting with family and friends.

Perhaps one of the reasons that there is precious little information about Lew Fields' personal life for this period is that he indeed had very little personal life. He had no close personal friends besides his partner Weber. Although he apparently felt great affection for his family, he was able to maintain only a nominal closeness. In family matters, it is likely that Lew confided in his brother Max, particularly when it involved the touchy subject of Lew's ever-increasing financial contributions.

The variety artist whose livelihood depended on "working the circuits" needed a spouse who understood the pressures of performing and booking, who accepted the long periods away from family and the drastic financial ups and downs that characterized most theater careers—i.e., someone eligible for sainthood. Then as now, marriages between theater professionals were common, since it was unreasonable to expect someone outside of the profession to understand—or even tolerate—their way of life.

But the idea of marrying one of the charming soubrettes or dancers he had shared the stage with did not appeal to Lew (or Joe, for that matter). Perhaps Lew was prejudiced by the stereotype of the actress as an unfaithful wife and indifferent mother. It is equally likely that he concurred with his parents' wish that he marry a respectable girl from a stable family (which by definition precluded an actress). One actor in the family was enough.

Neither did he seem to be susceptible to backstage romances. There is no evidence—either before or after his marriage—that he was ever romantically involved with an actress. Of course, the era's moral rigidity made it imperative to conceal such illicit liaisons. Lew's concern for social propriety would have made him a prime candidate for the "badger game," or the popular blackmail ploy of "seduction under the promise of marriage," which the shyster Abe Hummel plied so successfully on behalf of the city's single women—aspiring actresses, in particular. If Fields drew any conclusions from the sordid offstage situations he had observed during nearly a decade of touring—the alcoholism, infidelity, divorce, loneliness, insanity—it was that the exclusive society of theater folk was, in the long run, unhealthy.

Fears about the personal lives of actors notwithstanding, Lew formed several working friendships with his stage colleagues. Among them were John and James Russell, "foremost delineators of Irish chambermaids," who appeared on the bill with Weber & Fields at Pastor's in June of 1891. The Russell Brothers were a few years older than Weber & Fields, but they, too, had grown up on the Lower East Side (in an Irish neighborhood) and had made their professional debut as a blackface act in 1877. James was an extraordinary mimic of male and female characters. Both brothers were capable dancers. Johnny, the older brother, had a sweet singing voice, and could wring a bucket of tears out of a ballad, at which point James would burlesque the outpourings of sentiment with a ridiculous remark, thereby restoring the proper level of hilarity to the routine. Their characterizations of Irish servant girls were strongly influenced by the female impersonators in the minstrel shows. There was nothing inherently feminine in the physique or facial features of either brother, but the juxtaposition of their manly physiques with their letter-perfect costumes and makeup created a humorous parody before a word was spoken. Audiences implicitly recognized the fact that real chambermaids could be rather masculine specimens. Once, when the Russells' theatrical trunks were mistakenly delivered to their hotel, they had no choice but to dress in their room. Emerging from their room in their costumes, they were set upon in the hallway by two infuriated chambermaids—the real kind—flailing away with brooms. The attackers had just been fired by the hotel, and had decided to get even with the "girls" who had been hired to replace them. The Russells' dialect patter was full of non sequiturs and almost surreal imagery. "Mag-gie! Mag-gie!" James would bellow, his harsh, singsong falsetto reaching the farthest corner of the gallery, "Put the horse in the kitchen an' give 'im a bushel o' coal!"

By signing the Russell Brothers for the 1891–1892 season, Cromwell delivered on his well-publicized promise that the "new company . . . will be better and stronger than ever." John Russell also served as stage manager for the company. Cromwell made a point of mentioning that "better terms have been secured all around," implying that theater managers were willing to take a smaller cut of the gross because of Weber & Fields' impressive drawing power.

The rest of the company included Maud Huth ("clever singer of plantation melodies"), three teams of sketch artists (Lavender & Tomson, Dryden & Mitchell, Filson & Errol), a trio of comic gymnasts, a pair of eccentric musicians, and a club-swinger. The highlights of the program were, of course, "The Irish Lilies" and "The German Senators" (Weber & Fields' new label for their Dutch act). The Russell Brothers' turn included parodies of popular actresses Clara Morris, Kate Claxton, and Sarah Bernhardt, and in the afterpiece, they performed with other members of the company in a burlesque of the melodrama *The Two Orphans*, with John playing the role of Old Mother Frochard. The afterpiece was presented in four scenes, long by variety standards. This emphasis on extended sketches signalled a significant step in the aesthetic development of the variety format.

On August 31, Weber & Fields' second season opened to large houses at William's Academy of Music in Pittsburgh. The following week, at Kernan's Monumental in Baltimore, they "packed the house to the doors." Back to familiar ground in New York, the company played for two weeks (a booking rarity) at Tony Pastor's Fourteenth Street Theatre. The *New York Clipper* reviewers gushed:

> As was perfectly proper, a packed house gave a good old fashioned welcome to that tiptop organization of specialists known as Weber & Fields' Company. . . . The program was calculated to excite and enthuse the most jaded playgoer. . . . It is odds on that a majority had to employ seamstresses after it was all over. Such a howling, screaming, knock down and drag out conglomeration has no duplication on the contemporary stage. . . . The company easily ranks with the best vaudeville organizations of the day, and reflects a deal of credit on the owners and on Manager C. F. Cromwell whose able work has served to place the company on the highest pinnacle of success. . . .

There were higher pinnacles still to come. At the London, in Harlem, Brooklyn, and throughout the Northeast, the Weber & Fields Company continued to pack them in "like sardines." At Miner's Eighth Avenue, where six years earlier Weber & Fields had been last-minute replacements on the bill with the Adah Richmond Burlesque Company, "the business for the entire week has been one of the largest in the history of the house."

The standing-room-only houses in New York made Max Schanfield's job as advance agent that much easier. In many of the cities they visited, the Weber & Fields Company's engagement set new house records for gross receipts—a "banner week," in the trade vernacular. By the end of the season, Cromwell was boasting that Weber & Fields had played the most banner weeks of any touring company. Cromwell also surprised *Clipper* readers with the news that Weber & Fields had signed the veteran team of the Russell Brothers to a five-year contract. In a business where an unbroken season-long contract was a rarity, and the average lifespan of a touring company was two seasons, a five-year contract sounded like a fairy tale.

Signing top acts to long-term contracts—with guaranteed salaries—was a radical departure from the accepted business practices of the day, at least where vaudeville was concerned. For Weber & Fields, it was the first step in their plan to expand their influence as producers and managers. As it turned out, it was also a necessary step in counteracting the growing power of booking agents and theater owners.

During their second season, the Weber & Fields Company continued its crusade to spread the gospel of vaudeville as a respectable and profitable middleclass diversion. In Cincinnati, Weber & Fields borrowed a page from Tony Pastor's book and persuaded Colonel Jim Fennessey, owner of the People's Theater, to designate the Friday show as Ladies' Night. Fennessey was still running a stag house, and from a purely business standpoint, Weber & Fields considered this to be unnecessarily limiting to their box office receipts. At their suggestion, Fennessey papered the town with flyers announcing Friday as Ladies' Night—no smoking, no drinking, and a cut flower for every lady. Weber & Fields requested that the theater be thoroughly scrubbed, and that the lobby be filled with floral displays. It was the start of a Cincinnati tradition.[2]

Like Cohan's song-and-dance man, Weber & Fields were not ashamed to trumpet their successes. Halfway through their second season, they took out a large ad in the *Clipper*, proclaiming themselves "Undisputably America's Leading Vaudeville Attraction—pronounced as such everywhere." This boldfaced truth was followed by a statement to the theatrical profession explaining Weber & Fields' philosophy: "The marvelous growth and prestige that have attended this organization from its infancy can only be explained to those who fail to comprehend that you cannot make money by presenting indifferent entertainment. That day has passed. Give the Public, who are the best judges, what they demand and you are apt to meet with success. We present only the best. The question of price to obtain what we want never entertained. . . ." Nowadays, populist sentiments expressed by successful entertainers have a way of sounding self-serving. Considered in its proper historical context, however, Weber & Fields' statement reflects a subtle but significant shift in attitudes towards popular entertainment. The "Public," according to Weber & Fields, could no longer be treated like unwashed brats in need of moral instruction, or low-lifers too besotted to recognize an inferior product. Weber & Fields had only to consider their own families and their Bowery neighbors to realize that the vaudeville audience was increasingly composed of decent, hard-working men and women who sweated for the dimes to pay for their diversions. Whether they were shopping in one of the new department stores or going to a vaudeville house, they wanted goods that were "high-class," "high-quality," "refined," "the best of its kind," despite their limited means. The tired businessman and his family should not feel ashamed of his entertainments, or be short-changed.

The *Clipper* statement continued, culminating in an odd rhetorical flourish: "What Company has the majority of Banner Weeks to their credit this season? It won't require much guessing to arrive at the answer. We are out for the Shekels, and come pretty near getting our share. . . ." Mike and Meyer as vaudeville managers: in one brash and breezy sentence, Weber & Fields deflated the artistic and moral pretensions of their colleagues by putting the goals of Keith, Proctor, et al. on a par with those of a Lower East Side tailor or pushcart vendor. The deliberate ethnic reference was a sly reminder to the trade that two clever Jewish boys were now the top vaudeville attraction. There were already several successful Jews in theatrical management (e.g., Harry Jacobs, Abe Erlanger, Oscar Hammerstein), but Weber & Fields were acutely aware of the fact that they were, at the time, the only Jewish performers to attain such prominence on the variety stage.

Getting the shekels (or the dough), winning the girl (or the guy), beating out a competitor, striving for social approval and respectability: success preoccupied variety audiences, from Harrigan onward.[3] It was not simply that a large percentage of routines, sketches, and songs articulated the immigrant's quest for success; the performers often lived out rags-to-riches stories of their own. The successful vaudevillian was a Horatio Alger character in the flesh: the plucky kid from the wrong side of town who made it rich, succeeding against all odds by virtue of his (or her) perseverance and innate abilities. Unlike Alger's heroes, however, most vaudevillians did not get sanctimonious with success.

With Alger's popular myth in mind, it is interesting to consider the brief biographical sketches of Weber & Fields that appeared in the *Clipper* in December, 1892. Most likely, it was their manager Cromwell who prepared their bios, since he took such an active role in shaping Weber & Fields' public image. As befitted the purveyors of "thoroughly American" entertainment, both Weber & Fields claimed to be born in the United States. There was no mention of Fields' family name, although the *Clipper*'s bios often included this information for other vaudeville figures. The intended effect became obvious in the next sentence: "Weber & Fields are an excellent example of what Yankee perseverance and pluck can do." Apparently, the myth was more endearing when its heroes were native-born.

The bios also announced an early bid for theatrical respectability: "[Weber & Fields] will soon enter the field of legitimate comedy, Edgar Selden being at present engaged in constructing a play for them, in which they intend 'starring" in 1893–94." The play itself, *The Trolley System*, never lived up to expectations. It took Selden, who later became a leading Tin Pan Alley songwriter, two years to finish, and by that time, Weber & Fields were too busy with their touring companies to take on the lead roles. Nevertheless, this was the first indication of Weber & Fields' aspirations to anything beyond vaudeville. Going from vaudeville to the legitimate stage was the theater equivalent of leaving the tenements and moving uptown.

There were other indications of Weber & Fields' desire for social legitimacy. In July, 1892, Weber and Fields were initiated as members of Cosmopolitan Lodge No. 202 of the Knights of Pythias. The Knights of Pythias and the Elks had first appeared in the 1860's, but the proliferation of "secret societies" really began around 1880. In the years between 1880 and 1895, two hundred and sixty such organizations were founded, with membership rosters topping six million names by 1901.[4] In the early 1890's, the Knights of Pythias had accepted actors from the legitimate stage as members, but not variety artists, and certainly not Jews. Under these conditions, it must have been particularly gratifying for Joe and Lew to realize that their success and notoriety had overcome the club members' latent prejudices. A few months after joining, Weber & Fields entertained their fellow Knights at a banquet, with a performance of their newest comedy routine.

In their first two seasons as owner-managers, Weber & Fields had little time for developing new routines. Based on their box office receipts, it is clear that their audiences did not seem to mind. Vaudeville patrons were perfectly content to watch a favorite routine repeated. Even after memorizing the punch lines, they still applauded the style with which first-rate performers "put over" their act. In the days before records, films, and radio broadcasts, it was possible to build a career in vaudeville around one popular, well-executed fifteen-minute routine. With daily performances, the performers polished their acts to a high lustre; new lines and gags were added and discarded based on the audience's response, but the basic characters and situations remained the same. In this way, McIntyre & Heath's "The Georgia Minstrels," or the Russell Brothers' "Irish Servant Girls" were still getting laughs after twenty years on the boards.

Joe and Lew were objective enough to realize that despite their recent success, "The German Senators" routine was not strong enough to become a vaudeville perennial. Dressing up Mike and Meyer in evening dress, and having them argue (violently) about etiquette and topical matters while standing on their heads were really just embellishments of the same knockabout turn they had been performing since their last season with Gus Hill.

Perhaps it was the need to come up with new material, as well as the cumulative fatigue of their dual roles as performers and managers, that motivated them to refuse additional spring bookings and end the company's 1891–1892 season in March. Returning to their "office" in the poolroom behind Miner's Bowery, they spent the spring working up new routines. Joe was never at a loss for snappy one-liners and puns, but Lew wanted something more structured than the usual series of jokes and pratfalls strung together by dialect patter. While their company's vaudeville programs helped popularize the extended sketch or burlesque, Weber & Fields' own act—like most comedy acts—was still an escalating progression of quips and stage business with little narrative cohesion. As indicated by their announced intention to star in a farce-comedy, both Joe and Lew were actively looking for ways to expand their Mike and Meyer routines.

The recent success of two musical farces—Hoyt's *A Trip to Chinatown* and Harrigan's *The Last of the Hogans*—was a reminder that the subjects and methods of home-grown musical comedy were compatible with vaudeville and burlesque sketches. Both shows had episodic plots that unfolded in the streets of New York, with comic situations created by the main characters' pursuit of leisure-time activities. The loose plot allowed for vaudeville-style routines to be incorporated into the action. Take away the painted drops and stage effects, and the distance between the Hoyt and Harrigan shows and the burlesques presented by Pastor and various minstrel companies was not large. The main difference was that the musical numbers in Hoyt's *Chinatown*—most notable, "Reuben, Reuben" and "The Bowery"—were superior to anything written for the variety or burlesque stages.

Harrigan's continued popularity may have encouraged Weber & Fields to return to a familiar source for their inspiration: the struggles of the immigrant to adapt to American ways. Early in the summer, while working in the relative cool of Miner's back room, their brainstorming session was interrupted by angry German voices at a nearby pool table. Two of Miner's theater employees were involved in an increasingly disputatious call-shot pool game. Their heavily-accented insults and exclamations entertained an informal gallery of spectators, now joined by Joe and Lew. When the conflict escalated from threatening with cue sticks to hurling billiard balls, the spectators dove for cover. Underneath one of the pool tables, Fields grinned and whispered to Weber, "We've got it!"[5]

The new material was too precious to risk revealing to the covetous eyes of the actors and managers who frequented Miner's. During the next week, Weber & Fields worked up their routine on a battered pool table in a basement beer dive on a Bowery side street. They tried to use the love-hate relationship of Mike and Meyer to draw out the comic possibilities of the situation. The pool game was not merely a pretext for dialect jokes and knockabout; rather, they treated the pool game as a slice of life, a story about two immigrants getting acquainted with a typical American pastime. In shape and substance, it was closer to a scene from the Harrigan and Hart shows of the previous decade than to a contemporary vaudeville turn.

They continued to rehearse in secret for the rest of the summer. The prolonged rehearsal period and their uncharacteristic secretiveness are hints of the importance Weber and Fields attached to their new sketch. Although their company's 1892–1893 season opened in Pittsburgh on September 5, and moved on to Philadelphia and Baltimore, Weber & Fields did not perform "The Pool Room" in public until their first New York engagement at the end of the month. Appropriately, it was in the friendly confines of the London that Weber & Fields first presented the sketch that would be forever identified with them.

In the earliest versions of "The Pool Room," the sketch begins with a bet, for the typical pool room in the 1890's also served as a betting station for horse races. Mike and Meyer arrive and study the entries on the blackboard. They agree to place their money on a horse named India Rubber (a well-known thoroughbred at the time) because he is "good in the stretch." While they await the results (sent by wire from the track), Meyer suggests a game of pool. The following is based on Felix Isman's transcription[6] and the descriptions of contemporary journalists:

> MIKE: I don't know dis pool business.
> MEYER: Vatever I don't know, I teach you.
> MIKE: Dot seems fair.
> MEYER: To make der game more interesting, I bet you dot I beat.
> MIKE: Oughtn't you to beat? Ain't you biggest?
> MEYER: Brains in der head, not bigness, vins in pool.
> MIKE: Give me otts und I bet you.
> MEYER: Vat you mean, otts?
> MIKE: You should put up more money to my lesterest money.
> MEYER: I vill not! But I tell you vot I vill do. I vill put up five dollar to your ten dollar.
> MIKE: Dots what I mean.

Short and trusting, Mike places his ten dollars on the lower shelf of the ball rack. His tall, scheming buddy Meyer removes it immediately, and with his own five dollars, puts it on the top shelf. Seeing this, Mike stands on tiptoe, and discovers that he cannot reach the money.

> MEYER: Remember, now! Der one dot gets der money vins.
> MIKE: Let me understandt meinself: der one dot gets der money is der vinner, eh?

To decide who gets to shoot first, they measure hands on a pool cue like boys deciding the first batter for a baseball game. Mike wins and starts for the money.

MIKE: I vin! I vin!

MEYERS: Dumbskull! You don't vin der money. You chust get shot first.

MIKE: Pardon, please. I oliogepize.

Next, Meyer informs Mike that he must stand three feet from the table when he shoots; Mike's amply padded waistline already prevented him from reaching much beyond the table's edge. After taking a step backward, he takes a lunging cut at the cue ball, misses badly, then turns the cue around and aims with the large end. Meyer corrects him once again:

MEYER: Remember, you got to break der balls before you bust dem.

MIKE: *(confused)* I got to bust dem before I break dem?

Mike shoots the cue ball into the cluster of balls. The fifteen ball, by arrangement, drops into the corner pocket.

MIKE: I got him! I got him!

MEYER: *(replacing ball on table)* You didn't call it!

MIKE: I did call it! I did call it! I called it to meinself!

MEYER: Dots a bad habit, talking to yourselfs, und worser in pool. Don't do it some more. Now vot ball you play?

MIKE: Do I got to tell you?

MEYER: Sure, you got to tell me.

MIKE: Are you der mayor or somedings? I like to play dis one, only dot one is in de vay.

Meyer's frustration at his partner's inability to understand the rules was a good excuse to incorporate their familiar choking routine (with its violent declaration of eternal friendship) in the sketch. Thus reassured, they resume their game, with Meyer lining up a shot.

MIKE: Vot ball you play?

MEYER: Der round one.

MIKE: Round? All is round!

MEYER: *(picks up ball, scrutinizes it)* Dis one is rounder.

He replaces the ball on the table, but Mike picks it up to see for himself.

MEYER: Again! Once more, ain't I told you? Drop dot ball!

Meyer struggles to get Mike to relinquish the ball, manhandling him in the process. Meyer shoots and misses, driving the cue ball into a corner pocket. Both jump up and down excitedly.

MIKE: Hooray! A scratch!

MEYER: Sure! A scratch! Dot gives me four balls. Only best players can dodge all der other balls and get in der hole. I surprise meinself.

Mike ponders this while Meyer puts the four highest-numbered balls in his rack and prepares to shoot again. He calls his shot—"der colored one"—and misses. When Mike is about to shoot, Meyer interrupts:

MEYER: How many times got I tell you you got to name vat ball you shoot?

MIKE: Good! I name one Rudolph.

Meyer threatens Mike with his cue. Mike springs into classic fencing pose. They parry and thrust back and forth several times. Mike finally agrees to shoot the fifteen ball. They search the table in vain, moving several balls in the process. Meyer finds the fifteen ball in Mike's rack—the only ball Mike has managed to sink.

Meyer replaces the ball on the table. Mike shoots and scratches the cue ball into a side pocket. He dances jubilantly.

MIKE: Hooray! I vin four balls! Dots a scratch like you told me.

MEYER: Dots no scratch. Dots an itch. Scratches in the corner pockets, itches in side pocket. Itches is bad. One itch by you gifs me four balls more. . . .

Mike listens with growing dismay, and realizes that he has no chance of winning. Meyer bends over to line up his shot. Suddenly, Mike jumps onto the pool table, and using Meyer's back as a stepping stone, he leaps from there to the rack, grabbing the bet money as he falls past the top shelf. Meyer tries unsuccessfully to take the money back.

MIKE: *(triumphant)* Remember, der one dot gets der money vins de game.

Meyer drags Mike offstage by the scruff of his neck, with the latter still clutching his hard-earned cash.

To see Weber & Fields as their audiences saw them, we must try to imagine comedy before the advent of TV sitcoms, radio shows, revues, and silent-film clowns. The character types burlesqued by Weber & Fields were living and breathing neighbors of the theater patrons, and to a great extent, the audience sympathized with the social aspirations that Mike and Meyer caricatured.

Throughout the 1892–1893 season, wherever "The Pool Room" was performed, audiences were delighted by Mike and Meyer's novel interpretations of the rules, and by the trick shots made possible by the specially rigged pool table. As was customary, Weber & Fields continued to refine and augment their sketch at each performance, so that several reviewers mentioned new tricks, "side-splitters," and "breaks" when the company made its return engagements. The *Clipper* commentator recognized that Weber & Fields' new sketch was a significant development, saying that it provided "almost unlimited scope to their well-known comical contortion of the English language and their knockabout business."

"The Pool Room" established the formula that Weber & Fields would follow until they opened their music hall, when they turned to burlesquing theater rather than everyday life. Each of the next four seasons revealed the German Senators coming to blows in pursuit of another urban American pastime. For the 1893–1894 season, they presented "The Horse Race," a subject that was presumably of great interest to the duo, since Weber had recently invested in a trotter and Fields was often seen in the stands at Saratoga. The following season, they took on the latest craze—bowling—with less success, and returned to the pool table and horse race sketches after four or five weeks.

Shooting galleries (still a popular urban amusement) and Wild West Shows were the targets of Weber & Fields' sketch for 1895, "The Schutzenfest." A spinning wheel of electric light bulbs was set up on the stage. The prop man, hidden behind the target, exploded the bulbs as needed. As the competition between Mike and Meyer grew more heated, their shots became increasingly preposterous but never missed—impossible ricochet shots, blindfolded, behind the back, doing a headstand, and finally, without pulling the trigger. It cost five dollars a performance to replace the light bulbs, but the audience loved it. It was the same device that they had used to burlesque the magic act when they were with Gus Hill: stretching the credibility of an illusion beyond the breaking point, then revealing the mechanics of the illusion as the payoff to the gag.

Weber & Fields' encore routine was inspired by an incident they had witnessed in the Bowery involving two women customers who both wanted to buy the same article of clothing. Douglas Gilbert described the act:

> Returning before the drop [in front of the curtain], Fields would inquire of the violinist about his instrument. Oh, it was a violin, eh? And expensive? Uh huh. Could he see it? No, no! It was a valuable instrument, worth thousands of dollars. But they would be ever so careful. Couldn't they just see it, in their own hands, for a moment? The violinist finally yields, handing along the bow too. Whereupon the comedians handle it roughly, snatching it from each other; attempt to tune it and break the strings; get into preposterous arguments as to how it was made and how to play it. . . . As the quarrelling becomes more heated, Fields snatches the instrument from Weber's hands and smashes it over his head. Then, aghast at what they have done, they sneak out, and Weber, still holding the bow, runs hurriedly to the enraged violinist, hands it to him quickly and races off.[7]

During the long summer hiatus between the 1891–1892 and 1892–1893 seasons, Fields' attentions were not wholly occupied by the new comedy sketch. Since being reintroduced to Rose Harris at Tony Pastor's, he had corresponded with her on a regular basis. With the entire summer ahead of him, he became a frequent caller at her family's Brooklyn home. Rose worked in a Brooklyn department store, where Lew would meet her at the end of her shift. He had no trouble winning over her siblings: Jack, Bobby, Frances, and Madeline. Bobby admitted to stage ambitions of his own, and took advantage of Lew's visits to ask for pointers and to show off his dancing and Dutch dialect.

The courtship was lavish and proper. With the Weber & Fields Company tour set to begin September 1, the earliest possible wedding date would be late in the year, when the company was performing in New York area theaters. By then, Rose would be all of eighteen.

On the first day of 1893—also his twenty-sixth birthday—Lew Fields married Rose Harris at Congregation Khal Adath Jeshurun, 12–14 Eldridge Street, in an Orthodox wedding ceremony. The synagogue, built in 1886 in Moorish Revival style, with exquisite stained-glass windows and a vaulted ceiling, was the largest and most impressive in the neighborhood at that time. The interior walls were covered with murals, and the Holy Ark was made from hand-carved Italian walnut. Enormous brass chandeliers and candelabra cast a golden light on those assembled below.

Shortly after three o'clock, Lew and the Rabbi stood under the *chupah* (the traditional canopy, deep red velvet trimmed with gold lace), where they were soon joined by Rose and her father. From a brief article printed in the *New York Herald* (a rarity for Lower East Side weddings), we learn that the bride wore "a Bengaline silk dress with pearl passementerie trimmings," and that "her veil was of tulle and crowned with orange blossoms." The bridesmaids were Annie Schanfield, Madeline Harris, and Flora Klein, future wife of Lew's brother Charlie.

Rather than holding the reception and dinner in a nearby hall, the Schanfields hired Renwick Hall, uptown at Eighty-sixth Street and Third Avenue. In addition to a large number of family members, the guests included many of Lew's theater colleagues: Jim Donaldson, Tony Pastor and his wife, Edgar Selden, and managers Harry Jacobs, Max Klein, and Louis Lazarus. Joe Weber delivered a toast, as did Johnnie Carroll, who had recently joined the company. Harry Miner and the Russell Brothers sent congratulatory telegrams.

Interestingly, the *Herald* article did not mention Lew's profession, or that of his many well-known guests. As if to further downplay the connection, Lew was referred to as "L. Maurice Fields." Those who did not know better would have assumed that the groom was simply a successful businessman, an impression that no doubt pleased all concerned, Lew included. The name entered on the marriage certificate was yet another variation on the family name: Louis M. Schoenfields, a hybrid of Lew's stage name and the family's original name.

For the first year and a half of their marriage, Rose lived with the Schanfields at 199 East Broadway, on a block that was the unofficial center for garment contractors and tailors. Given Lew's touring schedule, it would have been considered the height of extravagance for Rose to live alone in a separate apartment. Rose did not choose to accompany her husband on tour. She had no intention of becoming "excess baggage"—vaudeville slang for a non-performing spouse who insisted on touring with the company. Perhaps it was in deference to her, or perhaps it was in response to a recent law banning manufacture in the home, but for the first time, Papa Schanfield moved his place of business outside of the family living quarters.

If Rose needed any firsthand stories about the tribulations of being married to a theater man, she had only to listen to Leah Schanfield, Max's wife. With a two-year-old son and another one on the way, Leah was struggling to maintain

Max's dressmaking business while he tried to establish himself as a theatrical agent. She had seen how Max's involvement with Lew's career had begun as nothing more than brotherly encouragement and advice. Before Max's involvement with the Weber & Fields Company as an advance man and business agent, he was a cutter, tailor, and dressmaker, and that was how Leah continued to think of him. He had opened his own shop in 1884, where he had labored steadily for six years. In the late 1880's, when Weber & Fields needed someone reliable to set up a benefit performance or negotiate New York area bookings, Max obliged, relishing the change of pace even more than the extra income. At first, Leah had believed her husband when he said that his dabbling in theater was done as a favor to his younger brother. Gradually, Lew's success opened Max's eyes to variety's financial potential, and Max began to envision a lucrative and exciting career for himself outside of the rag trade.

In many ways, Max Schanfield's vaudeville career was the flip side to his brother's success story, representative of all those who went bust panning for vaudeville gold. Max's listings in the annual New York City Directory tell the story of a man whose dreams of show business became a nightmare for his family. Over the next decade, Max's listing changed annually: dressmaker, showman, tailor, agent, clerk, agent. There was a new home address with each new listing. No listing appeared in the 1900 directory, but the listing for the following year tersely resolved Max's peripatetic career in showbiz: "Fields, Leah, widow Max, dressmaker, 748 E. 138th."

For the new Mrs. Lew Fields, however, there was no ambiguity about what line of work her husband was in. Their honeymoon would have to be postponed because Weber & Fields' Own Company had a matinee and an evening show for the day following the wedding. The booking at the New Park Theater (Broadway and Thirty-fifth Street) marked the first time that Weber & Fields would be playing in a Broadway theater.

It was a risky move to book a vaudeville show into the Park; the conventional wisdom insisted that uptown Broadway audiences would not attend. Weber, Fields, and Cromwell believed otherwise, convinced that a high-quality vaudeville program could appeal to the same people who bought tickets to farce-comedies and comic operas. The *Clipper* reported that the company "did excellently at the Park. . . . The firm proved that they and the members of their company are as solid on Broadway as they are on the two sides of town." Indeed, when they returned to the Park for two consecutive weeks in April, the *Clipper* pointed out that Weber & Fields' Company was "the first variety organization to play the house more than one week at a time." On the opening night of their return to "upper Broadway, . . . they got a welcome that they are not likely to forget in a hurry."

In May, 1893, Weber & Fields closed out their third season with two weeks in Chicago, hoping to take advantage of the crowds flocking to see the World's Columbian Exposition. For three years, the nation's most accomplished architects, engineers, and artists had worked together to transform a stretch of sand dunes on the Lake Michigan shore into the "White City." In the Court of Honor, awestruck visitors wandered among a dazzling landscape of fountains, Roman façades, and lagoons. For entertainment, visitors went to the Midway Plaisance for the giant Ferris wheel, and toured elaborate replicas of the streets of Cairo and other exotic marketplaces.

The Exposition's imperial style manifested itself in displays of pomp and false monumentalism at every level. Not surprisingly, popular theater was excluded from the official proceedings. The Exposition presented an idealized portrait of American culture; vaudeville and musical comedies caricatured that portrait, ridiculing the same grandiose impulses that the Exposition sought to celebrate. The only stage entertainment deemed worthy of the Exposition was Shakespearean plays, symphony concerts, and military bands.

The organizers could not prevent independent entrepreneurs from erecting circus tents and variety pavilions just outside the fairgrounds. It was here that the voluptuous Little Egypt introduced hootchy-kootchy dancing, boxing champ "Gentleman" Jim Corbett put on sparring exhibitions, and a young Florenz Ziegfeld exhibited Eugene Sandow, the Strong Man.

At first, this exclusive policy delighted Chicago's theater managers. Anticipating large crowds that would be hungry for the amusements denied them at the Exposition, theater managers booked the biggest attractions from all over the country: the Lillian Russell Opera Company, Buffalo Bill's Wild West Show, *The Black Crook*, Tony Pastor's troupe, and Weber & Fields' Own Company. By the end of the first month (May), however, it became clear that the visitors who gained inspiration from the Court of Honor and the Palace of the Fine Arts were not interested in going downtown to see comic opera, vaudeville, or extravaganzas.

In this unfavorable climate, on May 15, the Weber & Fields Company opened at the Vaudeville Theater. Although their program included most of the same acts that had made their season the most profitable yet, they played to limited turnout for their first week. For Joe and Lew, it was a strange feeling to look up from their pool table sketch and see empty seats. Attendance improved for the second week, as word of mouth about "The Pool Room" overcame the unsmiling pretentiousness that had suddenly infected Chicago's theater audiences. For the afterpiece, Weber & Fields added a farce entitled "Senator Myers." The only thing known about the sketch is that it contained topical jokes and satiric references. The World's Columbian Exposition would have been a deserving target.

Well before the end of their profitable 1892–1893 season, Joe and Lew were planning their next move. It was clear to them that the demand for their style of entertainment was still growing. But it was equally clear that to take advantage of this opportunity would sooner or later put them in direct competition with individuals and organizations whose resources far exceeded their own. With Cromwell's guidance, they incorporated under the name of Weber & Fields Amusement Enterprises. Buried within this pragmatic move was the symbolic recognition of the fact that the era of the itinerant actor-manager was over. The real bosses no longer worked onstage, or even backstage, but in plush offices attended by lawyers and accountants. Increasingly, the relatively simple relations between the seller (variety manager) and the buyer (theater owner) were being manipulated by a middleman: the booking agent. Moreover, the middlemen often owned several theaters themselves, and used their influence to bring formerly independent theater owners into line on issues of ticket prices, actor's salaries, and the content of the program. Gradually, performers and theater owners became little more than the chessmen and chessboards; the booking agents controlled the game. The era of the theater capitalist—of Proctor, Keith and Albee, Hayman, and Klaw and Erlanger—had arrived.

Although vaudeville and the legitimate stage remained separate spheres of economic endeavor, their business practices crystallized at the same time and along similar lines, in accordance with the principles of big business: centralizing control, absorbing and eliminating competitors, crushing labor opposition. Vaudeville acts who wanted to play the big-time had to come to terms with the Keith Circuit; the stars of musicals and dramas had to contend with the monopolistic policies of the Klaw-Erlanger Syndicate. By the middle of the 1890's, however, the unique character of Weber & Fields' entertainments cut across economic (and aesthetic) categories. As Weber & Fields Amusement Enterprises expanded, adding touring companies and eventually buying a Broadway theater, Weber & Fields found themselves engaged in sporadic battles with the corporate giants of both vaudeville and legit.

There was a slang expression for the performers who started in vaudeville and used it as a springboard to the legit stage. They were called "in-and-outers," and their ranks included Lillian Russell, Sam Bernard, Francis Wilson, George M. Cohan, and Fay Templeton. Weber & Fields were "in-and-outers" twice over, as performers and as businessmen. As performers, this gave them more power, but as independent managers, it made them more vulnerable. For Weber & Fields, the forces that were reshaping vaudeville and the legit stage—the rise of "continuous" vaudeville and the Theatrical Syndicate—were a growing threat to their artistic and financial independence.

Within a few days of Weber & Fields' Broadway debut at the New Park Theater, F. F. Proctor opened his Twenty-third Street Theater. Proctor's was New York's first continuous vaudeville house, beating out archrivals Keith and Albee, whose extensive renovations to the Union Square Theater were not completed until September. Prices were fifteen, twenty-five, and fifty cents. Six days a week, the matinees began at noon (in some theaters, 11:00 a.m.) and the entertainment continued until midnight. Headliners appeared twice a day (the "two-a-day" quickly became a synonym for the big-time), while the lesser acts performed as many as five turns a day. The ideal was to have every seat occupied for as long as the theater was open. To make room for patrons who arrived at odd hours—and many did, since the "continuous" format fit almost everyone's schedule—the managers placed a "chaser" (a weak, boring act) at the end of each cycle. The chaser usually succeeded in generating turnover when mere fatigue did not.

Proctor's intention was to make vaudeville a daily ritual for every urban man, woman, and child. His slogan, "After Breakfast, Go to Proctor's. After Proctor's, Go to Bed," was one of the classics of the early days of advertising. Like Pastor and Keith, Proctor saw the potential for profit in the "elevation" of popular entertainment. Discussing his reasons for introducing the continuous performance idea at the Twenty-third Street Theater, Proctor said, "My chief and fundamental motive was to attract to the theatre people who were non-theatre-goers, ladies and children more particularly."[8] The entire theatergoing experience had to be consistent with the audience's aspirations to gentility: the quality implied by the performers' high salaries, the increasingly capacious and lavish theater interiors, the use of legit houses for vaudeville, even the neighborhood the theater was located in.

Nobody understood this better than B. F. Keith, and his partner Edward F. Albee. They perfected the continuous format, which they claimed to have origi-nated with the opening of their Bijou Theatre, in Boston. Once Albee perfected this system, it was estimated that no more than two percent of the audience stayed to see a continuous performance more than once. Keith's managers could expect to sell out the house two and a half times a day on ordinary days, and four times a day on holidays. In effect, Keith had applied the "scientific" manage-ment principles of the leading industrialists to the popular theater. Continuous vaudeville became for entertainment what mass production was to consumer goods.

Having played at Keith and Proctor houses during their tours in the 1880's, Weber & Fields had no fond memories of the experience of being part of a con-tinuous bill. In their eyes, continuous vaudeville was not far removed from the exploitive practices of the dime museum days, when variety artists were required to perform ten or more times a day for low pay.

Weber & Fields had additional reasons for their dislike of continuous vaude-ville: as a format, it discouraged extended sketches. The constant comings and goings of audience members made it difficult to present material that depended on a storyline. The large size of the new vaudeville houses did not help the sketch artists either. Comedians had to fall back on one-liners and snappy repartee; man-agers preferred "dumb" acts (acrobats, magicians, jugglers) and animal acts to one-acts and sketches. As more vaudeville houses converted to the continuous format, Weber & Fields began to question whether vaudeville itself was still the most hospitable place to realize their own theatrical ambitions. It was yet another reason to look to the legit stage, to musical comedies and farces in particular.

It was the financial and marketing genius of Keith and Albee that made con-tinuous vaudeville into a social institution. For Albee, who ran the firm's day-to-day operations and who eventually emerged as the stronger partner, the furnish-ings of a theater were as important as the people who performed on its stage; the plumbing in the ladies' parlor was as important as the stage machinery. The costly imported marble, silk brocade, and Old World bric-a-brac reinforced the upscale impressions made by the legit actors whom Keith and Albee had lured into vaudeville with high salaries.

If any single event can be said to represent the legitimization of vaudeville, it was the opening of Keith's New Boston Theater on March 26, 1894. Located on Washington Street near Boylston Street in the heart of the shopping district, Keith's palatial vaudeville house surpassed most legit theaters in architectural splendor and engineering sophistication. The Boston *Evening Transcript* and the *New York Dramatic Mirror*—publications that had hitherto ignored vaudeville as a subject beneath their readers' interests—covered the opening and reflected the awe and excitement of the spectators. "Variety" made its debut in respectable society—scrubbed, perfumed, and draped in plush and satin—and became "vaudeville." The following year, the *Dramatic Mirror* gave its official imprimatur with the announcement of a new department called "The Vaudeville Stage." It was high time: vaudeville now accounted for over half of all theater tickets sold.

Having signed the Russell Brothers to a long-term contract, Weber & Fields decided to use the popular team as the nucleus of a second touring company for the 'ninety-three–'ninety-four season. The Russell Brothers' Comedians would be run according to the same operating methods as Weber & Fields' Own Company: one-week stands (no split engagements), big-time theaters, with quality acts signed for the length of the tour, and an emphasis on comedy sketches. Cromwell arranged the bookings so that the Russell Brothers' Comedians opened in Brooklyn (at Hyde & Behman's) and worked their way west, while Weber & Fields' Own Company began their season in Cincinnati (at the People's Theater) and worked their way east. The opening dates were staggered, with the Russell Brothers' troupe going first, so that Weber & Fields could personally oversee the program. In this way, Joe and Lew could spot the weaknesses in the performances or the sequencing of the acts and take immediate steps to remedy them.

Weber & Fields' ability to evaluate vaudeville acts, honed over a decade of touring, and their willingness to work with stars of equal or greater magnitude made it possible for them to assemble two remarkably strong and balanced companies. The Russells' company consisted of John E. Drew ("the Irish Aristocrat"), the Braatz Brothers (acrobats), Sam Bernard (German comedian, and Weber & Fields' childhood rival in the Bowery and Coney Island saloons), Bonnie Thornton (vocalist), Alburtus & Bartram (club jugglers), the Acme Four (comedy sketches), the Garnellas (acrobatic comedians), and Charles & Lottie Fremont (sketch artists), as well as the Irish Lilies themselves. For Weber & Fields' Own, they hired the only other two-act as durable and popular as the Russell Brothers—McIntyre & Heath, "the Georgia Minstrels." The troupe also included James & May Fanson (in the sketch "Our Childhood Days"), Capitola Forrest ("lofty dancing and sky-scraping kicks"), Johnnie Carroll (Irish song-and-dance), Marion & Bell (topical songs), James F. Hoey (imitations, burlesque song and dance), and Abuchi & Masand (acrobats). Weber & Fields reprised their poolroom sketch, and, according to the *Clipper*, "got excited over a horse race." The reviews also mentioned that the afterpiece, a long sketch entitled "One Price Only," gave the comedians in the troupe an opportunity "to dabble in the 'legitimate.' "

The season ended for both companies in April, with the Russell Brothers "attracting an audience of good size" in Baltimore, and Weber & Fields packing the house at all performances at the Lyceum in Chicago. It had been their most profitable season to date, and the next season's bookings for both companies were already in place. During the summer, Lew and Rose took a cottage "on the outskirts of Brooklyn," from which Lew would commute into Manhattan to attend to the business of auditioning and signing acts for the coming season. Meanwhile, Joe sailed to Europe with fellow managers Tony Pastor and Tom Grenier. Searching for "European novelties" to bring back to the United States, they stopped in England, Scotland, France, and Germany. (So much for "thoroughly American" entertainment.) Even Tony Pastor, who still refused to call variety by its French euphemism, recognized that foreign stars possessed a special cachet for his most faithful patrons. No doubt the recent opening of Keith's continuous vaudeville theater across the street (the Union Square, in September 1893) prompted Pastor's efforts to fortify his hold on the carriage trade.

There were now forty touring vaudeville companies; but the only managers besides Weber & Fields to own and operate multiple touring companies were Gus Hill and Sam T. Jack, and their outfits were usually divided between big-time and small-time vaudeville and minstrel shows. Weber & Fields' companies played strictly on the big-time circuits.

With return engagements, Weber and Fields' companies would account for twenty percent of the available bookings (as was the case in several New York–area theaters). Far from minding this disproportionate control, theater managers welcomed it, because Weber & Fields' companies consistently played to standing-room-only crowds. Indeed, in some theaters, it is likely that Weber & Fields' companies generated anywhere from one quarter to one third of the theater's gross receipts for a season. Theater managers also began giving preferential scheduling to Weber & Fields, hoping to book them for the peak weeks around holidays, and the start and end of the season. In some cases, the managers tried to accommodate the companies' eastward or westward travel, so that Weber & Fields' companies did not have to make long, costly "jumps" between cities or play a split engagement (less than a week) at any theater.

Weber & Fields' policy of signing popular vaudeville acts to season-long contracts meant that these acts were unavailable for individual bookings during the season. Naturally, booking agents disliked this practice, since they made a five percent commission for each week's engagement that they arranged for a performer. They also grumbled that vaudeville's premium attractions—the Russell Brothers, McIntyre & Heath, Sam Bernard, Lottie Gilson, and Maggie Cline, to name but a few—could only be booked as part of a Weber & Fields touring group.

During the 1894–1895 season, for example, Albee had used the growing strength of the Keith circuit to keep the big-time theaters in the Boston area from booking Weber & Fields' companies during the regular season. As soon as the season ended, Albee signed all of the acts from both companies—except for Weber & Fields—to appear at Keith theaters during the month of May. To Albee's way of thinking, if Boston fans did not see their favorite vaudeville stars at a Keith theater, they would not be able to see them at all.

In six years of touring, no Weber & Fields company ever appeared in a Keith theater. What may have begun as a simple inability to agree on the touring company's share of the gross receipts gradually escalated into a battle between two opposing business philosophies. Although there are no indications of a personal antagonism between Weber & Fields and Keith & Albee, their respective personal styles and business practices differed so dramatically that one may conclude that they did not have to meet in person to dislike each other. Of course, they had met before, in the mid-1880's, when Weber & Fields did eight shows a day in

Keith's museum for forty dollars a week, out of which they then had to pay six dollars to Mrs. Keith for the privilege of eating porridge and sleeping in the attic above the theater. In those days, Albee was the outside talker who worked the ticket booth in front of the museum, and he supplemented his salary by short-changing customers.

By personal choice and professional necessity, Weber & Fields affiliated themselves with the "opposition" managers—Proctor, Jacobs, Hyde & Behman—and, for a time, made it easier for these theater managers to remain independent. In the process, Weber and Fields earned the lasting enmity of Keith and Albee.

The continued growth of Weber & Fields Amusement Enterprises further impeded Keith & Albee's efforts to consolidate their control over vaudeville booking. Two months into their 1894–1895 season, Weber & Fields announced that they were going to put a third company on the road for the following season. For their Vaudeville Club, Weber & Fields lured Sam Bernard back from the legit stage and made him the stage manager and headliner. Around Bernard, they assembled a company of familiar performers (McIntyre & Heath, Lizzie Raymond, the Fansons, and Will H. Fox) with some newcomers, including one of the acts Weber found when he was in Europe the previous summer. With three touring companies, Weber & Fields were now providing anywhere from six to nine weeks of programming for each of the theaters on the Eastern and Midwestern circuit. In the New York–area theaters (downtown Manhattan, Harlem, Brooklyn, and Newark), where the Keith organization had not yet overwhelmed the independent theater managers, Weber & Fields' companies accounted for a total of thirty weeks of engagements. They also held the contracts for thirty acts; in effect, booking them for the season, or longer.

The economic threat of Keith-Albee was an added incentive for Weber & Fields to become "in-and-outers." If vaudeville houses became too difficult to book, they reasoned, why not try legit theaters? During the summer of 1895, articles in the *Clipper* announced that Weber & Fields' three companies would "play many legitimate theaters throughout the country," and that "many theaters are included in the route in which they will be the first vaudeville companies that have ever played."

On an artistic level, the idea of presenting Weber & Fields' shows in legit theaters made sense, both in terms of the style of comedy they were doing and the type of patron they wanted to appeal to. For Lew, the idea of performing on a legit stage had significance beyond his stated artistic and financial goals. It represented a major step towards fulfilling his yearning for social legitimization.

Considered strictly from a business standpoint, their decision to bypass the Keith organization by booking legit theaters was a questionable one. Indeed, this decision may have been the reason that Charles Cromwell resigned as the business manager of Weber & Fields' Amusement Enterprises when his contract came up for renewal in the spring of 1894. Weber & Fields were jumping out of the frying pan and into the fire. Booking for the legit theaters was already firmly controlled by the principal partners of what would soon become the Theatrical Syndicate: Al Hayman & Charles Frohman, Marc Klaw & Abe Erlanger, Sam Nixon & J. F.

Zimmerman. In 1895, when Weber & Fields began booking their companies into legit theaters, the Syndicate was still a year away from becoming an official business entity, but the Syndicate partners' combine was already considerably more organized and powerful in its field than the Keith-Albee booking office was in vaudeville.

For Weber & Fields, the crucial difference between Keith-Albee and the Syndicate partners may have been the latter's willingness to book "traveling combinations." Tours by legit companies headed by stars provided the majority of the partners' profits, particularly since partner Charles Frohman's brother Dan produced a steady supply of plays with big-name stars such as E. H. Sothern, Olga Nethersole, and the Kendals. Another factor may have been the persistent rumors that Hayman, Klaw, Erlanger, *et al.* were planning a way to pool their resources to gain exclusive booking control of all the important legitimate theaters in the country (which was, in fact, what the Syndicate actually achieved). From Weber & Fields' standpoint, if they intended to book their companies into legit theaters, their best hope was to act quickly, before the Syndicate consolidated its power.

To most managers and theater owners, the development of a central booking agency seemed inevitable and desirable, being the logical extension of the theatrical circuits that had sprung up all over the country during the 1880's. The cleverest middlemen—Hayman, Klaw, Erlanger, and Frohman—had realized that it was only necessary to control the attraction or the theater, and that by controlling either one of these elements, pressure could be brought to bear on the other.

In late 1895, while Hayman, Klaw *et al.* were developing their plan to get exclusive booking control of all the important legit theaters in the country, Weber & Fields were engaged in the more modest task of planning their first foray into legit production. Their long-awaited farce-comedy, "The Trolley Party," was set to open in Chicago on March 1, 1896, with the Garnella Brothers and Bettina Gerard in the featured roles, and then go on tour. "The Trolley Party" never left Chicago, closing after four profitable weeks, because Weber & Fields were unable to get bookings in other legit theaters so late in the season. (The tour finally went out the following season.) If the advantage of owning their own theater was not already apparent to them, the fate of "The Trolley Party" made it painfully obvious.

In the same way that the renter dreamed of buying his own home, or the cutter in a sweatshop dreamed of opening his own tailor shop, Weber & Fields dreamed of owning their own theater. Of course, it would have to be on Broadway, not downtown; this they had known ever since their appearance at the New Park Theater on Herald Square in 1893. They realized that to survive the competition from Proctor, Keith, and others, they could not open just another vaudeville house: there were at least half a dozen new vaudeville houses under construction in the New York area at that very moment. Weber & Fields knew that they would need something unique, something that nobody else could offer. Until now, owning a theater had been a purely symbolic goal for them. But with the rise of the theatrical trusts, it would become an economic necessity.

The 1895–1896 season ended March 28 for Weber & Fields' Own Company at Hyde & Behman's, where "even standing room could not be obtained at any price." Indeed, earlier in the season, the *Clipper* had commented that the appearance of a Weber & Fields show had "literally become synonymous with the words S.R.O." The Russell Brothers' Comedians closed their successful season in Cleveland, and the Vaudeville Club finished in late April at Hyde & Behman's. All three companies had operated at a healthy profit, and half of the bookings for the next season were already filled. Neither Joe nor Lew was contemplating any major changes. By nature, Joe was not inclined to tamper with success, and Lew was looking forward to spending more time performing now that their third company was running smoothly.

Yet both Joe and Lew had personal reasons for wanting to spend more time in New York and less time touring. For the past decade, they had spent anywhere from twenty-five to forty weeks a year on the road. The grueling pace had begun to take its toll of Joe's health; in the previous two seasons, he had missed performances due to illness for the first time in his career (including bouts with diphtheria and tonsillitis). And ever since his partner's marriage, Joe had a growing desire to follow suit. At a niece's birthday party in the spring of 1896, Joe met a petite brunette named Lillian Friedman, the daughter of a wealthy East Side real estate man. Her breezy charm and brilliant smile left Joe entranced, and in the eventful months ahead, he visited her whenever he could.

By April of 1896, Lew was a father twice over. His daughter Frances was born in early 1894 while he was on tour, and his son Joseph (named after Joe Weber) was born the following year, 1895, while Lew was in New York for an engagement at the London. It was after the birth of Frances that the Fields family finally made the long-awaited move uptown, where Lew rented an apartment in a fashionable building on Lexington Avenue and East Fifty-ninth Street. In fact, Lew's success made it possible for the entire Schanfield clan to move uptown *en masse*, leaving the Bowery behind forever.

Lew set up his parents in an apartment further up Lexington Avenue at East 106th Street. Papa Schanfield, now in his mid-fifties, refused to retire, and rented a storefront a few blocks away on Second Avenue for his tailoring business. Max, when he was not on the road with the Russell Brothers' Comedians, lived with Leah and their four children around the corner on East 107th Street. Living at 12 East 106th was their sister Annie, married since 1894 to Morris Warschauer, a cutter by trade. The Warschauers shared their apartment with Charlie Schanfield and his new bride, Flora. And in the coming year, brothers Sol and Nat, who had followed Lew into vaudeville, also followed him to the upper East Side, where the two aspiring comedians shared an apartment on East Seventy-seventh and Lexington.

At age twenty-eight, Lew had achieved what many immigrants spent a lifetime trying to accomplish: he had lifted himself and his family out of the slums. Although he had done it in the riskiest and, according to Papa Schanfield, in the least approved manner this side of crime, Lew's success validated his unorthodox choice of career. Lew considered it an honor when in the mid-1890's his brothers all changed their names from Schanfield to Fields; the eldest and youngest brothers, Max and Nat, began using "Fields" in 1895, and Charlie and Sol soon followed suit. A cynic may see only the exploitation of his famous name by family members trying to get ahead in the same business. Perhaps Lew preferred to recall that, when he was a child, his brothers had covered for him in the sweatshop while he was off rehearsing with Joe Weber. Or maybe it amused him to think that in his day, the reason most actors changed their names was to spare their families embarrassment. Here, his family changed their name to his out of pride.

In May, 1896, Weber & Fields were hired by Oscar Hammerstein I to perform at his gargantuan theater, the Olympia, which occupied the entire block between Forty-fourth and Forty-fifth Streets on Broadway. The Olympia, Hammerstein's fourth New York theater, opened on November 29, 1895, though the paint on the walls was not yet dry. Under one roof, it combined a huge music hall (seating capacity, 2,600), a theater for comic opera, a concert hall used as a lounging room for both auditoriums, a roof garden, an Oriental café, and a billiard room, all for a fifty-cent admission. Joe and Lew noted with satisfaction its address; that and their salary of $750 a week made it a pleasant way to close out the season in New York. A former cigar-maker, sometime inventor, and daring impresario, Oscar Hammerstein was an inspiration for Weber & Fields and an important early ally. At five feet four inches, he was no taller than Joe Weber, but his characteristic appearance—the pointy goatee, the ever-present cigar, Prince Albert coat, and striped trousers topped by a tall silk hat that he wore indoors and out—made him as recognizable to the general public as Teddy Roosevelt.

With his passions for opera and ballet, Hammerstein had a more "Continental" attitude towards what constituted "proper" popular entertainment. Unlike the vaudeville of Proctor, Keith, and Albee, Hammerstein's did not try to make a virtue out of censorship and false innocence; his music halls always included a bar, and featured more-provocative acts whose supposedly "Old World" origins provided an aesthetic justification. For example, a month before Weber & Fields appeared at the Olympia, Hammerstein introduced stylish New Yorkers to Fatima, "the original Oriental dancer" performing the *couché-couché* (hootchy-kootchy) dance. The previous year at Coney Island, there had been close to twenty "cooch shows" running at once, each claiming to have the original Fatima. (If anybody in the audience at the Olympia recognized the fraud, they did not care to admit how they knew.) In a similar vein, the program that featured Weber & Fields also included "Marblesques," voluptuous women posing in varying states of classical undress (backlit, with strategically placed shadows) to represent famous paintings—"Leda's Alhambra," "Diana," "The Rape of the Nymph," and so on.

For their appearances at the Olympia, Hammerstein asked Weber & Fields to reprise their poolroom sketch as part of a medley of their most popular routines, billing them as "The German Senators in 'English As She Is Speaked-d-d.' "

The featured performer—Fregoli, the multivoiced transformation artist—was another of the European sensations discovered by Hammerstein and paid exorbitant sums to make his American debut at the Olympia. As described in the *Clipper*, Fregoli appeared after the intermission, doing "quick character changes in a perfected state," playing anywhere from four to fifteen male and female roles in as many costumes and voices.

In "The Medallion," Fregoli did a comic imitation of a bandleader, then stepped over the footlights to take the place of the orchestra conductor, where he did a series of impressions of famous conductors—Rossini, Wagner, Verdi, among others—while leading the orchestra in their most famous works. The lightning changes were made with the help of wigs, false beards, and noses behind a small plush screen scarcely a yard from the front row. Five dressers stood in either wing to help him change costumes.

Fregoli's act was an instant success. Watching it during rehearsals, Joe and Lew were impressed with Fregoli's technical abilities, especially his ability to change completely from one character into another in mid-dialogue. Still, they could not help thinking about the quick-changes "from white to black in fifteen seconds" that they had performed in the Bowery museums in the early 1880's. Certainly, in terms of ability and polish, their old act did not begin to compare with Fregoli's. What they did was a coarse amusement; what he did was considered art. But the basic technique was the same, and for all Fregoli's elaborate costumes and dramatic posturing, Weber & Fields believed that the technique was inherently comical. Unfortunately, Fregoli, like most European artistes playing to American audiences, projected an air of superiority about the seriousness of his "art." He acknowledged the storms of applause from Hammerstein's patrons as further proof of his artistry. If ever an actor was an ideal target for burlesque, it was the self-important Signor Fregoli.

Fregoli proved to be a tough act to follow. "There's only one thing we can do to get attention," Fields decided, "and that's to burlesque this fellow." Eleven years earlier, at a crucial juncture in their budding careers, they had almost been fired for burlesquing the lead singer of Adah Richmond's company. Headliners—particularly "serious" actors—were understandably touchy about being ridiculed by somebody on the same bill. Joe and Lew were counting on the audience's response to overcome the backstage squawks that were sure to follow.

To help bring it off, Fields recruited his brother, Nat, and his brother-in-law, Bobby Harris. The two had worked together briefly in a vaudeville company as a Dutch act, using Weber & Fields' material without permission before Joe and Lew had prevailed upon a variety manager to shut them down. Nat was tall, like his brother Lew; Bobby Harris was close to Weber's size. With the right makeup and padding, they could easily pass for the German Senators.

Burlesquing his featured act was not what Hammerstein had in mind when he laid out his program. "Mr. Hammerstein was opposed to this change in our act," recalled Fields, "but we insisted upon doing it and he let us have our way."[9] After making-up Nat and Bobby as Mike and Meyer, they were dressed as a fat woman and a comic soldier, parodies of two of the characters in Fregoli's drama, *Cameleonte*. While the house was still abuzz with amazement over Fregoli's feats, Weber & Fields appeared on the stage apron in their familiar Dutch makeup and addressed the audience with their customary disregard for English grammar. Here is how Fields described the set-up:

> We opened our new act by my making the announcement to the audience that they had seen the wonderful work that Fregoli did, but for their information I told them that we had been doing these quick changes for years and we were going to give them an idea of just how quickly we could do it. The moment Weber and I walked off, on would come my brother and Bobby Harris, one made up as a fat woman and

the other as a soldier, and talk in Italian. The music would play furiously so that the audience could not hear them. The moment they came off I would go on made up like a old woman. Weber had changed into something else and would follow immediately. . . .[10]

Fregoli's changes required a slight pause, but Weber & Fields' required none whatsoever. With each change, the interval became shorter, until the rear halves of one team were still exiting while the front halves of the other team were making an entrance across the stage. The audience gasped, amazed and not a little bewildered.

At the end of it all, Mike and Meyer once again stood on the stage apron. There was stunned silence, then thunderous applause. Weber & Fields took several bows, then gestured towards the wings. Their doubles revealed themselves, and came forward to share in the credit. The audience let out a collective whoop of surprise, delighted at the trick, only now beginning to appreciate the full scope of Weber & Fields' burlesque. Hammerstein, patron of olios and arias, laughed until he cried. Weber & Fields had upstaged the Great Fregoli. American-style humor had routed the artistic pretensions of the Old World.

Hammerstein immediately extended the duo's engagement to correspond to the entire length of Fregoli's run. Fregoli was surprisingly gracious, even going as far as to give the boys pointers on how to make their changes quicker.

The enthusiastic response of the Olympia's patrons to the Fregoli burlesque surprised even Weber & Fields. Fields later said, "The way it appealed to the audience gave Mr. Weber and me the thought that real burlesque on different plays would be a capital thing to do in the theater."[11] If Fregoli could be successfully burlesqued, why not serious Broadway shows—Belasco, Fitch, or the current European import? Weber & Fields already knew how to assemble an all-star company, so why not put together a stock company of talented comedians, singers, and dancers to perform burlesques? Their fantasy of having their own theater suddenly acquired a concrete *raison d'être*—an artistic and commercial justification. It would indeed be more than just another vaudeville house.

In their six seasons as variety managers, Weber & Fields' profits above their salaries were probably in the neighborhood of fifteen to twenty thousand dollars—nowhere near enough to build a first-class theater, but perhaps enough to lease one. The proposition seemed like a natural for Hammerstein. After all, within the Olympia he had a theater, a music hall, and, with summer coming, a roof garden, which he needed productions for. He could lease them one of his theaters for the production of their burlesques with their own all-star company.

But Hammerstein turned them down, insisting that they were doing well enough already. They had three companies with good bookings, he counselled, so why gamble away a sure thing? For their own good, Hammerstein tried to discourage them. Who knew better than he how risky it was to own a Broadway theater? Coming from Hammerstein, the advice to play it safe struck Fields as being amusingly out of character. It was then and there, Fields recalled, "that we determined to do it ourselves." Night after night, the riotous applause at the Olympia provided all the positive reinforcement they needed.

One afternoon in late May, Joe was having his shoes shined outside 1162 Broadway, where the offices of Weber & Fields' Amusement Enterprises were located. An old acquaintance from the Bowery stopped to chat—a man named Louis Robie, manager of Miner's Eighth Avenue Theater, and the former director of amusements for Miner's Bowery. Robie was returning from a meeting with George Kraus, who leased the Imperial Music Hall on Broadway and Twenty-ninth Street from Henry Miner.

Kraus had opened his Music Hall in October, 1892, and modelled it along the lines of Koster & Bials' Twenty-third Street resort, with variety bills, burlesques (the racy kind), a saloon and a café. In the true spirit of the day, Kraus spent lavishly on the decor—Turkish red-velvet curtains and upholsteries, with rococo detailing executed in gold leaf—and stingily on the entertainment. The house acquired a bad reputation with straitlaced vaudeville patrons. Miner had advanced around $40,000 to Kraus, of which $35,000 was secured by a mortgage. By the spring of 1896, Kraus had managed to lose about $70,000 on his music hall, and Miner quietly started looking for a more reliable tenant.

As Robie described this situation, Weber listened with growing excitement. Reading between the lines, he realized that Robie was saying that Miner was having trouble finding anyone to take the theater. As Weber later described it, "it was a hoodo house"; i.e., it not only had a bad reputation with the public, but superstitious theater managers believed that the place was jinxed. Joe and Lew believed that the jinx had more to do with its management than with anything supernatural. Its location was ideal—the very heart of "the Rialto," next door to Daly's Theater and a block away from Wallack's; within walking distance of several major hotels (Gilsey House, Hoffman House, Fifth Avenue Hotel) and the Ladies' Mile (the city's most fashionable shopping district). Although the entrance was on Twenty-ninth Street, if they could negotiate the lease for one of the adjoining shops, they could put in a Broadway entrance. The situation seemed ideal if the up-front money were not too exorbitant.

On May 27, Weber & Fields met with Miner in the office of his attorney. Their long and cordial relationship facilitated the negotiations despite the fact that both Miner and Weber had reputations for driving a hard bargain. Miner took a paternal interest in seeing "his boys" get ahead, and Joe and Lew were probably relieved to be dealing with a sympathetic party instead of somebody like Al Hayman or Ned Albee. They concluded the deal in a matter of minutes. Miner offered them a three-year lease at $20,000 a year, with the first installment of $5,000 payable at the start of the season. Weber & Fields also agreed to pay $20,000 for the mortgage Miner held on the furnishings, properties, and scenery of the house.

It was only appropriate that Weber & Fields should lease their first Broadway theater from Henry C. Miner. After all, it was Miner who in 1882 had given them their first chance to appear in a variety theater instead of a dime museum; ten years later, his poolroom became the inspiration for their most famous routine.

The transaction was noted in the *New York Herald* the following day:

IMPERIAL CHANGES HANDS.

Weber & Fields Take the Music Hall off Mr. Kraus' Hands.
The Imperial Music Hall, in Twenty-ninth street, yesterday passed from the control of Mr. George J. Kraus and will henceforth be managed by Messrs. Weber and Fields, the variety comedians. [. . .]

The new management, which already has under contract such well known performers as Miss Lottie Gilson, John Kernell, Troja, Sam Bernard, "Bobby" Gaylor, the Russell Brothers and the Avilos, will open the house early in August as a first class music hall. They intend to make a few alterations in the interior arrangements and the cafe in the basement will probably be turned into a rathskeller. The name of the house will be changed. . . .

The *Clipper*'s article on the transaction also reflected the belief that Weber & Fields would bring respectability to a theater held in low esteem: [their shows] "will doubtless restore the prestige of this place of amusement with the theater-going public."

By 1896, Lew Fields—and vaudeville—had succeeded in moving uptown. Onstage and off-, he and his partner Joe Weber had been an influential force in taking variety out of the Bowery beer saloons and bringing it to a Broadway audience. Vaudeville, in turn, rewarded Fields handsomely for his missionary work on its behalf, and the money and status it bestowed provided him with the sense of social legitimacy that he longed for. Yet, at the very height of his fame as a vaudevillian, Fields' dreams of artistic legitimacy were far from fulfilled.

During the summer of 1896, while Weber & Fields busied themselves with renovations and rehearsals at their music hall, the future members of the Theatrical Syndicate—Hayman & Frohman, Klaw & Erlanger, Nixon & Zimmerman—were quietly meeting to hammer out an official agreement. On August 1, they signed a secret agreement pooling their resources and establishing an exclusive booking exchange for first-class theaters across the country.

On September 5, Weber & Fields opened their Broadway Music Hall amid much hoopla. In the coming years, the quiet events of August 1 would become as important to Weber & Fields as that clamorous September evening.

CHAPTER VII

Music Hall Days: "Such a Muchness"

They come in as society folk, and go out as if they had been attending a rough house.

Lew Fields, describing audiences at
the Weber & Fields Music Hall

WHETHER by sheer luck or calculation, Weber & Fields had chosen the ideal moment to launch their new enterprise. In the summer of 1896, when they opened the doors to their Broadway Music Hall, the American popular stage was in the doldrums. Typical of its time was the previous year's hit musical, *El Capitan*, with book by Charles Klein and music by John Philip Sousa. The towering De Wolf Hopper starred as a conquistador and Viceroy of Peru, in a complicated story of disguises, mistaken identity, and farfetched military adventure. Although Sousa's music and Hopper's performance distinguished *El Capitan* from the season's other musicals, it was a typical American musical in its ridiculous plot contrivances, exotic settings, and military posturings.

Not surprisingly, the English imports of the day, such as Ivan Caryll's *The Shop Girl* (1895), *The Girl from Paris* (1896), and *The Circus Girl* (1897), won the affection of fashionable urban audiences. At least the imports offered relatively straightforward love stories in modern dress. Most of their librettos seemed to be about the problems of trying to marry outside one's social class, usually resolved when the lower-class lover was revealed to be an heir or heiress. New York audiences liked the glimpses of Continental fashions and manners. In one respect, the popularity of English musicals may have been beneficial: American lyricists and librettists probably learned something from their English colleagues about how to write wittier lyrics and more-coherent books.

Even the once-thriving comic opera had gone stale. The era's leading composers—Reginald DeKoven, Gustave Kerker, and Ludwig Englander—created forgettable scores consisting of marches and tinkly, sentimental songs. Jefferson De Angelis, Lillian Russell, Della Fox, and Francis Wilson lent their talents to increasingly inferior material, and soon began to feel the consequences. With the decline of playwrights Edward Harrigan and Charles Hoyt, one could find more comic invention in any of the big-time vaudeville programs than in an entire season of comic operas or farces on the legitimate stage.

In 1896, the art forms and the physical forms of Broadway were still under construction. The ramshackle area around Broadway and Forty-second Street was called Longacre Square. The Hotel Pabst occupied the triangular sliver formed by the junction of Broadway and Seventh Avenue. It was not until 1902, when *New York Times* publisher Adolph S. Ochs demolished the hotel to make way for the Times Tower and the subway stop that the corner became known as Times Square, "heart of Broadway" and "crossroads of the world." With the exception of Oscar Hammerstein's Olympia Music Hall complex (1895), which covered the block between Forty-fourth and Forty-fifth Streets, the Rialto did not extend above Fortieth Street. The impressive facades of the Casino (on Thirty-ninth Street) and Charles Frohman's Empire Theater marked the theater district's northern frontier.

The change—from the fringe of the Rialto to its center—occurred with remarkable speed. In 1898, the New York *Dramatic Mirror* moved from Union Square to Broadway and Fortieth, and the fashionable Delmonico's relocated on Forty-fourth. George Rector's restaurant opened in a long, -two-storey yellow building between Forty-third and Forty-fourth Streets; it quickly became the favorite after-theater supper spot for Broadway's elite. Also on Longacre Square was Shanley's Lobster Palace, where an affluent businessman or "sport" might take a chorus girl to impress her. Aspiring actresses were soon joking about finding a "lobster" (sugar daddy) of their own. Being a loyal family man, Fields rarely frequented Rector's or Shanley's after the evening shows, but he knew that it was good for business when one of his stars or chorus girls "made a splash" there.

Broadway did not become "the Great White Way" until 1901, when a clever display designer invented the name to encourage the use of electric lights in advertising and marquees. The name caught on; it had snob appeal. "The Great White Way" evoked images of diamond-studded extravagance and Continental frivolity. Naturally, Broadway theaters and restaurants tried to offer fare worthy of the name.

By the time the Music Hall closed its doors in 1904, there were ten legit theaters in the Times Square area, including the Liberty, where Cohan introduced *Little Johnny Jones* (1904), and the New Amsterdam, where Ziegfeld produced the first edition of his Follies (1907). Neither the theaters nor the theatrical forms they showcased existed when Weber and Fields opened their music hall.

Nowhere in theater—popular or serious—was there the kind of creative foment that characterized American literature, architecture, and painting. There were no equivalents on the popular stage to Theodore Dreiser, Edith Wharton, or Henry James. Vaudeville's caricatures of urban life covered much the same ground as the realism of Sloan, Glackens, and Henri, but in a self-effacing, reassuring way that provoked no one. Richard Mansfield's productions of Bernard Shaws' *Arms and the Man* (1894) and *The Devil's Disciple* (1896) attracted considerable interest from Broadway audiences, but inspired no American emulators among Broadway playwrights. Writers and producers were cautious and complacent, the audiences undemanding and unsophisticated. The artists and patrons of Broadway did their best to forget the unexpectedly bitter election of 1896 (McKinley *vs.*

Bryan), which uncovered alarming class and regional antagonisms. They pretended not to notice tenements, the five-foot piles of garbage that lined many lower Manhattan streets, or the stench of corruption that produced these conditions. Two subjects captivated *fin-de-siècle* theatergoers: Parisian fashions and America's imperial destiny. The newspapers seized the popular imagination with tales of romance and adventure—wayward heiresses, Admiral Dewey's victory in the Philippines, Lillian Russell's new suitor, and the discovery of gold in the Yukon.

Broadway's craftsmen scurried to find theatrical equivalents. Theater interiors were changed every season, like women's fashions, with a similar emphasis on well-upholstered curves and extravagant, impractical materials. Meanwhile, the American writers and producers of the late 'nineties seemed to be pursuing their own version of the Open Door policy; in *The Caliph, The Geisha, In Mexico, Captain Cook,* and numerous other mediocrities, the typical plot involved a military man (usually in the Navy), finding romance, adventure, and vaudeville specialties in a foreign land. South America, Africa, Hawaii, the Philippines, the Orient—all the colonial world—were the settings for heroic and romantic Americans to fight a "splendid little war" (to borrow John Hay's description of the Spanish-American War), restore order, and win the girl. The exotic locales also made it easier to interpolate the "coon" songs and Tin Pan Alley ditties that had lately become all the rage, and to stage the Amazon chorus drills that passed for choreography in many of the musicals of the 'nineties.

If there was no one of any stature who dared to mount a frontal assault on this complacency, there was at least one Broadway institution dedicated to ridiculing staid theatrical conventions and the stuffed shirts who applauded them: Weber & Fields' Music Hall.

At first glance, Weber & Fields' decision to satirize theater rather than the everyday foibles of immigrants appears to be only an extension of their longstanding interest in the comic possibilities inherent in leisure-time activities. Pool, horse races, shooting galleries, bowling, and baseball had all been subjected to Mike and Meyer's mangling; so why not the most popular leisure-time activity of all?

In taking the step from vaudeville to the musical stage, Weber & Fields did not merely change subject matter—they changed targets. No longer were immigrants the prime targets of their humor. The Music Hall's resident ethnics—Dutch (W&F, Sam Bernard), Irish (John T. Kelly), Jewish (David Warfield)—were the means to bring the dashing soldiers, saintly women, and other society folk who populated the stage down a peg. With the aid of Faye Templeton's and Mabel Fenton's brilliant parodies of famous actresses, Peter Dailey's cutting asides and ad libs, and De Wolf Hopper's digs at the rhetorical style of leading men, the real targets were the dramatic establishment and, implicitly, the society it idealized.

Most likely, Weber & Fields' decision to lampoon the elite rather than the powerless was not based on deeply held moral convictions. They knew what made people laugh, and they knew what kind of audience they wanted in their music hall. Joe and Lew were, after all, a part of that early wave of immigrants or children of immigrants who were now coming up in the world, becoming educated, acquiring wealth, social standing, and political power. What could be more natural than to subject their new neighbors on Riverside Drive to the same kind of ridicule that they had inflicted on the citizens of the Bowery?

On Saturday, September 5, 1896, Weber and Fields' Broadway Music Hall opened with a first-class vaudeville bill (recruited from the two dozen acts they still had under contract) and a burlesque of a Belasco play. Weber and Fields made certain that the house was sold out in advance for the entire first week, personally peddling tickets to friends and longtime fans on the Lower East Side. When Broadway first-nighters discovered that there were no tickets to be had, they bought out the house for the second week. The fact that the music hall only seated 665 made the tickets even hotter. Ticket speculators did land-office business, and the scalpers in front of the theater became a public nuisance. Weber & Fields offered one hundred dollars for the best suggestion on how to suppress the scalpers.

The price scale of twenty-five cents to one dollar, and one-fifty for box seats, undercut Hammerstein's Olympia and Koster & Bial's Music Hall. With several high-priced stars on the payroll, Weber & Fields had to play to capacity houses every night of the week just to break even. Profits would come later, reasoned Weber & Fields, once they had secured their reputation. Meanwhile, their three touring companies would cover any short-term losses. To add to the financial pressure, Weber & Fields decided to depart from the traditional music hall practice of serving food and drinks during the show. Their bar and café would be open only before and after the show, and during intermission. This policy distinguished Weber & Fields' from its main competitors, Koster & Bial's and Hammerstein's Olympia, and it appealed to a higher class of patrons.

The opening night audience was, by New York standards, unusually heterogenous. The pouring rain discouraged nobody. Patrons arrived in every kind of conveyance—by two-wheel hansom cab, coach, trolley, and horse-car—and created a traffic jam in front of the Music Hall. The tiny lobby was filled floor to ceiling with floral displays. There was a shared sense of anticipation, from the "smart set" in silk hats and evening gowns in the luxury box seats, to the shopkeepers in derbies and shawls in the gallery.

After a brief inaugural address from a Tammany judge (which did not exempt him from being made fun of later in the burlesque), the olio began with Alburtus & Bartram in a comic club-swinging act. Next, Thomas J. Ryan, formerly of the knockabout Irish team of Kelly & Ryan, did a dance with comic patter. His erstwhile partner, John T. Kelly, had a featured role in the burlesque. Ross and Fenton, the era's best male-female sketch artists, followed. Ross was handsome enough to play the leading man on any legit stage, and his wife, Mabel Fenton, was a talented singer and mimic—even better, some claimed, than Faye Templeton, and certainly slimmer.

Another audience favorite and veteran of Weber & Fields' touring companies, Lottie Gilson, sang several songs, including her hits, "Don't Give Up the Old Love for the New," and "You're Not the Only Pebble on the Beach," which she encored repeatedly. When Meyer finally pushed Mike onstage, they were greeted with a standing ovation and calls for a speech before they were allowed to proceed with their poolroom sketch.

It was a solid vaudeville bill, but the venture would live and die on what came next: the burlesque of Belasco's Civil War melodrama, *The Heart of Maryland*, renamed "The Art of Mary Land." Although the burlesque's book was attributed to Joseph Herbert, variety veterans Bernard, Ross, and Fenton had quickly dispensed with his script after the first rehearsal, with Fields' blessing. What survived was a deliberately ridiculous plot in which Hawlin Hayrick, an effete commander played (with an Irish brogue) by John T. Kelly, must rescue his beloved, Mary Land, (Mabel Fenton), the creator of a culinary masterpiece called chicken à la Maryland, from the clutches of Colonel Warp (Charles Ross, who always looked good in uniform). Aiding in the mayhem was Sam Bernard as Sergeant Grunt (with Dutch dialect), Thomas Ryan in skirts as Mrs. McFadden, Yolande Wallace and Lillian Swain in trousers, and the Beaumont sisters, Rose and Nellie, leading the chorus. Reluctantly, Weber & Fields decided not to appear in the burlesque; their touring commitments necessitated their absence from the music hall for long stretches over the coming weeks.

Though the burlesque plot inexplicably overlooked the chance to parody Mrs. Carter's climactic swing on the clapper of the curfew bell ("This bell shall not ring!"), it did provide ample opportunities for sight gags, topical jokes, and songs. Among the targets were William Jennings Bryan, the Populists and their whiskers, Coxey's Army, and the Free Silverites. Four tramps, "Populist Army veterans," carried banners with the slogans "Free Trade," "Free Silver," "Free Lunch," and "Free Ireland." Chorus members were costumed as popular comic strip characters (the Yellow Kid and the tenement urchins of his Hogan Alley gang) to perform an Ivy League–style pep rally.

The arbitrariness of the dramatic conventions also came in for ridicule. When Mary protests, "Colonel Warp, I will not go!" he insists, "But you must! The plot demands it!" At the burlesque's climax, Hayrick is tied to a tree to await execution by Colonel Warp. Hayrick then delivers his final speech, moving melodramatically around the stage with a tree tied to his back. In the end, three factors saved the show from the fate its script deserved: the comic skill of the stock company, the engaging good looks and charm of the chorus girls, and John "Honey Boy" Stromberg's catchy melodies. Laughs, lookers, and songs—it was the same formula that has saved many a musical since then.

Weber & Fields had hired the thirty-six-year-old Stromberg on the strength of his one hit song, "My Best Gal's a Corker" (1895), and his work as orchestra leader for the Night Owl Burlesquers. Stromberg's first efforts for Weber & Fields were only fair when judged against his later work, but they sparkled when compared to the current Tin Pan Alley fare. For the next six years, he was the house composer and conductor, writing the music for ten shows. In marked contrast to other producers of the era, Weber & Fields rarely interpolated the work of other composers into their shows. Stromberg's music quickly became one of the most popular features of the Music Hall productions.

It did not seem to matter to the music hall patrons or the critics that the same play had been twitted earlier in the summer at the Casino. The *Dramatic Mirror*'s reviewer called Weber & Fields' burlesque "bright, breezy, and very much up to date," and praised the ensemble performances and Stromberg's music. Fields, however, was not satisfied. The show leaned heavily on topical jokes and local references, and not enough on the specific play and performances they were ostensibly satirizing. He immediately commissioned Herbert to write a burlesque of the new season's hit, *The Geisha*, by George Edwardes, which was playing right next door to Weber & Fields' Music Hall, at Daly's Theater.

Weber delayed by a week the start of the Weber & Fields' Own Company tour to give them time to supervise the rehearsals of the new burlesque. At the same time, they were working on an elaborate new Mike and Meyer routine, "At the Baseball Game." It would be their last routine created outside the Music Hall. The demands of their touring commitments were preventing them from appearing in the burlesques or overseeing the productions on a day-to-day basis—a frustrating situation for both of them. Over the next twenty-two weeks, Weber & Fields' Own Company played seventeen cities. The partners refused all repeat bookings.

Accustomed to running every aspect of their business by themselves, they feared losing control of their day-to-day operations. They appointed close friends or family members to most of the key positions in the Weber & Fields Enterprises: in addition to their old friend Sam Bernard, they enlisted the aid of Lew's brother-in-law, Leo Teller, an ex-retailer from Brooklyn, as business manager. "Muck" Weber (Joe's protector) and Charlie Fields ran the bar and cafe, while Max Fields continued as road manager for the Russell Brothers Comedians. Eighteen-year-old Nat Fields toured with the Vaudeville Club. In their reliance on family members, Weber & Fields were no different from many proprietors of immigrant enterprises of the time.

The new burlesque was called "The Geezer, A Respectful Parody," and replaced "The Art of Mary Land" five weeks into the season. It was an immediate hit, and much closer to the kind of entertainment envisioned by Weber & Fields. The title referred to Li Hung Chang, a Chinese viceroy who has come to America to find a rich American bride for his emperor.

The first scene was a meticulous re-creation of Doyers Street, in New York's Chinatown. A sign identified the laundry and tearoom of Two Hi. Several pretty chorus girls in Chinese robes sang about the arrival of Li Hung Chang. Herbert's lyrics were a clever send-up of the typically inane choruses that opened comic operas: "Hurrah! Hurrah! We laugh and sing / So loudly let the welkin ring / We must admit, though far from slow / What welkin is, we do not know. . . ."

John T. Kelly played the title role, with Sam Bernard as his companion, Two-Hi. Both wore identical robes and tan makeup, but Kelly spoke his lines in a heavy Irish brogue, while Bernard sputtered away in a bizarre amalgam of German and Chinese—"one piecee beer mit pretzels." The Western characters included Nellie Fly (Mabel Fenton), a spoof of the intrepid female reporter Nellie Bly; New York's police commissioner, Teddy Roosevelt, with an entire police department bearing his name (A. Roosevelt, B. Roosevelt, C. Roosevelt, etc.), thereby poking fun at his recent attacks on patronage. The chorus consisted of Ladies

Faith, Hope, and Charity, a reference to actress May Yohe, whose marriage made her Lady Francis Pelham Clinton Hope. As an auctioneer, Kelly enjoyed himself at Bernard's expense, whacking him on the head repeatedly with his auctioneer's mallet.

"The Geezer" also marked the debut of chorus girl Frankie Bailey, whose superb legs (often described by the curious accolade "symmetrical") made such a strong impression that they became a figure of speech. Wherever American men congregated, the mere mention of a woman's "Frankie Baileys" meant that there was a great pair of legs to be seen. Frankie Bailey and the Beaumont Sisters were among the first of the Music Hall's long line of eye-catching chorus girls.

There was never a definitive text to a Music Hall show; it changed from performance to performance. Throughout its run, new material was constantly being added to the burlesque, and old or flat routines deleted, so that the viewer who attended the opening and then returned in the sixth week saw a show that was greatly changed and improved. When, for example, "those wicked little Barrisons" (five sisters) scandalized New York with a generous display of lacy lingerie while singing or doing tricks on horseback, the skit "Five Embarrassin' Sisters" was appended to "The Geezer." The burlesque sisters displayed loud plaid petticoats stamped "Made in Germany," and sister "Lonely" (Lona) did several foolish tricks on a bony, spavined horse while she was suspended from an immense cable. Likewise, when Ziegfeld made a splash by publicizing Anna Held's penchant for milk baths, Sam Bernard and John T. Kelly used a large wash tub and created a pantomime-burlesque that was reportedly hilarious. Obviously, there were some advantages to a plot that was elastic, if not downright disposable.

"The Geezer" ran for nineteen weeks—long by the Broadway standards of the day—and probably could have lasted out the season, if Weber & Fields had not insisted on keeping up with the latest hits of the legit stage. It was during the successful run of "The Geezer," at the height of the holiday season, that Weber & Fields raised the top ticket prices: orchestra seats would now cost $1.50, and box seats, $2.00. Nobody complained. Reviewers continued to note that, "The cozy theatre was packed to suffocation, every seat and inch of standing room being occupied." Strong olios, including specialties from Weber & Fields' touring companies (the Russell Brothers, Lizzie B. Raymond, Caron & Herbert, etc.) also helped pack 'em in.

In addition to supervising the Music Hall productions, Weber had other reasons to forswear touring. He had asked Lillian Friedman to marry him. She was, in the jargon of Broadway, a "non-professional," and her bouncy demeanor and utter devotion to "Web" promised the same kind of domestic stability and warmth that Lew had found with Rose. (By contrast, their buddy Sam Bernard was in the midst of a messy divorce from another Weber & Fields company performer, singer Lizzie Raymond, who had not bothered to divorce her previous husband before marrying Bernard.) In Weber's eyes, the Friedmans had respectability and social status—exactly what Weber lacked as an actor from an immigrant family of very modest means.

Joe and Lillian were married on the evening of January 3, 1897, in a private ceremony at the Nineteenth Street Temple, with Lew Fields as best man. After a one-week honeymoon, the new Mrs. Weber accompanied her husband to Philadelphia, where Weber & Fields' Own Company started the second leg of their tour. Perhaps because the Webers never had any children, Lillian frequently accompanied Joe on tour in the coming years.

At the end of February, Weber & Fields left their touring company for a week to return to New York to oversee the production of the new Music Hall show, a burlesque of *Under the Red Robe*, which starred William Faversham at the Empire Theater. Herbert and Stromberg's "operatic burlesque" of *Under the Red Robe* featured Charles Ross in the Faversham role, playing his part almost straight. Originally set in France, the story was relocated to Gaily's (read "Daly's") gambling house in Long Branch, New Jersey. (John Daly ran a gambling house next door to Weber & Fields' Music Hall, and he had a similar establishment in Long Branch, New Jersey, for vacationers.) Sam Bernard once again travestied his role with a Dutch dialect, and sang the hit song of the evening, "Love Lorn Lobster." While animal novelty numbers were popular at the time, it is likely that the coy slang connotations of "lobster" accounted for its popularity.

The introduction of motion pictures at Koster & Bial's the previous spring had brought an epidemic of competing inventions: Vitascope, cinematograph, kineopticon, animatograph, etc. It may have been sheer silliness, or some lost meaning of the word, that inspired Weber & Fields to call their spoof of primitive motion pictures "The Lobsterscope." Early in the 1896–1897 season, Weber & Fields had tried an animatograph in their vaudeville olios, following the lead of Koster & Bial's, the Union Square, and Pastor's. Herky-jerky, flickering, and slightly fuzzy, the eye-straining images were good vaudeville chasers, but inappropriate for the Music Hall, where the olio preceded the burlesque. Weber & Fields' version was a living picture played in front of a black curtain. Opaque and clear screens were alternated rapidly in front of the calcium spot, illuminating the actors' antics—a dance by the Beaumont Sisters, a burlesque of the Corbett-Fitzsimmons prize fight, and a skit called "The Artist's Dream." Sam Bernard stood at the side of the stage and commented on the pictures like a cinematograph lecturer. Bernard and company invented new "lobsters" every week for the rest of the season. It was, incidentally, the first use of a device that later became known as the strobe. In a facetious reference to all the copyright and patent disputes between motion picture exhibitors, Weber & Fields ran an ad in the *New York Clipper* warning managers against copyright infringements on their "wonderful animated picture machine," the Lobsterscope.

Despite the fragmentary character of the entertainment, the Music Hall's box office continued strong through the close of the season on June 6. Weber & Fields, however, had lost patience with Joseph Herbert. Fields felt that Herbert's librettos were inconsistent, and the comedy strained. He was also dissatisfied with the storyless format of Herbert's last effort, "Mr. New York, Esquire"; it lacked the kind of structural integrity he admired in comic operas and the classic burlesques (such as *Evangeline* and *Adonis*).

There were other reasons, more concrete, for conflict. In April, Weber & Fields were chagrined to learn that Herbert had sold the rights to "The Geezer" to a London producer without their consent. Herbert would receive royalties of

$150 week, while Weber & Fields would receive nothing. Weber & Fields threat-
ened Herbert with legal action, without results. On a Sunday morning in early
June, Joe Weber and Joseph Herbert met in a Broadway restaurant to discuss a
settlement. The two men came to blows, with Herbert getting the worst of the
encounter before friends separated them. The case never came to trial; Herbert
eventually rewrote "The Geezer" and added a new act, and sold it without further
opposition. From this, Weber & Fields learned that they had to spell out their
joint ownership of the burlesques in the writer's contract. It was a valuable lesson; in the years to come, the franchising of the Music Hall shows became an
important source of revenue for Weber & Fields.

Inevitably, Weber & Fields' success as vaudeville managers, and now as proprietors of a Broadway theater, antagonized certain competitors and critics. Lean-
der Richardson, who wrote a theater gossip column for the *New York Mercury*,
spearheaded a campaign of unfavorable rumors and anti-Semitic commentary directed at Weber & Fields. In a series of articles in May, 1897, Richardson pur-
ported to expose "Weber & Fields' reckless malice towards other managers in
the vaudeville business." He successfully persuaded the *New York Mercury* not
to run advertisements for their music hall or any of their other enterprises. In
one article, he quoted with approval the comments of "one well-known manager":
" 'There are three kinds of persons in the faith to which I belong. They are Hebrews, Jews and Sheenys [*sic*]. No one will have any difficulty in reaching the
correct conclusion as to which class Weber & Fields most faithfully represent. . . .' "

Reading between the lines, it appears that what rankled Richardson (and his
unnamed supporters) was that two Jewish boys from the Bowery could become
so popular and successful on Broadway: ". . . They are conducting themselves
on Broadway upon the theories which characterized their conduct when they
were east side ragamuffins trying to break into show business an [*sic*] any possible pretext. I do not believe that their prosperity as managers along the main
New York thoroughfare can possibly continue . . . [unless] they mend their ways
and abandon the obviously erroneous idea that the methods of the slums from
which they sprang are applicable to the management of high-grade amusements."

One of the things that Joe and Lew had learned when they were "east side
ragamuffins" was not to respond to Jew-baiting, but Richardson's assertions about
their professional integrity were potentially damaging. Weber & Fields filed suit,
and in August, 1897, Richardson was indicted by a grand jury for criminal libel.
For Lew, and probably for Joe as well, the experience was an uncomfortable
reminder of the kind of prejudice that they hoped to avoid by downplaying their
ethnic heritage, both on and off stage.

The new connotations of the term "Dutch" may have actually helped Weber
& Fields downplay their own ethnic roots. Audiences in the 1890's recognized
Weber & Fields' Dutch act as the embodiment of the immigrant Everyman, and
not of any particular ethnic group. Increasingly, in the music hall productions,
Weber & Fields' characters were the blundering *arrivistes* trying to be a part of
polite society. To distinguish themselves from the stereotypical Jew, they often
included a "Hebrew" comedian in their olios (e.g., Frank Bush or Joe Welch), and

an identifiably Jewish character (usually played by David Warfield) in their burlesques. By the time the Music Hall closed, Lew Fields played Dutch roles only occasionally.

The Music Hall burlesques in the first season owed much in form and content to the lavish "reviews" (as revues were still being called) produced by George Lederer at the Casino Theater. Lederer's Casino productions were known for their elaborate staging techniques—impressive sets, large casts, and what was considered to be the prettiest chorus line in the country—and not for the quality of their material or performers. In May, 1894, Lederer had presented *The Passing Show*, with a book by Sydney Rosenfeld and music by Ludwig Englander. Rosenfeld burlesqued two Pinero melodramas, and used the characters from one of them to provide a storyline for the show. In addition to theatrical targets, Rosenfeld included topical references and lyrics.

The Passing Show, in retrospect, has been called the prototypical American revue. At the time, however, its only immediate influence appears to have been as a model for the Casino's summer shows during the middle 1890's. Two years later, the Weber & Fields' burlesques used all of the ingredients of the Casino revues and met with instant acclaim. One critic, writing about *The Passing Show*, may have diagnosed its problem when he commented that "the scheme [the revue format] had merit" but the execution was dull.[1]

Herein lay the primary difference between the Weber & Fields' early Music Hall burlesques and Lederer's Casino revues. Weber & Fields' performers were variety veterans, accustomed to the snappy pacing of the variety bill and the give-and-take of ensemble and improvisational performing. Lederer's stars were legit actors, handcuffed by the conventions of the legit stage and the primacy of the scripted word. Many of the Casino stars who went on to join Weber & Fields' Stock Company—Lillian Russell, De Wolf Hopper, David Warfield, Lee Harrison, and Louis Mann, to name but a few—had to make significant stylistic adjustments in order to perform the Music Hall burlesques. Lillian Russell credited the Music Hall with "changing the whole method of my line of work on the stage." Performing on the Music Hall stage revived Fay Templeton's career, and brought Warfield to Belasco's attention.

Of course, the "Weberfieldsian" style did not emerge fully developed overnight. The proof was the burlesque that opened Weber & Fields' second season. "The Glad Hand" was written by an Englishman, Kenneth Lee, a vaudeville sketch writer. Lee also assumed the role of director, his English haughtiness being mistaken for competence. He attended rehearsals in evening dress, with a linen handkerchief tucked up one sleeve. When an actor did not perform a line or gesture to Lee's satisfaction, he would tap his cane impatiently. Not surprisingly, the freewheeling Music Hall comedians chafed at his attempts to enforce the rehearsal methods of the legitimate stage. Veteran vaudevillians Bernard, Ross & Fenton, *et al.* were not used to being drilled on line readings before they had a chance to "work up" their stage business. Rehearsals, in their experience, were for learning cues and blocking routines, not for verbatim readings of the script.

To make matters worse, the script itself was stilted and convoluted. It did not survive the first day of rehearsals. Fields later recalled:

> . . . We all began to write our own parts. It was rather amusing as I look back, to think of that first rehearsal, everybody standing around waiting for parts and we handed them two or three lines, which in a few minutes were deposited in the waste basket. . . .

> . . . Peter F. Dailey, Charlie Ross and John T. Kelly sitting on one side of the stage scribbling away on the backs of envelopes and scraps of paper, Joe Weber, Sam Bernard and I on the other. . . . No one would tell the other what they were doing, what business they were going to put in. In fact, they never did until the dress rehearsal. . . .

Lee quit after four days. Lew Fields immediately began looking for a new librettist. The only serious possibility was Edgar Smith, who was already under contract to the Casino. Meanwhile, Stromberg salvaged Lee's lyrics, and the ensemble rewrote Lee's show in rehearsal.

Into this anarchy (for so their rehearsals seemed to the uninitiated), Weber & Fields brought Julian Mitchell, a former Shakespearean actor who had recently directed Charles Hoyt's musical farce, *A Trip to Chinatown*. Handsome, intense, and almost totally deaf, Mitchell's training was also in the legit stage. He, too, was a disciplinarian (a quality Weber & Fields thought essential in a stage manager), but his quiet manner and firsthand knowledge of acting made him easier to take. In rehearsals, to compensate for his deafness, he would lean against the piano to feel its vibrations as he directed the chorus. Wisely, he decided that the comedians would take care of themselves, and he concentrated on the chorus numbers, sets, and costumes. Later, he admitted that he expected the show to die in rehearsal. Until the dress rehearsal, he doubted that the various parts would fit together.

Working with the Weberfields, Mitchell and his innovative chorus work established the importance of the dance director in the creation of musicals. Each successive Mitchell show was more elaborate and complex, with increasing numbers of performers and scenic effects. He was the first to attempt to integrate chorus routines in the plot and visual design of the show, and he set new standards for the appearance and training of chorus members. His work on the cramped stage of the Weber & Fields Music Hall became the basis of Ziegfeld's revues: Mitchell directed the first *Ziegfeld's Follies* in 1907 and a dozen more thereafter.

With Mitchell came his wife, Bessie Clayton, the greatest acrobatic toe-dancer of her time. Lithe, petite, with an elfin charm, Clayton perfected an uncanny combination of classical ballet and the more athletic moves from popular stage dances. Unlike most of her plumper colleagues, she looks like a dancer to modern eyes; the development of her leg and foot muscles astonished turn-of-the-century viewers. Her professionalism was unique among the popular stage dancers of her day: from childhood, she engaged in a demanding regimen of physical conditioning (running four or five miles a day), flexibility exercises, and a controlled diet. She performed on pointe barefoot or in unlined, unreinforced slippers, and she never did encores. Critic Beaumont Fletcher described her as "a terrifying miracle of litheness and agility . . . some gifted composer should write her a ballet, something infernally and demoniacally beautiful." In Weber & Fields' productions, she did her toe dancing and back kicks to a Stromberg instrumental, between the opening act and the burlesque.

Beginning with their second season, Weber & Fields always scheduled their season openings on a Thursday—a superstition that harked back to the day of the week of their first performance together. On Thursday, September 2, 1897, they reopened their Broadway Music Hall, with a long but smoothly performed version of "The Glad Hand, or Secret Servants."

The targets of the evening were the Yukon Gold Rush, then at its height, and William Gillette's popular play, *Secret Service.* Weber, Fields, and Bernard made their entrance as "Klondikers" on the back of the saddest-looking nag that ever walked on four feet. Charles Ross parodied Gillette's mannerisms, and Frankie Bailey's "symmetrical legs, shown in two different sets of tights, caused the usual flutter among the Harrys in the front row." Stromberg's music and Mitchell's staging were singled out for praise. One critic noted that "the chorus girls all made individual hits"—a trademark of Mitchell's chorus lines. The olio featured McIntyre & Heath, and an English singer named Marie Loftus, whose popular appeal apparently did not accompany her across the Atlantic.

The inventive talents of the stock company's newest member—Peter Dailey—made certain that there would be no dead spots in the show, no matter how weak the material. Rotund but exceptionally graceful, perpetually smiling, Dailey never learned three lines in the proper order, nor all of the steps of a dance number. Audiences laughed from the first minute he walked on stage. His tendency to interrupt the scripted performance with impromptu jokes and gags was a nightmare to legit actors. His love of nightlife made it difficult for him to attend morning rehearsals, yet his performances were rarely less than inspired. For the variety veterans of the Music Hall, the biggest problem with Dailey was that he would make his colleagues on stage laugh as much as the audience. Dailey was the first of the Casino actors to defect to the Music Hall, perhaps because he had known Weber & Fields since their dime museum days. (They used to practice tricks together on the dock at the end of Twelfth Street.) It was Dailey, along with John T. Kelly, who served as master of ceremonies after the final curtain of a Music Hall show, when the appreciative audience called for speeches and filled the stage with bouquets of flowers for the performers. According to Fields, "every day was a birthday for Pete Dailey. . . . There was never a squarer or fairer man on earth." Dailey, like Fields, abhorred "star" pretensions and was a notoriously soft touch for colleagues in need.

With Dailey added to the roster of Kelly, Bernard, Ross & Fenton, *et al.*, it is not surprising that Weber & Fields were reluctant to give up performing on the Music Hall stage to fulfill their touring engagements. The partners offered to send the Russell Brothers and the Vaudeville Club in their place, but the theater managers refused. One cannot blame them: in the previous season, Weber & Fields' Own Company had done $8,000 worth of business in one week of two-a-day performances at the Olympia in Chicago. Receipts in the other cities on the tour were less dramatic, but still sizable. Theater managers, hard-pressed by a general falling off in business, counted on the revenue from Weber & Fields' engagements. The only solution would be to find a star whose drawing power rivalled Weber & Fields'.

Fields had heard about a bidding war going on between Hammerstein and Koster & Bial's for the American tour of Vesta Tilley, "London's Idol," and the era's greatest male impersonator. Her slight build and cheery manner reminded audiences of a teen-age boy trying to act like a man. In her portrayals of various male types, her speech patterns, gestures, and costumes were accurate down to the smallest detail. Vaudeville managers knew that her return to the States (she had toured with Pastor in 1894–1895) would be one of the most lucrative tours ever.

Over lunch with Joe Weber and Leo Teller at Shanley's, Fields said that he did not believe Hammerstein's claim to have already signed her. Both partners were already concerned about Hammerstein's efforts to imitate their success with a new music hall of his own. They asked Teller to leave for London immediately. As luck would have it, Teller's arrival in London coincided with a last-minute dispute between Hammerstein and Vesta Tilley's manager (and husband) Walter De Frece. Weber & Fields' offer of $1,250 a week for eight weeks was astounding, but was still less than Hammerstein's bid. Teller sweetened the deal with the promise of an all-star touring company. Within days, the Rialto was buzzing with news of a master stroke by Weber & Fields. Hammerstein was furious; he tried to get an injunction forbidding Vesta Tilley to appear at the Music Hall, even though he was the one who had abrogated her contract.

In late October, 1897, Vesta Tilley became the featured attraction on the olio at Weber & Fields' Music Hall. Using the publicity generated by her nine-week stint at the Music Hall as a foundation, Weber & Fields elicited interest from vaudeville managers in an all-star troupe to accompany her on tour. Weber & Fields did not disappoint the theater managers; accompanying Miss Tilley on tour were the Four Cohans and Lew Dockstader. The Cohans were glad of an opportunity to escape the iron grip of the Keith-Albee organization. George was by now writing extended sketches for his family's act; the tour would give him a chance to try out his new farce, "Money to Burn." Lew Dockstader was the reigning blackface comedian of the era, keeping alive the last vestiges of minstrelsy with political and topical gags sprinkled into his monologues. He was a former member of an earlier Weber & Fields road company, and the proprietor of his own minstrel troupe.

The company would need a reliable business manager, so Lew Fields persuaded his brother Max to resume his travels. Family pressures, and several bouts with an as-yet-undiagnosed illness, had limited Max's activities over the previous year, so that he worked only as advance man for the New York–area appearances of Weber & Fields' touring companies. His wife, Leah, was encouraging him to stay close to home and establish himself as an agent. Max, however, could not pass up the chance to manage the Vesta Tilley All-Star Company. Three months on the road would bring in more money than he had earned at home in the previous year. In late December, 1897, Max said goodbye to his pregnant wife and three children and left New York with the Vesta Tilley troupe for a thirteen-week, nine-city tour. It was one of the most lucrative tours in vaudeville history: Vesta Tilley was reported to have netted over $50,000.

Popular though she was, Vesta Tilley's appearances at the Music Hall were not the high point of the 1897–1898 season. In early November, Weber & Fields succeeded in luring librettist Edgar Smith away from the Casino with an offer of more money. The first product of a Smith/Stromberg/Mitchell collaboration was "Pousse Café, A Dramatic Impossibility in Two Acts," replaced "The Glad Hand" on December 2, and raised the art of burlesque a notch or two in the process. It was the prototype for the great Weberfields productions to come. The production's visual impact was impressive; rather than settling for cheap, exaggerated knock-offs of the original sets, Mitchell and Fields insisted on realistic reproductions. Weber announced to the press that the sets and costumes cost close to $10,000, a slightly inflated figure that nevertheless assured Music Hall patrons that they were attending a first-class theater and not a vaudeville house.

The first act of "Pousse Café" was set in Paris, on the "Boulevard," and was primarily a burlesque of *La Poupée*, starring Anna Held, about a monk who marries a lifelike doll in order to honor his holy vows and satisfy the terms of a bequest to the monastery. For good measure, Smith also threw in fragments from *A Lady of Quality*, *Lord Chumley*, *The Girl from Paris*, and *The French Maid*— all plays involving social climbers. The second act, set in the Parisian villa of a wealthy but socially inept Irish businessman (played by John T. Kelly), was a more focused travesty of Belasco's *The First Born*, entitled "The Worst Born."

The pieces were tied together by the misadventures of a naïve inventor named Herr Weilshaben (Sam Bernard) whose lifelike mechanical doll has attracted the attention of two scheming confidence men, Bierheister (Fields) and Weinshoppen (Weber). Fields and Weber organize a "skindecat" (syndicate) to swindle the inventor and sell his doll, La Pooh Pooh (Rose Beaumont), to the American vaudeville manager Abel Stringer (Peter Dailey):

> BERNARD: Vot is de meaning of dis skindecat peesness? I foinish my prains und my voik und my doll, und de whole shooting match. Vot do I git out of it?
>
> FIELDS: Don't you understand de meaning of vot "skindecat" vos? You are simbly de inwendor of de show. We show you how to show it to de beoble, und on aggoundt of knowing how to do dis, ve each take sixdy ber cend of de grocery receipts, und you git vot is left ofer und above.

In sharing the cost of transporting the doll to America, Bernard will be responsible for the ship, while the "skindecat" will supply the ocean. But Weber & Fields fear that Bernard is going to "skin the skindecat" by selling it directly to McCann, so they browbeat Bernard into signing their contract. Fields reads the terms of the agreement:

> FIELDS: *(reading)* It is hereby understood and mucilage agreed upon by and between the parties as it never was to hold up any such agreement as may or may not be, to see fit and necessary, to whom it may concern that if the circumstances make it otherwise, whereby we

are compelled to overreach ourselves and necessity comes to such
that everything must be arranged consequently, we leave things
stand as they never was above stated.

Fields' accelerating double-talk makes Bernard sputter with frustration. Some of
the stage business reportedly included "mending" (amending) the contract by
tearing off pieces, much as Groucho and Chico did in the contract scene in *A
Night at the Opera* thirty years later.

The contract scene from "Pousse Café" became one of the classic Music Hall
routines, funny enough to keep audiences screaming with laughter for the ten to
fifteen minutes it took to perform. Originally only three pages long, the scene was
"worked up" by Weber, Fields, and Bernard in rehearsals and extended in subsequent performances. While the basic comic premise stayed the same, Lew Fields'
rehearsal script (with pencil revisions in his own hand) shows that many of Smith's
lines were deleted and replaced with the words "bus[iness] w/ Web" or "ad lib."
Peter Dailey rarely even noted cue changes; like the early jazz musicians who
could remember incredibly complex "head arrangements" of their ensemble's songs,
Dailey remembered what he had improvised, or else made up something new.

"Pousse Café's" real targets, of course, were not the plays, but the men behind the "skindecat"—Klaw, Erlanger, Hayman, *et al.* A month before "Pousse
Café" opened, the *Dramatic Mirror* announced, "an anti-trust chain of theaters
is now in the process of being formed. Its purpose is to emancipate the theater
business from the Trust's thralldom and restore equilibrium of dramatic business
in America." By January, editor Harrison Grey Fiske's vociferous campaign against
the Syndicate provoked its principal members to sue him for libel. Weber & Fields'
parody in "Pousse Café" was equally corrosive, but legally unassailable. By holding the Syndicate up for public ridicule night after night for an entire season (and
then sending out a road company the following year), Weber & Fields kept the
issue in front of audiences and members of the theatrical profession at a time
when most newspapers were unwilling to risk losing the Syndicate's advertising
revenues. Klaw and Erlanger did not forget all the laughs that Weber & Fields
had at their expense. That Weber & Fields would oppose the Syndicate in the
business arena was an acceptable annoyance, but to hold these "respectable"
businessmen up for public ridicule was unforgivable. Abe Erlanger was not known
for his sense of humor; he looked forward to having the last laugh on Weber &
Fields.

"Pousse Café" became the hit of the 1897–1898 season, "one of the funniest
and most picturesque entertainments ever seen in New York," according to the
reviewer for the *Dramatic Mirror.* Other reviewers joked about the "B.R.O."
(Breathing Room Only) crowds that nightly jammed into the Weber & Fields
Music Hall. It ran for twenty-six weeks, longer than any of the season's other
Broadway shows.

In late January, Weber & Fields replaced the entire second act ("The Worst
Born") when it became clear that was losing its appeal. "The Wayhighman," tak-
ing off on the popular comic opera *The Highwayman*, by Reginald DeKoven and
Harry B. Smith, included Weber & Fields as a would-be robber and real robber,

respectively. The hit song from "The Wayhighman" was Stromberg and Smith's parody of "coon" songs, "How I Love My Lu," sung by Peter Dailey:

> Way down in old Phil'delphy,
> Where the cotton sprouts so free;
> And the luscious watermelon
> Grows on ev'ry tree.
> There, by the Hackensack River,
> Where the alligators roam,
> My heart is ever turning,
> For that's my Lulu's home.

Ten blocks away, at Frohman's Empire Theater, there was another melodrama ripe for the Weber & Fields treatment. *The Conquerors*, Paul Potter's dramatization of a de Maupassant story about the Franco-Prussian War, starred Viola Allen, William Faversham, and May Robson. On St. Patrick's Day, Weber & Fields once again changed the second act of "Pousse Café," from "The Wayhighman" to "The Con-Curers." Charles Ross played the cynical Prussian officer, Eric Von Roeshad, and Mabel Fenton played the brave French maiden defending her virtue. In the original, the Prussian officer commands the heroine to drink a glass of wine; instead, she throws it in his face, an insult for which he vows a horrible revenge. In the Music Hall version, Yvonne Grandpiano (Fenton) slaps a fresh lemon-meringue pie in Von Roeshad's face. Another character samples some and dies in agony. It was the first recorded use of a pie-in-the-face in a comedy routine.

At times, the humor bordered on the surreal. When the Prussian tries to force her to eat her own pie, Peter Dailey steals the pie and is about to bite into it when the pie begins to play a tune, prompting a burlesque of a minstrel show in which none but the oldest gags are used. A bust on a pedestal wears a military cap at a rakish tilt, and has a cigar in its mouth. There are muddy boots on the mantel, a saddle on the piano, and a small pig in a birdcage (the pig is being held as a POW for rooting for the enemy). John T. Kelly, as a German major with an Irish brogue, dips his pen in his beer, wipes it on his whiskers, and dries his whiskers with the blotter.

Critic Acton Davies concluded that "The Con Curers" was a great deal cleverer than the play it was based on. Such was the reputation of the burlesque that Weber & Fields were asked to give a special matinee for professionals, so that Faversham, Allen, and the rest of the Empire cast could see themselves travestied. They laughed heartily and gave the burlesquers a standing ovation.

Weber & Fields closed their season in mid-July with a month of sold-out performances at Chicago's Grand Opera House. Fields claimed that they could have played there the entire summer, but heat and fatigue had taken their toll of the actors. In another month, they would have to begin rehearsals for their next season. One newspaper reported that they returned to New York with "a bag of gold as big as any that has ever come out of the Klondike."

Money aside, "Pousse Café" represented a breakthrough in the format of Weber & Fields' productions, and it set the pattern for the next six seasons at the Music Hall. All of the shows started with a script, a framework within which the inventive Music Hall comedians developed their routines, director Mitchell staged his choruses and settings, and composer Stromberg wrote his melodies. The first act, which gave its name to the entire evening, was composed of a series of comic sketches interspersed with musical numbers, tied together by a tenuous plot line or theme. Between the acts, Bessie Clayton danced. The second act was a more extended burlesque of one specific Broadway hit, usually replaced after several weeks by a new burlesque. Meanwhile, the first act continued to be revised, becoming more polished and condensed. Fields had been pushing for more thematic consistency, and the new Music Hall format came closer to achieving this goal. Its musical score—written by a single composer with no interpolations—was a step towards the modern "book" musical. At the same time, its emphasis on comic specialties, pretty chorus girls, and lavish settings pointed towards the revue, particularly the Ziegfeld Follies.

Weber & Fields' insistence that they were creating a new brand of entertainment was not merely show business hype. No term existed for what they were trying to do; "burlesque" described only their style or point of view, without implying any formal or structural characteristics. Even today, their entertainments elude categorization. They were neither musical comedy nor revue, but they were a wellspring for these two incipient theatrical forms.

The success of "Pousse Café" made Joe Weber and Lew Fields celebrities for New York's chic theatergoers. Former president Grover Cleveland and Tammany boss Richard Croker (recently returned from exile in England) were seen at several performances, enjoying themselves hugely. When John Stromberg's orchestra struck up "The Star-Spangled Banner," millionaire William K. Vanderbilt would stand up in the box seats and sing, waving his handkerchief like a baton to encourage the crowd to join in. He had lately been studying Weber & Fields because he wanted to do an imitation of them at a society concert; his partner was rumored to be Wall Street financier Russell Sage.

Financiers, lawyers, and industrialists scouted the chorus lines of the Casino and Weber & Fields' Music Hall in search of a pretty wife or mistress. Gradually, the social biases against actors were being relaxed. Since vaudeville had cleaned up its act and many legitimate actors were appearing on the vaudeville stage, the more daring members of high society were now willing to patronize successful vaudevillians. The *Dramatic Mirror*'s "Matinee Girl" reported that "the society act is getting to be the correct caper for the actor." Peter Dailey was invited to pour tea at the Astoria. Weber, Fields, and Bernard were invited by Stanford White to perform the "skindecat" scene for his Tuesday Evening Club. White's Club had earned a reputation for decadent private entertainments, with rumors of naked showgirls popping out of giant Jack Horner pies. Fields was reluctant to accept White's invitation, despite the risk of offending influential members of their Music Hall audience. He may have been anxious about his own reputation, or he may have disliked being patronized. With Weber's consent, Fields named a ridiculously high price for their performance. The swells paid it without a murmur. In the end, Fields admitted to having a good time, and volunteered that he would be willing to do it again for nothing.

At age thirty-one, Lew Fields was making his debut in New York society. In his two years as a Broadway producer and proprietor, he had learned something about stylish appearance. His hair was fashionably long and wavy, and he disdained flashy displays of jewelry and bright colors. As befitted the son of a tailor, he was fussy about his clothes—elegant suits from the city's best tailor, and twenty-dollar silk shirts. Only when he was in street clothes did one notice the deep laugh lines around his mouth and eyes. In his offstage photos, he always looked tired.

In comparison with most well-known actors of his day, Lew Fields' stable and unspectacular private life furnished little grist for the gossip mill. He was not, after all, a womanizer or a drinker; he was unusually diplomatic with his colleagues; and he enforced strict rules of decorum in his companies. Instead of scandalous tales of backstage goings-on, the newspapers would report that Lew Fields threatened to fire an actor for swearing at a chorus girl, for showing up drunk at a rehearsal, or for refusing to rehearse. Not coincidentally, the behaviors that the public regarded as typical of show biz folk—profanity in mixed company, drunkenness, and prima donna-ism—were the only three things that ever caused Fields to lose his temper with his colleagues.

To be associated with such behavior was to be guilty of it, or so Lew feared. In regard to actors, the attitude of Lew's father, Solomon, with his Old World Jewish values, and the attitude of the typical middle-class businessman, with his Victorian rules of decorum, were surprisingly similar. Lew had spent the early part of his career trying to prove to his father that he could succeed as an actor without compromising his own moral character; now he had a personal stake in proving the moral legitimacy of his profession to respectable Americans in general.

With the success of the Music Hall, Weber & Fields became darlings of the press. Both Joe and Lew had already demonstrated their shrewdness at manipulating public relations, but that cannot account for the genuine affection that they seemed to have inspired in everyone from theater critics to society columnists. Ziegfeld, Belasco, and Cohan were better self-promoters, but none of them was as well-loved during his lifetime as Weber & Fields. Interviewers seemed to enjoy Weber & Fields' offstage conversations almost as much as their performances: Weber, sitting "tailor-fashion" in a big armchair, punning a mile a minute and heckling his partner; Fields, at his tidy desk, spinning stories laced with his quiet, dry wit, always hinting at bigger things yet to come.

Not surprisingly, reporters focused on the rags-to-riches aspects of their careers—sons of the Bowery, six dollars a week in the dime museums, the hard life of the road, and so forth. This naturally led to speculation about Weber & Fields' personal salaries (at the turn of the century, rumor had it that they were making twenty-five hundred a week each.) Modest, genteel, and unaffected, Weber & Fields were held up as role models for the "other half," living proof that Horatio Alger was right. They lived clean in a "dirty" profession, and their virtue had been rewarded with financial success. Although the Jewish immigrants of the Lower East Side were not a part of the Broadway audience, many of the younger ones took pride in the popularity and financial success of Weber & Fields, for it proved that the stage was one gateway to opportunity that did not exclude Jews.

More heartwarming still, as far as the press was concerned, was Weber &

Fields' enduring friendship, and the apparently untrammeled harmony that extended to their company members. Reporters began referring to their stock company as "the happy family." Implicitly, Weber & Fields were the benevolent parents, and their audience were made to feel like close relations. Of course, it did not hurt Weber & Fields' press relations that they were early allies of Harrison Grey Fiske, editor of the *Dramatic Mirror*, in his showdown with the Syndicate, or that William Randolph Hearst was an avid fan—or that they kept an open tab at their bar for journalists.

Lew Fields had two favorite diversions: theater and gambling. He pursued both compulsively, though their effects on him could not have been more opposite. His love of theater was predictable, and therefore not particularly newsworthy, although it was noted with some surprise that his personal tastes ran to Shakespeare, particularly the tragedies (*Hamlet* was his favorite), and to the era's most popular Shakespearean actors, E. H. Sothern and Julia Marlowe.

Fields' other pastime was considerably less benign. It is indicative of the era's naïve acceptance of gambling as a harmless social activity, as well as the press' particular affection for Weber & Fields, that Lew's gambling was depicted as the stuff of cute anecdotes. While on tour in Chicago, Weber described (in a comic manner) going to the track with Fields to save Fields from an array of hustlers, beggars, and stupid bets, beginning with the brakeman on their streetcar. As was generally the case with their humor, there was truth at its core. Weber also gambled on occasion—he even owned a trotter—but never with "such a muchness" as his partner.

To be sure, gambling in one form or another had always been a part of Lew's daily life. The Bowery of his childhood was dense with poker flats, faro parlors, pool halls (where pool was the most infrequent activity), and policy shops (numbers and lottery wagering). Card-playing—poker, blackjack, gin—was the preferred activity for actors killing time, on trains, in hotel rooms, or backstage. In the actors' green room at the Music Hall, there was always a pinochle game in progress, including Joe, Lew, Pete Dailey, and whoever else happened to be offstage. Not surprisingly, Weber & Fields found ways to work all manner of card games into their burlesques. Their audiences never seemed to tire of the repartee, the fool's bravado, the card shark's elaborate attempts to cheat his partners, or the know-it-all's botched explanation of the rules.

Although gambling was not legal according to the letter of the law, it was almost *de rigueur* for affluent men who wished to be part of chic society. John Daly, who ran the casino next door to Weber & Fields' Music Hall, reportedly paid a hundred thousand dollars a year for "protection," but still turned a healthy profit with his baccarat and roulette tables. Even more lavish than Daly's was Canfield's casino, strategically located near Delmonico's restaurant. Richard Canfield, "the prince of gamblers," spent over a million dollars decorating and furnishing his palatial establishment. His private art collection was rivalled only by J. P. Morgan's. The casino included a supper room in the basement, "public" gaming rooms on the second storey, and, on the third floor, a private room for patrons desiring to exceed the house limits. Canfield instructed his doormen not to admit anyone who was not known to be able to afford substantial losses.

Players in the public room were expected to begin by purchasing five hundred dollars' worth of chips, but most of the action was upstairs, in the private rooms, where some patricians lost as much as one hundred thousand dollars in an evening.[2] With his keen eye for theatrical spectacle and his love of high style, Fields could readily appreciate Canfield's casino.

When Lew Fields gambled, he preferred the most theatrical forms—horseracing and roulette. (By contrast, Weber liked the intimate showdowns of poker.) Fields practiced only in the most genteel environments, the settings with the highest production values—Daly's, Canfield's, and Saratoga. There, he socialized with the people who made his theater the "in" place to go—high rollers such as Jesse Lewissohn, Russell Sage, and Diamond Jim Brady. His chief interest, however, was not the camaraderie, but the game. Win or lose, Fields' expression never changed; warm and animated with friends and family, he wore a mask of imperturbable seriousness at the gaming table. It was the look of an actor testing his ability to control his reactions, or a devout man concentrating on a holy task.

Gambling may have had a metaphorical significance to Lew Fields, as it has for many actors. Asked why actors are superstitious, Lillian Russell concluded that it was inevitable for "those who live by chance." Fields the showman was an extension of Fields the high-rolling gambler. He recognized that his career (like that of any actor) was based on a series of wagers in which he risked his reputation and livelihood with each new undertaking. In their long apprenticeship, Weber & Fields had also learned the value of a good bluff, and when to call others' bluffs. When they were broke, they wore diamonds; when they lost a star from their company, they went out and purchased the contract of an even bigger star. They became known as the greatest "plungers" in theatrical history, but they always plunged to a profit—at least, they had so far. Weber & Fields were gamesmen, and each had the gamesman's belief that his own talent and passion would see him through.

No one knows the extent of Lew Fields' gambling losses during the years from 1896 to 1904. A magazine profile of Weber & Fields in 1912, on the occasion of their reunion, mentioned that his losses were heavy. Fields tried to shield his family from the worst consequences of his gambling. He tried earnestly to be a good husband and father, and he apparently was—as much as any man could be who worked twelve to fifteen hours a day, ten months a year. Rose had hoped that the end of Weber & Fields' touring commitments would mean Lew would be able to spend more time with her and their three young children—Frances, now four years old; Joe, a plump toddler; and one-year-old Herbert. But she soon learned that Lew's responsibilities as proprietor, producer, and performer left little time for a normal family life.

Rehearsals began at eleven a.m., but Fields often arrived an hour early to take care of business with Weber, or confer with Mitchell or Edgar Smith about production matters. If it was not the day of a matinee, there would be a break in the late afternoon, during which Fields would race home in a cab, eat a hearty dinner, and visit briefly with his kids before returning to the Music Hall. Curtain was at eight o'clock; in the first week or so of a new production, performances usually lasted until after midnight; otherwise, they finished around eleven-thirty.

After the final curtain, Fields, unlike many of his Music Hall colleagues, did not head for Rector's for champagne and a late meal. Occasionally, he had a quiet midnight dinner with Rose at Shanley's or Louis Sherry's restaurant. On most nights, Fields did not get home until one a.m; later if he happened to stop in at Daly's or Canfield's. The Irish servant-girl would prepare a cold supper for him, which he ate alone. He tried to catch up with his family on Sundays, when the theater was dark, or during the summer layoff, when they rented a vacation home at Long Branch, on the Jersey shore.

Weber & Fields' third season continued their evolution away from vaudeville. To accommodate longer burlesques, they drastically shortened the olios, intending to phase them out altogether by the end of the season. Obligingly, the New York dailies began listing the Weber & Fields burlesques alongside the legit offerings at the Empire, Daly's, and the Knickerbocker, rather than with the vaudeville houses. In their public's eyes, Weber & Fields had made the symbolic crossover from the Bowery to Broadway.

Weber & Fields underscored their aesthetic ambitions by signing two more veterans of comic opera, David Warfield and Fay Templeton. Buxom and dark-haired, with a sultry smile, Templeton was arguably the most versatile comedienne of her time, a far better actress than Lillian Russell from the standpoint of craft. Templeton came from a stage family; she made her first appearance on stage at three years of age, dressed as Cupid, singing fairy-tale songs. While still a teen-ager, she established herself as a romantic lead, then quit the stage at age twenty-two to marry a wealthy New Yorker. Upon the death of her husband eight years later, she made a triumphant return to the stage in *Excelsior, Jr.*, appearing at Hammerstein's Olympia at the same time that Weber & Fields were doing their Fregoli burlesque. She, too, had a knack for satirizing theatrical pretensions; her burlesques of grand opera and comic opera divas of the day were reported to be devastating. Vivacious and magnetic, Templeton was the female star the Music Hall had hitherto lacked.

With Sam Bernard leaving the Music Hall to play the lead role in the farce *The Marquis of Michigan,* Weber & Fields needed to find a strong ethnic comic who could hold his own with Mike and Meyer. David Warfield came to the Music Hall straight from the Casino Theater, where his versatility in a variety of comic roles had impressed Lew Fields. Warfield's specialty was his "Hebrew" characterization, based on the Polish Jews of New York's Lower East Side. His wily but tactless Jew contrasted nicely with Weber & Fields' Dutchmen. Warfield also had more serious acting ambitions, and in his years at the Music Hall, he played as many character roles as "Hebrews."

In the previous season, Weber & Fields had burlesqued Harry B. Smith's *The Highwayman;* now they hired him to assist Edgar Smith with lyrics and libretti. Harry B. Smith (no relation to Edgar) was the era's most popular and prolific author of comic operas and revues. He had attended the first night of "The Way-highman," and had subsequently admitted that the Music Hall version was more entertaining than his own operetta.

On September 8, 1898, *Hurly-Burly,* the new creation of Smith, Smith, and

Stromberg, ushered in the new season. Rather than a spoof of a current Broadway play, the storyline was a more or less a continuation of their previous season's hit, "Pousse Café." The scene was shifted from Paris to London, and instead of a mechanical doll, the scheming Weinshoppen and Bierheister (Weber & Fields) now own Cleopatra's mummy (Fay Templeton). Solomon Yankle (David Warfield) accidentally revives Cleopatra, and she brings them all back to ancient Egypt. Two Stromberg songs caught on, both of the "coon" variety: "Kiss Me, Honey, Do," sung by Peter Dailey, and "Keep Away from Emmaline," belted out by Fay Templeton in her characteristically deep, sensuous singing voice. Although Stromberg scores usually ran the gamut of popular styles—waltzes, ballads, novelty songs—Music Hall audiences were especially fond of his coon songs.

Musically, the coon songs were Tin Pan Alley's interpretation of ragtime. As developed by black composers such as Ben Harney and Scott Joplin, ragtime was an instrumental style characterized by an up-tempo, syncopated melody. In the hands of Tin Pan Alley composers, the coon song differed from ragtime more in spirit than in musical style.[3] What defined the coon song were its lyrics—the stereotyped plantation dialect and racial characterizations—which were almost always sung by whites. It was one of the last vestiges of minstrelsy, another case of a black art form reconstituted by white sensibilities. The era's most popular dance, the cakewalk, was another holdover from the days of the minstrel show.

Proof of the theatergoing public's taste for cakewalking and ragtime came in July, 1898, with the resounding success of the first all-black musical at a major New York theater (the Casino Roof Garden): *The Origin of the Cake Walk; or, Clorindy*, with libretto and lyrics by Paul Laurence Dunbar and music by Will Marion Cook. It was more a social landmark than an artistic one, since ragtime had already found its way onto the musical stage in the form of coon songs and as an accompaniment to the cakewalk. Nevertheless, the success of *Clorindy* prompted the producers of musicals to interpolate "darktown" songs and dances in their programs.

If the measure of a musical is the number of memorable tunes it contains, then Stromberg's work for Weber & Fields has been forgotten for purely extramusical reasons. The hit songs from the Music Hall—"Kiss Me, Honey, Do," "De Pullman Porters' Ball," "Come Down My Evenin' Star," "Ma Blushin' Rosie" (later recorded by Al Jolson and Judy Garland)—were among the most popular show melodies of the era; with very few exceptions, they were all coon songs. Lyrics aside, many of Stromberg's so-called coon songs have more in common with the songs of John Phillip Sousa and George M. Cohan than with ragtime. The fact that Edgar Smith's lyrics are objectionable to modern tastes has meant that Stromberg's melodic gifts have gone unappreciated.

Within a few weeks of its opening, *Hurly-Burly* had been cut down to two scenes, and a burlesque of a racy French bedroom farce added to the program. *The Turtle*, adapted by Joseph Herbert and produced by Flo Ziegfeld at the Manhattan, was a convoluted story of infidelity, sleeping potions, and compromising coincidences. Its main appeal seems to have been a scene in which the female lead undresses for bed, followed a short time later by the male lead. The *Dramatic Mirror*'s reviewer called the play "offensive. . . . The palpable straining for off-color insinuations, for lines of unwholesome suggestion, frequently passed the bounds of tolerance. . . . The disrobing episode plainly had been relied upon to create talk and to invoke transitory prosperity." Worse still, "there was nothing to laugh at, nothing to cause even a smile."

Weber & Fields changed that. Assisted by Rose Beaumont and David Warfield, they burlesqued *The Turtle*'s disrobing scene "in a most ludicrous manner." Weber & Fields had a gift for getting an audience to laugh at its insecurities. A decade earlier, the underlying issue for their vaudeville audiences had been ethnic differences; in the late 'nineties, the issue for their Music Hall patrons was morality. In direct contrast to the leg-show type of burlesque, the comic exaggerations of the Music Hall's resident ethnics made the indecent scene decent.

The secret of Weber & Fields' most successful burlesques was that they spoofed plays of dubious morality like *The Turtle*, *The Conquerors*, *Sappho*, *Catherine*, and *Zaza*, and so on. Broadway critics and society watchdogs warned against the immorality of plays of the Parisian school, but Broadway audiences came to see for themselves. In March, 1900, Clyde Fitch's *Sappho* became a *succès de scandale* for a scene at the end of the second act, during which the male lead carried the voluptuous Olga Nethersole up a spiral staircase to an unseen bedroom. Men in the audience went bug-eyed trying to see her curves through her flimsy nightgown. Police Magistrate Mott closed down the show at its first performance, but popular demand—and Miss Nethersole's declarations of high moral purpose—prevailed, and a more modest *Sappho* was allowed to reopen.

Billed as "a clean travesty," Weber & Fields' *Sapolio* turned the moral universe of the original play inside out. In the burlesque, Fanny Legrand, played by May Robson (on loan from Charles Frohman), engaged in a campaign to make Paris nice and clean. Hefty Peter Dailey played Jean Gaussin, the dashing leading man. The romantic interlude culminates with Fanny trying to carry Jean up the spiral staircase, with predictable results. Instead, she stuffs her lover in the dumbwaiter and hoists him upstairs. Ads for *Sapolio* boasted, "None of the Members of This Company has yet been Indicted."

Ever so sweetly, Weber & Fields' burlesques simultaneously ridiculed the audience's prurient interest, the playwright's "Continental" pretensions, and the producer's cheap sensationalism. Actually, the frank costumes of the chorus girls in these shows, or Bessie Clayton's acrobatic dance routines, were more revealing than any disrobing or seduction scene on the legit stage of that time. The Music Hall productions allowed their patrons to savor the extravagance of the Parisian settings while twitting the aspects of Continental morality that made them uncomfortable. By inverting the moral premise of those legit plays, by replacing implied vice with exaggerated virtue, Weber & Fields made the violation of social conventions seem laughable and less threatening. The net effect was reassuring. Intuitively, Weber & Fields understood that beneath his conspicuous displays of affluence and hedonism, the Broadway theatergoer was straitlaced, unworldly, and puritanical at heart.

Just as Weber & Fields based their Mike and Meyer routines on close observation of real-life situations, they built their Music Hall burlesques around carefully re-created elements from the original play. Initially, this had meant that Edgar Smith, Fields, and sometimes Weber, would attend performances of several current plays, and then decide on their suitability and which elements best lent themselves to parody. Beginning with "The Con-Curers," Julian Mitchell specified sets and costumes that were essentially "straight" reproductions of the original set, to serve as a visual foil for the actors' broad humor and the occasional incongruous prop or special effect.

Fields considered firsthand observation so important that he asked the principals of the stock company to see the plays they intended to burlesque. The traditional Wednesday matinee was switched to Tuesday so that the Music Hall company members could attend the original. This also made it possible for other Broadway professionals to see the Music Hall programs; Richard Mansfield—a great actor not noted for his sense of humor—often attended the Music Hall's Tuesday matinees. Some legit managers, however, feared that their actors would not be able to give a serious performance if they had seen their roles à la Weber & Fields, and so discouraged attendance at the Tuesday matinees. Critic Alan Dale complained that he could no longer watch a serious play without simultaneously wondering about how it would be manhandled by the Weberfields. It had become a badge of distinction on Broadway to be burlesqued by them.

Following the burlesque of *The Turtle*, Weber & Fields announced their intention to spoof Rostand's *Cyrano de Bergerac*, starring Richard Mansfield. As a rule, Mansfield allowed no visitors during his rehearsals, but for the Weberfields he made an exception. Other producers followed suit; henceforth, Weber & Fields' burlesques could open within a month of the original play.

Described by its authors as "a prominent feature, amputated from the French, and disfigured without permission," "Cyranose de Bric-a-Brac" opened on November 3, 1898. Lew Fields played the title role; Joe Weber was his buddy, Ragamuffin. Fields wore a trick nose that had a habit of tilting when its owner was insulted. In one scene, it glowed with electric fire, enabling him to read a letter by its light. The script was not one of Edgar Smith's better efforts (too literal a travesty, not enough comic opportunities). Among the bit players were Fields' brother Sol, making his New York stage debut, and Lew's sister-in-law, Sadie Harris.

Like many troupers, Fields believed in playing through an illness. Blessed with an iron constitution, he had not missed a performance due to illness or injury in twenty years. In mid-December, however, Fields was suffering from a flu virus. Despite the pleas of his wife and partner, Lew would not lay off, or even cut back the more demanding stunts in his role. As the swashbuckling hero in "Cyranose," he had to scale a trellised wall and swing onto a balcony. It was not the kind of stunt that would normally have given him any difficulty. But during the December 17 performance, Fields felt a sudden faintness as he tried to boost himself onto the balcony; then fell on his back with a sickening thud. A few members of the audience laughed, mistaking it for a pratfall. Fields tried to get up, but could not, and had to be carried from the stage. After a brief curtain, the burlesque continued, with Peter Dailey filling in as Cyranose. The injury to Fields' back, though painful, was not serious. *Hurly-Burly* limped along without him for three weeks, although the cast, as one critic noted, seemed ill at ease.

Even before his recovery was complete, Fields began working with Edgar Smith on a burlesque of yet another melodrama of French origin. Earlier in the season, Annie Russell had starred in *Catherine,* an unhappy story about a poor working girl who is exploited and humiliated by friends and family: Cinderella with a corrupt Prince Charming and no fairy godmother. Of course, her intentions are virtuous, but she is driven to compromise her honor. By inverting the play's moral dilemma and exaggerating the martyr-like qualities of the heroine, Edgar Smith and Harry B. Smith created a near-perfect vehicle for the Weberfields. Catherine Villun (Fay Templeton) is a poor but proud girl who is desperate to take more of the world's troubles on herself. The rest of the characters, caring only about her happiness, are only too willing to oblige. The curtain opens on a garret, where Catherine Villun gives sewing machine lessons to support her two bratty young brothers ("only rivals of the Katzenjammers," played by Weber & Fields), while her lazy father (David Warfield) bemoans his inability to do less to support the family, and her wicked sister (Rose Beaumont) tries to smoke herself sick to give Catherine somebody else to care for. Catherine attracts the attention of the penniless Duke de Coocoo (Charles Ross) and his scheming mother, the Duchess (Peter Dailey). Catherine loves George Mantlepiece (John T. Kelly), but decides to marry the Duke, because George only owes six thousand francs, while the Duke owes a hundred times that amount. The Duke vows, "I shall be good to her indeed. I shall let her work as hard as she likes for me, and if she's real good, I'll let her send her money to Helene, too." (Helene is the Duke's mistress.) All of Catherine's family move in with her at the Duke's estate, where she works at a gilded sewing machine.

For the first time in their careers, Weber & Fields performed without dialect, as did Warfield and Kelly. As the elderly father, Warfield wreaked havoc with scissors ("a cliptomaniac"); he starts by clipping coupons (which upsets Catherine), but in the next scene, he's trimming the ornamental fringe off the conservatory archways with a large shears, pausing only to snip at the dress of a passing baroness.

When George Mantlepiece comes to court Catherine, the bratty brothers blow spitballs at him from behind a curtain. Each time he draws back the curtain, they pretend to be asleep in a series of increasingly unlikely poses. Later, the Duchess interrogates the boys:

DUCHESS (DAILEY): I hope you are good boys. The Lord watches, you know.
FREDERICK (FIELDS): Lord who?
DUCHESS: The Lord, you know, follows you wherever you go.
PAUL (WEBER): Get out!
FRED: The Lord knows everything we do, does he? Does he know we played hookey from school today?
DUCHESS: Yes.
PAUL: Does he know I got whipped?
DUCHESS: Yes.
FRED: The Lord knows everything we do, and He goes everywhere we go?

DUCHESS: Most certainly.

FRED: Does the Lord go down in the cellar?

DUCHESS: Yes.

FRED: You lie! We ain't got a cellar!

The Duchess' costume (Dailey in drag) reportedly "kept the audience laughing for two minutes after his first entrance." In typical Music Hall fashion, many of the best lines were ad-libbed, or occurred when the actors stepped out of character. This comic device was especially effective for lampooning the grandiloquent style of many legit actors.

Unlike the original, the burlesque ends happily, with the entire cast on stage. The Duke promises to be more extravagant in the future. Helene promises to do all she can to steal the Duke from Catherine, "and if that's not enough, I'll let you support me, too." Frederick announces that their sister Blanche has finally succeeded in getting sick. A tearful Catherine exclaims, "At last my cup of happiness is filled. I have all the worrying I wanted. . . ." Stromberg led the orchestra in a reprise of the evening's hit coon song, "What, Marry Dat Gal?" as the ensemble cakewalked off the stage.

For reviewers and patrons alike, there was little doubt that the burlesque of *Catherine* was the Weberfields' greatest achievement so far. Some critics observed that the production was so consistently excellent that it was difficult to single out the individuals entitled to the most credit. Even the company's official "tailors"—Weber & Fields and Julian Mitchell—could find few lines to cut, alter, or add. For the first time, a Music Hall production played out its run without any major script changes.

On April 6th, after thirty weeks of *Hurly-Burly*, Weber & Fields presented their final bill of the season, *Helter-Skelter*. In the seemingly arbitrary and nonsensical titles he gave to the Music Hall shows, Edgar Smith evoked the salient qualities of Weber & Fields' invention: frivolous, irreverent, high-spirited, trendy, fast-paced. In the years to come, there would be *Whirl-i-Gig*, *Fiddle-Dee-Dee*, *Hoity-Toity*, *Twirly-Whirly*, and *Whoop-Dee-Doo*. The titles have a goofy lilt, manufactured from slangy expressions and words deformed in daily usage, so that even the stuffiest person could not speak them without sounding a bit silly. Taken together, the Music Hall titles were deliberately interchangeable, trademarks of a unique brand of entertainment, like the Marx Brothers' titles: *Duck Soup*, *Cocoanuts*, *Horsefeathers*, or *Monkey Business* twenty-five or thirty years later.

With "Catherine" anchoring the second half of the program, *Helter-Skelter* mopped up most of the remaining hits of the season: *The Great Ruby*, *Lord and Lady Algy*, and *Zaza*. In a devastating imitation of Mrs. Leslie Carter's speech, walk, and mannerisms, Mabel Fenton played Zaza, the "other woman" who goes to her lover's house to tell his wife to give him up. In the original play, Zaza is dissuaded by the young daughter's innocent small talk. The burlesque replaced the little girl with a large French poodle named Toto (played by Richard Garnella, a veteran of Weber & Fields' touring companies). Toto showed Zaza the error of her ways. When the philandering father (Peter Dailey) discovered Zaza's mission, he is outraged: "I could have forgiven you for speaking to my wife. But my poor, innocent little dog—never!" *Helter-Skelter* did SRO business until the end of the season on May 28.

Three days later, Fields and business manager Leo Teller embarked for Europe. Interest in Continental plays and vaudeville acts was stronger than ever. In this respect, American producers were following the lead of ambitious tailors and retail garment magnates, who made their fortunes by mass-producing "knock-offs" of European fashions for off-the-rack purchase. Fields (the son of a tailor) and Teller (a former retailer) planned to scout European talent for the Weber & Fields Music Hall and touring companies. The Music Hall had been a significant force behind the public's enthusiasm for "Parisian"-style shows; it was about time that its proprietors saw the real thing. The working title of Edgar Smith's and Harry B. Smith's new burlesque was "Paris in 1900." To observe the subject firsthand, Fields spent most of his time abroad attending Parisian music halls and theaters, and watching preparations for the city's upcoming International Exposition.

Fields returned to New York in early July, ready to spend a month relaxing with his family in the Adirondacks, only to find that pressing personal and professional concerns made relaxation impossible. In his absence, his brother Max's recurring illness had been diagnosed as tuberculosis. Max had managed the 1898–1899 tour of The Pousse Café Company (which included brother Nat and brother-in-law Bobby Harris performing Weber & Fields' routines). By the end of the twenty-plus weeks on the road, Max could no longer disguise his worsening condition. He suffered through a serious bout in May and June. By July, he felt strong enough to resume his business duties.

Lew was torn between his concern for Max's health and his dependance on Max's expertise. From the time of Lew's first performances in the Bowery dime museums, Max had been Lew's advocate within the family, his most ardent backer and trusted advisor. During the growth of Weber & Fields Enterprises, Max had become their most reliable road manager and business representative. Now they needed him to manage the *Hurly-Burly* road show; it would be their lone touring company for the 1899–1900 season. Over Leah's vehement protests, Max agreed to leave with the *Hurly-Burly* company in September.

By 1899, four out of Lew's five brothers were working in theater, either as businessmen or actors. The lone holdout was Henry, who never showed any interest in theater or Lew's career. Most recently, Lew's older brother, Sol, had been drawing favorable notices on the local vaudeville stage. Lew gave him a small role in "Cyranose," and encouraged him to attend rehearsals and learn more about stage-managing. Perhaps overwhelmed by the plentiful Fieldses, Joe Weber moved his older brother, "Muck," from the café to the Music Hall's box office.

Yet another Fields put in an occasional appearance backstage at the Music Hall. Solomon, Lew's father, had recently been persuaded to retire. Now that Lew's financial success had made an appreciable difference in the family's standard of living, Papa Fields (he no longer insisted on "Schanfield") found it easier to reconcile himself to his famous son's profession. To persist in his disapproval would have meant alienating five of his six sons. Perhaps the Music Hall's well-heeled audiences finally persuaded him that the popular stage was indeed a respectable diversion. Not only did he begin attending Lew's performances, but he would occasionally come by in the afternoon during rehearsals. In the unlikely setting of the Music Hall, Papa Fields, bearded and bespectacled, would button-hole performers and employees and engage them in earnest discussions about the differences between the customs of their faith and his own. Papa Fields was proud of the respect accorded his son by the company members. Lew was delighted by his father's presence and all it implied, despite the man's rather embarrassing preoccupation with religious matters. At bottom, however, these issues still separated father from son. Although Lew now lived in a spacious Riverside Drive townhouse, his parents preferred to live in a kosher household with their daughter Annie and her husband Morris Warschauer.

With the start of rehearsals for the 1899–1900 season only a week away, Weber & Fields revealed that they had lost their two female stars, Mabel Fenton and Fay Templeton. Mabel Fenton told the press that she was retiring to her farm on the Jersey shore, but there were rumors that she was dissatisfied with the kinds of roles she had been given. Templeton had appeared without permission in a summer entertainment at the New York Roof Garden, a Syndicate house, while still under contract to Weber & Fields. They were in no mood to be forgiving where the Syndicate was concerned. Having secured control of the booking for over three hundred of the first-class theaters across the country, the Syndicate had intensified its pressure on independents by outbidding them for stars and scripts. Weber & Fields decided not to renew Templeton's contract.

The prerequisites for a Weber & Fields comedienne were intimidating: she had to be a beauty, a distinctive personality or stage presence, a strong singer, and a versatile actress capable of imitating legit performers while handling the improvisatory style performance. It was Fields who dared to suggest Lillian Russell, considered at the time to be the "Queen of Comic Opera." Russell surpassed the requirements of the first three categories, and, Fields surmised, she had the talent and wit to adjust to the Music Hall style. At age thirty-eight, she was still a radiant beauty, and despite several unsuccessful shows, she was still the highest-priced actress on the American stage. Voluptuous yet angelic, strong-willed yet vulnerable, she was the notorious woman who rose above her reputation, like the more-sinned-against-than-sinning heroines of the 'nineties melodramas.

Even if Weber & Fields could afford her price, it seemed unlikely that this living legend would lower herself to appear in burlesque. But had they not seen her in the Music Hall audience, roaring with laughter? Wasn't she sitting with Jesse Lewissohn, the copper magnate? Fields knew Lewissohn from the racetrack and the plush casinos they both frequented. Weber suggested that Fields go to the Sheepshead Bay races and ask Lewissohn for an introduction.

One version of the racetrack meeting, perhaps apocryphal, has Lillian Russell, seated in Lewissohn's box, picking a winner by jabbing a hatpin into the program with her eyes closed. Fields suggested that if she used a fork, she could pick win, place, and show. The quip broke the ice, and Fields asked her if she would consider joining his company. This, too, brought a smile to her face. How could they afford to pay her price, with their small theater? Swallowing hard, Fields asked her to name her price: twelve hundred and fifty a week, a thirty-five week guarantee, and all costumes to be paid for by the producers. Drawing on all of the reserves of self-control he had learned at the roulette table, Fields calmly replied, "That's fine. We'll be expecting you at rehearsals in August." He shook hands with a surprised Lillian Russell, and the deal was sealed. For the next five seasons, that was the only contract they needed.

"We simply wanted to have the strongest company in New York, and no performer in the field is too high-priced for us," Weber explained to the press. "The salary we are to pay Miss Russell is a good deal more than the weekly remuneration of the President of the United States." It was, in fact, the largest salary on Broadway. The press predicted disaster, suggesting at first that the announcement was a joke, and then pointing out that "the fair Lillian was entirely unsuited for the line of business proposed and that . . . burlesque would scarcely be a forward step in her career." Moreover, Miss Russell had a reputation for being unreliable (missed engagements, broken contracts, attacks of tempera-ment). With Weber & Fields, however, she was a paragon of professionalism: prompt, cooperative, and very diligent.

The *Clipper* report speculated that Weber & Fields' signing of Lillian Russell was "a strategic move against the opposition management"; i.e., the Syndicate. In an effort to capitalize on Weber & Fields' popularity and cut into their business, the Syndicate had bankrolled the Weber & Fields imitators, the Rogers Brothers, in a series of musical farces and installed them in a new theater on Forty-second Street, the Victoria. Although the Rogers' entertainments were not burlesques of plays, they were never ashamed to recycle old Weber & Fields vaudeville rou-tines. For example, Weber & Fields' joke about predicting the 1890 Harrison-Cleveland presidential race on the basis of the campaign banners (Weber: "Ban-ners don't vote"; Fields: "But they show which way the wind blows") became the favorite line from the Rogers Brothers' 1900 show, with only the candidates' names changed.

The addition of Lillian Russell to the Weber & Fields stock company put their payroll close to $6,500 a week, not including the salaries of the owners themselves. Observers then (and now) wondered how they could afford it, given the small size of their house. Weekly gross earnings from the Music Hall (eight sold-out shows) were approximately $8,000. This, however, accounted for only a part of their income. Through the 1898–1899 season, Weber & Fields' road com-panies toured to a tidy profit, which was further augmented by the end-of-the-season tours of their stock company. Although the stock company did not tour in the spring of 1899, it set box-office records in August, playing *Hurly-Burly* for vacationers at Manhattan Beach. Weber & Fields also owned the leases for the shops adjacent to the Music Hall on Twenty-ninth Street, from which they col-lected substantial rents.

With the growth of the Tin Pan Alley music publishers, Weber & Fields saw the potential for further profit in the sale of sheet music and performance rights for the hit songs from their Music Hall shows. In September, 1899, they an-nounced the formation of Weber, Fields and Stromberg Music Publishers. At year's end, they sold their entire catalogue to one of the leading publishers, M. Witmark & Sons, for $10,000 plus a percentage of the royalties. In a revealing indication of their future plans, Weber & Fields retained the rights for stage use of their songs not only in New York, but in Boston and Chicago "in the event of an opening of The Weber & Fields Music Hall in those cities."

Thus they could afford an expensive renovation of their Music Hall—necessary to compete with the glamorous resorts opening uptown. The prevailing color for the 1899–1900 season at Weber & Fields' Music Hall was old rose: the chairs were upholstered in rose plush, the box seats paneled in rose silk, with rose-shaped and tinted enclosures for the incandescent lights. The trim was ivory and gold leaf. The center chandelier consisted of multicolored glass globes. Here was a theater worthy of the "Queen of Comic Opera."

So great was the demand for opening-night tickets that Weber & Fields decided to auction off all seats. For several years, they had been fighting a losing battle against ticket speculators, even going as far as to have them arrested in front of their theater. Peter Dailey and other company members served as auctioneers; all profits were donated to the victims of the recent, devastating hurricane in Puerto Rico. Jesse Lewissohn set the tone with a bid of $1,000 for two box seats in Weber & Fields' "Horseshoe Circle" (a joking reference to the Metropolitan Opera's Diamond Horseshoe Circle). Bids ranging from $500 for boxes to $100 for orchestra seats were tendered by Diamond Jim Brady, Stanford White, Boss Croker, restaurateur Louis Sherry, society tastemakers Mrs. Stuyvesant Fish and Mrs. Herman Oerlrichs, millionaire James R. Keene, and William Randolph Hearst, among others.

The demand for first-night tickets for Weber & Fields' shows was particularly curious when one considers that their productions were always weakest at the outset. Unlike the majority of Broadway shows then and now, the Music Hall productions were not polished in out-of-town tryouts before opening in New York. Weber & Fields firmly believed that only New York audiences could tell them what New York audiences would like, so they opened their shows "cold." The first-night program was rarely less than four hours long; inevitably, some lines fell flat, or a performer missed a cue (though this was difficult to detect, given the improvisatory skills of the comedians). The following day in rehearsal, Fields and Mitchell would go over their suggestions for cuts or changes with the company. By the end of the week, the deadwood had been trimmed, and reviewers consistently marvelled at how well the piece had come along.

Flaws notwithstanding, by 1899, first nights with the Weberfields had become gala events for the more daring members of New York's social elite. The gay and gaudy displays onstage were more than matched by the dress and behavior of the audience. After the final curtain, it took fifteen minutes or more for all the floral tributes to the performers to be brought up to the stage. At a time when two-thirds of the country's wage-earners made less than twenty-five dollars a week, attending a Weber & Fields first night was an exercise in conspicuous consumption (to borrow a term from Thorstein Veblen's book, *Theory of the Leisure Class*, published that same year).

For the members (and would-be members) of New York's leisure class, Weber & Fields opened their fourth season on September 21, 1899, with Smith and Stromberg's *Whirl-i-Gig* and a burlesque of *The Girl from Maxim's*. The setting was a hotel just outside the gates of the Paris Exposition of 1900; Russell played an adventuress, and Warfield was Sigmund Cohenski, "a wealthy Hebrew, President of the Matzo Trust," vacationing in Paris with his beautiful daughter, Uneeda (Irene Perry). (Uneeda was named for the "Uneeda Biscuit," which was a popular food among Jewish immigrants.) Cohenski is dismayed when Uneeda falls for a dashing U.S. Navy officer, played by Charles Ross:

> UNEEDA: The captain is my idea of a hero.
>
> COHENSKI: A hero! Is dot a business? A tailor is a business, a shoemaker is a business, but a hero? Better you should marry a bookkeeper!
>
> UNEEDA: A bookkeeper! I suppose you think the pen is mightier than the sword.
>
> COHENSKI: You bet my life. Could you sign checks with a sword?

Later, Cohenski treats Russell to an intimate dinner at a fashionable café. Fields played a snooty French waiter. Russell orders at length in flawless French. Russell finishes her order: "And you might bring me a demi-tasse." To which Cohenski adds, "Bring me the same, and a cup of coffee."

Russell made her first entrance on the Music Hall stage with an un-divalike little skip, looking much slimmer than in the previous few years (the result of her well-publicized fondness for cycling). Reviewers were, for the most part, pleasantly surprised by her performance, noting that "she had imbibed some of the ginger which her companions possess in such abundance." Critic Beaumont Fletcher was alone in his belief Russell was "an exotic that perishes when transplanted." In time, Russell would actually flourish on the Music Hall stage.

The second part of the program, "The Girl from Martin's," was a burlesque of a Parisian farce. The title referred to Louis Martin's, a chic nightspot near Times Square. As Fletcher correctly noted in his review, it is an ungrateful task to try to parody a farce. Edgar Smith, influenced perhaps by the more daring Parisian entertainments he had seen earlier in the summer, included several jokes that patrons found offensive. When the curtain opened to reveal Russell sitting in bed in what looked like a nightdress, wearing a plug hat, the audience gaped. When she stood up and showed herself to be wearing a low-cut evening dress, there were audible gasps, and outraged letters soon followed. Russell seems to have enjoyed pushing the limit, but Weber & Fields had no need for that kind of notoriety. They quickly deleted the offensive material.

Within a month, "The Girl from Martin's" gave way to a burlesque of *The Only Way*. Fields now admitted that even with her incredible box-office appeal, Russell could not replace Templeton and Fenton in the burlesques. "Airy-fairy" Lillian was a diva, not a comedienne; the impromptu banter and kittenish behavior that she developed on the Music Hall stage only emphasized her unique charm— charm that could not be suppressed in the service of a stage character. For Weber & Fields, she was certainly willing enough to try, but in the end, her fans would not allow it. For the next three seasons, she appeared only in the first half of the program.

Fay Templeton was unavailable, but Fields persuaded Mabel Fenton to give up rural life to play the title role in "Barbara Fidgety," to open in December. Smith's burlesque of *Barbara Frietchie*, a Civil War drama by Clyde Fitch, marked his return to top form. Fenton spoofed the voice and mannerisms of Fields' favorite legit actress, Julia Marlowe. Instead of a war, Smith substituted a battle between Republicans and Democrats for the mayoralty of Frederick, Maryland. David Warfield, as Barbara's mad suitor, forces his way into her home, and after a stormy discussion, is bodily thrown out of the house by the athletic heroine. Her true love, Captain Grumbler (Charles Ross, once again burlesquing the dashing leading man) arrives, but their meeting is interrupted by Mr. Fidgety (John T. Kelly) and a neighbor, Colonel Jagley (Peter Dailey). Kelly and Dailey played their role with broad Southern accents. Dailey's song, "For That They Made Me Colonel," was the hit of the evening, though Lillian Russell noticed that he never knew more than four lines of it. He never sang it the same way twice; often, the words he made up did not even rhyme, and then he would return to the refrain "For that they made me Colonel, tum-*ta*-tum." Audiences soon caught on, challenging him in the encores to come up with more impromptu verses. No matter what he came up with, it was always funny.

Weber & Fields played two Union soldiers with two big thirsts but only one nickel—enough for one beer. Fields wants the beer for himself, but he's worried that it will look bad if he doesn't offer to buy one for his buddy. He instructs Weber: "Ven I ask you vot you vill haff, you must say, kind of careless, 'Oh, I don't care for it.'" He rehearses Weber several times, insisting quite vehemently that Weber order something, and each time, Weber gives in, spoiling the scheme. Finally, Weber gets it right, and they disappear into the saloon while the burlesque continues. A short while later, they exit the bar, with Weber wiping his mouth on his sleeve and sighing contentedly. Fields blasts him for being a false friend. "Ven I ask you vot you vill haff, vot did you say?" Weber, all hurt innocence, replies, "I said vot you told me. I said, Oh, I don't care if I do." Several reviewers singled out this routine as one of the funniest Weber & Fields had ever done. (In 1912, Columbia Records recorded it and several other routines for their new 78 rpm flat disks). On paper or on record, the sketch seems more quaint than humorous. Yet a generation of theatergoers remembered it as hilarious.

Julian Mitchell's stage machinery included an elaborate version of the old minstrel show trick stairs built into the scenery. The elegant mansion's wide staircase became a slippery slide as soon as somebody stepped on it. Weber, Fields, Ross, and the ponderous Dailey all were victimized by it, much to the audience's delight. The evening ended with a medley of war songs, back in vogue thanks to the Spanish-American War.

Whirl-i-Gig played for 264 performance, the longest-running show on Broadway. Lillian Russell publicly declared that her time at the Music Hall had been the most pleasant she had ever spent, and that she would be delighted to return next year. Weber & Fields took the hint and signed her, and for good measure, Fay Templeton. The *Dramatic Mirror* reported that "the other members of the happy family . . . are so attached to this house and to each other that the very tempting offers they receive from other managers have no effect on them whatsoever."

On May 5, Weber & Fields closed their most successful season so far to embark on their spring tour. They hired a private train to transport a cast and crew of ninety, with scenery and costumes. They performed *Whirl-i-Gig* and either "Sapolio" (with May Robson) or "Barbara Fidgety," depending upon which of the original dramas had been presented in that city. The tour began with a week in Philadelphia, followed by two nights in Baltimore, and one night each in Washington, Buffalo, Toledo, Indianapolis, and Cincinnati. Their one-week engagement in Chicago earned them $21,000. After a night in Syracuse, they finished the tour with five nights in Boston. In these cities, they played to sold-out theaters two or three times as large as their Music Hall. One month on the road netted them more than thirty-three weeks in New York. Weber & Fields took note: the big money was on the road. But the Syndicate's control of a growing number of the first-class theaters across the country would make it increasingly difficult for Weber & Fields to take advantage of this.

Weber & Fields were, as a gambler would say, on a roll. In January 1900, they celebrated the twenty-first anniversary of their professional debut with a banquet on the Music Hall stage for their "happy family" of employees. On this occasion, the *Dramatic Mirror* lauded their careers as a triumph of the work ethic: "By talent, industry and strict attention to the smallest details of their business they have risen, step by step, until now they are the proprietors of the most popular music hall in America." At age thirty-three, Morris Weber and Moses Schanfield were the toast of Broadway.

At the gala first nights, when the enthusiastic Music Hall patrons clamored for speeches after the final curtain and deluged the actors with flowers, Weber & Fields waited backstage like proud parents and applauded from the wings. In part, this was genuine modesty in deference to their stars, several of whom had headlined their own companies before joining Weber & Fields. But this gesture was also a smart managerial tactic—"one for all and all for one," a show of generosity and humility that set the tone for the other company members. Similarly, even as proprietors of their own theater, Weber & Fields continued to share a dressing room. It was a space so cramped that they had to use the same mirror for putting on their makeup. (When Weber put on his "false front," he could not turn around. It was so cramped, Fields said, "we only used small words when we talked in there.") These were some of the ways (besides the generous salaries) that Weber & Fields kept their "family" happy.

Weber & Fields knew that for their all-star company to function as an ensemble, there could be no single company member commanding the center of the stage. "Never was another stage so cluttered up with high explosives of temperament," commented De Wolf Hopper, who joined the Weberfields for the 1900–1901 season. "Half a dozen stars managed by two other stars! . . . I do not say there was no jealousy; that would be absurd. Had there been no jealousy, there would have been nothing remarkable in the harmony. The astonishing thing was that everyone kept a tight rein and curb bit on his or her envy."[4]

What was true for the company as a whole was particularly true of the relationship between Weber & Fields. In its tone, as well as in its material, the Music Hall was a surprisingly direct expression of their personalities. Their harmonious relationship was reflected in the company's spirit of camaraderie and amplified by the press in stories about Weber & Fields' enduring partnership, their humble origins, and their happy family of stars.

But like any family's, the happiness of the Weberfields depended on the parents' own continued compatibility.

CHAPTER VIII

Music Hall Days (Part Two)

. . . There always seems to be a lot of mysterious feelings and adventures corked up in these two men, and of their intense joint life we catch only glimpses.

Newspaper article, 1904

AFTER twenty years together, the strength of the bond between Weber and Fields was something that they—and their fans—took for granted. Their close personal relationship had become a marketable commodity. In the early 1880's, when the young Weber & Fields were struggling to keep their jobs with Carncross' Minstrels, John Carncross had advised them to shake hands and hug after their knockabout routine to reassure the audience that it had all been in fun. Over the years, the well-publicized friendship of partners Joe and Lew added to their appeal, infusing the brutal onstage relationship of Mike and Meyer with an added pathos. The knowledge that the actors loved each other like brothers in real life somehow made the kicks and blows more humorous, even poignant. When Meyer choked Mike and said, "If you luffed me like I luffed you, den no knife could cut us togedder," the audience assumed that the sentiment originated with the individuals behind the masks.

If the deliberate conflation of their offstage and onstage personas had certain advantages, it also put a substantial amount of pressure on them to maintain their harmonious personal relationship, or at least perpetuate that perception for their "happy family of stars" and the public. Far more than that of most partners in business or on the stage, Weber & Fields' continued success was dependent on their continued friendship. Thus, they scrupulously avoided any public display of discord, limiting whatever disagreements they had to the privacy of their shared dressing room, or away from the theater, well out of range of their employees and the press.

In their apprenticeship, when Weber & Fields quarrelled, the issues were usually simple and petty, sometimes aggravated by the loneliness of the long tours, or the violence they wreaked upon each other on stage. The result would be a few days of the silent treatment. When conversation was unavoidable—in the dressing room, for example—they would address each other in the third person. Once, while touring with Gus Hill, a minor disagreement between Joe and Lew smoldered into a week-long silence and then exploded when Joe accused

Lew of hitting him unnecessarily hard on stage. After mutual recriminations, they decided that this was to be the end, and they returned to their room at Mrs. Adams' boardinghouse to divvy up their joint possessions. But who would get to keep the stage trunk they had shared? Fifty-fifty had always been the rule, inviolable to the bitter end. Weber borrowed a saw from a stage carpenter, and after arguing with Fields about how to determine the exact center, began sawing the trunk in half. As he watched Joe attack the trunk with the saw, Lew could not help but smile. He asked Joe what he was going to do with his half of the trunk, adding that the trunk halves would be equally useless to them both. Their sheepish glances culminated in a burst of laughter. It was a routine that was worthy of Mike and Meyer, but it contained a moral that for Weber & Fields was almost prophetic.

After four seasons as actor-producers on Broadway, Weber & Fields were facing issues that were no longer simple or so easily resolved. The phenomenal growth of Weber & Fields Amusement Enterprises meant that the partners had to divide the managerial responsibilities. Weber took charge of business affairs and scheduling, while Lew concentrated on production matters. Gradually, almost imperceptibly, the differing priorities of business manager and artistic director began to intrude upon their partnership. During the next four years, their friendship would be tested by competition from other stage formats and by their own changing artistic ambitions. Even the issue of finding a larger Broadway theater— something Weber & Fields started to do before they had finished their first season in the Music Hall—became charged with conflicting personal priorities. As leaders in the vaudeville actors' struggle against Keith-Albee and the Independents' opposition to the Theatrical Syndicate, Weber & Fields would find themselves fighting costly battles on two fronts. The stakes were now so high that petty personal provocations became increasingly difficult to laugh off.

With each new season came the burden of trying to top the previous one. Summer renovations had become an annual ritual, as essential as the writing of a new show or the signing of a new star. Befitting its new status as a Broadway institution, the Music Hall's Broadway entrance was aggrandized by the addition of two immense marble pillars on either side of the doorway. Inside, Weber & Fields reupholstered the lobby walls in green silk brocade with gilt trim. They replaced the rows of mezzanine boxes in the upper balcony with reserved seats, increasing the seating capacity by almost one hundred.

Attractive as the interior was, the little theater's cramped seating conditions created a level of physical discomfort that contrasted ironically with the mirth created onstage:

> . . . It is quite certain that many of the patrons wouldn't undergo so much to get into heaven. . . . To get to the seats one must squeeze and push and fight through the mob of standees with which—contrary to the fire laws we believe—Weber and Fields pack the passages of their music hall. . . . The construction of the building makes the temperature that of a Turkish bath and the air poison to the lungs. Should there be a fire or a suggestion of fire in this house during a performance—but there are some horrors *Life* prefers not to imagine. In spite of these things curious New

York gives Weber and Fields a patronage unequaled by that given any theatre in town.[1]

A fire inspector visiting Weber & Fields' Music Hall agreed that the crowding of the passageways was dangerous, but he found that its numerous exits made it "one of the safest theaters in the city in case of fire." In theaters across the country, the lack of adequate fire safety laws was widely discussed, yet nothing would be done until lives were lost.

On a tropical night in early September, 1900, Weber & Fields opened their fifth season with *Fiddle-Dee-Dee, An Entertainment in Two Exhibits.* As usual, the house was "packed to suffocation." Society reporters now accompanied theater critics to first nights at the Music Hall, describing "a hurrah, a jolly well met, happy family of 'first nighters' that you can't duplicate off Broadway." Among them were impresarios Fred Hamlin and Flo Ziegfeld (future partners of Fields and Weber, respectively), attorney Abe Hummel, Julius Witmark, and assorted commissioners, justices, and police chiefs.

Undeterred by the physical discomforts or dangers, they had come to see what many considered to be the greatest assemblage of talent ever seen on the popular stage: Lillian Russell, Fay Templeton (now returned to the Weberfields), David Warfield, Bessie Clayton, Weber & Fields, Charles Ross, and John T. Kelly, and a stunning chorus of forty-two. But the big news was the addition of another leading man to the all-star stock company—De Wolf Hopper.

With Peter Dailey's departure after the 1899–1900 season to star in a musical comedy, Weber & Fields once again turned to the ranks of Casino Theater veterans to fill the vacancy. For almost a decade, De Wolf Hopper had been one of the most popular leading men on the comic opera stage, appearing in such hits as *Wang* (1891), *El Capitan* (1896), and *The Charlatan* (1898). Yet he would forever be identified with an extraneous bit that he had inserted in the second act of the operetta *Prince Methusalem* twelve years earlier. The text was the poem "Casey at the Bat" by Ernest Lawrence Thayer, and for the rest of Hopper's career, there was rarely an engagement during which a few members of the audience did not insist upon a recitation, no matter how irrelevant or disruptive it might be.

Handsome and imposing (a solid six foot three), and justly proud of his rich baritone voice, Hopper departed from the self-important posturing of the typical leading man. His slightly self-mocking manner added a refined sexiness to the Music Hall stage; the perfect romantic foil for Lillian Russell. Like most legit actors appearing for the first time on the Music Hall stage, he was visibly nervous at the start of *Fiddle-Dee-Dee;* his entrance was greeted with loud applause, and, several patrons ("congenital idiots," according to the *New York Herald*'s reviewer) yelled "Speech! Speech!" the customary cue for a recitation of "Casey." Hopper graciously declined. Oddly enough, there is no record that Hopper ever recited his signature piece during a Music Hall production, even as a part of an encore or curtain call.

"Exhibit One" of *Fiddle-Dee-Dee* was set in the Rue de Paris, at the Paris Exposition, and at the Exposition's Swiss village. The Weberfields' preference for

Continental settings was in itself topical, a concession to the public's abiding interest in Americans abroad, like the turn-of-the-century New York dailies that included special Sunday sections with news of the Paris and London social scenes.

The curtain rose on a multinational crowd of revelers—the chorus—exercising their voices and their legs. An unctuous Irishman (John T. Kelly) sang of the woes of a man with a big pocketbook. Lillian Russell made her entrance as Mrs. Waldorf Meadowbrook, announced by the choristers in the proper comic opera manner, and sang of fashionable ennui in "I Sigh for a Change." De Wolf Hopper, as a nattily attired Wall Street magnate named Hoffman Barr, joined her on stage, and they sang a soprano-tenor duet, in which they spoofed the kind of roles they had performed in comic opera. Next, Weber & Fields became the victims of one of the Exposition's technological marvels, a moving sidewalk. With the help of a "Turko-Hebrew" magician (David Warfield), they decided to form a trust to fleece the good-natured Barr. Weber suggested that maybe they would be better off as a gang of thieves than as a trust. Fields replied, "What's the difference?" (a line that reportedly delighted William Randolph Hearst). An elaborate reproduction of the Exposition's Swiss village provided an unlikely context for the first of two Stromberg coon songs. Lillian Russell stood on a rock with moonlight shining upon her and sang "Come Back, My Honey Boy, to Me." Bessie Clayton closed the act with another astonishing blend of ballet and acrobatics, "La Danse D'Afrique."

Exhibit Two was a burlesque of the pompous historical drama *Quo Vadis*, which in music hall-ese was translated into "Quo Vas Iss?" In Edgar Smith's irreverent adaptation, the W.C.T.U. (Women's Christian Temperance Union) closed the saloon of Antium and threatened to burn Rum. Alarmed, the Emperor Zero (John T. Kelly) ordered the maiden Lythia (Fay Templeton) thrown to the wild borax. Her would-be rescuer, the strong-man Fursus, was Joe Weber; when deprived of his leopard skin, he was too weak to burst the chain that bound him— a chain of link sausages. Smallus (Lew Fields), an obnoxious Roman kid, was wise to Fursus and blackmailed him. Smallus' costume included a baseball bat and glove, and the team name of "Rome Juniors B.B.C." on his tunic.

Charles Ross played a debonair Roman, but he had to share the romantic spotlight with De Wolf Hopper, who played Petrolius, the lion tamer ("With the power of Croker / And my fame as a joker / I'm the boss and Chauncey Depew of old Rome . . ."). David Warfield was Hilo, the hobo-philosopher. Much fun was made of the original play's stilted pseudo-classical dialogue, and audiences found the juxtaposition of classical syntax and contemporary slang to be hilarious:

> SPOONICE *(Bonnie Maginn)*: My lord, I have brought you a ewer of bromus caffeinus. Thou must quaff it if thou wilt.
>
> PETROLIUS *(De Wolf Hopper)*: Nay, Spoonice, I am wilted enough. Last night's orgy was a peachus. I need not thy bromus caffeinus but anon I shall play the hose upon me.

Here in coarser form was the same verbal technique that Herbert Fields, Richard Rodgers, and Lorenz Hart used twenty-five years later, in Lew Fields'

production of *A Connecticut Yankee*. In "Quo Vas Iss?," Fay Templeton introduced one of Stromberg's most popular tunes, "Ma Blushin' Rosie, Ma Posie Sweet."
During rehearsals, a scrawny fourteen-year-old named Al Jolson came into the
Music Hall to try out as a chorus boy. Jolson was rejected, but Templeton's ren-
dition of "Ma Blushin' Rosie" so impressed him that he later incorporated it into
his repertoire.

In mid-October, Weber & Fields replaced "Quo Vas Iss?" with a burlesque of
the current season's hit, Augustus Thomas' *Arizona*. Hopper was Henry Cannedbeef (originally, Canby) the eccentric owner of the Aridvapor ranch; Russell and
Templeton played his daughters Sarsaparilla and Bonita. Sarsaparilla was married
to U.S. Army Colonel Bunjam (John T. Kelly), whose regiment was stationed
nearby. Weber & Fields were relegated to supporting roles; Fields as a German
sergeant whose comings and goings were regulated by self-given orders, and
Weber as his daughter Lena, an overworked servant in the Cannedbeef's household.

In the original, the Captain seduces his Colonel's daughter; in the Weberfields' version, he hypnotizes Sarsaparilla and teaches her to smoke. The sight of
Lillian Russell smoking in public—on stage, no less—enhanced her reputation as
an "emancipated" woman, and helped distract from the uneven script.

Having worked together for three seasons, Fields and Julian Mitchell had by
now developed a visual corollary for the Weberfields' brand of burlesque. In their
send-up of *Arizona*, they mocked the realistic pretensions of the original play's
rustic decor and costumes. In the second scene, for example, the interior walls
of the Cannedbeef's ranch house were covered with cowhide wallpaper. The ta-
blecloth was also of undressed cowhide, and all the dishes, saucers, and cups
were painted to resemble cowhide. Prominently displayed was a portrait of a
cow's head ("Old Bess"), wearing spectacles and a frilled cap. Loud Indian rugs
covered the floor. Only David Belasco, who was emphasizing realism as a new
way to dress up the melodrama, paid as much attention to details of decor and
costuming. Simultaneously, but for entirely different ends, Fields and Mitchell
and Belasco were using decor and stage effects to enhance characterizations. In
the decade to come, realistic details and effects would be as important to Fields'
musical comedies as to Belasco's melodramas.

Arizona's most striking production element, however, was not the decor, but
Mitchell's chorus line. The turn-of-the-century audience did not know what to
make of *Arizona*'s chorus: forty attractive young women, their faces smudged
with dirt, straggling onto the stage wearing shabby but tight-fitting National Guard
uniforms with strategically placed tears and patches. At a signal from the one
"soldier" in a neat uniform (Bonnie Maginn), the tired troopers snapped to attention and performed a complicated series of drill formations. Some Music Hall
patrons complained that they paid to see the famous Weberfields girls looking
glamorous, not bedraggled; a few clucked about the indecent ventilation of the
costumes. Fewer still recognized it for what it was: an innovative attempt to
integrate the chorus in the action of the play and give the girls a dramatic justification for their presence on the stage. From the start, Weber & Fields wanted
their chorus line to be the most attractive not simply by virtue of the girls' phy-

siques, but by virtue of their vivaciousness and talent. Shaped by their years in vaudeville, where every act had to carry its own weight, and influenced by the success of the Casino's chorus line, Weber & Fields wanted to make their chorus as much a feature of the play as the principals.

Like Weber & Fields, Julian Mitchell had been dissatisfied with the conventional usage of the chorus as a passive backdrop for the principals. In an era when the chorus was considered to be little more than a necessary evil of the musical, what impressed many observers about the Weberfields' chorus girls was their discipline and the precision of their routines, as well as their charm and good looks. Mitchell, like Fields, had a mania for rehearsing: "Our policy is to give the girls a typewritten copy of the lyrics and then . . . drum the airs into them by constant repetition. . . . It does not end with the first performance either."

Mitchell's pet peeve was what he called "the English chorus," as typified by the English imports that had lately become so popular on Broadway. In an interview entitled "Why the American Chorus Girl is Queen" in the *New York Herald* (January, 1902), Mitchell responded to criticism from the English composer Leslie Stuart, who had complained that the American chorus was too "restless" and showed too much "ginger:"

> It has been my experience that the American public want what has been termed the "restless" chorus and are opposed to the English variety, which may be termed the "listless" chorus. . . .
>
> They [English chorus girls] had practically little or nothing to do except to sing at the right time, and even then without pretending to interpret the lyrics. . . .
>
> The English chorus girl is pretty, after the English fashion, but that is all. She wears her clothes well and stands still, looking out at the audience to see if there is anybody in the house that she knows. A girl detected looking out at the audience at Weber & Fields' is at once discharged. It is not because she might be flirting, but because she shows a lack of interest in her work. . . .
>
> . . . This is my idea of what is called the "restless" chorus—the American chorus, snap, go, intelligent action. They are, in a word, a part of the play.

On stage, the Music Hall chorus girl was a full-fledged performer, not merely part of the scenery, or a moveable mannequin to model the latest fashions. Backstage, she was entitled to the same respect accorded the featured performers. When Fields overheard one of his male leads swearing at a chorus girl, he threatened to fire him unless he publicly apologized to the chorus girl. Weber & Fields' treatment of actors—not just big names, but every member of the company—was decidedly atypical in the days before effective unions or guilds. The Music Hall's egalitarian atmosphere nurtured Mitchell's aesthetic of the American chorus girl: ". . . . If I have been successful it is because I appeal to the intelligence of the girls and impressed them with the fact that their presence onstage should be understood by the audience . . . and that, above all things, they should interpret their songs so that the audience, even if they did not hear a word, could get the sense of the lyrics from the action of the chorus." Mitchell's deafness made him a good judge of how well the chorus "interpreted" the song.

It is difficult to conceive of Mitchell's experiments with the chorus occurring under the auspices of anybody but Weber & Fields. Most producers would not have been willing to spend the money to train and rehearse chorus girls, or to pay them enough to keep them once the women got some experience. In fact, Mitchell directed several Victor Herbert productions while working for Weber & Fields, but none of them elicited much excitement for their chorus work. Here one might discern Lew Fields' role as a creative partner and producer. Of their working relationship, Mitchell said, "I provide the pie crust, he [Fields] provides the filling." For Fields, the "restless" chorus was a way to integrate the wit and pacing of vaudeville with the dazzling scenery and costumes of extravaganzas. With the vaudeville bill as his point of reference, Fields wanted chorus routines that had as much snap and personality as the comic routines and song solos. It was a milestone in the development of his personal aesthetic, and a breakthrough for the American musical.

In his years with Weber & Fields, Mitchell not only redefined the role of the chorus girl in the American musical, he also redefined the role of the stage director. Henceforth, the stage director would be more than just a competent traffic cop and rehearsal master; he should also possess the ability to combine images, movement, words, and music into a coherent whole. In his Music Hall productions, Mitchell proved that the director of a musical could be the creative equal of the librettist and composer.

One English-style chorus that the American public did not seem to mind was the sextet in *Florodora*, a musical by Owen Hall and Leslie Stuart that became the biggest hit of the 1900–1901 season. The chief reason for *Florodora*'s popularity was a song performed by a chorus of six men and six women. The women stood in a row across the stage, tapped the boards with their parasols, swished their skirts imperiously, and posed. Aside from their smiles and twirling parasols, they looked like the "English" chorus as described by Julian Mitchell. The high point of the choreography came when the six women locked arms with the six men and they took a few steps in unison.

The play itself was the usual piffle about heiresses finding romance in exotic places (an island in the Philippines). Few pretended that the play was the thing anyway; Broadway swells such as Stanford White and Frederick Gebhard bought seats for every performance, but did not arrive until the second act, and left after the sextet's number. The women in the Florodora Sextet were pretty and projected a saucy charm; nobody expected them to be accomplished dancers or singers. The Florodora Sextet became a social phenomenon, and all six of the women went on to marry millionaires.

In December, 1900, Weber & Fields replaced "Arizona" with short burlesques of several hits of the current season, including *Florodora*. Naturally, they chose to spoof the Sextet, with Warfield, Weber, and Fields flirting with Bonnie Maginn, Allie Gilbert, and Belle Robinson. The women feigned complete indifference as the men bowed, stumbled, argued, and tried to outdo each other with exaggerated shows of gentility. Stromberg's parody of the song's melody was every bit as catchy as the original. And Mitchell had the satisfaction of ridiculing the "listless" English chorus.

Burlesquing the signature scene in a popular play was a well-established pattern at the Music Hall, but the *Florodora* material differed in several important respects. For the first time, the signature scene was a production number, not a dramatic or comic interlude. "Tell Me, Pretty Maiden" was the first hit show tune that was not sung by one of the principals. Yet, on the strength of this one production number, *Florodora* lasted over five hundred performances, almost twice as long as the season's next-most-popular show, *Fiddle-dee-dee.* Weber & Fields' burlesque of the Florodora Sextet became the hit of the show, and one reviewer correctly predicted, "The success of this song will probably show the management the advisability of having more work of this kind in future productions."[2]

For Lew Fields, the success of *Florodora* made it easier to justify to Joe Weber the increasingly large budgets for choruses and stage effects. It was also proof that a hit song and a show-stopping production number were as important as the romantic leads and comedians. In addition to the *Florodora* burlesque, "Exhibit II" of *Fiddle-dee-dee* included parodies of *The Gay Lord Quex* and *The Royal Family.* In the latter, Warfield as Queen Ferdinand, Fields as King Louis, and Weber as the Prince spoofed the banquet scene: the Prince's birthday cake exploded, provoking a food fight and other distinctly unroyal forms of behavior. As a Cockney manicurist, Fay Templeton did her best work since "Catherine," and her song, "I'm a Respectable Working Girl," brought down the house:

> I'm a respectable workin' girl and I've no time to dally.
> I'm none of your flirtin' actresses or ladies of the ballet,
> I'll give you a smack if you are an Earl, if you don't leave me go,
> For I'm a respectable workin' girl I'd 'ave you known.

The subsequent verses—about her escapades with gents at the beach, at a fancy restaurant, and at the Grand Opera—were not heard by the first-night crowd. Templeton was so certain that the song would not go over that that she did not bother to learn anything after the first verse, and had to repeat it three times when the audience demanded encores. Besides providing Templeton (and Music Hall patrons) with a respite from coon songs, it also expressed in a humorous manner the unfunny plight of the working girl. Her independence and refusal to be victimized echoed the new status of the chorus girls who accompanied Templeton on the Music Hall stage.

On the night before the burlesque of *The Royal Family* was due to open, Fields called for a company rehearsal after the evening show. This was not an unusual practice for the Music Hall when it changed its programs in mid-season, and the members of the stock company from Lillian Russell to the newest chorus girl usually accepted it without grumbling. On this particular night, however, Charles Ross declared that he was "up on his part" and was tired, and there was no reason for him to stay late. To allow Ross to miss rehearsal, however, would set a dangerous example for the rest of the company's stars. Fields told Ross to stay for the rehearsal or to leave for good. Without further discussion, Ross went upstairs to draw his final salary. With less than twenty hours until the opening performance, Weber & Fields frantically searched for a replacement for Ross. At two o'clock in the afternoon, Charles Frohman agreed to loan them Fritz Williams from his Empire Theater Company. John T. Kelly met Williams in a hansom cab, and for the next four hours they rode around Central Park while they rehearsed the part. Williams' performance that evening was flawless, and the following season he joined Weber & Fields Stock Company as a full-time member.

For the old-time trouper, the call of the playhouse—the near-sacred duty of the entertainer—was so powerful as to defy conventional logic and, sometimes, compassion. The old-time actors would not allow the vicissitudes of their private life to interfere with their mission—to divert their audience from their own daily tribulations. Shortly before Christmas in 1900, Lew Fields' seven-year-old girl, Frances, contracted diphtheria, then a common and untreatable childhood respiratory disease. In short order, it infected Joseph and Herbert as well, accompanied by scarlet fever. For several weeks, Fields would return home every afternoon filled with dread and longing—longing because Rose (who showed no symptoms) and the children were quarantined in the nursery. Lew could speak to his wife only through the closed door, and he could see his children only through the window. Late on the afternoon of January 8, 1901, while dressing for his evening performance, he heard a shriek from the nursery. He came running and broke through the door to find his wife holding little Herbert in her arms. The child was white as marble and spasming. Lew held the child while his wife phoned the doctor.

The doctor's diagnosis was bleak: he said that Herbert would probably not last the night, and that Frances would not be far behind. Lew and Rose stared at each other in shock. "The heart went out of me," was how Fields later recalled it. Rose finally took Herbert from her husband and gently suggested to him that he had to go to the Music Hall. He could not stay in the room and risk infection, she reasoned, and there was nothing he could do anyway. And Lew, dazed with grief, went to the theater.

There he was met by the callboy with more bad news. A telegram informed Lew that his brother Max had died. For the past eighteen months, Max had been convalescing in Denver, where the mountain air was supposed to be of therapeutic value in treating tuberculosis. Leah and the four children were still living in New York. Max was still young—a few months shy of his fortieth birthday—and with the enforced rest and change of climate, he had seemed to rally. His death had come suddenly.

Fields had lost the family member he was closest to, and his children were deathly ill, but he did not ask to excuse himself from performing that night. "I hardly realized what went on around me after that. It was the toughest performance of my life," he commented. "I had to go on stage and try to be funny." The audience that night found his antics as funny as ever.

The children confounded the doctor's predictions and recovered. Max's remains were shipped back to New York for interment. Lew probably offered to foot the bill, since he made similar gestures to employees and less affluent colleagues. It is equally likely that Max's widow, Leah, refused the offer. She had been vehemently against Max's last tour with Weber & Fields' Hurly-Burly Company. To Leah's way of thinking, it was Lew who had lured Max into the theater business, away from a stable career and the comforts of home. For the rest of her life, she insisted that "theater killed [her] husband." She forbade her son, named for Lew, to pursue a career in theater, and cut off relations with the Fields side of the family.

As superior a stock company as the Weberfields undoubtedly were ("the best burlesque company ever seen anywhere," gushed the *Dramatic Mirror*), they were also the recipients of some help at the box office from an unlikely source. The 1900–1901 season marked the outbreak of labor hostilities between vaudeville actors and theater managers, the latter led by Keith and Albee. The vaude-villians called their organization the "White Rats," after an English actors' union ("rats" being "star" spelled backwards). In response to Keith-Albee's exorbitant commissions and booking abuses, the White Rats staged a series of sick-outs and strikes against Keith-Albee houses throughout the spring of 1901. Not coincidentally, business at the Weber & Fields Music Hall, and at the theaters they visited in Chicago, Philadelphia, and Boston, had never been better.

In June, 1900, B. F. Keith and Ed Albee had brought the leading American vaudeville managers together in Boston for a series of meetings, including F. F. Proctor, Weber & Fields, Tony Pastor, Hyde & Behman, Kohl and Castle, J. D. Hopkins, and the fast-rising Orpheum Company (Morris Meyerfeld and Martin Beck). Between them, these managers controlled over sixty of the first-class vaudeville houses in the country. The subject was the creation of a professional organization to be known as the Association of Vaudeville Managers (A.V.M.), to be administered as two separate entities, one for the East and the other for the West. Although Weber & Fields and Tony Pastor owned only their own theaters in New York, their enormously popular touring companies (and the former's franchising agreements) made them influential forces.

Albee, who had spent the past year observing the methods of the Theatrical Syndicate, persuaded the managers that a centralized, efficiently run organization was essential to the continued growth of vaudeville. "Uncertainty" and "harmful competition" had to be eliminated. To offset the actors' loss of income, Albee pointed out that a centrally controlled booking office could guarantee forty or more weeks of bookings. Actors would therefore no longer need independent agents. For their services, the A.V.M.'s booking office would be entitled to a five percent commission from the actor. This arrangement would do away with the competition that enabled performers to pit theater against theater within a city, or the Eastern houses against the Western houses. Albee assured them that the organization was "in no sense a trust" or monopoly; no individual manager would put his own interests above that of the general benefit of the organization.

It is unlikely that Albee's assurances fooled anybody. Most of the managers knew that they could not beat Keith-Albee in the East or the Orpheum Company in the West, so they had little choice but to join. In effect, Albee was laying the

groundwork for the interlocking directorate that would dominate bigtime vaudeville for the next quarter century: the Keith-Albee and Orpheum Circuits. The
most vocal dissenter was F. F. Proctor, whose hatred of Keith and Albee almost
derailed the negotiations. Proctor refused to sign the final agreement in Boston
(Keith's turf), so an additional signing ceremony was arranged in New York.

Whether Fields accompanied Weber to these meetings is unknown. Neither
partner had any great affection for Keith and Albee; they had always preferred to
book through Proctor or the other independent managers. Weber, however, saw
no advantage to antagonizing Keith-Albee or any of his managerial colleagues.
The first public announcements of the Association of Vaudeville Managers included Weber & Fields on its roster. Meanwhile, the ambivalent partners quietly
redoubled their efforts to lease or purchase theaters in their prime markets: Chicago, Boston, and the New York area.

Down Broadway from the Holland House, where the A.V.M. was signing itself
into existence, a group of vaudevillians led by George Fuller Golden were meeting at the Parker House to form an organization of their own to protect them
from the managers. The actors considered the five percent booking fee to be little
more than a kickback extracted by the people who were hiring them, another
chunk of cash that came out of their pay, along with their agents' ten percent,
travel expenses, and the tips for stage doormen, prop men, and musicians. The
actors also feared that the A.V.M. would give Keith-Albee the power to apply its
infamous blacklist on a national scale. Starting with a core of eight members that
included vaudeville headliners such as Tom Lewis, Sam Morton, and the team of
Montgomery & Stone, the White Rats grew rapidly into the first actors' union.

For Weber & Fields, membership in the A.V.M. was a hedge. Business interests may have necessitated their early participation in the A.V.M., but their personal sympathies were with the White Rats from the start. How publicly they
should proclaim these sympathies may have been the subject of some private
debate. Lew, without Joe, posed for a publicity photo with the White Rats' "Star
Cabinet" (prominent vaudevillians) taken in the summer of 1900. Although Weber
& Fields' names did not yet appear on the White Rats' roster, they attended the
meetings. In September, at the White Rats' first testimonial dinner, Weber & Fields
gave $300, one of the largest donations.

By the beginning of 1901, a strike seemed inevitable. It was now clear to Joe
Weber that there was no longer any advantage to keeping a low profile. On February 3, Weber & Fields were officially initiated as members of the White Rats,
along with David Warfield and Harry Conor. To commemorate the event, Weber
& Fields gave the group the deed to a plot of land at Park Avenue and 147th
Street, valued at five thousand dollars, for the construction of a clubhouse. By
throwing their weight behind the White Rats, Weber & Fields set an example for
other vaude-legit figures: Sam Bernard, Edgar Smith, and Julius Witmark, as well
as the organization's first women, Lillian Russell, Fay Templeton, and Jennie Yeamans.

Thus, Weber & Fields became the only people ever to hold memberships in
both the A.V.M. and the White Rats. It was emblematic of their unique (and ambiguous) position in popular theater as actor-managers on the vaudeville and legit

stages. Weber, sensitive to the business ramifications, undoubtedly exercised a moderating influence on the partnership's initial response to the managers. Fields, less practical and more passionate by nature, pushed to act on the principles that he knew Joe shared.

Within a week of Weber & Fields' initiation as White Rats, Keith and Albee met with Golden and the White Rats' Board and offered to consider rescinding the commissions at the A.V.M.'s next meeting. Albee explained that the five percent commission had not been Keith's idea (true; it was Albee's) and that Keith had been against it from the start, but had been outvoted by the other managers (a lie). Besides, they had a constitution and by-laws, so no changes could be enacted before the next joint meeting of the Eastern and Western Association of Vaudeville Managers.

When no date was set for the meeting, the White Rats ordered its members not to appear for the Thursday matinee at Keith's theaters in New York, Philadelphia, Boston, and Providence. Albee met with George Golden and worked out a temporary truce, which stipulated that the five percent commission would be abolished immediately. The White Rats were jubilant, and returned to work.

But nothing changed. Keith and Albee were playing for time. By the beginning of March, the commissions were still in effect, and representatives of Keith-Albee had begun approaching individual actors and offering them large, long-term contracts to book through the A.V.M.. The White Rats responded by staging a series of sick-outs against theaters belonging to Keith, Proctor, Hyde & Behman, Percy Williams, Shea, and Lathrop. Singers and monologists showed up backstage with red flannel bandannas around their throats; dancers and acrobats limped in to deliver their regrets. The trainer of a dog act said his performers had cat scratch fever. The *New York Clipper* reported that the vaudeville managers "were greatly embarrassed" and that vaudeville patrons were complaining about the last-minute changes to the bills. Vaudeville patrons were not, by and large, sympathetic to the performers' strikes, any more than baseball fans during the Major League baseball players' strikes.

Keith and Albee used the newspapers effectively to stir up public resentment against the actors. Keith claimed that at the February 7 meeting he had promised to do away with the five percent commission. Albee even suggested that the strikers were mostly inferior acts who had trouble getting regular bookings, and that the leaders were political agitators. The White Rats responded with a statement signed by its most popular members. In it they described some of the real issues:

> The contracts offered by the Association of Vaudeville Managers are not equitable, yet they are the contracts which one must sign if one cares to work. The manager reserves the right to cancel the artist's engagement without giving them the same right. He further declares that he can cancel the player's contract if he (personally) does not like the performance. . . .

> [The White Rats' organization] is not controlled by Anarchists nor agitators, but by level-headed, God-fearing men, who, knowing their cause is just and right, intend to fight to the last ditch, and to that end, I, as a loyal White Rat, give my whole soul's support.

[signed] De Wolf Hopper, Joseph Weber, Louis Fields, Peter F. Dailey, Dave Warfield, John T. Kelly, Sam Bernard [and five others].[3]

The following day, Ed Albee threatened the White Rats' financial backers: "Some of the strikers of course we know are not responsible persons but then there are others who have invested their earnings and we will get them. . . . If it is possible, we will make them pay dearly." For vaudevillians such as George Fuller Golden, he was true to his word. Weber & Fields were beyond his reach.

Sporadic sick-outs continued until March 6, when the two branches of the Association of Vaudeville Managers reconvened (without Weber & Fields, it can be assumed) and abolished the commission. For the managers, the commission was a minor concession; the real issues were an actors' union and a rival booking agency. With the abolition of the commission, the actors proclaimed victory and returned to work. "We have got what we were fighting for," said a naïve Sam Bernard, "and I don't think there will be any more trouble." Meanwhile, Albee continued to tempt actors away from the White Rats with long-term contracts, targeting those he knew to be financially pressed or habitually scared of being blacklisted. Many of the new contracts included a five percent commission for booking.

By the end of the season, Albee's crafty behind-the-scenes maneuvering reduced the White Rats to token opposition. The naïveté of the White Rats and their inability to recognize Keith-Albee's duplicity were lessons that Lew Fields remembered when he and Weber took on the Syndicate during the next two seasons.

Practical jokes were as much a part of life backstage at Weber & Fields' as the ongoing pinochle games. Mixed in with the bundles of real mash notes that the Music Hall's actresses received every week were fictitious notes, such as the one to Lillian Russell supposedly from a denizen of Central Park known for his herd of goats. Stars like Templeton, Hopper, and Warfield became accustomed to bogus offers from famous producers, promising them ridiculously large sums of money to leave Weber & Fields. Naturally, when David Warfield received one such note from David Belasco, he ignored it. The real Belasco, however, was not used to having his offers ignored. At "Barbara Fidgety," Belasco sat next to Lillian Russell and exclaimed over Warfield's parody of the country boy gone mad: "How clever that man is! He has endless possibilities. . . ." After the performance, he went backstage and repeated his offer to Warfield in person.

Warfield had never made any secret of his serious ambitions, and Weber & Fields sympathized wholeheartedly. Had they not also aspired to be more than a variety act? But in leaving Weber & Fields, Warfield also abandoned comedy and song, and went on to star in Belasco melodramas, beginning with *The Auctioneer* in September, 1901. To Fields, Warfield's transformation from a Hebrew clown into an American tragedian represented an actor's apotheosis, the pinnacle of legitimacy, both artistic and social. After Warfield's crossover, Fields became increasingly dissatisfied with his own low comedy roles, and ultimately, with burlesque in general.

The opening night of *Hoity-Toity*, on September 5, 1901, was a long, hot, gala affair. To some enthusiasts, a Music Hall production was no longer just an entertainment—it was a form of therapy. As one reviewer expressed it: "No community in the universe, perhaps, has such a real need of healthful amusement as have the people of New York. . . . To such an exhausted, tried, careworn population Weber & Fields bring a tonic better in effect, quicker in remedial quality than all the learned doctors. . . . One evening's merriment at Weber & Fields' is worth more than two years of drugs to worn out New York. And *Hoity-Toity* goes on record as one of the best treatments that the good-natured managers ever prescribed. . . ."[4]

Continuing the trend begun the previous season, the extravagant production values of the first section made the burlesque (of *Diplomacy*) look weak by comparison. *Hoity-Toity* also had more of a plot than its Music Hall predecessors: an American billionaire, General Steele (De Wolf Hopper) brings his six pretty daughters to Monte Carlo, where they encounter Harvard Yale (Fritz Williams) and three East Side delicatessen owners played by Weber, Fields, and Bernard. The trio are in Monte Carlo to gamble with the fortune they earned by cornering the sauerkraut market. Lillian Russell was Lady Grafter, a wily society leader. The plot was flexible enough to include John T. Kelly as King Kazoo, an Irish cannibal, and Fay Templeton as Cho-Cho San in a brief travesty of *Madame Butterfly*.

With the able assistance of Sam Bernard, *Hoity-Toity* gave Weber & Fields their best comic opportunities since *Whirl-i-Gig*. The three sauerkraut kings argue about how to spend their money; Weber wants to sell sausages on the Riviera, but Fields and Bernard persuade him to open a bank. Weber protests, "But I know nothing about this banking business." To which Fields responds with glee, "So much the better; we would teach you." As penned by Edgar Smith, the routine lasted about five minutes; by mid-season, Weber, Fields, and Bernard worked it up to twenty-five minutes in length, the longest and funniest scene in the show. Evidently, audiences had not tired of Mike's and Meyer's shenanigans. Reviewers compared it to their parody of the "Skindicat," or their old pool table sketch.

Good as the comedians were, what drew the rave reviews was the sumptuous spectacle. The *New York Evening Sun*'s review of *Hoity-Toity* was subtitled, "The Most Expensive and Artistic Pageant That New York Has Seen." Will J. Barnes, the costume designer, was singled out, not just for the exquisite gowns he created for Lillian Russell, but for the way the entire cast's costumes fit the color scheme of the sets. (This kind of design coherence was unknown in turn-of-the-century musical theater.) For Julian Mitchell, *Hoity-Toity* was "a triumph of stage managing": "Imagine handling a company of sixty [more like fifty] people on the smallest stage but one in all New York and achieving spectacular effects worthy of the Academy of Music, while dances, groupings, marches and choruses follow each other in a succession that becomes positively bewildering." Mitchell's first act sets re-created the main boulevard of Monte Carlo. The second act took place on the Yale University campus, where a rowing crew takes Lady Grafter for a spin. While the audience watched, the scene changed to the river. Lady Grafter acted as the coxswain, and as she urged on the crew, large stereopticon

slides were projected, depicting the changing panorama of the riverbank and culminating in moonlight over the river. Gradually, the balance of the Music Hall
productions was shifting, with the emphasis on burlesque giving way to the more
elaborately produced musical portions—big production numbers interspersed with
comedy routines, loosely tied together by a plot. Under the guidance of Fields
and Mitchell, the Music Hall productions were shedding their vaudevillian qualities and beginning to take on more of the characteristics of musical comedy.

For a burlesque of Charles Hawtrey's *A Message from Mars*, Lew Fields
passed over the comic role and cast himself as the tramp inventor, a character
role. In the original, a selfish, nasty man is reformed by a visitor from Mars. As
usual, the Weberfields inverted the premise: the Martian, played by De Wolf Hopper, tries to cure Fritz Williams of his prodigious generosity. Hopper makes his
entrance via an explosion in the subway—a reference to the subway construction
that was shaking Broadway at the time with periodic underground blasts. New
wardrobes for Russell and Templeton had to be created after the first week to
replace the ones copied by Flo Ziegfeld for his production of *The Little Duchess*,
starring Anna Held at the Casino.

In an otherwise middling burlesque, the real surprise was Lew Fields' acting.
Stepping out from behind his Dutch dialect and makeup, Fields played the tramp-
inventor as an emotionally rounded character rather than as a clown. The *Evening Sun* called it "the artistic hit of his career." According to the *New York
Clipper*, Fields' performance "dispelled the idea that his ability is limited to the
mixing up of Dutch and English. . . . He gave as artistic a bit of eccentric character acting as has been seen on the local stage for some time." The *Herald* and
Dramatic Mirror also lavished praise on Fields' straight character portrayals, and
Broadway insiders openly wondered if Fields intended to follow in Warfield's
footsteps. Fields listened and believed what he heard. Many years later, Lillian
Russell described Fields' predicament: "He has greater talent than he has ever
had the opportunity to express, because the public always expects him to be
funny. He has a depth of feeling that, were he to have a play similar to those
which Belasco furnishes Mr. Warfield, would enable him to enjoy the same results
that Mr. Warfield enjoys."[5] The "discovery" of Lew Fields the actor was a decidedly mixed blessing. Over the years, it was not the comparison with Warfield that
gnawed at Fields; it was the knowledge that he had the ability to attain what he
considered to be true artistic legitimacy, but never the opportunity to prove it.
The knowledge would haunt him for the rest of his acting career. Periodically, he
would continue to insist that he had no interest in playing serious roles. Privately,
he waited for *his* call from Belasco. But while he was waiting, he gave stage
comedy a purposefulness and depth of feeling that it had hitherto lacked.

In 1902, Fields' immediate ambitions were more modest. Unquestionably,
Warfield's crossover showed Fields the possibilities in his own acting, but Fields
pursued it only within the context of the Music Hall's gradual shift towards musical comedy. He was tired of knockabout roles; after working with so many
accomplished actors from comic opera and musical farce, he wanted to try his
hand at something more sophisticated. To realize his ambition, however, would
mean taking roles that did not lend themselves to playing opposite a short, round,

excitable Dutchman. By replacing dialect comedians with comic characters, he was polishing the rough edges of a vaudeville specialty to make it fit more smoothly into the framework of a musical comedy. But he was also tampering with the delicate balance of his relationship with Weber, on and off the stage.

Joe Weber, who gave Warfield's plans his blessings, felt uncomfortable with his partner's artsy airs: "I don't think I am cut out to play Romeo, and I have my doubts what kind of a Hamlet you would make, Lew." This was in part Weber's cautious business sense—if it ain't broke, don't fix it. But there was an element of jealousy at work as well, aggravated by family members whose Iago-like whisperings played on the insecurities of the men who hired them.

Family members who had played a significant role in the rapid rise of Weber & Fields Amusement Enterprises suddenly began bickering with an intensity that threatened to destroy the organization more quickly than it was built. When Fields' performance in "A Message from Mars" was so strongly commended, Joe's closest advisors—his wife, Lillian, and his brother Muck—were alarmed. Muck warned Joe to beware of his partner's ambition to follow Warfield. The subsequent praise that Fields received for his character acting in the next travesties was proof that Muck Weber was right. Joe's wife, Lillian, picked up the refrain. To the jaundiced eye, it looked as though Fields was using his creative control of the Music Hall productions to provide character roles for himself rather than comic opportunities for Weber & Fields as a team. It may have been, as Lillian Russell described it, "nothing but boyish temper caused by listening to the foolish gossip of outsiders," but to Joe Weber, it looked as though his lifelong partner was leaving him behind.

Abe Hummel, Weber's attorney, recalled that after "A Message from Mars," "a marked coolness sprang up" between Joe and Lew. To their players and their public, however, the relationship between Weber & Fields continued to appear as warm as ever. In reality, their offstage public appearances were as artificial as their on-stage antics. Weber described it: "We were always seen together in the streets or in restaurants whenever we could be. It was a business necessity. We didn't want the public to get the idea that we were not good friends, and of course we kept right on using the same dressing room. That was for the benefit of the members of the company. Then they could only say to outsiders that apparently we were on the best of terms."[6] Their behavior resembled that of a married couple who know that their marriage is on the rocks. For the next two years, Joe and Lew would have no more face-to-face contact than was absolutely necessary. Under those conditions, it could not have been easy sharing the same makeup mirror every night.

The burlesque "The Curl and the Judge," based on Clyde Fitch's *The Girl and the Judge*, replaced "A Message from Mars" on January 2, 1902. It featured most of the male Weberfields in skirts and pretty Bonnie Maginn in trousers. Fitch's play was about the theft of a jeweled brooch by a "respectable" woman who turns out to be a kleptomaniac. In the Music Hall version, an old lady's false curl, carelessly dropped, was the cause of the trouble. Faye Templeton spoofed Annie Russell's role, as she had in "Catherine." Sam Bernard, sans dialect, played Mrs.

McKee Rankin's role of mistress of the boardinghouse. Her establishment was furnished in what Fields referred to as Louis-The-Fourteenth-Street style, including wallpaper that was printed with large red lobsters rampant on a bright green field. When Fields appeared onstage as Mrs. Tankton, the kleptomaniac, it took several minutes before the audience recognized him under his makeup, and reviewers once again singled him out for his fine character acting. Except for the scarcity of original music and the lack of a hit tune, "The Curl and the Judge" was considered to be the best since their burlesque "Catherine," which had become the standard by which all of their travesties were judged.

In fact, the thinness of the season's musical scores was symptomatic of another unfortunate behind-the-scenes development that the partners tried to keep quiet. Their composer and conductor, John Stromberg, had for several years been suffering from the progressively debilitating effects of rheumatoid arthritis. At times, the pain was so intense that conducting was impossible, and Stromberg would retire to his Long Island home for several days to recover. By the start of the 1901–1902 season, he was so incapacitated that he could spend only limited time at the Music Hall. Rather than interpolate the work of other composers— the norm among Broadway producers at the time—Weber & Fields decided to make the best of Stromberg's dwindling output. They hired William T. Francis to fill in as conductor. Towards the end of the season, Fields finally consented to an interpolation, though he did not look far afield to get it. The song, "When Mr. Shakespeare Comes to Town," was by the Music Hall's onstage accompanist, Jean Schwartz, who went on from there to a successful career as a Broadway songwriter.

The Music Hall season closed with a weak travesty of Belasco's *Madame DuBarry*, which starred Leslie Carter at the Criterion. Referring to the play's disputed authorship—Jean Richepin, a French playwright, was suing Belasco— the Music Hall program stated, "Any author who thinks he wrote 'Du Hurry' need not bother to enter suit. He is welcome to it." Broadway regulars recognized a dig at Belasco's colossal ego in the set decoration; every conceivable surface— walls, chairs, costumes—was covered with the monogram "DB", which stood for either DuBarry or David Belasco. Fields played the faithful servant, relying on his lines rather than on physical clowning. Weber's small part called for some acrobatic stunts. Bernard complained that his role was too small, and announced that he would be heading a company of his own next season.

Weber & Fields' 1902 spring tour began attracting attention months before the company ever left the city. The long-simmering hostilities between Weber & Fields and the Syndicate had reached a boiling point. In February, Weber & Fields proudly announced that they would not play in any Syndicate theaters during their upcoming tour. "Hey, Mike, We're Independents Now!" was the headline, as if their decision was the start of another Mike and Meyer misadventure.

The years 1897 to 1903 were not only the heyday of Weber & Fields but the Syndicate's greatest period of growth. In 1897, the Syndicate directly controlled fifty-three theaters; by 1903, they directly controlled eighty-three first-class theaters, including twenty in New York City and Brooklyn. Indirectly, the Syndicate controlled an additional four hundred theaters nationwide through booking con-

Joe Weber and Lew Fields in 1900. At age thirty-three, they were the owners and stars of Broadway's most popular theater. *(Special Collections Library, University of Southern California)*

Weber & Fields' Broadway Music Hall. The theater itself was on Twenty-ninth Street; they built the Broadway entrance for a more prestigious address. They depended on the lease money from the adjacent stores to help meet the huge payroll of their all-star company. *(Museum of the City of New York)*

The chorus girls' dressing room at the Music Hall. Weber & Fields' chorus line set new standards for beauty and talent. Members of the chorus were treated with the same respect as the stars. *(Museum of the City of New York)*

The Four Cohans (clockwise, at top): George M.; his sister, Josie; his father, Jerry; his mother, Nellie. They played in the first part of the Music Hall shows in 1897, then toured with Vesta Tilley under Weber & Fields' management. *(Variety Arts Theater Library)*

The Russell Brothers, James and John. Their characterizations of Irish chambermaids or "biddies" convulsed vaudeville audiences for over a quarter century. They starred in one of Weber & Fields' vaudeville companies in the early 1890's. *(Variety Arts Theater Library)*

"WHOOP-DEE-DOO."
Left to right: Lew Fields, Joe Weber, Lillian Russell and Louis Mann.

A SKIT ON CAPTAIN JINKS.
Left to right: Mr. Fields, Mr. Weber and John T. Kelly.

"THE GLAD HAND."
The first play in which Weber and Fields appeared at the head of their own stock company at the famous Weber and Fields music hall. Left to right: Mr. Fields, Mr. Weber and Sam Bernard.

"THE STICKINESS OF GERALDINE."
A skit on "Stubbornness of Geraldine."
Left to right: Mr. Weber, Mr. Fields.

"CATHERINE,"
One of the most laughable and popular frolics of the famous comedians. Left to right: Mr. Fields, David Warfield and Mr. Weber.

"TWIRLY WHIRLY,"

A FIRST NIGHT OVATION TO VESTA TILLY,

Scenes from Weber & Fields' Music Hall productions and some of their stars. *(Billy Rose Theater Collection, New York Public Library)*

Weber & Fields, as a pair of German Army deserters named Mike Schlaatz and Meyer Augsgrabben, made their entrance in an airship in *Twirly-Whirly* (1902). *(Billy Rose Theater Collection, New York Public Library)*

The "Poker Scene" from *Hokey-Pokey* (1912), with Lillian Russell, Joe Weber, William Collier, and Lew Fields. Russell's gown was studded with $150,000 worth of diamonds, pearls, and rhinestones and tinkled like a chandelier when she moved. *(Museum of the City of New York)*

On board the S.S. *Pneumonia* from "The Stickiness of Gelatine," a burlesque of Fitch's melodrama, *The Stubbornness of Geraldine*. Lew Fields is the hacker at the bass fiddle; Fay Templeton stands to his right. (*Billy Rose Theater Collection, New York Public Library*)

Broadway's biggest payroll: Weber & Fields' all-star stock company for *Hoity-Toity* and the 1901–1902 season. *(Special Collections Library, University of Southern California)*

The male Music Hall stars in a number with some of the most popular chorines. Left to right—Gertie Moyer, Lew Fields, Stella Moyer, William Collier, Bonnie Maginn, Joe Weber, Mabel Barrison, and the irrepressible Peter Dailey. *(Billy Rose Theater Collection, New York Public Library)*

Lillian Russell, David Warfield, Lew Fields, and Joe Weber don peasant garb to fit in with the Swiss village at the Paris Exposition, from *Fiddle-dee-dee* (1900). *(Billy Rose Theater Collection, New York Public Library)*

Fay Templeton, Lew Fields, and John T. Kelly, in "Du Hurry," from *Hoity-Toity* (1902) a burlesque of Belasco's *Madame DuBarry*. *(Billy Rose Theater Collection, New York Public Library)*

Marc Klaw and Abe Erlanger, the dominant pair behind the Theatrical Trust or Syndicate. The power-mad Erlanger dealt ruthlessly with anyone who refused his terms; for a brief while, Weber & Fields led the opposition. *(Special Collections Library, University of Southern California)*

Sheet music for "My Blushin' Rosie," one of the hits from the Music Hall composed by John Stromberg. Weber & Fields negotiated an innovative and lucrative licensing arrangement with publisher M. Witmark & Sons. *(Variety Arts Theater Library)*

tracts that gave it exclusive rights to provide attractions.[7] The theater owner or lessee who signed up with the Syndicate was relieved of the responsibility and effort of engaging attractions and the worry of local competition. Of course, the theater owner would have to give up a large chunk of his gross receipts, but he could offset this by giving a smaller percentage to the attractions.

Actors and independent producers found themselves being squeezed from both directions: the theater owners offered a smaller percentage of the gross, while the Syndicate's central booking office also insisted on a commission for making the booking. Erlanger unequivocally denied the latter charge: "This firm, and no representative thereof, ever exacted a large, small or any amount from any star or producer for making bookings."[8] Weber & Fields had abundant proof to the contrary. They had heard how James K. Hackett had to pay five percent to Klaw-Erlanger to get a route; and that Leibler & Company could not get a route for *The Christian* until they agreed to assign a one-third interest to Messrs. K. & E. David Belasco repeatedly (and unsuccessfully) brought suit against Syndicate members who insisted on exorbitant percentages as booking fees. Certain friendly and allied interests, such as the Frohmans and George Lederer, never paid anything. Whether an attraction had to come across, and with how much, also depended on their recent success and the general conditions in the theatrical market. From 1899 on, Weber & Fields' phenomenal popularity on the road gave them unusual bargaining power with the Syndicate. Even so, they preferred to book independent theaters, such as the Grand Opera House in Chicago and the Tremont in Boston. As Weber put it with characteristic bluntness, "What's the use of giving them a part of the money when we can get it all ourselves?"

Behind the businessman's bluster, however, were deeply held moral convictions. Although Weber & Fields were uncomfortable with the vaguely anti-Semitic tone of the attacks on the Syndicate by *Dramatic Mirror* editor Harrison Grey Fiske, they shared his outrage over the Syndicate's arrogance and duplicity. Beginning in 1899, Syndicate members tried to intimidate newspapers that printed negative reviews of their productions. The *New York Herald*'s critic was fired for interviewing Mrs. Minnie Maddern Fiske; when Norman Hapgood wrote a well-documented essay about the destructive effects of the Syndicate, Klaw & Erlanger withdrew their advertising from the *New York Commercial Advertiser* in an unsuccessful attempt to have Hapgood removed.

Every winter, Weber had the unpleasant task of going to 1440 Broadway to negotiate with Abe Erlanger for spring dates outside of New York. Erlanger was a squat, vulgar man whose graspingness was embodied in his big, meaty hands. Napoleon was his patron saint: busts, portraits, and memorabilia of the Little Emperor made Erlanger's office seem like a shrine. He was used to having his way, and he had a vindictive streak wider than Broadway. Even his partners (Joseph Brooks, Sam Nixon, and occasionally the Shuberts) were not immune to his bullying and deceit. Weber & Fields not only had the audacity to challenge his monopoly, but they had publicly ridiculed him and his colleagues in the Music Hall burlesques.

In January, 1902, Weber met with Abe Erlanger to discuss the spring tour. When Weber haggled about the Syndicate's booking fee, Erlanger remarked that it was too bad that Weber & Fields were so short-sighted. He knew that they were looking for a larger theater—like the ones he was planning to build on Forty-second Street. One of them, to be called the New Amsterdam, would have a roof garden and would be perfect for musical comedy. The other, the Liberty, was intended for Weber & Fields' Dutch *doppelgangers*, the Rogers Brothers. Think of what the Syndicate could do for Weber & Fields, if they would only consent to a "partnership."

It was the same strategy Klaw & Erlanger had used to win over the other leading actor-managers. In 1898, Nat Goodwin, Francis Wilson, and Richard Mansfield had made impassioned declarations about artistic freedom and principles, but all eventually yielded to promises of large amounts of cash, their own companies or theaters, and favorable routes. Mrs. Fiske was the only holdout. As Norman Hapgood put it, "In most cases, when the players who talked most about intelligence and freedom were offered more money, they became silent." [9] When Erlanger tried the same approach with Weber & Fields, they began to yell. In February, 1902, the *Dramatic Mirror* published Weber & Fields' response to Erlanger's offer:

> Weber & Fields are independent men, who have built up their great popularity by conducting their business in their own way. Apparently that way is not in line with the ideas of the Theatrical Trust. . . . When they [Weber & Fields] leave the city of New York this coming spring for their annual tour, they will play only theaters not controlled by the trust.
>
> Boston, Chicago and various cities will be visited, and the great burlesque company will not be crowded out of any of the places that it was the intention to visit before the rupture with the Trust occurred.

At the same time as their public support for the White Rats and their private backstage feuds, Weber & Fields were taking on the juggernaut of the theatrical world.

At least in the short run, their gamble paid off. After an SRO week in Brooklyn, Weber & Fields took one hundred members of their stock company on a private train to Boston, where they performed for four nights at the Tremont; to the Academy in Philadelphia for three nights; to one-night stands in Louisville, Cleveland, and Detroit; and to a week at the luxurious Duquesne Garden in Pittsburgh, where the orchestra seats were sold for a staggering $2.50 each, and the program stated that "the Weber & Fields trademark is in amusement matters such a guarantee as is United States Steel in trade or the Pennsylvania Railroad in transportation." By the time they pulled into Chicago for their final two weeks, the advance sales at the Grand were the largest in the theater's history.

In six weeks on the road, Weber & Fields reportedly grossed $142,000. With a payroll of over $7,000 a week and the expense of a private train, they probably cleared seventy to eighty thousand dollars for the tour. This was not the extent of their earnings, however. Not far from the Grand Opera House in Chicago was Miaco's Trocadero, a luxurious vaudeville resort along the lines of Koster & Bials' and Proctor's in New York. At the Trocadero and other theaters throughout the

East and Midwest, the Orpheum Extravaganza Company was performing *Hurly-Burly*, *Whirligig*, and other Weber & Fields shows featuring Nat and Sol Fields in the Dutch roles. Across the continent, in San Francisco, *Fiddle-dee-dee* was on its way to a run of over one hundred performances at Harry Fischer's Theater, with Maude Amber, Barney Bernard, and the Dutch comedians Kolb & Dill playing the roles originated by Lillian Russell, David Warfield, and Weber & Fields. From all of these franchise shows, Weber & Fields received royalties, although the exact amount and details of the arrangement are unknown. With the help of the Witmark Company, Weber & Fields were also able to close down several unauthorized productions of their work.

During their remunerative stay in Chicago, an interview appeared in the *Chicago Evening Post* with the multitiered headline: "Kings of Burlesque / Picturesque Personalities of Joe Weber and Lew Fields / Invented a New Comedy Mode." The newspaperman seemed impressed with the ways Joe and Lew did not fit the stereotype of the actor. Fields' language was "much above the average stage performer," and both were "shrewd-looking chaps, and neither wears diamonds." (Weber & Fields had evidently learned that gaudy displays of "ice" were inappropriate for sober businessmen).

The interview is both ironic and revealing in light of what we know about their differences behind the scenes. In one paragraph, Weber says that they have no intention of changing their style of entertainment. In the next paragraph, Fields contradicts him, and in his defensive and grandiose comments, unwittingly reveals more about his own ambivalence:

> Our errand is to provide amusement, not instruction, and it seems to us a perfectly legitimate one. While the entertainment we give is not educational, it is clean, bright and the highest of its class. We believe people will not tire of it for at least another year. When they do tire of it we are ready for them.

The more Fields spoke, the more obvious his ambivalence became to the reporter:

> Mr. Fields talked as if he rather deprecated the taste of the public . . . and intimated that he should welcome a change to something heftier. He gave no hint, however, that he and Mr. Weber, like their former colleague, Mr. Warfield, contemplated an excursion into Shakespeare.

Of course, no article about Weber & Fields was complete without mentioning their close personal relationship: "they are fond of each other, and each is authority for the statement that they haven't quarrelled once in their twenty-five years' connection." Rather than waiting for the reporter to draw the usual comparison with a "happy family," Fields invoked it himself: "Everybody is friendly, and we are just like a big family. . . . We all like each other and there is never more than the slightest difficulty." It was another brilliant performance by the parents of the "happy family."

Much of the rest of the interview was about the newest star to be added to Weber & Fields' company. In early May, while they were appearing in Brooklyn,

Weber & Fields had created a stir on Broadway when they paid $30,000—in thirty thousand-dollar bills—to manager Jacob Litt for the contract of a rising young comedian named William Collier. Turn-of-the-century critics compared Collier's breezy stage manner to that of George M. Cohan, and Collier's extemporaneous wit seemed suited to the Music Hall style. Weber & Fields needed someone of his stature to replace De Wolf Hopper, who was leaving to head his own company for the 1902–1903 season. With Collier came his actress-wife, Louise Allen Collier, and another hefty salary.

Fields announced that they had big plans for Collier: after he appeared at the Music Hall for one season, they would set him up in a theater of his own the following season. At the same time, they announced the return of Peter Dailey and the signing of Charles Bigelow, the principal comedian (playing opposite Anna Held) with Ziegfeld's company for the previous two season. The acquisition of all this high-priced talent (with the promise of more to come) represented another successful skirmish in the war with the Syndicate. Ziegfeld, a Syndicate stooge, had intended to star Bigelow the following season; Peter Dailey had become a major drawing card in Syndicate houses; Klaw & Erlanger coveted William Collier and his manager's theater, the Broadway. Weber & Fields realized that the Syndicate's monopoly of theaters and routes meant greater control over the stars and attractions as well. What would be the point of leasing or building their own theaters when they could not get the first-class talent and dramatic properties to fill them? Others wondered how long Weber & Fields could afford to outspend the Syndicate for actors when they had no place to play them outside their little music hall. Klaw, Erlanger, Hayman, *et al.* kept upping the ante, waiting for Weber & Fields to blink. For the last two years of Weber & Fields' partnership, every business move they made was in reaction to a Syndicate move.

Returning to New York in early June, Weber & Fields learned that organized opposition to the Syndicate was ready to announce itself, encouraged perhaps by the success of the Weberfields' tour. Led by Harrison Grey Fiske, Maurice Campbell (husband and manager of the actress Henrietta Crosman), and James K. Hackett (manager of two touring companies), the Independent Booking Agency had already established relations with two hundred theaters across the country and was arranging bookings for the 1902–1903 season. By August, they claimed to have agreements with 450 theaters. In effect, the I.B.A. was trying to organize its own chain. But by 1902, virtually all of the first-class houses were controlled by the Syndicate. The Independents hoped that they could make second-class houses sparkle with the reflected luster of the stars that played in them. Abe Erlanger reacted to the I.B.A.'s plans with characteristic contempt: "I think with thirty or forty million dollars, they would have no difficulty in establishing a rival circuit." [10]

Of more immediate concern to Weber & Fields was the deteriorating health of their composer, John Stromberg. In desperation, he had tried every cure anyone suggested to him, from carrying a lucky stone in his pocket, to sauna-style baking treatments. He still insisted on being at the Music Hall whenever possible, though this meant that on some days he had to be carried to and from his chair. Partway through the spring tour, he had to leave the company and return to his home in Freeport, Long Island. There was a tearful sendoff for "Honey Boy," as he was called by company members, at the Chicago train station. Working in pain and fighting a deepening depression brought on by his condition, Stromberg began composing the songs for the 1902–1903 season. Lillian Russell visited him, and he showed her a song he was working on. "Lillian," he promised, "I will write you the prettiest song you ever sang." His death, a few days later on July 5, was initially attributed to "paralysis of the heart." Several days later, it was revealed that he had committed suicide by poison while "temporarily insane." The poison—Paris green—was an insecticide that Stromberg had bought to use in his potato patch. His death must have been agonizing.

Finding a replacement for Stromberg would not be easy. The established stage composers were a decidedly uninspiring lot. At that time, the most prolific composers of comic opera and musical comedy were Gustave Kerker and Ludwig Englander. Their theater music was forgettable even to contemporary reviewers, and neither man was temperamentally suited to the Weberfields' brand of humor. Others, such as A. Baldwin Sloane and Raymond Hubbell, were younger but no more inventive. None of them ever demonstrated the melodic gifts, the wit, or the versatility of John Stromberg.

The only composer Weber & Fields could agree on was Victor Herbert. Modern audiences, accustomed to the sickly sweet MGM versions of Herbert's operettas, might think the idea absurd. Yet, several of Herbert's pre-1900 scores were written for comic opera stars such as Frank Daniels and Marie Cahill, neither of whom would have been out of place on a stage that featured Lillian Russell, De Wolf Hopper, and Fay Templeton. Moreover, Julian Mitchell's staging gave the Music Hall shows a scale and panache that would be the perfect showcase for Herbert's music. In fact, Mitchell had staged several of Herbert's comic operas in the late 'nineties, and it was through him that Weber & Fields had met Herbert.

At the time, Herbert was on hiatus from the theater, conducting the Pittsburgh Symphony Orchestra. Somewhat apologetically, Weber & Fields asked Herbert if he would consider taking over as conductor and composer at the Music Hall. Herbert graciously declined, although his reasons were not immediately clear. As a symphonic conductor, he had become sensitive to charges that he was a theater hack posing as a serious artist. The opposite was closer to the truth. Classically trained in Stuttgart and Vienna, he incorporated the European operetta tradition in the American musical vernacular. He also brought with him some decidedly Old World notions about artistic integrity and control. His insistence on the coherence and appropriateness of the musical score was but one aspect of his overall ambition to elevate the entire art form. As much as he respected Weber, Fields, and Mitchell, he feared that working in a glorified vaudeville house with the words "music hall" hanging over the door would damage his artistic credibility. Despite the Weberfields' best efforts, the stigma attached to their brand of entertainment persisted. For Victor Herbert, it would not disappear until they had closed the Music Hall and gone their separate ways.

With only two weeks until rehearsals were scheduled to begin, there was no time to search for a new composer. Weber & Fields decided to retain William T. Francis as composer and conductor for the coming season. When necessary, they would do what other Broadway producers did—buy songs from Tin Pan Alley to interpolate in their scores.

Stromberg had left three completed songs and notes for several others. One of them was found in his coat pocket at the time of his death: it was the manuscript with the music for the song he had promised Lillian Russell. According to Russell, the manuscript for "Come Down, My Evening Star" was covered with brownish spots, a disturbing reminder which she always recalled during her emotional performances of the song in the coming years.

With Stromberg's death, Weber & Fields had lost both a friend and a key collaborator. Its impact on the Weberfields was crushing, as if Harrigan & Hart had lost their composer David Braham, or the Princess Theater shows were suddenly deprived of Jerome Kern.

CHAPTER IX
Business Suicide

> JOE: . . . I believe it is a good thing to stick to success, and not go experimenting. . . . Our style of show has made us a good deal of money and a big reputation. Why shouldn't we stick to it?
>
> LEW: Oh, I don't know. I think the public has got sick of sidewalk conversation. . . . It has been overdone. . . . There is no acting in getting close together and talking into each other's face. . . . That's all right, but you must keep up with the times or you'll be left behind. . . .
>
> from an interview with Joe Weber and Lew Fields, 1904

B Y the time rehearsals for the 1902–1903 season began in August, Joe and Lew had worked out an agreement that formalized their division of executive powers: Joe would be supreme in all front office and business matters, while Lew would have the final say regarding productions. In practice, the arrangement had its shortcomings. Who, for example, would have the final say when the issue was hiring high-priced stars, such as the husband-wife team of Nat C. Goodwin and Maxine Elliott, at $2,500 a week? Fields argued that they needed the legitimate stars to compete with the shows being offered by Klaw & Erlanger, Charles Frohman, and the Shuberts; Weber pointed out that salaries were increasing yearly, and that they could not afford to keep adding to their already immense payroll.

By the summer of 1902, the obvious solution—move the stock company to a larger Broadway theater and raise admission prices—seemed too risky and expensive. Why Weber & Fields did not do this sooner is a mystery; they certainly had the financial resources to do so by the end of their second season. Their closest advisors argued that their unique style of entertainment would fail in a larger house. Actually, Weber & Fields had tried repeatedly to secure a larger theater on Broadway, as well as satellite stages in Brooklyn and Harlem. As far back as 1897, they negotiated unsuccessfully for the lease to the Fifth Avenue Theater. They tried to buy out Daly's casino next door, the Herald Square, and the Dearborn Theater in Chicago. At every turn, they came up against the Syndicate or those upstarts from upstate, the Shuberts. Between 1897 and 1902, the Syndicate assumed the leases of most of the available first-class theaters in New York City, expanding its local holdings from four to fifteen. The Shuberts picked up the leftovers—the Herald Square, the Casino, the Princess—while quietly ac-

quiring some choice Manhattan real estate. The only solution was for Weber &
Fields to build theaters of their own.

Twirly-Whirly reopened the Weber & Fields Music Hall on September 11,
1902, with the usual first-night fanfare and deluge of floral offerings, the air heavy
with tobacco and patchouli, the crowd a tapestry of laces, silks, diamonds, and
panne velvet. Returning favorite Peter Dailey acted as master of ceremonies, with
impromptu speeches at the opening and the final curtains.

Acutely aware of the latest trends in entertainment, Weber & Fields called
their new show a musical comedy. Set in Seville, it concerned a wealthy American broker (Charles Bigelow) and his widowed stepdaughter, Mrs. Stockson Bonds
(Lillian Russell). Mrs. Bonds invites the local nobility to a gala, but they turn up
their noses at the American *arriviste*. In their place, she invites a vaudeville
impresario (Peter Dailey), a mischievous monkey (Will Archer) and his keeper
(John T. Kelly, as a sailor), a Spanish opera singer (Fay Templeton) and a pair of
German Army deserters, Michael Schlaatz (Weber) and Meyer Augsgrabben (Fields).
The monkey, who terrorizes the locals with a seltzer siphon, was a topical refer-
ence to a recent fashion in dinner parties. Only two months before, Newport
society had been atwitter about the "monkey dinner" given by Henry Lehr for
Mrs. Stuyvesant Fish, where the guest of honor was "Jocko the Simian."

For their entrance, Mike and Meyer descended from above in an airship, with
Meyer dangling Mike by the scruff of his jacket outside the canopy. Their argument about how to land the airship, and later, how to liven up the stodgy soirée,
were the favorite scenes in the show. One reviewer gladly noted that Weber &
Fields had returned to their "old methods, using much physical force."[1]

If one of the identifying features of a musical comedy is songs that are integrated in the action and expressive of specific characters, then "Twirly-Whirly"
was a forward-looking effort. When Templeton appeared at Mrs. Bonds' party,
she delighted the audience with her parody of the hopeful chorus girl, who sings,
"I've a Particular Friend Who's an Intimate Friend of an Intimate Friend of Frohman." Lillian Russell, as Mrs. Bond, then presented her credentials with "The
Leader of Vanity Fair":

> You must take up the fad I start
> Whether it be racing or Delsarte
> Though it seems hollow, still you must follow
> The leader of the set called "smart."

Here was a character Russell could truly feel for. When she is snubbed by
the local nobility, she sadly observes, "the life of a society star is not a path of
roses. I envy the little stars up there. They can stay out every night and not lose
their sparkle." Cue the orchestra to begin "Come Down, Ma Evenin' Star," Stromberg's swan song:

> When from out de shades of night
> Come de stars a-shinin' bright
> I spy the one I do love, I recognize my true love
> Amid de tiny orbs of light. . . .

Show biz legend has it that on opening night, Russell broke down in tears before she could finish the song, overcome with emotion for the late composer. The truth was somewhat less dramatic. Actually, Russell had been unable to get through the song at rehearsals. As soon as the accompanist started the number, chorus girls began to cry. Julian Mitchell would say, "All right, pass that number today." The same thing happened at every rehearsal until the dress rehearsal, when Mitchell ran out of patience: "Now then, Miss Russell, we will have that song as you and the chorus are going to do it tomorrow night! See that you all sing it!"[2]

In their opening-night reviews, several critics mentioned how well Russell sang, particularly "Evening Star," but they use as much copy to describe her gorgeous gowns as her performance. Only the *New York Evening Sun*'s reviewer saw fit to mention her unusual rendering: "Miss Russell's voice shook as she sang the song and she seemed on the verge of tears. . . . As [she] sings it, it is destined to live for many nights."[3] For the few who noticed or cared, Lillian proved that she had soul as well as style. In that moment, she became the prototypical heroine of the modern musical, spirited yet vulnerable, singing from the heart and through the tears. Every time she sang that song, she remembered her last meeting with "Honey Boy" and the brown spots on the original manuscript. Perhaps she imagined a smitten Stromberg composing "the prettiest song you ever sang" as he waited for the poison to take effect. The image inevitably brought tears to her eyes and a catch to her voice.

Whether this was an intentional bit of "method" acting is beside the point. "Come Down, Ma Evenin' Star" was a coon song performed with the skill and conviction of a diva singing "Un bel di" or "Mi chiamano Mimi." Rather than the smarmy, condescending tone used by most coon singers, Russell's opera-trained voice throbbed with real emotion. The coon song idiom had come into vogue when the popular stage needed a way to disguise sentiment and longing. By investing the song so visibly with her personal emotion, Russell broke through the artifice and rendered it superfluous. In future years, she sang her trademark number with almost no trace of coon syntax. Producers and composers soon realized that they did not have to disguise their sentimental numbers or protect Broadway audiences from a range of emotions.

In late October, 1902, Weber & Fields announced the first step in their ambitious program of theater building and acquisition. They broke ground for the construction on a 1,700-seat theater in Boston's most fashionable shopping district (the corner of Washington and Beach Streets). Weber & Fields' Globe Theater was scheduled to open in time for the start of the 1903–1904 season. The theater's name was an indication of its owners' hopes and pretensions. At the same time, they also hinted that they were about to purchase a site in Chicago.

It was the start of an expansion program that would stretch their resources to the limit. In little less than a year, they would construct two new theaters (Boston and Brooklyn), break ground for a third (Chicago), purchase the West End (Harlem), sign four major legit stars and back five or more productions. At stake was not simply their own survival as independent producers, but the survival of the Independent Booking Agency. By defying the Syndicate, Weber &

Fields risked being cut off from the first-class theaters outside of New York. Competition for Broadway audiences was also intensifying: a new theater by Belasco on Forty-second Street, two new Shubert theaters (in addition to the three they already leased), and Klaw & Erlanger's New Amsterdam and the Liberty. At the same time, vaudeville barons Keith and Proctor introduced stock companies to play burlesque skits at their New York vaudeville houses. For Weber & Fields to stand pat would be fatal, but to expand meant a series of costly confrontations with the Syndicate that would in the long run prove ruinous.

Weber correctly foresaw the growing importance of profitable tours. The company's immediate survival depended on its road earnings, so that securing out-of-town theaters became a higher priority than finding a larger Broadway theater. Fields lamented the fact that the Music Hall's tiny stage was becoming a creative liability in terms of choreography, lighting effects, and stage machinery. True, Julian Mitchell had worked wonders on it, but how long would audiences continue to pack the Music Hall when Mitchell's techniques could be duplicated on a grander scale by Broadway producers with access to bigger stages?

The newest source of friction between Weber & Fields was in fact Julian Mitchell himself. It came as no surprise to Fields that Mitchell had become restless confining his directorial talents to the cramped Music Hall stage. During his first two years with Weber & Fields, Mitchell found the time to direct and stage three comic operas scored by Victor Herbert, as well as the spectacle *An Arabian Girl and Forty Thieves*, in which the stage effects included real water cascading into a moonlit glen, and a production number that combined the chorus and the corps de ballet. In 1900, Weber & Fields signed Mitchell to an exclusive contract, and for the next two and a half seasons, Mitchell focused his genius on bringing dynamic movement and the illusion of depth to the Music Hall's shallow stage.

Fields' love of lavish spectacle was fueled by Mitchell's creative vision, never mind the expense or the logistical headaches. Weber was willing to indulge them, up to a point, but they never could convince him that the Music Hall productions would benefit from a larger stage. Fields realized that he had more in common with Mitchell, at least artistically, than with his lifelong partner.

In the summer of 1902, after the Weberfields' season had closed in Chicago, Mitchell stayed on to direct *The Wizard of Oz* at the Grand Opera House. Mitchell and Fred Hamlin, owner of the Grand, were the show's producers. Although the libretto (by L. Frank Baum, the original author) and the score (by Paul Tietjens and A. Baldwin Sloane) were unremarkable, the show became the hit of the summer on the strength of its spectacular stage effects, notably the opening cyclone and the snowstorm that transforms the field of poppies, and the clowning of a pair of former minstrel men (Montgomery & Stone). So great was the show's success in Chicago that Hamlin and Mitchell decided to bring the show to Broadway as soon as they could secure a theater. Naturally, Mitchell planned to stage the New York production.

When Weber learned of this, he was incensed. Not only did Weber & Fields have exclusive rights to Mitchell's services, but Mitchell was now asking for time off to work on a production that would compete with the Music Hall—a production that many (including Fields) were predicting to be a major success. To make matters worse, Fields sided with Mitchell. Fields shared Mitchell's frustration at the limitations of the Music Hall productions, and he may have hoped to guide the Weberfields organization towards the Hamlin-Mitchell style of entertainment. Most of all, he feared losing Mitchell. He argued with Weber on Mitchell's behalf. Each accused the other of working against the best interests of the partnership.

At a meeting between Weber, Fields, and Mitchell after the last Saturday matinee in December, Weber exploded. Why, he asked indignantly, should Mitchell be allowed to get the best of it? Mitchell replied that rather than see Weber get the worst of it, he would resign from his employ. He then climbed the stairs to the third-floor office, informed treasurer Al Minehan where to forward his check, and exited the theater.

Fields threatened to quit on the spot. In the space of six months, he had lost his two closest collaborators. He missed several performances, reportedly because of a severe cold, but more likely out of pique. For the first time, Lew spoke seriously of dissolving the partnership. Family members lined up behind their respective relatives and amplified the discord.

The voices of reason came from an unexpected source: Weber & Fields' attorneys. Abe Hummel (for Weber) and Emmanuel Friend (for Fields) were inveterate first-nighters at the Music Hall, and they argued vigorously for the preservation of their favorite theatrical institution. They pointed out that Weber & Fields' assets were tied up in actors' contracts, theater leases, and construction projects that had to be honored even if they dissolved the partnership. In the end, it was business expediency—or the threat of financial disaster—that forced Joe and Lew to work out a truce. Hummel and Friend also recommended that family members be kept out of Music Hall matters in the future. Joe and Lew agreed in principle, but when faced with crucial decisions about hiring a manager for a new theater or licensing a road company, their clannish instincts continued to get the better of them. Insiders began to wonder which would give way first, their finances or their friendship.

In the wake of Mitchell's sudden departure, rumors flew up and down Broadway that Weber & Fields were quarreling. To squelch the rumors, Joe and Lew contrived a cunning public display worthy of a campaigning politician. The setting was the shoeshine stand that was across the street from their theater, and the main prop was a bag of peanuts. On a chilly February afternoon, they sat side by side on the raised chairs. Whenever they spotted a familiar face coming towards them, Joe offered Lew the bag of peanuts and Lew would take a handful and smile appreciatively. Broadway passersby saw the supposedly feuding partners chatting amiably and sharing peanuts from the same bag. Nobody lingered long enough to notice that Weber & Fields never once looked at each other ("I never looked at you because I didn't want to have anything to do with you," Fields later admitted to Weber). Nor did anyone wonder why the partners needed to have their shoes shined so many times. The important thing was, as Fields recalled, "the peanuts stopped the rumor that we were quarreling and that's all we cared about." On or off stage, they knew what their audience wanted to see.

Mitchell's last show at the Music Hall was a painful reminder of his capabilities. At the Garrick Theater, the audience for Clyde Fitch's *The Stubbornness of*

Geraldine had been impressed by a scene set on the promenade deck of an ocean liner. On December 18, the Weberfields christened their own vessel the S.S. *Pneumonia,* and treated their patrons to the burlesque "The Stickiness of Gelatine." Mitchell's reproduction of the promenade deck was regarded as more elaborate and detailed than the original. It was also a more complicated piece of stage machinery, rocking at various speeds as the story (or gags) demanded. As an English lord, Peter Daily smoked an immense bulldog pipe; when he took his constitutional on deck the ship listed heavily under his weight, sending passengers sprawling. Fields played a Hungarian violinist, while Weber retained his German dialect as Fraulein Krank, chaperon of Gelatine (Fay Templeton). Several reviewers also noted that the *Twirly Whirly* part of the show had shaped up nicely since its inauspicious beginnings. "Gelatine" stuck at the Music Hall for eleven weeks without a replacement.

Meanwhile, Weber & Fields busied themselves with plans for a major blow against the Syndicate. In late January, 1903, Weber & Fields were approached by George Blumenthal, manager of the West End Theater, a combination house at 125th and St. Nicholas in Harlem. Three years earlier, Abe Erlanger had ruined Blumenthal in a deal involving a proposed theater in Harlem, and Blumenthal had been waiting for a chance to even the score. He knew about Weber & Fields' anti-Syndicate sympathies and their booking problems. When the owner of the West End, Meyer Bimberg (affectionately known as "Bim, the Button Man,") hired Blumenthal to manage his new theater, Blumenthal proposed booking the first-class independent attractions that the Syndicate had frozen out of New York theaters. In short order, he lined up Weber & Fields, James K. Hackett, Henry Savage's Grand Opera Company, Mrs. Fiske, and David Belasco (who managed Mrs. Leslie Carter and David Warfield) for a total of twenty-three weeks of engagements in the spring and fall of 1903.

Bimberg's backers, however, were leery of head-to-head competition with the Syndicate, and when the stock market became erratic, they began to panic. Fearing a crash, they authorized Blumenthal to offer the theater for one-half of what they had invested in building it. The Syndicate tried to buy out the theater property, but Bimberg insisted on the stipulation that the contractual agreements with the performers had to be fulfilled. Meanwhile, Blumenthal convinced Weber & Fields that buying the West End would not only be a great deal but a way to further the cause of independent booking.

February, 1903, was a month for big announcements. On the ninth, Weber & Fields announced their purchase of the West End Theater (for $300,000), and said that they intended to spend $25,000 for redecorating and fireproofing. Leo Teller would return from Chicago to manage the house until September, when he would take over the Broadway, the new Weber & Fields theater being built in Brooklyn. A few days later, Weber & Fields also announced the signing of another comedian from the legit stage, Louis Mann. Fields was aware that Mann had a reputation for being pompous and fussy offstage, but Mann's skill at playing German roles was undeniable, and many considered him the most "artistic" of the German comedians. Weber & Fields planned to send Mann and his actress wife, Clara

Lippman, on the road for an eight-week spring tour in a revival of the farce *All on Account of Liza*. Blumenthal would manage the tour, and the first stop would be the West End Theater.

The momentous month ended with an exclusive agreement between Weber & Fields and the Independent Booking Agency. In return for booking Weber & Fields' spring tour, the I.B.A. would supply attractions for Weber & Fields' theaters. The I.B.A. now claimed that it was possible for independents to book time in every major city without booking through the Syndicate. In reality, many of their theaters were totally unsuitable for presenting first-class productions. Weber & Fields not only brought four first-class theaters to the I.B.A., but first-class attractions as well. Besides their own all-star company, they planned to create productions and touring companies for William Collier, Charles Bigelow, Louis Mann, and the dashing leading man Charles Richman (lured away from Charles Frohman's Empire Theater Stock Company).

After several years of skirmishes with the Syndicate, Weber & Fields finally made it official: they not only joined the opposition, they intended to lead it as well. In April, Fiske, Hackett, and Campbell acknowledged Weber & Fields' importance to the I.B.A. by appointing them to the organization's governing board. The appointment was more than an empty title; it carried with it the financial responsibility of contributing to the I.B.A.'s operating costs. Weber & Fields put teeth in the I.B.A.'s bite.

With Mitchell gone, it was up to Fields to direct the final burlesque of the season. Fortunately, he had the benefit of Edgar Smith's best script of the season. "The Big Little Princess" was described in the program as "a good natured kid of Mrs. Burnett's kid play," *The Little Princess*. Set in a girl's boarding school, the story afforded rich possibilities for the Weberfields comedians, most of whom assumed the garb of grade schoolers. Fay Templeton burlesqued the performance of the original's star, Millie James. Fields' performance as Specky, a Cockney slavey, was "touching and funny"; Charles Bigelow played Mrs. Pinchin, the shrewish schoolmarm; the outsized Peter Dailey was the precocious "baby" of the class; and Willie Collier's blue bow and auburn ringlets were delightfully at odds with his tough manner.

The quality of the ensemble performances in "The Big Little Princess" inspired the *Dramatic Mirror*'s columnist, the "Matinee Girl," to reflect seriously on the Weberfields' fun-making:

> . . . These players without exception give the most unique performance that is done in America today, and while some of us go because we laugh, there is a lot of thinking to be done when one sees this easy, apparently careless performance that has in it so much genuine art. . . .
>
> If Weber and Fields' theater was abroad, say in Vienna, and their names twisted into something unpronounceable, one could imagine the furor that America would make over them. As it is, we have them, they are ours and we accept them smugly and complacently. . . .

After fifteen years in variety, and seven in the Music Hall, Weber & Fields had become a Broadway institution.

On April 11, *Twirly Whirly* closed after its 247th performance, and the Weberfields embarked on their spring tour. The first stop was Weber & Fields' new theater in Harlem, the West End, for a week's engagement. It was the first time that the Weber & Fields Company had played in any New York theater other than the Music Hall. After the Saturday night performance on April 18, the company—125 strong—boarded a private six-car train and headed for Boston, where the Tremont was already sold out for the entire week. As a consequence of Weber & Fields' agreement with the I.B.A., most of their bookings between Boston and Chicago were one- or two-night stands, except for a week in Cincinnati. In Philadelphia, Toledo, Indianapolis, and Milwaukee, they consistently packed houses with tickets that were sold at "advanced" prices (meaning a more expensive scale, from $1.00 in the gallery to $2.50 for an orchestra seat). As usual, the two weeks they played in Chicago were the most profitable of all. Feeling flush, Weber & Fields looked over two possible sites for their Chicago music hall. Eventually, they purchased property on Michigan Avenue near Monroe, but the theater was never built, at least not by them.

As Weber & Fields' empire grew and their friendship crumbled, Fields' visits to the roulette table and the racetrack became more frequent. Gaming, however, was no longer the social lark it had been in the 1890's. Beginning in 1901, reformers in city and state government vowed to dismantle the Tammany machine and the illicit businesses that were protected by it. The flamboyant new district attorney, William Travers Jerome, targeted the New York City gaming establishments: not just the dives in the Bowery or Hell's Kitchen, but the gentlemen's resorts in the Tenderloin. In 1902, Jerome led a series of highly publicized raids on Daly's, Farrell's, and Canfield's, arresting employees and confiscating furniture, roulette wheels, and faro lay-outs. In each case, the patrons had been tipped off, but Jerome insisted that he would go after Canfield's clients, no matter how rich or famous they were, to secure an indictment against Canfield.

To make good on his threat, Jerome subpoenaed Jesse Lewissohn, Lillian Russell's companion and the man who had introduced her to Lew Fields. When Lewissohn refused to cooperate, he was arrested while at the races with Russell. Jerome also questioned other prominent businessmen known to frequent Canfield's, such as Reginald Vanderbilt, John W. Gates, and Eberhard Faber. For two years, the interest generated by Jerome's crusade made gambling stories a mainstay of New York newspapers.

Lew Fields was never mentioned in connection with Jerome's investigation, but his presence at various tracks and out-of-town casinos was often noted in the press. Rose, who was only now beginning to realize the extent of her husband's problem, found the publicity particularly unwelcome. She worried about what the neighbors would think. The Fields' home on Eighty-third Street (just off West End Avenue) was a spacious brownstone in one of the city's most fashionable neighborhoods. With their servants, chauffeured motorcar, and summer home, their affluent lifestyle was no more or less extravagant than that of the bankers, brokers, and attorneys who were their neighbors. Still, Rose was acutely sensitive to the low esteem with which many of them regarded her husband's profession.

"You must be polite to strangers," Rose would later tell her children, "because your father is an actor."[4]

Although Lew was equally sensitive to the possibility of public embarrassment, he did not—or could not—give up gambling entirely. The only effect of the crackdown in Manhattan was to force him to change his habits. He continued to play the horses, using a bookie who would visit him backstage at the Music Hall. He confined his casino visits to the summer resorts outside of New York, Canfield's Club House in Saratoga and Daly's in Long Branch.

Rehearsals for the Weberfields' 1903–1904 season began in early August under the direction of Ben Teal, whose qualifications included a falling out with his previous employers, Klaw & Erlanger. Despite his success as a director, Fields preferred to concentrate on acting and supervising the other productions that were going out under the Weber & Fields banner. In addition to their other theater holdings, Weber & Fields had leased the Bijou Theater, a block up Broadway from the Music Hall, for William Collier and his straight comedy, *Personal*. Earlier in the summer, Weber & Fields had purchased the American rights to an English musical comedy, *An English Daisy*, as a vehicle for Charles Bigelow and Christie MacDonald, the latter a rising young beauty with an exceptional voice. Fields believed that the libretto and music would have to be rewritten for an American audience. He began the search for hit tunes to interpolate, and he set Edgar Smith to the task of adapting the story.

In late August, Weber & Fields took a flying trip to Boston to check on the construction of the Globe Theater, which looked doubtful for its scheduled opening on September 12. The stage was to be one of the largest in Boston: more than fifty feet deep and sixty feet high, with a 210-foot proscenium arch, and a frame of 300 lights around the arch that could be turned on to permit a dark change onstage without lowering the curtains. Backstage, there were three storeys of dressing rooms (twenty-four in all), with hot and cold running water, gas, and electricity. To enhance the theater's acoustic properties, the Globe's architect, Arthur H. Vinel, designed the auditorium in the shape of an old-time speaking trumpet. In contrast to the gaudiness of other first-class New England theaters, the Globe was a model of restrained elegance, with not a trace of gilt or brass anywhere. In short, the Globe was everything the Music Hall was not: spacious, modern, technically sophisticated. Not surprisingly, it was the project Fields took the most pride in.

Curiously, Weber & Fields began their last season at the Music Hall with no more margin for failure than they had for their first season. Living close to the edge of financial ruin had become a way of life for Fields; the higher the stakes, the more personal it became. Weber may have let his partner's passion for the Independents overwhelm his own better judgement. (Years later, Weber admitted that it had been foolish to try to oppose the Syndicate.) With all of their resources tied up in their costly maneuvers against the Syndicate, Weber & Fields could only watch helplessly when the economy began to go sour in the summer of 1903.

In early 1903, the overexpansion and reckless (if not criminal) speculation that accompanied the growth of the monopolies provoked a panic on Wall Street that sent ripples through the theater world, much as the Panic of 1893 had done.

With two theaters nearing completion, one (the West End) extensively renovated, another leased, half a season's attractions booked for each of them, and a dozen high-priced stars under contract, Weber & Fields were in too deep to pull out.

Weber & Fields' last season seemed ill-fated from the start. Louis Mann and Peter Dailey raised $8,000 in the annual auction of first-night seats, but the opening had to be postponed for a week when Lillian Russell came down with tonsillitis. Russell's throat recovered in a matter of days, but Weber & Fields clung to their superstitious belief that the Music Hall season had to open on a Thursday night. Their superstition cost them dearly: a week's salary for the company—between six and seven thousand dollars—and a week's worth of box office receipts.

The delay also gave Weber & Fields' competitors (including *The Wizard of Oz*, which was still running, and the much-praised *Three Little Maids* by Paul Rubens) first crack at New York theatergoers, and many of them reacted to the Wall Street slump by becoming increasingly tightfisted. In Boston, James K. Hackett inaugurated Weber & Fields' Globe Theater with the Western melodrama *John Ermin of Yellowstone*, to an enthusiastic audience. In New York, a block away from the Music Hall, William Collier's new comedy, *Personal*, was already struggling.

Whoop-De-Doo, "a jumble of jollities in two whoops," finally opened on September 24. Both the spectacle on stage and the one in the audience lived up to the house standards. According to the *Dramatic Mirror*, the glittering first-night audience included "everybody who is anybody, as well as those who would like to be somebody." The wealthier women dressed to compete with Lillian Russell's extravagant costumes. The orchestra and box seats contained a stunning display of Paris gowns; many of the women wore their diamonds on the back of their necks and in their hair to show them off more effectively to those seated behind.

Russell confounded them all when she made her first entrance in male evening clothes, à la Vesta Tilley, then lit up a cigarette and sang a song. One nonplussed reviewer praised her "lighting and smoking of the cigarette . . . for true naturalism and ease."[5] Evidently, the idea of putting the era's epitome of femininity in male attire and allowing her to smoke a cigarette onstage made Music Hall patrons uncomfortable. When Russell reappeared "as her radiant self . . . in the costume of her sex," the audience seemed much relieved.

Once again, the setting was Paris. The curtain opened on a failing German beer garden owned by the anxious Herr Hoffbrau (Louis Mann), whose flirtatious waitresses refill the steins of the Heidelberg students and German officers for free. The setting evoked two of the previous season's hits, *Old Heidelberg* and *The Prince of Pilsen*, foreshadowing the operetta craze that would last for a decade or more.

Hoffbrau's guests include Peter Dailey as a ragtime impresario, and Carter De Haven as a gilded youth trying to become a reckless spendthrift. John T. Kelly was P. Dennis O'Shay, a New York subway contractor "enjoying the fruits of his crimes," accompanied by his pretentious daughter Bridget, played by Evie Stetson (an ample replacement, at least physically, for Fay Templeton). Much of the action satirized the philistinism of wealthy Americans, and their appetites for acquiring European art work. A student asks the Countess (Lillian Russell) whether it is true that the millionaire Russell Sage wanted to buy the Venus de Milo. True, says the Countess, "but he wanted it cut-rate because it was damaged."

Weber & Fields were, respectively, Michael Suppergreentz, "a grocer looking to invest," and Meyer Schmartzgeezer, "a financier with no money." In a variation on their "Skindecat" and "Starting a Bank" routines, Meyer explains to Mike how the stock exchange works. Hoffbrau recognizes the pair as potential suckers and decides to try to sell them his beer garden.

The hit of the evening was, appropriately, a new Weber & Fields routine that would be remembered as one of their greatest. The Countess (Russell) is interested in buying a marble statue of Roman gladiators in combat on display in the garden. Naturally, Mike and Meyer's inspection of it results in its destruction. To conceal their misdeed, they have no choice but to don short skirts and swords, paint themselves white, and pose as "The Dying Gladiators." Hoffbrau, who hopes to profit from the sale, instructs them: "Don't look so happy! You're about to be killed. Look dying! Look dying!"

The Countess, however, is wise to their scam and decides to have some fun with them. Inspecting the statue, she pinches, prods, and tickles the life-like figures. When they cannot suppress a sneeze or a cry, Hoffbrau pretends to make the noises himself. Mike and Meyer have difficulty holding their uncomfortable poses, and try resting whenever they think the Countess is not looking. The Countess is so delighted by the naturalness of the statue—"Isn't it grand, the expression of agony on the dying gladiator's face?"—that she invites her guests to join her for dinner in front of the statue.

Frozen on their marble perches, Mike and Meyer watch the diners enviously. When they think nobody is looking, they steal food from the table, but in between bites, they are forced to suspend their movements in increasingly ridiculous poses—fighting over a piece of bread, their cheeks bulging with food. Meyer spears a chicken with his sword, but before he has time to remove it, he must reassume his pose, with Mike apparently reaching for it. Seeing this, Hoffbrau tries to distract the Countess and retrieve the impaled fowl, but Meyer raises it out of reach.

Reviewers described "convulsions of laughter," and an audience "in fits." One critic claimed that the statue scene was so good that "few could adequately praise it." As for the music, William Francis' score was unremarkable; the two best tunes in the show were interpolations composed by the black ragtime masters Cole and Johnson.

What appeared onstage to be a harmonious teaming of talent—Weber, Fields, and Mann—was in fact bristling with hostilities almost from the outset. The frosty relations between Weber and Fields were still unnoticed, but Fields could not conceal his dislike for Mann. In rehearsals, Mann was arrogant and impatient. Backstage, he loved to tell of his lifelong struggle against the odds to become the well-educated and refined gentleman that he now fancied himself to be. In performances, he refused to share center stage with anybody. Since Lew Fields had attracted so much attention as a character actor, Mann tried to prove his superiority on a nightly basis: backing Fields upstage, crowding him, fidgeting while Fields gave his lines. Later in the season, the competition between Fields and

Mann erupted in a backstage fistfight witnessed by several members of the company.

Theater attendance worsened throughout the fall of 1903, especially in the East. The trade papers noted the hard times; by November, companies in Eastern cities were closing, putting over 3,000 actors out of work. At the Weber & Fields Music Hall, however, business was hearty as ever. The West End was also holding its own with serious plays, supplemented by Sunday concerts by Walter Damrosch and the New York Symphony Orchestra. In December, the West End presented Henry Savage's English Grand Opera Company, the first grand-opera season ever given in Harlem. Each week, they would perform two operas; the first week's bill featured *Otello* and *Carmen*.

For Weber & Fields' other ventures, the picture was considerably less rosy. Collier's *Personal* limped through a month at the Bijou and showed a loss. His next effort, a farce called *Are You My Father*, lasted six weeks with similar results. Weber & Fields sent him and a new production—aptly titled *A Fool and His Money*—to Boston to fill an open week at the Globe. With no attractions ready to replace Collier at the Bijou, Weber & Fields were forced to turn over the lease. By December, when Collier's company returned to play at the West End, Weber & Fields had lost close to $50,000 backing Collier. After agreeing on a buy-out fee, Collier released Weber & Fields from their contractual obligations and signed with Charles Frohman.

At the Globe, Weber & Fields had a modest success with *Captain Barrington*, a patriotic drama starring James Hackett. In bringing it to New York, Weber & Fields learned that what was big in Boston did not necessarily go over in New York. A similar fate befell their musical comedy, *An English Daisy*, after it played a strong month at the Globe. Weber & Fields felt certain that they finally had a hit. The story concerned two impoverished lodgers who are about to be evicted when one of them agrees to marry their landlord's homely niece. Somehow, the show's stars (Charles Bigelow and Christie MacDonald) end up exchanging their marriage vows in a cage with a real lion and lioness.

For its New York run, Fields added two more name talents to the cast: Templor Saxe and Truly Shattuck. He also tried to boost the score by interpolating a Cole & Johnson tune and three songs by a young unknown named Jerome Kern. For a variety of reasons, not all of them the fault of its creators, *An English Daisy* folded after only forty-one performances at the Shuberts' Casino, but not before giving Broadway's greatest composer his first public audition.

With ticket sales plummeting, any musical that did well at the box office was held up as an example. One of the most successful new shows, *Babes in Toyland*, opened at the Majestic in mid-October after four months in Chicago. Its producers, Fred Hamlin and Julian Mitchell, intended it as a replacement for *The Wizard of Oz*, only this time they commissioned a score by Victor Herbert. Mitchell's spectacle and Herbert's music more than compensated for Glen MacDonough's mediocre libretto. In scene after scene, audiences were dazzled by the visual richness of the staging and effects—the shipwreck, the Spider's forest, the street in Toyland, the Toymaker's workshop, and others. Herbert's score was, if anything, even more dazzling; songs such as "March of the Toys," "Toyland," and "I

Can't Do That Sum," (accompanied by the chorus tapping away on slates with chalk) gave *Babes* an enduring charm.[6] The show simultaneously looked backwards and forwards: its elaborate mounting harked back to *The Black Crook* and *Humpty-Dumpty*, but Herbert's lyricism and the integration of music and story set a new precedent for American musicals. To Fields, the Hamlin-Mitchell-Herbert production was the shape of things to come.

For the moment, he had to content himself with a new burlesque, only the second of the season at the Music Hall. The target of the season's initial burlesque, "Looney Park," was not a play, but another kind of popular amusement: the recently opened Luna Park on Coney Island, a cross between Disneyland and the old Bowery. The Weberfields' "Looney Park" was inhabited by characters from the Sunday funny papers: Little Buster and his dog, Happy Hooligan, Gloomy Gus, Lady Bountiful, etc. The *Times'* critic called it "very demented," which may not have been a compliment. Weber & Fields replaced it on December 10 with "Waffles," a travesty of *Raffles, the Amateur Cracksman*, Kyrle Bellew's hit drama about a society burglar.

For "Waffles," Fields insisted on copying without exaggeration the costumes and makeup of the original, while the props, lines, and stage business were burlesqued unmercifully. Fields (as the Cockney burglar) and Mann (as Captain Dedwood) were singled out for their character work and their mimicry: "Scratch a Weberfields," said the *Times* critic, "and you reveal an artist of the first water." By contrast, Peter Dailey and John T. Kelly apparently played their roles more broadly. As the French maid who confounded broken French with broken Yiddish, Joe Weber played his small part "with finish and restraint."

Was it simply the smallness of Joe's part that set the stage for Weber & Fields' final rupture? Or was it Lew's insistence on mixing high and low comedy styles that provoked another argument about the future policy of the Weberfields? The precise irritant was never made clear, but the disagreement that started with the production of "Waffles" led to the final breach.

No doubt the remarkably poor state of the theater business contributed to the tension. The trade papers reported failure after failure in the East, although business in Chicago and points west was close to normal. With touring companies losing money in the big Eastern cities, the one-night stands were booking two or three times more attractions than could possibly find profitable patronage. Naturally, the Syndicate tried to exert pressure on the managers of the one-night stands to exclude independent bookings. Many of these managers had been forced to pay a large fee to the Syndicate in return for a small number of attractions, so they were quick to rally behind the I.B.A. The most important of the one-night stands was the Stair & Havlin chain, whose popular-priced houses in the West and Midwest presented Minnie Maddern Fiske, Henry Savage's Opera Company, and most of the other first-class attractions bucking the Syndicate.

By Christmas of 1903, it was clear to Weber & Fields that drastic measures had to be taken. It was not simply the box-office slump, or the losses on the Collier and Richman productions and the anticipated costs of opening *An English Daisy* in New York. Weber & Fields, who were the only I.B.A. principals to control several theaters in addition to their own, were having difficulty filling the time at their theaters with first-class attractions. Business at the Music Hall was falling off. The idea of an extended tour—starting as early as March—seemed like the perfect solution.

The next step was painful but necessary. During the last week of 1903, Weber & Fields began negotiating a deal with Stair & Havlin. To raise some immediate capital (the exact amount was never disclosed), Weber & Fields would lease their three theaters—the West End, the Broadway in Brooklyn, and the Globe—to Stair & Havlin, with the stipulation that they maintain the existing policies and honor all of the bookings and contracts made by Weber & Fields. This included the contract with the I.B.A., which gave the I.B.A. control over Weber & Fields' houses for booking purposes for five years. In return, Stair & Havlin agreed to book Weber & Fields' extended spring tour into its Midwestern and Western houses for a modest percentage of the gross receipts.

The announcement of the deal in early January, with all it implied about the fortunes of Weber & Fields Enterprises, was chilling news to the members of the I.B.A., who had come to regard Weber & Fields as all but invincible. Nevertheless, Weber & Fields struck a defiant pose: "This does not mean that we are going to abandon all theatrical ventures except the Music Hall. Not by any means. We are in the business and we have no idea of getting out. . . . In fact, we are at this very time seriously thinking of taking up offers to build theatres in several parts of the country. This transaction was a peculiarly commercial one. Sentiment or change of policy was not concerned with it. We had these houses and could not use them to the best advantage. . . ."[7] Unfortunately, they were only jumping out of the frying pan. Between the inking of the deal and its announcement, a tragedy of shocking proportions shook the theater world; no one more than Weber & Fields.

Only once or twice a year was there a crowd like the one that jammed Chicago's newest theater, the Iroquois, on December 30, 1903. The occasion was the holiday matinee of *Mr. Bluebeard*, a musical extravaganza starring the great solo clown Eddie Foy. The Iroquois was Klaw & Erlanger's Midwestern flagship. In their advertisements, Klaw & Erlanger boasted that the Iroquois was "absolutely fireproof," a claim unrivalled for sheer hubris until the sinking of the "unsinkable" *Titanic* eight years later.

Into a theater built for 1,700, the Iroquois' happy managers packed approximately 2,000 people—mostly mothers and aunts with children, working girls with their chums, and college kids. The three hundred standees were herded to the rear of the orchestra seats and the first balcony. On the other side of the footlights were the 300 members of the extravaganza company, an equivalent number of backdrops and flies, and a "revolutionary" system of electric lighting. Between the audience and the stage was an immense asbestos curtain that could be lowered in seconds with the push of a button.

Early in the second act, a spark from one of the new electric floodlights ignited a piece of gauze scenery. The muslin border of the big drop acted like a fuse, carrying the fire from drops to flies to draperies. Within seconds, fingers of flame reached around the proscenium arch. Hearing screams and smelling smoke,

Eddie Foy came on stage clad only in tights and greasepaint and appealed to the audience for calm: "Don't get excited. Don't stampede. It's all right." He signalled to the assistant stage manager to lower the fire curtain, then called to the orchestra leader: "For God's sake, play and keep on playing!" Though the entire set above him was ablaze, the orchestra leader raised his baton and the few remaining musicians gamely played. Between two and three hundred people from the orchestra seats made it to a side exit before the roar of the fire, the stamp of rushing feet, and women's screams drowned out the music.

Backstage, somebody opened a door, letting in a gust of cold air that swept the flames into the audience. The asbestos curtain, billowing in the draught, came down only a few feet before it caught on a scenery rig. The switchboard exploded, leaving the house dark except for the flames. Slivers of glass rained down as the first of three skylights shattered, creating a chimney of hot gas and fire that incinerated scores of people in their tracks. Panic reigned; many jumped from the first balcony to the floor, their landing cushioned by the dead and dying. In the balcony and the galleries, the first to arrive at the exit doors found them locked. Those who succeeded in breaking through ended up forty or fifty feet above the alleyway on narrow iron platforms without any stairs or ladders. Bodies piled up like cordwood, twenty feet high, blocking the exits, spilling back into the aisles. In the upper galleries, many of the victims apparently gave up and never left their seats.

In less than fifteen minutes, over six hundred theatergoers were burned or trampled to death, and another four hundred injured. Shock waves of horror and indignation swept through the country. City administrators ordered thorough inspections of all theaters to check for the kinds of flagrant violations that had caused the Iroquois disaster: exposed wiring, narrow aisles, flammable scenery, inadequate fire exits, too many standees. New safety codes were hurriedly drafted and passed into law. In every city, theaters were closed down, some never to reopen. Within days of the fire, five thousand Chicagoans had been thrown out of work by the theater closings; similar numbers became jobless in Boston and the other major Eastern cities. Theater attendance, already slumping in the wake of the Wall Street panic, fell to its lowest level in a decade.

The conditions that led to the Iroquois inferno were widespread, but the public outrage focused on the Syndicate—specifically, on its unprepossessing leader, Abe Erlanger. Across the country, newspaper editorials denounced Erlanger and his money-hungry theatrical trust; the Syndicate's theater managers were accused of disregarding the safety of their patrons to save on construction and maintenance costs. *Life* magazine ran a vicious cartoon by their artist-critic James Metcalfe, showing a bloated Erlanger with the burning Iroquois theater behind him.[8] (It was Metcalfe who earlier in the year had complained about the crowded, unsafe conditions at the Weber & Fields Music Hall.)

The Syndicate's theaters were not in fact worse than many others. But Erlanger's reputation made him a likely villain, and the recent, highly publicized abuses of other trusts—beef, railroads, shipbuilding—fanned the flames of public resentment against the Theatrical Trust. As a result of the press' aggressive anti-Syndicate campaign, the Syndicate's influence in the theater world was seriously damaged.

Investors began looking for a viable alternative to Erlanger's monopoly. The Shuberts, who now positioned themselves as trust-busters and righteous under-dogs, saw their opportunity, and through their well-connected attorney, Samuel Untermeyer, began courting Wall Streeters. New theaters had to be built, and many of them would sign with the Shuberts.

Ironically, the electric spark that eventually brought about the downfall of the Syndicate also was responsible for the demise of the Weber & Fields Music Hall. Like the mayors of other cities, Mayor McClellan of New York ordered im-mediate inspections of every theater and music hall (sixty-two in all). McClellan's relative restraint was a tacit recognition of Broadway's increased economic im-portance: instead of closing down and fining violators, he encouraged "voluntary" compliance. Theater owners would have thirty days to begin to remedy viola-tions—install fire walls and asbestos curtains, widen aisles, add fire exits, and create unobstructed alleyways on both sides of the theater.

By the end of the first week of 1904, Weber & Fields knew that they would have to rebuild their music hall, or abandon it. Not surprisingly, Weber wanted to rebuild and retrench; Fields saw it as the logical time to move into a larger theater and implement his new ideas about musical productions. Two years of personal jealousies and feuding left them with little inclination to compromise. The only thing they seemed to be able to agree on was that they would finish the season before announcing their split. Until then, their plans had to remain a se-cret.

With the imminent closing of the Music Hall, and the poor business condi-tions in the East, Weber & Fields decided that their best bet was to start their spring tour early—two months early. The timing of the Stair & Havlin deal now seemed especially fortuitous. With their help, Weber & Fields were able to put together a tour of the West and Midwest, to begin in San Francisco in early February. The good news was that Charlie Ross and Mabel Fenton had agreed to rejoin the company for the tour, and that "Waffles" was to be replaced by the burlesque of *Catherine*, with Fenton playing the role originated by Fay Temple-ton.

At the evening performance on January 30, the Weberfields and their fans bid a rousing farewell to the Music Hall. Peter Dailey ad-libbed a half dozen new verses to his song to express his sorrow at leaving Broadway and the heaps of slush and garbage that encumbered it. Fields improvised a transcontinental dance, and Weber told sleeping-car jokes. Louis Mann got his German dialect tied up in a hard knot trying to tell how to go to the West Coast from New York. During the curtain calls, cartloads of flowers and presents were handed over the foot-lights. Afterwards, company members and friends gathered in the café down-stairs, where the banquet lasted until sunrise.

Company members and the rest of Broadway thought that the purpose of the tour was to allow time for renovating the Music Hall or procuring a new theater. Joe and Lew knew otherwise. Their attorneys had already begun discuss-ing how their assets were to be divided. At some point late in the evening, Fields (a sentimental guy) may have slipped away from the festivities to take one last tour of the little theater: from the dressing rooms behind the bar to a passageway, climbing the narrow stairway up to the left-hand side of the stage; crossing the shallow stage, its scenery already struck; staring out at the auditorium and remembering how shabby it had looked when he saw it for the first time eight years before.

Weber & Fields launched their farewell tour in San Francisco, the city where fourteen years earlier they had assembled their first stock company. This was Lillian Russell's third trip to San Francisco, and she was greeted like visiting royalty. After a week of capacity business at the Grand Opera House, Weber & Fields felt confident that they would quickly recover their season's losses. San Francisco showed no signs of an economic slump. The turmoil of Broadway seemed distant indeed.

Back at 1440 Broadway, the news for Abe Erlanger since the Iroquois Theater fire had all been bad—until he learned of Weber & Fields' deal with the Stair & Havlin chain. By relinquishing control of their theaters, Weber & Fields had in effect placed their immediate future in the hands of Stair & Havlin. Erlanger saw his opportunity, and pounced.

When the Syndicate had tried to muscle in on the one-night stands in the major Midwestern and Western cities, Stair & Havlin retaliated by booking first-class attractions, including many of the Independents. Having failed to intimidate Stair & Havlin with a frontal assault, Erlanger was suddenly quite eager to work out a compromise. He waited until Weber & Fields were 3,000 miles away, and then made his proposal to Messrs. Stair and Havlin. In the parlance of the day, it was known as a pooling agreement: the Syndicate would cease to compete with Stair & Havlin and would guarantee them control of the popular-priced field. The Syndicate would furnish Stair & Havlin with attractions that were "suitable" to its houses. In return, the popular-priced circuit had to agree to discontinue the presentation of first-class attractions, effective immediately.[9] One can almost picture Abe Erlanger rubbing his meaty hands together with anticipatory glee. With one masterful stroke, he was able to derail Weber & Fields' tour and cripple the Independent Booking Agency.

Weber & Fields were in the second week of their San Francisco engagement when they learned that their entire route had been cancelled, with the exception of their engagements at the Broadway, Globe, and West End late in the spring. Several of the Western theaters were suddenly closed for violating the new fire codes, while the managers of several other theaters decided to perform required renovations during the time Weber & Fields were scheduled to appear. Abe Erlanger's hand in these sudden closings was not hard to discern; he was hoping to force Weber & Fields to come to terms. Through his maneuvering, Weber & Fields were stranded three thousand miles from Broadway with a company payroll of over $7,000 a week and eight weeks of open dates to fill.

While Fields pored over maps and railroad timetables, Weber exchanged telegrams with almost every sagebrush opera house and music hall in the Southwest. An association of West Coast theater managers similar to the I.B.A. offered its theater in Los Angeles, but L.A. was still a backwater town in those days. From Denver and Omaha came word that other independents would welcome the Weberfields' bookings.

Between Los Angeles and Denver was a two-day, 1,400-mile jump, and only four real theaters, all Syndicate-controlled. Weber & Fields considered buying a tent (something the Shuberts did for Sarah Bernhardt two years later) but could not decide on where to pitch it. Within days, every bill-poster, advance man, and promoter in the West knew that the legendary Weber & Fields Company had open dates. In Los Angeles, a booster from Albuquerque, New Mexico, told Weber about a new theater in town, and offered a 60–40 split. Weber was suspicious—the total population of the town was under ten thousand—so he insisted on a $3,000 guarantee, enough to cover the expenses of the jump to Denver. The appearance of Weber & Fields Company became the biggest event in the territory, occasioning a parade and day-long festivities. The receipts for the one performance were $12,500. By insisting on a lump-sum guaranty, Weber & Fields lost $4,500.

It was during the scramble to reroute the tour that company members first noticed the tensions between Weber & Fields. Erlanger's stratagem undoubtedly provoked some finger-pointing between Joe and Lew, with Joe concluding that the whole mess could have been avoided if they had been willing to compromise with the Syndicate. Predictably, rumors that Weber & Fields were quarrelling found their way into print. The open hostilities between Fields and Mann intensified the gossip. Throughout the remainder of the tour, the partners were forced to issue periodic denials.

Nevertheless, Weber & Fields played for two immensely profitable weeks in March at the Shuberts' Chicago theater, the Garrick. The Shuberts booked the Weberfields between Chicago and Brooklyn. At the Broadway Theater in Brooklyn, a reporter described finding Weber & Fields together in their dressing room, "happy as two boys" upon hearing that the performance was sold out. Other company members were asked about the rumors. Dailey and Ross covered for their bosses and said that the tour was a picnic, and "the utmost fellowship prevailed." The reporter concluded, "The whole organization maintains the harmony that caused it to be known since its inception as 'The Happy Family.'"[10]

Speculation increased when Peter Dailey and John T. Kelly, loyal members of the Happy Family, quietly signed contracts with other producers for the next season. A rumor originating in Chicago said that Fields was going to appear in a Hamlin-Mitchell production. In Boston, where the Weber & Fields Company were setting box-office records at the Globe, the partners continued to issue denials. It was difficult not to be bitter, playing to capacity crowds on the grand stage of a theater they had built but no longer controlled.

On Sunday, May 1, Weber & Fields slipped away from Boston on the New York train. The following morning, they were joined by Fields' attorney, Emmanuel Friend, at the offices of Howe & Hummel, on Centre Street, across from the Tombs Prison. Abe Hummel, the favorite lawyer of the Rialto and New York's underworld, represented Weber.

The meeting proceeded with mechanical efficiency. Joe and Lew avoided looking at each other, afraid of betraying any emotion that might have weakened their resolve. In twenty minutes they reviewed and signed the agreement that dissolved their partnership of twenty-seven years. Weber kept the Music Hall, and Fields received a check for $40,000. All royalties and lease monies would be evenly split. The settlement left Weber with a net worth estimated at $500,000. Fields was said to be worth just over $100,000, the discrepancy coming from Fields' gambling losses and the costs of supporting a family.

Despite their clear-cut differences, the erstwhile partners were oddly ambivalent until the end. "Ten minutes before the papers were signed," Fields said, "I did not believe we would separate. All along I had a sort of an idea that we would stick together."

Two days later, Fields, possibly distracted, fell down a flight of stairs at the Lexington Hotel in Boston. Initially, it was feared that he had dislocated his right hip. Weber was ready to cancel the rest of the tour. Upon closer examination, the doctor concluded that Fields' hip was only bruised, and Fields insisted that he would be able to perform again in a matter of days. It was inconceivable that the Weberfields should disband before playing one more time in New York, even if it was not on Broadway. For their farewell engagement, the Weberfields were booked into the West End. Neither the Shuberts nor Klaw & Erlanger—not even the I.B.A.—was willing to provide them with a downtown theater.

Now that their breakup was common knowledge, Weber & Fields were subjected to a relentless barrage of questions and commentary, which they handled with characteristic patience and candor. While reporters badgered them for the personal details, Joe and Lew insisted that their parting was for "purely business reasons." "We couldn't agree as to the policy of the house or the firm's business," was Lew's explanation. When somebody asked if the problem had been relatives in the business, Fields replied, "That's a very touchy question," and refused further comment.

But when Weber & Fields tried to explain the "business reasons" for their separation, the discussion had the undertones of a long-standing personal feud. An interview in May 1904 revealed fundamental differences in character, and something more:

> LEW: I wanted to make a decided change in the style of entertainment.
>
> JOE: And I believe it is a good thing to stick to success, and not go experimenting. Experience has shown us where our strength is. . . . Our style of show has made us a good deal of money and a big reputation. Why shouldn't we stick to it?
>
> LEW: Oh, I don't know. I think the public has got sick of sidewalk conversation . . . , It has been overdone. . . . There is no acting in getting close together and talking into each other's face. Anybody can do it who can learn a quick dialogue with a few jokes in it. I tell you the public is educated beyond that sort of stuff. Why all we have ever done is to come out and I try to get your money. That has been the whole business in every scene we ever had.
>
> JOE: Well, we ought not to find fault with the bridge that carried us over. It is just that business and sidewalk conversation that has made the public laugh, has filled the theater, has given us a reputation, and, incidentally, a few dollars. We have never had a failure since we became known in that line. . . .[11]

Seen in its historical context, their argument embodied the artistic choices facing American showmen at the turn of the century: the differences between

vaudeville and musical comedy, *shtick* and character development, skits and coherent storylines.

Weber & Fields' farewell tour would have ended without a Broadway appearance
had it not been for the timely intervention of some influential friends. The friends
(one of whom may have been the real estate tycoon and future biographer Felix
Isman) put up the money to rent Klaw & Erlanger's New Amsterdam Theater for
two weeks. The only stipulation that Abe Erlanger attached to the deal was that
Ben Teal, Weber & Fields' stage director, would not be allowed in the theater.
The real difficulty came in persuading Weber & Fields to appear there.

Klaw & Erlanger's New Amsterdam had opened in the fall of 1903, the first
theater on the south side of Forty-second Street. Built expressly for musical productions, it was a monument to the musical's ascendancy to a position of artistic
and financial respectability. Behind its impressive pseudo-baroque facade were
two theaters: an 1,800-seat auditorium with the largest stage in New York, and a
1,200-seat roof garden with movable glass walls and a fully equipped stage for
fair-weather entertainments. The interior was truly stunning: vaulted ceilings, a
green onyx staircase, mahogany-panelled walls, art nouveau ornamentation, alle-
gorical murals, and terra-cotta reliefs depicting scenes from Shakespeare, Wagner, Faust, and Greek drama.

For two weeks, Erlanger gave Weber & Fields a taste of what might have
been theirs had they acquiesced to the Syndicate's terms. New York journalists
were quick to point out the irony of the situation. "Gossips of the Rialto are
amused," said the *New York Times*, "over the fact that Weber & Fields should
play their last engagement in a [Syndicate] house . . . after having been among
the leaders of the Independent Booking Agency."

It was difficult not to impute irony to Klaw & Erlanger's ads, which stated
that the management "takes pleasure" in announcing the last two weeks of Weber & Fields' association. The entire engagement sold out in two days, with the
final night—Saturday, May 28—selling out first. At a time when divorce was still
a spicy gossip item, here was an opportunity to witness what amounted to a
public divorce, the breakup of "the Happy Family."

For their part, Weber & Fields did everything in their power to downplay the
event. Perhaps they feared caving in to the emotionalism of the evening themselves. As usual, their behavior set the tone for the rest of the company. They
sailed through *Whoop-Dee-Doo,* by now polished to a high gloss, and the familiar
burlesque of *Catherine.* But the final curtain opened the floodgates of emotion
on both sides of the footlights:

> A demonstration unique in theatrical history marked the ringing down of the last
> curtain. An audience which filled the large auditorium and composed of represen-
> tatives of society, clubdom, the world of first night, the theatre and every walk of
> life, called for the curtain to rise again. . . .
>
> A Broadway audience is not particularly sympathetic, but the tears that streaked the
> paint and powdered faces of the stage were repeated many times in the audi-
> ence. . . .[12]

When the curtain rose again, the entire company was on stage. In front, the principals stood hand in hand, with Weber and Fields at opposite ends. Many of the chorus girls were already weepy. Those onstage seemed dazed by the volleys of applause that thundered through the huge auditorium. Repeated cries of "Speech! Speech!" became a rhythmic chant. Peter Dailey, the Weberfields' self-appointed emcee, stepped forward and gestured for quiet. "These boys were married in the dime museum and divorced on Broadway," he began. But after this promising start, his usual wit failed him, and all that he could manage was a simple statement about how sorry he was. What else can one say to someone who is getting divorced?

Dailey then called on John T. Kelly, who said that the eight years he spent with Weber & Fields were the happiest of his career. Louis Mann, never one to be upstaged, lied and echoed Kelly's sentiments. Dailey then called on Frankie Bailey, the company's "singing teacher" (a private joke referring to her piping singing voice); she tried to speak, but was overcome with sobs and had to leave the stage. Lillian Russell said that she hoped—"I hope a whole lot"—as she turned to look beseechingly at each of the partners. She, too, was crying.

Next, Mabel Fenton and her husband Charlie Ross mentioned that they were the first act to sign with "the boys" eight years earlier, and that it was a shame to see them separating. The boys were making a grievous mistake, said Ross; "I call it business suicide," to which the audience responded with vociferous cheers and exclamations of "Right! Right!" The cheering continued until Joe Weber and Lew Fields were led to the footlights.

As the two comedians humbly faced their public, all show biz pretense vanished. Fields tried to speak, but only gasped. In a voice that barely carried beyond the first rows, Weber murmured, "We can only say that we are sorry."

"Shake hands," came a voice from the audience. The erstwhile partners complied. Their former boss and mentor from their minstrel days, John Carncross, had been right all along: after all the onstage feuding, the audience needed to be reassured.

His voice quavering, Fields finally spoke: "I can only echo Mr. Weber's sentiments." He and Joe exchanged frightened looks, then turned their backs and rejoined their colleagues at opposite ends of the stage. The orchestra played "Auld Lang Syne" as the curtain rang down on a sad lot of play people.

After all the farewells had been spoken to company members, Weber & Fields climbed the winding stairs to their shared dressing room. The New Amsterdam had accommodations for a company of six hundred, but Weber & Fields would not use separate dressing rooms, even on the eve of their separation. More than a superstition, the shared dressing room was a reminder of their humble beginnings and a symbol of their enduring friendship. Neither partner ever revealed what was said in those painful last moments together as they scrubbed off their makeup and put on their street clothes.

The last day of Weber & Fields' Enterprises—May 28—was also the last day of the Independent Booking Agency. When the Syndicate succeeded in luring Stair & Havlin away from the independents, the I.B.A. was cut off from its largest chain of theaters. Since the I.B.A. was maintained solely at the expense of its members (it charged no booking fees or commissions), it could not survive without Weber & Fields' substantial resources. With no other course left to them, Campbell and Hackett returned to the Syndicate. Harrison Grey Fisk held out, renting the Manhattan Theater for Mrs. Fisk. In his bitterness, Fisk apparently blamed Weber & Fields—in specific, their deal with Stair & Havlin—for the failure of the I.B.A. Accordingly, Fisk's *Dramatic Mirror*, once Weber & Fields' most vocal champion, ran only a terse acknowledgement of their last joint appearance.

The possibility that either could be successful without the other offended the public's romantic sensibilities. For most of their lives, Joe Weber and Lew Fields had shared the same goals, fought the same battles, suffered the same setbacks. Their names were inextricably linked; like "ham and eggs" and "Dewey and Manila," one could not say "Weber" without evoking "Fields," and vice versa. Weber and his wife were introduced as "Mr. Weber and Mrs. Fields" on several occasions, while Lew Fields sometimes passed unrecognized in a hotel lobby or train station until someone whispered, "of Weber & Fields." A few years after their separation, Weber was quoted as saying that whenever he saw Fields' name on a show poster, he thought of a one-legged man.

Weber's plans reflected his belief that the Weberfields style of entertainment was not played out. He kept the Music Hall, and during the summer had it extensively renovated to bring it up to code. To play opposite him in German roles, he hired the "burley-cue" star Harry Morris, and to play the leading straight roles, Aubrey Boucicault. Weber's new partner, Florenz Ziegfeld, Jr., was arguably the only producer whose flair for spectacle and production savvy rivalled Fields'. Ziegfeld brought with him his talented wife, Anna Held, the era's hottest sex symbol after Lillian Russell. Still three years away from his first Follies show, Ziegfeld saw possibilities in the Music Hall format that Fields had overlooked. Unfortunately for Weber, Ziegfeld was a rather imperious and disagreeable collaborator, and even more prodigal than Fields. The partnership did not last out the 1904–1905 season.

Fields had no second thoughts about the wisdom of the split with Weber, nor did he ever express any doubts about his ability to make it on his own. He plunged ahead, announcing his new partnership on the eve of Weber & Fields' engagement at the West End. Effective May 15, 1904, Fields new partners were Fred Hamlin and Julian Mitchell, for whom he would become the featured player and director of the Lew Fields Stock Company. Their intention was to produce shows along the lines of *The Wizard of Oz* and *Babes in Toyland;* ones that would be "more consistent [than the Music Hall] and less on the happy-go-lucky order." Victor Herbert would compose the music. Oscar Hammerstein, who had given Weber & Fields their first Broadway engagement, was building a playhouse on Forty-second Street for the new firm, just a few doors west of the New Amsterdam. It would be named the Lew Fields Theater.

Vacationing with his family in a summer cottage in Allenhurst, New Jersey, Fields had some time to reflect on what had happened. He had split from the man he had been on the stage with for over twenty-five years, pioneered a new entertainment form, and built one of the most successful theatrical companies ever. The journey from the Bowery to Broadway represented a lifetime's work, but Lew Fields was still only thirty-seven years old. He had capital and prestige, and the sanguine temperament of a gambler on a roll.

If the sense of promise needed any reinforcement, it came in the form of a beautiful nine-pound baby girl, born on the afternoon of July 16. Lew and Rose chose to name their daughter after a heroine of the popular stage—Dorothy—a name made fashionable by the success of *The Wizard of Oz.*

As partners, Weber & Fields had to content themselves with a Pisgah view of the American musical theater. They were the most successful actor-producers of their time, but by the turn of the century, the primacy of the actor-producer was past. With the rise of the theater middlemen—the booking agents, touring circuits, theater monopolies—success on stage was no longer simply a matter of gauging public tastes. In the emerging struggle between the Syndicate and the Shuberts, Weber & Fields Enterprises was as out of place as a cavalry troop on a modern battlefield. But the image of the actor-producer was too hard-won for Fields to relinquish gracefully. In the years to come, his insistence on claiming the prerogatives of the old-style actor-producer would cost him dearly.

How do we judge the legacy of Weber & Fields and their Music Hall? It was on the Music Hall stage that the basic forms and techniques of the revue and the musical were assembled and tried out: from the minstrel show, the irreverence and zaniness of the afterpiece; from vaudeville, the vigor and precision of performances and love of vernacular; from extravaganzas, the eye-filling scenery and costumes; from the legit stage, realistic lighting effects and sophisticated stage machinery. To this hybrid they added a blending of classical and popular dance and song styles, and a new conception of the chorus line. It was also on the Music Hall's tiny stage that Julian Mitchell defined the creative responsibilities of the stage director, becoming the progenitor of American musical directors, from Ned Wayburn to Bob Fosse. John Stromberg composed all of the music for twenty-eight Weberfields shows; his work was early proof that the right composer could deliver hit tunes and lend thematic coherence to the action on stage.

All of the above was achieved for the ephemeral and seemingly trivial purposes of burlesquing the conventions of comic opera, melodrama, and turn-of-the-century society. Although most of their targets are dead and forgotten, the Weberfields' achievements are nonetheless impressive. Socially and aesthetically, the Weber & Fields Music Hall was the evolutionary link between the popular stage entertainments of the nineteenth and twentieth centuries.

As performers, Weber & Fields' most lasting contribution is the knockabout friendship of Mike and Meyer. The Dutch duo was the archetype for a long line of two-acts extending from vaudeville (Smith & Dale) through silent films (Laurel & Hardy) and sound (Abbott & Costello), and into television (Gleason and Carney in *The Honeymooners*). In the later Music Hall travesties, Fields departed from the broad caricatures of vaudeville to develop a style more appropriate to the new musical comedies and operettas he admired. Descriptions of Lew Fields' "character" performances in the Music Hall travesties suggest that he may even have been a forerunner of the great character comedians of the silent screen, Chaplin and Keaton. Indeed, in the middle 'teens, he was described as "the Chaplin of an earlier generation" for his poignant comic style. Fields' face, according to Helen Hayes, was "next to Chaplin's . . . the most perfect comic mask I know."

As for the direct influence of the Music Hall itself, we must rely on the appraisals of knowledgeable eyewitnesses. Shortly before his death in 1942, George M. Cohan wrote: "To my way of thinking the best musical revues ever produced in this country were the Weber and Fields shows at their old Music Hall. . . . Those were great shows at that little playhouse downtown, and there has never been anything quite like them. . . ."[13] Cohan, whose *Little Johnny Jones* (1904) is considered the first significant American musical, thought so highly of the Weberfields shows that he emulated them repeatedly throughout the first two decades of this century. That Cohan referred to the Music Hall productions as revues rather than as musicals suggests the aesthetic richness of the burlesque form as developed by Weber & Fields. In effect, the Music Hall stage was a common source and point of divergence for the development of both revue and musical comedy.

Flo Ziegfeld, generally credited as the inventor of the revue, owed much to the Music Hall. Using most of the techniques pioneered by the Weberfields, he enlarged the scale of his productions, broadened the scope of his travesties, eliminated the last vestiges of a storyline, and with the help of Julian Mitchell, created the Follies. Even more derivative of the Music Hall productions were the Shuberts' Passing Shows. Curiously, Fields had no hand in them, despite the fact that he was the Shuberts' most prolific and reliable musical producer for almost a decade.

Traces of the anarchic, irreverent style of the Weberfields' shows can be seen in the movies of W. C. Fields, the Marx Brothers, and even Preston Sturges. The Marx Brothers, in particular, with their well-defined comic personas, dialect routines, strong ensemble work, and loose-jointed plots may be the closest modern viewers ever come to seeing a Weberfields production.

To be sure, the burlesque tradition did not originate with the Music Hall, but it was Weber & Fields who radically reconstituted it. The artfulness and wholesomeness of their entertainments made the form itself respectable; in the Music Hall, the tired businessman and his family learned how to laugh at the foibles and pretensions of their peers. The Music Hall productions created a market for satire and travesty that is still thriving today. The advent of electronic vaudeville—the TV variety show—proved that the well-aimed barbs of the topical parody still have a wide appeal. The targets and techniques of *Your Show of Shows* or *Saturday Night Live* differ only by degrees from the Weberfields shows. Today, the tradition of ensemble improvisation—derived from the minstrel show afterpiece and perfected by the Weberfields—lives on in the work of Second City and Monty Python.

Within the limits of Victorian attitudes about good taste, nobody high or low was exempted from becoming the subject of a Weber & Fields burlesque. For the clerks and shopgirls in the gallery, for the Wall Street magnates and society stars in the orchestra seats, and for everybody in between, laughter at the Music Hall was a great social equalizer. They all found something to laugh at, though they were not necessarily laughing at the same thing for the same reasons. At Weber & Fields' Music Hall, the impulse to knock the pompous celebrity from his or her pedestal, or to ridicule social fads and conventions, entered the mainstream of American culture, where it remains a redeeming feature—perhaps the only redeeming feature—of mass culture today.

CHAPTER X

The King of Musical Comedy

> . . . Dashing on before us,
> We see the merry chorus,
> And everything they do you know's been done;
> You hear the same old jokes,
> That make the same old hit.
> The scenery's just the same
> But it's been painted up a bit;
> You can ask most any showman,
> Inquire of Charley Frohman,
> And he'll say there's nothing new beneath the sun.
> George M. Cohan

RECLINING in an old-fashioned armchair in the new offices of Hamlin, Mitchell & Fields, Lew Fields puffed on an Egyptian cigarette and tried to explain how his future productions would differ from his work with the Weberfields. "There was neither coherence nor consistency in anything I did, or what my associates did," Fields said. "We have simply been dragged on for a laugh, without rhyme or reason. . . ." As he spoke, his gaze periodically came to rest on the rare prints of famous theater folk on the wall over his desk. "I think the public will welcome an entertainment that has at least a semblance of a clever story capably worked out," he continued, "and I have a real ambition to play a character role in a bright musical play without feeling every time I walk on stage like an intruder."

In retrospect, it would seem to be a modest enough ambition, and eminently practical. But to follow this concept to its logical conclusion involved hidden dangers. Already, his "modest" ambition had led him away from the vaudeville clowning that had brought him from the Bowery to Broadway. Unlike his buddy David Warfield, however, Fields' desire to be an actor, "not just a performer," did not motivate him to desert the musical stage for the straight drama—not yet, anyway. Instead, Fields wanted to apply to the musical the aesthetic principles that he admired in serious drama and operetta.

"This is my principle theory of what the public wants. . . ." He reached for the reporter's pad and wrote in block letters C-O-H-E-R-E-N-C-Y. "Coherency. Don't forget that word, for I think it sizes up the entire situation. No more sidewalk conversations, slapsticks and nose-to-nose talks."[1]

In the end, it was more a statement of what he aspired to than a prescription

206

for change. He was searching for something that did not yet exist—a script in which the basic elements of the musical (star performances, choreography, spectacle, and songs) could be combined as an integrated whole within a more or less consistent narrative framework. There were no models for him to emulate. The only precedents for the coherent libretto and score were the operettas of Gilbert & Sullivan.

The problem, according to Fields, was the libretto. Without "the semblance of a clever story, capably worked out," coherency was impossible. Alone among his contemporaries, Fields recognized the importance of the musical's book. Unfortunately, he was working in an era of hack librettists. To be fair, there was little to attract talented authors to the musical stage. The attitudes of Fields' colleagues and collaborators towards the libretto ranged from disdain to despair. "The plot is a convenient hook on which to hang songs," commented the singer-comedienne Blanche Ring, and her sentiments were widespread among performers and producers. Librettos were dashed off in a week or two and sold outright for $100. The Shuberts, whose early reputation was built on fair treatment for actors, treated librettists with outright contempt. "A playwright ought to get a share of the producer's profit, not the gross . . . before the playwright gets any the producer ought to get back his investment," insisted Lee Shubert.[2] Actors are what matter most, he reasoned: "it takes more than printer's ink and electric lights to make a star."[3] Songs could be bought from Tin Pan Alley, chorus girls and scenery were inexpensive, choreography consisted of military drills and cakewalks, and the book was usually patched together in rehearsals. The crucial ingredient in the Broadway show was a star performer. Even Edgar Smith, librettist for the Weberfields and author of some of Lew Fields' biggest hits, was forced to conclude that American musicals were "built upon no sure foundation of story or plot and constructed of a varied assortment of elements which cannot be expected to assimilate." The typical producer assumed that the playgoer had no interest in story or plot, and assembled a cast and bought songs in advance, so that "the wretched author of the unborn libretto must perforce embody them all in his work, despite the fact that the cast may be totally incompetent for any sort of dramatic work, the music and songs unsuitable and the scenery both dramatically and geographically unadaptable."[4] To this day, the importance of a musical's book is consistently undervalued. Insiders know differently: composer Jerry Bock put it best in responding to the inevitable question, "What comes first, the words or the music?" Bock's reply—"The book."

Mediocre librettos, all-powerful stars, and interpolated scores—these were some of the obstacles facing the ambitious producer who wanted to promote coherency as an aesthetic value on the popular stage. But the biggest obstacle for Lew Fields was his own status as a star. "Giving the public what it wants"— a phrase that Weber & Fields were fond of using—was becoming an increasingly burdensome obligation.

In the eight seasons from 1904 through 1912, the unusual range of Fields' activities as an actor and producer suggests a man who was not quite ready to accept the audience's image of himself. During this period, his productions covered the broad middle ground between vaudeville and Viennese operettas: five operettas (four with Victor Herbert), three revues, nine musical comedies, two straight comedies with William Collier, and at the beginning and end of this period, five burlesque-travesties in the Weberfields tradition. Categories are deceptive, however; some of the shows that were advertised at the time as musical comedies conform to today's definition of a revue, or vice versa, and the distinction between operetta and musical comedy was often deliberately blurred by producers.

Throughout this period, there were constant rumors of the imminent reunion of Weber & Fields. Partly this was newspaper hucksterism pandering to a sentimental public, and partly this was the wishful thinking of producers who envisioned the mountains of coin a Weber & Fields reunion would surely bring. As long as Fields was successful in his ambitious solo productions, he could ignore the pressures to revive the Music Hall. But as every handicapper knows, there is nothing like a series of losing bets to make the promise of a sure thing seem irresistible. And when the crowds pack the theater time and again to see the same old show, the phrase "give the public what it wants" acquires a more cynical edge. By 1912, Fields would be facing painful questions about his relationship with his public.

Taken as a whole, Lew Fields' shows are representative of the promises—and failings—of the American musical stage during this period.[5] At a time when "musical comedy" was no more than a convenient label attached to ever-changing amalgams of vaudeville, farce, and extravaganza, Fields' attempts to define it in terms of specific aesthetic practices—acting style, stagecraft, and subject matter—were necessary steps towards achieving coherent musical shows. If he ultimately fell short, it was not so much a failure of nerve or taste as further proof that revolutions in musical comedy are made by collaborators, not by individuals acting alone.

July, 1904: In St. Louis, the Democratic Party gave the nod to conservative judge Alton B. Parker over William Randolph Hearst to oppose Teddy Roosevelt in the fall presidential contest. In Chicago, a strike against the meat-packing industry turned violent when packers refused to negotiate with unionists. It was the time when every parlor had to have a piano, and the sheet music on every parlor piano was almost certain to include "In the Good Old Summertime" and "Sweet Adeline." At New York's Polo Grounds, the Giants' Christy Mathewson, the "All-American Boy," was pitching his way to his second straight season of thirty or more victories. The Broadway subway line now ran between City Hall and 125th Street, stopping at the newly christened Times Square. A block away, Oscar Hammerstein was building a 1,000-seat theater for Lew Fields. Restless with anticipation, Lew Fields was shuttling between New York City and his summer home on the Jersey shore, where Rose was about to have their fourth child.

The new firm of Hamlin, Mitchell & Fields was scrambling to find a composer, librettist, and cast for the 1904–1905 season. A week after the birth of Dorothy Fields, the partners announced that they had engaged Victor Herbert to write the scores for all of their productions, Glen MacDonough to script the opening piece, and the popular singer-comedienne Marie Cahill to play the leading female roles opposite Fields. The show's working title was *The American Ambassa-dress*, later to be changed to *It Happened in Nordland.*

In the casino as well as the theater, Fields continued to be a "plunger." Shortly after Dorothy's birth, he was invited by some local touts to visit an exclusive casino in Deal Beach. There, in the company of theater manager William Brady, Fields asked to raise the house limits at the roulette table. In the course of two afternoons, he managed to win over sixteen thousand dollars. Showing uncharacteristic restraint, he left the casino without squandering his winnings. A few weeks later, he also won an undisclosed amount at the Saratoga races. The memories of such streaks were enough to inspire years more of unsuccessful betting.

His reputation as a theatrical spendthrift undoubtedly complicated negotiations with his featured actress. Auburn-haired, blue-eyed Marie Cahill was riding the crest of her popularity as a musical star in *The Wild Rose* and *Sally in Our Alley.* Her stage presence was like that of two other leading comediennes, May Irwin and Marie Dressler—plump and not particularly pretty, but with a robust charm and a strong voice. In the parlance of the day, Cahill was a "coon shouter," but she had pretensions to being a grande dame of the theater. Cahill believed, with some justification, that most Broadway librettists and composers were hacks. She correctly attributed her recent successes to the Tin Pan Alley tunes she had interpolated in otherwise mediocre musical scores, making hits of the songs "Under the Bamboo Tree" and "Nancy Brown."

Everybody knew that when Fields wanted an actress, money was no object. Daniel Arthur, Cahill's husband and manager, was determined that his wife should be treated like the diva she believed herself to be. Fred Hamlin offered $1,000 a week for thirty-seven weeks; the abrasive Arthur insisted on $1,200—about the same as Lillian Russell received at the Weber & Fields Music Hall. Moreover, Cahill insisted on the right to rewrite her part and interpolate the songs of other composers as she saw fit. This would not have posed a problem if the composer had been anybody but Victor Herbert. Herbert, however, customarily included a clause in his contracts prohibiting interpolations, a fact known to Hamlin from his contract with Herbert for *Babes in Toyland.*

Julian Mitchell advised against capitulating to Cahill's demands. It is difficult to believe that Fields would have knowingly agreed to such dictatorial terms. No decision, particularly where casting was concerned, would have been undertaken without Fields' consent. According to one report, Hamlin actually broke off negotiations with Cahill, but when Fields heard that his old partner, Weber, had secured the services of Anna Held and Marie Dressler for the Music Hall, Fields insisted that an actress of Cahill's stature was essential to his stock company. Did his need to compete with his former partner overwhelm his better judgement? Or was this an early example of Fields' carelessness in business matters, the kind of inattention to the fine print that would eventually come back to haunt him in his dealings with the Shuberts?

Fields' oversight matched an equally serious one by Herbert. The composer had neglected to include his "no interpolations" clause in his new contract with Hamlin, Mitchell & Fields. A landmark battle over the integrity of the musical score and the power of the star was about to begin, and Fields would be caught in the middle.

Rehearsals began in late August, although casting was far from complete. Marie Cahill finally agreed to play the part of Katherine Peepfogle, American Ambassadress to the Court of Nordland. Fields would be her long-lost brother Hubert. In supporting roles, Fields assembled an accomplished—and expensive— team of veterans: Harry Fisher (the Dutchman in Harrigan's farces), Harry Davenport (a romantic lead in legit drama and musicals), May Robson (from Dan Frohman's stock company), William Burress (a favorite supporting player), Bessie Clayton (danseuse extraordinaire, in a speaking role), and Joseph Herbert (an actor in comic opera as well as an occasional burlesque writer, and the loser in a fistfight with Joe Weber seven years earlier). One of the newcomers was Pauline Frederick, a bright twenty-year-old showgirl with a beautiful profile and an equally beautiful voice. Fields had hired her to play only minor roles, but he was impressed by her seriousness and dedication. During rehearsals, she stood in the wings and studied the work of the principal actors.

From the outset, it was clear that Marie Cahill intended to exercise the full prerogatives of her contract. During her scenes, Cahill's husband-manager stood in the wings and interrupted whenever he saw an opportunity to build up her part. When Mitchell tried to choreograph a chorus routine around one of Cahill's songs, she refused to interact with the chorus girls because she considered it demeaning. Exasperated, Julian Mitchell threw down his script and walked out of the theater; thereafter, it was up to Fields to direct her. Repeatedly, Fields argued with Cahill over her line changes, but she ended each argument by threatening not to appear in New York. She incurred the hostility of the rest of the company by her immodest scorn of her colleagues, including a nasty attack on Fay Templeton. To make matters worse, by early October, Fred Hamlin had become too ill to deal with the consequences of his contract with Cahill, or any other business. There was not even an understudy for Cahill. Fields' forbearance could only have been born of desperation; in the days of the Music Hall, he had dismissed featured players for much less.

Fields' diplomacy held the production together through its troubled tryouts. Victor Herbert's worst fears were realized when Daniel Arthur started bringing in tunes by outside composers for his willful wife. Stymied by his own flawed contract, Herbert nevertheless refused to be a party to Cahill's interpolations. Fields worked out a compromise: Herbert would continue to conduct the orchestra for all of his original music, but he would hand over his baton to the musical director, Max Hirschfeld, for any interpolated numbers. Cahill's behavior was a reminder that the shape of a Broadway musical was still determined by its stars, however much the contributions of Lew Fields, Julian Mitchell, and Victor Herbert looked ahead to the days when the musical would become the creation of a producer, director, or composer.

The first public performance of *It Happened in Nordland* took place at the New Lyceum Theater in Harrisburg, Pennsylvania, on November 21, 1904. Despite the backstage strife, the premiere was a rousing success. Local critics noted the exceptional quality of Herbert's music and Mitchell's chorus work and scenery, as well as the "fine, well-balanced" cast. One reporter, however, commented on the leading lady: "There was entirely too much of Marie Cahill. The management must give some one else besides their pet star a chance if they wish to hold the favor of their audience. . . ."

At the Trenton tryouts, Cahill raged, "I want to get out of this show. This management is a bunch of shines. You [supporting actors] are a lot of amateurs." To Victor Herbert, she said, "You're no composer, you can't write music and you never could."[6] Complaining that she had a sore throat, she excused herself from the next few rehearsals.

With *Nordland* scheduled to open in New York on November 29, Oscar Hammerstein rushed to put the finishing touches on the new Lew Fields Theater. The façade was in the French Renaissance style, in red brick and white stone. Hammerstein needed something that commanded attention, for his new theater would be the seventh one on the block between Seventh and Eighth Avenues. To construct a huge marquee for the Lew Fields Theater that extended from the theater entrance to the curb, he defied a building code and hired carpenters to work at night.

As usual, Hammerstein had designed the theater himself, and his unorthodox, sometimes innovative building techniques antagonized the heads of the Building, Fire, and Health Departments. Hammerstein was particularly proud of his fire-fighting innovation: a grid of iron pipes connected to two large water tanks on the roof, controlled by a pull chain backstage. He also improved upon the current stage machinery to facilitate quicker handling of scenery. Several other engineering details, however, became the subject of further disputes in the coming months.

The ailing Fred Hamlin had just returned from the South where he had been taking a rest cure for "a nervous debility." Two days before the opening, he collapsed and began hemorrhaging from the nose. He died the following day; an autopsy revealed tuberculosis. Out of respect for their late partner, Fields and Mitchell postponed the New York opening until December 5. The entire company—except for Marie Cahill—waived their salaries for the week of mourning.

Snow began falling a few hours before curtain time on December 5, as befitted a show called *It Happened in Nordland*. By evening, Forty-second Street was ankle-deep in slush, and the wet pavement in front of the Lew Fields Theater reflected the electric lights (hung that very day) on the oversized marquee. Near the door a gaunt, black-gowned, middle-aged woman stood selling matches. "Matches Mary" was a familiar Broadway character, plying her humble trade every night, rain or shine, in front of a different theater. Weber & Fields had accorded her one of Broadway's highest forms of recognition when they burlesqued her in *A Message from Mars*. Her presence on opening night was said to be a talisman of success.

The usual Weberfieldsian first-nighters were there—Abe Hummel, Stanford White, Jesse Lewissohn, Lillian Russell, the Witmark Brothers, and Richard Harding Davis, as well as interested theater colleagues—Lee Shubert, William Brady, and Bimberg the Button Man. Representatives of all New York, "from the book-maker at the tracks to boxholders at the opera,"[7] thronged to the opening per-formance to welcome Lew Fields without his "Siamese attachment."

From the opening notes of Herbert's overture, the audience was transported to a fantasyland of Central European customs and royal intrigue. The curtain rose to reveal the railroad station in Kronenberg, capital of Nordland. The first act unfolded on the promenade in Elsa Bad, and the second act took place the fol-lowing day, on the terrace of Queen Elsa's palace in Kronenberg.

The main characters in Glen MacDonough's libretto—an emancipated female diplomat from New York and her long-lost "Dutch" brother—were as American (and as topical) as a *New York Herald* cartoon. Dr. Blotz (Julius Steger), an itinerant dentist and beauty doctor, arrives in Kronenberg with his assistant, a waif named Hubert (Lew Fields). The capital, however, is in an uproar, because Queen Elsa has disappeared to escape an arranged marriage. If word of her dis-appearance gets out, Nordland will be bankrupted and will fall into political chaos. Fortunately, the new American Ambassadress, Katherine Peepfogle, looks exactly like the absent Queen. To save Nordland, Katherine agrees to impersonate the Queen. As the queen for a day and a night, she finds her scapegrace brother Hubert (Lew Fields) and saves him from execution by appointing him Secretary of the Navy. She also straightens out the court intrigues, and gives sage advice illustrated by stories of New York life. Brother and sister return to America, the latter as bride-to-be of Lieutenant von Arnim (Charles Gotthold), who has loved her all along.

The plot line was fairly typical of the era's musical comedies, but this was the only thing average about *Nordland*. Although the setting was Old World, Fields and Mitchell made sure that the pacing, characterization, and staging were pure New York: breezy, irreverent, bursting with energy and spectacle. The chorus of fifty women was "a beauty show . . . even in the last row," with various members arrayed in the court costumes of many countries, and others appearing as Indi-ans, "detective girls," "matinee girls," and the living "samples" exhibited by Dr. Blotz.

Mitchell's "stage pictures" (the combined effects of scenery, choreography, and costumes) elicited rounds of applause for the clever way they developed out of the play's dramatic and musical expressions. Mitchell used dance to evoke moods and not just to underline action, as in the routine accompanying the song "Absinthe Frappé." Dancers dressed in shades of pale green and yellow, against similarly colored backdrops, enacted the drink-induced reverie of a decadent no-bleman, Prince George (Harry Davenport). A "riot in 'greenery-yallery-ness' " one reviewer called it, while another found it "so weird and fascinating[ly] unhealthy that it remains in my mind." Herbert's music for this sequence did not merely accompany, it beckoned invitingly. "Absinthe Frappé" was a waltz with a playful rubato and a sinuous melodic line. It soon became one of Herbert's most popular tunes.

The show's most notable stage picture, however, was apparently the carnival scene in the second act, for which Herbert adapted his lively piano piece "Al Fresco" for chorus and orchestra. Unfortunately, no detailed descriptions of the staging of this sequence survive. "The Knot of Blue," a smoothly flowing waltz sung as a romantic duet, followed.

Marie Cahill's imperious manner suited her role. Her performance showed no trace of her offstage differences with Fields, and her scenes with him won her the most praise. Herbert supplied her with three numbers: "Business Is Business," "Bandanna Land," and "Commandress-in-Chief," the last a toe-tapping march for the first-act finale. Cahill supplemented these with two interpolations, described as "humorous ditties"—"Beatrice Barefacts" and "Ding Dong Dell." When these songs did not catch on, she substituted other extraneous tunes. Her pretensions to divahood did not escape the notice of several newspaper critics.

By contrast, Fields' first-act entrance in *Nordland* elicited considerable comment for its "modesty." The musical stars of the day typically made certain that their first entrance was big, regardless of whether or not it was dramatically appropriate. Fields slipped on stage unnoticed among a group of peasants who gathered to welcome Dr. Blotz (Julius Steger). The doctor, a notorious charlatan, comes on stage in his wagon amid shouts and a fanfare from the orchestra. In the Harrisburg tryout, the audience mistook Steger for Fields and applauded vigorously, as was customary for the star's first appearance. Fields insisted nevertheless that his approach was the correct one: "What license would a German boy, friendless, parentless, and penniless, have to be greeted with loud acclaim? None whatever, so I say that in this scene we have got down to what would naturally happen in real life. . . . They might have accepted a blaring welcome for me as consistent with stage traditions, but if they stopped to think they would have realized that it was not reasonable."[8]

A small step perhaps, but change in the musical occurred in tiny increments. As long as the star's entrance had to be heralded, how could the composer or librettist hope to maintain the integrity of their contributions? And if we give the star his or her big entrance, why not give him or her control over the score and the staging of the chorus numbers, as Cahill had demanded? To Fields, it was indicative of how the star's power superseded all other aesthetic considerations, a condition that was at odds with his ideal of a "coherent" shape for the musical.

Ever the diplomat, Fields made certain that his temperamental co-star shared his curtain calls following the opening-night performance. As the stage filled up with banks of flowers, he gestured for Victor Herbert, MacDonough, Mitchell, and Max Hirschfeld to join him onstage. A basket of champagne arrived, compliments of Lillian Russell; Fields helped fill the glasses. Although he usually avoided curtain speeches, he proposed a silent toast to the memory of Fred Hamlin.

Back in his dressing room, Fields submitted uneasily to his customary post-performance alcohol rubdown. Despite the thunderous reception, he was nervous about what the reviewers would say about his performance. It was, after all, his debut on the legitimate stage, and his first production without his longtime partner. Much to his relief, critics were unanimous in their praise of his performance in *Nordland:* "the best work of his career";[9] "it will prove that he is an actor and not merely a broken-English comedian."[10] If there was any negative criticism, it was that in Act Two he was "too generous to others, and these others . . . were not nearly so clever as himself." The comment that pleased him most was that he "did not stoop to slapstick." He was proud to point out that his comic scenes in *Nordland* were situational, dictated by the book, which was in turn held in line by the score.

Fields' personal need to legitimize his profession translated itself into an artist's zeal for redefining his medium. To create a story in which characters were not, as he put it, "dragged on and off stage without rhyme or reason," he looked to the approved Old World sources: comic opera and operetta. But his long experience as a popular comedian in vaudeville and the Music Hall had taught him what kept American audiences engaged: high spirits, topical references, brisk staging, dazzling spectacle, pretty girls, and catchy tunes. In effect, Fields' first solo flight as a producer was an attempt to reconcile the era's two most popular forms of stage entertainment, vaudeville and operetta.

What made this marriage of high and low possible was Victor Herbert's music. Fields wanted consistency and coherence and Herbert's score delivered it. "We have tried to unfold a real story in a natural way," Fields commented a few days after *Nordland* opened. The comment seems paradoxical until one considers the function of Herbert's score. Unlike the patchwork of interpolations that characterizes most of the era's musical scores, Herbert's score evokes a microcosm where it seems natural for songs and dances to reveal the inhabitants' hopes and fears. MacDonough's libretto was a serviceable vehicle for setting up comedy scenes and plot turns, but it was the music that gave form and substance to the characters' feelings.

The opening night program described *It Happened in Nordland* as "a musical comedy in a prologue and two acts," a structure that reflected Victor Herbert's unique treatment of the operetta form. The score for *Nordland* was not an imitation of the Viennese style; the numbers were shorter and simpler, less massively orchestrated, and written for non-operatic voices. While his sparkling lyricism evoked Old World sophistication, Herbert provided enough melodic hooks and stylistic variety—waltzes, marches, comic numbers, ragtime—to connect with American audiences. *It Happened in Nordland* was exceptional for its time because its score was the glue that held all the other elements in place.

Ironically, when theater historians today want to identify a "breakthrough" in the American musical, they ignore *Nordland* and focus on another 1904 musical that may be described as the ultimate one-man show. George M. Cohan's *Little Johnnie Jones* arrived at the Liberty Theater on November 7, 1904, about a half block away and a month before *It Happened in Nordland*. He, too, was working with a new partner: Sam Harris came well prepared for working with the pugnacious Cohan, having previously managed a game but undersized boxer. Cohan's approach to making a consistent, coherent show was not particularly original, but he was the only performer with the talent and audacity to bring it off. He made the entire production an extension of his brash, electrifying personality. As librettist, composer, producer, and leading man, Cohan created the ultimate star vehicle for himself, with supporting roles for his wife (Ethel Levey) and his parents.

The combined force of his theatrical instincts and his ego produced the most coherent American libretto Broadway had ever seen. The dialogue and humor were pure vaudeville. The fast-talking, slangy, wisecracking banter of Cohan the Vaudevillian dictated not only the rhythm of the dialogue but the pacing of the musical numbers. His guiding principle was "Speed! Speed! And lots of it. . . . Perpetual motion."[11] He embraced the rhythms of urban life as portrayed on the vaudeville stage. Fast and loud alternated with fast and soft. Cohan had no patience for the languid pacing or the frothy niceties of English comedies and Viennese operettas. He had learned his stage-craft from Harrigan & Hart's plays, in which the slambang, knockabout scenes were often resolved with the stage direction "general mêlée."

Cohan's first entrance as Johnny Jones presents an interesting contrast with Fields' first entrance in *Nordland*. Strutting briskly across the stage, Cohan repeatedly acknowledged his admirers on stage and in the audience with a hearty, "Hello, everybody!" No question, the star had arrived. There is no better example of the differences between the personality and sensibilities of these two showmen: the ex-vaudevillian who made everything he did an extension of his outsized ego, compared to the ex-vaudevillian who wanted to play a character role in a coherent musical without feeling like an intruder every time he walked on stage.

Although the verbal style and pacing of *Little Johnny Jones* were indebted to vaudeville and Harrigan's farces, the plot reflected Cohan's boyhood fascination with melodramas and dime novels. Cohan added a few melodramatic twists to newspaper accounts of Tod Sloan, an American jockey who rode in the 1903 English Derby. Cocky Johnny Jones is unjustly accused of throwing a race. He vows to stay in England to clear his reputation and that of his country, though later he journeys to San Francisco's Chinatown to rescue his kidnapped girl-friend.

Cohan's songs captivated the audience. It was not simply that he knew how to "put over" a song. His melodies rivalled the best of Tin Pan Alley—snappy and unpretentious—while his lyrics had a refreshingly conversational quality that made the singer seem all the more sincere. True, some of his rhymes were sloppy, and he was overfond of using catch phrases from other songs. But unlike most contemporary Broadway lyrics, Cohan's communicated the "I am" of the singer in the vernacular of urban Americans.

Unlike Cohan and the Tin Pan Alley songwriters, Broadway lyricists worshipped the same idols as Broadway composers—Viennese operetta. Not surprisingly, they concocted lyrics that scan like bad translations from the German, replete with awkward inversions, grandiose imagery, and vacuous sentiments.

In this context, Cohan's *Little Johnny Jones* was a revelation: a musical with the dramatic shape (and impact) of a melodrama, with songs in a vernacular that approximated the everyday speech of the audience. His unique blend of patriotism and sentimentality captured the fancy of a public thrilled by the real-life exploits of another brash little American battling for international respect—Teddy Roosevelt. "Cohan's genius," observed Oscar Hammerstein II, "was to say simply what everybody was subconsciously feeling."

Although the first Broadway run of *Little Johnny Jones* lasted only fifty-two performances, Cohan continued to improve the show during its road tour. He brought it back to New York in May, 1905, for four months, and again in November, for a total of over 200 performances. Only *Nordland* and the Shuberts' *Fantana* had more.

In its conception and execution, *Little Johnny Jones* was more of the same, only done better: a showcase for the star performer. It simultaneously confirmed the conventional wisdom about musicals (that they should be extensions of the star's personality) and proposed an impossible model. To emulate the relative coherence of *Little Johnny Jones*, one needed a star with the triple-threat talents of George M., but there has never been another stage figure who combined these abilities.

It Happened in Nordland proposed a more practicable model. As collaborators, the team of Fields, Mitchell, MacDonough, and Herbert "built" *Nordland*. The spine of the production was Herbert's strong score and MacDonough's weaker story; these elements dictated the star turns, chorus routines, and stage effects. The show bore Fields' imprint as a producer without becoming a showcase for him as a star. In *Nordland*, he defined a working relationship between the producer, director/choreographer, librettist, and composer that anticipated Broadway creative teams of the future.

The box-office appeal of *It Happened in Nordland* continued unabated throughout the spring of 1905. Its success prompted one reporter to comment that everybody connected with the production seemed to be wearing a beatific smile. Actually, the smiles concealed no small amount of anxiety. Marie Cahill continued to interpolate songs ruthlessly, which kept her quarrel with Herbert simmering away just below the boiling point. Fortunately, Herbert had little direct contact with the show on a daily basis after the first week. Conductor Max Hirschfeld had to bear the brunt of Cahill's complaints and last-minute substitutions. Fields and Mitchell subjected the production to their customary pruning and revisions, but they made certain that no changes were made to Herbert's score without his approval.

In late March, Fields scheduled a special Thursday matinee for members of the profession. The audience was a show in itself, as everybody grinned and posed and waved frantically at everybody else, stars and soubrettes and relatives of stars. The crowd included Amelia Bingham, David Warfield, opera star Fritzi Scheff, former Weberfields dancer Bonnie Maginn, and one ill-fated couple, Harry Thaw and Evelyn Nesbit. Joe Weber arrived with Marie Dressler. For the first time since their farewell performance, Joe and Lew were seen talking together in public. Fields may have considered the applause of his colleagues, including that of his old partner, as his validation as a solo performer.

It was evidently an emotional event for Fields, for he went to great lengths to mask the depth of his feeling. During twenty-seven years on the stage, Fields had never made a curtain speech, except for the pitiful few words he had mumbled at Weber & Fields' final performance, and the toast he proposed in honor of the late Fred Hamlin after the opening of *Nordland*. When the matinee's final curtain rang down, and the audience called for Fields to make a speech, he appeared with a stagehand carrying a Victor phonograph. They set up the machine and cued up the flat disk. Out of the horn came the voice of Lew Fields thanking the crowd and welcoming his ex-partner. Surprised and delighted, the audience applauded enthusiastically while Fields smiled silently and bowed. It was perhaps the earliest use of a phonograph as a practical stage prop.

When conductor Max Hirschfeld was hospitalized with an eye infection in mid-April, Victor Herbert took over the conducting chores. He still refused to conduct interpolated songs; during performances, he handed his baton to the concertmaster, and returned when Cahill's song was finished. Cahill believed that Herbert's hand-off was becoming increasingly (and deliberately) ostentatious. She had lately added two new interpolations, "Any Old Tree" and "Ma Hindoo Man," and was in the habit of adding extra verses without warning the orchestra.

It was during the last performance of *Nordland* in New York (April 29) that Cahill struck the final blow. Her first song was the interpolated "Any Old Tree," for which Herbert handed over the baton to the concertmaster. Part way through the second stanza she stopped, stamped her foot, and began to sob. She asked the audience to excuse her and left the stage. Hearing an eerie silence, Fields rushed from his dressing room. Cahill complained that Herbert's orchestra was sabotaging her songs, but Fields persuaded her to finish her performance.

The audience applauded when she returned to the stage. "You are very kind," she said. "I will try to sing without the orchestra, it is so intentionally bad." When she resumed her song *a cappella*, members of the orchestra began to hiss, but they were silenced by cries of "Shame! Shame!" from the audience. Cahill's song ended with calls of "Speech!" and she obligingly bared her soul to her doting public: "I do not wish to inflict my personal troubles upon an audience. . . ." ("Please do!" was understood.) "But it is hopeless for me to continue under the conditions which have been forced upon me." Loud applause.

Why shouldn't the star choose what he or she wants to sing? What did Joe Blatz (Cohan's name for the typical theatergoer) care about the integrity of the score? If, as Fields had claimed, coherency was what the public now wanted, they did not seem to know it yet. When it got down to cases, a star could do no wrong.

Having demonstrated that her public was behind her, Cahill gave Fields her ultimatum: she would not open in Boston on Tuesday unless Herbert was banned from the theater. Furthermore, Fields had to affirm publicly that Herbert was the cause of the dispute for violating her contractual right to insert songs. Behind Cahill's threat was the assumption that the show could not succeed without her. Perhaps she also hoped that as a fellow actor Fields would sympathize with her plight.

Much to her surprise, Fields chose to support his composer. In the end, Fields believed in the hitherto unproven theory that a good musical was bigger than its featured actress, and he was willing to play his hunch that there were any number of actresses who could fill Cahill's role.

In Boston, Fields was gratified (and embarrassed) to receive a standing ovation on his first entrance. To fill the role of the American Ambassadress, he promoted "Billie" Norton, who had been appearing as the Ambassadress' secretary. At the Grand Opera House in Chicago, *Nordland* broke house records for summer attendance, lasting ten weeks. The Opera House's larger stage allowed Fields and Mitchell to expand the size of the chorus. Nobody missed Marie Cahill.

Fields and company returned from their successful Chicago run in mid-August, only two weeks before their Broadway season was due to open. He took a week to make his annual pilgrimage to Saratoga, where he was joined by Rose without the children. There he made out almost as well as he did in Chicago. An earnest interviewer asked about his Art, but Fields preferred to tell him about his luck at the track and the roulette wheel: "Do you know, I just couldn't lose after the first twenty-three bets. First twenty-three went against me, but after that, it was all velvet, and they paid me first and last a thousand dollars a day for the time I might have drunk the waters of the Spa if my thirst had been built that way. . . ."[12]

Lew Fields was not the only producer bringing a hit show back to Broadway for a second season. The return of Weber's *Higgledy-Piggledy*, the Shuberts' *Fantana*, Cohan's *Little Johnny Jones*, and Belasco's drama starring David Warfield, *The Music Master*, indicated a widespread belief that the 1905–1906 season would be a profitable one. Fields explained his show was returning because it "did not outlive its welcome last year," and not, as he was quick to add, "because I have any fear of risking my money"[13]—as if such fear in a producer was cause for embarrassment.

Of all the returnees, *Nordland* was the most changed. While the show was touring, Fields had been content to use talented unknowns to play the American Ambassadress. For Broadway audiences, however, only a star would do. A week before *Nordland* was due to reopen, Fields signed the exuberant ex-vaudevillian Blanche Ring. Curvaceous, assertive, and impulsive, Ring rose to stardom in George Lederer's Casino musicals. Like Cahill's, Ring's success as a singing comedienne came from the songs she interpolated, including such hits as "The Belle of Avenue A," "Bedelia," and "In the Good Old Summertime." Although Ring was less pretentious than Cahill, leaning more towards vaudeville than grand opera, she was no less temperamental. Fields took no chances; he made certain that their contract did not allow her to rewrite her role or include interpolations. At the same time, he recognized her talent and stage appeal, and signed her to a three-year contract under his management.

No sooner did Ring became comfortable in her new role than Fields substantially shortened *Nordland*, keeping all of the Victor Herbert music but cutting the libretto in half. Three weeks into the season, Fields and Ring opened in "The Music Master," a burlesque of the Charles Klein melodrama of the same name. Joseph Herbert wrote the burlesque and included references to another Klein melodrama, *The Lion and the Mouse*, which gave him the excuse to play the part of a villain who bore a strong resemblance to John D. Rockefeller. The score, in contrast to *Nordland*'s, was a patchwork of interpolations, with songs by Hans Linke, Joe Howard, and C. M. Chapel.

Fields was no doubt attracted by the opportunity to send up the part of Herr von Barwig, played to so much acclaim by David Warfield. In the burlesque, Herr Barewig, "a professional assassin of melody," has been reduced to living in a shabby Houston Street boardinghouse. He loses his job and family at the hands of the Chairman of the Auto Oil Trust, the eccentric multi-millionaire Henry Canting.

Cheery Blanche Ring was "the wise child who does not know her own father." Barewig is forced to give music lessons to hopeless hacks. He asks one would-be diva if she has any talent. "Ah yes," she replies, "a very prominent manager once told me that I had a beautiful voice for wearing tights."

In one clever transformation scene, the dingy boardinghouse room was turned into the gaudy drawing room of the Canting mansion "with the lights up and in the twinkle of an eye." Fields worked out the design and hired several stage carpenters to build it. All the furniture and fixtures in the Houston Street boarding house had reversible sides except the chairs, which were covered with rusty brown cloth to hide their gilt. Stage hands turned walls on pivots; an ice box became a gilt and glass cabinet containing Helen's doll collection, vases of flowers sprang from sudden corners, and by turning down its sides, the old piano was turned into a cabinet with panels depicting Watteau pastoral scenes. At one performance, stagehands took bets to guess the time it took to complete the change; the lowest estimate was seven seconds. They timed the transformation with a borrowed stopwatch: three seconds.

Despite Fields' higher ambitions, burlesque still beckoned—at least financially speaking. The breakup of Weber & Fields had left New York audiences with a hunger for high-class burlesque that Weber alone had been unable to satisfy. The opening of "The Music Master" burlesque coincided with the hopeful announcement of a rapprochement between the estranged masters of burlesque. Weber's olive branch came in the form of an offer to Fields: a five-year contract that guaranteed $1,000 a week for thirty-five weeks each season. Flush with the success of his first year on the legitimate stage, Fields graciously declined.

The double bill of *Nordland* and "The Music Master" lasted until late November (for a total of 254 New York performances, as well as the ten weeks in Chicago), but not without additional fireworks. As a vaudevillian, Blanche Ring had acquired the habit of breaking character and engaging in side-talk and in-jokes. Fields strongly disapproved of "guying" on stage, and told her so. Ring persisted, nonetheless, perhaps believing (as many actors did) that nobody had the right to interfere with her special relationship with her fans. During a Saturday evening performance in mid-October, her willfulness became intolerable. Disregarding the fate of her predecessor in *Nordland,* she interpolated a song in the Herbert score. Fields, furious, could barely contain himself until the final curtain, when he blasted her behavior in a bellowing voice that could be heard through several closed doors. Ring threatened not to show up for Monday's performance unless Fields apologized, and stalked out.

The following day, Fields spoke with Ring's representative, Fred MacKay, and offered what he thought was an apology: "Let this be a case of forgive and forget, and consider the incident closed." MacKay thought that the apology would be acceptable. Upon arriving at the theater Monday evening, Fields discovered that Ring had removed her costumes and had left word that she would not appear. An hour before curtain time, a frantic Fields asked Ring's understudy, the twenty-one-year-old Pauline Frederick, if she was up on her lines. Frederick, having watched every performance from the wings for the past year, was calm and confident. The costumes did not fit her properly, but her performance was so

polished that nobody noticed. Her voice—a clear soprano covering three oc-
taves—was superior to Cahill's or Ring's. And unlike her predecessors, she played
her role along straight dramatic lines.

Fields meant it as high praise when he told her that the part had never really
been *acted* before. By playing it straight, she not only brought out the comedy in
her own role more effectively, she also strengthened Fields' role. Several established actresses expressed a desire to take over the part, but Fields was so impressed with Frederick that he told her the part was hers for as long as she
wanted it. She stayed with the show until it left New York in December. Her
experience in *Nordland* launched her on a long and illustrious career in dramatic
roles.

Newspaper accounts of the Ring incident were evenly divided about the cause
of Fields' anger: interpolation or "guying." From Fields' standpoint, both behaviors were equally disruptive of the kind of musical theater he envisioned: interpolation was to the score what guying was to the libretto. Having already made
public pronouncements about coherence and the star's entrance, Fields wrote an
essay for *Broadway* magazine called "Guying and Guys on the Stage" which appeared about a month after Blanche Ring's sudden departure.

Fields explained his objections in the language of commerce rather than
aesthetics. When a theatergoer buys a ticket, he reasoned, the producer "stipu-
lates that for value received this man [the ticket-holder] shall enter into posses-
sion of a certain fictitious life, known as a play, presented by a body of salaried
people under the title of actors. For the evening under date . . . all that pertains
to the production are the properties of the ticket holder's senses. . . . If he is
deprived of his rights . . . he is as absolutely cheated as if a hand were slipped
into his pocket to rob him of his greenbacks or his gold watch." The actor was
"honor bound to become the fictitious personage which the audience has paid to
see." In polite society, Fields observed, to be excluded from a joke was a sign of
disrespect, but for an audience, it was a "heinous" offense. The "pernicious trick
of carrying on side talk between the lines" was not the same as the "fine art of
taking the audience into one's confidence. . . ." Guying resulted in "insincere or
frivolous" performances, which not only insulted the audience, but demoralized
the company. Fields vowed that any principal who thought he could afford "to
be half himself and half his role" would be "firmly and speedily called down."

"Guying," he concluded, "is contrary to the ethics of true dramatic art, and
as such, should be ruthlessly stamped out from every production whose manager
enters into an honest contract with the public." Few of his colleagues had given
such serious thought to acting styles, or any other aesthetic values, for musical
comedy. As he was the boss of the largest cast on Broadway, Fields' preference
in acting styles carried weight. After what happened to Blanche Ring, nobody
doubted that Fields meant what he said.

With *It Happened in Nordland*, Fields began to develop the notion of the
musical as a delicate balance of music, libretto, performance, and spectacle. Cahill and Ring had threatened this fragile equilibrium. In the quest for "coherency"
in the musical, a consistent acting style purged of vaudevillian self-consciousness
and preening was as important as a continuous storyline or a cohesive musical

score: *more* important, as it turned out. Over the course of the next decade, Fields rarely had the luxury of a strong libretto or score.

Even before *Nordland* left New York for its road season (twenty-six cities in twenty weeks), Fields' future plans were the subject of considerable speculation. Rumor had it that he and Mitchell were wearying of the management and administrative duties that they had assumed with the sudden death of Fred Hamlin. An article in mid-October, headlined "Shuberts Covet Mr. Lew Fields," announced that "Lee Shubert made Mr. Fields a definite offer of a large sum—the largest sum ever offered a star, so the story goes—to take the lead of a musical comedy to be written for him. The Casino Theatre figures in the offer. . . ." [14] Fields and the Shuberts refused to comment because the *Nordland* tour had been booked through Klaw & Erlanger. A month later, the Shuberts took over the lease of the Lew Fields Theatre. Fields himself now became the prize in a bidding war between the Syndicate and the Shuberts.

Tiny, energetic, and shyly engaging, Sam Shubert had masterminded the Shubert brothers' meteoric rise from the Syracuse streets. In the early days, there were three: Levi (Lee, the eldest), Sam, and Jacob (J. J.) were from a desperately poor Jewish immigrant family. Sam entered the theater business at fourteen as a ticket seller in a local opera house after landing a walk-on part in a road production of Belasco's *May Blossom*. During the 1890's, Sam obtained leases on theaters in Utica, Albany, and Syracuse. With backers, he leased a theater in Rochester. By that time, his brothers Lee and J. J. were a part of the organization, serving as the managers of the road companies and various theaters. In 1900, Sam and Lee leased their first Broadway theater, the Herald Square, on the northwest corner of Broadway and Thirty-fifth. To survive as producers, the Shuberts signed an agreement with the Syndicate (run by Abe Erlanger) even though they did not care for the organization or the man. Erlanger soon judged them to be a threat to his monopoly and attacked them in the courts and in the press.

Lee Shubert was Sam's faithful lieutenant, his childhood protector, and his closest advisor. Sam had the charm and the drive, but Lee plotted their business strategy and found the necessary financial backing. When Sam was killed in a grisly train wreck in May, 1905, Lee was so devastated that he seriously considered selling the family business. Sam's will left everything to Lee, charging him with the care of their sisters and mother. The will did not mention J. J., who never got over being treated as the unreliable little brother.

Open warfare between the Shuberts and the Syndicate began after Sam Shubert's death. Over the next two years, Lee Shubert directed the greatest expansion in theater history. Belasco, Harrison Grey Fiske, and the Shuberts joined forces to create the Sam S. Shubert Booking Agency. The new combine controlled players and plays such as Ada Rehan, Henry Russell Opera Co., David Warfield, Mrs. Fiske, Leslie Carter, Jefferson DeAngelis, DeWolf Hopper, Eddie Foy, Henry Miller, Margaret Anglin, *Babes in the Wood*, *The Darling of the Gods*, *The Heart of Maryland*, and *Wang*. Two months later, with the backing of Cincinnati financiers George S. Cox (a Republic party boss), Max Anderson, and Congressman Joseph Rhinock, they chartered the Sam S. and Lee Shubert Corporation with an initial capitalization of $1,400,000. During the fall of 1905, when the Shuberts took over the lease on the Lew Fields Theatre, they also acquired the leases for twenty-two other theaters.

Lee's penchant for collecting real estate also began to pay off. When there were no suitable theaters available in a given city, the Shuberts would build one. A steady stream of stars and managers defected from the ranks of Klaw & Erlanger. By the end of the 1905–1906 season, the Shuberts had built up a circuit of over fifty theaters. About two-thirds of these were owned by the Shuberts or their financial backers, and the rest were under the control of their allies.[15]

They not only fought the Syndicate for money, theaters, and productions, but for public opinion as well. Posing as the champions of art and freedom against the Syndicate forces of commercialism and tyranny, the new Independents proclaimed their own "open door" policy (a deliberate appropriation of a popular political catch-phrase). All theaters were to be open to all worthy attractions, without prejudice or favor. Of course, when the Shuberts eventually reached their objectives, the open door was slammed shut; but in the meantime, they captured the sympathies of actors, managers, and audiences. Erlanger's arrogance fed their propaganda campaign; when the Shuberts booked the aging Sarah Bernhardt for one more American farewell tour, Erlanger refused to allow her to play in any Syndicate house (much as he did to Weber & Fields in their final tour). Lee Shubert rented tents from Barnum & Bailey (as Weber & Fields had done in Albuquerque), which accommodated three times as many people. Their gross was over $1,000,000, but the publicity was priceless; newspapers coast to coast attacked Erlanger and extolled the Shuberts.

Lew Fields was particularly susceptible to the Shuberts' trust-busting image. Out of necessity, he had booked *Nordland*'s spring tour through Klaw & Erlanger, for they still controlled most of the one-night stands and first-class theaters in the smaller cities. The high point of the tour came in January, at the National Theater in Washington, D.C., where Fields staged a special performance of *Nordland* for President Roosevelt and his family. A few weeks later, Abe Erlanger offered Fields $3,000 a week to reunite with Weber for a summer tour. Fields rejected the offer and continued his backroom discussions with the Shuberts.

For the Shuberts, an alliance with Fields would be an important step in their battle with the Syndicate to control talent as well as theaters. Fields was not only one of the top comedy stars, but his experience as a producer-manager made him especially useful. Although the Shuberts already had contracts with several leading musical comedy stars (DeAngelis, Foy, Lillian Russell), their musicals had suffered from uninspired and inconsistent production quality. Neither Lee nor J. J. had much savvy when it came to staging musicals, although J. J. later pretended to. Fields would bring his own considerable expertise and a host of valuable collaborators: directors, designers, librettists, composers, and performers eager to work with him. The Shuberts wanted Fields to do for musicals what Belasco was doing for serious drama. Not to be overlooked was Fields' value in vaudeville, for Lee Shubert had designs on the vaudeville market as well.

The relationship between the Lee Shubert and Lew Fields was built on more than just their anti-Syndicate stance. Their personal styles were compatible. Both men valued restraint and gentility in their day-to-day affairs, although in private they sometimes gave vent to their volatile tempers. They could work eighteen hour days for weeks at a time, and they imposed their workaholic habits on their employees. They disliked profanity, in marked contrast to J. J., who seemed incapable of expressing himself without it. Both men were fastidious dressers: Fields the dapper one, Lee more prim. Lee, who fancied himself a bit of a raconteur, enjoyed Fields' limitless supply of stories, and tried in his faintly accented, high-pitched voice to emulate the actor's polished delivery.

In each other they recognized themselves—Polish-Jewish immigrants from large families, working from an early age, with little or no formal education, and a boyhood fascination with theater. The longing for legitimacy and respectability was even more acute in Lee Shubert, exacerbated by the need to overcome his family's humiliating poverty (which he and his brothers blamed on their alcoholic father), and by his vow to carry on the work begun by his dead brother. Both Lew and Lee were self-made men who reinvented their pasts for similar reasons and by using similar methods: the Americanized names, the American birthplaces, the avoidance of overt "Jewishness," the Horatio Alger tales about their childhood that were embellished with each retelling.

In the early days of their relationship, Lee Shubert treated Fields (older by a decade) deferentially. The fact that Fields was one of the first Jews on stage to become popular with Gentile audiences enhanced his stature in Lee's eyes. Although both men shared a sense of shame at their lack of education, Fields had worked hard at acquiring a veneer of sophistication. His English was unaccented, his vocabulary large, he read books (Shakespeare most nights before bed), and he was learning to speak French. In casual conversation, Fields would mention stage trivia—describing the intricate machinery used in fifteenth-century religious plays to simulate thunderbolts and falling stars, or the first stage earthquake, used in *The Virgin of the Sun* at Covent Garden in 1812—that Lee would later garble when he tried to impress journalists and show girls. Lee liked being around a cultured man who did not make him feel like an illiterate.

In actuality, one did not really work for or with "the Shuberts"—associates and employees were either "Mr. Lee's" or "Mr. Jake's." So great was their antagonism that the brothers operated in two semi-autonomous fiefdoms, competing for profits and publicity but sharing in the expenses. Each regarded the other's associates with suspicion, and, in Jake's case, open disdain. If in the end they seemed to operate as a united entity, it was because there was no disputing the bottom line—profitability.

As the "other" Shubert brother, J. J. was still trying to stake out his territory, which included musical production and talent. He had two reasons for disliking Fields. Not only was he "Lee's boy," but J. J. believed that Lee hired Fields to keep control of the Shubert musicals. If J. J. wanted to produce his own musicals, fine, but they would be compared artistically and financially with Fields' productions. As long as Fields kept producing hits, J. J. could not shake Lee's faith in Fields. But J. J. knew that it was only a matter of time before Fields produced a flop, and then J. J. could rant about how much Lee's misplaced sympathies had cost the Shuberts.

On March 8, 1906, Lee Shubert cabled an offer to Lew Fields at the theater in Omaha where he was appearing in *Nordland:*

> Dear Lew: I am in position to obtain the Herald Square Theatre which you know is situated on one of the best corners in New York City and could easily be made into a first class music hall. . . .
>
> . . . I would be willing to make an arrangement with you whereby we could make an improvement on the old Weber & Field *[sic]* shows. Surround yourself with a first class competent company and give reviews and burlesques of all the latest plays. So far as the business arrangements are concerned, I would be willing to have you go in half on the lease and draw a salary as an actor, and we share the burden of the profits and losses together, half and half.
>
> . . . I will be willing to listen to any other proposition that you have to make, as it is getting late and we ought to do something for next season. Yours truly, Lee Shubert[16]

Shubert's offer contained two hidden assumptions worth noting. First, his primary interest was to resurrect the Weber & Fields Music Hall, not to continue in the theatrical style developed in *It Happened in Nordland.* Second, his offer is not as generous as it sounds when one considers that the Shuberts would also be getting a sizable chunk of the theater's gross, not only in New York, but in every out-of-town theater (in which Fields had no financial interest). The arrangement bound Fields to the Shuberts as a co-lessee of their theater and as an employee; it also meant that even as he provided his production expertise, he had to supply one-half of the financial backing *and* share in the risk.

Apparently, Fields had no objections to the gist of the offer. With the help of his brother Charlie, he negotiated a contract with Lee Shubert. Among the terms: incorporation as the Lew Fields–Shubert Company, with capital stock of $20,000 split in half, the directors to be Lew Fields, Charles Fields, Lee Shubert, and J. W. Jacobs (note the exclusion of J. J.). Fields would appear as "star actor" for at least fifteen weeks a year at a salary of $750 a week until the break-even point, and $1,000 a week thereafter. Sixty percent of the gross receipts would go to the Fields-Shubert Co., forty percent to the theater. Fields would have full control of the stage, while the Shuberts would control the front of the house, management, and road bookings. The theater would henceforth be known as Lew Fields' Herald Square Theatre, and Fields would retain the option for a half interest in a new theater the Shuberts were promising to build for him.

In the long run, Fields' involvement with the Shuberts was a slow and inescapable quagmire. The more active he was as a Shubert partner, the stronger their hold on him. When Fields began his partnership with the Shuberts, he had enough capital to cover his share up front; later, Lee would have him sign promissory notes for his share, or take a portion of some new venture; finally, when the only asset Fields had left was his salary, he found himself working for the Shuberts to repay the debts he had incurred as their partner.

Fields never had much patience for the details of financial arrangements, and saw only the opportunities his association with Lee Shubert would afford him: a savvy business partner who would not meddle with his productions, a strong booking office, the backing to expand his activities as a producer and manager. The contract was signed in late May in the café of the Lew Fields Herald Square Theater. Fields, his brother Charlie, his new press agent William Raymond Sills, and Lee Shubert launched the new venture by smashing one bottle of champagne on the bar rail and drinking the other. They decided to expand the café and to allow smoking in the theater. Renovations had already begun—twenty thousand dollars' worth, for which Lee persuaded Lew to share in the costs. They raised a toast to "a music hall of the highest order."

That Fields actually intended to return to the style of the Weber & Fields Music Hall seems curious, especially in view of his public statements and the success of *Nordland*. There was evidently some question in his mind about what kind of entertainment to present in his new theater. At the end of May, quite suddenly, he decided to sail to London to secure the rights to a musical—not the logical course of action for a man intending to produce burlesques. He joined the spring exodus of American producers (led by Charles Frohman), who regularly raided the London stage to compensate for the dearth of good home-grown musical scripts.

On board the *Oceanic*, Fields tried to sign Vesta Victoria, the plump British songstress who had just completed a successful American tour. He stayed in London only three days, just long enough to determine that the play he intended to buy was unsuitable. At the new Gaiety, he saw another musical, *The Orchid*, by Ivan Caryll and Lionel Monckton, about a bumbling explorer who discovers a rare orchid, loses it, and then finds another in a florist shop. He purchased the rights for the Fields-Shubert Company, but by the time he disembarked in New York, he had decided that *The Orchid* was not for him, either. Late in the 1906–1907 season, they made it into a vehicle for Eddie Foy, Trixie Friganza, and Irene Franklin (in her debut) at the Lew Fields Herald Square.

Fields' assessment of the London stage ran counter to the conventional wisdom of his fellow producers, who were buying up every English farce, musical, and serious drama that they could find. "I didn't see anything in London that would be a big success in America," he said. "We are badly off for musical shows in America, but we certainly beat them over there."[17] Rather than adapt an English musical, he chose what he considered to be the lesser evil: "sketches" along Weberfieldsian lines. A few years later, after refusing several other English adaptations suggested by the Shuberts, Fields commented: "I have never produced an English musical comedy and I cannot understand why some managers cross the water for material when we have so much better stuff on this side. . . . Our big department stores, drug stores, railroad stations and other places where people are wont to gather in great numbers afford endless opportunity for musical comedy treatment."[18] His productions over the next two seasons, *About Town* and *The Girl Behind the Counter*, proved that he had the courage of his convictions. During an era in which English musicals and Viennese operettas overwhelmed the Broadway stage, Fields continued to expand the possibilities of indigenous stage forms with productions that defied categorization, each show being a slightly different blend of vaudeville, revue, musical comedy, and spectacle. Working without the benefit of strong, consistent scores or coherent librettos,

Fields created delightful entertainments on the strengths of the comic performances and the spectacle. In doing so, he seemed to turn his back on many of the values he had championed in *Nordland:* the integrity of the musical score, a "coherent" story, and the de-emphasis of star turns.

On the evening of August 30, 1906, the Lew Fields Herald Square theater opened with *About Town.* The renovated interior featured red satin on the walls of the orchestra level and a new painting over the proscenium entitled "Aurora." Though billed as a musical comedy, *About Town* was essentially a revue held together by a slender plot, as were most revues of that time. The book and lyrics were by Joseph Herbert, who also ended up playing a supporting role when another actor dropped out. What little plot there was concerned a brash cab driver nicknamed Baron Blitz (Fields) who is forced by circumstances to impersonate the president of the All-Night Bank. He comes to the aid of his new colleague, the Duke of Slushington (Lawrence Grossmith), who must choose between a saucy adventuress (Edna Wallace Hopper) and a pert Gibson girl (Louise Dresser).[19]

Few if any legit actors of the day were as diligent as Fields in preparing for a role. He researched his role as a cabby by observing a real one who picked up late-night fares in front of Shanley's Restaurant. Fields followed him around every night for a week. To perfect his impersonation, Fields rented a cab and spent an evening and early morning driving around the Tenderloin and picking up Broadway nightowls.

Lee Shubert had told Fields to "surround [him]self with a first class competent company," and Fields willingly complied, putting together a cast of talented (and expensive) veterans and promising newcomers. The veterans included three leading ladies with three names, Louise Allen Collier, Elita Procter Otis, and Edna Wallace Hopper (DeWolf's former wife), who had played leading roles in *El Capitan* and *Florodora.* Among the newcomers were Jack Norworth and his wife, Louise Dresser. Norworth, a darkly handsome singer and songwriter (composer of "Take Me Out to the Ball Game," and "Shine On, Harvest Moon,") was one of several performers Fields had hired away from the vaudeville stage. With him came his wife, Louise Dresser, a tall, blonde vaudeville singer with a tender voice and expressive features. Dresser was, depending on which accounts one reads, the sister or the adopted daughter of the songwriter Paul Dresser, and she used to introduce his songs in vaudeville. Later in the season, after Norworth left the company, he made headlines when Dresser accused him of adultery with a plump comedienne named Trixie Friganza. (Norworth and Dresser were subsequently divorced; he went on to marry Nora Bayes, and the new couple appeared together in later Lew Fields shows.)

Fields took a particular liking to a gangly young Englishman in the chorus who was appearing in his first Broadway show. Vernon Castle Blythe had recently graduated from the School of Engineering at Birmingham University, but he came to the United States to try his luck as a comedian, at the urging of his brother-in-law, Laurence Grossmith. Castle's long legs and suppleness made him a standout eccentric dancer. Even in the midst of the most foolish pratfall, he maintained an air of grace and elegance.

Fields saw the makings of a good character comedian, and spent extra time working with him. Castle was soon substituting for his brother-in-law in the role of the foppish lord. The young man with the crazy legs and the shy smile became a mainstay in Fields' productions over the next four seasons, playing increasingly important roles. Castle came to regard Fields as his mentor, and Fields loved him like a son.

The score for *About Town*, by Raymond Hubbell and Melville Ellis, convinced Fields of the need to interpolate. He raided Tin Pan Alley, purchasing songs by Gus Edwards, Albert Von Tilzer, Gustave Kerker, A. Baldwin Sloane, and Victor Herbert (who did not mind having his work interpolated in somebody else's score). The closest thing to a hit was "I'm Sorry," (Von Tilzer) sung by Louise Dresser, and Jack Norworth's renderings of "The Great White Way" and "When Tommy Atkins Marries Dolly Gray."

As if to compensate for the weak score, Fields and Julian Mitchell devised some striking chorus routines. Interspersed with the star turns were curvaceous cadets, Gibson girls, nursemaids (in polka dots) and Dutch Boys (led by Edna Wallace Hopper, blowing smoke rings from a Dutch pipe) dancing and singing. The settings, including one called "Le Jardin Fin-de-Siècle, Paris" (a satirical reference to Ziegfeld's theater) were the work of scenic artist Arthur Voegtlin, just before he was "borrowed" by Jake Shubert to design the fall spectacle at the Hippodrome.

One of the chorus routines was quite daring. A group of girls ("French wives") in red frocks and black stockings dance on and attempt to "steal" the male escorts of a group of girls in blue. The chorus boys then had to choose between the two groups of girls; Fields instructed them to make their choice spontaneously at each performance. The girls who were not chosen became jealous and incited a quarrel that culminated with them ripping off the frocks of the other group of girls. The dresses were made of paper, and the girls' lingerie not at all immodest, but the stunt drew gasps and appreciative applause at every performance. It made the famous double sextette from *Florodora*, with its coy banter and lockstep choreography, seem quite tame by comparison.

When the first month's receipts for *About Town* did not live up to Lee Shubert's expectations, Fields once again turned to the tried-and-true formula of the Music Hall. He commissioned Glen MacDonough to write a burlesque of the season's hit, *The Great Divide*, a melodrama that celebrated the virtues of the American West. The story involved a Boston socialite who longed to find "an unfinished man." To mock the roles originated by Henry Miller and Margaret Anglin, Fields added two irrepressible and expensive comedians to his payroll, Peter Dailey and Blanche Ring.

For three days, Fields' theater was dark while he rehearsed the new burlesque. As usual, Peter Dailey failed to make it to a single morning rehearsal, but Ring was much more cooperative than in her previous stint with Fields. On November 15, Fields reopened to present "The Great Decide" and an abbreviated version of *About Town*.

Mitchell drew his share of praise for his staging of "the Indian spirit dance, picturing one of the legends of the Mojave tribe," during which a warrior, betrayed by a beautiful maiden and taunted by the spirits of his ancestors, leaped to his death from the cliff that was also their trysting place. The illusion of a fatal plunge had been used in melodramas, but Fields and Mitchell staged it strictly for laughs. The novelty hit of the evening, however, was not exactly a piece of stage action. The second scene was a primitive motion picture in which Ruth (Blanche Ring) used a lariat to drag Steve (Dailey) across the alkali plains to the Justice of the Peace (Fields) to be married, with Steve protesting to the bitter end.

Receipts improved, but Lee Shubert was uncomfortable with how much it was costing. In a note dated November 26, Lee wrote: "I wish you would go over the situation of your salary list, and see where we can cut the expense down. Go over it and let me know if we cannot get this down to a paying basis."[20] In Shubert-speak, "paying basis" did not mean breaking even; it meant paying a profit. In his years with the Shuberts, Fields would receive hundreds of similar notes, which became less polite and more directive over time.

About Town closed in New York in late December after 138 performances and began a six-month, eighteen-city tour of Shubert houses. Because *The Great Divide* had not played outside of New York, they replaced "The Great Decide" with "The Music Master" burlesque. The tour was extended for four weeks; Fields became the first of the Independents to play in Syndicate houses under a new pooling arrangement with the Shuberts. *About Town* split a week between Minneapolis and St. Paul, then worked its way back to New York playing Klaw & Erlanger one-night stands.

Based on information gleaned from the Shubert files and from the *New York Clipper*, it would appear to have been a profitable six months for the Fields-Shubert partnership. Yet, somehow, Fields managed to come out in the red. Fields signed a promissory with the Shubert for $10,937.70 (which was still unpaid four years later) to cover his share of the production and losses on *About Town*. Odder still, the Shuberts' business manager, J. A. MacMartin, instructed Fields to sign and return it without informing Fields' business manager, F. C. Langley, "who knows nothing whatsoever of this deal."[21] Sometimes, the surviving documents only make Fields' business arrangements with the Shuberts seem more inscrutable, though the overall thrust is distressingly clear.

By the time Fields finally returned home in June, he had been away from his family for a total of twelve out of the previous eighteen months. He tried to be dutiful, calling almost every day, sometimes making quick trips home between road bookings: taking an overnight train from Pittsburgh, for example, and arriving in time for an early Sunday dinner with Rose and the kids before catching an eight o'clock train to his Monday engagement. Little Dorothy (now two years old) seemed to barely recognize him. Once, when Fields came home in costume for a meal between a matinee and evening performance, she burst into tears and ran away, frightened by the strange man in the house.

On another occasion, he rushed home so that he could take the family out driving in "the steamer," only to find that the recently repaired vehicle needed further repairs. He then proposed taking out the trotter and runabout, but Rose told him that the liveryman had called to say that the horse needed new shoes and the buggy a new tire. "Then I was mad," recalled Fields, "and I guess for about five minutes I said a few things to the furniture." He was still muttering when nine-year-old Herbert handed him a piece of paper on which were scribbled these lines:

> Everybody's working father,
> Since he went on the road,
> Everybody's working mother,
> All cons on her they load.
> Father's touring the cities,
> Mother's wearing a frown,
> Everybody's working the both of them,
> Since Pop left town.

Lew joked about how nice it was to have a librettist in the family so that he would not have to pay royalties. Someday, Herbert would provide his father with the best librettos the old man ever had. Rose found it less amusing, having leaned heavily on the older children, Joe and Frances, to cultivate other interests besides theater.

Presumably, it was his desire to spend a quiet summer with his family in Far Rockaway that led him to refuse an astounding offer from the United Booking Office (the Keith-Albee combine). The U.B.O., which had enjoyed a virtual monopoly in vaudeville for nearly a decade, was now being confronted with a powerful new challenger. In April, 1907, Abe Erlanger and the Shuberts had suddenly forgotten their implacable enmity and joined hands as partners in the United States Amusement Company, capitalized at $1,000,000. They called their product "advanced vaudeville," and they signed longtime U.B.O. foe William Morris to a five-year contract as chief booker. Within three months, Morris had secured U.S. Amusement Company contracts for a million and a half dollars' worth of vaudeville acts. Salaries escalated as the competition for big stars became desperate. The cost of putting on a first-class vaudeville show in New York went from $1,900 a week to $10,000.

Naturally, the U.B.O. sought to steal their rival's prized commodities. On behalf of the U.B.O., M. S. Bentham offered Lew Fields $2,500 a week for thirty weeks. Fields' terse reply—"Not enough"—could be read as both ironic and equivocal. On one hand, he had no desire to work for Keith-Albee or play in vaudeville, much less spend the summer away from his family; on the other, he had just lost over $10,000 on his last show (according to the Shuberts' bookkeeping).

By July, Fields was already immersed in rehearsals of his new musical comedy, an English import that he and his Music Hall colleague Edgar Smith were rebuilding from the ground up as a showcase for Fields' comic talents. The only elements that Fields kept were the title, *The Girl Behind the Counter*, and a few of the musical numbers (by Howard Talbot). In actuality, it was the man behind the counter, played by Fields, who became the center of the show. Fields conceived of the main character—a butcher named Henry Schniff—as a henpecked but unflappable husband. His role model was a newsdealer whose stand was near

Fields' summer home in Far Rockaway. Every time Fields used to go by the newsstand, he would overhear a heated but one-sided argument between the dealer and his hefty wife. The dealer never answered back, but instead clasped his hands, smiled at passersby, and was forever tidying his displays. After studying him for several days, Fields offered to buy the newsdealer a new coat in exchange for the one he was wearing. The old coat was what Fields reportedly wore at the start of *The Girl Behind the Counter*. Edward Harrigan, author, producer, and star of the Mulligan farces *Reilly and the Four Hundred* and *Old Lavender*, had a similar interest in the clothes of his real-life role models, and considered the acquisition of authentic garb an essential part of building a stage character.

Taking no chances on the kind of weak New York opening that had hurt *About Town*, Fields scheduled three weeks of out-of-town tryouts before returning to New York at the end of September for a week of polishing. At each performance, Fields stood in the wings with a script and pencil and watched the audience. If they laughed at a line, he underlined it. If they did not, especially when he thought it was funny, he made a note of it. After the show, he studied his markings, deciding to shift a conversation or give a line to somebody else. If it still failed to "get over," he deleted it.

For the female lead, the Shuberts had signed the English comedienne Connie Ediss during their annual spring raid on the London stage. Fields had no objections; Ediss, a veteran of the Gayety Theatre musicals, was a perfect choice for the role of the Cockney landlady who wants to break into society. More massive than the Maries (Cahill and Dressler), Ediss' overbearing, voluble vulgarian was the ideal foil for Fields.

Several members from the previous season's company returned (without new contracts, as Lee Shubert was horrified to learn). Louise Dresser played Millie, Mrs. Schniff's daughter from a previous marriage. George Beban was cast as an excitable Frenchman, and Vernon Castle returned in dual roles, as a loose-jointed waiter and an absent-minded fop. Other returnees included Joseph Ratliffe, May Naudain, and Topsy Siegrist. Though this was to be Fields' star vehicle, he still insisted on surrounding himself with talented supporting players, even if the resulting salary list created friction with his partners.

In the incidental role of Merri Murray, "America's leading chorus lady," Fields cast a petite brunette with luminous eyes, a mischievous smile, and a flawless figure. Lotta Faust was working behind the dry-goods counter at Abraham & Strauss when she was discovered by Fred Hamlin. As Trixie, the Queen of the Emerald City in *The Wizard of Oz*, she gained a Broadway following; when she sang her hit "Sammy," she picked out a bashful-looking man in one of the lower boxes and directed the song to him. Vivacious and generous to a fault (she was perpetually lending and borrowing money), she became not only the darling of the stage-door johnnies but the idol of the chorus girls. Her dancing was superb, her singing voice passable; under Lew Fields' tutelage, she developed into a magnetic comedienne. She, too, became a regular in Fields' stock company, playing "soubrette" roles.

By the standards of the day, her offstage behavior was considered bohemian; she smoked cigarettes, she wore only white or black, and she created a new fashion stir by wearing half-hose in warm weather. That she was also unaffected and totally guileless only added to her allure. It is no wonder that she became a personal favorite of Fields, and he came to be as close to her as his rigid standards of propriety would allow.

When *The Girl Behind the Counter* opened at Lew Fields' Herald Square Theatre on the evening of October 1, 1907, New Yorkers welcomed it as the funniest, fastest, and slickest musical comedy in recent memory. In many ways, Edgar Smith's plot harked back to Harrigan's farces. Instead of the Bowery, the first act was set in a large department store, with a soda counter at one side, a flower counter at the other, pivoting storm doors at the back, stairways leading to a mezzanine floor, and a commotion of salesgirls, cashiers, and customers. Fields played Henry Schniff, a former butcher, who is chased on stage by an irate cabby (a reference to Fields' role in *About Town*). Schniff has married his landlady to avoid paying four years' back rent, only to learn that he has inherited a fortune. Mrs. Schniff wants to get into society at all costs; she shops relentlessly and arranges for her shapely daughter (Louise Dresser) to marry a titled Englishman. At the department store, where she is stocking up for a grandiose reception to celebrate her daughter's engagement, she pauses to admire "a crushed raspberry cloak with poisoned lamb's fur," and asks to have the Schniff family crest— a dog rampant on a frying pan, with a border of sausages linked, and the motto, "Cave canem"—set in diamonds and spitfires.

Her long-suffering husband follows her around and desperately searches for ways to curtail her extravagances. At the same time, he tries to facilitate his stepdaughter's romance with an American boy. To keep tabs on his wife, Schniff disguises himself as different employees. He becomes the store detective, and then pretends to be a floorwalker. Fields based his characterization on a real floorwalker he had seen at Macy's, just across the street from his theater, whom he encountered when he went in to buy a toy for one of his children.

Schniff's next disguise, as a soda jerk, provided Fields with the inspiration for one of the best routines of his career. Turn-of-the-century sodas came in colors as well as flavors; the inexperienced Schniff borrows a rack of neckties from a nearby counter and has his customers pick out their color, then he takes the tie and runs along the bottles until he matches it with a syrup. One haughty young man tries to stump Schniff by handing him a striped tie, but the resourceful soda jerk duplicates it, much to the audience's delight. In the process, he discovers that the soda comes out of the dispenser with enough force to blow the customers out of their seat. Eventually, Mrs. Schniff arrives at the soda fountain. Without recognizing her husband, she asks for something that will put her on her feet. The results were predictable, but the anticipation was delicious.

The second act unfolds at Mrs. Schniff's society ball, where Schniff is in charge of a quintet of mismatched waiters. Once again, Fields drew inspiration from a scene he had witnessed. While on tour in Kansas City, Fields came into the hotel restaurant for an early dinner and saw the head waiter drilling a group of inept and unprepossessing recruits. Fields hit upon the idea of stage waiters as a chorus of grotesques; he sent his brother Charlie to scout for likely candidates in the Bowery and the Tenderloin. Four out of the five were non-actors:

one had bushy side-whiskers ("Galway sluggers") and a sarcastic demeanor; the second was a jolly fat man with a baby smile (a masseur Lew found at the Murray Hills Baths); the third was a four-foot tall bootblack; and the fourth was a glowering, unshaven thug. Vernon Castle, the human stringbean, played the fifth waiter.

Schniff lines up his sorry crew and proceeds to instruct them in the duties of waiters:

> Always remember, the first duty of a waiter is to look insulting. Never go near a customer until ten minutes after he has come in. If he goes like that *(snaps fingers)* don't pay any attention to him. If he gets excited and jingles on the glass with his knife, go out in the kitchen where you won't hear him. In about ten minutes come around and brush the crumbs into his lap. Then, if he asks you for a programme [menu], look at him as if you pitied him, give him a glass of ice water and walk away. When you come back, he has found his programme and knows what he wants. Then you take out your pad and write it down—and then go in the kitchen and order something else. . . .[22]

Schniff gives individual instructions to each waiter; he tries repeatedly to shake the good nature out of the fat man, and he assigns the midget to be "the finger bowl waiter." He avoids saying anything at all to the thug, who glowers and flexes every time Schniff passes by. The Terrible Tenderloiner, however, turns out to be a simpering softie, and Fields discharges him for being unqualified for the job.

The waiter routine became the most talked-about scene of the season. "Mr. Fields never did anything in the course of his stage life that was funnier than his tending of the soda fountain and his drilling of the forces of waiters," gushed the *New York Clipper*'s critic. "He has progressed a long way beyond the Germanic-English dialect dialogue of give and take stuff," observed another.[23] One astute critic commented on the difference that a good libretto made. Others noted the refreshing absence of the sentimental and foolish dialogue so common to musical comedies.

Julian Mitchell's staging and chorus work were clever and relatively restrained. "You mustn't sacrifice the story," insisted Fields, "by lugging in a chorus for the sake of a dance or a song or a bunch of beauty."[24] Mitchell's specialties came more naturally out of the story than those in *About Town*. In the first act, he transformed the Pony Ballet (a team of precision dancers between five feet and five feet five inches tall) into a human xylophone. In the second act, where Fields suggested a romantic interlude, Mitchell created a summer arbor at night, with tiny, moving electric lights to simulate fireflies. The stage picture was charming at first glance, but fell flat when nothing dramatic followed. A song was needed; something on the order of "Absinthe Frappé." Fields was already concerned in rehearsals that his score did not include a likely hit song.

Edward Marks, a Tin Pan Alley music publisher and Saratoga gambling buddy, suggested that Fields interpolate a German song called "The Glow Worm" by Paul Lincke. Fields was reluctant; the song was already a hit and there was a stage superstition about disturbing a success. Mitchell was also opposed to the idea. Fields jokingly asked if Marks would pay him $1,000 to insert the song in the summer arbor scene. Marks, quite serious, said no, but he would pay Fields

$1,000 if it was not the hit song of the show.[25] Marks proved correct. As sung by the fetching May Naudain, "The Glow-Worm" became an even bigger hit, and helped *The Girl Behind the Counter* to a thirty-eight-week New York run.

After reading the opening night reviews, Fields could not help boasting that, for the first time in fifteen years, all the Broadway critics were unanimous in their praise of a musical comedy. He attributed it to the book: "I like to think that the praise is given us because we are exploiting a consistent story—a slight one, it is true, but none the less a continuous one."[26] *Everybody's* magazine called it "one of those highly sophisticated and satirical entertainments that appeal particularly to . . . the class whose leisure is passed in theatres, restaurants, and automobiles. It shows more skill than any show of its kind that has been seen in years."

Early in 1908, the *New York Globe* hailed Fields as "The King of Musical Comedy." *The Girl Behind the Counter* had averaged $15,000 every week since its opening, which, in the eyes of the anonymous author, entitled Fields to royal respect: "He wore a herringbone sack suit of greenish gray, a purple tie, and green socks with a thin red stripe—truly a gorgeous person. But his face is his fortune . . . smooth and pink from shaving and grease paint . . . a long nose tobogganing from his forehead to his Indian bow smile (always in a parentheses of deep wrinkles); bright brown eyes, ears in full sail, and hair like a woof of glossy black silk. . . . It's a face unlike any you ever saw. Laughter has left its stamp indelibly upon it. Laughter is its trademark."

A knock on the door interrupted the interview. Fields opened the door, and the reporter noted a dramatic change in his manner, as if he were putting on armor. A girl, veiled in the shadows of the hallway, handed Fields a letter. "From the Shuberts," she said. Fields measured her with a quick glance, and scanned the letter. In a tone as hard and cold as hers was hopeful and warm, he told her that he would see her the following day. The coldness observed by the reporter was how Fields masked his distaste. Fields had learned that there was a protocol to the Shuberts' referrals: when the Shuberts were recommending a serious prospect, they sent a note by messenger requesting that Fields or an associate watch a performance in which the aspiring showgirl was appearing. When a would-be chorine arrived with a personal note from Lee or Jake, it usually meant that the girl was a victim of Jake's or Lee's casting couch. Fields was stuck with the responsibility of giving her the promised audition. Whether Fields hired her or not, the Shuberts had lived up to their end of the bargain.

Two major events—one theatrical, one financial—overshadowed the success of *The Girl Behind the Counter*. Three weeks after its opening, a Viennese operetta arrived that would radically redefine the American musical. Following its premiere in Vienna in 1905, Franz Lehar's *The Merry Widow* had swept west through the European capitals, influencing fashion and social behavior in its wake. By the time Henry Savage brought it to American shores, the show had already attained legendary status.

When *The Merry Widow* opened at the New Amsterdam on October 21, it was as if a spell had been cast on American producers and audiences, which would only be broken by the clamor of world war. Donald Brian, a handsome hoofer who had appeared in *Little Johnny Jones*, played Prince Danilo, and Ethel Jackson was the wealthy widow, Sonya. The libretto told a familiar story of royal romance and intrigue in a contemporary setting: reluctant Prince Danilo is ordered to marry Sonya to keep her millions in the country. When he falls for her, he must convince her that he loves her for herself, not for her money. What made the evening extraordinary was Lehar's score: seductive melodies such as "The Merry Widow Waltz" and "Maxim's" gave renewed life to the waltz in an age besotted by ragtime. The music lent an air of elegance and nostalgia to the libretto, emphasizing the romance rather than the comedy.

Where critics praised *The Girl Behind the Counter* for reversing the general order of things by having "more and better fun in it than music," three weeks later they revised their standards for musical comedy yet again in light of *The Merry Widow:* "Coming at the end of an epoch of inane musical comedies—grant that it is at an end!—the operetta is twice welcome, on account of its own excellence and because it may start a new era in musical entertainment."[27]

Its success spawned four road companies and countless burlesques (including one by Joe Weber, with Charles J. Ross playing Prince Dandilo). Overnight, broad-brimmed, elaborately feathered hats for women became the rage. The resurgence of the waltz sparked an interest in new dance styles on and off the stage; after the waltz came the tango and the turkey-trot, popularized by stage performers and imitated by fashionable men and women across the country.

Meanwhile, American producers rushed to acquire the rights to French, German and Austrian operettas, or they commissioned imitations of their own. Over the next seven seasons, Broadway was flooded with pseudo-Graustarkian entertainments. Following in *The Merry Widow*'s footsteps were *The Gay Hussars, A Waltz Dream, The Chocolate Soldier, The Count of Luxembourg, The Dollar Princess, The Slim Princess, The Merry Countess*, etc., etc.

Few producers dared to buck the trend; the three who did so most consistently and successfully were Cohan, Ziegfeld, and Fields. In July, 1907, Ziegfeld had launched the first of his Follies, with a book by Harry B. Smith, direction by Julian Mitchell, and backing by Klaw & Erlanger. Between 1907 and 1914, Ziegfeld avoided musical comedy and concentrated on redefining the revue in his annual summer entertainments. Meanwhile, Cohan split his talents between musical comedies (seven in all), straight plays, and attempts to revive the Weber & Fields–style revues. During that seven-year period, Lew Fields produced or acted in twenty-eight Broadway musical entertainments, not including his forays into vaudeville or straight comedy; of these, over half were musical comedies. No American producer or actor was more productive, more innovative, or more deserving of the title "the king of musical comedy."

Despite the instant success of *The Merry Widow, The Girl Behind the Counter* continued to be strong at the box office for the entire 1907–1908 season, with a phenomenal average gross of $15,000 a week for thirty-seven weeks. For the Shuberts, it was the only bright spot in an otherwise dismal year. The day after *The Merry Widow* opened, the Knickerbocker Trust Company was forced to close, setting off a wave of bank closings. In New York, the resulting panic was worse than the crash of 1893. Fearing that the panic would spread to the rest of the country, out-of-town theater managers canceled road bookings for Broadway shows.

The timing could not have been worse for the fledgling U.S. Amusement Company. The Shuberts' chief contribution to the partnership had been many less-than-desirable theaters acquired in their war with the Syndicate. Albee's first countermove was to instigate salary inflation among vaudeville performers to lure away the best stars and to force the challengers to overextend themselves. The U.S. Amusement Company soon found itself forced to book vaudeville bills that were too costly for the second-rate houses that were available to them. By November, Erlanger and the Shuberts realized that they could not win. For a lump sum pay-off of $1 million, Klaw & Erlanger transferred their vaudeville acts to Keith-Albee's United Booking Office and pledged to stay out of vaudeville for ten years. William Morris was hung out to dry, left holding a season's worth of expensive talent and no place to book them.

The Shuberts' share of the pay-off was reportedly $125,000; that, and the profits from *The Girl Behind the Counter* were their major sources of revenue during the 1907–1908 season. Fields' stock with Lee Shubert rose, and the latter listened more closely to Fields' ambitious plans. Their interests became so intertwined that they even co-produced benefit shows. Together they bought a half-interest in the Arverne Pier Theater (Long Island) and remodelled it; there they staged annual benefits for the families of ill or indigent actors, and for various Jewish charities (the Sanitarium for Hebrew Orphans, the Young Women's Hebrew Association, etc.). Lew and Lee became active fund-raisers for Jewish social programs, despite the fact that they were so assimilated that they exchanged Christmas presents and Easter plants.

On the evening of December 1, the entire Fields/Schoenfeld clan assembled in Vienna Hall to celebrate the golden wedding anniversary of Lew's parents, Solomon and Sarah. Witnessing the elderly couple's exchange of vows (in English rather than German) were their five sons and two daughters. Also present were Max's three children, though his widow could not bring herself to attend. Lew, who was "all over the place in his desire to please everyone," repeatedly explained, "My parents were married in Germany in 1857 and lived happily ever after." He was proud to have been able to contribute materially to their happiness.

Despite Fields' success after breaking with Weber, there were still many people on both sides of the footlights who would not accept that the Weber & Fields partnership was over. Every few months brought rumors of possible reunions, even though the erstwhile partners were barely on speaking terms and were doing quite nicely on their own. Producers and booking agents tried to tempt them with tremendous salaries; stage colleagues looked for excuses to bring them together. In May, 1908, the recently formed Friars' Club scheduled their first annual benefit performance at the New York Theater. Among the stars who volunteered their services were Victor Herbert, Eddie Foy, George M. Cohan, and Louise Dresser.

News that Weber and Fields would revive their German Senators routine "for this date only" boosted ticket sales over the $15,000 mark.

Halfway through the show, a Friar came out and introduced two "amateurs," begging the indulgence of the audience. There was a commotion backstage, and then the familiar reedy-voiced complaint, "Don't poosh me, Meyer" as Fields backed Weber onto the stage. The audience exploded into cheers so loud that the performers had to stop their act. "The large audience simply went wild over them," reported the *Clipper*, "and it was fully nine minutes before they were permitted to speak their lines." During this ovation, Joe and Lew looked distinctly uncomfortable. They had not performed the sketch for over ten years, but they felt no need to rehearse. The performance was "as funny as of old." At the climax of Meyer's abuse of Mike, Fields surprised everybody, including his partner, by kissing him. But the *Clipper* was overly optimistic when they wrote, "The kiss had the ring of sincerity about it." Perhaps, but Weber and Fields continued to pursue their separate careers.

Fields had originally planned to take *The Girl Behind the Counter* on the road in April, but the financial panic and the poor receipts from the Shuberts' other New York shows convinced Lee that it would be wiser to keep Fields' show in New York for as long as possible. Meanwhile, J. J. wanted to do a summer show at the Casino to compete with *Ziegfeld's Follies of 1908*, which was rehearsing in Atlantic City prior to its New York opening on June 15. Not to be outdone, J. J. rushed his summer show into rehearsals in Atlantic City. He had a title, *The Mimic World*, several cast members, two composers (Ben Jerome and Seymour Furth), and no book.

How *The Mimic World* ended up a Lee Shubert–Lew Fields production is unclear. After leaving Atlantic City, the show had laid off for a week and then spent a week in Philadelphia under Fields' supervision, where "various things that did not suit in the first place have been rectified."[28] *The Mimic World* was aptly titled: Fields now found himself in the curious position of trying to imitate Ziegfeld's Follies, which was in part derived from the Weber & Fields burlesques. Fields brought in Edgar Smith to concoct a series of sketches, and he strengthened the cast with the addition of several vaudeville acts. (One of them was a young vaudeville hoofer named Seymour Felix, who went on to become a noted choreographer in the 1920's and 1930's, for Fields' productions with Rodgers and Hart and in Hollywood.) For his salvage work, Fields received an unspecified salary (probably around $500 a week), as well as twenty percent of the net for his scripting and the use of his name in connection with the show.[29] Lee Shubert realized that Fields' name on a musical had become a valuable asset.

One key collaborator he could not hire was Julian Mitchell, who had just signed an exclusive contract with Flo Ziegfeld. Mitchell had grown tired of the Shuberts' constant attempts to cut his expenditures for choruses and stage effects. Ziegfeld, like Fields, had a reputation for spending lavishly on productions. Unlike Fields, nobody was looking over his shoulder. To replace Mitchell, Fields sent for thirty-four-year-old Ned Wayburn, a director and choreographer working in Chicago on a local hit musical, *The Honeymoon Trail*. (Wayburn would replace Mitchell yet again, in 1915, when Mitchell left Ziegfeld.) The inventiveness of Wayburn's vaudeville features for Hammerstein and Klaw-Erlanger had impressed Fields immensely. A large but graceful man (six feet two inches, over two hundred pounds) with a kindly face, Wayburn was no less exacting a director than Mitchell, but had a far more sophisticated knowledge of dance and stage movement. He elevated the choreography of the chorus line to an art, and the training of chorus girls to a science.

Born in 1874 into a family of industrial inventors, Edward Claudius Wayburn was educated in Chicago as an architectural draftsman and a musician. A stint in the Hart Conway School of Acting, where he learned military drills and the aesthetic gymnastics of François Delsarte, turned his love of precision and symmetry to the possibilities of the musical stage. By some accounts, he then ran away to pursue a stage career, appearing in a Dutch-Irish duo at Middleton's West Side Museum. By the turn of the century, he had performed in New York as a ragtime pianist. Wearing blackface, he became known for setting familiar classical tunes to ragtime syncopation. Around 1903, Wayburn attached metal plates to dancers' shoes, creating tap dance as an alternative to the old clog dances. A few years later, he was creating feature vaudeville acts and lively chorus lines. With Lew Fields, Wayburn began to develop the techniques for training and choreographing the chorus that would revolutionize the staging of the American musical.

With Wayburn and the vaudevillians, Fields set to work in the stultifying summer heat to save *The Mimic World.* After several postponements, the show finally opened at the Casino Theater on July 9. The hard work paid off. One reviewer observed, "The whole affair goes off with such a swing that the thinness of the music is largely concealed." Others praised the lavish costumes and the presence in the cast of so many "clever people" (what vaudevillians were called when they appeared in Broadway shows). The program called the entertainment a "review of the successes of the current season with no pretense of a plot." Indeed, it had less plot than any Weberfields program, or anything Fields did on his own. All of this was consistent with Shuberts' original intent—to compete directly with the Follies.

Among the stage characters parodied were Henry Schniff, Mr. Disch (Joe Weber), George M. Cohan, Kid Burns (Victor Moore), and Prince Danilo. The Salome dance, the titillating new dance craze popularized by Gertrude Hoffman, and the exotic ballet of Genée, were more precisely rendered. Fields wrote several of the sketches, and he coached actors Charles Sharp and Sam Sidman in their imitations of Weber and himself. Wayburn created another of those quick transformations that so delighted audiences of the era; a dozen boys and girls of the chorus appeared carrying dress-suit cases which they open up on stage to make the interior of a Pullman dining car. Lotta Faust danced and sang in a daring gown with the lowest-cut back ever seen on a Broadway stage. A young painter in the audience named Malcolm Strauss fell in love with her back and proposed to her face, though she was still married to tenor Richard Ling. The charms of *The Mimic World* outlasted the sultry weather, and the Shuberts sent the review on tour in the fall.

Before the summer was over, an era came to a sad end when Tony Pastor, the Father of Variety, lost the lease on his Fourteenth Street Theater and had to close it down. For the past decade, he had watched in dismay as the theatrical center shifted farther and farther uptown, and the stars he nurtured on his stage jumped to Broadway at the first opportunity. Still, he stuck by the little playhouse that he had made famous, lowering prices, adjusting the bills to include more sketches, circus acts, or dancers, and searching for bright new talent. His goal was to present first-class, wholesome entertainment, but with the rise of the Keith-Orpheum Circuits and the overreaching U.S. Amusement Company, vaudeville (how he hated that word!) had become too expensive.

Belatedly and reluctantly, he added motion pictures at the beginning and end of the program. More and more patrons, however, were stopping a few doors away from Pastor's at the Automatic One Cent Vaudeville arcade. The partners in this profitable enterprise included two ex-furriers named Adolph Zukor and Marcus Loew. Here, for a penny, viewers could watch primitive "flickers" such as "In My Harem," "Creeping Jimmie," or "Her Beauty Secret" in the peek machines that lined the walls.

Within a week of the closing of his theater, the seventy-one-year-old Pastor was reported to be gravely ill. Doctors could not determine the cause; he lingered for almost two weeks before he finally expired from what could only be described as a broken heart. Unlike the vaudeville titans who capitalized on his invention, Tony Pastor died with an estate of less than $9,000—and the love and respect of thousands of performers and patrons.

Word of Pastor's death reached Lew Fields in Chicago, where *The Girl Behind the Counter* was preparing to launch its season-long tour. Fields cabled his condolences but could not leave to attend Pastor's funeral. He later offered to organize a benefit performance.

The Girl Behind the Counter resumed in August at the Garrick in Chicago with the same popular acclaim it had enjoyed in New York. The show had been newly costumed by Melville Ellis, and Charles Judels replaced George Beban in the cast. Dainty and dangerous Lotta Faust rejoined the company from *The Mimic World*, bringing with her Salome's Dance of the Seven Veils. The gasps of the Chicago audiences grew louder with each successive veil, a response Lotta evidently enjoyed. "I am always thrilled and excited when I perform the dance," she admitted in an interview. "Especially tonight, when I saw a fat man walking down the aisle. I thought it was a policeman." A few days later, she performed with so much "exquisite abandon" (as one reviewer put it) that she was arrested. The following day, escorted by Fields and the manager of the Garrick, Lotta appeared before the judge to plead her innocence. She came dressed in white, with a white sailor's cap and a black silk bow tied around her throat. The judge dismissed the charges, but Fields decided to retire Salome for the rest of the tour. As William Sill said in a note to J. J. (who wanted to keep the dance), "It's a great show, even with Salome omitted."[30]

After playing six weeks in Chicago to capacity crowds, Lew Fields' All-Stars (as the Shuberts called the company) embarked on an extended tour of Shubert houses, crisscrossing the East and Northeast several times. Often, Fields would not be informed of booking changes until the last minute. The road show visited twenty-nine cities (besides Chicago) in twenty-six weeks, ending up in Springfield, Ohio, on March 31, 1909, for a one-night stand. The show played in New York and Brooklyn theaters during December, so Fields was able to spend several weeks with Rose and the children.

While the gross receipts were consistently high, so were the expenses. Fields' two shows—*The Mimic World* and *The Girl Behind the Counter*—cost one and a half to twice as much as the other Shubert shows on tour, and *The Mimic World* ended up losing money. Almost daily came wires from both Lee and J. J. on how to cut costs; the messages usually came through Frank Langley, the company's business manager. Lee, for example, insisted that the cast should only get half salaries the week before the election (supposedly a slow week for the box office); J. J. questioned Langley about the excessive number of calcium lamps, and the savings on royalty payments if a certain song was dropped from the show. Through Langley, Fields pointed out that the song in question—"I Want to Be Loved Like a Leading Lady," sung by Louise Dresser—had become the hit of the show.

During this period, Fields repeatedly spoke of his plans to become a producer "on a really big scale, like in England"—producing several new shows each year, supervising touring companies, managing leading performers, and building productions around them. With Ziegfeld and Cohan under contract to Klaw & Erlanger and Weber threatening to join them, the Shuberts could not afford to let Fields look elsewhere to satisfy his ambitions. On November 21, 1908, in the morning before a performance in New Haven, Connecticut, Lew Fields and Lee Shubert met secretly in New York to negotiate a contract.

Fields had heard that Jacob Litt was giving up his lease for the Broadway Theater. The Broadway could be refurbished to accommodate the big musicals that he envisioned, and it was better located (at Broadway and Forty-first) than the Herald Square. Lee Shubert promised to put up half of the lease money if Lew would act as the stalking horse in securing the lease. The owner of the theater was Felix Isman, a Philadelphia real estate tycoon who managed stars such as William Faversham and Louis Mann. Isman agreed to lease Fields the theater if he could become an equal partner in Fields' productions for the Broadway. Possibly, Isman was hoping to cash in on a Weber & Fields reunion if there was one; he had already made one attempt in partnership with William Morris to interest Joe and Lew in a reunion tour.

The resulting contract between Fields and Lee Shubert would be the determining factor in Fields' creative output for years to come. In return for providing half of the lease money, the Shubert Theatrical Company became equal partners with Fields for the lease. Given the expense of Lew Fields' productions, the Shuberts were anxious to minimize their financial exposure, so Fields, Lee Shubert, and Isman agreed to split three ways the profits and expenses from all Broadway Theater productions. Of course, the Sam S. Shubert Booking Agency would be the sole agent for the theater and any production originating there. Isman and the Shuberts would share the cost (estimated at $50,000) of refitting the theater for large-scale musicals "with the conveniences of a music hall" (i.e., a café and bar). At the same time, Lee Shubert extended his original employment contract with Fields for an additional five years (until September 1, 1914). Fields would

continue to be the lessee of the Herald Square Theater, and in a separate agreement, he promised to appear there as a performer at least once every season.

To supply two New York theaters with musical shows on a regular basis
meant a dramatic increase in Fields' activities as a producer and manager; in the
early part of 1909, Fields was planning two (possibly three) projects with Victor
Herbert, one with the team of George Hobart and Silvio Hein, another featuring
the veteran comedian John Slavin, in addition to the summer show that would
reopen the Broadway. What this meant to the Shuberts should not be underesti-
mated: now they could fill more of the time in their theaters more profitably with
Shubert-originated productions, instead of making costly deals with Syndicate
touring companies. Moreover, the cachet of a Lew Fields production would open
the doors of Syndicate or independent houses in cities where the Shuberts did
not yet have a first-class theater. The Shuberts' vaunted "open door" policy worked
best when it was the competitor's door that was kept open.

It would be several months before it would be clear to outsiders just how
closely Fields' future would be intertwined with the Shuberts'. When it was learned
that Fields was taking over the lease of the Broadway, *Variety* circulated more
rumors of a Weber & Fields reunion. Indeed, Fields was frequently seen around
Broadway with a short sidekick, only it was not the outgoing and endearing Joe
Weber; it was the quiet, calculating Lee Shubert. They appeared together to lay
the cornerstone of the new Shubert Comedy Theater (108 West Forty-first Street).
No larger than the Weber & Fields Music Hall, it was to be reserved for comedies
and intimate dramatic presentations.

In the spring of 1909, Lee Shubert had at least one compelling reason to back
Fields' ambitious plans at the Broadway. For the previous two years, Klaw &
Erlanger's summer attraction at the Jardin de Paris had proven that a well-staged
"review" (the French spelling was not yet common usage) could draw the lucrative carriage trade during the months when most theaters were closed. Messrs.
K. & E. had the foresight to back Flo Ziegfeld's Follies, and now enthusiastic New
Yorkers were touting it as the perfect summer show. The phrase "summer show"
described a subspecies of musical, part vaudeville and part "leg show," a fast-
paced and mindless entertainment designed to distract playgoers from the heat.
In the days before air-conditioned theaters, when no gentleman would be seen
without a coat and tie even in the dog days of summer, it was believed that the
mental effort required for watching serious plays produced an uncomfortable rise
in body temperature: "the slightest mental effort makes [the playgoers] perspire
and a respite from the dramatic will be granted by every manager alive to his
own interests."[31] Today, Hollywood's "summer releases" continue that tradition,
with far less justification.

Until Ziegfeld hit upon the idea of opening his *Follies of 1907* in July (subsequent editions opened in mid-June), the summer show was a little more than a
sideshow to attract tourists, a sloppy and haphazard production done on the
cheap. From the late 1890's, the preferred venue for the summer show was the
roof garden, a well-ventilated auditorium atop a regular theater. Its decor typically featured lush foliage suggesting an oasis or European garden. In the better
roof gardens, such as the Madison Square, the rows of seats were replaced with

tables where patrons could order light meals and sip cool drinks while they watched the show. It was at the Madison Square Roof Garden that the jealous millionaire Harry Thaw shot and killed the Garden's architect, Stanford White, for love of Evelyn Nesbit. Ziegfeld called his theater the Jardin de Paris; located on the top floor of the New York Theater, its original furnishings were far from glamorous— wooden folding chairs and a tin ceiling—but the French pretensions promised a hint of wickedness that was seductive indeed.

Initially, the only things that mattered in a summer show were girls, and lots of them. Critic Charles Darnton observed that "the sight of frilled and smiling femininity was enough to cool the fevered low-brow and high-brow alike."[32] (Apparently, as long as the girls wore frills and smiles, nobody in the audience got overheated.) Comedy was secondary; comedians who wanted to earn a few extra dollars for the summer were hired to perform monologues and sketches between the chorus routines. "Managers went into the beauty market," said Darnton, "for the best specimens that money can buy and crowded the stage with them."

Flo Ziegfeld did this better than anybody. Working with Julian Mitchell, he adapted the staging techniques of the Weberfields' chorus line, replacing the good-natured innocence of the Music Hall's girls with the artful devices of the Continental coquette. Except for singer Nora Bayes (still a rising star), the early editions of the Follies featured a grab bag of so-so vaudevillians and tired sketches by Harry B. Smith. Ziegfeld put his money into the trappings that would glorify his showgirls—the revealing costumes with outlandish headgear, the tasteful decor, the elaborate props. He was less concerned with other production elements—hiring the talent, writing the sketches, composing the music—and he usually left crucial creative decisions to a few trusted associates. But it was Ziegfeld's knack for turning pretty women into objects of public delectation that made the Follies a hit from the start.

Neither Lee nor J. J. could stand by idly while Klaw and Erlanger cornered the market on classy summer entertainment. *The Mimic World* had been J. J.'s botched attempt to lure away the Follies crowd. Fields' salvage job convinced Lee that J. J. had the right idea but the wrong man for the job. Fields, however, had little interest in parroting Ziegfeld's approach; he had his own ideas about how to produce a summer show. Lee Shubert did not mind as long as Fields could put two dollars in every seat.

To get a jump on Ziegfeld, Fields began rehearsals in mid-April for *The Midnight Sons*, the inaugural production for the renovated Broadway Theater. The book, by Glen MacDonough, and the music, by Raymond Hubbell, contained few clues to the show's rousing reception when it finally opened on May 23. The eponymous offspring were the four playboy sons of a rich, publicity-hungry politician, Senator Constant Noyes. At a "stag" banquet given in his honor (he is leaving on an African safari at the invitation of Teddy Roosevelt), he warns his sons that they must find productive occupations by the time he returns or risk losing their inheritance. Dick opens a shoe store (because all American millionaires start on a shoe-string) but fails. Harry builds a theater for his favorite chorus girl, Merri Murray, and loses money staging a benefit performance. The other two brothers, Tom and Jack, open up a resort hotel in Florida, and with the help of

Harry's and Dick's earnings as bellboys, scrape together enough cash to impress their father.

The libretto was piffle, and Fields knew it. Nobody expected much of a plot from a summer entertainment; nevertheless, Fields wanted to find an organizing principle that would give the illusion of a coherent shape to his production. Fields decided (as many Broadway producers have since then) that the only substitute for a good libretto and score was a rousing display of showmanship; i.e., visual and comic craft unfettered by content or story considerations (also known as giving 'em the sizzle without the steak.) Stymied by the lack of capable librettists and composers, Fields developed *The Midnight Sons* and its sequels around strong comedy ensembles and dazzling stage effects. In the process, he helped redefine the stagecraft of the Broadway musical.

Fields' cast was a judicious mixture of first-rate talent from straight drama, musical comedy, and vaudeville stages. From his unofficial stock company, he featured Lotta Faust (as Merri Murray, "America's leading chorus lady"), Vernon Castle (as Lushmore, a perpetual souse who can't find his way home), and Harry Fisher and Joseph Ratliff (as two of the Senator's spendthrift sons). Fields also hired George Monroe, a plump comedian who specialized in bossy Irish housemaids, to play Pansy Burns, an irascible cook who won't cook for just anybody. Broadway veteran George Schiller played the Senator, and Music Hall alumnus Fritz Williams played another one of the Senator's sons. A week before opening night, Fields signed Blanche Ring to a three-year contract under his management. With only five days to learn her role, she stepped into the part of the widow Carrie Margin and brought with her two song interpolations that saved Hubbell's mediocre score. She stayed for the summer run of *The Midnight Sons* while Fields had another piece prepared for her.

The blending of the chorus work of Ned Wayburn and the scenic effects of Arthur Voegtlin gave the show its sizzle. As a stage director, Ned Wayburn was as meticulous and demanding as Julian Mitchell, but more inventive and sophisticated in his routines. The chorus for *The Midnight Sons* consisted of twelve to fifteen men and forty or more women, the most that Wayburn or Fields had ever used. Fields argued with Lee Shubert that the cost of a larger chorus line was justified: making it possible for quicker and more dazzling scene transitions, including the visible changes that so delighted summer audiences. For the first time, Wayburn was working with a producer whose creative vision and ambition complemented his own and who was not afraid to spend the cash to make it real.

On his opening night program, Fields called *The Midnight Sons* "a musical moving picture in eight films." At first glance, it was a peculiar choice of labels; the typical subject matter of movies of the day and of Fields' productions could hardly have been more dissimilar. To the audiences of 1909, "films" meant silent one-reelers and nickelodeon shows—adventures, melodramas, and costume epics. In contrast to most theater productions, films provided fast-paced action and movement in a startlingly realistic context. It was this "realism"—the camera's ability to reproduce real objects, actions, and locations—that fascinated the early filmgoers, including Lew Fields. When Vitagraph released its version of *Uncle Tom's Cabin*, their advertisements boasted: "It will be the real thing in every respect—real ice, real bloodhounds, real negroes, real actors, real scenes from real life as it really was in the antebellum days!" Moreover, films were short, self-contained narrative units, usually no more than ten minutes long (early filmmakers believed that viewers would not sit still for anything longer). In its discontinuity and its emphasis on discrete novelties, the experience of attending a moving picture show more closely resembled a vaudeville bill than a legit play.

When Fields called his pioneering summer show "a musical moving picture in eight films," he was comparing its formal characteristics to those of early films. Wayburn supplied the speed and movement, Voegtlin, the realistic pictures, all presented within the framework of eight related but discontinuous scenes. "Musical"—as in comedy and extravaganza—was what made it better than a film, worth the extra $1.90 for admission.

Arthur Voegtlin's settings for *The Midnight Sons* were chosen more for their visual and comic potential than for their narrative logic. As the scenic designer for the mammoth productions at the Hippodrome, Voegtlin had established himself as a master of complex stage machinery and large crews, mounting cavalry charges on horseback, naval battles in a huge tank, and auto races. His sets for Lew Fields' productions were of necessity less epic in scope but cleverer in conception. All of the sets for *The Midnight Sons* were detailed replicas of actual locations familiar to the audience, the idea being that the staging and comic performances would be more effective playing off "realistic" settings—the same principle developed in the later Weberfields burlesques.

The Scene One curtain revealed the Sportsman's Room of the Hotel Insomnia (read "Astoria"), where a farewell banquet for Senator Noyes is taking place. The Senator, his four sons, and twenty-four guests (all male) are seated at a horseshoe-shaped table, with an additional fifteen guests seated at tables on a platform behind them. In the opening chorus Wayburn inserted a specialty act, an eccentric dance by Vernon Castle, as the sentimental drunk, Lushmore. Singing "Call Me Bill" ("Never mind my real name now . . ."), the rubber-legged Castle performed a "drunk dance," stumbling from one waitress–chorus girl to another, using a conventional One-step or Hesitation Walk as an excuse for the swaying, dips, and trip steps that characterize a drunk.[33]

Later in the scene, Merri Murray (Lotta Faust) saunters in, wearing another daring backless gown, and sings "The Soubrette's Secret," while she and the French waitresses are lifted onto the tables to dance. Merri accidentally drops her handkerchief near Dick; he kneels to retrieve it just as Merri finishes her dance. She steps from table to floor, using his shoulders as a step. Harry tells her of his plans to name a theater after her where she can appear in a new play every year and speak the one line that has made her famous: "Oh, Goils, the royal body guards is passing." When Harry's play flops, Merri is sure that it is because he neglected to include her line.

The settings for Scenes Two and Three reproduced the exterior and interior of a Fifth Avenue Shoe Store. After a comedy bit trying to find shoes that fit Pansy Burns (George Monroe) and her ugly, amorous friend (the gangly comedienne Lillian Lee), enter Rose Raglan, a country girl who has become a vaudeville headliner. Dick's shoe store is supposed to make the slippers for Rose and her

Ten Owlets, so they have come to be fitted. Naturally, Rose ends up demonstrating her act, a novelty rag about "a cynical owl . . . once a jovial fowl" who perches in a tree outside a summer hotel. Every night "ten or twelve pairs of lovers he'll view . . . but in twenty odd years / He hasn't heard anything new." During the first verse, curtains on the upstage window raised about eighteen inches, revealing the feet and ankles of ten showgirls standing in the window, with their feet on shoe stands. As the solo refrain begins they step down from the window and move into their positions on stage.

Scenes Four and Five contained the kind of up-to-the-minute technical tricks that Fields (and audiences) loved. The setting was the Grand Concourse at Grand Central Station, where Senator Noyes is being met by two of his sons. Amidst a bustling crowd of travelers and redcaps, Tom runs into the pretty widow Carrie Margin, and he proposes to her on the spot: "It's the true American method. Fall in love at first sight, propose in ten minutes, get married in an hour and go around the world in thirty days." If Carrie is willing, they can get married right away and leave together on the Honeymoon Express. It will be "love at a mile a minute." As Tom sings "On a Yankee Honeymoon," six couples enter chasing a parson, who is finally persuaded to marry the couples, including Tom and Carrie. At the end of the dance, bride and bridegroom board the Honeymoon Express—a Pullman observation car at the back of the departing train—where they join the other newlyweds in a final chorus. Voetglin used film footage projected behind the observation car windows to create the illusion of accelerating movement. The audience watched in fascination as the scenery of the New York Central line hurtled by. The Act One curtain came down on trains, whirlwind romances, moving pictures, and choruses. Fields' thoroughly modern musical showed love and everything else at a mile a minute. *"The Midnight Sons,"* concluded critic Acton Davies, "travels at the pace that kills. It was all the audience could do to keep up with it."

Voegtlin's setting and Wayburn's staging also overcame the usual problem of regaining momentum at the start of the second act. With the rise of the curtain, the audience found itself face to face with a similar audience on stage, consisting of 300 actors, chorus people, extras, and wax dummies filling the boxes, orchestra, balcony, and gallery seats. The dummies were made up to resemble famous first-nighters such as Lillian Russell, Diamond Jim Brady, and Alan Dale. Onstage, an orchestra is making music, and ushers are showing latecomers to their seats. The imaginary audience has gathered at the Merri Murray Variety Theater to watch a hastily arranged benefit performance. Separating the two audiences is a narrow strip of stage, and the footlights of the imaginary stage illuminate the first few rows of the real audience. The scenery elicited a spontaneous burst of applause when the audience realized what they were seeing.

The performers—an English Pony Ballet, a trapeze artist, a toe dancer, and a singer (Blanche Ring as Carrie Margin)—played their specialties with their backs to the real audience. Led by Pansy Burns (George Monroe), who won't remove her "peach basket" hat, unruly patrons of the benefit interrupt the turns. Wayburn's staging of this show-within-a-show accommodated the insertion of individual specialties without interrupting the flow of the story. To circumvent the fact that the setting required performers to play with their back to the real audience, Wayburn choreographed the turns so that the sight lines were equally favorable from any angle.[34] The sets for the Merri Murray theater were so massive ("quite the biggest piece of stagecraft" ever seen in a Broadway house, according to the *Clipper*) that they required an intermission to put them in place.

The final scene unfolded at a garden fête at the brothers' resort hotel, the Pounceuponham, in Palm Beach, Florida. Voegtlin's garden fête setting reproduced a veranda and lawn, with tables and chairs scattered around and a set of stairs in the center back. Once more, the show-within-a-show format afforded Wayburn and Fields the excuse to insert a series of specialty acts and solos. Chief among them was the evening's hit song, "I've Got Rings on My Fingers," sung by Blanche Ring, about an Irish castaway who lords it over the natives and offers to make his lady love the queen: "Sure I've got rings on my fingers, and bells on my toes, / Elephants to ride upon, my sweet Irish rose, / So come to your nabob, and on next St. Patrick's Day, / Be Mistress Mumbo Jumbo Jijiboo Jay, O'Shea." Ring delivered these infantile lyrics in a winsome Irish "come-all-ye" style, and the song became identified with her for the rest of her career.

Merri Murray, humbled at having to give a turn at a hotel garden fête, imagines herself "Carmen the Second." Wearing a short skirt and backless blouse, Lotta Faust drew raves, gasps, and applause with a fervent Spanish dance.

There was little effort to tie up the plot's loose ends until the last page, when a crucial dramatic question was raised and disposed of in a few lines. Was this "the semblance of a clever story capably worked out" that Lew Fields had said the public wanted in 1904? *The Midnight Sons* had less plot than *The Girl Behind the Counter*, which had less plot than *It Happened in Nordland*. No matter— audiences and critics loved Fields' summer entertainments. Like a mythical Eastern potentate, he overwhelmed them with his lavish gifts. "A show of class, a show of infinite novelty, a show of bigness . . ." wrote Rennold Wolf in the *New York Morning Telegraph*. Acton Davies *(Evening Sun)* used similar terms: "a production which is colossal in its proportions, prodigal in its extravagance and unequalled in its long cast of musical and dramatic celebrities." Ditto the the *Dramatic Mirror: "The Midnight Sons* sets a new and more extravagant standard for musical comedy pretentiousness, quantity and quality. It is immense." With the production of *The Midnight Suns* and its successors, *The Jolly Bachelors*, *The Summer Widowers*, and *The Hen Pecks*, Fields redefined the summer show; putting, in Charles Darnton's words, "this class of entertainment on a whole new footing. Lew Fields . . . has gone in at breakneck speed for a typically American entertainment in which the element of vaudeville predominates. . . . If you had time to think you would realize that he is giving you glorified vaudeville till you can't rest.[35] The term "glorified vaudeville" was not necessarily pejorative when one remembers that "musical comedy" was merely a commercially appealing label: everybody used it but nobody could define it. As Fields himself had come to realize, musical comedies were something less than the sum of their parts. Fields' innovative stagecraft, his comic style, and his subject matter all tended to blur the distinction between vaudeville and musical comedy. To describe a program made up of the moments that exude the essence of showmanship—the Honeymoon Express or the Merri Murray Theater in *The Midnight Sons*, for example—there was really no better term than "glorified vaudeville." William Morris went as far as to suggest that musical comedy was vaudeville's apotheosis: "The day of distinction, or line of differentiation by theatre patrons has not only passed, but it is so completely submerged that there is no discriminating between legitimate musical comedy and the better kind of vaudeville."[36] Eighty years later, "glorified vaudeville" is still a fair designation for what happens to a musical when showmanship substitutes for narrative integrity.

"This is my principle theory of what the public wants . . ." declaimed Fields in 1904, "coherency." Absent consistent scores and librettos, there was only one way to ensure coherency. Showmanship substituted for it and disguised its lack. As an actor, Fields wanted "to unfold a story in a natural way . . . to play a character role in a bright musical play without feeling every time I walk on stage like an intruder." *The Midnight Sons* was a play in which he would have felt like an intruder; it did not have a story that unfolded "in a natural way." In his first major outing as a producer, Fields put aside his actor's ambitions and made showmanship the ultimate goal.

Comparisons with Ziegfeld were therefore inevitable. Critics applied the generic label "review" to both Ziegfeld's and Fields' summer shows. Nevertheless, there were substantial stylistic differences. Fields' summer shows always had a book, though in the weakest of them, the plot was only a tissue-thin pretext for vaudeville specialties. Ziegfeld's entertainments were plotless, organized around topical themes, "the follies of the day." Fields' shows were comedy sketches tied together by chorus routines; Ziegfeld made his choruses the evening's *raison d'être*. Fields' motto was "Make 'em laugh"; Ziegfeld's, "Make 'em stare."

Behind these stylistic differences were two men whose sensibilities could not have been more dissimilar, and their productions carried their distinctive moral imprints. Lew Fields' summer shows were, in the words of Charles Darnton, "as thoroughly American as popcorn." Ziegfeld chose to emulate the French music halls; his reviews came "as close as near as the law will allow to the type of summer show one sees in the open air resorts of Paris.[37] Fields admitted to being scandalized by Parisian summer shows. Though no prude by American standards—had he not presented the Weberfields' chorus, Salome dances, and chorus girls ripping off each other's frocks on stage?—he roundly condemned the Parisian revue: "No sane man with any regard for himself or his family can extract any real pleasure from the unlovely items that constitute these Parisian programmes. . . . A lady simply cannot enter them. . . . Nothing depends upon imagination. They do not stop within a thousand miles of decency. . . . I used to think that my own experiences on the Barbary coast in San Francisco in the old days were rough enough, but they were Sunday school picnics in comparison to what goes on in Paris."[38] It especially pained Fields to discover that the Parisian music halls were packed with Americans, and that native Parisians referred to their tawdry summer entertainments as "the American season."

Having spent the better part of his life trying to obtain social legitimacy for the actor's profession and the popular stage, Fields' comments are perfectly understandable. His role model, Tony Pastor (also known as "Tony the Puritan"), had criticized variety shows of the 1870's and 1880's in much the same terms. Where Fields sought to preserve the rigid moral standards of the Victorian society he aspired to, Ziegfeld made a career of provoking them. After all, Ziegfeld began by promoting sensuous "freaks": the strong man, Sandow, whose muscles were stroked after the show by society women; and Anna Held, whose fame derived from her tiny waist, kissable lips, and legendary milk baths.

Nowhere were the contrasts more apparent than in their attitudes towards the chorus girl. There had always been a certain ambivalence about the Weber-fieldsian chorus girl. Like Miss America, she had to be admired for her charm and her talent as well as her looks, but her sexual availability was officially suppressed. Still, Weber & Fields traded on glimpses of voluptuous figures and shapely limbs. In contrast to the screwball innocence of the Weberfieldsian chorus girl, the Ziegfeld girl exhibited a more frankly sexual provocation. At heart, however, Fields was a moralist, like all satirists, whether they are performers or writers. Ziegfeld was an unabashed hedonist; he promoted indulgence, not just impertinence; which is one reason why Ziegfeld's sensibility strikes us as more modern.

Two weeks after the successful opening of *The Midnight Sons*, Fields felt confident enough to leave New York for a brief vacation with Rose in Atlantic City. On the boardwalk, they posed for a photograph against a painted backdrop of the shore. Rose, seated stiffly, wore an elaborate Merry Widow hat and held her beaded purse primly in her lap, while Lew leaned casually on the arm of her chair, dapper in his three-piece suit, Arrow collar, and straw hat. The picture was reproduced in a New York paper under a curious but apparently truthful headline: "The first picture taken in years of Mr. and Mrs. Fields together," with a caption describing them as "a devoted couple . . . never happier than when having a good time with their attractive young children." It was evidently deemed newsworthy when such wholesome sentiments could be attributed to a stage celebrity. One cannot imagine a similar description caption for a photo of Mr. and Mrs. George M. Cohan or Mr. and Mrs. Flo Ziegfeld.

Fields' trip to Atlantic City was not strictly for relaxation. As Rose had sadly learned by now, their vacation destinations were determined in part by Lew's business interests. During this unusually mild and rainy June, what drew Fields to Atlantic City were the tryouts for *The Follies of 1909*. He wanted to see first-hand the difference between his summer show and Flo Ziegfeld's.

CHAPTER XI

The King of Musical Comedy (Part Two)

A megalomania in the inflation of musical plays seems to possess Mr. Fields and his collaborators. . . .

from an article in the *Boston Transcript*, Nov. 1, 1910

O N the afternoon of June 10, 1909, Lee Shubert and the Shuberts' press representative, a man with the wonderful moniker of A. Toxen Worm, took the five-hour train ride to Atlantic City to check on their rivals' summer production, *The Follies of 1909*, then in its tryouts. Shubert and Worm met Rose and Lew Fields at their hotel in Atlantic City for a light supper. Rose knew what Lee Shubert's presence meant; he had a habit of showing up on short notice at the Fields' summer homes, vacation spots, even on their overseas cruises. Nevertheless, she was flattered by Lee's courtly manners. A perfect gentlemen, he always remembered Rose and the children with lavish Christmas gifts, a gesture that further endeared him to Lew as well. And she would not begrudge Lew the company of one of his few close friends in the business.

At about eight o'clock, Shubert, Worm, Rose, and Lew presented themselves at the Apollo with orchestra seat tickets purchased earlier in the day. As they entered the theater, Fields saw Ziegfeld and the Apollo's manager, Fred Moore. They traded polite nods. Also present, but waiting backstage, was Abe Erlanger, who had come down to oversee the preview performances. The Shubert party (as the press would later refer to them) had been seated for ten minutes when Moore, accompanied by the special house officer, approached them with an urgent message from Mr. Ziegfeld and Mr. Erlanger: the curtain would be held until Mr. Shubert left the theater. Bristling with indignation, Shubert and Fields refused to leave. The audience, growing restive over the unexplained delay, began to sense that something was wrong. The manager returned with Ziegfeld, who delivered the same message in person, but added that Mrs. and Mrs. Fields were welcome to stay because he "[had] nothing in the world against them." Fields, however, would not stand by while his friend was publicly insulted. By now, most of the audience was aware of the increasingly loud argument in the front section of the orchestra seats. The house officer then reappeared with two burly stagehands and said that he would remove the party by force if necessary. Audience members seated nearby began to shout in support of Shubert and Fields.

According to Fields' account, the threat of force made Rose uneasy, and out of deference to the lady, Shubert agreed to withdraw. Later that evening, Ziegfeld approached Fields in their hotel lobby and tried to explain. Fields would not forgive him for "the humiliation to which Mrs. Fields had been subjected," and walked away.

The reporter for the *New York Herald* put it in its proper perspective: "There was a spirited skirmish between the rival theatrical camps here to-night. . . ."[1] The Shuberts' agreement with the United States Amusement Company had expired in May, and hostilities between the Syndicate and the Shuberts were heating up once more. J. J. boasted that the Shuberts could now book forty weeks coast-to-coast, and that during the coming season they would control over a hundred attractions, sixty of their own and forty of allied producers (a quarter of these belonging to Lew Fields). Alliances between producers, players, and theater managers shifted almost daily, but more and more theater managers were declaring themselves for the Shuberts' Open Door.

Shortly after the incident at the Apollo, Erlanger retaliated by signing a deal with Joe Weber that made them joint operators of the former Weber & Fields Music Hall. The five-year contract also specified that Weber would book his road companies in Syndicate theaters. Weber, whose feistiness and business acumen had finally contributed to a rupture with the Shuberts, publicly praised Klaw & Erlanger and said that he now regretted the independent stand that Weber & Fields had defended so vehemently. The possibility of a Weber & Fields reunion now seemed remote indeed.

During the summer of 1909, rumors about Fields' ever-expanding activities filled the theater trade journals. In support of his plans to produce from six to nine musicals in the coming season, he was busy signing some of the biggest talents in vaudeville and legit to appear under his management. Shortly after Blanche Ring rejoined Fields, he signed the brilliant comedienne Marie Dressler to a three-year contract. The terms were generous: $500 per week for thirty weeks a year, guaranteed, plus ten percent of the gross. By the end of the season, his management roster included Andrew Mack (Irish singer and comedian), Joe Welch (Hebrew comic), John T. Kelly, Irene Franklin, William Collier, Blossom Seeley ("the Queen of Syncopation"), Stella Mayhew, George Monroe, and Fritzi Scheff, the opera star who had crossed over to operetta and musical comedy.

Fields' reputation among his colleagues made him a magnet for stars. They knew him to be as generous in his salaries as in his willingness to share top billing. Moreover, they knew that he had the ability to build productions that would showcase their talents. Many of them signed with Fields when they would not have been willing to sign directly with the Shuberts. Proof of this came when J. J. would try to borrow them for his productions, and the performers would often refuse. Lee also found it advantageous to invoke Fields' name when he was trying to negotiate with a performer.

The scope of Fields' theatrical endeavors could be measured by his office's cluttered new letterhead. To the right of his name (which was capitalized in bold-face type) were the addresses of his two theaters, the Broadway and Lew Fields' Herald Square; to the left he crowded the names of his productions for the 1909–1910 season:

The Midnight Sons
Blanche Ring, in *The Yankee Girl*
Andrew Mack, in *The Prince of Bohemia*
Marie Dressler [in an as yet unnamed musical]
The Rose of Algeria
The Winter Review—*The Jolly Bachelors*
The Girl Behind the Counter [touring company]
and
Lew Fields, in *Old Dutch*

Before the season ended in June, there would be a ninth Fields production as well—another summer spectacle, *The Summer Widowers*. All told, Fields' shows accounted for twenty-five percent of the new musicals produced on Broadway during the 1909–1910 season.

Yet, even as he seemed to be making efforts to corner the market on mirth and melody, Fields admitted that he was "tired of being laughed at."[2] In an interview with a female reporter, he complained that, hard as it is to make a reputation as a comedian, it was harder still to keep it up, and "many times it is very much of a bore to do so." It was an extraordinarily candid expression of Fields' growing ambivalence. He sounded resigned to the idea of being a comedian, and spoke of it as if it were a family or social obligation. "All comedians get tired of [being laughed at]. But it is our business in life and we keep on with it because we know that our bread and butter and a few other things depend on it"—such as an upper West Side town house, live-in servants, chauffeured cars, private schools, twenty-dollar silk shirts, and summer trips to Saratoga.

The timing of these utterances—at the start of the most ambitious season ever attempted by any Broadway musical producer—was odd, to say the least. "People are willing to pay me for laughs, so it would be foolish of me to offer them tears. I'm tired of laughing though, tired of it." Such comments fueled the rumors that he would retire as a comedian, and that he would act in and produce "heart interest" dramas. But his participation in twenty musical comedies and revues during the next three seasons was not the kind of behavior one would expect from a man who claimed to be "tired of laughing."

Although Fields seemed to be an indomitable force during the 1909–1910 season, he was swimming against the tide. Broadway audiences had developed pretensions to sophistication. Viennese operetta was at the height of its influence, and fashionable theatergoers surrendered themselves to its idyllic entreaties. Whereas the musical comedy was chaotic, flippant, sometimes even corrosive, the operetta, with its more coherent stories and soothing melodies, promised an orderly world where romance ruled and sentimental gestures were taken seriously.

While the "Fields touch" was discernable in all of his productions, his shows possessed a stylistic diversity that did not suggest a definite trend or aesthetic direction, at least to the audiences of the day. In fact, this medley of forms was itself becoming the Fields trademark. Performers from the minstrel show and the Met, stage devices from vaudeville and Belasco, American social types in comic opera settings—Fields' style was a constantly changing collage of borrowings and found fragments, a hybrid of high and low stage traditions and techniques, all in the service of musical comedy. There was something inherently irreverent about his pluralism, suggesting the methods of a man who would apparently do anything (and spend everything) for a laugh.

Two Viennese operettas set the tone for the entire season. *The Dollar Princess*, with a score by Leo Fall, and *The Chocolate Soldier*, with music by Oscar Straus and a book based on Shaw's *Arms and the Man*, opened a week apart in September and went on to almost three hundred performances in New York. The only home-grown musicals to come close were Cohan's *The Man Who Owns Broadway* (128 performances), and three of Fields' productions: *The Midnight Sons* (counting its summer run, 264 performances), *The Jolly Bachelors*, and *Tillie's Nightmare*. It is worth noting that Fields' longest-running shows were the ones that least resembled Viennese operetta.

The two Fields productions that opened the season—*The Rose of Algeria* and *Old Dutch*—were the ones that most closely resembled the fashionable imports. Both had scores by Victor Herbert. Fields had been eager to work with Herbert again ever since the triumph of *It Happened in Nordland*. Early in 1908, he commissioned Herbert to compose the music for an operetta to be called *Regina*. In the contract, Fields agreed to the unprecedented stipulation that no part of the resulting work—book, lyrics, or production numbers—would be produced apart from Herbert's music. The contract reflected Fields' respect for Herbert, as well as Herbert's unhappy experience with Joe Weber on *Dream City*, which ended with Herbert suing both Weber and the librettist, Edgar Smith. *Regina*, however, never materialized.

Instead, Herbert finished the score for a "musical play" for producer Frank McKee. Called *Algeria*, it had a libretto by *Nordland* author Glen MacDonough, whose creative contributions were generally held to be responsible for *Algeria*'s closing in September, 1908, after only forty-eight performances. Sultana Zoradie is enamored of a poet she has never seen, and a French captain (actually the poet) is in love with a "girl of the desert" (naturally, Zoradie in disguise) whom he meets in the marketplace. War is threatening, and the peace treaty with France depends upon identifying the poet. Zoradie must deal with three imposters before she finally discovers her true love.

Herbert's score was one of his best, full of passionate melodies and grand chorale arrangements. His songs emphasized the romance and downplayed the comedy; rather than burlesquing the overblown fervor of opera, he celebrated his character's romantic yearnings. When Zoradie first reads / sings the poem "Rose of the World," she is in disguise and must struggle to conceal her amazement. The Act One finale depicts American nurses receiving overseas mail; they waltz to illustrate the love letters they know they are handling. Herbert's vibrant opening for Act Two evoked an Algerian carnival (similar to his Act Two opening chorus for *Nordland*), followed by the Captain's quiet musings in "Love Is Like a Cigarette" ("a cigarette may last as long"), which was originally a part of the 1905 edition of *Nordland.* Zoradie answers with the atmospheric "Twilight in Barrakeesh." Even in the lighter numbers, such as "Ask Her While the Band Is Playing," romantic concerns took precedence over comic effects.

Still, Herbert's beautiful score could not stand alone. MacDonough's book was coy and broad when it was not simply dull. The New York critics, unanimous in their praise of the music, condemned the story, its principals, even its comedians. According to Herbert's biographer, Edward Waters, the quick failure of *Algeria* was one of Herbert's greatest disappointments.

Lew Fields believed that a new cast and a rewritten book would turn the show into a success, so, shortly after *Algeria* closed, he bought the rights. He made the mistake, however, of assigning Glen MacDonough the task of revising his own book. Fields asked MacDonough for several minor script changes as well as for more visually exciting settings—not just the typical one set per act. Herbert's score remained virtually intact, except for the deletion of one minor song, and the addition of two other songs and orchestral interludes.

During the summer of 1909, Fields made frequent trips to Herbert's summer home in Lake Placid to discuss the other two productions they were collaborating on, *Old Dutch* and *When Sweet Sixteen.* Approaching Lake Placid one afternoon, Fields and William Sill came upon a pickup game of baseball. Fields asked the cabby to pull over so that they could watch for a few minutes. There was a runner on first, and the batter hit a sharp grounder to a stout, mustachioed man playing second base. With surprising grace, the rotund second baseman fielded the ball and tossed it to the shortstop covering second base, who relayed the ball to first for a double play. It was not until the inning was over and the second baseman was being congratulated that Fields realized that he had just seen America's greatest stage composer start a double play. Herbert declined an offer to play on Fields' Broadway show team.

By the end of the summer, Fields had at least three shows in rehearsal and two others being scripted, with *The Midnight Sons* continuing at the Broadway. It was on the reshaping of *Algeria*—now renamed *The Rose of Algeria*—that he lavished the most energy. Together, Fields and Herbert supervised the out-of-town tryouts for *The Rose of Algeria*, and their personal involvement was indicative of their high hopes for the show. Fields spent money on it recklessly—his own, apparently, and not Lee Shubert's (the Shuberts booked and managed the show's tour, but there is no evidence of other financial involvement). A Pittsburgh newspaper referred to Fields affectionately as "the theatrical spendthrift" and reported how he "squandered" $25,000 for cast and stage effects to give "his friends the public the best that he can buy."[3]

For the role of Zoradie, Fields imported a German light-opera star, Lillian Herlein, whom he had heard during his last trip to Europe. Touted as "the nightingale of Berlin," she insisted on a "huge" salary with a thirty-week guarantee and a bonus. One of her costumes, a court dress, was an exact duplicate of a robe made for an East Indian princess. It reportedly cost $1,500, half of that sum going to pay for the dress train, which was made from pure gold thread. Fields believed that the audible murmurs of the audience when Herlein swept on stage justified the cost.

To play the Governor-General, he ransomed the veteran basso Eugene Cowles from a Klaw & Erlanger contract. Cowles, now approaching the end of his career, had been a member of the Bostonians, generally considered to be the greatest American comic-opera company of the late nineteenth century. For what Fields paid to buy out Cowles' contract, Klaw & Erlanger were able to equip an entire new production. The Shuberts were not pleased. Likewise, Fields secured the contractual release of the vaudeville team of Ethel Green and Billy Gaston by guaranteeing them forty weeks at a rate that surpassed their vaudeville salary. Several of the players had no written contracts at all, reflecting their trust in Fields and Fields' own casual approach to business. (This inattention to financial matters alternately infuriated and delighted the Shuberts; when Lee Shubert took over management of the tour, he was able to use the lack of contracts to his advantage.)

If nothing else, MacDonough's revision did give Wayburn the pretext he needed for his ambitious stage pictures. For the Act One finale, Wayburn returned to the same device he had used in *The Midnight Sons:* rear-screen film projection as a background for live performers and three-dimensional sets. He put the two co-medians in a storm-tossed rowboat as the duo struggled to escape the enemy on shore and the "moving picture" breakers crashing around them. The effect was judged to be "startlingly realistic and took repeated encores" (an interesting con-cept for a stage effect) at its New York opening.[4] For this one-minute effect, Fields reportedly paid "several thousand dollars and a large weekly royalty" to the inventor, Frank D. Thomas, because Fields wanted to have the exclusive rights to the patent. To modern playgoers, it may seem like mere gimmickry, but in the context of the era's stagecraft, it was an innovative attempt to incorporate the latest technological advances in the staging of a musical. Still, one may question whether this essentially comic scene had the right emotional tone, given the un-abashedly romantic intent of Herbert's score. It is perhaps a clue to why Fields' musicals during this period seem to be at odds with the public's taste for the imported Viennese confections. He could not resist using comedy to subvert or dilute romance, while the Broadway public wanted their romance undiluted, in all its sickly sweetness.

When *The Rose of Algeria* opened at Lew Fields' Herald Square Theater on September 20, it was with Victor Herbert conducting an augmented orchestra (fifty, instead of the usual forty musicians). Reviews of the sold-out first night were positive but not glowing; the new cast, Wayburn's staging, and, of course, Herbert's score all received favorable mention. The best that could be said about MacDonough's book was that it was changed. One reviewer noted that there were "no storms of applause. . . . no roars of laughter" for the libretto. Most agreed that the production was nothing more than "old wine in a new bottle," even if the refurbished version was "a delightful entertainment."[5]

Fields' second mistake (after hiring MacDonough to revise his libretto) was opening the show barely two weeks after *The Dollar Princess* and a week after

The Chocolate Soldier. Despite a musical score and staging that were arguably superior to either of the hit shows', *The Rose of Algeria* could not overcome its foreign competition or the poor reputation of its libretto. It folded after only forty performances in New York. The ill-fated *Rose* toured Eastern theaters through the rest of the year; in mid-December, Lee Shubert halved the company salaries, and in early January, the show finally closed after a dismal week in Detroit.

How much money (if any) Fields lost is unknown. It clearly did not matter to him; *The Rose of Algeria* was a labor of love. Under less than promising circumstances, Fields produced the show for the most romantic of reasons: he loved the music, and wanted to give it the staging it deserved. For the record, the show was hardly the failure—artistically or financially—that theater historians have made it out to be.

Autumn of 1909 was a time of frenetic activity for Fields, and the beginning of the most productive phase in his career. The Monday following the opening of *The Rose of Algeria*, Fields started rehearsing his second Herbert collaboration of the season, *Old Dutch*, in which he also had a leading role. Victor Herbert, along with librettist George Hobart and lyricist Silvio Hein, was working on yet another musical for Fields, *When Sweet Sixteen*. Meanwhile, Fields also had four other shows in the early stages of production. In rehearsals were *The Prince of Bohemia*, with Andrew Mack; the Marie Dressler vehicle, *Tillie's Nightmare;* and *The Jolly Bachelors*, Fields' giant winter "review," with an all-star cast of vaudevillians surrounded by a Wayburn chorus and a messy, half-formed book by Glen MacDonough. *The Yankee Girl*, starring Blanche Ring, had already opened at the Savoy in Atlantic City on September 23. Fields moved it at once to Philadelphia, where it played to capacity business.

Fields did not simply lend his name to a production; he involved himself in every aspect except its business matters (where he was notoriously erratic). The press could not decide whether to call him a producer or a manager, so they often called him "producing manager." In nineteenth-century stage lingo, a manager had the hands-on responsibility for shaping the show. But Fields also supervised scripting and revisions, the hiring of principals and chorus girls (for the latter, Wayburn provided him with candidates from his dance school), the selection and placement of interpolated songs, and the set design. And like the Shuberts, he had money of his own invested in the shows.

Unlike the Shuberts, who ran a growing entertainment empire backed by Wall Street investors, or Felix Isman, who was a real estate tycoon quite apart from his theater ventures, Fields' only business was making musicals. Two or three box-office flops would not break the Shuberts or Isman. But with each of the increasingly extravagant entertainments that Fields produced, he was staking his personal fortune on continued success. He may have been an equal financial partner with Isman and the Shuberts, but the stakes for him were considerably higher.

Once rehearsals began, it was Wayburn who assumed many of the day-to-day responsibilities. He developed solutions within guidelines set by Fields, and then Fields approved or modified them. From 1909 to the end of 1911, Wayburn was Fields' closest collaborator, and it is impossible to say where one's contributions ended and the other's began. In the summer of 1910, Wayburn moved his offices into Fields' Broadway Theater, and they were frequently seen getting a late meal together after an evening performance. Through thirteen productions in three seasons with Fields, Wayburn had the freedom to develop the artistic ideas that would eventually bring him acclaim in Ziegfeld's Follies.

In the autumn of 1909, theater columnists began to refer to Lew Fields as "the busiest man on Broadway." True, he had always been a tireless worker, but now he seemed driven. One journalist compared Fields to Teddy Roosevelt, and doubted that the latter had ever "been forced to unleash as much nervous force and energy."[6] Rarely did Fields sleep more than four hours a night. Every time he checked his watch he seemed to be running late. He bemoaned the lot of the theatrical father who "can only kiss [his] family by telephone or telegraph," and he joked that he had to look in the telephone book to remember where he was living. Still, his pace did not slacken. In the course of the coming season, he began to resemble a demonic juggler who keeps adding balls to see how many he can handle, until he falters—or drops from exhaustion.

A typical day for Lew Fields—say, a Wednesday in October, 1909—began at 8:30 a.m. (an ungodly hour by theater standards), when Fields arrived at his suite of offices at the Broadway Theater.[7] In cold weather, he wore an overcoat with a mink collar, a symbol of power and status on Broadway, worn by those who could make things happen with a nod of the head or a wave of the hand. Immaculate in his custom-tailored suit, with cuffed trousers and nipped-waist jacket, topped by a fedora (worn sportsman-style with right brim curled up and the left brim pulled down), he cut a dashing, almost rakish, figure. He looked through the previous day's late correspondence—over thirty letters waiting for a response. He dictated answers to about half of them, then sent a diplomatic telegram to a featured singer who was threatening to resign because her name was not in large enough type in the ads.

At nine o'clock, he auditioned thirteen women (graduates of Wayburn's Institute of Dance) applying for places in the chorus, and hired one of them. A comedian from one of Fields' productions pleaded tearfully for a $200 advance to pay his insurance premium. Though Fields did not believe him, he approved a check anyway.

By nine thirty, he was in a taxi with Ned Wayburn, heading for a read-through of *Old Dutch* at Amsterdam Hall. All the principals were there—Alice Dovey, John Henshaw, Ada Lewis, Charles Judels, John Bunny, Vernon Castle—and Fields went through his part with the same care as the others in the cast. About an hour into the read-through, Victor Herbert and George Hobart arrived to listen to the chorus work. Fields and Wayburn then took a taxi back to the Broadway to listen to a reading of *Tillie's Nightmare*. He was greeted by the booming voice of Marie Dressler: "How well you are looking, Mr. Fields," as if the curtain has just come up on her vaudeville act. "Same to you, Miss Dressler, and many more of them," Fields replied with a smile. He huddled with Marie Dressler for a few minutes, listening and nodding, then whispered with Wayburn, author Edgar Smith, and composer A. Baldwin Sloane, and huddled with Dressler again. She was regarded as a tough customer who required special handling; she did not like being directed in front of the other actors, and she often had good suggestions for line changes. Fields got on fine with Dressler as long as they were not sharing the same stage.

Next stop—the Lyric Theater, where Andrew Mack was rehearsing his songs for *The Prince of Bohemia* with the chorus. While waiting for composer Sloane to finish at the Broadway, Fields and Wayburn lay prone on the ground studying scene plots with the author J. Hartley Manners. Wayburn would glance up every now and then to tell this girl to kick that way or to keep up the tempo; Fields nodded approvingly.

Shortly after noon, Fields and Wayburn were on their way back to see Victor Herbert to listen to the score for *When Sweet Sixteen*. An article in the "Stage" section of the *New York Herald* (Aug. 30, 1909) said that Fields had named the play after his eldest daughter, Frances; they even ran a picture of her looking sweetly affluent in a Merry Widow hat. The story was that Fields returned home one night and found his daughter "celebrating her sixteenth birthday with a throng of friends," and then telephoned Herbert excitedly to tell him the new title. Actually, the party was for Frances' fifteenth birthday. Fields was returning from a preview of *The Rose of Algeria* in Trenton and had not only forgotten the date of her party, but how old she was.

After a fifteen-minute stop at Childs' for griddle cakes and coffee, Fields and Wayburn stopped by at the Broadway to peek in at the matinee of *The Midnight Sons*. Fields noted with satisfaction that the house was filled, and that the laughs still came at all the right places. They stayed through Vernon Castle's "souse" dance, then grabbed a taxi to the Herald Square to check on *The Rose of Algeria*, where the attendance was surprisingly strong. Suddenly, Fields remembered that he was supposed to be at the photographer's studio to pose for new promotional material. He hated posing and called it "a terrible bore," perhaps because it forced him to stand still. He called his office and told them to reschedule, then headed for Lyric Hall with Wayburn for the rehearsal of *The Jolly Bachelors*.

The *Bachelors'* cast was so large that it occupied several rehearsal rooms. Pandemonium reigned in the room where the show's principals were trying to persuade the librettist, Glen MacDonough, to include more of their specialties in his script. At this stage of rehearsals, the cast included Stella Mayhew, Joe Welch, Josie Sadler, John T. Kelly, Emma Carus, Topsy Seigrist, Gertrude Vanderbilt, and Ed Begley, all of them vaudeville headliners. Fields arrived and the room grew quiet. He spoke first with MacDonough, who complained that the vaudevillians were wrecking his libretto. The performers believed that they were saving it. Fields reminded his all-stars that this was not a benefit bill and that there was a script to follow.

Someone opened the hall door and called out: "Mr. Fields, will you please step over to the chorus rehearsal in room one?" Fields walked quickly down the hall, but was waylaid by the proprietor, who told him that Rose had called. Fields usually returned such calls immediately. His press agent, William Sill, overheard: "All right, if you prefer red wallpaper for the dining room, I'm agreeable. . . . What's that? Joe wants to see the football game in New Haven? All right, I'll get tickets. . . . Dorothy what? Why certainly, yes, yes. . . . I'll send the flowers. . . . Can't possibly say when I'll be home, but as quick as I can . . . no, not before midnight I'm afraid. . . . Good-bye . . . kiss children. . . . Yes, I'm feeling all right. . . . No, not a bit tired, just busy, that's all. . . . Good-bye. . . ."

Down the hall, Wayburn was putting forty-eight chorus men and sixty chorus girls through their paces. The *Bachelors'* chorus was to be the largest ever in a Broadway musical. Fields watched, tilting his head to one side, and began pacing. Wayburn turned to ask Fields what was troubling him, and Fields explained, gesturing with his hands.

Just then, Arthur Voegtlin arrived with the set models. Fields' eyes lit up like a child in a toy store, and he got down on his knees on the dirty rehearsal room floor and studied the models from all angles. Wayburn joined him, along with the stage carpenter and electrician. Wayburn asked Voegtlin about the steepness of the steps on the deck of the ocean liner, and Fields asked about the colors of the drugstore interior. Meanwhile, costumer Melville Ellis and an assistant lined up the chorus men and women and began taking their measurements. Fields called Ellis over to look at the set models.

A few more minutes of excited discussion—producer, director, set designer, costumer, even the librettist joined in—then Fields checked his watch and gasped: ninety minutes to get back to his office, look over his mail, and catch the 5:55 train from Jersey City for Philadelphia, where he intended to watch Blanche Ring in *The Yankee Girl.*

Back at his office, he glanced through a foot-high stack of memos and telegrams (mostly from the Shuberts), dictated several letters, went over the previous night's box-office statements with his general manager, Frank C. Langley. Charlie Fields (Lew's business manager) would send the office boy out to get coffee and cigarettes for Lew. There were countless logistical and business details: a message from the railroad ticketing agent about the cost of taking *The Jolly Bachelors* company to New Haven (three coach cars and three sixty-six-foot baggage cars, a block ticket for two hundred people, round trip, $2.25 per capita), with an addendum from J. J. asking if all these people were necessary. Voting trust agreements from the Shuberts for stock in their new co-ventures. Notes due on bank loans. Referrals for would-be chorus girls and stagehands. Requests for benefit performances.

Among the day's crises was a visit from a representative of the A.S.P.C.A., concerned over the condition of Lightnin' Charlie, a spavined old delivery horse being used onstage in *Old Dutch* (a clever use of greasepaint made the horse look almost skeletal). Another earnest do-gooder, this one from the Gerry Society, had appeared at the rehearsal for *Old Dutch* earlier in the week to check up on the activities of the children in the show. Fields, who never forgot his own youthful problems with the Gerries, assured the man that he cared for these children as if they were his own, and that they would not be called upon to sing or dance.

The 5:55 express was just pulling out of the Jersey City station when Fields swung himself aboard the rear of the observation car. Settling in, he realized with a start that he had forgotten to tell Rose that he would not be coming home. He sent a bouquet of roses with a note of apology from Philadelphia. En route, he went over his lines for *Old Dutch*, perused MacDonough's new scenes for *The Jolly Bachelors*, and ate dinner. Perhaps he even dozed off.

He missed *The Yankee Girl's* opening curtain, but it was obvious to him from his first minute in the packed theater that the show was going over well. He watched from backstage, then went to sit in the audience, all the while scribbling notes. The Philadelphia reviewers called Ring's opening night performance "a triumph," and claimed that she received "the greatest ovation ever given a musical star in Philadelphia."[8] Still, Fields had a lot to say about how to improve the show, and it was 1:30 a.m. when he finally bade goodnight to the company.

Exhausted and alone, he retired to his usual hotel, the Bellevue-Stratford, only to find that conventioneers had booked every available room. The night clerk, however, would not hear of turning Mr. Fields away; he ordered a bed and other necessities to be moved into the gold ballroom. The ballroom was typically ornate, decorated to represent the wealth of the Indies, which made it remarkably similar to one of the sets for *The Yankee Girl*. In a room 160 feet long and 98 feet wide, Fields fell asleep on a trundle bed so short that his feet dangled off the end.

A few precious hours later, he was at the Broad Street Station to catch the 6:55 a.m. express back to New York; and so began another day for the busiest man on Broadway.

Old Dutch was Fields' first New York stage appearance in eighteen months. In it, he transformed what would have otherwise been a broad caricature of an ethnic type into a character role with self-referential undertones. "Dutch" was slang for an old-fashioned, unassimilated immigrant from Central Europe; "Old Dutch" was the nickname of the self-effacing main character played by Fields. It also stirred memories of Fields' old two-act with Weber.

Over the years, Edgar Smith had become Fields' most consistent and sensitive librettist; by 1909, Smith understood better than anybody Fields' abilities and ambitions as an actor. Working closely with Smith, Fields was able to express many of his own preoccupations through the character "Old Dutch."

Smith's plot for *Old Dutch* was a door-slamming farce of mistaken identity. Actually, the uncredited source for the book was a German farce brought stateside by Lee Shubert. In Smith's reworking, Fields played the part of Ludwig Streusand, a famous Viennese inventor who wearies of the honors showered on him and steals away to the Tyrol with his daughter Liza (Alice Dovey) to rest. Travelling incognito, he unwittingly assumes the name of a local swindler, Leopold Muller, and uses it to register at the hotel. While pursuing his favorite pastime, butterfly collecting, he loses his wallet containing all his money and identification. The wallet is found by the real Leopold Muller (John E. Henshaw), who is accompanied by a runaway music hall singer (Ada Lewis, known for her "tough girl" roles). They use the wallet to check into the hotel as the inventor and his daughter. The bogus Streusands are accorded every honor by the villagers, while the real inventor and his daughter are compelled to do menial service in the hotel.

"Old Dutch" must shine shoes, carry luggage, and groom horses for the money he needs to wire Vienna to prove his identity.

While undergoing various humiliations, Streusand can only watch helplessly while the imposters receive the credit he has earned. As a valet, porter, and hostler he is hilariously inept, leading him to conclude: "I never knew before how rotten a fellow could be outside his regular business. . . . Every man is a foolishness when he's out of his right place." The speech had an air of self-justification to it, spoken in twisted "Dutch" dialect by the actor who had sworn some time ago that he was through playing Dutch roles. But audiences paid to see the Lew Fields Dutchman, so for Fields to appear as anything but a Dutchman would be a "foolishness."

Victor Herbert's musical score for *Old Dutch* was uneven at best, and the fact that he was not on speaking terms with the librettist may have had something to do with it. Herbert detested Edgar Smith for the latter's role in rewriting *Dream City* without Herbert's music. When Fields told Herbert that Smith would be collaborating with them on *Old Dutch*, the composer threatened to quit. Fields managed to work out a compromise: he hired George Hobart as lyricist, so that the composer and librettist would not have to meet. Hobart was already in Fields' employ for *The Yankee Girl*, and a friend and fellow member of the Lambs' Club. As a lyricist, Hobart was as competent—and as uninspired—as Smith, MacDonough, or Sloane.

The Philadelphia previews of *Old Dutch* gave every indication of a hit in the making. The Shuberts were more worried about the show preceding it at the Lyric—*The Jolly Bachelors*—which looked like it might fold before ever reaching Broadway. Lee reminded Fields that this was the most expensive show they had ever done, and asked him if he was "on top of it."

Fields was not. In late October, Rose's mother died after a lingering illness. Mrs. Harris' death made an orphan of Rose's youngest brother, Herbert, who was about the same age as Joe Fields (fourteen). Lew and Rose brought Herb Harris to live with them. The addition of a fifth child may have prompted their move to a more spacious townhouse at 307 West Ninetieth Street.

After watching a preview of *The Jolly Bachelors* in early November, Fields decide to take drastic measures: he shut down the production, directed Glen MacDonough to create a new book from scratch, and dismissed some of the stars (others left when they decided that their roles were too small). Rehearsals resumed around November 21 without John T. Kelly, Joe Welch, Ed Begley, Emma Carus, or Elfie Fay.

On the evening of November 22, Lew Fields' Herald Square Theater was sold out and the audience applauded enthusiastically for the New York debut of *Old Dutch*. The critics were less impressed. Several reviewers found fault with Herbert's music; one complained that in places, the drums and brass ran away with the score, while another compared Herbert's score to the kind of "potboilers" a gifted author writes to generate income between more serious works.

Smith's book was treated to the lion's share of the blame for its derivative nature and its lack of comic opportunities for its stars. Critic Acton Davies summed up the general opinion of his colleagues when he concluded that Fields' presence carried the play "by the sheer force of his own personality and popularity." To be fair, Wayburn's chorus—composed of "the prettiest and most striking girls of the approved Weberfields type"—helped ease Fields' burden, as did Melville Ellis' tasteful costuming. Vernon Castle appeared as the Honorable Algernon Clymber, "in the Tyrol for his health," and he once again proved to be hilariously agile, particularly in a scene with a coffee percolator.

Playing opposite the lanky Castle was a large, moon-faced comedian, John Bunny, whose excessively slapstick characterization of Alfred's wealthy father was not well received. During the day, Bunny's activities included sneaking off to the Vitagraph Studios to make movies. He would arrive at the theater thoroughly exhausted, sometimes falling asleep between his scenes. He also had a reputation among the rest of the company of being a "stuffed shirt." When Fields found out about his extracurricular activities, he took a childlike delight in tormenting Bunny—giving the dozing comedian a hot foot, or announcing the presence of the Governor or Ziegfeld in the audience.

The biggest hit in *Old Dutch* was not made by any of the principals, or even the specialty acts. Early in the first act, Alfred and Liza sang "U, Dearie," a sentimental duet that Fields found dreary and unappealing. To liven it up, he hired two nine-year-olds, a boy and a girl, to perform a solemn pantomime of the lovers' behavior. Fields guessed correctly that by their very seriousness, the children would give this otherwise cliché scene a distinctive humor and charm. Their bit earned the most encores of the evening.

Fields had created the bit for the girl, a remarkably poised little blonde named Helen Hayes. Three years earlier, when he was on tour with *It Happened in Nordland* in Washington, D.C., he had spotted little Helen doing an imitation of a Gibson girl in an amateur show at the Belasco Theater. The child's poise and concentration so impressed Fields that he wrote a note to her parents saying that if they were interested in a stage career for Helen they should contact him.

On a hectic summer afternoon before the start of the 1909–1910 season, Fields was meeting with Lotta Faust in his office, unaware that Helen and her mother, Mrs. Catherine Brown, were waiting nervously in the reception area to see him. It was not unusual for Fields to be ambushed as he emerged from the elevator by ambitious stage mothers with their prodigiously talented charges in tow. Wanna be's and hopefuls haunted the halls of the Broadway, much as the young Weber & Fields had lurked for hours outside Tony Pastor's to catch the attention of the great showman.

For Mrs. Brown, Lew Fields was the last resort. She had already taken Helen to see every other major Broadway producer, but she had been unable to get past the office boys. The patrician Mrs. Brown avoided going to see Fields because she did not entirely approve of musical comedies, and she did not want her daughter associated with that kind of entertainment. Fortunately, a stage director she knew persuaded her that Fields was worth seeing; Fields was not only a respectable man, but he "could get the Shuberts to do anything."

After his meeting with Lotta Faust, Fields escorted the petite soubrette to the elevator. When Fields finally returned to his office, Mrs. Brown was ready.

She stood up, holding a photo of Helen as the Gibson girl, thrusting it at him and saying, "Do you remember this child, Mr. Fields?" Fields looked from the photo to the nine-year-old standing before him. "My, my," he said with a smile, "I'm glad you brought her to me. Come right in . . ." and he ushered them into his office.

Fields signed Helen to a contract that same afternoon. For thirty-five dollars a week, she would join the cast of *Old Dutch*. The talent for mimicry that she displayed in the amateur show inspired the pantomime bit that Fields invented for her. (Did he perhaps also recall the devastating pantomime that he and Weber had performed with the Adah Richmond Burlesque Company, when the boys stood behind the male and female leads and mimicked them?) Never, he told Mrs. Brown, had he seen anything "as funny as that baby's poise" in the amateur show.[9] In later years, Fields said that hiring the nine-year-old Hayes "was the most brilliant decision I ever made."

Helen become his special ward. She was a shy and serious child; unlike most child actors, she did not try to be cute or obsequious. Mrs. Brown insisted that Helen maintain a professional reserve, but Fields' warm smile and easygoing manner drew her out. For her first rehearsal, Fields took her hand and introduced her to the company members. Before her arrival, he had described her to them as "the greatest child comedienne he had ever seen." He also warned them that they had to be on their best behavior around Helen and the other children in the cast. This meant hats off for the men, and fines for any person overheard using coarse language in her presence.

Little Helen did not impress in her first rehearsal. Wayburn told Fields that she was "no good" and to let her go because she could not project. Fields turned around to where Helen was sitting, looked at her a moment and smiled. "I think she's a little like me," he said. "There's a little of the Jew in her. She has to see two dollars in every seat before she can act."[10]

Fields gave his brother Charlie the responsibility of seeing that Helen and her mother got safely to the streetcar after evening performances. Charlie was a fortyish, fun-loving fat man who used to play games with Helen, including late-night snowball fights while waiting for the streetcar. Vernon Castle looked out for Helen when Fields was not at rehearsals. At performances, Castle would wait for her backstage and then carry her on his shoulders up the steep iron stairs to her dressing room.

Of course, Mrs. Brown accompanied Helen everywhere. Stage mothers can be one of the banes of backstage life, and Mrs. Brown was the quintessential stage mother. Fields had had his fill of stage mothers in the last two seasons of the Music Hall, where the mothers of the adolescent Carter de Haven and the McCoy Sisters seemed to compete for the title of Most Meddlesome. Aside from the daily formalities, Fields rarely spoke with Mrs. Brown, and generally pretended that she was not there. But when Helen arrived, he would smile warmly, pick her up and hug her and ask her what she had been doing that day before she came to the theater. Sometimes he would tell her a story about his daughter Dorothy, who was four years younger than Helen. When touring, Fields would occasionally rent an automobile for long rides in the countryside (he was a man in motion even when relaxing); Helen and Mrs. Brown were his frequent guests.

Fields recalled: "She [Mrs. Brown] protected eight year-old *[sic]* Helen something fierce. Nearly every grown-up female in the cast had a sugar daddy who'd regularly send her flowers and diamond bracelets. Even though little Helen was right in the middle of such goings-on, she probably was better safeguarded then some kid in Grand Rapids. Even her crush on Vernon Castle was babyish."[11]

In his own way, Fields was as fiercely protective as Stage Mother Brown. Having been a child performer himself (and in much less sheltered circumstances), he had seen firsthand the peculiar hardships and temptations of stage life that so often corrupted young actors. In her autobiography, Miss Hayes remembered Fields as "old-fashioned and strait-laced . . . the conscience of the company."[12] When Fields discovered that Pat Neaves (a chorus girl in his company) had moved in with George Monroe (one of the leads in *The Summer Widowers*), he sent word that the couple were to be fired. Ironically, it was Mrs. Brown who pleaded on behalf of Neaves, even threatening that she would "remove Helen from such an uncharitable atmosphere." Fields was flabbergasted, protesting that he was only trying to uphold these moral standards for the sake of Helen and Mrs. Brown. He gave in, and Neaves moved in with Helen and her mother for the rest of the season to satisfy Fields' sense of propriety.[13]

Helen Hayes played in four of Lew Fields' productions over three seasons, with increasingly large roles in each show. What delighted Fields about Helen was that her comedy was unselfconscious and unstressed. He also instructed Wayburn to leave "the baby" (his pet name for Helen) alone. His methods during rehearsals indicate his great respect for her dramatic instincts; before giving her a direction, he would ask her how she would do it. If he thought that what she said or did could be funnier, he would say, "Suppose you try it this way," and then would demonstrate. To be able to change one's stage business without first telling the director was usually the prerogative of only the most experienced comedians, but Fields allowed his little star to do just that.

"He loved me like a daughter," commented Helen Hayes in a 1937 interview, "and Vernon Castle he loved like a son." In terms of affection and special attention, she was not exaggerating. For extended periods between 1909 and 1913, Fields spent more time with Hayes and Castle than with his own children.

At the same time that he was taking the young Castle and Hayes in hand, he was actively discouraging his real children from any involvement with theater. On the few occasions when Joe tried to come by the Herald Square or the Broadway after school to watch a rehearsal, his father would chase him out of the theater, chastising the boy for not having something better to do with his time. Behind Fields' paternalism was the unshakable belief that the theater life posed a moral threat to impressionable youth. Here was a man who truly deserved to be called, with all due affection, "Old Dutch."

To the arbiters of taste in the orchestra seats, *Old Dutch* may have seemed like an old-fashioned show about an old-fashioned guy—a throwback to comic opera—compared to the self-conscious modernity of *The Dollar Princess* and *The Chocolate Soldier*. Although it may seem odd to today's playgoers, the costumes, manners, music, and subject matter of these two operettas were, in their day, decidedly trendy.[14] *Old Dutch* played for eighty-eight break-even performances without ever generating the kind of enthusiasm in New Yorkers that it had in its out-of-town tryouts. It could probably have lasted another month or more, but for another of Fields' shows, *The Yankee Girl*. Blanche Ring's star vehicle had been such a money-maker on the road that the Shuberts were anxious to bring it into the Herald Square.

Sadly, *Old Dutch* was the last Fields-Herbert collaboration to make it to the boards. Fields put *When Sweet Sixteen* back into rehearsals in the fall of 1910 with Christie MacDonald slated to play the lead (she backed out when her salary demands were not met), but he was still dissatisfied with the book. After a month of rehearsals, he withdrew as producing manager and eventually sold the rights. Fields also acquired the rights to George du Maurier's novel *Trilby* as a vehicle for Fritzi Scheff. In June, 1910, he commissioned Victor Herbert to write "an operatic version" of it. Joseph Herbert was hired to write the libretto, and he worked with Fields and the composer at the latter's home in Lake Placid, but the project never went into production. Despite these misfires, Victor Herbert held Fields in high esteem. He still maintained that Fields was "one of the greatest, if not the greatest, producers of musical comedy in the world."[15]

Just because a musical was roundly panned in its tryouts, Fields saw no reason to give up on it. The reformed Jolly Bachelors Company reconvened in Philadelphia the day after *Old Dutch* opened in New York. Fields approved MacDonough's revised book, which returned to the semblance of a plot. Gone from *The Jolly Bachelors* cast were the vaudevillians whose desire to shine in their own specialties played havoc with the story. In their place, Fields cast men and women trained in musical comedy and amenable to Ned Wayburn's direction. Among the newcomers were Elizabeth Brice and Lew's youngest brother, Nat, who had spent the last five years playing Weber & Fields burlesques in the Midwest and South. Fields gave the versatile Melville Ellis the title of music director, and charged him with finding some good Tin Pan Alley songs to interpolate in Hubbell's mediocre score.

For the featured role, Fields brought in vaudeville's most popular songstress, the same one he had tried to see with Lee Shubert when they were forcibly expelled from *The Follies of 1909*. Nora Bayes and her adoring husband and sidekick, Jack Norworth, broke their contract with Ziegfeld to join the *Bachelors*. Ziegfeld went to court in an unsuccessful attempt to enjoin the couple from performing in Fields' production. Few performers could put over a song the way that Bayes did, though her voice was far from memorable. She did not have the flawless good looks of stage heroines such as Lillian Russell or Christie MacDonald, which gave her the freedom to play a wider variety of roles. Bayes was what was known as a serio-comic. Photos of her reveal her fascinating changeability—by turns inviting, imperious, glamorous, and downright plain—hinting at a temperament that, by all accounts, was equally changeable. Her husband, Jack Norworth, was a gifted songwriter, an adequate singer, and a limited actor with all-American good looks. Together, Bayes and Norworth were known as "The Happiest Married Couple of the Stage," though their relationship would visibly deteriorate by the end of their time with the show.

On the eve of the New York opening of the biggest production he had ever undertaken, Fields called for a midnight rehearsal. His busy schedule had prevented him from seeing a run-through of the revamped *Jolly Bachelors* from beginning to end. There were, of course, no union rules regulating the working hours of actors, musicians, or stagehands, though the last were generally paid by the hour. Anyway, Fields maintained that tired actors gave better performances and were easier to direct. Lee Shubert complained about the added expense for the crew, electricity, and heat for the theater. Fields agreed to forego heat in the house. Shubert expressed doubts that the show could be salvaged. Fields bet him a dinner for fifty at the new Café de l'Opéra that *Bachelors'* first week would gross as much as *The Midnight Sons.*

Shortly before midnight on a frigid Wednesday night, Fields settled into the front row of the Broadway Theater to watch what he hoped would be the final run-through of *The Jolly Bachelors.* His face showed his fatigue—he had played two performances of *Old Dutch* that day—but the excitement of being able to have a first-night production all to himself seemed to revive him. Behind him, his partners Lee Shubert and Felix Isman hunched in their seats.

Act One unfolded without a hitch. By 3:00 a.m., Fields made a quick trip to an all-night beanery and returned with a sandwich in one hand and a tin pail of steaming hot coffee in the other. Behind him was Lee Shubert with two enormous bundles of sandwiches, which he distributed to cast and crew as he walked down the aisle. Fields' relaxed demeanor was a sure sign of approval. Those not required onstage made a picnic in the seats and watched the second act in jolly spirits. After the final curtain, Fields and company filed out into the predawn chill of Broadway, where the bakery wagons were beginning their deliveries. It was nearly 5:00 a.m.

When *The Jolly Bachelors* finally opened at the Broadway on January 6, 1910, reviewers who had seen the earlier version were astonished: Fields had turned an overstuffed variety show into a worthy successor to *The Midnight Sons.* As an entertainment, *The Jolly Bachelors* was the polar opposite of operettas, Viennese or otherwise. Ironically, it lacked many of the values that Fields aspired to in a musical: a coherent story, consistent characters, a strong score with songs rooted in the logical unfolding of the plot. It was high-class vaudeville on a grand scale, and it was a hit. Fields won his bet with Lee Shubert; their dinner guests included Victor Herbert, Felix Isman, and Winthrop Ames of the New Theatre.

The chief merit of MacDonough's revised book was that it provided ample excuses for comic specialties, chorus routines, and scenic effects. The curtain opened on a Red Cross bazaar in the garden of a suburban Westchester residence, where showgirls in evening dress flirted with businessmen to sell them raffle tickets. The heiress Astarita Vandergould (Nora Bayes) desperately wants to find "just one man whose heart wouldn't make a noise like a cash register." To hide her identity, she takes a job as a cashier in a pharmacy, where she attracts the attention of three feckless men-about-town. Distracted, she mistakenly gives a lethal prescription (a potion to kill a murderous circus elephant) to a customer who asked for a hangover cure. She enlists the help of her beaux, including Jack Norworth as a slick realtor, in tracking down the customer before he cures himself permanently.

Bayes performed the hit song of the evening, an interpolation called "Has Anybody Here Seen Kelly?" (purchased by Melville Ellis) and a duet that she co-wrote and sang with Norworth, "Come Along, Mandy." Al Leech, a vaudevillian known for his eccentric dancing and acrobatics, played Chase Payne, the pharmacist who is perpetually "under the influence" of one or more of his wares. Buxom Stella Mayhew appeared in blackface as Veronica Verdigris Jackson, "a colored chorus girl" and belted out "Stop Dat Rag" by Irving Berlin. Another Berlin tune, "Make-A Rag-a Time-a Dance Wid Me," which did for (to) Italians what his "Yiddle on His Fiddle" did for (to) Jews, was dropped when Emma Carus was replaced.

The spectacular scenic effects and chorus ensembles were at least as important as the stars or the songs. The most novel effect was a variation on the Honeymoon Express from *The Midnight Sons:* it showed the flight of an airship with passengers visible on board, sailing through the clouds with a moving panorama of river scenes. Other elaborate settings depicted the dormitories of a college campus, where Norworth led the chorus in a medley of college songs, and the decks of the ocean liner *Insania.*

Less spectacular but equally novel was the pharmacy interior, done in various shades of brown and tastefully coordinated with the costumes. This was the work of the versatile Melville Ellis, who was proving himself to be an invaluable member of the Fields production team. Wayburn's choruses also won high praise from the *Evening Sun*—"Finer ensemble work has never been shown in a Broadway musical piece," and the *Dramatic Mirror*—"the company is admirably rehearsed and the dances go like clockwork."

"Huge," wrote Acton Davies, "is the best word to describe *The Jolly Bachelors.*" Other critics were equally enthusiastic: "It takes you out of the doldrums by the magic of its spectacular display, its rapidity of movement, its rhythm and cleverness. It is folly unfrocked and let loose with cap and bells." [16] In reconstructing *The Jolly Bachelors*, Fields applied the formula that he had developed for *The Midnight Sons*, and built himself an unqualified hit. He proved to the Shuberts that the summer show could have its winter uses.

With *The Midnight Sons* leaving on an extended tour, *The Jolly Bachelors* continued the box office bonanza at the Broadway. On January 28, the directors of the New York Broadway Theater Company—Lew Fields, Felix Isman, and Lee Shubert—voted themselves a handsome bonus. "For additional services rendered," each of them graciously accepted $10,000 in cash.

The departure of the Midnight Sons Company was not the joyous occasion it might have been, however, for they left without one of their most beloved members. Within days of their final New York performance, Lotta Faust underwent a "minor" operation at a private sanitarium for an undisclosed ailment. Faust had recently divorced her first husband, tenor Richie Ling, and was engaged to marry Malcolm Strauss, a society artist. The discrete lack of details about her illness, and her marital circumstances, suggest the possibility of a miscarriage or an abortion.

For two weeks after the operation, her recovery was reported to be normal. Then an infection set in, and her condition quickly deteriorated. For several days she was delirious. In the final stages, she threw back the covers, sat up in bed, and burst forth in the "Carmen II" song that she performed in *The Midnight Sons*. After trilling the last few notes, she sank back and called for the nurse. "Please go and tell Mr. Fields," she whispered, "I will return to work in two weeks and that I hope he isn't angry at my staying away so long." Fifteen minutes later, she was dead.

Fields was devastated. Only a month before, he had spoken with Lotta Faust about featuring her in a straight comedy, encouraging her to go beyond the soubrette roles she had played in musicals to become a real comedienne. Her insouciant charm, generosity, and wholesome beauty forever endeared her to him. When her distraught fiancé broke down in Fields' office and asked for help with funeral expenses because her medical bills had drained him, Fields immediately offered to pay for the funeral. His partners Isman and Lee Shubert were out of town at the time, but Fields told his business manager, Frank Langley, that he would pay for the funeral himself if they were not willing to split it with him. In the end, Shubert instructed Langley to charge the funeral expense to Fields' production account, the Midnight Sons Company, rather than to the New York Broadway Theater Company.

For a day and a night, Lotta Faust's white-gowned body lay in state at the Stephen Merritt funeral home. Close to two thousand theater colleagues and fans attended the service; the crowd was so dense that police had to close down Eighth Avenue for one block on either side of the funeral home. A telegram from Marie Dressler, who was out of town for the tryouts of *Tillie's Nightmare*, spoke for many: "We have lost the kindest heart, the prettiest face, and the brightest jewel of our profession." Besides Lew Fields, the pallbearers included his brother Charlie, brother-in-law Bobby Harris, Lee Shubert, Victor Herbert, Edgar Smith, and Glen MacDonough.

Fields had little time to grieve. Earlier in the week, the Rose of Algeria Company had limped home from its road tour. The following day Fields and the Old Dutch Company boarded the train for Pittsburgh, the first stop on their nine week tour. Later in the week, Blanche Ring in *The Yankee Girl* would open at Lew Fields' Herald Square after a profitable pre-Broadway tour of three months.

Fields' responsibilities as a managing producer did not cease because he was on the road; actually, the logistics became more complex. While touring with *Old Dutch*, Fields was also working with Glen MacDonough on the book for his annual summer show at the Broadway. *Tillie's Nightmare* had already begun a long pre-Broadway tour, and its star and librettist were already squabbling over the script. The problems began on Christmas Eve when Marie Dressler rewrote the script after a series of poorly received performances in Albany. Edgar Smith was outraged and insisted that Fields and the Shuberts shut down the show. Fields caught up with the show in Pittsburgh, and much to Smith's chagrin, was enthusiastic about Dressler's version. Although Fields generally resisted the willful exercise of star power, he had to admit that, in this case, the performer was right. Fields also backed up his road manager, who had complained to Lee Shubert to no effect about the shabby costumes. Soon after Fields' visit, the entire company was fitted for new costumes under Ned Wayburn's supervision, though Shubert considered it an unnecessary extravagance.

It may have been the rigors of the road, or the cumulative effect of his killing pace throughout the summer and fall of 1909, but those closest to Fields noticed a change. In a letter to Lee Shubert, William Sill (who travelled with Fields) observed: "Lew seems to be just a bit down-in-the-mouth. . . . He has had a pretty hard season when all is said and done, but God Almighty could have taken a day off without hurting his conscience, after he made Lew Fields. . . ."[17]

Certainly he was tired, but the death of Lotta Faust also weighed upon him heavily. He did not respond to several memos from Lee Shubert about finding a permanent replacement for her. While still on tour, he organized a benefit performance for her mother at the Broadway Theater, to occur immediately upon his return to New York. Performers included Bert Williams, the great black vaudevillian who was just then coming into his own; Blanche Ring, Irene Franklin, Stella Mayhew, Nora Bayes, Jack Norworth, Al Leech, Melville Ellis, George Monroe, and Fields himself. Rounding out the bill were several dance and acrobatic specialty acts. The May 1 benefit raised almost $4,000 for Lotta's mother. In the lobby, Malcolm Strauss hung his painting of Lotta Faust as Carmen II in *The Midnight Sons*.

Unlike *The Jolly Bachelors*, in which Nora Bayes was brought in to save a failing production, Fields had *The Yankee Girl* and *Tillie's Nightmare* tailor-made to suit the talents of their respective female stars, Blanche Ring and Marie Dressler. For *The Yankee Girl*, George Hobart used the brashly winsome personality of Blanche Ring as the starting point, and concocted a thin story of international intrigue in a South American banana republic. The heroine, Jesse Gordon, saves her father's business from a corrupt native president and a treacherous Japanese mastermind. Naturally, the U.S. Navy assists the heroine and her father at the crucial moment. Hobart's book was less notable for its competence than for its unwitting display of contemporary prejudices—gunboat and dollar diplomacy, latent fears of women and ethnics in decision-making roles, and "the Yellow Peril."

Silvio Hein's score was equally unimpressive. "All the one-finger composers of musical comedies . . . have grounds for action for petty larceny against Silvio Hein," commented one discouraged reviewer."[18] Ring, who knew the importance of a hit song in a musical, appealed to Fields for help; she knew better than to interpolate without his permission. He gave her carte blanche to interpolate whatever songs she wanted, which indicates the low regard he had for stage composers other than Victor Herbert. Ring reprised her hit "I've Got Rings on My Fingers" from *The Midnight Sons*, and found a Sousa number, "The Glory of the Yankee Navy."

After twelve strong weeks at the Herald Square, Blanche Ring and the rest of the Yankee Girl Company retired for a well-earned vacation. In August, they resumed their profitable peregrinations at Asbury Park, New Jersey, and worked their way west to the Pacific Coast.

On May 5, Fields' star vehicle for Marie Dressler, *Tillie's Nightmare*, replaced *The Yankee Girl* at the Herald Square. Rave reviews from its road engagements persuaded Lee Shubert to bring it to New York before the warm weather set in. For once, the tastes of the out-of-town audiences coincided with those of Broadway.

Edgar Smith's starting point was a character he had created five years earlier for a Weber & Ziegfeld production, *The College Widower*. In it, Marie Dressler played Tilly Buttin, the homely but hopeful daughter of a boardinghouse keeper. For *Tillie's Nightmare*, Smith enlarged the character and the role into that of Tillie Blobbs, an elephantine Cinderella from the hick town of Skineatales, New York. As the maid-of-all-work in the boardinghouse of her tyrannical mother, Tillie looks forward to a weekend outing with her fiancé (a "Rube" shopkeeper) and the other boarders. But when Mother Blobbs learns that they are planning to go to a vaudeville house, she forces Tillie to stay home. The despondent Tillie falls asleep by the fireside while reading the colored supplements in an old Sunday paper. She dreams of wealth and all the marvelous things she would do with it. Each of the six scenes that followed provided new opportunities for Dressler's broad clowning.

Trading her plain gingham dress for silks and velvets, Tillie is almost trampled at the corner of Broadway and Forty-second Street in New York. To escape, she goes into a huge department store whose owner is none other than her country beau, now transformed into a merchant prince. Her attempt to masquerade as a saleslady turns the establishment upside down, but things are smoothed over when she marries the owner in his own store. For her honeymoon, Tillie and her new husband cruise on a private yacht named for her, but she gets seasick. Somebody suggests that she drink champagne to cure her seasickness, and the resulting "jag" (which sends her overboard) was widely considered to be the funniest scene in the show, if not in Dressler's entire career. Sobering up, she visits an amusement park and is invited by a friend to go up in an "aeroplane." Her bulk makes it difficult for the plane to take off and for her to settle into her seat comfortably. As the overloaded plane sputters through the clouds, it lurches back and forth, finally sending Tilly hurtling downward.

She wakes up flailing and screaming in the dreary boardinghouse. The boarders (all of whom appeared in her dream in more refined guises) return from the vaudeville house in high spirits, and the curtain closes with the raucous voice of Blobbs *mère* yelling "Tillie! TIL-*LIE!*" from the kitchen, just as she did in the opening.

For nearly two and half hours of what almost amounted to a monologue, Dressler's eccentric, often bizarre characterization of a boardinghouse drudge had the audience in stitches. The supporting players, all more than competent, were simply used as straight men to set up Dressler's gags. "She has a peculiar[ly] masculine sense of grotesquerie," noted the *Dramatic Mirror*'s critic, referring perhaps to the unladylike physicality of her clowning. Like Weber & Fields, her comedy was broad but never vulgar, with an underlying pathos. When the riotous applause brought her out for a curtain speech after the first act, she curtsied modestly and said, "I wish I could tell you in my own way how I feel—but I'm afraid of the police."

The song hit of the evening came early in the first act, when Tillie sang "Heaven Will Protect the Working Girl," accompanying herself on the piano with painful ineptitude. It was the closest A. Baldwin Sloane would ever come to writing a memorable tune. Later, in "What I Could Do Upon the Stage," she travestied various dramatic actresses, including Mme. Tetrazzini's singing in *La Traviatta* and the new dance crazes popularized by Gertrude Hoffman and Ruth St. Denis. Voegtlin's scenic work for *Tillie's Nightmare* combined an appropriate amount of whimsy with the detailed naturalism that was now a trademark of a Lew Fields musical.

Traditionally, late May was when the Broadway season began to wind down, but Lew Fields' amazing season was far from over. While other producers were trying to eke out a few more performances or announcing their vacation plans, Fields was in rehearsal for his summer review at the Broadway, *The Summer Widowers*. He kept the nucleus of the cast from *Old Dutch*—Alice Dovey, Charles Judels, Ada Lewis, Vernon Castle, Helen Hayes—along with several performers from his other shows—Walter Percival, William Burress, Maud Lambert, Willis P. Sweatnam, and Music Hall veterans Fritz Williams and Will Archie. Fields himself would also appear in the cast, "quietly and without display, listed . . . on the program in the same sized type [as] his co-workers are billed." [19]

For the leading role, Fields signed another of vaudeville's leading ladies, Irene Franklin. Two years earlier, she had been voted "Most Popular Woman Vaudeville Artist," beating out Eva Tanguay, Vesta Victoria, and Marie Dressler. In 1896, when Weber & Fields opened their music hall, the twenty-year-old singer and impersonator was already an established vaudeville performer. On the vaudeville stage, she was known primarily for her "kid" songs ("I'm Nobody's Baby Now") and her satires of such social phenomena as the suffragettes. [20] Red-haired and slender, with an angelic face, soulful eyes, and a dimpled chin, she could convey compassion for the targets of her satire—most often, the ordinary working woman or working-class children. With her came her husband and accompanist, Burt Green, who composed songs for her and accompanied her on piano.

For weeks before its opening, a cryptic question covered the advertising placards outside the Broadway: "What Are the Wild Waves Saying About *The Summer Widowers?*" On the evening of June 5, 1910, wave after wave of eager first-nighters tumbled into the theater lobby until the police had to be called to restore order. For the first time, Fields would be performing in a Broadway Theater production. His popularity was at high tide.

In keeping with the traditions of the summer show, the plot for *The Summer Widowers* was not demanding. Librettist Glen MacDonough elaborated on gossip-column speculation about what all those "tired businessmen" did in the summer while their wives and children went off to the country or the seaside. It was the same social phenomenon that inspired two of Irving Berlin's 1909 hits, "My Wife's Gone to the Country (Hurray! Hurray!)" and its sequel, "I Love My Wife But Oh, You Kid." In MacDonough's version, three dutiful husbands leave their wives in Atlantic City and return to New York on business. The doting wives wager on their husbands' devotion to them and hire a slang-slinging female detective (Irene Franklin) to prove that they are right. The husbands are pursued by a man-hungry widow (Ada Lewis) with a mischievous son, and they are invited to a "bohemian" party by a prima donna named Fritzi Fluff (Maud Lambert), which provokes some comic misunderstandings. The prima donna was a parody of the temperamental operetta star Fritzi Scheff, who was under Fields' management at the time.

Fields took the role of the flaxen-haired Otto Ott, a retired druggist and the

father of one of the summer widowers. For the first time, one of his Dutch characterizations was described as being "a German Hebrew." Whether this description reflects a different shading in Fields' characterization or a growing confusion
over ethnic types (Jewish comedians were just then coming to the fore in vaudeville) is difficult to determine. What can be said with certainty is that Fields'
scenes were once again considered to be the funniest in the show. Posing for a
photographer, Ott tries with great difficulty to look unhappy so that he can prove
to his wife that he misses her. As a temporary clerk in a deli, he takes a chisel to
a petrified wheel of cheese and then has to chase after pieces that walk away
under their own volition. When a lady comes in and whistles for her lost dog, a
plate of sausages come to life, the links forming the semblance of a canine with
a wagging tail. Later, Ott has some fun with a recent innovation, the pneumatic
tubes used for delivering messages within retail outlets throughout the city.

Despite Fields' efforts, the comedy in MacDonough's script did not measure
up to *The Midnight Sons* or *The Jolly Bachelors*. Some critics began to wonder
why Fields seemed content to play variations on the same old Dutch roles: "Mr.
Fields deserves richer material and finer opportunity than he and his collaborators make for him in their musical plays. . . . His public, however, insist now
that he shall characterize no one but middle-aged Germans bewildered of mind
and tongue . . . incessantly harassed by the blows and perplexities of circum-
stance. . . ."[21] Fields was asking himself the same questions, as evidenced by
some surprisingly candid statements he made over the next few years. Was he
afraid of discovering, in the words of Old Dutch, "how rotten a man could be
outside his own business?"

The real stars of *The Summer Widowers* were Ned Wayburn and Arthur
Voegtlin. Subtitled "A Musical Panorama in Seven Views," the show was the most
elaborately staged of Fields' productions so far, with more emphasis on three-
dimensional sets and movement. The first-act curtain revealed a replica of the
boardwalk in Atlantic City. Action proceeded simultaneously on the boardwalk,
on a terrace above it, and in a photographer's studio alongside it. The scene
ended with a song and chorus number, "Flying High," during which illuminated
aeroplanes were sent darting all over the theater on invisible wires. After a brief
scene on a New York City street, we go inside the well-stocked delicatessen of
Salve Di Mora, with its animated cheese and sausages and its deadly pneumatic
tube. Act One concludes with a surf-bathing scene at the Atlantic City shore;
Frank Thomas' rear-screen motion picture footage of girls frolicking in the waves
was seamlessly combined with painted flats and sets reproducing the pier and
beach in the moonlight. Acrobatic chorus girls in bathing suits dive off a springboard, yelling with glee as the salt spray flies into the air, while a laughing crowd
watches them from the shadows of the pier. "Nothing more realistic in stage
mechanism has ever been seen here," wrote the *Times*' critic. Acton Davies agreed,
"As a scenic effect, [it] excels any illusion New York has seen."[22]

For the second-act "topper," Voegtlin took Fields' idea of a dollhouse cutaway and created one of the most massive sets on any legitimate stage of the era.
His cutaway showed the third, fourth, and fifth floors of the St. Vitus Apartments
on Riverside Drive. The large and ostentatious apartment houses and residential

hotels on Riverside Drive had lately become the most fashionable addresses for New York's smart set. This was Fields' neighborhood—he lived just off Riverside Drive, on Ninetieth Street—and returning home late at night, he could peer into the windows, many of them still lit, and see that many of his neighbors were up and about. Voegtlin's marvel of a set was the perfect opportunity to stage a travesty of fashionable New York apartment life.

Fields' idea was that there should be "something doing" on every floor as the curtain rose, and that their activities should be interwoven throughout the scene. On the third floor, the prima donna Fritzi Fluff is throwing a "bohemian bash" at which the "summer widowers" will come to grief. On the fourth floor, the room at the right is occupied by a man reading; in the center room, a poker game is in progress; the left room has Fields trying to shave before a mirror on a folding bed in which Vernon Castle is hiding. On the top floor, the three rooms display a group of girls sewing, a band rehearsing, and a cook in a kitchen being chatted up by a friendly policeman. The mayhem unfolded over a period of thirty minutes. (The elaborate and heavy scenery had other unforeseen consequences. During the summer, a significant amount of structural damage to girders beneath the stage was discovered, enough to inspire fears that it would not pass the city building inspection. The Shuberts argued with Felix Isman throughout the fall about who was responsible for paying for the repairs.)

The finale of *The Summer Widowers* took place at an amateur night being staged in the Folderol Roof Gardens, with the rooftops and night skyline of New York visible around it. Here was the obvious pretext for the specialty acts Wayburn was so good at inserting: Arabian dances, Russian dances, and acrobatic dances, interspersed with songs by the summer widowers and the lady detective. Wayburn created more opportunities for Vernon Castle's eccentric dance routines. Fields himself danced in a trio with Fritz Williams and Vernon Castle and demonstrated that "as a dancer, he is second to none."[23]

For the first time, however, there were some criticisms of Fields' approach to staging musical comedy. In the midst of an otherwise favorable review, the *Times'* critic called *The Summer Widowers* "a sort of three-ring-circus affair, with so much going on all the time, that it is difficult to know how to describe it. . . . Action and noise are often the main essentials, and the human element gets lost." A Boston reviewer observed: "A megalomania in the inflation of musical plays seems to possess Mr. Fields and his collaborators. . . . The sheer bulk and multifariousness of *The Summer Widowers* clutter and choke it."[24] He pointed out that beginning with *The Girl Behind the Counter*, Fields' shows had been getting bigger and faster and more lavish—which would be fine if Fields were manufacturing trains instead of plays. But few other critics or playgoers seemed to mind.

The success of his Broadway Theater productions, and the relative failure of *The Rose of Algeria* and *Old Dutch*, were valuable indicators of his public's expectations. Given a choice between "the semblance of a clever story, capably worked out" and an elaborate vaudeville show, Fields' public seemed more interested in seeing the latter. Instead of a coherent libretto and a consistent score, he should build his musical entertainments around a series of pleasing effects held together by comic performances. His summer shows demonstrated an essential principle of Broadway producing, one that still holds true today. When the show's book is weak and its score is unremarkable, make it big, make it loud, keep it moving, and make it sparkle.

In fact, "a megalomania in the inflation of musical plays" could be said to have possessed Mr. Fields and his collaborators even before the opening of *The Summer Widowers*. On May 19, Shubert architect William A. Swasey filed blueprints for the reconstruction of a well-known Manhattan landmark, the American Horse Exchange, occupying the entire block on Fiftieth Street between Broadway and Seventh Avenue. The Shuberts proposed to build for Lew Fields a new music hall modelled after the Winter Garden in Berlin, "the first place of amusement of its kind in New York."[25] The new stage would be the largest in New York: 45 feet deep by 108 feet wide, with a proscenium 30 feet high. Total seating capacity: 1,750, with 1,200 on the pitched parquet floor.

The transformation of the American Horse Exchange into an American winter garden was symbolic of the changing landscape of the city as it left behind two more nineteenth-century traditions. North of Forty-second Street had been the center of the horse and carriage trade, but the proliferation of automobiles made this old enterprise seem obsolete. And it was equally clear that the days of high-class theaters south of Forty-second Street—such as Lew Fields' Herald Square—were numbered. Fields also realized this; his contract with Lee Shubert specified that in the event of the closing of the Herald Square, he would have the option of a fifty percent interest in any new theater built for him by the Shuberts. In the spring of 1910, Lee told Lew that his Herald Square Theater would be razed after the next theatrical season.

Having discovered that Fields' "summer" shows were big box-office in all seasons, the Shuberts decided to create an elegant roof garden environment that could be a year-round venue. Just as B. F. Keith built his New Boston Theater to be the embodiment of "refined" vaudeville, Fields and the Shuberts designed their winter garden to embody the carefree, expansive spirit of their Broadway Theater offerings: "The entire auditorium will be finished to give the effect of open air trellis construction, on which vines will be interwoven. . . . The entire audience will appear to be witnessing a theatrical performance on a roof high above the city sidewalks and in the open air, protected from the sky by a huge pergola with trellised roof."[26]

In its original conception, the Winter Garden was an intermediate step between the old Atlantic Gardens in the Bowery and the theater-restaurants and cabarets that arrived on the scene over the next few years (the first of these, Jesse Lasky's and Henry Harris' Folies-Bergere, opened in 1911 two blocks away from the Winter Garden). The main entrance to the theater was to be on Broadway, with a spacious lobby, chandeliers, and marble floors. Unlike most Broadway theaters of the era, which often contained a small café or rathskeller in an out-of-the-way corner, the Winter Garden would give over almost as much of its area to serving up food and drink as to laughter and song. The balance of the Broadway front and the entire Fiftieth Street side was to be occupied by a café and restaurant. The Broadway corner would have a two-storey cafe fifty by seventy-five feet, done as a courtyard of an old Holland inn, with balconies overlooking the court. Opening onto this courtyard was to be the main dining room, paneled entirely in Flemish oak. Thus, it would be possible to provide an entire evening's divertissement under one roof: before the show, a light supper in the café, where one could watch the comings and goings on the Great White Way; after the show, an elegant dinner in the restaurant, or in one of the private dining rooms.

From the outset, Fields' involvement with the Winter Garden was to be a source of heartache (and headaches) for him. The confusion and contradictory information began with the first public announcement: *Variety* reported two very different sets of plans filed with the Building Department.

The major difference between this and previous Fields-Shubert undertakings was the role of J. J. Shubert. Until now, there had been an inscrutable logic to the Shubert brothers' division of labor: Lee had authority over the Hippodrome productions, while J. J. had supervised the Casino shows. Along with Fields' Broadway Theater shows, Lee's Hippodrome extravaganzas had been among the top money-makers every season, while the Casino shows were frequent targets of the critics' scorn. On a personal level, J. J. resented Lee's success, especially when it was a musical. He seized every opportunity to point out areas where Lee's people were wasting the firm's money. Fields' prodigality was a particular sore spot, but J. J. could not argue with the box-office results.

From the start of negotiations in December, 1909, the Winter Garden was J. J.'s project. It is doubtful that J. J. wanted to involve Fields in the Winter Garden, but Lee (who controlled the Shubert Theatrical Company) probably insisted on it. Fields had the reputation and the expertise; he had arguably the best production personnel in the business—Wayburn, Voegtlin, Ellis, composers, writers—as well as a long list of performers under his management. During the summer of 1910, J. J. could only hover impatiently in the background, peering over Fields' shoulder and hoping for an excuse to step in.

The Summer Widowers was sufficiently popular to deny Fields and his company a summer vacation, but the show's box-office net was significantly lower than its predecessors' at the Broadway. Almost certainly, its large initial production expenses (rumored to be as much as $36,000) and its payroll of high-priced vaudevillians were responsible. Competition that summer was stiff; the *Follies of 1910*, for example, with Fanny Brice and Bert Williams, was Ziegfeld's best production yet. And Fields was in the curious position of competing against himself for the summer audience. In addition to his own *Tillie's Nightmare* (which closed in mid-July for a three-week layoff), he was half-owner of the new show that opened at the Casino on July 18. *Up and Down Broadway* was described in its program as "a more or less incoherent résumé of current events, theatrical and otherwise." In contrast to Fields' musical comedies at the Broadway, which were referred to as revues, *Up and Down Broadway* really was a revue, though it called itself a musical comedy.

Eddie Foy starred as Momus, a janitor to the Muses and Immortals of Parnassus and sent by them to investigate reports of lowbrow, frivolous activities on Earth. Accompanying him is the serious-minded Melpomene (Emma Carus), who vows to reform the theaters and the people who go to them. She succumbs to

their charms after witnessing and participating in several specialty acts and burlesques of current shows. The specialty acts included La Petite Adelaide, a daring,
classically trained toe dancer who went on to fame in vaudeville as part of the
team of Adelaide and Hughes. A pair of young composers, Irving Berlin and Ted
Snyder, performed two of their own songs, "Sweet Italian Love" and "Oh, That
Beautiful Rag."

Lew Fields and Ned Wayburn had little or nothing to do with the staging of
the production, and it showed. The patchwork quality of the program, as well as
the silliness of several of the specialty acts (including an "Apache Chinese" dance),
bore the creative imprint of J. J. Shubert.

The preparations for the Winter Garden and the production of *Up and Down
Broadway* brought Fields and J. J. into close working proximity, and it did not
take long before their distinct personal styles came into conflict. When Lee questioned one of Fields' creative decisions (which was surprisingly rare), he did so
respectfully and in private. J. J., however, would reverse a decision without further discussion, and Fields would find out about it in the newspaper or through
a subordinate. In J. J.'s eyes, Fields was a "hamfatter" (J. J.'s term for an actor)
who made his reputation as a producer by spending a lot of Shubert money. It
did not help matters that Fields was also Lee's personal friend. To J. J's way of
thinking, the Shuberts should have the right to any of the talent that Fields managed. Unfortunately, several of the performers who signed with Fields refused to
be loaned out for other Shubert productions. J. J. had wanted Stella Mayhew for
Up and Down Broadway, but Fields wanted her to be rested for the tour of *The
Jolly Bachelors* beginning in August. When J. J. needed some additional chorus
girls at the last minute, he thought that he should be able to borrow some from
Fields' overblown *The Summer Widowers* and save that show some money at
the same time. Fields and Wayburn, it can be assumed, protested vehemently,
and William Wilson (the Casino's stage manager) had to cast his own chorus girls.
Wayburn and Voegtlin had had their differences with J. J. in the past, and wanted
no part of the Casino show. (Two years later, J. J. punched Voegtlin and bodily
ejected him from the Hippodrome for refusing to "lend" him some musicians for
the Winter Garden.)

The war between the Shuberts and the Syndicate—at its peak in 1910—was
being fought in the daily and trade papers as well as in the box offices and
booking agencies. Lee and J. J. had long since soiled their mantles as the white
knights of the Independents. Their business practices looked increasingly like
those of their adversaries, and sometimes even worse. They threatened to withdraw advertising from newspapers suspected of having Syndicate sympathies.
They began barring critics who wrote unfavorable reviews of Shubert shows:
Channing Pollock (a former Shubert press agent) and Rennold Wolf of the *New
York Telegraph*, Percy Hammond of the *Chicago Post*, and later, Heywood Broun
(the *New York World*) and Alexander Woolcott *(New York Times)*. Conversely,
Charles Darnton *(Evening World)* reviewed Shubert shows so gently that many
believed that he was on the Shubert payroll, and the Shuberts put excerpts from
his reviews up in lights. To give their shows a fair chance in the press, the Shuberts set up their own weekly newspaper, the *New York Review*, in 1909.

The Shuberts' blacklist put Fields in an awkward position. Pollock, Wolf, and Hammond were friends since the days of the Weberfields; Wolf was also the toastmaster of the Friars' Club, to which Fields belonged. These critics, and others who were often unpopular with the Shuberts, such as Acton Davies *(Evening Sun)* and Alan Dale *(New York Journal)*, had always dealt fairly with Fields. He refused to enforce the Shuberts' blacklist,and the journalists continued to treat him with respect and sympathy, even when they found fault with his productions.

This tangle of hostilities and hidden alliances inside and outside the Shuberts' organization makes it difficult to separate truth from rumor—or malicious gossip—in the coverage of Fields' activities during this period. In mid-July, *Variety* and several dailies announced an impending "rupture" between the Shuberts and Lew Fields: "The opening of *Up and Down Broadway* at the Casino, July 18, will decide Mr. Fields' course, it is said. Fields does not think it clubby of the Shuberts to land another 'revue' on Broadway to oppose *The Widowers.* . . ."

Fields' emphatic denial followed quickly. He pointed out that he was half-owner of *Up and Down Broadway*, and that the Shuberts were similarly involved with *The Summer Widowers* and *Tillie's Nightmare*, "so it is on the face of it ridiculous to think that they would do anything to injure an attraction bearing my name."[27] Ridiculous on the face of it, perhaps, but not unlikely—neither Shubert brother minded when he could make one of his projects look good at the other's expense. And because the Shuberts controlled bookings, Fields was particularly vulnerable. For example, the Shuberts could cancel the final leg of a Fields company tour and fill its bookings with a more profitable Shubert road company. Or, when Fields didn't have one of his own plays at the Herald Square, J. J. Shubert could swap a money-making production at Fields' theater for a turkey from the Lyric. The costs to the Shuberts were negligible, while Fields would lose thousands of dollars in potential ticket sales. One of the only times press agent Bill Sill ever heard Fields curse in public was when Fields was informed of a sudden theater switch; after uttering "a very naughty word," Fields ordered Sill to "festoon the office photograph of Jake Shubert with quinces." Fields prefaced his denial of a rupture with a statement about the lasting friendship between himself and Lee Shubert. The implications were clear enough to savvy observers of the Broadway scene: the dispute had been between Fields and J. J., and Lee had smoothed over the differences. The pattern that began with *Up and Down Broadway*—news of internal discord, then denials followed by vows of friendship—was symptomatic of J. J.'s growing prominence in Shubert affairs. The symptoms would become chronic through the autumn of 1910 as Fields and J. J. Shubert wrestled for control of the Winter Garden. J. J. wanted to be the "artistic" producer of Shubert musicals, and he knew that his brother was first and foremost a smart businessman. All friendship aside, Lee's support for Fields was directly proportional to the net profits Fields generated.

CHAPTER XII
Tailor's Tricks

Sometimes these big ambitions have to be put up in alcohol and preserved on the shelf. They won't always do for the box-office.

Lew Fields, 1911

TO describe the changing tastes of Broadway audiences, a line from *Naughty Marietta*, the most significant new musical of the 1910–1911 season, seemed to say it all: "Tis love and love alone the world is seeking"—not laughs, or dialect clowns, or spectacular stage effects. The three hit musicals of the season confirmed the supremacy of Viennese operettas. *Madame Sherry*, by Otto Hauerbach (later Harbach) and Karl Hoschna, *Naughty Marietta* by Victor Herbert and Rida Johnson Young, and *The Pink Lady*, by Ivan Caryll and C. M. S. McClellan, were all made in the U.S.A., but their foreign-born composers clearly were emulating the Old World form.[1]

The acclaim that greeted Victor Herbert's *Naughty Marietta* was welcome indeed after the tepid reception accorded his 1909 collaborations with Fields. Barely a month after Fields hired Herbert to write *Trilby* for Fritzi Scheff, Arthur Hammerstein commissioned Herbert to write a score for Emma Trentini. It was not unusual for Herbert to work on two or even three scores at once. According to his biographer, Herbert would choose a different kind of wine to drink with each score, and the taste of the wine would put him in the right mood to resume work on that score. Perhaps the *Trilby* score remained unfinished because the wine he chose was too young. Most likely, Herbert was inspired by the grand-opera staging and stars promised by Oscar Hammerstein; the dauntless impresario bankrolled *Naughty Marietta* with the money that the directors of the Metropolitan Opera had paid him to retire from the grand-opera field.

Rida Johnson Young's libretto for *Naughty Marietta* put aside comedy, and banished all topicality. Instead, she told an intricate love story that brought together three romantic adventurers in eighteenth-century New Orleans: Captain Richard Warrington, who is searching for the daring and elusive pirate Bras Pique, and Marietta, an impulsive young woman of noble origins, who has come to New Orleans to escape an unhappy marriage. Marietta attracts the attention of the buckskinned Captain Dick. She feels strangely drawn to him, but neither admits their feelings for the other. Meanwhile, another suitor, Etienne Grandet, the son of the Lieutenant Governor, falls in love with Marietta and agrees to accept

276

her despite her past. Captain Dick reveals that Etienne is actually the buccaneer Bras Pique. Just as Zoradie, the heroine of *The Rose of Algeria*, had consecrated her love to the unknown poet of "Rose of the World," Marietta vows to give herself only to the man who can finish a mysterious melody she hears in her dreams. In the cathartic finale, Marietta and Captain Dick sing "Ah, Sweet Mystery of Life" together.

With *Naughty Marietta*, Victor Herbert created his most melodically inventive score: the macho "Tramp! Tramp! Tramp!" to introduce Captain Dick, the youthful vigor of "The Italian Street Song" as Marietta recollects her life in Naples, the stirring confession "I'm Falling in Love with Someone." Bits of the melody that haunt Marietta are played (and sung) throughout the show, and it accumulates nuances and insinuates itself into the subconscious, so that when Marietta finds the man who can finish the melody, it fulfills a yearning made palpable to us through the score. In the romantic sweep of its music and themes, *Naughty Marietta* set a pattern for operettas that held the stage for two decades.[2]

Naughty Marietta epitomized everything that Fields' summer shows were not. In Fields' shows, to paraphrase the *Naughty Marietta* lyric, " 'Tis fun and fun alone the world is seeking." The microcosm of *The Midnight Sons* or *The Summer Widowers* was the urban hurly-burly, where smart-aleck young men and women out for a good time are thrown together with success-crazed ethnics and would-be entertainers. Speed there was a virtue in itself: it propelled the banter, the staging of the choruses, the rage for novelties, the ragtime rhythms. The cross-section of the St. Vitus Apartments from *The Summer Widowers* was the ideal metaphor: a mosaic of fragments, nine slices of life unfolding simultaneously, like an entire vaudeville bill on stage at the same time. It was too much to take in all at once. No wonder these shows had so little romance; love slows things down, impedes the pursuit of fun. Love among the Midnight Sons and Jolly Bachelors becomes enjoyable at a mile a minute (the Honeymoon Express) or as a badge of success. But what had once been exhilarating can with repetition become oppressive; there is no escape from the ceaseless comic patter, the topical references, the frenetic pacing, and the gigantic scenic effects. In Fields' summer shows, the members of the Leisure Class could only laugh at themselves—but in operettas, they could dream.

Seven touring companies of Lew Fields' productions took to the road in the fall of 1910. *The Yankee Girl*, two companies of *The Midnight Sons*, and *The Jolly Bachelors* filled Shubert time in first-class theaters from coast to coast. Ed Rush (partner in a booking agency with Weber's nephew, L. Lawrence Weber) booked a condensed version of *The Girl Behind the Counter* in vaudeville houses throughout the South. Sam Bernard's brother Dick played Lew Fields' role, but when Dick fell ill, the stage manager (Lew's brother Sol) stepped in without a rehearsal and "scored an emphatic hit." Lew Fields and the Summer Widowers Company left New York at the beginning of October for a nine-week tour. *Tillie's Nightmare* lasted through November at Lew Fields' Herald Square; Marie Dressler did not want to tour, but when a bad investment forced her to declare bankruptcy, she decided to take her act on the road. The only new Fields productions before the opening of his Winter Garden would be the Victor Herbert operetta, *Trilby*, and a straight comedy starring William Collier, *I'll Be Hanged If I Do*, written by Collier and Edgar Selwyn.

Fields started the 1910–1911 season already exhausted. His explosive temper, hitherto unleashed only on the rarest occasions, became more apparent to balking colleagues and family members. Backstage, he appeared more nervous, giving long lists of directions, and double-checking to see that they were carried out. He so rarely took a day off that when he did, it was news to journalists and family alike. An article published on August 6 recounted how Fields took his first day off in three years, spending the day at his Edgemere, Long Island, summer home, playing in the sand with his daughter Dorothy. Rose marked the event with a telegram to Herbert and Joe at camp at Paradox Lake: "Dear Boys, Papa is taking an afternoon off." By return wire came the disbelieving reply: "Dear Mother, Hate to dispute you, but tell us an easier one. Wire that the Giants won 3 straight from the Cubs."

A few months shy of his forty-fourth birthday, he began to feel the effects of the killing pace he had set for himself. In the four years since his last vacation, he had produced thirteen new shows (acting in five of them) and organized their road companies. He was a partner in the management of three theaters, and was trying to supervise the construction of the mammoth Winter Garden, for which he was to produce and star. By most accounts, he was one of the largest employers of theatrical talent in the world. Including his road companies, it is estimated that he had approximately two thousand people on his various payrolls. Stretched to the limit as a producing manager and performer, he had neither the time nor the temperament to attend to the administrative duties required by his vast enterprises.

Once a Fields production went on tour, it was up to the Shuberts to do whatever was necessary to make it profitable. This was known in Shubert-ese as "cutting it down to a living basis." They would start by reducing the number of chorus people and stagehands. Naturally, with fewer stagehands, the sets had to be simplified, but this, too, saved money in erecting, striking, and transportation. If these measures did not generate enough profit, then actors were asked to take salary cuts, or play extra shows, or were replaced with less expensive performers. And depending on which theaters and cities had been booked, the Shuberts could lower the top ticket price from $2.00 to $1.50 to attract a less selective audience. It was all that Fields and his stage managers could do to keep their productions from being slashed beyond recognition when they were cut down "to a living basis."

The size and expense of Fields' touring companies made them irresistible victims for the Shuberts' paring knife. Lee and Jake monitored expenses and receipts through each company's business manager and the theater manager (Shubert employees). Among the thirty or forty letters waiting on Fields' desk every morning, there were usually a dozen or so communications from the Shuberts and their lieutenants.

When the 1910–1911 road season got off to a weak start, Lee's anxieties deepened. Summer temperatures continued through September and October in

much of the Midwest and East, discouraging theater attendance. Ticket sales in
the one-night stands were also hurt by the proliferation of movie theaters—9,500
by 1910—and the continued growth of vaudeville. Lee pleaded with Fields:

> Dear Lew:
> You will notice that the business around the country has been very bad and some
> of our shows are so expensive that it is absolutely impossible to live. As I do not
> want to interfere with anything back of the stage, I wish you would kindly take up
> the matter of "The Jolly Bachelors" as regards cutting this show down. I think Lucy
> Weston could be replaced by a woman at $75 a week. She has no draft and is not
> particularly good in this show.
> What do you think about it?
> Yours very truly,[3]
> Lee Shubert

Fields was impractical enough to fret over what these cuts would do to the artistic integrity of the show. He would recommend some cuts, but rarely enough to
satisfy Lee.

At times, Lee and J. J. worked on Fields the way a "good cop–bad cop" duo
interrogate a suspect. In the end, the Shubert brothers both wanted the same
thing; they just used different means to get it. With Fields, Lee always played the
good cop:

> Dear Lew:
> I want to call your attention to the expenses of the "Midnight Sons" Company and
> to the fact that they are carrying 90 people. It is absolutely throwing away money to
> carry such a large show. I can use some of the chorus in a half dozen shows now
> rehearsing and it is much better to do this than carry them around the country and
> pay their railroad fare home. Won't you please give this matter your serious consid-
> eration.[4]

J. J., of course, played the heavy. He disliked Wayburn, and he was livid
when he learned from one of the road company's business managers that Wayburn had refused to make the cuts. In an irate letter to Fields, he called it "an
insult and we are not going to stand for it." "We" referred to the Shuberts; J. J.
made it very clear who had the final authority over Fields' road companies:

> My dear Lew:
> . . . This is not the first time that we have been belittled by people working for us
> and getting our money. We are better able to take care of the business departments
> of the shows, when they are away from New York, than anyone else . . . the one
> point in view being to save all the money we possibly can and to make money,
> instead of waste it.
> Mr. Wayburn or anyone else could not take any such stand with me. We must
> either be masters of our business, or not be in it at all.[5]

Fields did not have the time to argue with the Shuberts over every cut, but
he resented J. J.'s tone. He was learning how little control he had over his companies once they went out on tour. Although Lee gave lip-service to the notion
that the Shuberts would not "interfere with anything back of the stage," it was

clear that whoever controlled the box office and bookings could effectively dictate the production decisions.

Meanwhile, construction on the Winter Garden was behind schedule, and
Fields was becoming increasingly disturbed by the prospect of J. J. Shubert's
making crucial decisions in his absence. Already, Fields had argued with the architects about the seating plan. The Shuberts instructed the architects to plan for
a disproportionate number of orchestra seats—1,200 out of a total seating capacity of about 1,700—which would ensure higher gross ticket sales, since orchestra
seats traditionally cost more. The drawback to this arrangement, from Fields'
standpoint, was that those sitting in the back rows of the orchestra seats and the
small gallery overhead would be too far from the stage to read the actors' faces.
This was irrelevant if the intention was to present vaudeville or revues, which
depended on broad comedy, large choruses, and specialty acts. Fields envisioned
more refined entertainments; for the Winter Garden, he had commissioned two
operettas, *The Violet Widow* and *The Singing Teacher*. In the end, neither made
it to production.

Fields made plans to be in New York to supervise personally the final month
of preparations for the opening of the Winter Garden. He hired the veteran Dutch
comedian Charles Kolb (of Kolb & Dill, a team of Weber & Fields imitators) to
replace himself in *The Summer Widowers*, beginning in mid-November. After a
profitable engagement in Philadelphia, the Summer Widowers Company spent
equally successful weeks in Washington, D.C., and Pittsburgh. On Monday, October 31, they opened at the Grand in Boston. The show was still being described
as snappy and brisk, even though it ran for over two and a half hours. In response
to earlier criticism that there was not enough comedy, Fields had built up his
role, and he played it with his customary vigor. Wednesday was matinee day,
which meant that Fields performed his most physically demanding role twice in
one day.

He collapsed in his hotel room the following morning. The physician who
examined Fields called it a "physical breakdown" brought on by overwork, and
prescribed bed rest. Weak and almost incoherent, Fields' first concern was to get
somebody to replace him for the evening performance. When he heard that Charles
Kolb had been contacted in New York and would arrive in Boston the following
day, he let himself be sedated and put to bed. There was no Thursday performance, and the company was kept in the dark about Fields' absence for several
days. Meanwhile, the dailies traded rumors about Fields' mysterious illness.

By Friday evening, he was back in his own bed, tended by Rose, who was
distraught and not a little angry. She knew that a body does not reach the point
of a physical breakdown without some warning signs. Lew had ignored these
signs and laughed off her own pleas. Now she had one more proof of the hazards
of life in the theater: the unsuccessful actor kills himself for peanuts, the successful actor kills himself to stay successful. Either way, it was his family who
would suffer most.

In his collapse Fields saw his most ambitious plans crumbling. Unwittingly,
he had facilitated the very situation he had worked so hard to avoid. With good
cause, he feared what would happen in his absence. When the family physician

recommended a month's vacation, Fields would only agree to two weeks. On November 5, Lew and Rose boarded the steamship *Saratoga*, bound for Havana. As the steamship passed Charleston, South Carolina, Fields sent a wireless message to Lee Shubert, "Feeling much better. Wish you were here"—an ironic reference to Lee's habit of accompanying the Fieldses on their vacations.

Shortly before Fields' return, *Telegraph* critic Rennold Wolf wrote of the unique affection that Broadwayites felt for Fields: "It is not easy to think of another manager in this city whose loss would cause more general and profound regret that that of Lew Fields. If he has an enemy in the theatrical profession that individual has not yet appeared. . . . Mr. Fields is more than an excellent comedian. He is one of the most capable producers of musical plays in America. Moreover, he is generous to a fault, liberal in all his ideas and policies, sympathetic, straightforward and of a most genial personality." Lee Shubert tried to play down the seriousness of Fields' condition, planting the absurd story that Fields had not "broken down" but had decided suddenly to take his wife on a brief vacation after "a lively summer" and a busy fall. He calmly announced that Fields would not return to the stage for at least four weeks, but would devote his time to rehearsing the Herbert-Hobart light opera, *When Sweet Sixteen*, and preparing for the opening of the new Winter Garden.

Meanwhile, J. J. made the most of Fields' sudden absence. After all, somebody had to step in and take charge of the Winter Garden, not to mention all of those expensive road companies. J. J. sent for the architects, and apparently insisted on several design changes that contradicted the instructions left by Fields.

On the Monday following Fields' collapse, a notice appeared on the call board of the Boston theater where *The Summer Widowers* was playing: the company's season would close on Saturday, the end of their Boston engagement. Many of the players had been with Fields for several years; because of their trust in him, they had no written contracts for the season. The Shuberts took advantage of this, as well as the vague wording in several other contracts that spelled out guarantees for "the season." By declaring the season to be over and officially disbanding the company, the Shuberts were under no further obligation to these high-priced performers. The company remained closed for one week, while the Shuberts had Glen MacDonough rewrite the libretto (presumably for legal as well as budgetary reasons). They then reopened with a "reorganized" cast.

Upon his return on November 15, a robust and sunburned Lew Fields greeted the press at his home on Ninetieth Street. One look at him and any doubts about his health were put to rest. "I left New York rather tired," he admitted, "but I am back, refreshed, and honestly I haven't felt so good in years. Mrs. Fields and I had a real, regular vacation. I feel like a boy about to cast his first vote."

But his good humor turned to indignation when he learned about the reorganization of *The Summer Widowers*. When he visited the site of the Winter Garden and saw how far they had deviated from his plans and specifications, he was livid. His dream of making a Continental music hall—a classy, inviting place to spend an evening—had been ruined. In its place, he now saw an oversized auditorium that as he put it, "possessed as much luxury and elegance as a roller rink."[6]

J. J.'s hand in these maneuvers did not surprise Fields; what upset him most was Lee's complicity. Fields felt betrayed. How could Lee let this happen? Lee mumbled something about "business conditions" and "the need to make some economies." Fields then delivered an ultimatum: adhere to the original plans or he would withdraw from the project and take with him the talent he had signed, the scripts, and his production team. Wisely, Lee backed down. The construction changes that Fields was insisting on would delay the opening of the Winter Garden at least until mid-February. By then, the Shuberts could assemble their own production if necessary.

Fields was not naïve enough to believe that the matter was settled. He took several precautionary measures of his own: he abandoned work on *When Sweet Sixteen*, which seemed doomed to failure with or without a prima donna on the order of Christie MacDonald or Fritzi Scheff. If he was not going to go into rehearsals for the Winter Garden opening, he had to come up with another production to use all the players he had under contract. He pushed Glen MacDonough to complete the book for *The Hen Pecks*, which was to be the next big summer production at the Broadway. Rehearsals began with a partial script in mid-December using most of the principals signed for the Winter Garden. Fields instructed Wayburn and Voegtlin to incorporate the scenic ideas that they had been saving for the Winter Garden.

Rumors about Fields' involvement with the Winter Garden were flying up and down the Rialto throughout December. Early in the month, Fields reportedly had a "heart-to-heart" talk with Lee Shubert and expressed his continued dissatisfaction with the renovations of the Horse Exchange. Impatient with Lee Shubert's vague assurances, he was overheard to say in the most emphatic terms that he would take no further part in their scheme, and would erect a music hall on another Broadway site that was available to him. Lee knew that this was no idle threat, but he remained strangely passive in the face of J. J's machinations.

On the day before Christmas, the Shuberts announced a new opening date for the Winter Garden, and omitted any mention of Lew Fields' involvement. On New Year's Day—Fields' forty-third birthday, his eighteenth wedding anniversary, and the day he had hoped to open his Winter Garden—it was made official: Fields had signed over his interests in the Winter Garden to the Shuberts.

At the same time, Fields let it be known that he had not abandoned his original plan for a Continental music hall. Perhaps, he hinted, he would convert the interior of the spacious Broadway. First, however, he wanted to see the outcome of Harris & Lasky's new enterprise, the Folies Bergere. (Harris & Lasky's theater-restaurant failed, but it sparked an interest in a new type of popular entertainment: cabaret.) Meanwhile, Fields was negotiating for "a new modern music hall . . . not a thousand miles from Broadway and 47th Street"[7]—in other words, in Chicago. His new partner remained a secret.

Not surprisingly, Fields came away puzzled and hurt by Lee's behavior. Giving Lee the benefit of the doubt, perhaps Fields saw it as proof that blood is thicker than water; J. J. wanted to use the Winter Garden to imitate Ziegfeld's Follies, and Lee did nothing to stand in his way. Lee claimed to want Fields to produce the Winter Garden shows, but Fields would have to do it on J. J.'s terms.

When Fields refused to participate or allow his performers and production team to participate, he was punished.

The real mystery was not why Fields and the Shuberts quarrelled, but why he continued to be their partner. Two possibilities, not mutually exclusive, stand out: the friendship between Fields and Lee Shubert was strong enough to endure despite certain business differences; or, Fields' financial affairs were by now so inextricably entwined with the Shubert organization that to attempt a total severance would have been ruinous (to Fields).

Rather than entertaining offers from the Syndicate, as so many of the other independents had recently done, Fields insisted that there was no strain in his relations with the Messrs. Shubert. Instead, he announced that out-of-town tryouts for his new production, *The Hen Pecks*, would commence in late January at the Shuberts' theater in Albany. When asked why he withdrew from the Winter Garden, he said only that the work of preparing his own productions and appearing in *The Hen Pecks* was too pressing to permit him devoting any time to the new enterprise.

Perhaps the only good to come out of the reorganization of the Summer Widowers Company was that it created an opening for Vernon Castle's fiancée, a willowy, ambitious beauty from New Rochelle named Irene Foote. When the new cast opened at Brooklyn's Majestic Theater in mid-November, Irene Foote played one of the wives. She had three lines and no dancing; the little girl who shared her dressing room (Helen Hayes) had a much larger part.

Irene's stage debut was the result of a long campaign. For months, Vernon tried unsuccessfully to get his mentor to agree to an audition. Fields' reluctance was understandable; for five years, he had been teaching Castle the tricks of the trade, grooming him to be a stage comedian—a far loftier (and more lucrative) ambition, to his way of thinking, than to be one half of a dancing act. Having taken a strong paternal interest in young Castle, Fields may have also feared that Irene was trying to lure Vernon away from comedy to further her own professional aspirations.

Vernon and Irene finally auditioned for a harried Fields in September, 1910, a few weeks before Fields' collapse from physical exhaustion. According to Helen Hayes, who watched the audition from the wings, the Castles had to dance in near darkness because Fields refused to turn on any lights except for the work light onstage. Out of the shadows of the empty Broadway Theater, Fields' voice commanded, "So—go ahead, Vernon." Vernon asked for some more light. "Go ahead, Vernon. I'm waiting." "But you won't be able to see what I've worked out!" Fields replied wearily, "I came. I'm seeing." He watched them dance—they were competent but had not yet developed the innovative steps that would make them famous—and he left without saying a word. A short time later, he offered Irene a position in the chorus of the Number Two Midnight Sons Company (then touring the West) but she refused. When Fields returned from his forced vacation, Castle persuaded him to put Irene in *The Summer Widowers*, which was about to begin a two-week stay in Brooklyn, followed by a week at the West End, and then a Northeast tour after the first of the year.

Irene Castle's first professional engagement was short-lived. For some mysterious reason, the Shuberts finally shut down *The Summer Widowers* right before the holidays (normally the most profitable weeks for musicals).

The Hen Pecks was unique among Fields' Broadway Theater spectacles in that it did not use the peccadilloes of the leisure class as its point of departure. The story grew out of a vaudeville sketch about a vengeful barber, for which both Fields and Ned Wayburn claimed credit. Fields said that he got the idea for a barbershop scene the previous summer, when he met Bernard in the barbershop in the Times Building. Watching his old friend undergo a shave and a haircut while trying to talk business alerted Fields to the situation's comic potential. At the same time, he saw possibilities for chorus effects with barbers, manicure girls, and customers.

With the help of Wayburn and Voegtlin, Fields transformed what had started as a crude vaudeville sketch into a feast for the eyes. The first-act curtain of *The Hen Pecks* rose to reveal a dazzling stage picture: a realistic representation of a Long Island farm at sunrise, complete with live chickens, ducks, geese, and pigs. Roosters crowed on cue; a farmhand feeding the animals discovered a tramp and set a dog on him to chase him away. In the curtained window of the farmhouse, a female silhouette was visible as she washed her face and got dressed. (The device that made this possible was called a "Shadowgraph," presumably another use of the rear-screen projection system that Fields held the rights for). Colored lights simulated the sunrise, the first of several "astonishing color effects" during which colored lights were coordinated with the scenery and chorus costumes.

As the name suggests, farmer Henry Peck (Fields, struggling with a "down east" accent) is bullied by his tall virago of a wife, Henrietta (Lillian Lee). Henry gets even in his own way, with sad-but-true quips about his put-upon condition. Henrietta, daughters Henoria, Henelia, and Henolia, and son Henderson are eager to be citified. They want Henry to sell off the farm to a real estate hustler who plans to build a suburban town. When Henry refuses a generous offer, they decide that he is crazy, and they threaten to have him committed.

Meanwhile, his favorite child, Henoria, becomes enamored of a glass-eating magician she saw at the Melodeon Hall. "Professor Zowie, the Monarch of Mystery" (Vernon Castle) has beautifully coiffed golden hair, which Henoria finds so irresistible that she vows to follow him to New York. Henry goes after her, and the entire family seizes the opportunity to leave the farm.

New York, or getting there, provides a wealth of scenic and comic possibilities. At the railroad station, Henella, an aspiring chorus girl, ponders whether to be a first-class actress or a happy wife. She opts for the former: "I'm going to stick right where I belong—close to the music cues," and then climbs up on a table and belts out "Toddlin' the Todalo" in a brassy voice. The exuberant singer was San Francisco–born Blossom Seeley, familiar to the Western vaudeville circuits as the Queen of Syncopation, but hitherto unknown to Broadway audiences. Fields had her dance on the table to show off her shapely legs, and she used the platform to launch a dance craze. As an encore to the Todalo, she performed the Texas Tommy, a dance originated by black vaudevillians in San Francisco's Barbary Coast. Theater critics were generally nonplussed by the way she toddled and shook, but Broadway audiences loved it. "Toddlin' the Todalo" and the Texas Tommy focused the attention of well-to-do New Yorkers on the casual pleasures to be found in modern social dancing, especially to a ragtime rhythm. Blossom Seeley made these dances seem like such fun that it was not long before "everbody's doin' it" (to borrow an Irving Berlin refrain from the same year). Soon, New York nightlife was transformed by chic couples clutched in tight embraces, performing barbaric-sounding dances called the turkey trot, grizzly bear, and bunny hug.

The second scene of the first act showcased the comic genius of Lew Fields and Vernon Castle. In fact, few "bits" in any musical comedy of the era could compare with the barbershop scene in *The Hen Pecks*. In it, Fields temporarily put aside his pretensions to more sophisticated kinds of humor and returned to the knockabout methods of Weber & Fields. In so doing, he discovered a new generation of theatergoers with a taste for the rough stuff, a taste that movies had only just begun to exploit.

The Hen Peck's barbershop was realistic in almost every detail: twelve real barber chairs, porcelain sinks, compressed air, a heating device for towels. The entire shop was several steps below street level, with a long window at sidewalk level revealing the legs of passersby. Henry, wearing a black wig with long sideburns, masquerades as an Italian barber. He is hiding from his wife and searching for "the narrow man with the hair" who has abandoned his daughter Henoria in the city. Sooner or later, most of the characters from Cranberry Cove pass through the barbershop. Henolia, on a shopping expedition, stops by to lead the chorus in a topical number, "It's the Skirt," to illustrate the changing fashions in women's wear. The chorus begins in crinolines, which are soon discarded to reveal lacy undergarments, which in turn give way to more form-fitting and colorful outfits. Meanwhile, E. Ray Goetz's lyrics extoll the rule of "the skirt," though it is unclear whether the metonymy referred to the burgeoning women's movement (which decried the restrictive Victorian fashions) or to men's susceptibility to feminine charms.

When Zowie enters the shop, Henry can barely contain his glee. Fields and Vernon Castle "worked up" the barber-father's revenge in rehearsals in the time-honored manner of a Weber & Fields routine. As a foil for Fields, Castle was getting the opportunity to prove that he was a full-fledged comedian and not just a talented eccentric dancer and bit player. Castle responded as the dutiful apprentice, writing down the "steps" of the routine in his notebook.[8]

Once Henry has the glass-eating philanderer in his barber's chair, he inflicts the most sadistic come-uppance ever presented in a Broadway show. For fifteen minutes, the unfortunate Zowie is terrorized and manhandled by the vengeful Italian barber. For reasons that are never made clear to the victim, he is shoved, jabbed, strangled, blinded, forced to eat shaving cream, scalded, set afire, hosed, and blown out of his chair. The nature of the personal relationship between Fields and Castle added another interesting subtext to the act; as Helen Hayes observed, Fields "loved Castle like a son," but this son had of late been questioning his father's plans for him.

By all accounts, the barbershop routine put 1911 theatergoers into paroxysms of laughter. Audiences did not seem to mind the overt sadism; in fact, they seemed to revel in the extreme skillfulness of Fields' cruelty, and the cleverness with which it escalated. Of course, they were innocently unaware of the Freudian implications of the scene. Most critics agreed that it was Fields' funniest routine ever, better than the soda fountain scene in *The Girl Behind the Counter* or his famous bits with Joe Weber. One of them even judged Fields' sustained act of physical cruelty to be a kind of public service: "Any man who can succeed in making his fellow-man laugh as did Lew Fields at the Broadway Theatre last night need not feel that he has lived in vain."[9]

No actor ever tires of applause, and the success of *The Hen Pecks* must have been reassuring to Fields. Yet, he was acutely aware that it was his least ambitious productions that had garnered the greatest acclaim. The productions with the best scores and most coherent librettos, *The Rose of Algeria* and *Old Dutch*, had barely broken even, while *The Summer Widowers* and *The Hen Pecks*, the latter featuring a knockabout routine that recalled the pre–Music Hall antics of Weber & Fields, played to consistently full houses. Fields had always believed that it was his duty as an entertainer to give the public what it wanted, but by the spring of 1911, he had come to regard that duty with a marked ambivalence.

Contemplating the successful run of *The Hen Pecks* and his plans for the next season, he was moved to make some rather startling observations about musical comedy and its audience: "Of course, a producer has to fall in with the ideas of the time, but I work to keep some originality in my shows. In the main, the public want pretty much the same old thing from year to year, but they want little changes and little surprises hitched on to the old situations and lines. You like to see your old friends dressed up in smart new clothes each season. . . ."[10] The resourceful tailor who must make a ballgown out of hand-me-downs and glad rags—that is how Fields now saw his job. In a metaphorical sense, he was still practicing his father's trade.

At first glance, Fields' comments smack of condescension. Coming from Lew Fields, however, they were nothing more than a frank and accurate appraisal by the era's most successful showman. Like the best popular artists, he was sensitive to how the audience perceived him. Had he not spent most of his life seeking self-affirmation in his public's approval? His comments reflected a certain resignation, perhaps, and a battle-scarred pragmatism, but no condescension. To be sure, it was a considerably less enthusiastic assessment than his comments of seven years earlier, right after he broke with Weber, when he said, "coherency is what the public wants now," and "the semblance of a clever story capably worked out."

The interview continued with a description of his next production, *The Never Homes*, "a musical show of the same sort, except it has more of a story. . . ." He always intended to have "more of a story," but the exigencies of musical staging intervened:

> You see, an attraction of this kind can't get by on a story, although we always start with one at the first rehearsal. Then the composer will complain that the numbers are not placed properly, and the changes that suit him will probably interfere with

the plot. Then the manager will find fault with the movement of the lyrics because they don't give a chance to move the show girls around, so the songs have to be overhauled. . . . And so it goes. When it is all over, consistency of the narrative is a thing that was.[11]

Unlike most musical producers of the time, Fields' sympathies were with the most maligned member of the production team, the librettist: "As it is, the author gets blamed for a lot of lines he never was guilty of. At rehearsal some day, the comedian will say, 'Here, I want to put in this line. It is always good for a scream.' In a weak moment, the manager consents, and then the audience grunts, 'Oh, rot! The same old gag. Give me something new.' " But the audience's idea of "something new," according to Fields, meant dressing the same old joke in "a new overcoat." In other words, more tailor's tricks.

The interview concluded with the familiar refrain: "I am trying to give the public what it wants." Only now, the refrain did not sound so convincing, and Fields could barely conceal hints of weariness and disappointment: "In the Broadway Theatre, everything must sound big. We must have the biff-bang stuff, for the little love things would drop dead. People never tire of laughter and music, so that is what we hand out, with all the improvements that we can devise."

Fields had realized that his own artistic ambitions were no longer necessarily synonymous with what his public wanted. Henceforth, he would be forced to choose.

The immediate success of *The Hen Pecks* made it easier for Fields to get over the Winter Garden affair. From what he had heard about J. J. Shubert's planned production, he saw no reason to expect that it would be any better than the revues J. J. staged at the Casino. When the Winter Garden finally opened on March 20, 1911, the sumptuous new theater almost upstaged the entertainment. The garden motif encouraged a festive atmosphere. Patrons crowded into the Dutch Café and the Wine Room, and brought their refreshments back to their seats. As J. J. had planned all along, there was an unusually large number of orchestra seats—nearly 1,200—which swelled the gross ticket sales.

The Musical Review of 1911 consisted of two parts; first was a bit of ersatz culture, J. J.'s notion of "class"—*Bow Sing*, a one-act "Chinese" opera by Manuel Klein. The main event was the two-act *La Belle Paree*, accurately subtitled "A Cook's Tour Through Vaudeville with a Parisian Landscape." Two performers salvaged the otherwise haphazard program: Stella Mayhew, the buxom ragtime queen, and a wiry blackface comedian who had made a name for himself with Lew Dockstader's Minstrels and in San Francisco's vaudeville houses. Al Jolson had been signed by J. J. as a supporting player and appeared late in the program. As Erastus Sparkler, "a colored aristocrat," he sang a ragtime duet with Stella Mayhew, "Paris Is a Paradise for Coons," and later returned to give his monologue and another song. By the second performance, Jolson's crowd-pleasing abilities were so obvious that the Shuberts rewarded him with an earlier spot on the program. His exuberant banter with the audience, his anything-to-please manner, and his uninhibited song delivery quickly made him a favorite attraction. For the next fifteen years, the Winter Garden shows would be built around him, and it was on the Winter Garden stage that the Jolson legend was born.

Undoubtedly, J. J.'s success with the Winter Garden altered the balance of power in the Shubert organization. The "other" Shubert brother had proven that the Shuberts did not have to rely on anybody else to produce successful musicals. Lee no longer had any justification for questioning J. J.'s production acumen. Henceforth, J. J. would take a more active role in supervising musical productions—not just road bookings and travel plans, but creative decisions such as costumes, composers, and chorus numbers. Unlike Lee, J. J. did not even pay lip-service to the notion that the Shuberts would not interfere with Fields' authority in back of the stage.

Five days after the opening of the Winter Garden, a horrific fire in a supposedly fireproof building on Washington Square claimed 146 lives and left the city in a state of shock. The fire began in piles of discarded cloth in the ninth-floor workroom of the Triangle Shirtwaist Company. The panic-stricken employees—most of them young Jewish women (called "shirtwaist girls") from the Lower East Side—discovered that the supervisors had locked the fire-exit doors. A single ladder running down eight stories to a rear courtyard was the only accessible fire escape, but this was soon blocked by a pile of bodies. The elevator boys saved hundreds until fire melted the cables. Dozens of workers crowded onto window ledges and leaped, with hair and clothing ablaze, to their deaths on the pavement below. Others were incinerated in chimneys of flame fed by rolls of silk and linen.

The tragedy struck home with Fields and the Shuberts. They identified with the victims; these unfortunates could have been their neighbors and relatives on the Bowery or in the tenements of Syracuse. Temporarily, Fields and J. J. Shubert put aside their differences. For the first and possibly only time, J. J. Shubert joined with his brother Lee and Lew Fields in sponsoring a benefit performance. On April 7, Fields and a roster of Fields and Shubert performers appeared on the stage of the Winter Garden to raise money for the survivors and the families of victims of the Triangle Shirtwaist Fire.

The Shuberts were not nearly so supportive of Fields' benefit activities for the Friars' Club later in the month. There were three social clubs for actors and other theater professionals: the Players, the Lambs, and the Friars. The differences between them were summarized in a popular quip: "The Players is a group of gentlemen trying to be actors, the Lambs is a bunch of actors trying to be gentlemen, and the Friars is a bunch of guys trying to be both."[12] Fields belonged to the latter two, though his frenetic schedule left him little time to enjoy their company. Still, he frequently attended their honorary dinners and always made himself available for their benefits. In May, 1909, he and ex-partner Joe Weber had accompanied the Lambs' All-Star Gambol on a one-week whirlwind tour to raise money for a clubhouse. The tour was organized by Abe Erlanger and his syndicate associate, William B. Harris, so the Shuberts tried to discourage Fields and Eddie Foy from participating.

In late April, 1911, the Friars tendered a dinner for Fields' friend Willie Collier. Weber also attended, and the two dusted off their chin whiskers, abdominal pad, and Dutch dialect to entertain the Friars. Assisted by Collier, they performed their old choking routine. The laughter and applause were so loud that nobody could hear their lines, but it did not seem to matter. Following the after dinner speeches, Fields turned to Abbot John Rumsey and volunteered his services for the Friars' Frolic (their annual spring tour). A moment later, Rumsey asked Weber if he, too, would like to participate. Weber looked across the table at Fields and said "sure." Sentiment and peer pressure had accomplished what the promises of a fortune had failed to achieve.

"For the last time on any stage" read the ads for the Friars' Frolic that announced the reunion of Weber & Fields as Dutch comedians, playing at the theater where their partnership had ended, Klaw & Erlanger's New Amsterdam Theater. On a bill that included George M. Cohan, Lew Dockstader, John Barrymore, Carter de Haven, Gus Edwards, Eddie Foy, and George Beban, Weber & Fields performed the choking routine with the help of William Collier. They received a thunderous ovation, moving one reporter to comment, "If in that night of continuous hits any players may be said to have loomed above their associates, then first honors should go to Joe Weber and Lew Fields in combination."[13] What had Fields said about the public wanting "the same old thing year after year"? Something about how the public wanted to see their "old friends dressed up in smart new clothes"? Well, he was only half-right. The public simply wanted to see their old friends in their old familiar outfits.

Fields closed *The Hen Pecks* in June, not for financial reasons, but because Rose was holding him to his promise. It was not easy for Fields to close down a profitable production, but he had promised Rose after his collapse that he would take the family on a real vacation after the season was over. Except for the odd weekend at their summer home in Long Branch or Edgemere, Fields had not been on vacation with his kids for almost four years.

During this time, the oldest two had all but grown up. Frances was now a demure seventeen-year-old, an aspiring debutante trying to decide whether to go to Wellesley or Vassar (she did not end up going to either). Any inclination she may have had for a theater career had long since been eradicated. Joe, at sixteen, was a strapping six-footer, serious-looking but outgoing. At DeWitt Clinton High School, he had already demonstrated a talent for journalism, drawing and painting, and football. Lew and Rose were trying to guide him towards more "serious" pursuits—preferably, law school. Herbert, in contrast to his older brother, was a slight and sensitive thirteen-year-old. His way with verses and quips was already evident. He was an avid participant in the weekly plays put on by the older boys at Camp Paradox (led by future lyricist and collaborator Larry Hart), mostly as a performer, which gave him the excuse to indulge his love of costumes. Regarding Herbert, Lew admitted he "shows symptoms of being funny, but I am in hopes that he will outgrow it."[14] Little Dorothy, a self-confident seven-year-old with beguiling dark eyes, was Daddy's little angel. Within the coming year, she became the keeper of Pop's scrapbooks, at first saving only the positive reviews—and in those days, most of them were.

On June 24, 1911, the Fields family, including Herb Harris, boarded the *Lu-*

sitania and were shown to their first-class quarters, and then returned to the deck, where a large crowd of well-wishers, consisting mostly of journalists and show people, bade them bon voyage. It was too much to expect that Fields would completely set aside his work. For one thing, Lee Shubert had been a late addition to the passenger list; he may have hoped to salve some of the wounds inflicted by his brother. Also on board (going and returning) were Glen MacDonough, A. Baldwin Sloane, and E. Ray Goetz, to work with Fields on their next Broadway Theater offering, *The Never Homes*. Willie Collier remained on board until the last minute to discuss his next play. Even as the ship was leaving the pier and being guided down the bay, Fields was already tending to business.

From London, the Fields family began a five-week motor trip that took them through Paris, Berlin, Vienna, Dresden, Leipzig, Munich, and Amsterdam. Just because Lew was on vacation did not mean he would take it slow. Days were spent sightseeing, nights, dedicated to attending the theaters or music halls of whatever city they happened to be in. Fields was, in his own words, "in search of transportable commodities"; i.e., new talent and a Continental musical "with a punch," one that would stand up to a Broadway adaptation. He went to most of the music halls alone, without Rose and the children. In Paris, he was shocked by the salacious jokes and displays; in London, he was disappointed by the heavy-handed humor and schoolboy suggestiveness of English variety shows. Berlin he found to be the most beautiful city in the world, but its music hall comedians relied too much on coarse puns that were untranslatable. He saw several operettas as well, but nothing that he considered worth buying. In the end, he came to basically the same conclusion he had the last time he was in Europe, five years earlier: "I did not bring back any musical plays from Europe. To be perfectly frank, I saw nothing which I considered worthwhile. During my stay abroad I was convinced more than ever that America is capable of producing its own librettists, composers and lyricists." [15]

His faith in American talent was endearing, but for the upcoming season at least, hopelessly misplaced. Over forty new musicals would open on Broadway in the coming season—the most ever—but the surge in quantity coincided with a depressing slump in quality. [16] Roughly one-third of these were imports or adapted from foreign musicals, and few homegrown productions fared well with the critics or the public. Where were all the gifted librettists, composers, and lyricists Fields claimed were working on the American stage?

Early on the morning of August 4, Lew Fields and family, accompanied once again by Lee Shubert, landed in New York. By ten o'clock, they had cleared customs; by eleven, Fields was working with his shirt sleeves rolled up, leading a rehearsal of *The Hen Pecks*. The cast was essentially the same, except for the addition of Irene Foote—the new Mrs. Vernon Castle—in a bit part.

His collapse the previous season had not made him any more modest in his ambitions. "I expect to have nearly a dozen plays running before the end of the year," Fields predicted, though he only mentioned seven. After he reopened *The Hen Pecks* at the Broadway on August 7, *The Never Homes* would go into rehearsals, followed almost immediately by *The Wife Hunters* at the Herald Square, and Collier's *Take My Advice*. Blanche Ring was to star in a new musical, *The*

Wall Street Girl, for which Fields signed a young vaudevillian who did rope tricks, Will Rogers. Two other Fields productions, *The Bigamist* and *The Singing Teacher,* were announced, but never went into rehearsal.

Oddly absent was any mention of the road companies of Fields' previous Broadway Theater productions. Bookings for another extended of tour Marie Dressler in *Tillie's Nightmare* were announced, cancelled, then reinstated. (Dressler was refusing to attend rehearsals, and Lee Shubert asked Fields to persuade her to cooperate.) Fields' announcement that he intended to present only new musical comedies in the coming season did not seem to make good business sense, and his decision to dispose of the rights to *The Midnight Sons,* *The Jolly Bachelors,* and *The Summer Widowers* raised some eyebrows. Next, he sold his interest in Blanche Ring's new show to her manager, Frederic McKay. Insiders speculated that Fields was trying to raise some quick cash for a new venture, but for what, and with whom?

The answer came in late August, from Chicago, where the American Music Hall announced "a Weberfields policy" for the coming season. The theater's new owner, Marcus Loew, said that he and his unnamed partners would renovate the interior and establish a permanent musical stock organization to produce travesties. A few weeks later, the partners' names were revealed: William Morris and Lew Fields. The enterprise seemed custom-tailored to the demand for "native" musical theater, and the theater's name was modified accordingly. When the "electrics" above the entrance were switched on, they read "Lew Fields' American Music Hall."

Fields had known William Morris since the mid-1880's, when the teen-age Morris had bluffed his way into a job with George Liman, a leading variety booker. In 1910, among the pictures covering his office wall, Morris kept a framed contract from 1889, in which Weber & Fields agreed to appear at Rockaway Beach for fifty dollars a week and board, playing three shows daily and appearing in the afterpiece.

Marcus Loew was a more recent acquaintance, another child of the Lower East Side. Fields met the mild-mannered ex-furrier through his friend David Warfield, who was the financial mainstay of Loew's early ventures. Warfield also introduced Loew to Adolph Zukor, with whom he opened his first nickelodeon. Unlike most of the other theater and movie moguls, Loew was known for being "on the square"—honest and fair in all his business dealings. In 1908, somebody inside the Shubert organization tipped off Loew that the Shuberts had acquired several New York–area theaters that were too small-time for their attractions. Loew called on Lee Shubert, who was happy to unload four unprofitable theaters in upper Manhattan and Brooklyn, which Loew quickly converted into successful nickelodeons. About a year later, when Loew was in the market for his first big motion-picture house, Fields told him about a seedy theater in Brooklyn called Watson's Cozy Corner. Watson's specialized in leg shows, and in getting raided by the police. Through his brother-in-law, Leo Teller (still managing Brooklyn's Broadway Theater) Fields heard that Watson's could be had cheaply. Loew bought it, changed the name to the Royal, and reopened with an Italian dramatic company playing Shakespeare, "to get the stink off the joint."

For the use of his name and services in connection with his American Music Hall productions, Fields would receive a weekly salary plus twenty-five percent of the net profits. For the first time in five years, the Shuberts did not figure directly in a Fields deal, but they were not exactly outsiders, either. Loew's activities seemed to complement the Shuberts'; Loew already had fourteen theaters, with three more under construction, and he was expanding into vaudeville and movie production, two areas Lee Shubert was eager to get involved in. In 1910, with $5 million capital, Loew formed Loew's Theatrical Enterprises. Its board of directors included Joe Schenck (Loew's manager), Joseph Rhinock (a major Shubert backer), and Lee and J. J. Shubert.

To give the opening of his American Music Hall an authentic flavor, Fields hired the Weberfields' favorite librettist, Edgar Smith, who gave his script a typically Weberfieldsian title, *Hanky Panky*. For the stock company, Fields hand-picked an ensemble of the most talented performers from his other productions: Gertrude Quinlan, Flora Parker, Mona Desmond, Max Rogers, Harry Cooper, Hugh Cameron, Bobby North, and Carter De Haven. (North, a comedian and Hebrew monologist, and De Haven, a handsome song-and-dance man, would eventually make their marks as producers in Hollywood.) For the leading comedienne, Fields hired Adele Ritchie. The director-choreographer was Gus Sohlke, famous for his Chicago chorus lines. Fields showed his growing confidence in his brother Sol by rewarding him with the position of stage manager.

By late September, it was becoming increasingly apparent that coordinating his preparations for the American Music Hall with his Shubert productions was not going to be easy. *The Hen Pecks* barely lasted to the final week of the month, closing after several losing weeks. On September 25, *The Never Homes* had its first public performance in Albany. The evening did not go well; the chorus numbers and specialties were uncharacteristically sloppy. Fields concluded that the show was under-rehearsed, for which he blamed Ned Wayburn, and postponed its New York opening. In addition to his responsibilities to *The Never Homes* and *The Wife Hunters*, the hard-working director had staged a revue for Harris and Lasky's struggling Folies Bergere, entitled *Hello, Paris*, which opened September 22. Wayburn took offense at Fields' criticism—Fields himself was preoccupied with rehearsals of *Hanky Panky*—and walked out, leaving Fields to finish polishing *The Never Homes* alone. A few days later, they shook hands and made up, but the incident pointed up the fact that both men had spread themselves too thin.

Subtitled "a musical kinemacolor in six scenes," *The Never Homes* seemed to be just another in the series of Broadway Theater "summer entertainments." In fact, the target of *The Never Homes*—the women's suffrage movement—was as central to its time as the ethnic clashes portrayed by Edward Harrigan or the breakdown of class barriers lampooned in Weber & Fields' Music Hall productions. By 1910, the participation of women in activities outside of the home was affecting almost every aspect of everyday life, from diet to politics. Approximately one quarter of American women over ten years of age were now bread-winners, though their income averaged less than seven dollars a week. Membership in women's organizations had surged dramatically. In some communities, the women's club was the only organization devoted to civic improvement.[17] Yet, only a handful of states (all of them in the West) allowed women to vote. Leaders of the women's suffrage movement began calling for more militant tactics.

To be sure, *The Never Homes* was no progressive tract, but it did not shy away from the issues. For opening night (October 5), the lobby and auditorium of the Broadway were decorated with flags and banners proclaiming "Votes for Women!" and yellow streamers (the women's rights color) hanging from the gallery. At the rise of the curtain, the town of Lilydale is in the throes of election night mayhem, and an uncivil war between the sexes. Two antagonistic crowds—one male and the other female—have gathered in front of the newspaper office for the balloting results. In the confusion, a policeman arrests little Jimmy Louder (Will Archie) but cannot send him home because there is nobody there. Bulky George Monroe played the suffragettes' political boss, Patricia Flynn, giving a performance that put a new twist on the old minstrel tradition of female impersonators. When the Super-Suffragette Ticket prevails, the new Mayoress breaks up her daughter's romance with the dashing Webster Choates (Joseph Santley), "an enemy of the cause." The Mayoress' first official act is to appoint a female supporter to be police chief, and Patricia Flynn the fire chief. The men relinquish their power and seem delighted with their newfound freedom. Each side vows not to have anything further to do with the other.

The only tenderness between the sexes comes in an encounter between the neglected Jimmy, and charming Fanny Hicks (Helen Hayes). Jimmy offers Fanny a bite of his raspberry tart; she tries it, then argues with him about what flavor it is, whether it's good for her, etc. She takes a few more bites to prove her case, until the tart is gone. To show her thanks, she wipes her sticky fingers on his sleeve. Jimmy is enthralled, and together they sing "There's a Girl in Havana," an Irving Berlin interpolation (though he took no credit for it) and, not surprisingly, the show's best tune. It was reprised several times throughout the evening.

The effects on Lilydale of "petticoat rule" occupied the rest of the plot. At the police station, the jail cells are redecorated, and the same married men are arrested every night. A chambermaid is made chief inspectoress of the street cleaning department, leading the Mayoress to complain that she sweeps everything under the front steps and forgets to dust the lamp posts.

As usual, the topper was saved for the last scene in Act One. The setting was a realistic reproduction of a fire station, including real horses and a steam fire engine, on which the fire ladies (in varying stages of undress) make taffy while waiting for an alarm. When Fire Chief Patricia gets a phone call about a fire, she turns to her crew and calmly remarks, "Why girls, what do you think of that? There's a fire!" Whereupon she wants to know if it's a large or a small fire, and announces if it isn't out by tomorrow the company will come around, as "it's a very damp day today and will be bad for the horses." Finally, the fire alarm sounds. In a flurry of activity, the fire ladies shed their pajamas and put on their uniforms, slide down the brass pole, while others hitch the horses in place. With sirens howling, they jump onto the engine and speed off, but in the excitement, they have forgotten to ask where the fire is. A colorful simulation of the fire provides the finale: a mass of tinsel ribbons dropped the full length of the proscenium with yellow and red lights playing upon them, as the orchestra played "There'll Be a Hot Time in the Old Town Tonight."

An epidemic of love breaks out and brings the warring sexes to a compromise. The women of Lilydale give the city back to their menfolk, having learned an important lesson: "What's the use of working hard to run a town when you can run the men who run the town without working at all?" In the end, "the Never Homes" of the title was an indictment of both sexes.

MacDonough's libretto (especially the first act) was so far superior to those of any of the previous shows in the series that one wonders why Fields did not take his librettists on transatlantic cruises more often. Broadway critics, who were carping loudly about the sorry state of musical theater, generally applauded the relative cohesiveness of the book: "the main idea . . . is very well maintained,"[18] and "more consistency than is usual in such pieces. . . . There was much more definite purpose seen in *The Never Homes*. . . ."[19]

Audiences, however, did not seem to notice or care. Attendance was strong through Thanksgiving, but then began to show signs of anemia in December, along with most of the other musicals on Broadway at the time. Two factors may have accounted for the show's surprising lack of staying power: the absence of Lew Fields from the cast and the absense of any extravagant scenic effects on the scale of the farmyard or apartment cross-section.

By the end of October 1911, Fields' inability to be two or more places at once was compromising both the commercial and artistic quality of his productions. Two days after the opening of *The Never Homes* in New York, Fields began a two-week engagement in Philadelphia in *The Hen Pecks*, which was followed by a week in Pittsburgh. At considerable expense, the companies of *Hanky Panky* and *The Wife Hunters* joined him for rehearsals in those cities, with Sohlke directing the former and Wayburn the latter.

Fields' commitment to *The Wife Hunters* was ambivalent, at best. The Shuberts had been carrying several promissory notes on the Fields Producing Company that had fallen due. Instead of paying off a portion of them, as was customary, they proposed an arrangement for Fields to pay them back. They wanted him to adapt *Three Million Dollars*, a straight comedy that had toured but never made it to New York; they would hire him as the producer-manager for a weekly salary and a share of the profits, and then deduct this from what he owed.

The script for *The Wife Hunters* was mediocre, and Fields had neither the time nor, one suspects, the inclination to rewrite it. To compensate, Fields gave free rein to Wayburn to create elaborate stage effects and chorus routines. In his usual lavish manner, Fields ordered scenery, costumes, wigs, and so on, without keeping tabs on his expenditures. After its tryouts in Albany and Pittsburgh (where "the show went over big" according to a cable from Fields), he decided to make some cast changes, which meant delaying its New York opening. He left it to Wayburn to supervise the final week of rehearsal and its Broadway premiere.

Fields had to sort out a more pressing schedule conflict. William Morris had scheduled the opening of Fields' American Music Hall for Tuesday, October 31; J. J. Shubert had booked *The Hen Pecks* to open at the Garrick in Chicago on the evening of Sunday, October 29. Neither would back down to accommodate the other. *The Hen Pecks* closed in Pittsburgh Saturday evening; J. J. figured that the production could load out by 3:00 a.m. Sunday (unlikely for so large a show). The company would then travel by special train to Chicago, arriving around 1:00 p.m., which left only six hours to set up two tons of scenery, rehearse and check music and lighting cues, etc. Fields insisted that he needed at least ten hours, and asked J. J. to postpone the first show at the Garrick until Monday evening. Shubert refused.

Fields was now faced with the prospect of opening against himself, and not having adequate time to polish either production. The company was already running late by the time they pulled out of Pittsburgh. Fields took the extra precaution of carrying some extra stagehands to help set up once they arrived in Chicago. En route, he rehearsed his music hall company. The company arrived with only five hours before the opening curtain was supposed to go up, and then discovered that several of the sets had to be cut down to fit onto the Garrick stage. The curtain rose only thirty minutes late, but the performance was beset by the kinds of problems created by hurried staging: mechanical miscues, ragged chorus work, slow set changes. "It was *awful*," Fields later admitted with a shudder to an interviewer. As soon as the final curtain was rung down, he informed his weary company that there would be an immediate rehearsal. Most of them were too exhausted to argue, and the rest knew better than to try.

It was 6:30 a.m. when they finished. With a sense of dread, Fields bought the morning papers and read the reviews. Although the opening night was sold out, the comments of disappointed reviewers would guarantee a falling-off in attendance.

At eight o'clock, when the Western Union office opened its doors, Fields sent a terse message to J. J. Shubert: "I told you it couldn't be done and it wasn't we killed our opening tonight." Later that day, adding insult to injury, J. J. Shubert sent word that he would not help pay for the extra stagehands Fields had hired.

On October 31, *Hanky Panky* inaugurated Lew Fields' American Music Hall with a capacity house. Like the first Weber & Fields Music Hall shows, the first part of the program was a vaudeville olio that was changed weekly. The idea was to give Chicagoans "a second edition of the Weber & Fields playhouse in New York. . . . It will become their patent 'blues' destroyer. . . . Tired businessmen and weary women can go there and forget their troubles in one long laugh."[20] Fields dropped all pretense to plot or a cohesive score. Edgar Smith's script reconstituted various plot elements from old Weberfields' productions. Bobby North and Max Rogers, as Herman Bierheister and Wilhelm Rausmitt, played the Weber & Fields parts; Carter DeHaven assumed the DeWolf Hopper romantic roles; Adele Ritchie took on the Lillian Russell–Fay Templeton leading ladies. Gus Sohlke, as director and choreographer, updated Julian Mitchell's chorus work. A. Baldwin Sloane's score could not measure up to John Stromberg's best, but Fields supplemented it with interpolations by Irving Berlin, Jean Schwartz, and others.

A reporter who interviewed Fields after the second or third performance of *The Hen Pecks* was surprised at how different he looked from his stage character. As Henry Peck, he appeared "short and scrawny, with fishy blue eyes, and a bald head with an aura of blonde fuzz around it like a baby's." In person, he was "rather tall, rather well-built. He has dark hair . . . a perfectly lovable smile . . . and heaps of beaux yeux." Instead of the vigorous eccentric from the stage, she saw a "nice man" who looked "tired" and "worn to a frazzle." His well-being worried her enough that she ended her article with an expression of concern: "Goodness knows I hope he takes care of himself."

She also asked him why, with all his responsibilities as a producer and a manager, he did not give up acting. "I'll tell you why," he said, leaning forward, "I act because I have to. There is always something I want to do myself. Not that I think I can do it better than anybody else, but because I happen to do it to suit myself. I love the stage. . . . Why can't I do what I love to do?" [21] Despite his successes as a producer, Fields remained an actor at heart. One wonders how much more he might have accomplished as a producer had he not loved acting so much.

When *The Wife Hunters* opened at Lew Fields' Herald Square in New York earlier that same week, his absence from the cast, and, apparently, from an active role backstage, was conspicuous. In previous Fields shows, even if the plot was weak, there was plenty of comedy. Not so in *The Wife Hunters*. Ned Wayburn's "stage pictures" and chorus ensembles, including a resurrected English Pony Ballet, provided most of the evening's novelties. While Emma Carus sang a coon song, "Mammy Jinny," the hedges and walls of a log cabin descended from the flies and were assembled by "appropriately clad" chorus girls. Other scenic effects were equally elaborate if not a little silly: chorus girls as "cohorts of living daisies, white and yellow, black and brown" danced down a grassy bank. Then, on the green slope over which they had just trod, "human marguerites sprung out of the ground. . . ." [22]

Less than a week after the show opened, Wayburn resigned as Fields' permanent director and stage manager and signed with Charles Dillingham. *The Wife Hunters* lasted only thirty-six performances. Lee Shubert watched the opening night and wrote Fields that "it was a mighty good show but the papers did not seem to take to it. Any musical show at this time in New York has a hard game, as there are fourteen here now. . . ." But when the Shuberts tallied up the bills for the extra scenery and costumes that Fields had ordered, they insisted that he share in the losses. This was how he came to lose $16,000 on a show for which he was not supposed to share in the risk.

By the end of his first week in Chicago, Fields had just managed to smooth out the kinks in *The Hen Pecks* when he received a message that forced him to close down the production altogether. On the afternoon of November 7, a wire came from New York informing Fields that his father was dying. He left immediately on the Twentieth Century to New York, along with brothers Charlie (business manager for *The Hen Pecks*) and Sol (stage manager of the American Music Hall). Nat was on his way from Duluth, where he was touring in another Lew Fields road show.

Their father, now seventy-one years old, had been ailing for several months with a kidney problem that was not considered serious. Solomon Fields, as he now called himself, had long since ceased to be the stern, disapproving patriarch. Around 1901 or 1902, he had put aside his needles and pinking shears for good, thankful and not a little surprised that his stage-smitten son should have become the family's financial mainstay. "Foolishness for foolish people," was how Papa Schanfield used to refer to the theater. He had learned to accept it as one of the oddities of the New World that one could turn fun-making into a thriving industry just like making clothes or automobiles.

The one thing that Solomon could never reconcile himself to was his children's indifference to Jewish traditions. Only his daughter Annie and her husband Morris Warschauer kept a kosher household. The others seemed to be in a race to see who could assimilate the quickest. Lew's eldest son, Joe, began study for his bar mitzvah, but the ceremony apparently never took place. (The rabbi who was supposed to teach him would, upon arriving at the Fields' townhouse, call out from the front steps, "Choe! Wanna loin?" setting off a chorus of snickers and imitations among Joe's upper West Side playmates.) Solomon was shocked when Lew and Rose bought a Christmas tree and Christmas gifts for their children. He stepped up his activities at the orthodox synagogue on West 161st Street, and soon became its president. He also belonged to the local Masonic lodge.

Lew and his brothers did not make it back in time from Chicago to see their father alive. With Henry, Ray, Annie, and his wife Sarah at his side, he expired with barely a sigh, a man so diligent and proper even at the end that he folded his own hands on his breast before he died. In accordance with Jewish law, the funeral was scheduled for one in the afternoon of the following day, November 8. Although the services were announced to be private, the Fields' spacious apartments at 600 West 150th Street were thronged with mourners, many of them members of Solomon's synagogue or Masonic lodge, as well as several theater figures, including Joe Weber and William Collier. With the entire family at the bier, the rabbi conducted the service in Hebrew and German, and then addressed the mourners in English.

After the services, the funeral party drove to Washington Cemetery in Long Island, where the last rites were performed. As the cortège passed the synagogue on West 161st Street, the doors were thrown open to reveal hundreds of burning candles, and the rabbi, with bowed head, spoke a benediction.

On the way back from the cemetery, Weber rode with Lew Fields and his family. Weber knew better than anybody how hurt Lew had been by his father's early disapproval and how proud Lew had felt when his father had finally accepted Fields as the family name. Recollections of Papa Schanfield gradually gave way to stories of their Bowery days, of museum man George Bunnell (who had just died the previous month), Miner's Saloon, and the Music Hall, where Lew's father finally came to see them perform. Lew asked if it was true that Weber was considering giving up the Music Hall. Weber was having difficulties finding attractions that drew well enough to pay the rent; with the theater district now extending north of Forty-second, the Music Hall was well out of the flow. Maybe he would try running moving pictures there. The prospect made them sad.

On impulse, Fields said, "We ought to go together again, Web." There is no evidence that Fields had been considering a reunion; had it not been for his father's funeral, it would have been months before he would have crossed paths with his old partner.

Weber was cautious. In the years since splitting with Fields, he had had his share of successes. Except for his collaboration with Victor Herbert, *Dream City/ The Magic Knight,* which lost money on the road and ended in a lawsuit, Weber played it safe, alternating between Music Hall–style productions and imported musicals such as *Alma, Where Do You Live?* (1910), and *The Merry Widow Burlesque* (1908). His productions, if not terribly inspired, were always well cast and well mounted. The same year that Fields' *The Midnight Sons* dazzled Broadway with the largest musical production of its time, totalling over 300 people in the cast and crew, Weber quietly made a small fortune on the smallest production of the season, *The Climax,* a straight comedy with a cast of four. Though the gross receipts for the hit *The Midnight Sons* were considerably higher, Weber's low production expenses gave him the biggest net profit. Booking through Klaw & Erlanger, he sent five companies of *The Climax* on tour. It was this kind of business acumen, and along with some good real estate investments, that had made him a millionaire.

Fields' impulsive statement reminded Weber of a promise they made when they parted. "It's like this," Fields explained later. "We agreed that, no matter what we were doing, if for any reason whatsoever, one of us needed the other, the other was to respond."[23] Weber, however, had no pressing need for more money. He had just refused an offer of $250,000 for the Music Hall property. Unlike Fields, he had no burning desire to continue acting; his only performances in the past two years had been the Lambs' and Friars' Club benefits. If there was a need, it was Fields'. Financially—and, perhaps, emotionally—he needed a sure thing. A Weber & Fields reunion would be a sure thing.

Weber indicated that he was agreeable if the details could be arranged— details like how to handle Weber's contracts with the Syndicate and Fields' deals with the Shuberts. Joe and Lew had sealed the deal in the same informal manner that they dissolved their partnership seven years earlier. Weber asked, "Is it on?" Fields replied, "If you say so." "Then shake on it," said Weber, and they shook hands. Theater critic and fellow Friar Rennold Wolf served as the intermediary when Fields left New York to rejoin *The Hen Pecks* in Kansas City. In his absence, the show had been shut down, wiping out the entire second week of its Chicago engagement.

While Fields completed his tour with *The Hen Pecks* (Kansas City, St. Louis, Milwaukee, Indianapolis, Columbus), he and his spokesmen denied all rumors of a reunion. Meanwhile, his need for one increased. The American Music Hall was doing enviable business, but at an enormous expense; Fields was required to increase his outlay. Morris asked Ed Bloom, who had just finished managing the blockbuster tour of the British vaudevillian Harry Lauder, to go to Chicago to try to cut costs. At the same time, the Collier production at the Fulton, *Take My Advice,* was losing money. At almost every stop on the tour, Fields found letters from the Shuberts' business manager containing another promissory note that had fallen due and needed his signature for partial payment and renewal. By the time he returned to New York in early December, he had signed new notes totalling over fifty thousand dollars.

At first, Fields had simply envisioned a Weber & Fields reunion, with the pair fronting a first-rate vaudeville bill for a short season in New York and a profitable road tour similar to what Harry Lauder had just done. It was William Morris who came up with the idea of reassembling the Music Hall's principals. Broadway insiders considered this next to impossible: many of them were busy in musical comedy or vaudeville. Their combined salaries alone would make it unprofitable. Moreover, Lillian Russell was about to marry Colonel Alexander Moore, a Pittsburgh newspaper publisher, while Fay Templeton had been happily married for several years to another wealthy Pittsburgher, W. J. Patterson, and had retired from the stage. Warfield had become Belasco's biggest star, and was committed to a long run in *The Return of Peter Grimm.* Peter Dailey, Louise Collier, and John Stromberg were dead.

Weber guessed that if they could get Lillian Russell, the rest of the company would fall into place. Shortly before Christmas, both partners paid her a visit at her home on West Eighty-ninth Street, around the corner from Fields' place. As soon as she saw "the boys" together, she knew why they had come. "Pay me what you like," she said. "We'll make Pittsburgh the last stop on the tour and you boys can come to my wedding." On December 30, she signed a contract with Weber & Fields that guaranteed $2,000 a week for twelve weeks. The following day, the major New York newspapers announced the most eagerly awaited theatrical event of the season: the Weber & Fields Jubilee, opening in early February.

Fay Templeton, George Beban, Willie Collier, John T. Kelly, Ada Lewis, Frankie Bailey (she of the symmetrical legs)—all signed on enthusiastically in the coming days. Danseuse Bessie Clayton returned from England to join the reunion; in the spirit of the event, she was reconciled with her estranged husband, Julian Mitchell. Edgar Smith started on the libretto—a two-part program featuring a pastiche of favorite Music Hall sketches and a new burlesque of a current Broadway hit. By vote of the company, the entertainment was entitled *Hokey-Pokey.*

When Fields announced that chorus girls who had been in the original Music Hall company would be given preference for positions in the new production, his office was besieged by pretty young hopefuls. Surveying the beauteous crush, he compared it to the long passenger list of the *Mayflower.*

In the Shuberts' offices at 1416 Broadway, and upstairs at the New Amsterdam Theater, where Klaw & Erlanger had their headquarters, the mood was anything but jolly. Abe Erlanger put Weber "on the pan" for going into combination with a Shubert ally. Weber replied that they intended to make it an independent venture. In that case, replied Erlanger, you can place it in any Syndicate theater you want. The Shuberts were applying similar pressure on Fields; because they were equal partners in all Fields' attractions, they figured that they were entitled to take their share out of the Jubilee's gross receipts. Weber quite bluntly stated he had made not such arrangement, and that if Fields had to declare the Shuberts "in," it would have to come out of Fields' share. Fields may have mollified Lee Shubert when he and his Hen Pecks Company attracted a sold-out house for the dedication of the new Sam S. Shubert Theater on Forty-fourth Street. Lee was very sentimental where his departed brother was concerned.

The Syndicate-Shubert wrangling looked like it would sabotage the reunion,

until William Morris helped work out a compromise. In New York, the Weber &
Fields Jubilee would play at Fields' and the Shuberts' Broadway Theater, and on
the road, it would be booked into mostly Syndicate houses, since theirs tended
to be the largest theaters outside of New York.

According to the tradition established by the Music Hall, the Weberfields'
season began with a ritual of conspicuous consumption: the auction of first-night
tickets. The Jubilee would be no exception. On the afternoon of February 1, William Collier welcomed a well-heeled audience to the Broadway: "The last thing
Joe and Lew told me was to keep the prices down and get all I could." Bidding
for the first box began at $15 and quickly climbed to $900, for which it was sold
to a man representing William Randolph Hearst. The six second-tier boxes brought
$2,285; purchasers included Broadway stars, department store magnates, finan-
ciers, and a Supreme Court justice. The four lower boxes were reserved for the
families of Weber, Fields, the Shuberts, and Felix Isman. (Fields later refused an
offer of $2,500 for his box.) By the time the final gavel sounded, the total was
$11,926. Seventy-one seats were reserved for the press, and the remaining 1,400
seats went on sale the following day at the standard two-dollar scale.

The rehearsals were loose but frenetic. Fields revived the Weberfieldsian
habit of ensemble improvisation and tinkering with Edgar Smith's lines. "We can
get anybody to speak lines for $50 a week," he commented to a reporter who
stopped in at a rehearsal. "We are paying [them] ten, twenty times that much.
. . . I want to see how witty and inventive they can be."[24] Unlike the book musicals Fields had been producing for the last seven years, Fields agreed "it would
never do to have things rehearsed letter perfect before the opening performance."[25]

The evening of February 8, at the Broadway Theater, was more a celebration
of long-lost friends than a performance, a delirious and at times almost hysterical
homage to a pair of beloved burlesquers and their famous colleagues. It was
"Broadway's night of nights," and something more. The Weber & Fields Jubilee
seemed to provoke a nostalgia that was almost frightening in its intensity. "New
York is itself again," wrote one otherwise stolid critic. "It has the favorite Weber-
Fieldsian fun and dance, joke and jingle. Are not these enough to restore the city
to its ancient pride of life?"[26] Public affection for Weber & Fields had grown
since their split; while other familiar emblems of *fin-de-siècle* life had been ov-
ertaken by disturbing signs of modernity, memory had endowed the Weberfields
with magical properties.

It was a bitterly cold night, but ticketholders started arriving at 6:30. Within
half an hour, the lines from the balcony and gallery entrances on Forty-first Street
extended around the corner and a block and a half down Seventh Avenue. Broadway was a mass of vehicles and striving pedestrians. Once inside the theater, the
faithful had to wade through a forest of floral offerings that filled the lobby and
overflowed up the stairways leading to the balcony. The boxes and proscenium
were smothered in American Beauty roses, their petals contrasting richly with
the glittering gowns and shirtfronts. There could be no doubt that a considerable
event was about to take place. Adversaries temporarily put aside their differences: J. J. Shubert did not try to eject Flo Ziegfeld; Ralph Pulitzer could look

across the hall and see William Randolph Hearst; Tammany pols sat across the aisle from reformers. Lillian Russell's fiancé, Colonel Alexander Moore, sat several rows behind Diamond Jim Brady. Sitting in Joe Weber's box were his wife, brother Muck, and their ninety-three-year-old mother. It was the first time she had seen Joe on stage since Weber & Fields' first performance at Turn Hall, thirty-five years earlier. In the corresponding box across the hall, Rose Fields sat with Frances, Joseph, Herbert, Dorothy, and several of the Harrises. The younger Fields children were seeing for the first time the two-act that had made "Pop" famous.

At 8:20 p.m. the orchestra began its overture, a medley of Stromberg tunes that provoked sighs and renewed applause as each melody was recognized. The curtain rose to reveal a replica of the Place de l'Opera, Paris, and a drill team of chorus girls in short skirts. Leading them was Frankie Bailey, clad in lemon tights that proved that her famous legs were as shapely as ever. Seeing this, the audience cheered for two minutes—one minute for each leg—while Frankie blushed and smiled and thanked them in her tiny voice.

Next, John T. Kelly rolled out of the wings, reprising his familiar role as Jeremiah McCann, the parvenu Irish-American tourist. He was appropriately outfitted—checked suit, green plush vest with soda-cracker buttons, red necktie, with a thick stogie clenched between his teeth—prompting comments of "Doesn't he look natural!" In a thick brogue (which had been banned in Boston), he observed, "Paris has it all over Syracuse." Wheezing slightly (he had gained a few pounds), he sang "If It Wasn't for the Irish and the Jews," including one verse that was as true in 1912 as it had been in 1898: "I really heard Belasco say / You couldn't stage a play today / If it wasn't for the Irish and the Jews. . . ." When McCann's daughter, Clorinda (Helena Collier Garrick), arrived, they argued about whether the museums or the department stores offered the most edifying cultural displays.

The chorus girls returned with their arms full of roses, and the celebrants knew that Lillian Russell was on her way. Encased in a white chiffon gown studded with $150,000 worth of diamonds and rhinestones, she sounded like a tinkling chandelier as she advanced towards the footlights. She carried a staff with a crooked handle wrapped around with a string of diamonds. Ample and radiant as ever, still in good voice, she sang, "The Island of Roses and Love." While she sang the verses, chorus girls dressed as artists sat at easels and painted, and at the final refrain, reversed their canvases to reveal portraits of Russell. Later, she sang her signature number, "Come Down My Evenin' Star," which still choked her up, and there were many moist eyes in the audience as they listened to John Stromberg's swan song.

A blare of brass and a petite majorette announced the minstrel parade, led by William Collier (as a talent agent) in a silver plug hat and a long white coat. He sang "De Pullman Porter's Ball," and did a ten-minute dance routine that left him so breathless that he had to decline the insistent requests for an encore. He was rescued by Lillian Russell, the socialite-adventuress Mrs. Wallingford Grafter, and the two immediately left the script behind and traded banter for five minutes. Frankie Bailey returned as a gendarme and tried to arrest Collier, and Kelly mistook Russell for the cook he was supposed to interview. Stagestruck Clorinda McCann told Collier, "Jake Shubert thinks I have marvelous ability as an actress." To which Collier replied, "You may be a success in spite of that."

Those who weren't laughing too hard then noticed Fay Templeton "peeking" around the corner of the scenery; she was making light of how much harder it was now for her to hide her girth after four years of domestic life. "Well, it looks natural to see you all again," she said after the applause died down. "Same old crowd. Paired off somewhat differently perhaps, but. . . ." She tore into "The Singer and the Song," and "Ma Blushin' Rosie," and threw in a few coloratura stunts to show that her voice was better than ever.

A thump, a crash, and the sound of a scuffle in the wings—then the familiar complaint, "Don't poosh me, Meyer! Don't poosh me!" Just like in the good old days, Mike came stumbling out backwards, propelled by Meyer's impatient shoves, and the audience was on its feet, whooping with joy. For the better part of the next ten minutes the applause was deafening. Their names were shouted from all parts of the house, like the stampede for favorite sons at a national political convention. Time and again they tried to start their lines, but had to give it up. Both doffed their fried-egg hats, and Mr. Weber tossed his artificial stomach around in the most reckless manner. As they waited for the applause to die down, their eyes wandered to the boxes where their proud families were seated.

Fields started right in where he had left off a decade before, choking his partner and jabbing him in the eyeball to prove how much he loved him. "You're strong after your seven years' rest," said Weber between assaults. They bully-ragged their way down the sidewalk to the entrance of a café, where Fields began another favorite routine: "Are you thirsty?" (Cheers of recognition.) Weber said no, and Fields, who was very thirsty, responded, "I could luff you for dose words—I have only five cents." And then, after elaborate instructions and several aborted attempts ("somedings in my heart tells me dat you are not going to do as you say," Fields concluded gravely), they enter the café. Of course, Fields' well-rehearsed plan goes awry.

All of the above was crammed into the first scene of *Hokey Pokey*, which did not end until ten o'clock, after Bessie Clayton toe-danced to "Au Clair de la Lune." In Scene Two, Weber & Fields argued about "the Skin-de-cat" and, aided by Collier, set up the old corporation whose only purpose was to relieve Weber of his bankroll. They decided that Weber's circular letter of credit was no good because it was printed on a square piece of paper. With Mrs. Wallingford Grafter (Russell) as a fourth, they sat down for a poker game.

Then came another of the evening's unrehearsed moments, perhaps its most dramatic. Looking up from his five aces, Fields glanced into the wings and saw a shabby-looking Jewish peddler, smiling and rubbing his hands together. It was David Warfield, in his pre-Belasco garb. He had rushed through his performance as the ghostly Dutchman in Belasco's *The Return of Peter Grimm* to drop in on the Jubilee. "It's . . . it's the return of Petie Grimm!" cried Fields as Warfield shambled on stage. There was a stunned silence as the audience tried to decide whether this was a stunt. Then Warfield spoke, "I'm not in this. I'm just here to call, bine gollies!" The spectators, on stage and off, exploded in cheers and applause. Turning to Weber & Fields, he said, "I'm happy to see you together. Dat's nice . . ." and the three traded hugs until Weber & Fields began plucking out tufts of Warfield's fake beard and putting them in their pockets to keep as souvenirs. Warfield then whispered something to Fields, and the two marched into the wings and dragged out a very surprised David Belasco. His protests were part of his act; he was known for his timid and obsequious curtain calls. "Golly, I'm glad to be here. It's a great night," he said before hastening off stage. Before the first-act curtain came down, Weber & Fields once again found themselves in the predicament where they had to disguise themselves in whitewash, short skirts, and galoshes to pose as the "Dying Gladiators" statue.

Act Two of *Hokey Pokey* was Edgar Smith's burlesque of the Scottish hit comedy, *Bunty Pulls the Strings.* Though it did not get under way until 11:30, it was no afterthought. "Bunty Bulls and Strings" ranked with the best of the old Music Hall travesties. Templeton, as Bunty, once again demonstrated that she was still the era's most versatile comedienne. Bunty was so frugal that she boiled her family's dinner with the wash. Later, she sang a clever novelty number— "Alexander's Bagpipe Band"—by Sloane and Goetz that spoofed a hit tune by Goetz's brother-in-law, Irving Berlin. Templeton was assisted by a fetching chorus of lassies in kilts, which included Music Hall alumnae Hazel Kirke, Edna Chase, and Gertie Moyer. Collier played the dour Scot, Tammus Biggar, who gets walloped by his son Rab (Joe Weber) for listening to a turkey trot on the Sabbath. Fields was the lugubrious Weelum Grunt, whose talent for palming coins came in handy when the collection plate was passed.

It was 1:00 a.m. by the time the final curtain came down and stayed down and the last bouquet had been handed over the footlights, and all the principals had given their speeches. Overwhelmed by the ovation, exhausted, and relieved, Weber and Fields had tears in their eyes as they trudged up the narrow iron stairs to their two little adjoining dressing rooms. (Fields had given his usual dressing room in the Broadway to Lillian Russell, and Collier had the other star accommodations.) The reunion that the two erstwhile partners had avoided for eight years had succeeded beyond their wildest expectations.

The fifteen thousand dollars spent for first-night tickets to the Jubilee was a new record for an American musical entertainment. It was as if the first-nighters at the Weber & Fields Jubilee—the theater figures, publishers, sporting men, politicians, lawyers, bankers, merchants, industrialists, socialites—were trying to buy the last innocent pleasures of a simpler age. They came away satisfied, because for a few hours the Jubilee put the lie to the cynics who claimed that there was no turning back, that divorces cannot be healed and once-happy families reunited, that past joys can never be recaptured.

The record-breaking attendance at the Broadway went on for 110 performances, producing gross receipts of over $300,000 before the company embarked on a thirty-six-city tour of one-night stands. Wherever they played—from Brooklyn to Omaha, Detroit to Louisville—they met with the same kind of public adulation. Their whirlwind tour brought in an additional $105,000. If the successful actor can be said to rule over his own little kingdom, then Weber & Fields in the spring of 1912 commanded an empire.

Three days after their triumphant opening, Weber & Fields were the guests of honor at a Friars' Club dinner at the Hotel Astor. Seventeen hundred men attended, filling the ballroom's banquet tables, while an additional five hundred women (including Lillian Russell) sat in the gallery boxes. Entertainment was provided by George M. Cohan, Raymond Hitchcock, John T. Kelly, and Irving Berlin. Every prominent performer and theatrical manager was either there or represented, with two notable exceptions: Lee and J. J. Shubert. Sitting with Weber & Fields at the head table were Charles J. Ross, Daniel Frohman, Marc Klaw, John Drew, De Wolf Hopper, Edgar Smith, a congressman, the sheriff, a judge, and Enrico Caruso. Elsewhere throughout the banquet hall was practically every member of the Fields/Schanfield/Harris clans.

The custom of good-natured raillery by the speakers (what later became known as the "roast") was already established. Enrico Caruso, who used to visit backstage at the old Weber & Fields Music Hall in its last season, offered one of the best: "At the Metropolitan Opera House we study so hard all our lives to learn to sing. Mr. Gatti-Casazza gives you an all-star cast. We sing like angels and you pay $10,000. But Fields here, who sticks his finger in Weber's eye, plays to thirteen-fourteen thousand dollars. How is that?"[27] Rennold Wolf introduced Joe Weber as "the only comedian in captivity who can speak Scotch with a German dialect and count the house in Yiddish at the same time." William Collier was supposed to introduce Fields, but he was too ill to attend. He was replaced by the much-married Nat C. Goodwin, who questioned whether Fields was truly an actor, for he was still married to his first wife after eighteen years. This, according to Goodwin, was especially remarkable, given Fields' expertise in the selection of chorus girls.

The Friars' Club celebration of Weber & Fields brought together in one room representatives of show biz past—Gus Hill, Jerry Cohan, Hurtig & Seamon, Percy Williams, and Henry Miner's sons—and show biz future—Ziegfeld, Berlin, Marcus Loew, Adolph Zucker, Cecil B. De Mille, Joseph Schenck, Harry Cohn, and Samuel Goldfish (soon to be Goldwyn). Which way was Lew Fields looking? In a nod towards the future, he and Joe agreed to make some phonograph records of their most famous routines for Columbia, and they no longer dismissed out of hand the suggestion that they put some of these routines on film. Still, Fields could not ignore the fact that he had made the biggest hit of his life reviving the "good old days."

Coming on top of a theatrical season that had an unprecedented proportion of failures, the overwhelming success of the Weber & Fields Jubilee deepened Fields' ambivalence about his direction. Popular acclaim seem to be reserved for the tried-and-true musicals of the past. The Shuberts and William A. Brady had revived Gilbert & Sullivan with comic opera stars such as De Wolf Hopper and Christie MacDonald, and even George M. Cohan had fallen back on a revival of *Forty-five Minutes from Broadway*. Moreover, the appetite for Fields' musical spectacles was showing signs of satiation. A week before the Jubilee opened, an article in the *Dramatic Mirror* on theatrical trends included the observation, "In New York, lavish settings for plays and colossal salaries for actors appear to have reached their limit."

It was time, Fields concluded with some reluctance, for his big ambitions "to be put up in alcohol and preserved on the shelf," for the simple reason that "they won't always do for the box-office." Of course, it was the public, through the box office, who were the final judges. If Fields wanted to continue as a popular entertainer, he had to give his public what they wanted. The man who had eight years earlier talked about bringing coherency to the musical and consistency to the musical score, and had expressed his desire for character roles in a play "with the semblance of a clever story capably worked out," now claimed that "he was never more contented than he is to-day, playing Meyer, the eccentric German, to Weber's familiar Mike."

During Ren Wolf's speech at the Friars' Club dinner, he delighted the attendees by revealing what had hitherto been a secret: the real names of Joe Weber and Lew Fields. Both boys, he confided, had originally been named Moishe, the Hebrew version of Moses. It had a satisfying ring about it; in a manner of speaking, "Moses" Weber and "Moses" Fields could be said to have led American popular theater during its wanderings in the wilderness. And over the next few years, it would begin to seem as though Fields was destined to share his namesake's fate.

Fortunately, by the time Fields put aside his pursuit of coherency, others were ready to pick up the banner. Coherence as an aesthetic value would become the goal of a new generation of Broadway producers, composers, and librettists in the coming decade. Lew Fields' new goal would be to survive.

CHAPTER XIII

Spendthrifty

MIKE: There's only one trouble with you. You are too spendthrifty with
the money. You pop it around as if you were a king or an emperor.

MEYER: I can't help it, Mike. You see, you have not got it in your nature
the delicatessen thing that I have got in mine. You are a business
man, plain and simpleton, while I—I am like a butterscotch, I
flitter from flower to flower . . .

Weber & Fields, "Racehorse Scene," 1912

THREE palace cars, three sleepers, a dining car, an observation car, and two
baggage cars—the private train bearing the Weber & Fields Jubilee Company on its 1912 tour was no less sumptuous and extravagant than the
show itself. One hundred people travelling in the height of pre-war luxury, they
were the high-profile ambassadors of a high style that would disappear within a
few short years. On board were the eighty members of the cast and crew, a
handful of newspapermen, and the principals' families—Lillian Russell brought
her sister, Collier brought his new wife and their adopted son, Willie Jr. ("Buster").
Joe and Lillian Weber were, as usual, inseparable.

Lew Fields had by far the largest contingent: Rose, the five kids, and a governess. It was a continuation of the spendthrift habits that Fields had developed
for the tours of *The Midnight Sons* and *The Summer Widowers*, a kind of deferred compensation for all of the cramped nights in coach, the spartan boardinghouses, and the stale cheese sandwiches from the station lunch counters. No
wonder actors loved him and the money men despaired. The pomp and circum-
stance of a private train and special venues were a form of advertising, a means
to distinguish the Weberfields from the typical touring vaudevillians, who were
still viewed as being in a class with vagrants and other lowlifes.

Though the trappings were extravagant, the Jubilee train was a remarkably
efficient money-making machine. In one month, the Weber & Fields Jubilee Company performed thirty-seven times in thirty-two cities, going as far north as Detroit and as far west as Kansas City, covering nearly five thousand miles. Even
with the "advanced" admission prices ($2 or $3 top), demand for tickets was so
large in some cities that Klaw & Erlanger rented the local armory or convention
hall, or pitched a circus tent in the biggest park to accommodate the crowds. The
tour's gross receipts came to almost $200,000, with Weber and Fields splitting a

cool $40,000 between them. Fields' bounty helped offset the $16,000 loss assessed by the Shuberts for his share of *The Wife Hunters*.

While the Jubilee was still in New York, one journalist observed: "Few heroes returning from victorious battle have ever been the recipient of more adulation outwardly expressed than greeted these two young veterans of the footlights."[1] What had been true in New York turned out to be equally true in every city they visited. By the time the tour ended in Pittsburgh on June 11, the fame of the Weberfields among urban audiences of the East and Midwest was greater than it had ever been in the days of the original partnership. The day after the tour ended, as a fitting finale to their legendary journey, the Weberfields attended the wedding of their queen, Lillian Russell, to a dapper knight of industry, Colonel Alexander Moore. Seven-year-old Dorothy Fields was the flower girl.

For the half million or so Americans who saw the Weber & Fields Jubilee Company in New York or on tour in the spring of 1912, the show became one of the most enduring memories of the pre-war era. Like people claiming descent from the original occupants of the Mayflower or those purporting to have been there when Babe Ruth hit his called-shot home run against the Cubs in 1932, in the years to come, an impossible number would tell how they had been there when the Weber & Fields Jubilee came to town.

The Jubilee also left an indelible impression on at least four youngsters. Until then, the Fields children had rarely seen their famous father at work. This was to be their longest sustained exposure to the heady professional world in which their father was a leading figure. Moreover, they were seeing him at the zenith of his popularity and box-office success—day after day of S.R.O. houses, thunderous ovations, and newspaper interviews. Frances, now an eighteen-year-old debutante ("the princess," her siblings called her) took all the attention in stride. Joe, who had inherited his father's somber looks and deadpan wit, enjoyed the camaraderie of the actors; he had one more year to go at De Witt Clinton High School and claimed to be interested in law and football, but he seemed to enjoy painting and writing more. Herbert, fifteen, already idolized his father and was hopelessly stagestruck. Dorothy was the company pet and the keeper of Pop's scrapbooks.

On the Jubilee tour, the children finally saw Lew Fields the showman, and they were awed. For the first time, they saw the striking difference between the public man and the private man, the performer and the father. It was a distinction that Fields had cultivated with great care. He resented the assumption that he was a comedian offstage as well as on, or that his private life was as broad and boisterous as a burlesque: "If you ask me if I am a comedian in my private life, do clowning in my house, at my dinner table, no! I am very serious. . . . I come to the theater and do my job with the tools of my profession, which I keep [there], just as the mechanic goes to work and uses his tools."[2]

At home, Lew played rather a passive role, deferring to his wife on most matters (whence, perhaps, came the inspiration for the henpecked husbands he so often created on stage). Out of necessity born from Lew's frequent absences, Rose ran—or more accurately, ruled—the household. She was the benevolent queen, capable of dispensing justice with a few well-chosen words or a cutting quip. Lew's passivity added to his mystery; he was physically very affectionate, but he could on occasion fly into a towering rage at the slightest provocation. Rose tried to insulate the children from his moods, just as she later tried to conceal the financial difficulties brought on by his Broadway failures and his gambling.

It was at Rose's insistence that the children were discouraged from theater careers. Over the years, Lew's public statements on the subject seemed to support Rose's position, but his actions were more equivocal. The one month on the Jubilee train probably did more to undermine Rose's careful guidance than any direct encouragement from Lew could have. Lew's notoriety, his long and frequent absences from his family, and his unpredictable demeanor at home combined to make him a larger-than-life figure to his children. For the younger children—Herbert and Dorothy—the Jubilee tour seems to have confirmed an idealized image of their father that would persist long after it ceased to reflect his true stature in the theater world.

Behind all of the cheering, however, there were more than a few wistful sighs. The reunion of the Weberfields uncovered a nostalgic longing in its well-heeled audiences that made it seem as if it had been a generation since the days of the Weber & Fields Music Hall instead of a mere eight years. The Jubilee show was called "a classic of its kind," "reviving gay old days," "like old home week," "a night of memories and sentiment," "the return of the Happy Family." It became a symbol of a simpler, happier time, a roseate revision of the days before progressivism, labor unrest, women's suffrage, income taxes, and foreign entanglements. In their enthusiastic applause for their old favorites, Jubilee audiences were saying farewell to an era.

In a sense, the Weber & Fields Jubilee was also the coda for an earlier era of show biz: it marked the effective end of all-star stock companies, the power of actor-managers and independent producers, cheap railway travel, lavish stage salaries. The Weberfields' burlesques were best enjoyed by audiences familiar with the Broadway originals, and with the rise of vaudeville and motion pictures, it had become increasingly difficult to predict what theatergoers outside of New York had seen. Burlesque, as practiced by the Weberfields, had become a problematic genre; by 1912, the melodramas that had been their primary targets no longer dominated the legitimate stage. Movies had taken over the stuff of melodrama, and were presenting it more effectively for a fraction of the price.

At the same time that the Weber & Fields Jubilee was a kind of sentimental send-off for the *ancien régime* of show business, the reunited partners were already making their first forays into the age of recorded sound and pictures. A month after the opening of *Hokey-Pokey*, Weber & Fields presented themselves at the studios of the Columbia Phonograph Company. They were feeling rather smug: for the sum of $10,000 plus royalties, they had agreed to talk ten of their most famous routines into the recording machine. How long could that take? A few mornings perhaps. It would be "gravy," they thought, easy money.

Since introducing the first two-sided 78 rpm record disk in 1904, the Columbia Phonograph Company (pooling patents with the Victor Talking Machine Company) had been waging a desperate battle with Edison's Amberola cylinders for the American market. Both companies recorded popular stars of musicals and vaudeville performing their hit songs, but it was the great opera stars (Caruso, Lina Cavalieri) and classical orchestras that generated most of the sales.

Weber & Fields' earliest recordings are quaint and revealing examples of a live performance tradition's first encounter with modern recording devices. On the March morning when Weber & Fields first presented themselves at the recording studio, they were totally unprepared for the problems resulting from the primitive recording techniques or the aesthetic demands of the new medium. First, there was the problem of the performance space. The engineer instructed Weber & Fields to stand completely still, shoulder to shoulder, no more than a foot from the two flared horns—"ether tubes," Weber called them—they had to speak into. On a raised platform, in a semicircle immediately behind them, was an eight-piece brass band, which played a few bars at the beginning and end of each routine.

Physical give-and-take and hand gestures were out of the question, and their positioning in front of the horns and the necessity of speaking every line directly into them made eye contact very difficult. "We were practically in strait jackets," commented Weber. Overlapping lines and interruptions—an essential rhythm of the sidewalk conversation—had to be kept to an absolute minimum. It also seems likely that their thick dialect and distortions of English were toned down to make them more understandable on the low-fidelity equipment.

Both comedians concluded that the physical restrictions had a drastic effect on their delivery: Weber said, "You would be surprised at how difficult it was for us to give the proper voice inflections, and all other elocutionary tricks, without using our hands and feet." Fields agreed, "It is hard for me to be eloquent with Joe without choking him." Weber also complained that he felt naked without his customary padding, but his barrel-sized belly would have put him too far away from the recording horn. Worst of all, there was no audience to play to. Performers like Weber & Fields, trained in the variety and minstrel traditions, tailored their presentations to their audience, improvising or adjusting their material in mid-course based on the audience response. For later recording sessions, they brought their own audience.

Making records turned out to be a much more arduous process than Weber & Fields had envisioned. It took the team three mornings a week for six weeks to record their first six sides; they were only half joking when they said that it was as tiring as a forty-week tour. They were unable to complete their contractual commitment of ten sides until after the Jubilee tour.

In addition to the limits placed on their delivery, the new medium also wreaked havoc on their material. Savvy craftsmen though they were, Weber & Fields evidently did not stop to consider how much their routines relied on sight gags and physical business. Their first four sides were full of familiar bits from their stage performances that misfire and sound flat when deprived of their visual accompaniment.

Their first recording, from March 7, 1912, was issued as "The Etiquette Scene," but it bore no resemblance to their earlier routine of the same name. Instead of Meyer upbraiding Mike for his ignorance of etiquette ("Who et a cat?" Mike had formerly responded), they made fun of each other's taste in clothes. Meyer accuses Mike of being "too negligée," which he translates as "neglected." Mike mocks Meyer's new coat:

MEYER: It's a great style, my boy.
  MIKE: What d'ya call it?
MEYER: You don't know what it is?
  MIKE: What?
MEYER: It's a three button cutaway.
   MIKE: Three button cutaway? [Laughs] One more cut and it vould be undershirt. . . .

Then Mike claims that Meyer does not know the meaning of a true friend. Meyer is hurt: "A true friend is a man who knows that you're no good and is able to forget it, and that's what kind of friend I am to you." Here, Weber & Fields aficionados would have expected the famous choking scene, with Meyer protesting his eternal friendship while throttling his sputtering partner. The recording, for the reasons outlined above, yielded not even a gurgle; without the physical assault, Meyer's verbal insistence that "with my heart, I tell you that I luff you" sounds pathetic and misplaced. A scene recorded a week later—"The Hypnotist ('Tipnotister') Scene"—was more coherent, but suffered even more from the absence of the routine's visual components. As Meyer tries to hypnotize Mike, he asks "Do you feel somethings?" Mike's response—"You got a hose in your mouth?"—makes no sense on record unless the listener already knows the gag; as Meyer tries to put Mike under, his patter splatters Mike with saliva. But without the pantomime, the verbal elements of their routine barely elicit a chuckle. Trying to get a sense of a Weber & Fields routine by a sound recording was like trying to judge counterpoint with one of its melodic lines missing.

Weber & Fields learned quickly from their mistakes. On the morning of March 22, eight days after they made the ill-conceived "Hypnotist Scene," they recorded two sides that indicated their growing understanding of the properties of the medium. "The Mosquito Trust" (Columbia A1168) and "Hymie at College" were reworkings of the stage routines that emphasized verbal devices such as dialect puns, malapropisms, and double talk. In "Hymie at College," Mike wants his son to go to Shale University, where the boy will be "so well-edumacated that when he speaks, no one will understand him."

Meyer's explanation of the Mosquito Trust is a tour de force of populist satire. The scene begins in mid-argument, with Mike wanting to know where Meyer "investigated" his (Mike's) money.

MIKE & MEYER—"THE MOSQUITO TRUST"

MEYER: As a friend, I vill tell you. I investigated your money in the Mosquito Trust. [. . .]
  MIKE: What's the idea of this Mosquito Trust?
MEYER: The same as any other trust—to bleed the public.
  MIKE: And I've investigated my money in mosquitos?
MEYER: Yes.

MIKE: Now I know I'm gonna get stung. [. . .]

MEYER: You don't *own* the mosquitos. You've only got an interest in them.

MIKE: Dot's the first time I ever took an interest in 'em. But how comes the profits?

MEYER: Ah, that's the point. You see, there's a farm in New Jersey, with incubators for mosquitos to lay eggs in. [. . .] In a short time we will be able to control the market. And if anybody wants any mosquitos, they'll have to come to us and pay us our price.

MIKE: Vell, how can ve control the mosquitos?

MEYER: Our mosquitos will do anything they're told. You see, they're trained. And besides, the agent goes from house to house, and says, "Good morning, would you like some nice fresh mosquitos today?"

MIKE: Do any of them bite at it?

MEYER: Of course not!

MIKE: Vell, den vhere comes the profit?

MEYER: If they say no, den we sign a contract with them for five hundred dollars a year to keep the place clear of mosquitos.

MIKE: And yet I don't see it. . . .

MEYER: Then we go to the head mosquito and give him the names and addresses of all the people who don't sign. And the next day, a flock of mosquitos go up there and give them a nasty bite. [. . .]

Mike begins to warm to the idea.

MIKE: Say, couldn't I pay a little more money and buy a couple of lightnin' bugs so I could see what our mosquitos are doing at night?

MEYER: We don't want any lightnin' bugs! We can't afford to throw any light on our business! [. . .]

Financial activities dominated the subject matter of Weber & Fields' records. Trusts, syndicates, corporations, insurance, the stock exchange—Mike and Meyer's "investigations" (investments) seemed to be their favorite topics of conversation, supplanting their famous travesties of leisure-time activities. Business matters lent themselves to the kind of verbal give-and-take that worked best on records, while the pool game, poker, and the shooting gallery depended on sight gags and visible actions. Their second effort, in March, 1912, concerned a racehorse and Mike & Meyer's plan to get even with the guy who gave them a bum tip, but the scene was notable only for how personal some of the jibes were:

MIKE: There's only one trouble with you. You are too spendthrifty with the money. You pop it around as if you were a king or an emperor.

MEYER: I can't help it, Mike. You see, you have not got it in your nature the delicatessen thing that I have got in mine. You are a business man, plain and simpleton, while I—I am like a butterscotch, I flitter from flower to flower. . . .

Weber & Fields did not return to the recording studio again until August, 1915, and then only to record four sides, two of which were rejected. There was a session in June, 1916, their last for Columbia, or anybody else for that matter, until 1933, when they made four sides for Victor, "At the Firehouse, Parts 1 and

2," and "At the Football Game, Parts 1 and 2." "Firehouse" was never released, but the "Football" sides reveal the positive effects of their radio experience in the late 1920's and early 1930's.

All together, only nine Weber & Fields records were ever released. Perhaps the partners realized how much the medium diminished them. Neither of them was terribly proud of their recordings; they seemed to regard it as a necessary bit of public relations. Anyway, by the end of August, 1912, Fields was thoroughly sick of them; he complained that wherever he went in Far Rockaway that summer, he heard a Weber & Fields record playing on somebody's parlor gramophone. One well-meaning neighbor unwittingly tormented Fields by cuing up the record every time he saw Fields returning from his morning constitutional.

Having put aside his big ambitions for the musical, Lew Fields concentrated on reaping the profits to be had from the public's renewed interest in the Weberfields style of entertainment. *Hanky-Panky* lasted out the season at Fields' American Music Hall in Chicago with strong attendance, thanks to some judicious trimming and recasting. Nevertheless, the show closed its Chicago run at the start of May almost $40,000 in the red, mostly because of its disastrous opening and the inflated salaries of its initial cast. Marcus Loew's confidence in the show and in Fields, makes a dramatic contrast with the Shuberts; had *Hanky-Panky* been a Shubert production, the brothers would have closed it long before and added Fields' share of the losses to his burgeoning debt. Instead, Loew sent *Hanky-Panky* on tour, where it made up for its Chicago losses in a month. By the time it closed in Boston in mid-June, it was showing a profit. Loew and Fields decided to chance a New York run, and booked it into the Broadway beginning August 5. To promote the New York engagement, Loew advertised it on lantern slides projected on the motion picture screens of his small-time theaters in the New York area. During the movies, he instructed the accompanists to play songs from *Hanky Panky*.

The critics' remarks about *Hanky-Panky* were unusually patronizing for a Fields summer production, perhaps reflecting their customary disdain for any musical originating in Chicago: "just about what the thoroughfare expects from such offerings";[3] "it may for a time please the inhabitants of the hinterland who are summer visitors to New York."[4] Most had to agree that it lived up to its subtitle, "a jumble of jollification."

Nevertheless, the show's staying power indicated that it appealed to Broadway natives, who applauded the return of Max Rogers (in a Dutch role opposite Bobby North) appearing on Broadway for the first time since the death of his brother Gus. In particular, they cheered the antics of another of Fields' recruits from vaudeville, an effervescent dancing comedienne named Florence Moore. Every night, Miss Moore created an uproar when, at the climax of her act, she came out into the audience, singing and chatting with them, and planting kisses on the bald pates of men fortunate enough to sit near the aisle, while her husband, William Montgomery, vented his eccentricities at the piano. One night, however, her crowd-pleasing act backfired: one of the bald heads she bussed was that of an ingenious process server whom she had managed to elude for four months. The process server thanked her for the kiss and handed her a summons, but had to make a hasty exit amid much hilarity when Montgomery bounded from the stage and began to chase after him threateningly.

Hanky Panky averaged around $14,000 a week at the Broadway until the beginning of November, when it moved uptown to the West End for a final two weeks, and then departed for another thirty-two weeks on the road. Ironically, this mélange of old Weber & Fields burlesques and new vaudeville turns, which made no money for its first six months, eventually became the most profitable of Fields' productions, excluding the Jubilee.

Though the Shuberts had initially scoffed at Fields' plans for the American Music Hall, they were now eager to get a piece of it—doubly so, since they had been cut out of the bookings for the Weber & Fields Jubilee tour. To their way of thinking, the American Music Hall only needed good, sound management (i.e., somebody to keep Fields' spendthrift ways in check) to make it a lucrative enterprise. J. J. Shubert offered Loew a reciprocal booking arrangement, in effect making Fields' American the western branch of the Winter Garden, and booking the Winter Garden's touring companies into the American.

Fields was understandably wary. One of the reasons he had gone into partnership with Loew was to get away from J. J. and his meddlesome lieutenants. But Lee Shubert knew how to persuade his old friend: the promise of a new theater, one to take the place of the Herald Square (which Loew had purchased for movies and small-time vaudeville). In May, 1913, the Shuberts had three theaters under construction in Manhattan, and they suggested that the largest, occupying an entire lot between West Forty-third and Forty-fourth Streets, should become the New Weber & Fields Music Hall. In addition, Fields could have a roof garden theater atop the music hall for his summer productions. Weber, who had just leased his theater to a movie exhibitor, liked the Shubert plan.

The first star they hired for their new music hall stock company was the estimable (and unpredictable) Marie Dressler, who had spent a restive three years under Fields' management touring in *Tillie's Nightmare* when she was not trying to sue him or quit. She remembered fondly her two seasons with Joe Weber, and she professed enthusiasm for the chance to be the featured comedienne at Weber & Fields' New Music Hall.

A decade earlier, Weber & Fields had been able to hire the biggest names simply by offering them the most money; by 1912, the salary scale had become so inflated that they could not hope to outbid the market. Still, the partners recklessly offered Metropolitan Opera diva Lillian Nordica $5,000 a week to take over the Lillian Russell roles. Fortunately, Nordica was forced to decline. She was already under an exclusive contract with J. J. Shubert to appear only at his Winter Garden. Attempts to sign Fritzi Scheff ($4,500 a week) and Blanche Ring also failed. Finally, Fields lured Jack Norworth and Nora Bayes back from vaudeville. Fields wanted Julian Mitchell to return to stage the musical numbers, but Ziegfeld would not release him from his contract, nor were they able to buy it out. They did succeed in signing Mitchell's wife, Bessie Clayton; she and Helena Collier Garrick were the only holdovers from the Jubilee company.

The decision to stay together for another season was no simple matter for Weber and Fields. Both were now in charge of large producing organizations with

competing interests and, on occasion, conflicting philosophies. Weber, in agreements with his nephew, L. Lawrence Weber, sent out touring companies on the
small-time vaudeville and burlesque circuits, as well as producing American adaptations of foreign operettas (such as *Alma, Where Do You Live?*) for Broadway.
Together, Weber & Fields planned to produce *A Scrape of the Pen*, a Scottish
comedy drama by Graham Moffat, whose previous play, *Bunty Pulls the Strings*,
had been the main target of the Jubilee burlesque. Having spent years splintering
the English language into German bits, they now decided to wreak further ven-
geance by importing what some called "the Scotchest play ever seen here."

Like a roulette fiend who spreads his chips over as many numbers as possible, Fields' own plans for the 1912–1913 season covered almost every popular
stage style, as well as one new form that was still taking shape. With the help of
Edgar Smith and E. Ray Goetz, he was producing a Viennese operetta called *The
June Bride*. At the same time, Fields would begin rehearsals for *The Sun Dodgers*, a musical spectacle starring vaudeville siren Eva Tanguay. A month later,
The Singing Teacher, a musical comedy by Glen MacDonough, was scheduled to
begin rehearsing. Later in the season, he also planned to produce another straight
comedy with William Collier. What sparked the most interest, however, were rumors of a new Fields-Loew partnership to produce a series of "tabloid" shows
(short musical sketches) for Loew's vaudeville circuit.

Compared to their next season, the Weber & Fields Jubilee of 1911–1912
was an affair of the heart, having been prompted by the death of Fields' father
and fueled by fans' sentimentality. While genuine emotion seems to have prompted
their reunion, it was the pragmatism of the pocketbook that motivated Weber &
Fields to remain together for the 1912–1913 season. Their own success in the
Jubilee notwithstanding, the previous season had been a surprisingly poor one
for American musical comedies and for Weber in particular. In a rather muddled
assessment of the problem, the *Dramatic Mirror* did manage to discern certain
trends, and these trends did not bode well for the kind of show that had made
Fields' solo reputation:

> Simplicity of effect, studied, perhaps, has hit the public fancy, as a natural reaction
> to garish ostentation. . . . Beyond this, demand for eccentric comedy has largely
> been converted into a demand for adequate singing. . . .

> If producers are as eager to learn from experience as they assert, we ought to have
> a season of really artistic musical comedies next year. Simple, straight-forward plot,
> capable singers, light, tasteful comedy and easy romance are the elements that have
> won favor lately. . . .[5]

Clearly, the plethora of Viennese operettas and other foreign imports during
the past five years had shaped public expectations of musical comedy. The new
season would bear this out: the three most significant musicals were an import
and two American emulations that surpassed their European models. The import,
Oh! Oh! Delphine, was an adaptation of a French farce with a score by Ivan
Caryll; it titillated Broadway for 248 performances with the carryings-on of reserve officers and their wives and mistresses at a hotel in Brest. The next-longest-

running musical, Victor Herbert's *The Lady of the Slipper*, was a star vehicle for the elfin Elsie Janis and the team of Montgomery & Stone, based on the Cinderella fairy tale. Another Cinderella story—this one in contemporary dress—was the basis of the season's most enduring musical. *The Firefly* was Rudolf Friml's first score; Arthur Hammerstein hired the classically trained composer when Herbert quit in a dispute with the show's star, Emma Trentini. While Hauerbach's libretto was adequate at best, Friml's score and Trentini's soaring soprano were widely praised.

After years of championing American librettists and composers, Fields finally jumped on the Viennese bandwagon. He had, after all, always regarded it as his duty "to give the public what it wants." *The June Bride* featured music by a Edmund Eysler, an Austrian composer whose previous effort, *The Immortal Ten*, lasted over two hundred performances in Vienna. The story told of a tulip grower who becomes a servant in a pension to satisfy the conditions of his rich uncle's will. Although *The June Bride* was announced as a joint Weber & Fields production, it would appear that the former shared only in the booking and the losses. Fields supervised the adaptation (Edgar Smith rewrote the script, and E. Ray Goetz, the lyrics), the casting, and the staging.

Rehearsals began in mid-September at the Shubert in Boston, with a cast that included Arthur Aylesworth (who had recently married Rose's sister, Sadie Harris), Amelia Stone, and Helen Hayes (in her last role under Fields' benevolent aegis). After a weak tryout in New Haven on September 21, Fields came to Boston for a week of rewrites and restaging. He built up the plot in the first act and inserted a Russian ballet and some new dances, but his attempts to apply the methods of the Broadway extravaganza to an operetta revealed a surprising indifference to the characteristics of the foreign medium. The "easy romance" that audiences now wanted in a musical was not something that came naturally to Fields. Pathos he could deliver, but sweeping romantic gestures and the ache of true love were almost completely absent from his productions. The irony and streetwise irreverence that made him a great comedian prevented him from creating romance in his musicals. *The June Bride* folded in mid-October after a week in Pittsburgh.

Vaudeville-derived entertainments were by far the better bets. Though both *Hanky-Panky* and the Weber & Fields Jubilee were ostensibly "book" shows, their methods and many of their performers had roots in vaudeville. Evidently, the crucial distinctions between vaudeville and musical comedy, and vaudeville and revue, were still evolving.

A case in point was the *The Passing Show of 1912*, which J. J. Shubert created to capitalize on the success of Ziegfeld's Follies. The Shubert version, however, more closely resembled a Weberfields production than a Ziegfeld revue. The first edition of *The Passing Show*, like the Weberfields' show, was a double bill. The first part was intended to be the "class"—an English mime–dramatic ballet. The second part had the "sass"—burlesques of the current Broadway hits. Unlike the Weberfields', who usually concocted a slim storyline to tie together several burlesques, the burlesques in *The Passing Show* were brief, discrete sketches. Still, the types of performers were basically the same. There was even a team of outstanding dialect comics from vaudeville to lead the fun: Willie and Eugene Howard, the best of the "Hebrew" comedy pairs. The elaborate realism of the sets—an ocean liner and, in later Passing Shows, an airship and the steps of the U.S. Capitol—continued the aesthetic fostered by Fields' Broadway Theater productions. Indeed, internal correspondence between the Shuberts and Fields suggests that J. J. appropriated several of the expensive sets created for Fields' summer shows.

So why didn't the Shuberts simply hire Lew Fields to produce *The Passing Show?* Twice before—with *The Mimic World* and *Up and Down Broadway*—Fields had salvaged J. J.'s botched attempts to outdo Ziegfeld. There is even some evidence that Lee wanted Fields to produce, and possibly perform with Weber in *The Passing Show*, but J. J. probably persuaded his brother that it would be too expensive.

Most likely, the real issues were more personal. Ever since the Winter Garden affair, J. J. considered musical productions to be his domain. Fields, as we have seen, would not work as a hired hand for J. J. Moreover, Fields seems to have been oddly resistant to the idea of doing a modern—i.e., plotless—revue. Though his plots were often perilously thin by the time the curtain rose on opening night, he always started with "the book."

When the more established stage formats proved temporarily uncongenial to Fields' unique abilities, he helped to create a new one. During the summer of 1912, Fields spent relatively little time preparing for his more conventional musicals, or even for the new Weber & Fields show. The majority of his time was lavished on his new venture with Marcus Loew, yet another type of vaudeville–musical comedy hybrid known as "tab shows," "tabs," or "tabloids."

Tabs, like so many other popular stage formats, were originally developed as an entrepreneurial concept—a new way to package and market existing material—without much thought for their aesthetic possibilities. Businessmen such as Loew, Big Tim Sullivan, and Alexander Pantages created tabs as a way of avoiding the heavy hand of the Keith-Albee and Orpheum Circuits. By 1912, Keith-Albee had consolidated its monopoly of big-time vaudeville east of the Mississippi, and Martin Beck, through his Orpheum Circuit, controlled the West. Keith-Albee and the Orpheum Circuit were tied together by common stock ownership and interlocking directorates. Angered by the high-handed tactics of Keith-Albee (which still included taking commissions from both the actor and the agent, as well as peremptory cancellations), vaudevillians began to desert the big-time for other fields: musical comedy and the "small-time" chains of Loew, Pantages, and Sullivan-Considine.[6]

"Small-time," it should be noted, did not necessarily mean low-quality entertainment. The small-time was primarily characterized by a lower admission charge, usually a 10-20-30 cent scale, instead of the big-time scale of $1 to $1.50. The lower scale dictated a high volume (three to six performances a day instead of two a day), lower production costs (one-half to one-fifth of big-time), and lower salaries. Nationally known stars or headliners played small-time theaters only occasionally; the bill was usually composed of local favorites and talented but unheralded acts. Big-time theaters ran the same show for a full week and never presented more than one "photoplay" on the bill, while small-timers ran a split week (two or three different shows a week). There was, however, little difference between big- and small-time theaters in construction, stage equipment, or capacity. Big-time houses often had more elaborate furnishings, although some of Loew's theaters, such as the National in the Bronx, were as plush as any of Keith's.

Faced with increasing competition from the circuits of Keith-Albee and Orpheum, and rising railroad rates and salaries for headliners, Loew and his small-time colleagues needed a program that looked classy enough to rival the big-time at a fraction of the cost—"big flash" for not much cash. For several years prior to 1912, Loew and Sullivan had noticed the travelling "girl acts" that performed musical comedy sketches with scaled-down choruses on the Southern and Western small-time circuits. The acts included ten to fifteen performers: a two- or three-man vaudeville team, a prima donna, a leading man, a dancing soubrette, and anywhere from five to ten chorus girls. Scenery was carried in one large trunk, costumes in another.

The earliest tab shows were abbreviated Broadway musical comedies (most of them at least five years old); among them were units playing authorized and pirated versions of old Weber & Fields Music Hall burlesques. Then, in the fall of 1911, a small travelling musical comedy company organized by a pair of Weber & Fields imitators hit on the formula that would make the small-time circuits profitable: the travelling tab was rehearsed to play two or three different sketches and then booked into a small-time theater for a full week, where they changed their shows two or three times during that week. Attendance increased and producers saved on transportation as well. Suddenly, for the mere pittance of thirty cents or less, a small-time vaudeville theater could offer a ninety-minute program that rivalled the "high-class" bills in the big-time: one or more sketches, two or more vaudeville acts, and one or two photoplays.

In the summer of 1912, when Sullivan and Loew approached Lew Fields about producing a few tabs for their circuits, the tab show was still an unproven innovation. They knew that Fields had already turned down several very generous offers from big-time promoters to appear in vaudeville. First, Loew had to convince him that an inexpensive entertainment was not inherently "cheap." It had been thirty years since anybody had been able to pay as little as a dime to see Lew Fields perform. Of course, Fields would not actually be performing, but his name would draw in customers, and he had a reputation to uphold.

In many ways, Fields was the ideal tab show producer. He could recruit and train actors and chorus girls, pick songs, supervise choruses, and direct actors. Best of all, he supplied his own material—sketches based on popular bits from his own productions, or on comic ideas he had not been able to find a place for in a full-length show. Loew originally hired Fields to produce four tabs for the Sullivan-Considine circuit, but by the end of the summer of 1912, *Variety* reported that he would produce fifteen or more. In other words, Fields would be supplying nearly all of the headline acts for the Sullivan-Considine circuit during the first half of the season.

With his brother Sol as stage manager and brother Nat as an occasional performer, Lew actually produced ten tabs for Loew-Sullivan-Considine. The first of "Fields' Fun Acts," as they were called, was "Fun in a Barber Shop," derived from the famous scene in *The Hen Pecks* in which Fields shaved Vernon Castle. Other Fun Acts took place in a cabaret, a deli, a restaurant (the waiter scene from *The Girl Behind the Counter*), a Turkish bath, a pharmacy, a courthouse, at the seashore, and aboard an ocean liner.

The tabs caught on quickly, in large part because musical comedy pros such as Fields, Ned Wayburn, and Gus Edwards were hired to produce them. By the fall of 1912, around thirty theaters had abandoned traditional vaudeville olios and offered nothing but tabs and photoplays. During the week of September 27, 1912, the program headlined by Fields' "Fun in a Barber Shop" broke the house record at the Empress. With a total capacity of 2,200, and admission at the usual 10-20-30 cent scale, the gross for the week totaled $6,080. Salaries and expenses came under $1,000 a week for Fields' tabs; others cost even less. Box office receipts for other tab shows were less dramatic, but still impressive. Playing at a 10-20-30 cent scale, they netted more than road shows that charged $1.50 for admission, with profits of anywhere from $2,500 to $3,000 weekly.

By the beginning of 1913, *Variety* reported that "the tabloid style of entertainment appears to have taken hold on everyone in show business." Legit producers and the big-time circuits were frantically trying to get in on the action. The most influential factor at the box office, tab show managers had learned, was a famous name or title. Weber & Fields sold the rights to a dozen of their old music hall hits—*Hoity Toity, Fiddle Dee Dee, Pousse Café*, etc.—to the American Theatrical Exchange, to be produced as tab shows and routed for fifteen week tours.

Tab shows remained a mainstay of big- and small-time vaudeville until the late 1920's. Fields praised tabs as a way "to give [aspiring actors] their schooling at the same time they were getting actual experience in vaudeville," an outlook that proved to be farsighted indeed. Many of vaudeville's greatest performers were products of the tabloid school of hard knocks: Eddie Cantor, George Jessel, George Price, and Lila Lee broke in as child actors in Gus Edwards' Kid Kabaret. One of the most popular tab acts was called "The Duke of Bull Durham," featuring the Four Marks (later Marx) Brothers, capably managed by their mother, Minnie Palmer. During one of their early tours on the Pantages circuit, Harpo Marx saw a wonderful comic in a Sullivan-Considine tab sketch, "a slight man with a tiny mustache, a cane, a derby, and a large pair of shoes." It was the young Charlie Chaplin, touring in a tab show at fifty dollars a week.[7]

Ironically, the success of the tab shows ended up hurting Fields in the long run, making it more difficult for his extravagant Broadway musicals to make money on the road. Later, the Shuberts would remind him of the economies of his tab shows with Loew whenever they thought he was spending too much for an actor or scenery.

Had he only been interested in financial gain, he would have continued producing tab shows instead of returning to full-blown musical comedies at the first opportunity. But the hard-won prestige of being a Broadway producer, and the thrill of being the mastermind of a spectacle that engulfed its audience in delight, were too compelling to put aside for mere money. Even before he had finished

A long way from the Bowery, a proud Lew Fields poses with his family outside their new home just off Riverside Drive in 1910. Dorothy (age 6), Lew, Frances (16), Rose, Joseph (15), and Herbert (13). *(Billy Rose Theater Collection, New York Public Library)*

The Fields brothers in 1910: Nat ("Duke"), Solly, Lew, and Charlie. Nat performed Weber & Fields material in small-time vaudeville, Solly became a stage manager for the Minskys, and Charlie was Lew's business manager. Their eldest brother, Max, died in 1901. *(Billy Rose Theater Collection, New York Public Library)*

When Fields went solo in 1904, Oscar Hammerstein I built this theater for him at 254 West Forty-second Street. It opened with Fields' production of *It Happened in Nordland,* with music by Victor Herbert. *(Billy Rose Theater Collection, New York Public Library)*

Interior, the Lew Fields Theater. Hammerstein's design included several innovations: twenty box seats arranged in staggered tiers flanking the stage, and a grid of fire sprinklers activated by a pull chain. *(Billy Rose Theater Collection, New York Public Library)*

The waiter scene from *The Girl Behind the Counter*. Lew Fields (at left) instructed his new crew: "Always remember, the first duty of a waiter is to look insulting." The string-bean at right is Vernon Castle. *(Billy Rose Theater Collection, New York Public Library)*

From *Old Dutch* (1909): Ludwig Streusand (Lew Fields, center) denounces Leopold Muller (John Henshaw) for assuming the former's name and position. John Bunny, at extreme right, moonlighted as a movie comedian and soon gave up the stage altogether. *(Billy Rose Theater Collection, New York Public Library)*

Victor Herbert was the first important composer for the Broadway musical, adapting the Viennese-style operetta to the American stage. When Fields split with Weber, he teamed up with Herbert and director Julian Mitchell. *(Museum of the City of New York)*

Ned Wayburn, the most prolific and influential dance director before 1930. He developed his innovative approach to chorus numbers and staging techniques in Lew Fields' Broadway Theater musical extravaganzas, then brought his magic to the Ziegfeld Follies. *(Museum of the City of New York)*

Marcus Loew, "the Henry Ford of show business." A mild-mannered ex-furrier, he built an empire of movie theaters and small-time vaudeville houses. He bought his first theater (in Brooklyn) at Lew Fields' urging and later became a partner in several of Fields' ventures. *(Variety Arts Theater Library)*

The younger Shubert, J. J., in 1911. Although Lew Fields was an important early ally of the Shuberts, J. J. found reasons to resent him: musicals were J. J.'s private domain, and he resented Lew Fields' friendship with brother Lee. *(Variety Arts Theater Library)*

Apartment house cutaway set from *The Summer Widowers* (1910), designed by Arthur Voegtlin. Fields' Broadway Theater productions used realism on a huge scale to underscore the social satire in his musical comedies. (*Billy Rose Theater Collection, New York Public Library*)

Leading Ladies from Lew Fields' Productions

Nora Bayes was a brilliant song stylist and one of the biggest (and most temperamental) stars in vaudeville; Jack Norworth was a gifted composer and, for a while, her husband. The couple appeared in Fields' *The Jolly Bachelors,* and Bayes later toured with Weber & Fields. *(Variety Arts Theater Library)*

Blanche Ring, singer and comedienne. She appeared in five Lew Fields productions, and it was under his management that she became a star. *(Variety Arts Theater Library)*

Marie Dressler was one of the few female comics to succeed using the broad physical clowning popularized by Weber & Fields. She joined Weber's company in 1904, but made her biggest stage hit as the boardinghouse drudge in Fields' *Tillie's Nightmare* (1910). *(Variety Arts Theater Library)*

Lotta Faust, in Salome's Dance of the Seven Veils, from *The Mimic World.* Guileless and alluring, she was on her way to stardom in Lew Fields' stock company when she died tragically. *(Billy Rose Theater Collection, New York Public Library)*

From Lew Fields' *The Midnight Sons*. When the Act II curtain rose, the audience found itself facing its double on stage, with the seats filled by actors, extras, chorus people, and wax dummies made up to look like famous first-nighters. (*Museum of the City of New York*)

Weber & Fields in their classic attire, during the Weber & Fields Jubilee (1912). Most of their routines involved Meyer inventing schemes to separate Mike from his money. *(Billy Rose Theater Collection, New York Public Library)*

producing the last of the tab shows (and while he was preparing for *The June Bride* and the new Weber & Fields show), he was starting rehearsals for another musical extravaganza, this one starring Eva Tanguay, the woman dubbed (by *Variety*) "vaudeville's single greatest drawing card." She was certainly the most expensive—her contract with Fields for $2,500 a week was low by her standards—as well as the most temperamental and outrageous.

Eva Tanguay's electrifying appeal is impossible to appreciate from her photos or recordings. She was homely and plump, even by the well-padded standards of the day, with a mass of frizzy blond hair, and her costumes exaggerated her tacky sensuality. She sang suggestive songs in a voice that alternated between coy and brassy while she pranced about the stage and gyrated her ample torso. Her most famous song, "I Don't Care," summarized her attitude towards producers, critics, and her theater colleagues. Another of her songs gave a hint about how carefully she cultivated her reputation for being crazy: "There's method in my madness / There's meaning in my style; / The more they raise my salary, / The crazier I'll be."[8] In short, she was exactly the sort of leading woman who was guaranteed to clash with Fields.

He knew this, but hired her anyway. A distressingly large number of American musical comedies had flopped in the last two seasons. He had little confidence left in the established Broadway composers or librettists, or, for that matter, in Broadway audiences to recognize an innovative score if one appeared. Hiring vaudeville's most notable headliner to star in an expensive musical production was a perverse kind of insurance policy, as were the lavish stage effects.

Edgar Smith's libretto for *The Sun Dodgers* was right in keeping with his other parodies of leisure-class behavior written for Fields. This time, he told of a group of affluent young men who seek their pleasure by night and sleep all day. Wakeleigh Knight learns of a millionaire aunt, Mrs. Honoria O'Day, from Butte, Montana. He asks her for money for a "can't miss" real estate venture: the conversion of a farm in Long Island into Sunless City, an exclusive development for those who prefer the nightlife (a concept that today sounds remarkably less farfetched than it did at the time). When the development fails, they return to Manhattan and open an automat ("because everybody in New York already has built a theater or a moving picture show . . ."). From the start, Mrs. O'Day was conceived as a character for George Monroe, and O'Day's husband–financial adviser was written for Harry Fischer. Tanguay's role, "a footlight goddess of the vaudeville persuasion," was relatively minor; inflating it to fit her billing distorted an already tenuous plot beyond recognition.

A few weeks before *The Sun Dodgers* began rehearsing in Philadelphia, Fields was quoted as saying that there would be "no more $40,000, $50,000, or $60,000 productions presented under the Lew Fields banner." Henceforth, he vowed to limit the initial investment in his musical comedies to under $30,000.[9] Nevertheless, *The Sun Dodgers* began its tryouts with fourteen principals, including Tanguay, Monroe, and blackface clown Willis Sweatnam, fifty chorus girls, and sets for seven scenes. Fields was evidently too busy producing tabs in New York and patching up *The June Bride* in Boston to supervise rehearsals in Philadelphia, and he never was terribly good about keeping track of expenses. The difference this time was that the Shuberts were not there to remind him—or to share the losses.

When he finally had time to oversee *The Sun Dodgers* in early October, the first thing he did was to hire the team of Jerome & Schwartz to write some new songs to supplement the feeble score by Sloane and Goetz. He replaced several of the more expensive principals with lesser-known actors (e.g., his brother Nat, who played a "rube"). Mostly, he tried not to lose his temper with his diva Eva. For almost two weeks, he managed to restrain himself, as Tanguay threw temper tantrums, abused the stagehands, and stormed out of rehearsals, only to return an hour or so later. She refused to take direction, even after a mediocre preview in Albany on October 18.

By the end of the following week, in Pittsburgh, Fields could tolerate it no longer. Borrowing a page from the Shubert management handbook, he closed the show, thereby ending its "season" and releasing him from any contractual obligations to Tanguay. After a two week layoff for rewriting and recasting, rehearsals would resume with Bessie Wynn in the lead, several new songs by Irving Berlin, and Ned Wayburn directing. Fields turned his attention to the new Weber & Fields production opening at the end of November.

When *The Sun Dodgers* finally opened at the Broadway on November 30, most critics treated it with surprising indulgence: "If *The Sun Dodgers* disappointed last night's audience, Mr. Fields has himself to blame for having set his own standard high and then having failed to approximate it." [10] In fact, the show dragged in long stretches, and some of its jokes were stale. The stage effects and choruses received the most praise: tiny electric lights were fastened to the shoes and caps of the female chorus while they danced in near darkness. A moving picture was projected on a transparent gauze screen, behind which the chorus sat, while in front of the screen a couple danced and sang "At the Picture Show." Said one critic, "[It] has the handsomest lot of show girls with the most sumptuous costuming that has been seen on Broadway this season." But, as the same critic was quick to point out, spectacle was no longer enough: "Mr. Fields, if he is looking for novelty, might make a ten-strike . . . by securing a real composer to supply the music. That experiment remains to be tried by some enterprising manager looking for something new with which to beguile the jaded taste of his patrons." [11] Evidently, Irving Berlin, who ended up supplying almost half the score, was not yet considered "a real composer." The "jaded" patrons seemed to agree with the critics, and *The Sun Dodgers* closed on December 14 "for reorganization" after just eighteen performances. Broadway audiences, having tasted the melodic confections served up by operetta, had little appetite for the pablum offered by A. Baldwin Sloane. One critic described him as "one of the best of the one-fingered Beethovens on Broadway." [12]

Fields, who had been so sensitive to public taste throughout most of his career, did not get the message. He seemed to think that good comedy and spectacle could still compensate for a mediocre score. J. J. Shubert questioned this in one of his periodic critiques of why Fields was not making more money: "You do not realize when you produce a show that all you need are situations which you are in and a little good music, but you cannot get just any tinpan musicians to write the score for you. . . ."[13]

The spotty career of *The Sun Dodgers* did not end when its run at the Broadway was over. Fields had the show rewritten again and he hired Nora Bayes and Jack Norworth, who had decided not to accompany the Weberfields on tour. The revised production opened on Christmas Day in Boston, where it played to full houses. Loew decided that it was worth bringing back to New York, and booked it into his American Music Hall. Miraculously, receipts for the first three weeks averaged around $11,500 before falling off dramatically in the fourth week. By then, rumors of discord in the company were running rampant; Wayburn had quit the show at the beginning of its New York run, reportedly because of disputes with Bayes. More disruptive still was the growing hostility between Bayes and Norworth; they had been squabbling since the season started, and they could no longer confine it to offstage. As a duo, part of the charm of their act was a kind of Nick and Nora Charles–style romantic banter. In *The Sun Dodgers*, their scenes together took on an increasingly nasty flavor, with ad-libbed lines that disconcerted the other actors as well as the audience. *The Sun Dodgers* closed for good at the beginning of February; a few weeks later, Bayes and Norworth were granted a divorce.

A dozen tab shows, a new Collier farce opening November 12, an operetta in trouble, a musical extravaganza in even bigger trouble—all this, and the opening of the new Weber & Fields Music Hall, too. In accordance with tradition, there was an auction of first-night tickets. Although the opening of new theaters in Manhattan had become almost a routine occurrence, the opening night at the Shuberts' new theater for Weber & Fields brought out the biggest crowds of the season. Onlookers lined the sidewalk across the street in front of the Hotel Astor, and filled the spacious new arcade that ran along the east wall of the theater between Forty-third and Forty-fourth Streets. Weber & Fields had considered naming their new theater the Palace, for it was indeed palatial, especially compared to their old music hall. Its total seating capacity was over 2,000, with an auditorium that was broad rather than deep, so that the rear seats were not too far from the stage (similar to the seating plan Fields had wanted for the Winter Garden). The aisles were wide and the sight lines were especially good; there were no pillars or obstructions from the ten boxes on either side of the proscenium, or from the mezzanine. The decor was simpler and less ornate than that of most first-class theaters of the day. Upstairs, still under construction, was the Lew Fields' Roof Garden, a 1,200-seat theater being readied for his summer shows. Downstairs, there was a bar and rathskeller.

"Gags, Girls, Glare; Oh! Such a Gladness!" was how the usually reserved *New York Times* critic, Adolph Klauber, described the evening. The glare was the huge sign of incandescent bulbs listing the stars' names—Bayes & Norworth, Marie Dressler, Frank Daniels, Bessie Clayton, Weber & Fields, Arthur Aylesworth, Helena Collier Garrick—over the show's title, *Roly Poly*. There were so many lights, one reviewer commented, that it looked like they were telling the plot of the show on their sign. In a sense, he was right.

The first part, *Roly Poly*, placed Mike Schmaltz (Weber) and Meyer Talzmann (Fields) in the resort town of Raatenbad, where they have come to take the waters. They encounter a bumbling merchant named Hiram Fitzsimmons (Frank Daniels) who is trying to marry off his daughter, Bijou (Marie Dressler) and track down his son (Jack Norworth), supposedly a student at Heidelberg. When Weber & Fields first appeared, they received a full three minutes of applause, during which they lovingly poked each other in the eyes.

Along with the old familiar contract scene, with its satire of legal double-talk, were several new ones that went over well. Bayes and Norworth appeared in a scene depicting a stream (with real water) meandering through a misty meadow and sang the sentimental "In My Birchbark Canoe"; their exit brought on Mike and Meyer in a rowboat (Mike rowing, of course), bristling with fishing gear. "Let's stop here," said Meyer. And Mike, having no further use for the oars, throws them overboard, saying he will pick them up on the way back. Meyer then tries to teach Mike "the rules of angling," just as he had tried in the past to explain pool or baseball, and with similar results. (In real life, Weber was an avid fisher-man, who spent his summers fishing at his house in the Thousand Islands. The previous summer, Weber had taken Marcus Loew and Fields out on a boat to teach them to fish.)

Weber & Fields hired Frank Daniels for the type of role that Sam Bernard, Warfield, and Louis Mann had once filled. Daniels was a veteran of Victor Her-bert's comic operas in the late 1890s, and his appearance in *Roly Poly* was touted as a comeback after an absence from the Broadway stage for several years. Per-haps it was his legit background, or his layoff, that made his performance seem tentative. He apparently had some difficulty with the rough stuff dished out by Dressler, Weber, and Fields, as well as their propensity for ad libbing.

The talented Marie Dressler quickly filled the void. Much of the humor was at the expense of Dressler's formidable heft. When Mike drives a miniature jalopy into her at full speed, she stops it dead and scratches absently at the point of impact. Bijou, Mike, and Meyer then fight over the best seat, causing the car to rear up and flip over. Later, Mike is subjected to more physical abuse when, at Meyer's suggestion, he plays dead to avoid marrying Bijou. Meyer gets his come-uppance in the finale, when the colossal Miss Dressler falls plump on him and flattens him. Fortunately, her role was not confined to fat jokes: early in the program, she revived her impersonation of various opera divas in the song "The Prima Donna," which included excerpts from *Faust* and *Die Walküre*.

Unlike *The Sun Dodgers*, *Roly Poly* was crammed full of serviceable tunes—eleven in the first part of the evening, as well as several instrumental interludes for dances by Bessie Clayton and the chorus. A. Baldwin Sloane and E. Ray Goetz were listed as the composer and lyricist, but the best songs came from elsewhere. Frank Daniels sang a sad ballad, "I Cannot Drink the Old Drinks Now." When they were not trading inside jokes and jibes, Bayes and Norworth could always be counted on to provide one or two good interpolations. "Apple Blossom Time in Normandie" made up for their smug insistence that they were, as one reviewer described it, "simply themselves, and lest the audience should forget it, they told them so."[14] Other first-nighters seemed to be similarly uncomfortable with the tone of the duo's patter.

The second part of the program—a burlesque of Bayard Veiller's successful thriller, *Within the Law*—showed that time had not dulled the Weberfields' satiric edge. "Without the Law" featured Fields as the grey-haired forger Joke Arson, mimicking the performance of the original's creator, Andrew Mack. Once again, critics cited Fields' abilities as a character actor, and one went as far as to say that Fields was "the best travesty actor the American stage has ever seen."[15] Weber impersonated the hero, Police Inspector Burke, rechristened Inspector Bunk. Dressler played Merry Urner, the persecuted shopgirl. Audiences howled when Dressler came on stage handcuffed to Weber; under arrest, she became agitated as she pleaded her case and literally swung Weber through the air like a rag doll.

The opening-night curtain did not ring down until well after midnight, but the show was not over yet. The happy, exhausted patrons tumbled out of the theater to the blare of a brass band. Atop a large sightseeing car across from the theater, Willie Collier led a group of serenaders made up of actors from the Lambs' Club. The second night's performance finished by 11:20; Fields trimmed another twenty minutes from the show over the next few days.

During its profitable eight-week run, *Roly Poly* was not simply trimmed and polished, it underwent constant changes. Not all of the changes were motivated by a desire for novelty. Weber & Fields were scrambling to accommodate several long-simmering backstage disputes. Bayes and Norworth announced that they would be leaving the show at the end of December, their future together undecided.

Marie Dressler's sudden resignation caught them by surprise. In her autobiography, *In the Life of an Ugly Duckling*, Dressler claimed that Fields insisted on occupying the center of the stage for every scene that he was in. Then he cut her scenes because she got a bigger laugh than he did. She believed that the show was most important, while he believed that the star (himself) should get all the laughs. Her descriptions of Fields' behavior were so uncharacteristic that one must question either her memory or her motives. For years he had allowed the best lines to go to the other principals in his productions; often critics had chided him for being too generous to his co-stars. Fields had shared center stage with talents equal to or greater than Dressler for most of his career. It does not make sense that he would suddenly become so jealous of a co-star, especially to the detriment of his own show.

Having previously agreed to remain with the company through its upcoming tour, Marie Dressler gave her two-week notice on December 21, then quit and walked out later that evening. She then brought suit against Weber & Fields for $24,000 (the remainder of her salary for the season), claiming to have been fired after giving her two-week notice. Weber stated that she "withdrew voluntarily," and that he for one was quite willing to continue her according to the terms of her contract. Fields brushed it off, pointing out that Dressler dismissed herself in front of the entire company. And, he added, Dressler's husband still owed him $3,500 for his share of the last *Tillie's Nightmare* tour.

Dressler's departure, and its effect on the box office, may have been a factor in Weber & Fields' decision to put *Roly Poly* on the road after only eight weeks in their new New York theater. A bitter strike by New York garment workers made it difficult to produce and maintain the company's elaborate costumes. Weber hurriedly put together a tour of the South—unexplored territory for the Weberfields. The growing urban centers of the Bible Belt had only recently begun to be receptive to vaudeville-style entertainments. The Weber & Fields Company tour began in Norfolk on January 27, 1913, and played in thirty-one cities in forty-eight days. Except for a week in New Orleans, and three-night stands in San Antonio and Memphis, they played one-night stands exclusively: Muskogee, Tulsa, Fort Smith, Hot Springs, Pine Bluff, etc. Despite the disapproval of the local reviewers in many Southern cities, *Roly Poly* played to capacity houses throughout its tour.

The tour finally closed in Harrisburg on March 15. It was followed almost immediately by four weeks in Boston, Brooklyn, and Philadelphia. Instead of performing *Roly Poly*, however, they presented *Tid Bits*, a "best of" program consisting of the most popular routines from their productions interspersed with chorus routines and songs. No extended burlesque was included. *Tid Bits* was, in effect, a Weber & Fields revue.

After *Roly Poly*, Weber & Fields never did play together again in the new theater bearing their name. In attempting to explain its short-lived success, some theater historians have concluded that Weber & Fields New Music Hall was too large for their "intimate" style of entertainment, and that the public had tired of it anyway. The facts prove otherwise: the Jubilee tour had played in some of the biggest indoor venues with smashing success. *Roly Poly* filled one of New York's largest theaters night after night, and nobody complained about the size of the theater (except those who thought it was still too small). The popularity of productions such as *Hanky Panky*, *Roly Poly*, Fields' tab shows, and the Shuberts' *Passing Show* suggests that the public's appetite for Weberfieldsian amusements was still strong. Anyway, Weber & Fields were resourceful enough to adjust for shifts in taste—if that had indeed been their aim.

More likely, Weber & Fields' New Music Hall fell victim to its hastily recruited mix of stars. Their freewheeling musical burlesques had always relied on an ensemble of experienced and multifaceted performers who did not mind sharing the spotlight. The players at the old Music Hall had been composed of a carefully balanced group of talents and personalities, known affectionately as the "the Happy Family." The Roly Poly Company was anything but happy: Norworth and Bayes were on the verge of divorce, Frank Daniels was intimidated by the knockabout, Dressler was complaining to the press that Fields was cutting out her role. In addition to Dressler's suit, Daniels also later brought suit against Weber & Fields. At issue were physical damages he said were caused by stage business in which his nose was repeatedly pulled; "impairment of facial beauty," was how his attorney phrased it. Photos of Daniels suggest that he should have considered a similar lawsuit long before.

As is so often the case in an unhappy company, the disharmony started at the top. The sentimental reunion of the two partners had cooled into a marriage of convenience. Weber and Fields were not feuding, publicly or privately; they simply could not agree on the kinds of shows they wanted to produce together. Already a millionaire, Weber had no pressing need to continue being the target of Fields' physical abuse on stage. Unlike Fields, Weber nurtured no big ambitions as an actor; performing was something he could take or leave. Now in his mid-forties, he found the physical demands of his role and the grind of touring increasingly unpleasant.

After the hoopla surrounding the new music hall died down, there were no more public pronouncements of friendship rekindled. While their onstage chemistry was stronger than ever, the daily contact gradually uncovered some of the same old tensions. Fields could not content himself with being one of a pair of "low" comedians, even if they were the most celebrated duo of their day. The longer he played Meyer, the more he seemed to need to prove that he was a true actor. While still officially in partnership with Weber, he purchased or commissioned several scripts that would give him the opportunity to play a character role. Ever the cautious businessman, Weber declined to back Fields in these ventures.

In the upper West Side neighborhood where the Webers and the Fieldses lived, the latters' free-spending attitude was much more prevalent. Most of those who lived in the Gilded Ghetto, as the neighborhood was known, seemed to share the Fieldses' belief that there would always be millions to be made. The Fields themselves were a shining example of upward mobility: twenty years before, when they were first married, they shared a tenement apartment with Lew's family at 181 Clinton in the Lower East Side. In January, 1913, they moved into a large flat at 230 Riverside Drive and filled ten rooms with English period furniture and knickknacks. Servants were essential; to help her run the household, Rose had a cook, a maid, a governess, a chauffeur-handyman, and a laundress coming in two days a week. Around the corner on Ninety-sixth Street were new tennis courts, and Lew took up the game enthusiastically, later playing doubles with Adolf Zukor, Marcus Loew, and Lee Shubert.

The partners' eight-year separation did nothing to diminish the antipathy between their wives, and their reunion revived the antagonism. If Lillian happened to overhear Joe complain about production costs or a late box-office payment from Fields' office, she was likely to attribute it to the Fieldses' "extravagant habits" or Rose's "wasteful spending." Rose, for her part, did not hesitate to make snide references to "those cheap Webers" in front of her children, while Lew listened in silent discomfort. He did not disagree, probably because Weber steadfastly refused to loan him any money—out of concern for their friendship, Weber insisted. "Those cheap Webers," Rose would say, "they still have the first million they ever made," thus illustrating both her knack for non sequiturs and the free-spending philosophy she shared with her husband.

According to an article by Rennold Wolf written during the Jubilee, Rose had insisted that Lew quit gambling, and he had given his solemn promise.[16] What Wolf—and Rose—did not know was how desperately Lew was struggling to keep his word. Although there is no mention of Fields' appearance at the racetrack or the casino during this period, the impulse to gamble was never completely extinguished. Bookies or their runners were everywhere—at stage doors, candy stores, the butcher shop, or the local bar. Fields would bet on anything; baseball games, boxing, the success of a vaudeville turn. Standing on a street corner with Weber, he would play automobile poker, betting that the license numbers of the second car rounding the corner made a better poker hand than those of the first car. Weber knew the extent of Lew's compulsion better than anybody; relaxing with his partner backstage before the show, he persuaded Lew to play checkers instead of playing his preferred games (poker or pinochle). For a time, Lew was able to limit his most serious gambling to the backing of his own shows.

The summer of 1913 found the two sometime-partners pursuing their favorite activities: Weber was fishing in the Thousand Islands and Fields was producing and starring in a new summer musical in partnership with the Shuberts. The billing revealed a subtle but significant change in the balance of power—instead of "Lee Shubert and Lew Fields present," it read "Messrs. Shubert present a Lew Fields production," indicating the growing importance of J. J.

All Aboard inaugurated Lew Fields' Forty-fourth Street Roof Garden, which resembled a wisteria arbor on a grand scale, with balcony and boxes screened with growing plants. His crew included his three brothers: Sol as stage manager, Charlie as business manager, and Nat playing a supporting role.

Dissatisfied with the more-established librettists and composers, Fields hired young unknowns, Mark Swan and Malvin Franklin, teaming the latter with veteran lyricist E. Ray Goetz. What the Franklin-Goetz score lacked in quality it made up for in quantity, providing seventeen musical numbers. Fields interpolated two additional tunes by Irving Berlin, "Take Me Back" and "Monkey Doodle." The latter number, aptly named, featured a real simian perched on the shoulder of each chorus girl. According to a memo from J. J., the monkeys gave "the house a very unhealthy smell and will bring the Board of Health down upon us." His suggestion to use prop monkeys was ignored. If Belasco could have a real cat walk on stage, Fields would present an entire barnyard (*The Hen Pecks*) and a chorus of monkeys.

Newcomer Mark Swan did his job better than his more-established colleagues, providing Fields with his best vehicle in years for displaying his acting ability. Fields played an aging Dutch sailor, Jan Van Horn, who is determined to make his little daughter proud by returning to Holland with a captain's gold braid on his sleeves. In a ragtime nightspot, two bunco men sell him a worthless captain's certificate and swindle him out of his savings. At the docks, he discovers the scam. Alone and dejected, he is overcome by the narcotic effects of a shipment of poppies. Van Horn's dream of being captain of an ocean liner becomes the pretext for a series of humorous misadventures. It was a hackneyed dramatic device, having been used for *Tillie's Nightmare*, *The Wizard of Oz*, and numerous lesser musicals over the past decade.

Fields' unusual performance and clever staging breathed new life into it. His hand in the script was obvious; his personal memories became the basis for his character's dream escapades. References to a musical on an ocean liner began shortly after his trip to Europe in 1911, which included a stay in Holland. Early in Act One of *All Aboard*, Fields created a "novel electrical and scenic effect" using rear screen projection to re-create the night skyline of Manhattan as seen from ocean liner cruising down New York Harbor. Later, an elaborate chorus routine, staged by William Wilson, was set in a Dutch tulip garden, and featured dancers in exaggerated Dutch costumes. Carter De Haven, with his hair slicked back and elegantly attired, danced with his wife, Flora Parker De Haven, and sang "In the Garden of Eden for Two."

Fields also incorporated more distant memories: on board Van Horn's dream steamer was a troupe of circus freaks. As he watches the Armless Wonder eat a custard pie, he comments that there are but two feet between the armless one and starvation. Then, despairing over the perversity of human nature, he asks "Why, why did he have to pick custard pie?"

Van Horn's dream voyage made ports of call in Spain, California, the Balkans (where he encounters a female anarchist), China, and the future, before arriving in Holland. The future is a male chauvinist's nightmare—the year is 2013, "When Women Rule." This interpolated skit (credited to Ned Joyce Heaney) simplified the premise of *The Never Homes:* in the twenty-first century, the roles of men and women have been completely reversed. Women not only have the vote, they occupy all the political posts. The burly cross-dresser George Monroe imperson-ated a female ward boss, and Carter De Haven, in a "Little Lord Fauntleroy" suit, was her effeminate son. Zoe Barnett (a last-minute replacement for Jose Collins, who was lured away by Ziegfeld) played the leading candidate for mayoress of New York. Lew Fields, wearing a veil and trousered widow's garb, played a broken-hearted dressmaker—"a man with a past." He is forced to dance a tango with Boss Mahoney before he is allowed to talk to the candidate. On the eve of the election, he confronts the would-be mayoress with her shameful past. She offers restitution, but Fields cries, "Keep your miserable money. You cannot restore my good name." At the climax of the scene, the wronged man rushes to the balcony and, addressing the clamoring voters below, identifies his despoiler: "This woman is the mother of my child, and I—I have no wedding ring!"

Audiences found this double-edged satire of suffragism and melodrama to be side-splittingly funny. Much of its charm, according to the *Dramatic Mirror*, came from "the complete consistency of the interpretation," and "the striking absence of horseplay." Fields and company played it straight, without vaudeville mugging: "the acting was as true as if the scene had represented an episode from *East Lynne.*" The nightmare ended in a chorus routine that was "a riot of color and music," as the dreaming sailor was buffeted and bewildered by a world where cubism ruled, as he searched for "My Cubist Girl."

All Aboard was a departure for Fields not just in its acting style but in its choice of subject matter. Rather than taking off from a current Broadway hit, Fields' targets were a topical miscellany: women's suffrage, Balkan revolutionar-ies, cubism, Asian tensions, the tango craze. Although the critics alternated be-tween calling it a musical comedy and a revue (Fields begged the question, call-ing it "a musical panorama in two acts"), the influence of the Ziegfeld revues is apparent. Curiously, J. J. Shubert's *The Passing Show of 1913* hewed more closely to the old Weberfields formula, burlesquing *Within the Law, Oh! Oh! Delphine*, and even *The Wizard of Oz;* using the storyline of another, *Peg o' My Heart*, to tie it all together.

All Aboard held its own quite nicely against the *Ziegfeld Follies of 1913*, which opened eleven days later at the New Amsterdam. In addition to hiring away Fields' leading lady, Jose Collins, Ziegfeld also included parodies of cubist painters and the suffragette movement. Although both were praised for their sumptuous staging, the initial cost of Fields' production was a modest $15,000, compared to $35,000 for the *Follies*. Ziegfeld's weekly payroll ($7,500) was only slightly more than Fields', suggesting how much more emphasis the Great Glorifier put on sets and costumes. *All Aboard* averaged gross receipts of $13,000 for six performances a week for fifteen weeks—remarkable for a summer show—outlasting the *Follies* before embarking on an extended tour.

The tour was not nearly so successful. In mid-September, *All Aboard* played in Brooklyn for a week of surprisingly lackluster attendance. At Fields' American Music Hall, in Chicago, where the Shuberts had counted on a profitable six-week run, business was similarly unimpressive. Fields attributed it to a well-attended series of post-season exhibition baseball games between the White Sox and the Cubs.

In fact, several changes in the cast and production may have accounted for the falling off. George Monroe had summarily quit before the show began its tour, saying that he needed a vacation. The chorus was cut back, and several of the scenic effects were eliminated. On October 6, Fields wired Lee about a set he needed $250 to build: "Wish you would come to some decision regarding air ship. Show is suffering here for lack of finale." Evidently, in the revised terms of his partnership with the Shuberts, Fields no longer could authorize additional production expenditures. Fields also questioned the way the Shuberts had renovated the theater.

Meanwhile, J. J. complained about the salary list: "I have gone over the salary list and it is absolutely impossible. How in the world can any (road) show make any money when you have a salary list of $5000?" He urged Fields to replace Carter De Haven and his wife, Lawrence D'Orsay, and Zoe Barnett. Fields tried out another actor in De Haven's role, but concluded that without Carter, he "would not have a soul who could get a song over if (he) let him go." J. J. found Fields' resistance baffling: "I am only citing these instances for your own personal good. It is pretty nearly time that you made some money after all the hard work you do. . . . I think you understand fully that our only desire is to make some money. . . ."[17]

Therein lay the problem: it is questionable whether Fields' "only desire" was to make some money; that usually became his "only desire" when he was on the verge of financial ruin.

In March, 1913, a new competitor for the two-dollar ticket had opened its doors with much ballyhoo on Seventh Avenue between Forty-sixth and Forty-seventh Streets—the heart of Shubert country. The newcomer was not a theater for musicals or drama, it was a million-dollar vaudeville house built by Martin Beck, head of the Chicago-based Orpheum Circuit. The clever Beck and his partner Morris Meyerfield had taken advantage of a franchise agreement between Keith and Hammerstein that had given the latter exclusive rights to all U.B.O. acts in the midtown theater district. When Keith learned of Beck's plan, he bought back the Hammerstein franchise for $200,000. Then, through machinations that have never been entirely clear, he managed to buy out Meyerfield's share of the Palace. By the time the Palace opened its doors, Beck's role had been reduced to that of minority partner.[18]

In an era of unabashed hype, the Palace lived up to its name: it was the handsomest, most comfortable vaudeville theater ever built. Its two-dollar top ticket price also made it the most expensive—two times the top price at Hammerstein's Victoria, the other leading purveyor of high-class vaudeville in New York. In contrast to Keith's continuous vaudeville policy, the Palace would present only two shows a day. In time, playing the Palace became the highest vaudeville honor, akin to making it to the World Series or the White House. To be able to "wow" the Palace crowd, the toughest audience in the nation, guaranteed a lucrative season on the big-time circuit.

Its Olympian reputation with performers and audiences was hard-earned, however, for its first month and a half of existence was disastrous. "The poorest big-time vaudeville show that New York has ever seen," said *Variety* of the Palace's opening night bill, and their judgement was echoed by the rest of the show business trade journals and by vaudeville patrons. Insiders predicted that it would not be able to compete with Hammerstein's Victoria. The predictions would have come true had it not been for yet another farewell tour by Sarah Bernhardt, booked by Beck before he lost control of the Palace.

Hammerstein's Victoria, and Bernhardt's engagement at the Palace, were proof that high-class vaudeville could sell two-dollar seats just as well as "legit" productions. It must have occurred to the Shuberts that high-class vaudeville was what Lew Fields had been serving up all along. Suddenly, they had a craving for a piece of the vaudeville pie.

Now, Fields' successful ventures with Marcus Loew—the American Music Hall, the late-blooming *Hanky Panky*, and the tab shows—suggested a way the Shuberts could have their piece of the vaudeville pie. It would be vaudeville by another name: "music hall." The Shuberts would not be billed as the producers; it would be "a Lew Fields production." The tab shows had demonstrated that Fields was even more valuable to the Shuberts as a producer of music hall attractions than as a performer. Moreover, there was a shortage of first-class acts for big-time vaudeville and revues, and Fields had at least twenty performers under his management for the season. And there was always the possibility of another reunion with Weber.

The Shuberts maneuvered carefully to keep their involvement in the background. Their first step was to take over Loew's share of the lease on the American Music Hall. Over Fields' objections, J. J. Shubert had it renovated, adding tables in the rear with meal service, a dance floor in the balcony, and a band that played after the show for dancing. In August, 1913, *Variety* reported that both the American Music Hall and Fields' Forty-fourth Street Theater would be under the personal management of Lew Fields, and that "two other houses in eastern cities will also pass to that producer shortly . . . he intends placing musical comedy stock companies in each house, transferring them at regular periods." Rumors circulated that a major vaudeville booking agent, H. B. Marinelli, was signing foreign acts for Fields. Gleefully, *Variety* pointed out that the combination of Fields' music halls, the Shuberts' theaters, and Loew's small-time circuits could be the opposition that would break the United Booking Office's monopoly on big-time vaudeville.[19]

In mid-October, the announcement of the opening bill at the Lew Fields Music Hall (the renamed Forty-fourth Street Theater), was an open challenge to Keith and Hammerstein: Match this if you dare. For $1.50, Fields was offering *A Glimpse of the Great White Way,* featuring Sam Bernard in a forty-five minute sketch called "The Modiste" (a condensed version of his full-length *All for the Ladies*), and a vaudeville olio hosted by Frances Demarest as Miss Manhattan. The acts she introduced included the *Carmen* ballet, a contortionist named Mado Minty who performed on a gigantic spider's web that filled the proscenium, and the Schwartz Brothers in their "broken mirror" routine (one brother danced in front of an invisible mirror while the other mimed his reflection). Bernard's skit was no piker's one-act, either; it had a cast of forty-four, while the *Carmen* ballet corps numbered over eighty dancers. The entire program cost $9,400 a week, including salaries, about the same as the weekly expenses at the Palace.

The magnitude of Fields' opening night at his new music hall sent the U.B.O. managers into a frantic series of meetings. The following week, prices at the Palace were reduced to the music-hall scale. According to *Variety,* "Not a vaudeville show in New York this week could stand up against the array at the Music Hall." All vaudeville (except for the Keith-Albee organization) was rooting for Fields' Music Hall because they hoped that it was the beginning of the end of "the Keith brand of vaudeville." Privately, however, the Shuberts were considerably less sanguine about its prospects.

The key to the music hall's future was the versatility of Lew Fields as a producer, manager, and occasional performer: "It attempts something vaudeville has never seen" commented *Variety,* " 'produce' every act. This is Mr. Fields' original idea and it will be carried out much further when he is able to give it his personal attention."[20]

When that would be was anybody's guess. Though Fields had carefully selected the turns that went into the opening bill, he was too far away to personally supervise *A Glimpse of the Great White Way* or select the new acts that were supposed to change weekly. Instead, he was in Chicago with *All Aboard,* on a tour scheduled to last another two months. He was doing what he liked best—producing and starring in his own show.

Desperate to bring Fields back to New York to supervise the Forty-fourth Street Music Hall, J. J. Shubert tried to persuade Fields to abort his tour. Interestingly, J. J.'s private assessment directly contradicted the published reports about business at the music hall.

> My dear Lew,
>   You know by now that our opening at the Music Hall has not been very auspicious. First of all we did not get started properly, and the next thing it needs some-

body's attention every day and every night. . . . With your energy and attention to it it ought to be the biggest thing in New York.

There is no use continuing on tour with *All Aboard* as they do not seem to want it. We made a mistake, let's pocket the loss and go at something else where there is an opportunity of getting our money back. I am sure that the Music Hall with proper supervision and attention paid to it can be made the biggest proposition in America. You can knock out from $3,000 to $5,000 per week once you can get it started. . . .[21]

Fields' response was sent from Kansas City, a long and vehement rebuttal. He reminded J. J. that it was "the beer garden and dance hall surroundings [that] drove away the high class people." As for the Music Hall, Fields saw it as a time-consuming venture: "you can't expect me to go in at a moment's notice with a lot of old stuff and build it into the big proposition that you seem to think it will be. I have my own ideas as to the music hall in New York and must have time to work them out." As for *All Aboard,* he totally rejected J. J.'s assessment: "You say the public don't want *All Aboard.* That is a matter of opinion. I think they do. . . . Papers and public claim here it is the best musical show that was ever in Kansas City . . . Of course, you can close if you want to, it's up to you, but what is to become of me? As you are aware, with the obligations I have I must have a steady income and I can't afford to lose any time laying off and don't want to go into the music hall unless I have something new to offer and something that will draw some money. . . ."[22]

Was it only the telegram's format—three pages of unpunctuated block letters—that gave it a distinctly hysterical tone? What were these "obligations" that seemed to have him running scared? The final paragraph of Fields' telegram not only reveals his rocky relationship with the Shuberts but also suggests the precariousness of his own emotional and financial condition. Fields continued touring with *All Aboard* through January, drawing consistently strong attendance and reviews but barely eking out a profit. The Forty-fourth Street Music Hall productions disintegrated into chaos. Without Fields' participation, the Shuberts were unable to secure enough first-class acts or to "produce" them with the same panache as Fields would have. By mid-December 1913, the Shuberts' attempt to establish their own big-time vaudeville circuit had collapsed. Insiders found Fields' lack of enthusiasm puzzling; the Shuberts found it infuriating. It made no sense to them: Fields was paying rent on the Forty-fourth Street theater anyway, so why could he not do for the Shuberts what he had done for Loew? Fields had consented to let them use his name as a cover to circumvent the "Advanced Vaudeville" agreement with the U.B.O., and he had even helped get the project off the ground. But he never had any intentions of putting aside his other plans, even though he had once again overextended himself.

His other plans included continuing to produce musical spectacles along the lines of *The Summer Widowers* and *The Never Homes,* with or without the Shuberts. Flush with the success of *Hanky Panky,* Marcus Loew agreed to back Fields in his biggest revue ever, *The Pleasure Seekers.* Fields took the principals from *Hanky Panky* (which had just completed its second year of touring), added two more stars, Dorothy Jordan and dancer George White, and built up the chorus to eighty chorus girls and forty-five men. Few stages in New York could accommodate such a host; for the first time, the Shuberts made their Winter Garden stage available to a show that they had no hand in producing. Wisely, Fields retained the house director, William J. Wilson, to stage the production.

As if to acknowledge the link with *Hanky Panky*, Fields' new extravaganza was subtitled "Another Jumble of Jollification." While the plot was indeed a jumble, there was little jollification, and that consisted mostly of stale rehashings of old Weber & Fields routines. Max Rogers, Bobby North, and Harry Cooper portrayed a trio of Jewish salesmen who give two upstate buyers a bon voyage banquet and then impulsively decide to accompany their clients to Paris. The lack of fresh comedy can be directly attributed to Fields' absence during the tryout period. E. Ray Goetz' tunes were only slightly better than the book. The song that drew the most comment was an interpolation, "Get Out and Get Under" (about the joys of automobiling), sung by Bobby North.

Fields was apparently counting on the spectacle to put the show over. The settings by Arthur Voegtlin, Fields' favorite designer, were as extraordinary as the comedy was uninspired. Each of the two acts contained five different scenes, beginning with a reproduction of the banquet room of the Ritz-Carlton and a cutaway of three decks of an ocean liner. The show-stopper came at the end of Act One, with an Alpine scene during which chorus boys and girls in bobsleds careered down the mountain from the fly galleries, while others indulged in a snowball fight with the audience. Several hundred snowballs made out of tightly rolled cotton were thrown back and forth. This proved to be the most exciting moment of the evening.

By the time *The Pleasure Seekers* had its preview in Albany on late October, it had been in tryouts for almost five weeks and had accumulated expenses of close to $75,000. Despite wildly successful previews in Albany and New Haven, the oversized stage pictures and choruses were not enough to satisfy New York audiences. "Scenery never made a play yet," Acton Davies pointed out. Fields knew this, but chose to ignore it. Without the benefit of his deft comic touch as a performer or his hands-on supervision, *The Pleasure Seekers* was basically an expensive vaudeville show afflicted with gigantism. The Shuberts had repeatedly warned Fields that such pretentiousness was no longer profitable; Fields' own assessment of his shows since *The Never Homes* should have told him as much. It was further proof that he was losing touch with popular taste.

The Pleasure Seekers lasted eight painful weeks at the Winter Garden, then spent twelve weeks in early 1914 on the road in the Midwest and Northeast, where the less sophisticated audiences seemed to appreciate it more. Loew and Fields lost heavily; it was the last time that Loew backed Fields in a show, or backed any stage production on a similar scale.

Losses from *The Pleasure Seekers* may have been the reason that Fields accepted the Shuberts' offer to book a Weber & Fields All-Star Company for a tour in the spring of 1914. The fact that Lee Shubert had secured another $10,000 loan for Fields and discounted several others probably influenced his decision as well. Certainly, Joe Weber had little enthusiasm for going out on the road, but he agreed to it for the sake of his old friend, insisting that it would be their farewell tour. The company featured Nora Bayes (assisted by her new boyfriend, Harry Clarke), George Monroe (who had apologized to Fields for jumping ship during

All Aboard), George Beban (in a one-act tear jerker, "The Sign of the Rose"), and vocal gymnast Dorothy Toye, along with fifteen chorus girls and several vaudeville acts. Because they were playing in Shubert theaters in Chicago and St. Louis, it could not for legal reasons be called a vaudeville program, though it could hardly have been mistaken for anything else.

Advance ticket sales in Chicago were the largest on record, and they quickly arranged for a return week there after St. Louis. Audiences in both cities had not tired of Weber & Fields' most familiar routines, the pool table and the Dying Gladiators statue. Younger patrons who knew of the famous Dutch comedians only by reputation laughed just as hard as the oldtimers in the crowd.

With grosses totalling around $75,000 for the four weeks, Weber was persuaded to continue the tour, and he masterminded their new strategy. Unlike Fields, Weber was guided solely by pragmatic considerations of where the biggest profits lay. Not in the big cities, he figured, for they had all been visited by various Weber & Fields companies within the past two years. Furthermore, big-time vaudeville had been in a slump, thanks in part to competition from Loew's burgeoning small-time circuits and motion pictures. (One topical joke making the rounds at the time asked, "Do motion pictures harm children?" The answer: "They do if their parents are in vaudeville.") Weber concluded that the most profitable new markets for vaudeville were in the cities with populations under 100,000.

With these facts in mind, Weber & Fields revived their Jubilee production, *Hokey Pokey*, engaging a company of lesser-known performers and arranging a tour of one-night stands. Instead of Lillian Russell, Fay Templeton, and William Collier, they offered the statuesque Amanda Grey, the petite Mona Desmond, and the elegant Larry Ceballos. Instead of playing in Philadelphia, Pittsburgh, or Chicago, they tanked through Terre Haute, Peoria, and Kalamazoo, hitting thirty-six cities in thirty-eight days.

Despite capacity houses at every stop, Fields was still in financial straits. From Danville, Illinois, he sent a night letter to J. J. pleading: "Will you please see that I get renewals for 60 days on state bank paper. There isn't a chance in the world of my meeting it now I haven't got it. Please do this for me. Make answer Terre Haute. Will send check for interest."[23] Where, one wonders, was all the money going?

The whirlwind tour ended in Boston, where Weber & Fields had not played together since 1904. Though it was a "big-time" city—it was the original headquarters of Keith-Albee—Weber & Fields shocked the trade when they announced that they would be playing at the cavernous Boston Theater at "small-time" (popular) prices for two weeks, from May 24 through June 6. In addition, there would be three special matinees each week at a top price of fifty cents. The theater's daring manager, William Wood, who earlier that spring had been unable to get the Syndicate to renew his lease, offered Weber & Fields a substantial guarantee *and* a percentage agreement if receipts were large enough.

The opening night brought the biggest window sales in the history of the theater. The fact that Weber & Fields were performing old material and fronting a cast of second-stringers did not seem to matter. Gross sales for the two weeks at popular prices topped $16,000. At the end of the two weeks, Weber & Fields turned down additional offers to continue the tour and returned to New York, weary but happy.

Upon their return, there were whisperings that Weber & Fields would go into a straight comedy in the fall. But Weber, having spent thirty-eight years being knocked about the stage, would have no more. He had none of Lew's lofty ambitions to be an actor. At age forty-eight, with a million dollars or more to keep the wolf away, Joe Weber announced his retirement from performing. Henceforth, he would devote his energies to his various managerial and business interests. In his retirement announcement, he commented on how much show business had changed since "the old days": "You know, it isn't like it used to be at all, when one could stay all season in New York. At the present state of things a player is lucky to be in New York eight or ten weeks out of the season. The rest of the time is catching trains and missing meals on the road. Lew and I were out last season for a time, but now I'm through."[24] And he meant it, too—until the next time Lew needed him for another farewell tour. Ironically, Weber would be more active over the next five years as a producer of musical comedies than his erstwhile partner.

By the end of the 1913–1914 season it was clear to Fields and the Shuberts that their second partnership was not working out any better than their first. The Shuberts had wanted Fields for his ability to produce highly profitable variety shows and revues, while Fields wanted the Shuberts to back his ambitions to be a legitimate actor-producer. Eventually, Fields' indebtedness to the Shuberts to back his ambitions to be a legitimate actor-producer. Eventually, Fields' indebtedness to the Shuberts gave them more leverage over his choice of projects, and that may have been why he produced so few musical comedies between 1914 and 1919. A memo from J. J. to his business manager in May 1914 reveals that Fields owed the Shuberts so much money that they decided to renew a $50,000 life insurance policy on him even though they did not expect that he would continue working with them.[25]

Adding to the confusion was Fields' own ambivalence about his priorities as a popular artist. Over the next five years, as he bounced between the legit stage, silent film, and vaudeville, his motivations became increasingly contradictory and incompatible. He spoke less often about "giving the public what it wants," because he had had enough flops to make him question his own judgement, as well as the public's. In some things he did, he seemed to be seeking artistic accomplishment, and then he would complain about being a slave to public expectations. Just as often, he fell back on past triumphs and familiar formulas in order to ensure commercial success. Then he would once more make statements such as "burlesque is the highest form of the dramatic art," or, "my greatest joy is in making people laugh."

Two forces seemed to sustain him during these difficult years: his undying love of performing (with the underlying need for applause) and the fear of financial failure. The love and the fear fed each other, so that Fields felt compelled to rely on his reputation as a performer (and not as a producer) to maintain his financial well-being and self-respect.

By 1914, it had become particularly important to the Fields family to maintain at least the façade of affluence. Frances, now twenty, was being courted by a young banker named Charles Lionel Marcus, a vice-president at the Bank of the United States and a graduate of Columbia Law School (Class of 1909). Charles' father, Joseph, had founded the bank. In the 1890's, Joseph Marcus owned a large clothing store at 102 East Broadway; around 1900, he opened his own bank by setting up a cashier's desk and putting an advertisement in the Yiddish papers. Marcus' reputation as an honest, reliable businessman made his Public National Bank an immediate success with immigrant Jews, many of whom were intimidated by the impersonal and discriminatory services offered by more-established banks. In 1913, Marcus incorporated as the Bank of the United States, a name that led many immigrants to believe they were banking with a government institution. By 1930, the bank had fifty-nine branches in the New York area.

Almost certainly, the Schanfield family knew of Joseph Marcus on the Lower East Side even before he founded his bank. The Marcuses had moved uptown at about the same time as the Fieldses; their home was at 315 Riverside Drive, about ten blocks away. Charles Marcus' pedigree was everything Lew and Rose could have hoped for for their eldest daughter—from a family of affluent, assimilated Jews (with their own bank!), Columbia University, a law degree, a young bank vice-president who would someday succeed his father as president. Having Charles Marcus as a son-in-law would set a good example for the Fields boys, and would perhaps provide them with some important opportunities when they were ready to begin their own careers. It was the kind of social union Lew and Rose Fields had been grooming their children for, the reward for insulating them from the taint associated with the theatrical profession.

Privately, the Marcuses sniffed condescendingly at the source of the Fieldses' affluence, an attitude that later became more overt when Lew's fortunes flagged and the other three children chose stage careers. Frances' unworldly charm and sunny disposition won over the Marcuses, however, as did her father's judicious display of wealth at the appropriate times. The engagement reception was held on June 7, the day after Lew Fields returned from Boston. Naturally, Fields booked a room in one of New York's most exclusive and elegant social venues—Delmonico's. With its ornate Beaux Arts building and lavish interior, as well as its esteemed chefs, Delmonico's had become a symbol of gilt-edged respectability.

Joe, Herbert, and Dorothy observed the hoopla with bemused detachment. Responding to all the careful planning, publicity, and elaborate social events surrounding the union of Charles Marcus, banker, and Frances Fields, daughter of the famous actor-producer, they began to refer to the marriage as "the merger." The groom's rather stiff manner contributed to the effect; though basically a personable young man, he maintained an air of formality that led one close family member to remember him as "the kind of man who wore a three piece suit to the beach."

On August 24, 1914, the day before Lew Fields was to open his new production, Frances and Charles were wed. Once again, the ceremony was held at Delmonico's, this time in the Gold Room in the presence of 200 guests, with Rabbi Eiseman from Temple Beth-El presiding. Under a huge floral canopy of white hydrangeas and pink roses, Fields, with tears in his eyes, gave his daughter away. Charles was attended by his younger brother Bernard, who in a few short years would push Charles out of the family business. A boys' choir sang in the musician's gallery, hidden behind a screen of smilax.

After the ceremony, Delmonico's head chef served the wedding banquet. Dancing continued until late into the night, though the bridegroom declined to dance. The newlyweds left for an extended honeymoon in Yellowstone Park and California resorts. Originally, they had engaged passage to England on the *Aquitania*, but the European war had changed their plans.

For most Americans, little inconveniences like changed travel plans and fewer foreign vaudeville acts were the only day-to-day reminders that Europe had been plunged into war since the assassination of Archduke Francis Ferdinand on June 28, 1914. Few people believed that the conflict would last more than a few months. Newspapers devoted more ink to the exploits of Pancho Villa and the aftermath of the American seizure of the port of Veracruz. American readers were more interested in the evangelist Billy Sunday, the five-month-long coal strike, the newest dances demonstrated by Vernon and Irene Castle or Maurice and Florence Walton, and the newest installment of *The Perils of Pauline* and *The Adventures of Kathlyn*.

Although it is only perceptible in hindsight, the American musical theater was among the first institutions to feel the effects of the war in Europe, primarily because so many of its plays, playwrights, and composers had their roots there. After the 1914–1915 season, it became increasingly difficult for American producers to procure European plays. This, and growing sentiment against the Central Powers, and in Irish-American and German-American circles, against England, made Broadway more receptive to the efforts of a new generation of American stage talents.

The 1914–1915 Broadway season quickly revealed itself to be the most dismal season since 1901–1902. Only twenty-three new musicals were produced, and half of them were European imports. Broadway and vaudeville slumped badly at the box office, and producers blamed each other for over-construction of theaters. In New York, after producers had just spent $8,870,000 for new theaters the year before, only six out of thirty-six legit houses made any money.[26] Box office was so bad that many managers shut down entirely two weeks before Christmas. And, contrary to the traditional pattern, receipts on the road were equally poor.

The only musical to prosper during the box office slump was *Chin-Chin*, a puerile musical fairy-tale starring Montgomery & Stone. *Chin-Chin* repeated the decade-old formula of *Babes in Toyland*, only instead of a Victor Herbert score, it featured interpolations of already popular songs such as "Goodbye Girls, I'm Through" and "It's a Long, Long Way to Tipperary."[27]

Yet in this otherwise dismal season there were glimmers of hope—at least three glimmers. Two of them were direct descendants of the musical burlesques-cum-revues presented by Fields with Weber and on his own. Irving Berlin, already well established as Tin Pan Alley's master tunesmith, dubbed his first full score "a ragtime opera." *Watch Your Step* had the wispiest of plots by Harry B. Smith, but it was the freshness and vitality of Berlin's slangy, syncopated songs that held it together. Berlin's score was a showcase for the nation's favorite dance team, Vernon and Irene Castle, who together and separately performed all the latest steps from the tango to their own patented Castle Walk. Fields was embarrassed to recall how four years earlier, he had been reluctant to allow them to dance together for even one number in *The Summer Widowers*.

George M. Cohan's *Hello, Broadway,* which opened on Christmas Day, 1914, (seventeen days after *Watch Your Step*), seemed to embrace the old Weberfields' aesthetic, but was actually a landmark in the development of the revue. Forswearing the elephantine lavishness of the Follies and the Passing Show (and Fields' own Broadway Theater shows), Cohan staged a fast-paced series of skits that satirized American institutions and Broadway shows. Playing opposite Cohan was Music Hall veteran William Collier, and the small dimensions of the Astor Theater recalled the beloved bandbox of the Weberfields on Twenty-ninth Street.

Unlike the Weber & Fields productions, Cohan's dispensed with any semblance of a plot, and boasted of it. Nevertheless, Cohan apparently regarded this as entirely consistent with his show's Weberfieldsian roots. In January, 1916, he announced that the permanent policy of the Astor Theater would be "reviews along the lines of the old Weber & Fields Music Hall." The cast of *Hello, Broadway* would become the nucleus of a stock company. Though Cohan's plans never materialized, his vision of a less opulent, more intimate style of revue looked forward to the revues of the post–World War I era even as it acknowledged the roots of the modern revue in the Weber & Fields Music Hall.

The season's third ray of hope came from a production that on its face could not be more opposite to Fields' outsized musical spectacles or the Weberfields' raucous burlesques. In 1903, Weber & Fields had included in their production of *An English Daisy* an interpolation by a previously unknown writer named Jerome Kern. For most of the next decade, Jerome Kern composed interpolations for the steady stream of English musicals imported by Charles Frohman. Among the seven tunes that Kern created for Frohman's 1914 show, *The Girl from Utah,* was a fascinating melody called "They Didn't Believe Me," which became the show's smash hit. So popular was the tune that producers F. Ray Comstock and Bessie Marbury hired Kern to score the low-budget musical they were planning for the Princess Theater, an adaptation of an English musical with the unwieldy title of *Mr. Popple of Ippleton.*

The Princess Theater was struggling; budget limitations and the small size of the house necessitated a scaled-down production. With this end in mind, Comstock and Marbury took Joe Weber's production of *The Only Girl*, one of the season's early hits, as the model for their "intimate" entertainment. *The Only Girl* had a solid Victor Herbert score and a clever book by Henry Blossom, but what impressed Comstock and Marbury were its small cast, simple sets, the absence of extraneous chorus personnel, and specialty acts. Kern and his librettist, Guy Bolton, made a virtue of necessity, and with frank good humor gave it the title deserved by so many musicals before and since, *Nobody Home.* Marbury promoted it cleverly, promising Broadway audiences something new: "It is said of 'Nobody Home' that there is a real story and a real plot, which does not get lost during the course of the entertainment."[28] The "real plot" involved society dancer Vernon Popple (read Castle) who wants to marry Violet but must win the approval of her snobbish aunt and the aunt's excitable Italian boyfriend.

Nobody Home was the first, and by no means the best, of the Princess musicals; in it, Kern and Bolton reasserted certain aesthetic values for the musical that had been all but forgotten. They attempted to tell a coherent story in dialogue and songs using the vernacular of contemporary Americans. The third member of the team, the British novelist P. G. Wodehouse, brought a new level of wit to lyric writing. Their subsequent efforts, such as *Very Good Eddie* (1915), *Oh, Boy!* (1917), and *Oh, Lady! Lady!!* (1918), came closer to achieving these goals. Statements by Bolton and Kern left no doubt about the shortcomings they sought to remedy: "It [*Very Good Eddie*] was the first of its kind to rely on situation and character laughs instead of clowning and Weberfieldsian cross-talk with which the large-scale musical filled in the between musical scenes."[29] And: "From start to finish it [*Oh, Boy!*] was a 'straight' and consistent comedy with the addition of music. The plot was connected, and every song and lyric contributed to the acceleration of the action."[30]

Bolton and Kern would have been surprised to learn that Lew Fields had expressed similar ambitions for the musical as far back as 1904, when he had bravely declared, "For a long time I've been convinced that the public wants coherency and naturalness in musical show." As it turned out, he was wrong about the public, and he eventually stopped trying, worn down by commercial pressures and the need to make a buck. Ten or more years later, the public's reaction to the Princess musicals was more encouraging, but the groundbreaking qualities of those productions still had little immediate impact on Broadway musicals.

If Lew Fields had no direct influence on the Princess Theater musicals (except as a symbol of an outdated style), the Princess shows had an immediate influence on Lew Fields. The Kern-Bolton-Wodehouse shows proved that a Broadway musical did not have to use elaborate sets, vaudeville specialties, and big choruses to do well at the box office. To potential backers, Fields' style had become a liability. Actually, he did not disagree with Bolton and Wodehouse, but their prescription for the ailing musical did not make him any more enthusiastic about producing and acting in them.

The Princess Theater musicals also had an indirect effect on Fields that was in the long run more beneficial. The Princess playgoer was younger, more sophisticated, and more affluent than the average playgoer. The tiny theater exuded an air of exclusivity which was reinforced by the play's subject matter—elitist (contemporary) stories in elitist (contemporary) settings. It was at the Princess that the teen-aged Gershwin brothers and Richard Rodgers became enthralled with the possibilities of the musical score through the work of Jerome Kern, and Larry Hart would rub his hands together and beam in satisfaction at Wodehouse's lyrics. And it was here that Herb Fields first encountered a witty, literate libretto for an American musical. Lew Fields' children took full advantage of the courtesy passes that he received from almost every New York theater. The only ones they ever argued about were the passes for the new Princess Theater shows. Emulating the Kern-Bolton-Wodehouse shows, the team of Herb Fields, Richard Rodgers, and Larry Hart wrote the musicals that eventually revived the career of Lew Fields.

So it was in the 1914–1915 season—the season of *Watch Your Step, Hello, Broadway,* and *Nobody Home,* and a big box-office slump—that Lew Fields finally gave up trying to make the great American musical. The influence of his past achievements was everywhere, but he could not find a place for himself. In the fall of 1914, his two productions were adaptations of foreign plays, and one of them was not even a musical.

After years of Fields' not-so-subtle hints about his desire to play character or dramatic roles, a Broadway producer finally decided to take him up on it. Al Woods had made his first million on melodramas and thrillers that were sent on the road as trunk shows. A rough-hewn, plain-spoken son of the Bowery, he turned a boyhood passion for dime novels into a career. He started with no money, but he had what he thought was a gripping title, "The Bowery After Dark." He persuaded a printer to create a lithograph, and he found a sick, discouraged German émigré to write a play to fit the title. His productions of *Nellie Went Away, Bertha the Sewing Machine Girl,* and *The Belle of Avenue A,* and many others, crisscrossed the country in the 1890's and early 1900's. Around 1909, when it seemed as if stage melodramas were losing popularity, he switched to bedroom farces and slapstick comedy. By the fall of 1914, he had thirty-two theatrical companies, including eight troupes on the road playing 1913's most popular comedy, *Potash and Perlmutter* (about the misadventures of a contentious Jewish pair, similar to Weber & Fields' Dutchmen).

Woods owned the rights to *The High Cost of Loving,* a straight farce adapted from the German by Frank Mandel, and he thought that Fields would be ideal for the lead. Fields' initial enthusiasm turned to dismay when he read the play and found the subject matter to be in questionable taste. Woods overcame Fields' priggishness, and then worked out an agreement with the Shuberts for Fields' services as producer and star.

The Shuberts and Woods would be equal partners in the production; Fields would be guaranteed a weekly salary of $1,250, and would be entitled to half of the Shuberts' share of the profits. This latter sum, however, was to be applied "against any debts or monies which you [Fields] owe the Shubert Theatrical Company and Sam S. & Lee Shubert, Inc., until such debts have been paid in full."[31] The signees later amended the contract so that if *The High Cost of Loving* was not a "success," Fields would agree to go into vaudeville. All the money he earned in vaudeville was to belong to him, and the weeks he worked were to count against the number of remaining weeks guaranteed by the contract. It was an agreement based on mutual need: Fields needed the guaranteed income, and the Shuberts needed performers who could be counted on to turn a profit in vaudeville.

The High Cost of Loving opened on August 25, the day after Frances Fields' wedding, at Belasco's Republic Theater. By the standards of the day, it was indeed a coarse story, but, as the *Times* critic pointed out, "it is cheerfully, frankly coarse." Mandel changed the original German small-town locale to Milwaukee,

where Ludwig Klinke (Lew Fields), a respectable and prosperous mustard man-
ufacturer, lives under the benign tyranny of his wife, Emma. Klinke appears to
be a pillar of propriety, except for a youthful indiscretion with a dancer from a
road show of *The Black Crook*. For twenty-five years, she has been blackmailing
him into sending forty dollars a month for child support. She is also blackmailing
three of Klinke's pals, all of them staid, middle-aged businessmen. Each supposes
that he is the father of an illegitimate son, but, of course, they do not share their
secret. Emma, who is the leader of the local Purity League, announces that a
certain highly respected but unnamed citizen is under investigation by her league.
Klinke's pals are also members of the Purity League, and he decides to join to
deflect suspicion.

Complications arise when the blackmailer decides she wants to increase her
allowance, and she hires a lawyer to oversee her plan. The lawyer, however, falls
in love with Klinke's daughter, and the scheme begins to unravel. In the end, the
blackmailer dies. The lawyer reveals that she has been receiving, not four, but
fourteen checks each month, and has left all her fortune to an orphan asylum,
"because the one great sorrow of her life has been that she never had a child."

Almost without exception, the New York critics complained about the show's
vulgarity while lauding Fields' performance. In fact, they used Fields' own squeaky-
clean reputation to excuse his play's subject matter. "Just because Lew Fields is
Lew Fields, *The High Cost of Loving* entertains without offending," summarized
on reviewer. Another analyzed it more thoroughly: "[Lew Fields] brings to the
role of a case hardened old reprobate such an atmosphere of wholesome fun that
all the sordidness and vulgarity of the play seem to evaporate into the geniality
of his personality." [32]

At least one critic felt that Fields played it too safe in his first attempt at
straight comedy: "*The High Cost of Loving* is a farce that falls only too easily
within the range of Mr. Fields' gifts. It would take a much more ambitious work
to test them." [33] Fields was already looking for one.

As *The High Cost of Loving* settled in for what looked like a profitable stay
at the Republic, Fields began rehearsing his imported operetta, *Suzi*. For a week,
he commuted every day between New York and Providence, drilling his company
from ten in the morning until two in the afternoon, then hopping on a train and
getting back to Manhattan just in time for the opening curtain at the Republic. A
hit in its native Budapest, *Suzi* was typical of the operettas imported as a result
of the sensational success of *The Merry Widow*. But it had been seven years
since the arrival of Lehar's waltzing lady, and the dozens of inferior imitations
that followed had begun to test the patience of American theatergoers. This, and
Fields' oft-stated dislike for foreign musicals, made *Suzi* an odd choice for him
to produce. Contracts and programs provide one possible clue: the production
was presented by "Sam S. and Lee Shubert" (Lee's production company) rather
than "The Messrs. Shubert" (which J. J. was directly involved in). Quite possibly,
Fields was persuaded to undertake *Suzi* as another means to repay his debt to
Lee.

To rewrite the book and lyrics, Fields hired Otto Hauerbach. In the best of
his previous libretti—*Madame Sherry*, *The Firefly*, and *High Jinks*—Hauerbach

added some new twists to the typical romances by creating ingenious settings and predicaments for his romantic leads. His adaptation of *Suzi*, however, was unimaginative and surprisingly humorless. Stephen, the son of a Hungarian count, is in love with Suzi, a prima donna, but he is compelled to forsake her for a lady of his own aristocratic standing. Suzi believes that Stephen is in love with the Countess Rosetti. The Countess understands Stephen's true love and arranges to bring them together, though not without the usual contrivances of misunderstandings and mistaken identity.

For the role of Suzi, Fields stole Jose Collins back from Ziegfeld. Her sultry beauty and sparkling singing voice were unanimously praised. As the Countess, Fields cast Connie Ediss, the corpulent English comedienne who had been a star in his *The Girl Behind the Counter*. Tom MacNaughton and Lew Hearn played comic roles, and were blamed for trying too hard to supply the humor that was missing from the script. To be fair, Hauerbach may not have found the score by Aladar Renyi to be too inspiring. Fields evidently believed that the score needed a boost, interpolating songs by Franz Lehar and Paul Lincke into the last act. Except for a langorous waltz number ("Oh, Fascinating Night") by Renyi, the interpolations were superior to anything in the original score.

Burdened with a mediocre book and score, *Suzi* was further crippled by the scheduling of its opening for November 3, 1914, at the Shubert's Casino Theater. November 3 was election night, a notoriously bad time to open a play. The previous night, two superior musical comedies opened: *Papa's Darling*, with an Ivan Caryll score and staging by Julian Mitchell, and Joe Weber's production of *The Only Girl*.

Critical reactions to *Suzi* were decidedly mixed. The outbreak of hostilities in Central Europe was a factor, making it a patriotic act to pan the show: "If *Suzi* is representative of the musical entertainments the Austro-Hungarian market is at present providing, it could scarcely result in disaster were American producers to follow our manufacturers in adopting the " 'made in America slogan.' "[34] The comment must have struck Fields as ironic; had he not championed American-made musicals, at times almost single-handedly, for years?

Reactions to *Suzi* foreshadowed Americans' growing discomfort with operetta during the next few years. Reality had intruded: the mythical realm of royal romance and noble gestures promised by Viennese operettas could not be separated from the geographic locale where an Archduke had been assassinated and bloody warfare now reigned. Still, it is likely that a strong book and score would have overcome the political sentiments, as was the case the following year in Romberg's *The Blue Paradise*.

While most of the New York reviewers dismissed *Suzi* as harmless, Adolf Klauber of the *Times* labelled it "hopeless" and denounced almost every aspect of the production. It was probably the nastiest review of any Lew Fields production ever. The resumption of open warfare between the Shuberts and the Syndicate may have had something to do with it. (A few months later, J. J. Shubert banned the *Times'* new critic, Alexander Woollcott, forbidding him to set foot in a Shubert house.) Fields' name was not mentioned in the review, but for the first time in his career, he felt the need to answer a critic. Such intensely negative criticism was a new experience for Fields. In a letter to the editor of the *New York Times*, he wrote: "it appears rather strange that *The Times'* reporter should be the only one to find fault with everything in the production." He supplied excerpts from favorable reviews by Alan Dale *(The American)*, Charles Darnton *(The Evening World)*, and Carl Van Vechten *(New York Press)*. Conveniently, Fields overlooked some of the other negative reviews, which also pointed out the mediocrity of both the libretto and the score.

It was Fields' first (and only) public rebuttal of a bad review, and it came at a time when he must have realized that his reputation as a leading musical producer had begun to slip. Interestingly enough, he had no immediate plans to produce another musical comedy. He announced two new productions: *Blood Will Tell* and *Let Them All Come*. The former was a straight farce, the latter a revue, and neither was ever produced.

In mid-November, with Broadway reeling from the impact of the box office slump, Woods closed *The High Cost of Loving* after twelve weeks. A somber Fields earnestly promised the cast that it was only a layoff. He then purchased Al Woods' interest in the show, and organized a tour to begin after Christmas. The tour lasted through the first week of April and was well received in every city, yet Lee Shubert's final tally showed a net loss. According to his contract with the Shuberts, Fields was entitled to fifty percent of the Shuberts' profits; in Lee's mind, it was only fair that Fields be charged for fifty percent of the losses.[35]

Suzi did not fare any better. Lee Shubert closed it in late December, after fifty-five performances, and then booked it into Eastern theaters for a six-week tour. The tour was accompanied by the usual outraged memos to Fields about his salary list, instructing him to cut salaries and the number of chorus girls.

The unprecedented number of box office failures on Broadway only deepened Fields' own uncertainty. Once the "king of musical comedy," Fields had become an unwilling harbinger of the changes afoot on the popular stage. Operetta appeared to be moribund, and musical comedy was suffering from terminal gigantism (which Fields had contributed to) and competition from vaudeville (also thanks to Fields). The best vaudeville performers were deserting vaude for revues. And the Shuberts and other producers, sensing the public's anxiety about the war in Europe, were becoming increasingly wary of serious dramas. The best bets were vaudeville and the new "plotless" revue, but Fields' interests lay elsewhere—at least until his money began to run out.

Chapter XIV

The Man Who Stood Still

> It makes me sad to think of all the good comedians who have retired,
> gone into picture work or are languishing in burlesque and vaudeville.
> They are the victims of themselves. . . .
>
> Lew Fields, 1916

FOR the established stage performer in 1914, motion pictures offered a new and highly profitable means to capitalize on their talents. This windfall was an unintended benefit of the leading motion picture producers' attempt to monopolize the technology.

Repeating the now familiar pattern, the most successful purveyors of a new form of popular amusement had combined in 1909 to form a trust. On the afternoon of December 17, at the Hotel Brevoort on lower Fifth Avenue, where the bosses of Edison, Biograph, Vitagraph, Selig, Lubin, Essanay, Kleine, Kalem, and two French firms, Pathé and Méliès, agreed to pool their patents and their claims to special rights. Out of this meeting, the Motion Picture Patents Company was born.[1] The Patents Trust, as it was called, immediately entered into an exclusive agreement with Eastman Kodak to sell raw film stock to licensed members only. Henceforth, every theater owner or exhibitor would have to be licensed by the M.P.P.C., who charged rental fees not only for the films, but for the projectors as well. The latter fee alone would bring the trust over $1 million yearly.

Just as every new amusement created its own trust, so, too, did it generate an opposition. The opposition to the Patents Trust was composed of former nickelodeon managers from the urban ghettos of Chicago and New York—men who came from the same immigrant background as the nickelodeon audience. Carl Laemmle, a former clothing store manager from Oshkosh, organized the Independent Motion Picture Company (I.M.P.), and he made a deal with the firm of Lumière to supply raw film stock. He also struck a blow for star power in motion pictures when he "stole" Florence Lawrence, Biograph's most popular actress, by promising her $125 a week. Until then, she had been known only as "the Biograph girl" because the producers thought it unwise to give too much importance to individual performers.

Once the Independents demonstrated that star power gave them an edge in the nickel theaters, the companies within the Trust had no choice but to follow suit. The ensuing competition for the services of stars such as Mary Pickford and directors Thomas Ince and D. W. Griffith raised salaries tenfold, then a hundred-fold. In 1910, a writer for a motion-picture trade journal admitted, "the people playing in them [movies] are very sensitive about having their identity become known. They have the impression that the step from regular stage productions to the scenes before the camera is a backward one."[2] Two years later, the average performer in vaudeville or the legit stage found that the bigger paydays offered by the movies made it easier to put aside their artistic disdain for the medium. Still, for the stars of the stage who were used to catering to the cultural tastes of the "better classes," motion picture acting had the stink of the great unwashed immigrant hordes who composed most of its audience.[3] Many musical and vaude stars also feared that they would be competing with their own shadows if they succumbed to the lure of the screen.

This explains in part why Weber & Fields were so cautious about involving themselves in film production. No doubt they were aware that movies had become the target of highly publicized moral crusades. Weber's Theatre ran *Traffic in Souls,* one of the most notorious "sexers," supposedly based on the Rockefeller White Slave Report. It played to thirty thousand spectators in the first week.

Such notoriety made Fields uncomfortable. The low esteem in which films and filmmakers were generally held was a particular drawback to a star of Fields' sensitivities, given his lifelong concern for the status of the actor, his efforts to make the popular stage a respectable entertainment for middle-class patrons, and his own compelling need for social legitimacy. It took the genius of a close friend of similar background and temperament—his tennis buddy Adolph Zukor—to give movies the air of legitimacy that Fields required.

Like his former partner, Marcus Loew, Zukor had been a successful furrier before becoming a penny-arcade operator. Zukor's differences with the Patents Trust began when they refused to distribute *Queen Elizabeth,* a four-reel French film starring Sarah Bernhardt, which Zukor owned the American rights to. The Trust opposed multi-reel films, claiming that anything more than ten or fifteen minutes long exceeded their audience's attention span, though the real reason was simply that multi-reel films cost more money to make.

Together with Daniel Frohman (who supplied the actors and plays) and Loew Enterprises (who supplied the theaters), Zukor formed the Famous Players Film Company. Its motto, "Famous Players in Famous Plays," summarized Zukor's innovative approach. Edwin S. Porter directed stage stars such as James O'Neill and James Hackett in feature-length versions of their theatrical hits, and Zukor found an enthusiastic middle-class audience willing to pay a one-dollar admission. Others—Griffith at Biograph, and Cecil B. DeMille with Lasky Feature Plays—followed Zukor's lead. The popularity of multi-reel films added the "tired businessman and his family" to the ranks of moviegoers and forever changed the face of the film industry.

Zukor's aim, according to his biographer, was "to kill the slum tradition" in movies.[4] In this way, Zukor did for motion pictures what Tony Pastor and Weber & Fields had done for vaudeville more than a decade before. Weber & Fields had helped break down the social barriers between the vaudeville/burlesque player and the legit actor. Similarly, Zukor overcame the prejudices of famous stage stars (and audiences) who looked on motion pictures as beneath them. Laemmle's "theft" of Florence Lawrence and Mary Pickford had the same symbolic significance as Weber & Fields' success in luring Lillian Russell away from the legitimate stage a decade earlier. As was true in the theater, the institution of star salaries in movies not only raised the status of the actor but sent an appealing message to the audience. This message—that "nothing is too good for our patrons . . . no expense has been spared"—was identical to what Weber & Fields used to put in the ads for their music hall.

Not surprisingly, it was Zukor's Famous Players Company that made the first serious offer (in June, 1913) to Weber & Fields to appear in movies. The deal fell through for several reasons; most notably, they could not find a script that fit the Famous Players' format. (Too bad nobody thought to film Weberfieldsian burlesques of the pretentious dramas—e.g., *Camille* and *Madame Sans-Gene*—that were being adapted to the screen).

Apparently, Weber & Fields were also holding out for a more lucrative arrangement, which they found later that summer with the Kinemacolor Company. Kinemacolor held the American rights to the color motion picture process patented by Britishers Charles Urban and G. Albert Smith in 1908. Theirs was a two-color process involving red-orange and blue-green filters in the camera and projector. Its first releases were travelogues of exotic locales, as well as the coronation of King George at Delhi as Emperor of India. Kinemacolor exhibited in its own theater on Fortieth Street in New York, just around the corner from Fields' Broadway Theater. By 1912, the Kinemacolor releases were so popular that they were headlining vaudeville programs.

Out of necessity, Kinemacolor allied itself with the Independents. The M.P.P.C. were making millions with black-and-white pictures at ten cents a foot, and they did not own the patents on the color equipment. Color would only cut profits and create new problems for exhibitors, who would have to buy the color projectors as well. The exhibitors who had the temerity to show both M.P.P.C. and Kinemacolor pictures found their licenses cancelled by the M.P.P.C. Projectors unaccountably broke down, and projectionists misaligned the machines so that the red and green images were distorted. In some cases, Kinemacolor prints burned mysteriously or were lost in transit.[5]

For Fields, motion pictures were initially little more than high-tech scenic effects for theatrical spectacles. As early as 1906, Fields had inserted a brief film sequence into his burlesque of *The Great Divide*. Beginning with the Honeymoon Express scene in *The Midnight Sons* (1909), almost every one of his productions used motion pictures to dazzle the audience with the realism of a familiar location reproduced on stage. Lacking sound and color, films seemed to hold little potential for Fields as a vehicle for dramatic expression. Were it not for their commercial success, he might never have considered them as anything more than a scenic device.

In September, 1913, Kinemacolor announced a new series entitled "Popular Players Off the Stage." Footlight favorites Lillian Russell, Anna Held, Raymond Hitchcock, Bessie McCoy, Eddie Foy and the Seven Little Foys, and Weber & Fields were to be featured in "natural color motion pictures [that] portray the actor as his friends know him."[6] Lillian Russell made "How to Live 100 Years" (beauty tips and regimen for the well-groomed woman), but most of the other stars never got around to posing for their backstage film portraits.

Weber & Fields had bigger plans. In October, 1913, with a half million in capital, they formed the Weber & Fields-Kinemacolor Production Company to produce "a full evening's entertainment" on film. The first in the series was to be *Mike and Meyer Around the World.* Roy McCardell, humorist for the *New York World,* wrote the scenario: deli owners Mike and Meyer are bought out by the Deli Trust, so they use their newfound wealth to go globe-trotting. Crossing the ocean on board the steamship *Imperator,* they fall overboard. Their adventures under the sea would use Kinemacolor footage taken from a submarine "with real fish and aquatic animals."

For over a year, the start of production was repeatedly postponed while Weber & Fields fulfilled their stage commitments. By the time Weber & Fields finally began shooting at Kinemacolor's Whitestone Landing Studios on Long Island, the scale of the project had been drastically reduced, and it is doubtful that it was even photographed using the two-color process. The war in Europe had made it increasingly difficult to obtain raw color stock from England, and the war with the Patent Trust had seriously damaged Kinemacolor's distribution capabilities.

Based on descriptions in newspaper reviews, the only part of the original Kinemacolor scenario to be used was a reworking of the deli sketch, in which Mike and Meyer argued over the deli and divvied up its contents by hurling them at each other. Weber divided their cash by stacking it up and cutting it with a cleaver. Audiences mourned the absence of mangled English: "subtitles of comedy dialogue . . . fall far short of the sparkling dialogue spoken by these masters of comedy."[7] They responded enthusiastically to the slapstick action, especially when Meyer demonstrated how much he "luffs" Mike. To fill up the 2,000 feet of celluloid dictated by the two-reel format, Weber & Fields introduced a subplot, a romance between Meyer's daughter and Mike's son. Both parents disapprove; the lovers elope, and the irate parents give chase. Reportedly, these scenes were grossly overdrawn.

In February, 1915, Marcus Loew secured the rights to the "Mike & Meyer" serial and played it in all of his Western theaters. A few months later, *Variety* reported that the Weber & Fields–Kinemacolor firm had sold its entire stock— three one-reelers—to the World Film Corporation. Evidence exists suggesting that World re-edited them into a two-reeler and rereleased it as "The Children of Mike and Meyer Elope" in June, 1915. Weber & Fields thought so little of these early film efforts that they expressed the hope that the reels would be burned.

Fields nurtured higher hopes for his solo film career. In December, 1914, while laying off from *The High Cost of Loving,* he made daily trips out to the Peerless Studios in Fort Lee, New Jersey. There he starred in a film version of *Old Dutch,* the Victor Herbert comic opera that he had produced on the stage in 1909. Directed by Frank Crane, co-starring Vivian Martin (a Mary Pickford clone) and George Hassell from the *High Cost of Loving* cast, the film preserved only the shell of the original plot. The setting was switched from the Tyrol to Palm

Beach, where the eccentric inventor Ludwig Streusand and his daughter lose their wallets and identity papers to a pair of larcenous vaude-villains.

Facing jail for nonpayment of his hotel bill, Streusand must work odd jobs while awaiting proof of his real identity. His odd jobs give him ample opportunity to revenge himself on his usurper, and to incorporate several of Fields' most popular stage routines. As a bootblack, he blacks the man's trousers instead of his pants. As a barber, he subjects his tormentor to the same treatment that Vernon Castle received in *The Hen Pecks*. As the head waiter, he instructs his freakish underlings in how to be rude to customers.

The film *Old Dutch* was, in effect, a medley of Fields' greatest stage comedy hits, and nobody complained about the material being stale. Indeed, reviews were unanimously enthusiastic; one reviewer (for the staid *Dramatic Mirror*) went even further: "Here we have a comedy photoplay that excels anything the Keystone Film Co. has ever turned out." No print of *Old Dutch* survives to demonstrate whether there was any merit to this rather unlikely judgement.

Fields' increasingly precarious financial condition meant that he could not refuse any offers. Arriving in Chicago in March, 1915, for a month of performances in *The High Cost of Loving*, he was greeted by Joe Weber. They had just come to an agreement with the World Comedy Star Film Corporation to appear in fifty-two one-reelers to be released at short intervals over the next two years. The announcement was exactly the kind of brash, watch-me-now publicity trick that Lewis Selznick, World's new general manager, used to upset his competitors and win over exhibitors.

A former jeweler with a fondness for classic literature, Selznick acquired a film-importing enterprise in 1914 and immediately started trying to attract capital. He found it on Wall Street, most notably in the support of George Cox, the financial bulwark of the Shubert organization. On the board of the newly formed World Film Corporation were Lee Shubert and theatrical manager William A. Brady. The Shuberts and Brady would provide players, plays, and theaters for World, much as Frohman's participation had done for Zukor's Famous Players. Selznick, like Zukor, was an avid proponent of star merchandising, and his first move was to sign on Vitagraph's biggest star, Clara Kimball Young. He also persuaded Lillian Russell to appear in the film version of her stage hit, *Wildfire*, which finished shooting just before Fields began *Old Dutch*.

With the success of Mack Sennett's Keystone comedies, exhibitors all over the country were clamoring for more of the same. Selznick created a subsidiary to World Film, the World Comedy Star Corporation, to compete with Keystone. He ordered a script for Weber & Fields in which they would play—what else?—cops. And instead of shooting in a studio, he adopted the Keystone practice of using actual locations; in this case, the streets of downtown Chicago.

"Two of the Finest" featured Fields as a motorcycle cop, complete with white cap and leggings. In his first day on the job, he arrests ten speeders, but the judge refuses to divide the fines with him. He decides to go into business for himself and recruits his buddy (Joe Weber) to help him. They are getting rich with fines when a burglar breaks into the police station and steals their loot.

Weber & Fields insisted on putting a few "finishing touches" on the script, which meant that by the end of the first day, they had completely rewritten it, much to the director's dismay. Cutting capers on Chicago's busiest thoroughfares, they caused gigantic crowds to gather. Every day, thousands of people watched their stunts, sometimes standing ankle deep in slush and snow to see the legendary Weber & Fields at close range. One young actor, playing the part of a motorist caught speeding, had to do take after take of a scene in which Fields manhandled him. Finally, the young man could take it no longer, and he aimed a haymaker at Fields' jaw. Fields ducked, and crew members grabbed the overwrought young man and led him away.

Weber described the joys of motion picture work: "[It] is delightful. We get up at six in the morning, we take a narrow breakfast and then we rush to the studio. Then we sit around until noon, and the director calls us to do a scene. We work five minutes, then we rest an hour. And so on until we are totally exhausted."[8]

Of the ballyhooed fifty-two-film contract, only "Two of the Finest" and one other story ever went before the cameras. The second, referred to variously as "Two of the Bravest" and "The Fireman and the Policeman," was never released and may not have been completed. A shooting script bearing the title "Weber & Fields as Mike and Meyer in The Jail Breakers (2nd Installment)" appears to pick up the narrative where "Two of the Finest" left off.

As a team, Weber & Fields made no more movies for World because, as Fields said sourly, "something happened to the financial arrangements." They had apparently made the kind of mistake that would have embarrassed them when they were still neophytes on the dime museum circuit. Selznick had dazzled them with the promise of a fantastic sum, and they had not bothered to find out if he could really deliver it.

Fields finished touring with *The High Cost of Loving* in late April and returned to New York. He no longer had any excuse to avoid producing the revue he had been promising the Shuberts since January. Lee Shubert reaffirmed their complicity by making a $12,500 loan to Fields, perhaps to cover Fields' share of the new show's production costs.

Hands Up was to be Fields' annual summer show; in it he cast himself and a host of familiar performers: Fanny Brice and her brother Lew, Bobby North, George Hassell, Arthur Aylesworth, and the suave dance tandem of Maurice (Mouvet) and Florence Walton. Second in public favor only to Vernon and Irene Castle, Maurice and Walton were idols of the early cabarets and had been a major force behind the popularization of ballroom dancing. In contrast with the clean-cut image of the Castles, Maurice was often represented as a sensual and dissolute Latin (though he was born in Brooklyn), perhaps because he had initially gained attention performing the notorious Apache dance.

Maurice and Walton were counting on *Hands Up* to do for them what *Watch Your Step* had done for the Castles, and therein lay the trouble. Edgar Smith's book had a typically thin plot about a stolen ruby necklace, a fake detective, and a lot of oddball suspects. Fields was to star as the fake detective; his investigation was the pretext for the dance numbers that featured Maurice and his wife, as well as the other vaudeville turns. It was not much of a plot, but it was clearly driven by Fields' character.

Fields' recent bout with motion pictures provided him with new burlesque material and some novel staging techniques. His performance as the sleuth was to be a burlesque of movie detectives, and Edgar Smith incorporated several running gags spoofing the melodramatic clichés inherited by movies. Periodically, the stage would go dark and a spotlight would appear on "the Snitching Hand" as it filched another piece of jewelry or wallet.

During its out-of-town tryouts, Fields used a film sequence as a kind of prologue or overture, in which the more exotic scene settings were introduced: a beach resort, the Panama-Pacific Exposition in San Francisco, Sing Sing Prison, the Palais de Dance. Other characteristic Fieldsian touches were also in evidence: Sing Sing was the site of a hilarious sketch spoofing prison reform and the *thé dansant* craze: the Warden served afternoon tea and looked on affectionately as his prisoners learned knitting and the latest dance steps.

In the long tryout period, Fields addressed a less desirable characteristic of his productions—a weak score, this time provided by E. Ray Goetz and Sigmund Romberg. To bolster the score, Fields bought several songs from a young unknown named Cole Porter, whose only previous experience had been as leader of the Yale Glee Club. At a time when most Broadway and Tin Pan Alley composers and lyricists were immigrants or graduates of the School of Hard Knocks, Porter's patrician WASP background made him an anomaly. Porter met Fields through agent-producer Bessie Marbury, whose musical taste and social connections no doubt impressed Fields. He bought several of Porter's songs. According to his biographer, Charles Schwartz, the fact that a Broadway producer of Fields' stature had paid money for his songs was worth writing home about. Porter immediately wired his sister: "Tell Granddad that Lew Fields gave me $50 for each song I sold him and [eventually] 4 cents on each copy [of published music]." How many songs, and which ones they were, is undetermined: at the *Hands Up* preview in New Haven on June 6, Porter was credited with "many of the lyrics," but by the time of the Albany performance a week later, only one Porter tune remained. "As I Love You" was written for a Yale show; retitled "Esmerelda," its refrain barely hinted at the playful sophistication of his mature style: "Esmerelda, / Then Griselda, / And the third was Rosalie. / Lovely Lakme / Tried to track me, / But I fell for fair Marie. . . ."[9]

Porter's other songs may have been casualties of the battle between Fields and Maurice & Walton. The dance team complained to the Shuberts that they were not getting enough opportunity to showcase their talents. Fields tried to accommodate them within the elastic framework of his musical comedy format, but the results were so unsatisfactory at its Albany performance that Fields cancelled the rest of the previews and brought the company back to New York for extensive revisions, including a new cast and scenery.

The new delays meant that *Hands Up* had to open after the *Ziegfeld Follies of 1915*, which meant trouble at the box office. J. J. Shubert was furious at what he considered to be Fields' stubbornness. He second-guessed Fields at every turn;

he complained there were too many "Hebrew" comedians for modern audiences, so Fanny and Lew Brice were fired and Bobby North was made to play in blackface. Meanwhile, the rest of the actors were getting understandably impatient because the show had now been rehearsing for eight weeks. Actors were not paid for the time spent in rehearsal.

Rumors quickly spread that Maurice had quit or been fired, and that Fields had hired Clifton Crawford to replace him. This was repudiated the next day when it was learned that Maurice and Walton had purchased an interest in the show from the Shuberts, making them partners with Fields. With the Shuberts' connivance, Fields had been outflanked. Rather than remain as a comedian doing a vaudeville turn within a dance revue, he withdrew from the production.

As far as Fields was concerned, his nine-year partnership with the Shuberts—the longest of any producer-manager of that era—was over. Unlike his separation from Weber, there were no tears shed by a saddened public. If anything, there was a sigh of relief. According to one Broadway corner jockey, Fields was reported to look "ten years younger since he escaped from the tribulations of *Hands Up.*"[10] Within days of the rupture, he was deluged with offers. Fields declined to discuss his plans except to admit that he planned to go to southern California "and reap a fortune in film production." He and Weber had just signed an exclusive three-year contract with the newly formed Triangle Film Corporation to appear in comedies produced and directed by Mack Sennett at his Keystone Studios. The *Clipper* called it "the biggest contract ever entered into between a manufacturing company and players," though the figure that they quoted—$600,000—was a grossly inflated estimate of Weber & Fields' salaries and their films' box office receipts. Even so, it had to be an exceptional amount to lure Weber back as a performer.

The Keystone contract had more value as a public relations ploy than as a binding legal commitment. One immediate and calculated effect was to raise the bidding for Weber & Fields' services on the vaudeville stage. By the end of July, they had concluded negotiations with Keith-Albee's United Booking Office for a twenty-week season at $4,000 per week. The first two weeks would be at the Palace in New York, and their remaining eighteen weeks would be fulfilled in the spring after finishing at Keystone.

At the same time that he was negotiating lucrative film and vaudeville contracts, Fields was trying to find a backer for his fondest dream—to become a "serious" actor. Upon the announcement of his break with the Shuberts, persistent rumors began circulating that Fields would sign with a legit producer: "David Belasco, it is said, greatly admires Fields' talents—which proves again that Mr. Belasco's judgment is sound—and has found a play exactly suited to him."[11] The rumors proved to be correct. Belasco agreed to back Fields in his efforts to become a second Warfield.

Movies, big-time vaudeville, and legit drama—in July, 1915, Fields mapped out his future. Only three years before, he had been the most prolific producer of musical comedy on Broadway. Now musical comedy did not figure in his plans.

In August, 1915, Weber & Fields headlined a bill at the Palace Theatre that would have seemed perfectly satisfactory to the patrons of Miner's Bowery twenty years earlier. Derkin's Dog and Monkey Troupe started the program, followed by the song-and-dance team of John Corcoran and Tom Dingle. The Schwartz Brothers performed their "Broken Mirror" sketch, mostly as pantomime. After a soubrette in the Lottie Gilson tradition came the feature of the first half of the bill, a freak act combining sleight-of-hand and contortions. Harry Houdini swallowed needles and had them pulled out on a single thread by a member of the audience. He escaped from sealed sacks, locked trunks, a straitjacket, and a "punishment suit" used to restrain criminals.

After intermission, tramp comedian Joe Jackson opened up the second part of the bill with a hilarious bit using an abandoned bicycle. Madame Paulina Donalda added some notes of high culture to the proceedings by singing excerpts from *Faust* and *Carmen*, and as an encore, "Coming Thro' the Rye." The applause for Mme. Donalda gave way to whispers of "They're next!" and "The old boys are coming!" Fields strode out, with his little companion in the stuffed vest trotting to keep up with him. They waited impatiently for several minutes while the applause died down, fiddling with each other's costumes, and gouging each other's eyes. Once under way, they did nothing new. A clog dance, the sidewalk conversation about forming a corporation, the choking scene, the pool game, and the "Dying Gladiators" statue—with the exception of the last-named sketch, everything they did was from before their music hall, and therefore at least twenty years old. Their old plaid suits, the "fried egg" derbies, and the huge boutonnieres had become emblems of an earlier era in entertainment—good-natured reminders of the bad old Bowery—but the men in the suits proved that their comedy was still up-to-date. If the applause that greeted them was tinged with auld lang syne sentiments, the ovation at the finish showed that Weber & Fields were "not just a couple of old hacks being applauded to cheer them on." The applause was for two men who were "as amusing in today's vaudeville as they were in that old-time variety."[12]

Things backstage were also much the same. Joe and Lew shared a dressing room. On Sundays, the theater manager brought the boys their pay envelope. At the Palace, however, the envelope was considerably thicker, for it contained $3,800 ($200 was subtracted by the U.B.O. for its booking fee). Fields looked inside the envelope and deadpanned, "Look, here's our wages," as he tossed it to his partner. Feeling its weight as he caught it, Weber could not help smiling. This, too, reminded them of their variety days.

The real difference between their variety days and their big-time vaudeville debut was in the surroundings. To see Weber & Fields in a variety show in the early 1890's was like going slumming; their debut at the Palace was treated the same as any Broadway first night at a legit theater. Even the audience was the same, including New York's most notable first-nighter, Diamond Jim Brady. Within that quarter century, vaudeville had travelled from the Bowery to Broadway, and Weber & Fields (together and apart) had helped make that uptown trip possible.

In an industry populated by clever hucksters and brash entrepreneurs, Harry Aitken was filmdom's most daring financial equilibrist. Ousted as president of the Mutual Company in June, 1915, it took him less than one month to mastermind the creation of the Triangle Film Corporation. The apexes of Aitken's Triangle were the three leading directors of the day: D. W. Griffith, Thomas Ince, and Mack Sennett, the last having brought with him his Keystone Company and its studio. Aitken, like Selznick, was an admirer of Zukor's "famous players" philosophy. Not only did Aitken sign Broadway stars for unheard of sums, but he created a sensation by announcing that Triangle releases would be shown in legit theaters at legit prices—two dollars a seat.

Weber & Fields were among the first Broadway comedians to show up at Sennett's Keystone lot under his Triangle contract. For the young, status-hungry film colony, the arrival of Broadway's most famous comedy team had symbolic significance. Stepping off their train at Union Station in Los Angeles in early September, Weber & Fields were greeted by Mack Sennett and most of the Keystone players, along with a brass band and a gang of reporters. By all appearances, Weber & Fields were visiting royalty.

Behind the cheers and welcoming smiles, however, not everyone in Hollywood was so enthusiastic about the influx of Broadway stars. Many of the Hollywood players resented the Eastern interlopers who were signed for salaries ten to twenty times larger than the average film actor received. Weber & Fields, for example, were paid $3,500 a week, not including first-class travel and living expenses, which worked out to a bigger individual share than what either Chaplin or Pickford was getting at that time. On Sennett's Keystone lot, Mabel Normand was the only player receiving more than $250 a week. The disproportionately large salaries were bitter reminders of the elevated status of the legit stage performers.

The snobbish airs of some Broadway stars did nothing to lessen the resentment. During the fourteen weeks it took to shoot *Tillie's Punctured Romance*, prima donna Marie Dressler argued constantly with director Mack Sennett, condescended to her co-stars Chaplin and Normand, and snapped at the hapless crew. On another Triangle set, Eddie Foy insisted that custard pies and water fights were beneath his dignity as a performer.

The tension between the stage stars and "mere" Hollywood actors became the subject of a thirty-minute comedy, "Fatty and the Broadway Stars," in which Weber & Fields, Willie Collier, Joe Jackson, and Sam Bernard all had cameos. Keystone's most popular film actor, Roscoe "Fatty" Arbuckle, was the director and star. Fatty played a clumsy but well-intentioned studio janitor who keeps breaking up the scenes the various stars are performing in. Rebuffed, he falls asleep and dreams that the studio catches fire, a scene for which Sennett actually burned down a studio building. In his dream, Fatty is the brave hero who rescues the beautiful girls, earns the gratitude of the stars, and is rewarded by being made a star himself. Upon awakening, he discovers that his discarded cigarette has set fire to a pile of rubbish. Instead of being made a star, he loses his job.

At the heart of Arbuckle's film was the Hollywood player's insecurity about how the influx of Broadway stars would affect his own situation. Ironically, "Fatty and the Broadway Stars" proved to be the most popular of the Triangle releases. When the vast majority of the Broadway stars turned out to be flops on film, movie players felt vindicated, and their brand of acting began to be accorded some respect. The ridiculous sums paid by Triangle to Weber & Fields, Foy, Bernard, *et al.* made it that much easier for the most popular film performers to demand even higher salaries the following year.

Unaccustomed to the stop-and-start rhythms of film production, with the long periods of waiting between scenes and then seemingly endless repetitions, the legit performers were alternately bored, impatient, and bewildered by life on a movie set. Film crews quickly tired of pretending to be an appreciative audience for stage actors who could not perform without the promise of hushed attention and loud applause. Supporting film players could drive the legit stars to distraction by making little mistakes that forced additional takes.

Weber & Fields were the exception. Genuinely modest and good-natured, they quickly won over the film workers. Their innocent curiosity about filmmaking was endearing. Between scenes, Joe and Lew entertained the Keystoners with jokes and reminiscences. In turn, Mack Sennett told how he had once been a chorus boy in the Weber & Fields Music Hall (though there is no evidence to back this up), and little Chester Conklin described how as a boy growing up in St. Louis he had been inspired by Weber & Fields to try a knockabout Dutch act. Perhaps Mabel Normand even heard the story of the first pie in the face (in the Weberfields' burlesque of *The Conquerors*), a gag she later took credit for inventing. On Saturday afternoons, Weber & Fields would join the other company actors at the local "plunge" (swimming pool), which was next to their dressing rooms. Unlike most of their Broadway colleagues, Weber & Fields never complained about the spartan studio facilities. The long, arduous days reminded the duo of their dime museum days.

Of all the comedians signed by Aitken for Sennett, Weber & Fields appeared at first glance to be the closest to Keystone in their comic methods. In practice, Keystone's brand of slapstick was based on the knockabout tradition perfected by Weber & Fields for the variety stage. Sennett claimed inspiration from a loftier-sounding source, the French Pathé films featuring Max Linder, but his performers learned their tricks from American vaudeville. Despite these commonalities, however, the effects of knockabout's stylized brutality were not the same on the silent screen as on the stage. Lacking the verbal component (the mangled dialect and crossfire banter), the violence in Sennett's comedies became more prominent, more ingeniously sadistic, and more impersonal.

Weber & Fields, as we have seen, used the physical violence as counterpoint to their declarations of friendship and their twisted explanations. When Meyer choked Mike and said, "If you luffed me like I luff me, den no knife could cut us togedder," the cockeyed poetry of his utterance played off the physical assault. Compared to the typical Keystone figures, Mike and Meyer had complex personalities. Sennett's ideas for character nuances were casual acts of mayhem—flooding a house and driving cars off a cliff, for example. Large-scale pie fights and bumbling cops falling out of speeding cars were plot developments. Keystone comedians had "specialties" (the bully, the bum, the flirt) rather than characters, which is precisely why Arbuckle was never really able to show his true ability with Keystone.

Combine the cruelest aspects of Weber & Fields' knockabout *and* their burlesque methods, and you would come up with something resembling Sennett's

slapstick. The satirical spirit of the Weberfields' burlesques had a relatively narrow focus; they were sharpshooters aiming at social pretensions and incongrui-
ties. Sennett used the art of ridicule like an automatic weapon, spraying every
target within range; his Keystone comedies were punctuated by anarchic outbursts leading up to brilliantly choreographed chaos.

Weber & Fields already knew how silent movies diminished their art, but for
$3,500 a week plus royalties they were willing to adapt. The more serious prob-
lem was in the Keystone production process. Sennett adhered to a rigid production schedule; each production unit was responsible for producing a two-reeler a
week. Not surprisingly, the results often looked slapdash, which may have complemented the Keystone ethos, but it discouraged more ambitious comedians. By
contrast, for his twenty-six-minute film *The Immigrant*, Chaplin shot as much
footage as Griffith did for his two-and-a-half-hour epic, *The Birth of a Nation*.[13]
At Keystone, there was simply no time to try to "work up" a routine through
rehearsals, much less polish it. Anyway, most film directors disliked improvisa-
tions on the set because departures from the script jeopardized their schedules.

Worse still, Weber & Fields found that they were not in control of the production. They were hired players whose opinions could be ignored. Not that they
had any trouble satisfying the harried director on the first or second take, but
this left too little time to try something new. Muzzled by the technical limitations
of the silent film, handcuffed by Keystone's rigid working methods, Weber & Fields'
performances in their Triangle films could not live up to the standards of their
vaudeville appearances.

By far the most painstaking part of any Keystone production was the stunt
work, particularly the car chases. By the end of his first two weeks at Keystone,
Fields complained that he had more bruises than he had ever had in the heyday
of knockabout. ("Now you know what it feels like," commented Weber.) Weber
& Fields' knockabout was usually limited to stage acrobatics and one-on-one assault with nothing more elaborate than a cane; Sennett's slapstick called for violence and destruction on a far grander scale. Sennett's favorite props—projec-
tiles, breakaway walls, moving vehicles—greatly increased the risk of injury to
the actors. Accidents were not uncommon. Most of the Keystone Kops had suffered serious injuries over the years and accepted it as an unpleasant part of the
job.

Weber & Fields came very close to learning about this firsthand during the
shooting of their first Keystone two-reeler, "The Best of Enemies," in early October. The scene called for the duo to be seated in a taxi with the camera in the
front seat when a speeding racing car collides with them. Sennett loaned his 120-
horsepower Fiat for the occasion. Director Frank Griffin instructed the driver of
the racing car to miss the taxi by no more than twelve inches, and reprimanded
him when he did not come close enough in rehearsals. The driver promised to
do better with the cameras rolling. Griffin yelled, "Camera!" and Weber & Fields
watched helplessly as the Fiat raced towards them at fifty-eight miles per hour
and struck the taxi a glancing blow across the front fender, overturning the taxi
and throwing its passengers to the ground. Miraculously, no one was seriously

hurt. The driver, unconscious, and the comedians, dazed and bruised, were rushed to the studio hospital.

Through thirty-five years of knockabout, Weber & Fields had survived with nothing more serious than a few stitches and some bad bruises. They were understandably reluctant to risk their lives for a movie stunt, and talked of quitting on the spot. Sennett spent hours with them, trying to persuade them to stay. Eddie Foy stopped by to offer reassurance: "I'm the father of a large family and I'm taking the same chances you are, so cheer up. They haven't killed me yet."[14]

Weber was not convinced, and spoke longingly of the safety of Broadway. Fields felt the same way, but he could not afford to leave. At that very moment, he was the defendant in at least five different lawsuits. One of them put his Triangle contract in immediate jeopardy: the Peerless Features Film Company tried to get an injunction preventing him from going in front of the Keystone cameras, claiming that he had broken a contract to make at least two films for Peerless before acting in the movies for any other firm. The Peerless contract, signed in April, 1915, provided Fields with a $5,000 advance, and stipulated that he was responsible for securing the rights to the plays he acted in. Director Frank Crane began production on a film version of *All Aboard*, but it was shut down when it was discovered that Fields was not the sole owner of the rights. The judge in the Peerless case refused to issue an injunction but ordered Fields to file a $12,000 bond. Most likely, Fields used his advance from Triangle to pay this.

Simultaneously, in another case, Fields was ordered to pay royalties and damages to producer Edward Rush for *Suzi*. Though the judgement was for a relatively modest sum (around $4,000), Fields' finances were so tight that he had to pay Rush $500 a week out of his Keystone wages.

Upon his arrival at the Keystone Studios, Fields had asked for a substantial advance on his salary. To his dismay, he discovered that Triangle's highly speculative approach to financing meant that there were frequent cash flow problems. Fields' share of the weekly salary was $1,750, but after the first few weeks, Keystone was unable to pay him the full amount. This resulted in some very lean weeks when he did not have enough to meet his family's needs, much less satisfy his grumbling creditors.

Among the grumblers were the Shuberts, still angry over Fields sudden departure from *Hands Up* and his vaudeville deal with Keith-Orpheum. In September, several notes fell due on loans to Fields with Lee Shubert as guarantor. For years, it had been the elder Shubert's habit to discount Fields' notes with a small payment to renew them. Now that Fields had left the Shubert fold, however, Lee may have felt that he was no longer entitled to such indulgences. Perhaps Lee decided that Fields needed to be taught a lesson in gratitude. The Shuberts refused to renew the notes and the debt was turned over to the National Surety Company for collection.

Fields began receiving urgent telegrams from Lee Shubert warning of the consequences if the debt was not paid immediately:

> Lew—National Surety Company are going to attach you and make a lot trouble. Would strongly advise you to raise money and pay, as it would mean disaster in end. Take my advice, as they can hurt you a great deal in the future with everybody. . . .
>
> Lee Shubert[15]

In other words, Fields would be unable to get loans for future productions. But Fields was worried about the present, not the future, and his reply indicated the extent of his predicament:

> Lee—Am up against it. Help me out. Keystone people deducted money, left me very short. . . . Hope to [get] advance on next week's salary. Can hear you hollering now but can't help it. . . .
>
> Lew Fields[16]

These exchanges escalated in urgency and desperation as the weeks went by. Fields: "Am doing the best I can with one salary. Many others pestering me to death. . . ." Shubert: "Have held bank off until Saturday. Unless you remit money before then, they will proceed against you. . . ." Fields: "Lee—Won't you please arrange for bank to accept $250 for three or four weeks. . . . It would help me greatly and means nothing to you. . . ."

It was not to Lee's advantage to let Fields go under. The wily producer stalled the banks at several critical junctures while trying to keep the pressure on Fields. Meanwhile, Fields' desperate promises of "a day or two" or "next week" seemed to be daring the banks to do their worst. He agreed to pay $250 a week, then reneged: "Sorry I am again compelled to beg-off. I realize what I promised but things break so badly for me I just can't help. It cost me over five hundred dollars for lawyers and depositions. . . ."[17]

By mid-December, Lee Shubert wired him that the notes were being protested and that the bank would take action unless Fields paid $1,000 by the end of the week. Once again, Fields had to beg off. His communications with Lee had taken on the tone of a pathetic supplicant: "I don't know what to do or say. My affairs are in such a terrible condition. I'll do the best I can."[18]

So precarious was his financial condition that he decided that he could no longer conceal it from Rose. Together, they agreed to do everything possible to keep this potentially disturbing (and embarrassing) news from the children. Somehow, word of their difficulties reached the ears of Charles Marcus, Frances' husband. It was during this period that "the merger"—having just passed its first anniversary—paid its first dividends. Charles Marcus made the first of several personal "loans" to help his new in-laws.

Meanwhile, Lee Shubert somehow managed to fend off the bloodthirsty bankers for another few weeks, because on January 3, the same threats from his December 14 telegram were repeated in somewhat more emotional terms:

> Lew—Unless substantial payment of thousand dollars made immediately and continuous payment made thereafter to bank, they will foreclose end of this week and take judgement against you and your wife. This means bankruptcy for both. Have done everything I could. You are treating me shamefully and taking care of everyone but myself who have been your friend. . . .[19]

He was wrong on one score: Fields had not taken care of everyone. Among his many creditors was ticket broker Joe Leblang, the father of one of Dorothy's school chums. Fields had borrowed $2,000 from Leblang and did not get around to repaying it until Leblang took him to court six years later.

What saved Fields—from bankruptcy as well as deadly Keystone stunts—was his vaudeville contract with Keith-Orpheum. Weber & Fields still had eighteen weeks of prime bookings waiting to be filled. On the last day of their Triangle contract (around December 7), Weber & Fields worked for eighteen hours without a break to finish "The Worst of Friends." Still in their makeup, Weber & Fields were rushed to Union Station at the last possible minute to catch the late train to San Francisco, where they were to open the following day. It seemed perfectly fitting that their Keystone careers should end with them sitting nervously in the backseat of a car careering through the streets of Los Angeles.

As predicted, Weber & Fields' Keystone exposure boosted their box office receipts when they returned to the big-time vaudeville circuit. Both men were relieved to be in front of a live audience—especially Fields, since the applause these days translated into a large and steady paycheck. He was grateful to vaudeville but could not wait to leave it.

Returning to New York in April, 1916, Fields was reunited with his family after a separation of nearly five months. He announced another homecoming as well—his return to Broadway in a musical comedy. And, just like old times, his partners in the production were to be the Shuberts. Lee had welcomed him home with an idea that he was certain would help Fields erase his debts to the Shuberts and make some money, too. A remake of Fields' 1908 hit, *The Girl Behind the Counter*, would be "sure thing."

Though Fields had already agreed to star in a straight play produced by Belasco, he may have felt obliged to his old friend for (as he saw it) warding off the banks during his recent financial difficulties. He decided to make it up to Lee Shubert, and maybe even regain a measure of financial security as well. In conversation with Rennold Wolf, Fields talked about how lucrative his film and vaudeville junkets had been. Now, Fields joked, he was going to take up producing again because he had accumulated another sinking fund. "And I don't know an easier way to sink it than to put it in musical comedy."[20]

Fields, however, was hedging his bets. He went back to Edgar Smith, the librettist for *The Girl Behind the Counter*, and asked him to update the script. Fields' famous turns as Henry Schniff, "a soldier of misfortune," were left intact: the soda-fountain scene and his instructions to the mismatched group of waiters were, after all, surefire crowd-pleasers. As a performer, his one concession to changing tastes was to drop the heavy dialect. One younger reviewer now identified the softer inflections as Yiddish. Apropos nothing in the story but the current popularity of dance in revues and cabarets, Fields retitled the show *Step This Way*. Gone were the lavish sets and elaborate scenic devices. Reflecting the impact of the Princess Theatre musicals, there was only one set per act, and no large choruses.

Step This Way opened in New York at the Shubert Theatre on May 29, 1916. Audiences and critics were so eager to welcome Fields back to the musical stage that they overlooked the show's shortcomings. On opening night, the loudest applause came from his erstwhile partner, Joe Weber, seated in the front row. Lee Shubert cheered Fields on from backstage.

Fields was not nearly so enthusiastic as his audience about his return to musical comedy: "The public pays for the entertainment, and the public must be allowed to judge for itself what it wants. Most actors are only too glad when the public is interested enough in us to care what we do. So, although there are many things that I can do that the public knows about, and a few that only a few of us know about, still, the selection must be made by others than myself." [21]

Having lived by the maxim "give the public what it wants," he now seemed to resent them for it. On tour with *Step This Way* in Chicago, he expressed his discontent in more melodramatic terms: "The galley slave chained to an oar is in no whit better position than the actor who has come to be accepted in a certain line of character parts."

Still, he did not blame the public for the state of musical comedy, in contrast to the way some highbrow critics of the day blamed the proverbial Tired Businessman. In Fields' judgement, the real problem was that nobody knew how to write a good musical comedy any more. In an August 1916 essay called "The Renaissance of True Comic Opera," Fields discussed the future of the musical. "Laugh fashions change like the styles in hats," Fields wrote. Now that the vogue for burlesque-revues and musical spectacles had passed, he predicted a return "to the old school of entertainment that is opera and is still comic." He also explained his absence from the musical stage: "For more than two years I have been looking for such a piece to produce."

The renascent comic opera would bring fresh glory to those old stalwarts, the prima donna and the comedian, but it would bring the greatest rewards to the authors:

> The composer who has not to halt the flight of his musical imagination to fit a ragtime ditty into his score, the author who may contrive a plot and develop it unhampered . . . will certainly hail the opportunity the new regime will bring. . . .
>
> I look then for the development of a class of men who shall do for America what Offenbach and von Suppe, what Halevy and Strauss did for Paris and Vienna; what Balfe and Gilbert and Sullivan did for England. The public is waiting for the men who shall do that for the stage. [22]

Several of these authors of the future were closer at hand than he could have imagined. While he was waiting for these men (women, evidently, need not apply), Fields would not produce another musical comedy. Instead, he continued to pursue his ambition to be a serious actor.

William A. Brady, head of production for the World Film Company, had once been at a party with Fields where the actor had performed a lengthy dramatic recitation to settle a bet. The instigators wagered that because of Fields' reputation as a comedian, his performance would provoke laughter rather than tears among the partygoers. According to Brady, within minutes, every face in the room was rapt with melancholy, even if no tears were flowing. Brady made a note of it; two years later, he offered Fields the leading role in the film version of *The Man Who Stood Still*. Fields was so delighted that he almost shed real tears.

The play was by Jules Eckert Goodman, a promising playwright who perished in the sinking of the *Lusitania*. Originally a hit stage vehicle for Louis Mann, Fields' old Music Hall colleague and sparring partner, the story was built around the idiosyncratic personality of an old German jeweler who refuses to adapt to modern business methods. Herman Kraus risks losing his East Side shop because he "stands still" while his competitors forge ahead. No doubt the strength of Fields performance derived at least in part from his empathy with his character. Kraus is also intransigent when it comes to forgiving his daughter for the vicissitudes of fortune that have befallen her, including an illegitimate child. In the end, Kraus' grandfatherly sentiments overcome his moralism and the family is reunited.

The symbolic significance of the role as it related to Fields' own situation did not escape him. "The actor is hedged in—as by fire—with tradition," said Fields, barely a week after completing the film. "When trying to jump out of the ring he sometimes gets burned! But—if he doesn't jump, if he lacks the courage, he'll stay right in one spot."[23]

Director Frank Crane began principal photography on *The Man Who Stood Still* in early August at the Paragon Studios in Fort Lee, New Jersey, while Fields was still appearing in *Step This Way*. Goodman's script provided ample opportunities for Fields to showcase his seriocomic abilities. There is a touching scene in which the worried Kraus gets together with his buddy Spiegel around the kitchen table to practice on flute and trombone. Later, they bring their instruments on a picnic where they charm a balky horse into prancing to their martial tunes. One critic singled out Fields' scenes with his infant granddaughter, describing a series of close-ups in which his expression of disapproval changes to curiosity and then delight as he watches the squirming bundle of humanity in his arms.

Whereas Fields' film work with Weber attempted to exploit their past stage hits, descriptions of Fields' solo film appearances during this period indicate his growth as a dramatic actor for both stage and screen. Fields applied the same habits of close observation and physical preparation to his serious roles that he had to his comic roles, only without the exaggeration. For the first time since he was twelve years old, Fields played his part without a wig, letting his thinning, greying hair serve the character. He walked with the slight stoop of a man who had spent the better part of his life hunched over a bench. The deep lines in his face and brow gave him the look of a man overburdened with worries. It was a startling contrast to the foolish comic mask he donned every evening to characterize Henry Schniff in *Step This Way*.

Critics expressed surprise at Fields' versatility. The reaction in *Variety* was typical: "Lew Fields proves what he has long felt but hesitated to insist upon— that he is master of the art of bringing tears to the eyes of theatregoers. . . . Lew Fields has yearned for a play which he could portray a human being instead of a caricature. Perhaps the screen appearance in a legitimate role will be a wedge that will pry open some managerial door. His film portrayal of Herman Krauss certainly entitles him to a chance."

Sadly, none of Fields' seriocomic film performances survives. Early in the summer of 1917, Fields made *The Barker*, a ten-reeler for Selig in Chicago with a script by Charles K. Harris. Set in a circus, a milieu that must have been rife with memories for Fields, its storyline was similar to that of Warfield's star vehicle, *The Music Master*. Descriptions mentioned "a strong heart interest" and "plenty of atmospheric comedy and the employment of the well-known wild animals which have been utilized by the Selig people in other releases." [24]

In one scene, Fields did a series of well-executed cartwheels. He had recently celebrated his fiftieth birthday, and he may have wanted to give the lie to the articles that were describing him as an "Old Timer" and "the aging showman." He also made it clear that he had no thoughts of retiring: "I do not believe in retirement for an actor except when he is physically incapacitated for his work. Acting keeps me feeling youthful and is a healthy exercise. The old actor feels young again just as soon as he gets out on the stage in front of an audience." [25]

Later that summer, Fields fulfilled his obligation to Peerless as the star of *The Corner Grocer*, a five-reeler co-starring Madge Evans. Once again, Fields played a careworn father in financial straits. Charles Wendel, a whimsical grocer, has centered his life on his feckless son, Ralph. He uses his life's savings to send the boy to college, but the boy gets in with bad company. He is duped by "an adventuress" into forging his father's name on a check. The old man makes good on the check; broke and brokenhearted, he turns out his son with orders not to return unless he "makes good." After struggling for some time, Ralph returns to his father and makes full restitution. Of Fields' performance, most reviewers agreed with *Variety* that he once again proved that he could "portray the more serious emotions with quite as much facility as the broad fun with which he has long been associated."

As records of Fields' abilities as a performer, *The Man Who Stood Still*, *The Barker*, and *The Corner Grocer* would have been invaluable. While it is unlikely that any of these films qualifies as a lost masterpiece, they were the most ambitious of Fields' film projects and the focal points of most of his creative energy during a time when he had all but withdrawn from the Broadway stage as a producer or performer.

Using the hot weather as an excuse, Fields and Lee Shubert closed *Step This Way* in early August after eleven weeks. The production opened well in Chicago, but by the end of its seven-week run it was losing money. J. J. Shubert repeatedly asked Fields to trim the payroll—halve the salaries of Bergman and Clark, cut the Pony Ballet's rate by ten dollars a week, get one of the actors to double as assistant stage manager. When Lee insisted that Charley Mitchell (who played one of the oddball waiters) be reduced to half salary, Fields replied that he would rather pay him the difference out of his own (empty) pockets than go back on his word. Fortunately, box office receipts improved as *Step This Way* crisscrossed the Midwest, and the "sure thing" began to pay off.

In late October, at the beginning of an engagement in Davenport, Iowa, Fields made a minor cast change that he was able to justify as a money-saving move. For the role of the rubber-kneed waiter (the same role that the young Vernon

Castle had played), he hired his eighteen-year-old son, Herbert. The move came as a surprise to those who knew Lew Fields, for they knew that he had forbidden his children to pursue stage careers.

Herbert had never been seriously interested in anything else. At DeWitt Clinton High School, he wrote for the school paper and belonged to the swim team, the Good English Society and the French Society, but most of his time outside of class was spent inside a theater, either as a spectator or a participant. He memorized songs and dialogues from Gilbert and Sullivan, and welcomed any excuse to perform them. Slender, intense, possessed of an acid wit that belied his rather prim and delicate appearance, he was an excellent student without ever having to work very hard at it. Attending Columbia University in 1915, Herbert joined the Dramatic Society, where he became close friends with Larry Hart and later met Richard Rodgers.

Over the years, Herb gradually wore down his famous father's resistance with frequent displays of talent as a writer, critic, and performer. In high school, Herb tricked his father into coming to see a performance of the dramatic club. "I've got a friend I want you to see act," Herb said, "and he would be glad if you told him what you think of his work." Herb pretended to have a backstage job. Lew, who was always on the lookout for new talent, agreed to attend. The play was an adaptation of *Oliver Twist*, and Herb was Fagin. Lew's initial surprise gave way to anger at being duped. Herb's ruse, however, was no worse than many that the young Lew Fields had used, such as telling George Bunnell about the one-eyed Chinaman. The quality of Herb's performance turned his father's anger to delight.

A sad consequence of Lew's financial problems in late 1915 and early 1916 was that he could no longer afford the tuition for Herb at Columbia. Charles Marcus helped Herb through the spring 1916 semester, but after that Marcus was beset with problems of his own: his brother Bernard was forcing him out of the management of the family's bank. Although Herb was genuinely chagrined to have to leave Columbia, his father's guilt feelings may have been the final reason that he acceded to his son's stage ambitions. Rose was bitterly opposed, but she could not prevent it. Lew assured her that it would only be a year or two before Herb would "get it out of his system." He told a Broadway columnist, "I had hoped to make the boy a bank president or a Wall Street giant, but if he wants to be an actor, I'll have to make the best of it."

A letter from Lew to Herb, written in January, 1916, at a time when bankruptcy threatened, represented a dramatic turnaround in the elder Fields' thinking. The letter was a response to one in which the young man had expressed the belief that he had inherited some talent and that he wanted the chance to exploit it. It was a subject that sent his mother muttering from the room, and he had not dared to discuss it with his father in person. Surprisingly, Lew gave his blessing to his son's ambitions: "Some people say there is something in heredity, and I think that there is more in you than has yet appeared. . . . I am aware of the restlessness in a young boy's heart when he is ambitious. I approve your going on the stage, for you wouldn't be happy until you tried." Lew's letter also offered sage advice:

I haven't much confidence in stock work. You must learn to create. People in stock are given parts that have been created by other actors and only suffer by comparison. . . . Stock is a place where a great many bad actors go before they die. . . .

And now my dear son, I want to tell you—there are two roads when you enter the theatrical profession: the *never succeed* and the *sure success.* You know a few that have taken the never succeed, I don't have to mention any names [probably referring to his brother Nat and his brother-in-law, Bobby Harris]. . . . If you have the ability, all you want is the opportunity. If you haven't the ability, opportunity will only shorten your theatrical career. . . .[26]

Herbert finished out the tour with *Step This Way*, returning to New York in early December. Though he was not nearly so good an eccentric dancer as Vernon Castle (few were), he was a competent comedian. His time backstage—observing the principals perform night after night, watching the stage manager and choreographer, experiencing his father's relentless rehearsals—was even more valuable than the time he spent onstage.

Emboldened by the praise showered on his dramatic performance in *The Man Who Stood Still*, Lew Fields was eager to start rehearsing for his debut in a David Belasco production. So eager, in fact that he turned down a guarantee of $45,000 from producer Charles Dillingham to reunite with Weber and head a big musical revue. Dillingham offered to put the entire amount in a New York bank before the show opened so that Weber & Fields could draw $3,000 a week for thirty weeks whether or not the revue was a success. For that kind of money, Weber said that he was willing to come out of retirement.

The big revue turned out to be *The Century Girl*, co-produced by Flo Ziegfeld. The score was written by Victor Herbert and Irving Berlin, the sets designed by Joseph Urban. Such was Fields' obsession with proving that he was a serious actor that he turned down a financial windfall and an opportunity to star in the most opulent musical entertainment of the year. Burns Mantle was incredulous: "He [Fields] honestly believes that had he quit clowning ten years ago and taken to semiserious drama, he would have been as great, and as rich, as Dave Warfield is today. . . . Mike [sic], I luff you, but beleef me, you ain't got it in your soul."[27]

Fields had good reasons to believe otherwise. For over fifteen years, he had been hearing about his potential as a serious actor from newspaper critics, columnists, and theater colleagues. In May or June, 1915, Frank Mandel (author of *The High Cost of Loving*) came to Fields and said: "I have a comedy which calls for a cast of only eight people and one set of scenery." Fields, who was feuding with the Shuberts over *Hands Up*, responded, "Give it to me quick." Within a month, he had struck a deal with Belasco to co-produce the play at his Liberty Theatre. Finally, Fields would have his long-awaited opportunity to make 'em laugh *and* cry in the same evening.

The comedian who yearns to make audiences cry is a stock character in the history of the stage, but few comedians ever get the opportunity to try, and fewer still succeed. Two of the most esteemed comedians of the period, Francis Wilson and Nat Goodwin, had tried and flopped. Unlike these two, however, Fields' fame as a comedian rested on his burlesques of melodramas. Now he aspired to that which he caricatured.

It was more than the vanity of a celebrated clown. No matter how artistically it was presented, "low" comedy would always bear the muddy paw prints of its origins; musical comedy was a step up, but it was still, aesthetically speaking, a mutt, though an increasingly well-groomed one. It was why the pictures on Fields' office wall were not of famous comedians, but tragedians—Kean, Forrest, Booth, Garrick, Irving. Starring on the legitimate stage was, for Fields, the final step in the long climb towards social legitimization.

It is easy to see why the story of Mandel's *Bosom Friends* appealed to Fields, with its themes of parental sacrifice and the tribulations of two middle-aged friends brought into conflict by the misdeeds of their children. Sebastian Krug, a schoolmaster of Pennsylvania Dutch origins, has for many years shared a home in upstate New York with Dr. Aaron Mather, a rural physician. Krug is blessed with a daughter, Mather is cursed with a son; daughter and son are planning their wedding at the start of the play. Young Mather is a promising inventor, but he is lured to wicked New York City by a clever vamp who tricks him into signing over the rights to his invention. She then induces him to forge documents, steal, and generally misbehave. He returns home penniless, disgraced, and a fugitive from the law. The fathers debate whether to pool their life's savings to save the boy from arrest. Krug refuses, insisting that his first responsibility is to protect his daughter's welfare, and the two old comrades quarrel. The wedding is called off, and Krug's daughter is inconsolable. The simple schoolmaster then manages to trick the streetwise vamp into surrendering the incriminating papers, and the two families are reconciled.

After rehearsing in New York in December, Fields began the new year with tryouts in Albany, Detroit, and Cincinnati, followed by a more extended stay in Chicago. Until he reached Chicago, the reviews of Fields' performance were unanimously favorable. In Albany, Fields was said to have "achieved the triumph of his life in the character of Rev. Sebastian Krug."

The Chicago critics were more skeptical, even if the patrons were not. Amy Leslie, who first championed Weber & Fields in the early 1890's, observed sadly that "the long, lean, virile clown Lew is exchanged for a gentle, pious, tender Mr. Fields." She found the play itself to be quaint, talky, and worn out. Krug's scenes with his daughter were "platitudes bald and fringed out with the wear and tear of all old plays. . . . the old Lew Fields does not show through the obvious veneer."[28] Chicago patrons, however, voted with their seats, and all the shows were sold out despite the near-zero temperatures outside. This was all the validation that Fields needed. He sent a representative to New York to try to line up a Broadway theater.

David Belasco booked *Bosom Friends* into his Liberty Theater, a Klaw & Erlanger house, for an April 9 opening. During the intervening month, Fields replaced everybody in the cast except Matthilde Cottrelly (Anna, the motherly housekeeper). His new cast included some of the most respected and expensive legit actors around: Irene Fenwick (Gretel Krug), John Mason (Dr. Aaron Mather), Richard Bennett (Henry Mather), and Helen Ware (the vamp, Mrs. Carsairs). The stage director, Robert Milton (who staged the Princess Theatre shows), was rehired to work with the new cast. Suddenly, the simple comedy with eight characters and two sets had a weekly payroll as bloated as any of Fields' spectacles'. The price of orchestra seats at the Liberty was raised to $2.50.

Fields' philosophy was that New York audiences would not tolerate an inferior cast in an ensemble piece. In an interview, he pointed out that ever since the Music Hall he had always believed in giving the public the best cast that money can buy.[29] Burns Mantle uncharitably suggested that Fields was surrounding himself with a list of respected names to convince the audience that he was indeed a good actor, and that the scheme was an elaborate bit of self-promotion.

When *Bosom Friends* finally opened on April 9, first-nighters had been primed to expect a fiasco. Instead, they saw a first-rate ensemble of actors making the most of an antiquated, sentimental comedy-drama. For Fields, there was surprised, almost relieved, praise; for the play itself, almost universal disdain. Fields was credited with instilling a tone of wistful humor in the proceedings—"ten laughs to every tear" was his formula—that was a far remove from the kind of breast-beating pathos associated with Warfield. Several critics pointed out the daunting challenge of facing an audience that was used to seeing him poke and choke his friends instead of engaging them in homely discourses. There were repeated references to two old trees whose roots have interlocked (to separate them is to kill both), which was the playwright's attempt to create a poignant motif *à la* Ibsen.

Bosom Friends lasted seven weeks, not quite long enough to break even. Fields then took his powers of pathos to the Peerless lot, where he starred in the film *The Corner Grocer*. *Bosom Friends* had been a costly indulgence. It may have proved that Lew Fields had the ability to be a "serious" actor, but it did not convince his theater colleagues that audiences would rush to the theater to see Lew Fields the serious actor. Outside of his films for Brady, no offers of straight roles were forthcoming.

While there was some question of whether *Bosom Friends* was the right play for Lew Fields, there was no question that the timing of his production could not have been worse. Three days before its New York opening, the United States declared war on Imperial Germany. For the previous two and a half years, Broadway—like most of the country—had gone about its business with only an occasional acknowledgement of the continued carnage across the Atlantic. The torpedoing of the *Lusitania* in May, 1915, temporarily tore through the curtain of make-believe, for among its victims were the beloved producer Charles Frohman, actress Rita Jolivet, and playwrights Charles Klein and Jules Goodman. The outrage subsided quickly, however, replaced by a generalized distaste for visible symbols of European politics and culture.

By the end of 1916, President Wilson, who had just won re-election because "he kept us out of war," was preaching "preparedness." The Shuberts and other producers predicted that unsettled Americans would seek relief in escapist fare. The Palace prospered, and musicals and revues were sold out weeks in advance. American sentiment was turning against the Germans, exacerbated by reports of spies, German submarine warfare, and the mysterious explosions that levelled munitions plants in Jersey City. Anything German became suspect: German performers were booed, *The Prince of Pilsen* was reset in a French beer hall, and the Federal government confiscated waterfront property in Hoboken from private owners with German surnames. It was during this time that Lew Fields and his siblings began referring to their parents' origins as Polish or Russian rather than German.

Dutch comedians found that they could no longer get bookings in vaudeville or burlesque, while their Hebrew, Italian, and blackface colleagues were enjoying boom times. Nat Fields, recently remarried and scrambling for work, worried about his future: "My greatest fear is that we will become embroiled in a war with Germany, and then what will all of us German comedians do?" Some of them went north to Canada and became Irish comics. Nat went south instead with a travelling burlesque company which he called "Weber & Fields Musical Comedy Company." Nat, whose first appearance on stage was as a double for his brother in the Fregoli quick-change skit, had made a career out of playing Lew's hand-me-down roles; perhaps he had performed his brother's material for so long that he thought he was entitled to use it without prior approval. Charging one-dollar admission in a 3,000-seat theater, he presented *Fiddle Dee Dee* and *Hokey Pokey* to the bored soldiers at the Army camp in Chattanooga. Anti-German sentiments aside, a Weber & Fields entertainment was *sui generis*, and Nat Fields did land-office business.

Lawyers hired by the real Weber & Fields finally caught up with Nat Fields in Charleston, where the U.S. District Court issued an injunction forbidding the unauthorized use of their name. Lew had to disavow publicly any connection with Nat's production, which contained more blue material than any Weberfields show, and apologize to Joe Weber, who had warned him about family members' using their material. Lew's youngest brother had embarrassed him professionally and personally, which Lew never entirely forgave him for. Nat Fields' second-rate career foundered without his famous brother's support. Dutch comedy was never the same after the war, and Nat spent the rest of his career working in the seedier "burly-cue" joints. Nicknamed "Fashion Flash Fields," he would boast about his wardrobe rather than his stage exploits. His claim to fame was that he had "a thousand neckties and a suit for every hour of the day."

Within a month of the formal declaration of war, most of the country had joined the frenzy of mobilization. The entertainment industry was squeezed from all directions until political leaders realized its value as a propaganda vehicle. Even before the United States entered the war, the federal government had been assuming greater control of the railroads, reducing passenger service, and discouraging civilian freight with stiffer rates and taxes. Touring managers such as the veteran trouper Gus Hill had to cancel their road shows. Among the two million draftees were five thousand actors, which thinned out casts as well as audiences. Musical comedies eliminated chorus boys, and backstage crews were shorthanded. Theatrical supplies became expensive and scarce. When the government froze steel supplies, theaters under construction were left unfinished. Theater tickets were taxed, and patrons were encouraged to spend their cash on Liberty Bonds instead of frivolous expenditures. "Four minute men"—government teams pledged not to speak longer than four minutes—were allowed to sell bonds between acts. The Gay White Way went black every night at 10:45 to conserve fuel; a few months later, all theaters were ordered closed on Tuesdays for the same reason. By the fall of 1917, the war effort had sent box office receipts plummeting.

For Lew Fields, whose financial and professional status were already precarious, the war brought even greater anxiety and uncertainty. Returning from an eerily dark Broadway, he came home to a nearly empty house. His son Joseph and foster son Herb Harris gave up their successful poster advertising business to enlist in the military, Joe in the Naval Reserve and Herb Harris in the Army infantry. (Herbert tried to enlist by lying about his age but was found out). Frances, who had been living right around the corner on Riverside Drive with her husband, Charles Marcus, was in Switzerland doing Red Cross work.

Personally and professionally, Fields was more isolated than ever before. He had parted ways with the Shuberts, and his erstwhile partner Weber was scoring big as a producer of Victor Herbert musicals. Fields had gambled on a new career as a dramatic actor and had lost a small fortune, and some professional credibility as well. This time, when Charles Dillingham approached him about starring in a new revue at the Century, *Miss 1917*, Fields accepted eagerly—on condition that Dillingham's co-producer, Flo Ziegfeld, promise not to eject him from the theater. Ziegfeld treated his older colleague deferentially; when Ziegfeld announced Fields' participation in the revue, he mentioned that Fields would also be the "artistic advisor" for the comedy portions of the show. For this, Fields would be paid $1,750 a week, with a thirty-week pay-or-play guarantee. This was considerably more than what the Shuberts had paid him to produce and star in *Step This Way*. The fact that he would be a featured performer in a Klaw & Erlanger production was regarded as a slap in the face for the Shuberts.

It is doubtful that any wartime musical show had as much talent onstage and backstage as *Miss 1917*, except possibly one of the patriotic benefits. Intending it as a successor to their hit *The Century Girl*, Dillingham and Ziegfeld put together a dream team of old and new stars: music by Victor Herbert and Jerome Kern, book and lyrics by Guy Bolton and P. G. Wodehouse, staging by Ned Wayburn, scenic design by Joseph Urban, costumes by Lady Duff Gordon. The cast was equally stellar: Lew Fields, Irene Castle, Bessie McCoy Davis, Cecil Lean, Savoy and Brennan, Van and Schenck, Marion Davies, Ann Pennington, George White, Vivienne Segal, Elizabeth Brice, and Charles King. In a minor role was Herbert Fields, who told Ziegfeld that he was there "to keep Pop from being lonesome."

The production also reunited Fields with a former collaborator and a favored old employee. Since leaving Fields, Ned Wayburn had perfected his trend-setting choreographic style in his own *Town Topics* and in two editions of the Ziegfeld Follies. Back in 1911, Wayburn had told Fields not to hire Irene Foote, but Fields had anyway, mostly to satisfy her future husband, Vernon Castle. Now she was one of the stars of *Miss 1917*, while her husband was a captain in the British Royal Flying Corps. A decorated hero with 150 missions in France, Vernon Castle had just been transferred stateside—to Fort Worth, Texas—as an aviation instructor. During rehearsals, Fields frequently asked Irene for word of her "brave husband."

Miss 1917 had something for almost everybody. Though the book's authors, Bolton and Wodehouse, had publicly scorned the Weberfields style of show, its scale and structure owed much to the oldsters' productions. The opening sketch established the thread of a plot that reappeared sporadically throughout the evening. Set on a pickle farm owned by Hiram Askem (Lew Fields), it burlesqued a popular drama, *Turn to the Right*, and satirized a film production shooting on location. There were frequent references to the war effort, even if the show itself exhibited not a trace of wartime economies.

For sentimentalists, there was a medley of old favorites from Tin Pan Alley and Broadway: "In the Good Old Summer Time," "Under the Bamboo Tree," and "Dinah," with Cecil Lean impersonating Peter Dailey. The Weberfields' veteran Bessie McCoy Davis sang "We Want to Laugh," about modern audiences who were "tired of those strutting leading men / And posing juveniles." Bolton and Wodehouse's refrain suggested why Fields' attempt to become a second Warfield had failed: "We want to laugh. We want to laugh. / Of lovesick heroes weary we've grown / We like Lew Fields, and funny reels / And love to see Fred Stone." The Act One finale exploited a typical Wayburn device: a throng of beauties clog-dancing down a steep stairway that extended from the rafters to the stage.

In Ziegfeld's revues, the comedy sketches were typically the least consistent ingredient. In the cavernous Century, comedians were at a particular disadvantage. By all accounts, Fields' presence put the comedy on a level with the spectacular ensembles and the song-and-dance specialties. As Hiram Askem, proprietor of the near-bankrupt pickle farm, he also appeared as a bartender in "The Deluge" saloon, where he mixed wartime drinks, measuring out the booze with an eyedropper and keeping the sugar in the cash register. He reprised his famous role as a sadistic hairdresser, only this time he was working in a hotel beauty salon where he tried to put a permanent wave into the carrot top of female impersonator Bert Savoy.

Fields' return to comedy met with enthusiastic approval, and the entire revue was strongly praised: "Sets a new mark . . . seldom has an entertainment of this sort been so profusely liberal, so evenly balanced and sustained"; "A brilliant revue"; "The triumph of *Miss 1917* was not a matter of doubt from the first scene to the last."[30] So it came as a great surprise to performers and critics alike when *Miss 1917* was rumored to be in trouble by early December. Feeling the first ripples of America's entry into the war, theatrical attendance went into a sharp slump just as *Miss 1917* was opening. Already, half of the year's seventy-five productions had failed; with no touring possibilities, borderline shows closed early. December set a new record for poor box office in almost every part of the country. By Christmas, the principal backer of *Miss 1917*, Otto Kahn, had decided that it was a losing proposition and withdrew his support. The revue closed January 4, 1918, and Ziegfeld and Dillingham's company, the Century Amusement Corporation, was placed in receivership.

Of the principal actors, Fields was the heaviest loser; he had been paid for only nine weeks of a guaranteed thirty-week pay-or-play contract. Through attorney Max Steuer (a Shubert lawyer), Fields filed suit for breach of contract in the amount of $21,500. The receivers quickly discovered that the Century Amusement

Corporation possessed a capital stock of but $5,000. Fields was unable to recover any of the money owed him.

It was Fields' bad luck that when he finally acted in somebody else's musical show, it was for the one producer who was an even more prodigal spender than Fields. Later, in a conversation with librettist Harry B. Smith, Fields complained about how Ziegfeld had duped him, and commented: "The fact is we are in a dirty business—dirty, but fascinating."[31] Lew Fields was finally waking up to the truth about modern show biz.

Two nights before *Miss 1917* closed, Lew and Rose celebrated their silver wedding anniversary, a subdued affair with the two remaining children and a few other members of the immediate family. Counting on his large weekly salary from the Century show, he had promised his creditors that he would make regular payments. Once again, he was forced to make excuses, cajole, apologize, and look for new lenders.

For the first time since he arrived on Broadway in 1896, Lew Fields was without a production even in the planning stages. January 1918 was not a good time to be trying to get a new production under way. A nationwide coal shortage had prompted theater closings; train service was cut drastically, and a temporary ban had been put on travelling theatrical companies. With the lights-out curfew policies being strictly enforced, Broadway was now being referred to as "the Late White Way." One journalist described the Rialto as "one long strip of gloom."

For Fields, the bad news in the coming weeks must have confirmed that impression. On February 15, Vernon Castle was killed in a collision of biplanes during a training flight over a Texas aviation field. Flight instructors usually sat in the second position in the trainer planes, but Castle had been riding in the front seat. He died twenty minutes after the crash; his trainee suffered only bruises.

Irene Castle, in their home in New York, did not believe the news for an hour after the first telephone call; Vernon had been reported dead once before over France. When she received a telegram from Castle's fellow officers, she realized it was true and collapsed. "It was a brave man's death, and it is not a woman's part to complain," was all that she could say.

Fields, who according to Helen Hayes, "loved Vernon Castle like a son," was understandably distraught. Funeral services for the actor-aviator were held on February 20; soldiers and theater folk packed the actor's church, "The Little Church Around the Corner." As an actor and dancer, Castle's face had been pale and thin, but mourners that last day saw him looking tanned and rugged, with the Croix de Guerre pinned to his breast. Outside, over two thousand mourners stood in a cold drizzle until the coffin draped in British and American flags passed, carried by six soldiers.

Another blow later that same week sent Fields reeling. His brother and business manager, Charley, was diagnosed with tuberculosis, the same thing that had killed their older brother, Max. For several weeks, the normally robust Charley had been weak and often feverish. He was admitted to Miss Allston's Sanitarium, but there was little hope that he would recover.

Since the days of the Weber & Fields Music Hall, Charley had been Lew's right-hand man. Given Lew's remarkable ineptness in his business dealings, it would seem logical to blame Charley for not being more circumspect. In fact, Lew would not let anybody else, including Charley, make decisions for him. Sometimes Charley would not even know a deal was on the table until Lew informed him of his decision. More factotum than manager, he faithfully tried to hold together the fraying patchwork of his brother's business ventures. The true measure of Charley's abilities was that he kept Lew from financial ruin for so long.

Lew's renewed gambling activities did nothing to help his financial condition. Since his return from Hollywood, he had become a member of the Partridge Club, a group of prominent Manhattan businessmen and lawyers who met weekly for dinner and poker, and once a month for an evening of *chemin de fer*. When Fields first joined, they were meeting at the Hotel Knickerbocker, but police crackdowns on gambling in hotels forced them to move to the Ritz, and finally to the Hotel Imperial.

Shortly after the club's January 26 meeting, Assistant District Attorney Swann announced that club members would be subpoenaed to testify in his inquiry into gambling establishments in New York. State law provided for gambling fines of five times the amount won or lost. First called was the club's president, an attorney named George Bauchle, who cooperated fully by providing a membership list consisting of over "one hundred names of prominent men." Among the stockbrokers, attorneys, and doctors were two commanders of the Russian Navy, one judge, a former commissioner to Mayor McClellan, one playboy playwright (Wilson Mizner), and Lew Fields.

Also on the list were at least two well-known professional gamblers, Arnold Rothstein and his partner Nat Evans. These men, said D.A. Swann, "are using the club . . . for purposes of getting at men of wealth and social standing."[32] Actually, "A. R.," as Rothstein was called, was quite wealthy already; his townhouse was around the corner from the Fieldses, on Riverside Drive and Eighty-fourth. A. R. laughed off D.A. Swann's inquiry. The following year, Rothstein and Evans masterminded the fix of the 1919 World Series, otherwise known as the "Black Sox scandal."

As one of the most visible club members, Fields could not avoid the scrutiny of the court of inquiry. On March 5, he and several other members were subpoenaed to testify. Fields begged off, claiming that he had a rehearsal; he promised to come at an hour's notice if called by telephone. Meanwhile, D.A. Swann and Judge Wadhams had become figures of public ridicule in the press because they could not understand the rules for *chemin de fer* (Mizner had facetiously testified that the game required no intelligence, "only bull strength"). No further action was taken against the Partridge Club. Nevertheless, the exposure had been embarrassing to Lew Fields, for it held up to public scrutiny the extent of his gambling habits. In so doing, it damaged his credibility with lenders; potential backers would think twice before putting up thousands of dollars to be managed by a known gambler. The publicity did nothing to endear Fields to his son-in-law, Charles Marcus, who had already lent the family a substantial amount.

A few days before Castle's death, the new Jolson revue, *Sinbad*, opened at the Winter Garden. By some unknown contrivance, Fields and his family were given house seats in the same box as Joe Weber and his family. Perhaps it was Lee Shubert's hope to reunite the two old partners under his management; or perhaps Fields himself asked Lee to arrange it. Desperate for work, Fields used the coincidence to suggest that they lunch together the next day. The sight of the two together in public brought so many well-wishers to their table that they could hardly finish a sentence. Over lunch, Fields casually speculated about the two of them getting back together. Weber, like everybody else on Broadway, knew of Fields' misfortune in *Miss 1917*, so he may have been half expecting to run into Fields. Would Web be willing to come out of retirement one more time?

Reluctantly, Weber agreed, perhaps more out of sympathy for his lifelong friend than from any desire to return to performing. Underscoring the urgency of Fields' financial situation, they chose a musical already produced on the West Coast rather than waiting for a new show to be written for them. *A Peck of Pickles* had been a musical comedy vehicle for the foremost Weber & Fields imitators, Kolb & Dill. The fact that Weber & Fields were looking to their imitators for material should have been a warning sign.

Weber & Fields brought in two veteran Broadway hacks to rework the property: Louis Hirsch to compose a new score, and George Hobart to update the libretto. The opening scene unfolded in a New England village where Weber was a deli owner and Fields was a shoemaker. Both are about to be expelled from the village, Weber for selling liquor illicitly and Fields for gambling (!). After a chorus number and dance specialty, a city "drummer" (travelling salesman) sells spiked candy to the villagers. The entire populace is induced to misbehave, going on a "ragtime jag." Finally exhausted, they fall asleep. The second act is their collective dream—inexplicably, Washington, D.C., at the time of the Civil War.

In most ways, it was a pitifully old-fashioned entertainment, further weakened by Weber & Fields' softened dialect and knockabout and the absence of burlesque targets. Though the book contained almost no topical references, Hobart was instructed to find a place to "show the Kaiser up in a bad light." He obliged with a scene in which Weber's character was being taunted by his friends until he blurted out, "To hell with the Kaiser!" This was presumably a surefire crowd-pleaser of a line.

The casting was equally problematic. Instead of name talents, they went for glitz. The featured performers were the Dolly Sisters, Rosie and Jenny, Hungarian-born identical twins who danced a little and sang even less. The Dolly Sisters had become vaudeville's favorite clothes-horses. Elegant and beautiful, they were wined and a dined by the world's most eligible bachelors. What they lacked in talent they made up for in glamour and attitude. Observed a *Variety* reviewer, "The Dollys are the Dollys, and people accept them in that way."

In rehearsals, Fields found the Dollys less easy to accept. Instead of a mélange of humorous patter and familiar dance steps, they were given real parts, with real dialogue and stage business. The constant changes to the book upset them, and they resented the long rehearsals. By the time *Back Again* began its previews in Philadelphia, the Dolly Sisters were becoming contentious, their tempers easily ruffled and frequently placated.

The Shuberts had tentatively agreed to book *Back Again* into one of their

New York houses for the summer. After seeing the Philadelphia tryout, however, J. J. had second thoughts. The wartime economy had created a sudden theater shortage, and shows that would have previously been given an extra few weeks to develop an audience were being packed off to the warehouse. Fields, driven by his desperation for a paycheck, wanted to try to salvage the show, and Weber reluctantly agreed. They recast several of the principals and worked with Hobart to rewrite the book, but Weber soon concluded that the show was hopeless. It closed in Philadelphia after playing barely a month, with losses of over $25,000.

Still, Fields persisted: he announced that the book and score would be completely revised for the fall season in New York, and he hired Ned Wayburn, on loan from Ziegfeld, to stage the new numbers. What the show needed, *Variety* agreed, were specialty acts; Fields signed two of the most expensive, Adele Rowland and the team of Clark and Bergman.

By the time *Back Again* was finally shelved, Weber was so annoyed with his spendthrift partner that he would not speak to him. Since the closing of *Miss 1917* and Charley Fields' illness, Lew's personal finances had deteriorated to the point where he was often short of cash for daily expenses. Hoping to a certainty that *Back Again* would turn a profit (hadn't all of his previous reunions with Weber been moneymakers?), he borrowed from Peter to pay Paul. Weber warned employees in his organization not to lend Fields any money, but Lew's warm smile and sad brown eyes had their way with Weber's business manager, William Oviatt, who became a $600 touch and had to sue Fields to recover it.

Actors were among the most enthusiastic and generous in their support of the war effort, despite the dire effects of the war on their livelihood. Broadway stars such as E. H. Sothern and Elsie Janis brought songs and sketches to American soldiers overseas. George M. Cohan renewed his claim to being Broadway's most fervent flag-waver with "Over There," a song inspired by the first three notes of a military bugle call. Laurette Taylor, Chauncey Olcott, Ethel Barrymore, and John Drew toured the country for the Red Cross, and Harry Lauder gave them his salary from three shows each week. For the Second Liberty Loan, the Palace Theatre alone turned in $750,000. Producers such as Klaw & Erlanger, Albee, and the Shuberts contributed hundreds of thousands of dollars to the Liberty Loan drives, as much to forestall further governmental restrictions on the theater as to express their patriotism.

With free talent and backstage labor, actors and producers in uniform organized large-scale revues for civilian audiences in Broadway theaters. For some young men aspiring to a show business career, it was their first professional experience. In November, 1917, Fields' foster son, Private Herbert H. Harris, in the Army's Rainbow Division, organized a benefit performance for the 107th Infantry at Camp Upton. Ironically, military service now gave Harris and Fields' eldest son Joe an excuse to indulge in the one activity their father had previously forbidden.

Located in the potato fields near Yaphank, Long Island, Camp Upton was a major staging area for troops being shipped off to France. It was a dull and desolate place to await marching orders. What was needed was some healthy form of diversion—say, a motion picture theater. Private Harris had all the right connections to set up a benefit performance to raise the necessary funds. Through his stepfather, he arranged for the use of the Forty-fourth Street Theater (the former Lew Fields' Theater), and an all-star cast: the Dolly Sisters, Elsie Janis, boxer Jim Corbett, Bessie McCoy, Frank Tinney, Donald Brian, and Lew Fields. The one-time-only performance raised $14,000 for the Camp Upton movie house. Harris was permanently bitten with the theater bug; he became the Fields family "angel" for the Rodgers-Hart-Fields productions in the 1920's and for Joe Fields' Broadway hits with Jerome Chodorov.

In a similar fashion, Ensign Joe Fields of the U.S. Naval Reserve took advantage of his military service to work in show business. With 250 of his shipmates from the Pelham Naval Training Station, he mounted a massive revue called *Biff! Boom!* at the cavernous Century Theatre in May, 1918. Joe contributed several sketches, and appeared as a "stevedore show girl" (he was a hulking six-footer) in one of the revue's all-male kick lines. Broadway audiences considered it a novelty and flocked to it for its run of two weeks.

The theater slump in late 1917 had passed like some freak storm, and by the summer of 1918, Broadway box offices were prospering—despite ticket taxes, bond drives, railroad restrictions, and the "lights-off" curfews. Lee Shubert's prophecy notwithstanding, Broadway was inundated with war plays by the spring of 1918: *Billeted, Three Faces East, Watch Your Neighbors, Allegiance*—and *Friendly Enemies*. To be sure, they were more like propaganda pieces than dramas exploring the subject of war. The typical plot featured naïve or misguided Americans who learn of the insidious workings of the Kaiser's minions. In *Friendly Enemies*, the season's most popular war play, authors Sam Shipman and Aaron Hoffman spun a familiar tale of two longtime friends who came to the United States in early life to escape German oppression and made good. Karl Pfeiffer retains the *kultur* of the Fatherland, while his pal has become completely assimilated. Though still great friends at heart, their constant wrangling over their differing political outlooks is, at least initially, comic in its intensity.

The charm of the play reportedly came from the characterizations of the two old friends, for the roles called for a wide range of emotional shadings, from comedy to pathos. The result was a crowd-pleasing blend of humor and melodrama wrapped in homilies, and patriotic and topical references.

Producer Al Woods offered Fields the leading role, but he declined "out of respect for my sons in uniform," for the role required that he deliver several pro-German speeches. When Fields turned down the role, Woods hired Louis Mann to play opposite Sam Bernard. After the show's strong Broadway opening, Woods tried to persuade Weber & Fields to star in a London production. Weber, however, was still angry over Fields' behavior during *Back Again* and refused to share a stage with him. (Others suggested that Weber knew his limits as a performer and would not undertake a serious role.) For the Western territory, Woods organized another company around Jess Dandy and Sam Sidman. Woods' corner on Dutch comedians was almost complete when Fields finally saw the opportunity for what it was and agreed to star in the Eastern company tour. With the war drawing to a close, *Friendly Enemies* became the apotheosis of "Dutch" comedy, and its swan song. Low "Dutch" comedy had been absorbed (and effaced) by the legit stage just as its German-American models had given up their *kultur* and become assimilated in the American mainstream.

On August 26, 1918, Lew Fields opened in *Friendly Enemies* at the Plymouth Theatre in Boston. Playing opposite him was Charles Winninger, an up-and-coming comedian who had risen through the ranks of burlesque and vaudeville. In 1912, Fields had cast Winninger in *The Wall Street Girl* in a role supporting Blanche Ring. (Later, Winninger and Ring had a brief marriage). In 1927, Winninger became the original Captain Andy in *Showboat*, a character who bore certain similarities to the henpecked but wise, foolish-fond fathers that Fields had perfected a decade earlier.

Fields' ability to play serious material was still a revelation to most audiences, despite *Bosom Friends* and his solo film roles. In *Friendly Enemies*, Fields had perhaps the best role of his career for demonstrating the breadth of his acting talent:

> In the lighter moments there were reminders of the days agone in the methods Mr. Fields employed to enrich his comedy, but in the more subtle moments he displayed a skill and depth of thought. . . . Mr. Fields has this gift [to express deep-seated emotion], although heretofore he has never been afforded an opportunity of demonstrating it.[33]

And:

> In his hands, Karl Pfeiffer becomes a real human being. His antics, beliefs, arguments, furies, make the audience laugh to the point of hysteria, while the next moment his pathetic speeches draw tears.[34]

The *Herald*'s reviewer singled out for praise the scene in which Fields' character hears of his boy's death on the bombed transport. The scene was no stretch for Fields to play; his son Joe's Naval Reserve unit was on active duty in the North Atlantic, and foster son Herbert Harris had been sent to France.

The quick success of *Friendly Enemies* made it possible for Lew Fields once more to stave off financial ruin. The show opened barely two weeks after his brother Charley's death from tuberculosis. Lew's business affairs had been in serious disarray since before Charley had entered the sanitarium in February. He had failed to recover even a fraction of the salary owed him for *Miss 1917*, and two of the principals from *Back Again* were suing him for breach of contract.

Based on the box office returns in Boston and Philadelphia, Fields and Woods had every reason to expect a long and profitable tour. Events prevented it from living up to its promise. In the summer of 1918, a virulent strain of influenza— dubbed "Spanish"—broke out in the military camps in the East and Southeast. Initially, government authorities downplayed its seriousness because they feared the publicity would damage the war effort. Meanwhile, military personnel unwittingly dispersed the bug. By early September, the epidemic had spread nationwide. The known medical treatments—poultices, camphor oil rubbed on the chest, mercury preparations—were useless. For many of the victims, the virus proved fatal in less than thirty-six hours. In some New York neighborhoods, wakes were as common as milk deliveries, and funeral crêpe became the predominant foliage.

By the beginning of October, authorities were closing all places of amusement throughout the country. Many touring companies were temporarily stranded. College football games were played, but no spectators were allowed in the stands. By the end of the month, the epidemic had killed 196,000 in the United States alone. Woods postponed bringing *Friendly Enemies* back to New York, then booked it for the Hudson. In early November, as the epidemic seemed to abate, many theaters reopened just in time to feel the effects of a second wave of the Spanish influenza. The euphoria surrounding the end of the war depressed theater attendance for the rest of the month. Managers and owners yanked war plays from the boards, convinced that the public wanted to forget the war.

Only two war plays survived the flu epidemic and the peacetime amnesia: *The Better 'Ole,* and *Friendly Enemies.* In mid-December, Woods sent the latter on the road, where it prospered well into the new year, finally returning to New York in January for a nine-week run, and then brainstorming the Eastern and Midwestern one-night stands until May. As a manager, Al Woods was a genius at milking every dollar out of a road company. Woods always did well by Fields, and vice versa. For Fields, however, acting in somebody else's show was only a temporary expedient.

CHAPTER XV

Broadway Broke

In his broadest burlesques, [Fields] preserves a glint of infinite sadness. . . . Not even Walter Hampden in *Hamlet* is so successful in suggesting the infinite gap between the reach of a man and his grasp.
Heywoud Broun, *New York Tribune*, June 11, 1919

RESTORED to box office popularity and financial solvency, Fields was eager to produce and star in another musical comedy. It had been three
years since *Step This Way* (a mere reworking of his hit of 1907, *The
Girl Behind the Counter*) and six years since *All Aboard*. The Broadway landscape had changed significantly since the last time a Fields musical had scored a
hit there. The war effort had pulled the plug on the Gay White Way, but after the
Armistice, the lights of Broadway returned, more garish and plentiful than ever.
Around Times Square, huge illuminated billboards for Wrigley's Gum, Lucky Strike,
Four Roses, and Pepsi-Cola outshown the electric marquees for theaters and movie
palaces. The most elaborate of these advertisements—six giant marionette soldiers performing their drill for Wrigley's Gum, the scantily clad White Rock nymph
sitting near her reflecting pool, and the playful kitten batting at the spool of
Corticelli Silk—were mechanized tableaux that used the façades and roofs of
theaters, restaurants, and other buildings as a stage for providing free spectacles
to the public. The once-chic Hotel Knickerbocker, where Lew Fields and Lee
Shubert still dined, looked quaint in the midst of the towering electrical displays
and the steady stream of taxis and streetcars.

Forty-second Street between Broadway and Eighth Avenue was now thick
with theaters. Theatergoers who could not get tickets for the newest hit could go
next door or across the street and find a satisfying evening's entertainment at
another theater. The brothers and sisters of Lew Fields' Midnight Sons, Sun Dodgers,
and Pleasure Seekers flocked to the cabarets and nightclubs that proliferated up
and down Broadway. These nightspots offered interactive diversions with a delicious tinge of criminality—boozing (soon to be illegal), social dancing to "Negro"
or "jazz" music (the word "jazz" itself carried sexual overtones), racy revues that
brought chorus girls into the audience, and earthy performers such as red-hot-
mamma Sophie Tucker and the queen of the shimmy, Gilda Gray. The evening
might begin at the theater, but a midnight visit to Maxim's, Reisenweber's, or the

375

Palais Royale was replacing the Broadway show as the quintessential New York experience.[1]

One had to be young and affluent to keep up the pace. Youth, rather than maturity, became the model. It was no longer incongruous for sober-minded businessmen—"butter-and-egg men"—to emulate the leisure-time pursuits of Hollywood celebrities, college boys, and sports heroes. Adult women took their fashion cues from the flappers, whose juvenile, angular figures and bobbed hair (popularized by Irene Castle) became the feminine ideal. In the cities, the tired businessman and his wife were looking to their well-heeled sons and daughters for lessons in how to have a good time.

The purveyors of popular entertainment—for stage and screen as well as in the cabarets—adjusted their presentations accordingly. On the Broadway stage, the cult of the flapper led to chorus girls who were more lithe, agile, and frankly attired, while the popularity of social dancing encouraged producers to emphasize more-demanding choreography and more-athletic dance turns in their shows. Movie producers exploited racy new ideas about romance, marriage, and personal expression. To satisfy daring urbanites as well as the more tradition-bound rural audiences, filmmakers used the slightest pretext to include scenes of wild nightlife—but then also showed the grim consequences of urban sin.

The giddiness and self-indulgence of prosperous city dwellers was not simply a celebration of an end to wartime austerity. It had a defiant air. It was a challenge to the old social order as typified by the members of the Anti-Saloon League—White Anglo-Saxon Protestants and their small-town lifestyle, with their Victorian morals and xenophobic social attitudes. For tired businessmen since the turn of the century, the pleasures of the theater, lobster palace, and nightclub were the city's rewards for success and hard work. Now these pleasures were being threatened by "reformers" mobilized and empowered by the war effort. They were no longer merely the eccentric hicks and dour zealots who had been such easy targets for parody on the popular stage. (Fields had satirized this sensibility in *The High Cost of Loving*, in which the fear was inspired by the local Purity League).

The infamous Eighteenth Amendment did not officially go into effect until January 16, 1920, but wartime restrictions on alcohol sale and consumption had already raised the specter of national alcohol prohibition. The same patriotic zeal that had darkened theaters and taxed tickets had put a curfew on cabarets and banned the sale of liquor after 1:00 a.m. In October, 1919, the Volstead Act made it clear that Prohibition would include beer and wine as well as distilled spirits. Both the "wets" and the "drys" understood the link between liquor and other urban diversions such as gambling, dancing, ragtime, and jazz. As Irving Berlin pointed out in his song for *The Ziegfeld Follies of 1919*, "You Cannot Make Your Shimmy Shake on Tea."

Urbanites regarded the drive for a national ban on alcohol sales and consumption as the last gasp of small-town Protestants trying to control city life. And they were right: Prohibition forced many cabarets and the Broadway lobster palaces to close. In so doing, the Prohibitionists turned the activities associated with these resorts into "fashionable" crimes appealing to vast numbers of Americans of all classes.

The Prohibitionists' "noble experiment" was but an early symptom of a growing contagion of intolerance. At its most absurd, it manifested itself in a ban on jokes and disrespectful references to Prohibition on the stage and screen. But the intolerance was rarely so laughable. The nationalistic passions that had been directed against the wartime enemy were redirected against foreigners in general, particularly Eastern and Southern Europeans and Japanese. Two weeks before Prohibition went into effect, Attorney General A. Mitchell Palmer ordered the arrest of 3,000 allegedly alien radicals and held them without hearings. Congress began debate over bills to restrict immigration along ethnically discriminatory lines. When it was revealed that 2,000 of the 7,000 union musicians in the New York City local were not United States citizens, the Federal government ordered all alien musicians to take out citizenship papers or face deportation. At its most extreme, the intolerance manifested itself in the revival of the Ku Klux Klan and the prosecution of two Italian radicals, Sacco and Vanzetti, for an alleged murder.

Booze, bolshevism, racially impure immigrants, gangsters, sexual permissiveness—small-town moralists could impute every contemporary evil to the big cities, particularly New York. Most of the major social conflicts seemed to fit into the opposition of country and city: drys versus wets, Victorian morality versus sexual freedom (the "new woman"), Americans of Aryan stock versus the "new" immigrants, even old versus young. Within the city, the cabaret was the symbolic site where many of these social issues converged and found a clear articulation. If "puttin' on the ritz" by going to a cabaret was one of the most cherished rights of the urbanite, then the new social sanctions had to be circumvented. Make no mistake, the tired businessman (now more tired than ever) was still firmly committed to a world where respectability and appearances mattered. In his leisure time, however, he craved the image of irresponsibility and indulgence. The cabarets and speakeasies catered to this directly, while the stage and, to a lesser extent, movies, presented it vicariously, at a safer remove.

For the tired businessman and his midnight sons and daughters, this meant a dual or compartmentalized existence: a private realm of illicit fun and personal expression that existed quite apart from the public realm of productive commercial pursuits. These conflicting goals could only be realized by a double life. The hard-working broker or shopkeeper by day became the insatiable pleasure seeker at night, not accountable for his activities after dark. "My candle burns at both ends," was how Edna St. Vincent Millay described it in a famous stanza.

Few postwar musicals embodied these elements more completely than the show that marked Fields' return to Broadway as a producer and star. *A Lonely Romeo* opened on June 10, 1919, at the Shubert Theatre with a plot and production numbers that revealed as keen an understanding of the follies of the day as any of the Music Hall burlesques.

Fields' character, Augustus Tripp, *is* burning the candle at both ends: by day a middle-aged hatter and a henpecked family man, he turns into a "cabaret fiend" after dark, disguising himself as a younger man to indulge his dancing prowess with the young women he meets. Tripp's innocent philandering leads to comic complications when he pretends to be his own son from a fictitious first marriage. Caught in the rain at 4:00 a.m. with Maizie, his dance partner (Frances Cameron), he gallantly offers her shelter in his Fifth Avenue hat shop. Maizie falls asleep in his private office, and Tripp finds a comfortable spot in his show window, where he is found the next morning by his prospective son-in-law (Alan Hale). When Tripp's daughter Sybil (Violette Wilson) and wife Alexina (Octavia Broske) show up, Tripp must invent every sort of stratagem to keep them from discovering who is in his office, including increasingly quick costume changes. By the third act, his final lightning change takes under ten seconds, during which time he changes wigs, coat, vest, collar, tie, and shoes with spats. The Act One closer was a made-to-order comedy bit. Like the soda fountain, the barbershop, and the delicatessen, it was built around a prop and an uncooperative customer. In this case, it was a hat, or series of hats, and the customer was one Ichabod Wintergreen, a large, cantankerous Westerner who just so happens to be Maizie's uncle. Wintergreen arrives at closing time, when Tripp, after an especially trying day, is eager to leave. Every hat is either too large or too small. Exasperated, Tripp places a pearl-colored derby over Wintergreen's ponderous dome while telling him how handsome it looks. The derby, much too large, keeps falling over the irate customer's eyes except when Tripp puts his thumb in the back of the hatband. Not easily persuaded, Wintergreen wants to try it on one more time. It was not a particularly original bit, having been used in vaudeville many years earlier, but Fields' unique characterization had the audience in stitches.

Fields managed to top the hat scene in the Act Two finale. In his disguise as Augustus Jr., he visits the candy shop owned by his daughter Sybil's boyfriend. There he opens a suitcase and hands out samples of liquor-laced confections to the customers. It is not long before the marshmallow highballs and nougatine Manhattans have the customers soused and singing rag lines and competing with each other in a "cutting" contest for ragtime dancing honors.

Fields had used the same "spiked" candy bit in *Back Again*, but the intervening months had given a special urgency to the premise. Now, instead of being a mere pretext for some eccentric dancing, it reminded the audience that the enforcement of Prohibition (the Volstead Act) was only weeks away. Moreover, the spiked candy—a metaphor for innocent indulgence—seemed more appropriate to Fields' characterization of Augustus Tripp.

To the tune of "The Candy Jag," dance director Jack Mason built the souse routine to a frenzied pitch by featuring specialty dancers, some of the best from vaudeville, alone or in couples. The climax of the routine came when the fifty-two-year-old Fields, who had been looking on and ad-libbing in a genial fashion, performed a half dozen handsprings across the stage. The audience erupted in applause and wild cheering. Their response called for a speech.

Fields stepped forward, perspiring and breathing hard, shy as ever of curtain speeches, and admitted that he had just enough breath left to say "Thank you." On opening night, he then performed two more handsprings in honor of his new grandchildren—twin boys born to Frances and Charles Marcus a few days earlier.

In the third act, set in suburban Pelham, Tripp untangles the romantic knots he unwittingly created. Heeding the advice of his son Larry (Harry Clarke), Tripp agrees to end his double life by faking the drowning of his "son" (his alter ego) in the Long Island Sound. Henceforth, Tripp intends to act his age. He confesses his deception to Maizie. Removing his thick red wig to reveal his thinning grey locks, he jokes that he was an "evening edition" in the one, and a "morning edition" in the other. Adds Maizie with a sly wink, "and a sporting edition the rest of the time." At the final curtain of *A Lonely Romeo*, Augustus Tripp is neither remorseful nor lonely.

A Lonely Romeo was also Fields' debut as a credited author. His co-author was Harry B. Smith, musical comedy's most prolific librettist. Smith had become the theater critics' favorite whipping boy; they invented the adjective "harry-b-smithed" to describe his facile, cliché-ridden style. Fields and Harry B. had worked together once before, on the Music Hall production of *Hurly Burly*, twenty years earlier.

Reviewers naturally found fault with the book, attributing the most clichéd aspects of the story—the philandering husband and the comedy built on mistaken identity—to Harry B. Smith. What made the show a hit was Fields' ability to refurbish this shopworn comic opera premise with up-to-the-minute accessories. The strengths of *A Lonely Romeo* were Fields' strengths: his "genuinely human humor" (as one critic described it) and his staging, particularly his use of dance. The sharpness of the social observations, the comedy tinged with pathos, the crisp pacing, and the youthful delight in a new dance or a new mechanical device all bore the Fields imprint.

An early draft of a script belonging to Harry B. Smith reveals that almost every one of Fields' lines in the first act was rewritten, presumably with Fields during rehearsals.[2] The opening scene, for example, was changed in rehearsals from a theater exterior to the exterior of an all-night restaurant-cabaret. Not only did this provide a more effective way to establish Tripp's character, it also allowed Fields to use a characteristic staging device. The first-act curtain opens to reveal the exterior of the Shimmering Pheasant Restaurant, a two-storey façade with stained glass windows on the first floor and dancing couples visible through the open windows upstairs. The merry revellers—men and women of the chorus—are dancing to frenetic ragtime (or "jazz," to use the newest lingo). Rain begins to fall, but the dancers are unfazed; waiters lower the window sashes so that the audience can see only the dancers' legs and feet. Fields and Ned Wayburn had used the same technique for staging a chorus routine in *The Midnight Sons* (the shoe store scene), but here, in the window of a cabaret, the lighting and framing emphasized the agility and exuberance of the youthful limbs. Coming at the start of the program, it also announced that this was a show about people who "gotta dance." Apart from Fields' masterful performance, it was the dancing that provoked the most favorable comments.

By enacting the story of a youth-obsessed middle-aged man, Fields himself seemed rejuvenated. As Fields himself had said in a 1916 interview: "The very element which makes the musical stage what it is, high spirits, laughter, melody, song, dance and gaiety, are tonics for the jaded intellect of age and put new blood into withered and infirm limbs. And it is these elements which insure the permanency of musical comedy. It is only required of the light form of musical show that, like a newspaper, it be up to date and in the fashion of the day."

In the six years since *All Aboard*, it appeared as though Fields had lost touch with "the very elements which make the musical stage what it is." Behind his back, his employees (and his children) had begun referring to him as "Pop" Fields. Then came *A Lonely Romeo*, and Fields was the producer, co-author, and star of a musical that captured the spirit of the emerging Jazz Age. Who or what accounted for Fields' revitalized vision?

The inspiration may have come from an unlikely source. Among the supporting players in the cast of *A Lonely Romeo* was twenty-one-year-old Herbert Fields. Ever since the elder Fields' financial problems had made it impossible for his son to finish at Columbia, the stagestruck young man had been pursuing a full-time theatrical career. In addition to playing bit parts in *Step This Way* and *Miss 1917*, Herbert had been writing sketches, directing, and choreographing amateur musicals for the Akron Club, whose other members included his sister Dorothy, Larry Hart, and seventeen-year-old Richard Rodgers.

In *A Lonely Romeo*, Herbert originally played Milton, a bit part that gave him the opportunity to "feed" his father a few laugh lines. "They looked alike and talked ditto," observed one reviewer; "[Herbert] has a quiet, easy manner, a good comedy method," said another.[3] Later, Herbert replaced Harry Clarke in the role of Larry, Augustus Tripp's son, who learns what his old man is up to and chastises him for not acting responsibly. Despite the good reviews, Lew tried to steer Herbert away from the footlights. According to one account, Fields Senior was rather blunt about it; after seeing Herbert perform in another play, he reportedly said, "Now I *know* you should be an author."[4] Lew's vote of no confidence effectively ended Herbert's acting career.

Herbert's value to his father lay elsewhere. Herbert, and to a lesser extent, Dorothy, were becoming their father's eyes and ears on the changing popular tastes. Their enthusiasm for the Princess Theatre musicals, jazz, and the latest in fashions, dances, and slang brought Lew into contact with these developments on a daily basis. Like the emblematic tired businessman of the Jazz Age, Fields was looking to the younger generation for lessons in how to have a good time.

Whether observing German tradesmen in the Lower East Side or his *nouveau riche* neighbors on the Upper West Side, Fields' most inspired characterizations were based on the people closest at hand. Herbert, Dorothy, and their many friends became his new models. Eschewing the cold detachment of the satirist, Fields empathized with his characters' foibles, hence the "glint of infinite sadness" observed by Heywood Broun. He understood what would delight the Tired Businessman because he was one himself. In *A Lonely Romeo*, Fields enacted some of the fondest fantasies of the Tired Businessman: Tripp was hip, he was tireless, and he had his pick of the young women. To cut loose, all he needed was a cocktail, some hot jazz, and the right dance partner.

In the guise of Augustus Tripp, Fields could escape his own fear of aging as a middle-aged man who succeeds, if only for a time, in impersonating a fictitious son. The fact that Lew chose to have Herbert play Tripp's real son could only have strengthened Lew's identification with his role. Everything in and around the show conspired to remind Lew of his advancing age: the subject matter, his recent failures, his son's presence in the cast, the birth of his first grandchildren.

When Fields turned handsprings in the Act Two finale, he did it to prove that the youthful vigor he exuded in his role was no mere artifice.

Sarcastic, sophisticated, a snappy dresser, and, like his father, a prodigal spender, Herbert Fields was the epitome of the young urban hedonists whom the Anti-Saloon League was trying to suppress—and whom Augustus Tripp was trying to emulate. No wonder Fields looked to Herbert and his peers as the inspiration for a new kind of musical comedy. Though there is no hard evidence that Herbert wrote a word of *A Lonely Romeo*, his involvement in all of Lew Fields' successful musicals over the next decade supports the notion that his presence was a significant factor. The influence worked both ways; in the unrepentant Augustus Tripp, we have the spiritual father of the street-smart hedonists in Herbert's books for Rodgers & Hart in the 1920's.

Apart from his skills as a writer, Herbert was useful to his father as an unofficial talent scout, bringing to his attention promising young performers and creators. On Herbert's recommendation, Lew would go to an out-of-the-way theater or an amateur production to appraise a "rough diamond." Herbert was able to tap resources that were unfamiliar to Lew. For the most part, the new generation of musical comedy creators came from universities and music schools instead of the Bowery saloons and vaudeville houses. The young men and women in Herbert's own circle of friends were mostly college-educated, second-generation Jews, equally conversant with the works of Wagner, O'Neill, Sophie Tucker, and the Original Dixieland Jazz Band. A remarkable number of them went on to make significant contributions to the musical stage: George and Ira Gershwin, Arthur Schwartz, Dorothy Fields, Oscar Hammerstein II, Libby Holman, Richard Rodgers, and Lorenz Hart.

Herbert's first encounter with Larry Hart was in his early teens, either at Camp Paradox or on the staff of the DeWitt Clinton High School newspaper. At Columbia, Larry did a profile of the Fields family for the student newspaper. Larry was Herbert's senior by two years, and for most of their early lives, they travelled parallel paths and shared the same interests. Despite Hart's diminutive stature (under five feet tall) and odd appearance, he commanded the affection and respect of his peers with his wit, erudition, and limitless energy. People clamored to be around him just to hear him tell stories, during which his eyes would sparkle as he rubbed his hands together with glee. Like Herb, Hart was a frustrated actor and a profligate spender. Unlike Herb, he was a bohemian in his personal habits, sleeping little, drinking much, and generally neglecting his health.

It was Phil Leavitt, a mutual friend of Herb's and Hart's, who introduced Hart to Richard Rodgers early in 1919. During the spring and summer, Rodgers and Hart wrote some songs together and came up with a few that they thought were saleable. Phil Leavitt heard them and took it upon himself to arrange for an audition with a producer. That summer, the Leavitts were renting a cottage on Franklin Street in Far Rockaway, next door to the Fields family. In addition to being a friend of Herb's, Leavitt was also sweet on Dorothy. In late July or early August, Leavitt asked Dorothy to persuade her father to audition Rodgers and Hart. According to another version, he asked Lew directly.[5]

The summer heat had taken its usual toll at the box office, and the Shuberts had moved *A Lonely Romeo* to the Casino, a smaller house. Fields was exhausted from the physical rigors of performing the role of Augustus Tripp. He lamented his decision to do handsprings in the Act Two finale, for he found that audiences at every performance now expected it. According to Leavitt, Fields was "too tired to say no when I suggested he listen to the hottest pair of songwriters since Gilbert and Sullivan." What Leavitt did not realize was that Fields was also struggling to keep his show from being closed down with the rest of Broadway: the Actors' Equity strike had begun on August 6.

On a sweltering Sunday afternoon in August, Richard Rodgers was greeted at the door by Lew Fields. (Hart, who disliked "selling," stayed home with a splitting headache, leaving Rodgers to sing to his own accompaniment.) Expecting an audience of one, Rodgers was surprised to see the entire Fields family, including Frances, assembled around the piano in the living room. Rodgers recalled that fifteen-year-old Dorothy had the most dazzling eyes he had ever seen, and that all of them did their best to make him feel comfortable.[6] Evidently, Lew wanted to see how the songs went over with an audience. He knew his family to be a knowledgeable and demanding audience. They "are all dramatic critics, and I am their favorite victim," he had once joked. "When I can please Mrs. Fields and the children I know that I have made good."[7]

Rodgers led off with "Venus," the song Hart judged to be their best. There were polite murmurs from various family members. Lew asked Rodgers to play a few of their other numbers. One of them was a bouncy melody with a chug-chugging train rhythm and a clever compilation of place names in the lyrics:

> From old Virginia,
> Or Abyssinia,
> We'll go straight to Halifax.
> I've got a mania
> For Pennsylvania,
> Even ride in London hacks. . .
> . . . Oh, for far Peru!
> I'll go to hell for ya,
> Or Philadelphia,
> Any old place with you.[8]

After the audition was over, Lew praised the team's efforts, and casually announced that he would like to buy "Any Old Place with You" to use in *A Lonely Romeo.* Rodgers was, in his own words, "stunned and slightly hysterical."

Of course, it was not unusual for Fields (or any producer at that time) to interpolate a new song in an already running show. Fields planned to use "Any Old Place with You" in place of the duet in Act One, "You Never Can Tell," sung by Eve Lynn and Alan Hale. According to Rodgers, Fields launched the professional career of Rodgers and Hart with the August 26 matinee of *A Lonely Romeo.*

There were, however, no performances of any Broadway play on that date, except for the Theatre Guild's *John Ferguson.* On Saturday, August 23, with a full house at the Casino Theatre waiting eagerly for the opening curtain, the stagehands and musicians had walked out of *A Lonely Romeo* and forced its closing. Until then, the ticket sales at the Casino were booming as never before, for the Actors' Equity strike against the Producing Managers Association had already closed down almost every other Broadway show.

The walkout surprised Fields and embarrassed him. He had already refused to become a member of the Producing Managers Association, and his long-standing sympathy for Equity's cause was well known. Indeed, his insistence on treating actors with decency and fairness was the source of many of his conflicts with the Shuberts. Over the years, most of the strikers' demands—no extra matinees for free on holidays, a limit to unpaid rehearsals, courteous treatment of choristers, costumes paid for by the producer, no summary dismissals without compensation—had been the subject of disputatious memos between Fields and the Shuberts.

A week into the strike, Fields went on record regarding his attitude towards the P.M.A.:

> In answer to innumerable inquiries regarding myself and my company in "Lonely Romeo," I wish to state that I am not a member of the Producing Managers' Association, nor will I become a member of the P.M.A.
>
> In all my experience as an actor and a manager my choice under the circumstances is to remain an actor. My son, Herbert Fields, is a member of the A.E.A. and the entire company, including myself, are working under 100 per cent Equity contracts.
>
> [signed] Lew Fields[9]

Equity officials had assured him that his show would be exempted from the strike.

Ironically, it was his association with the Shuberts that ultimately told against him. In late May, when *A Lonely Romeo* began its tryouts in Atlantic City, the program had listed the Messrs. Shubert as "presenting." By the time it opened in New York on June 10, there was nothing indicating who or what was producing the show, except for the phrase, "The entire production under the personal supervision of Lew Fields." *Variety* speculated that Fields owned the show himself, with financial backing from an unidentified "angel" in Philadelphia.

Actually, the out-of-town backer was a businessman who was fronting for the Shuberts. It is entirely likely that the wily Shuberts, covering their bets in the event of an actors' strike, decided to take advantage of Fields' pro-Equity reputation as a means of concealing their own interests. In the spring of 1919, Actors' Equity were threatening to join the American Federation of Labor, and members of the Producing Managers' Association feared the worst. The Shuberts were one of the main targets of the actors' complaints, and the ones who stood to lose the most by a union contract.

So Fields' idealism became the Shuberts' opportunism, and Fields could not afford to act otherwise. Between August 6 and the twenty-third, during the time when all of the Shuberts' other productions were closed down, *A Lonely Romeo* played twenty sold-out shows. When his show was shut down without warning, Fields questioned why they had to embarrass him before a capacity audience, but the real embarrassment was the revelation of Fields' complicity in concealing the Shuberts' interests.

The strike not only put Fields at odds with his fellow producers (including Joe Weber, Al Woods, and William Brady), but he also found himself opposing many of his older acting colleagues. The proposal to join the A.F. of L. brought out the actors' insecurity about their social status. Although the actor had fewer rights or protections than the plumber, the engineer, or, for that matter, the stage-hand, many actors—particularly legit stars—thought that membership in a trade union was beneath their dignity as artists. Amelia Bingham, for example, resigned from Equity to express her disapproval of "trade unionism," a buzzword at the time that had not only a note of snobbery but a reference to the supposedly un-American (i.e., Bolshevist) character of the labor movement.[10]

Like Fields, George M. Cohan was an actor and producer caught in the middle. Nobody had crusaded harder than Cohan to protect the rights of actors, but no-body reacted more vehemently when actors challenged his paternalistic author-ity. When Cohan vowed that if Equity won, he would quit the theater and run an elevator, his friend Eddie Cantor retorted, "Somebody'd better tell Mr. Cohan that to run an elevator he'd *have* to join a union."[11] Cohan formed the Actors' Fidelity League ("Fido" to Equity members), backed it with his own considerable re-sources, and began negotiating with the producers. He was joined by David War-field, Otis Skinner, E. H. Sothern, Julia Marlowe, Mrs. Fiske, Willie Collier, and Louis Mann. Cohan also resigned from the Managers' Association when he learned that they were about to concede a closed shop to Equity.

A handful of actors of Fields' age and stature lined up behind the Equity banner: Eddie Foy, Lillian Russell, Francis Wilson, Marie Dressler. The bulk of Equity's support came from the younger generation of performers—Ed Wynn, Ethel and Lionel Barrymore, Eddie Cantor—who had paid their dues in the sweatshops of the Syndicate and the Shuberts.

The strike lasted exactly one month, and the public was hugely entertained, with marches down Broadway, all-star benefits, and cutting quips (example: "An empty taxi drew up in front of the Friars Club and Louis Mann got out"). Total losses were estimated to be $500,000 a week, not counting the sixty shows that were in rehearsal or were unable to open. Actors' Equity won the right to bargain for stage people, and some modest concessions: half-pay for the chorus after four free weeks of rehearsals, minimums for choristers in New York and on the road, regular pay to all actors for extra matinees.

These additional costs came on top of already growing production costs: fifty to sixty thousand dollars for a musical comedy or revue; fifteen to eighteen thou-sand for a burlesque show. The price of an orchestra seat in a Broadway theater went from two dollars to three or even four dollars.

The strike's immediate impact was as much symbolic as financial. Actors had become an official part of the working world, a step up from their position as the bullied bondsmen of the Syndicate and the Shuberts. In retrospect, one could see that the actor had had a better chance for a square deal in the chaotic days of the actor-managers. But the era of the actor-manager was long gone. The success of the middlemen—the commercial managers, agents, and booking pools—had made the hyphenate role an awkward anomaly. If the strike proved nothing else, it was that one had to choose sides. One was either an actor or a producer; labor or management. Hyphenates Lew Fields and George M. Cohan ended up on opposite sides of the dispute more because of differences in personal style than because of philosophy. They were anachronisms; their approach to show biz belonged to the age of the bustle and the cavalry charge. Fields' position on the actors' union may have proven once and for all to the Shuberts that he was at heart an actor and therefore not to be trusted.

The *Romeo* company closed on Broadway on October 10 after eighty-seven performances and headed to Boston, where it received strong reviews and did good business. Extended engagements in Brooklyn and Philadelphia kept the company on the road until Christmas. The tour would have continued into the new year, but the show was closed when Malvin Franklin and Frederick Bowers, its composer and lyricist, attached the theater box office for $2,400 in unpaid royalties. Why Fields had not paid them is unclear; perhaps there was confusion with the Shuberts over who was responsible for keeping track of it. What is clear is that the Shuberts made no attempt to save Fields or his show, as they had in the earlier years of their partnership. The legal action in Philadelphia that closed the show was a professional embarrassment to Fields and a blow to his credibility as a producer.

From the anomalous adventures of a middle-aged man imitating youthful activities, Fields turned his attention to a protagonist who could embody youth itself—the chorus girl. By 1920, the chorus girl had become as familiar a type to popular stage audiences as any of the ethnic characterizations. The stereotypical chorus girl was in her early twenties, lithe (like the girl next door) rather than voluptuous (like the vamp or fallen woman), self-reliant, a bit impudent. She was exciting and not to be taken seriously as a person; she was the perfect playmate.[12] Either she was a "Dumb Dora" (a young woman of astounding stupidity) or, more frequently, a gold digger. The term "gold digger" came into use during World War I; in 1919, playwright Avery Hopwood made it a part of the national idiom with his farce *The Gold Diggers*. The gold digger usually came from a working class background (thus she was uneducated and coarse in manners), and she had no qualms about using her sex appeal to attract affluent men and manipulate them into providing the trappings of success—jewels, furs, expensive meals, maybe even a nice apartment.

The chorus girl, whose thirst for social mobility brought her to the city and led her to display her physical charms onstage, was almost by definition a gold digger. She could not help but be the product of her corrupt environment—the theaters and cabarets where she worked and the city where she lived. In its 1918 annual report, an organization of elite Republican reformers concluded that the chorus girl was "open prey for the disreputable patrons who, demoralized by drink, force their attentions upon her." In the stereotype of the gold-digging chorus girl one can see many of the prejudices and anxieties about the Eighteenth and Nineteenth Amendments (Prohibition and women's voting rights). As the exploits of cunning chorus girls became a staple of the popular press, they became emblematic of the shopgirls, clerks, and secretaries who had lately joined the work force. In fact, any unattached young woman working in the big city was liable to be called a gold digger.

The reality behind the myth was much less glamorous. Chorus work was physically demanding, with long hours of rehearsal with (until 1919) no pay, the constant threat of summary dismissal, and almost exclusively male bosses, many of whom were verbally abusive. Although the chorus offered a select group of young women a taste of independence and big-city living, many of them lived at home and were supporting parents or other family members with their meager earnings. Often, the working chorus girl had neither the energy nor the money for the high life. Opportunities for individual advancement were slim; few chorines lasted more than three or four years. They either changed jobs, moved up, or got married and quit work. In this sense, the chorus girl was indeed similar to the secretary and the clerk; their autonomy was temporary, and its best possible outcome was marriage.

From the days of Adah Richmond and her beefy burlesquers, the chorus girl had always fascinated Lew Fields. His interest was characteristically straitlaced (repressed, some would say). He was as concerned about their treatment offstage as on. In the Weber & Fields Music Hall productions, the chorus girl had become an active participant in the entertainment, not just a decoration. At the same time, she also became a desirable marriage mate for the affluent men in the orchestra seats. Weber & Fields—with Julian Mitchell—legitimized the chorus girl socially and aesthetically; Ziegfeld—with Mitchell and then Ned Wayburn—took it one step further, "glorifying" her with expensive peek-a-boo costumes that made her into the ultimate luxury item. Ziegfeld made the chorus girl sexually dangerous once more, but as a symbol of high class glamour that appealed to both men and women.

Though Fields was considered an expert judge of pulchritude and dancing ability, he avoided the libidinous *luxe* of Ziegfeld and the transparent tackiness of the Shuberts. As we have seen, examples of sexual suggestiveness and romantic passion in Fields' work were rare indeed, even by the rigid standards of his time. From the time of the first Weber & Fields Company, he maintained a Victorian sense of propriety and gentility, particularly where women were concerned. It was old-fashioned propriety that caused him to fire the Music Hall actor who swore at a chorus girl; he made the actor apologize to the chorine in front of the entire company. And it was his old-fashioned gentility that led him to insist on fair treatment for chorus girls and to support Actors' Equity. These same traits emerged in a 1916 interview, when he attempted to dispel the gold-digger image of the chorus girl:

> I have known dozens of girls who have left the stage in order to nurse and comfort an aged or decrepit father, mother, brother, or sister. The chorus girl doesn't do anything half way: she is ever the little brick, who when she makes a sacrifice, does it without grumbling, and completely, and finely. . . .

> . . . .It is generally supposed that this [her ambition] consists in a desire for multitudes of broiled lobsters and seas of sparkling wine. This is but another of those silly notions regarding this public pet. . . .

. . .The point is, the chorus girl is not the average feather head that she is supposed to be. The best thing you can say about a girl is that she made a good wife [!], and this can truthfully be said of a large number of girls I've known. . . . The stage has left no perceptible taint.[13]

The stage may be "a dirty business" (to repeat Fields' own description), but most chorus girls resisted being corrupted by it. His regard for their inherent wholesomeness was accompanied by a growing respect for their professionalism. By 1919, Fields noted a big improvement in the quality and dedication of chorus girls, who were now "bubbling over with ambition."[14]

In April, 1920, *Variety* announced that Fields was about to begin rehearsals of a new two-act musical comedy with a book by an unknown, Adeline Leitzback, and a score by a pair from the Shuberts' Winter Garden productions, Al Bryan ("Who Paid the Rent for Mrs. Rip Van Winkle?") and George Meyer ("Where Did Robinson Crusoe Go with Friday on Saturday Night?"). This time, Fields was unusually finicky about the realization of his artistic intentions: within the next three months, a total of five credited writers, two more songwriting teams, three directors, and three sets of romantic leads would come and go.

In the end, Fields was once again the co-author of a musical and took the auteurist credit for personally supervising the entire production. At first, it was rumored that he would feature himself as in *A Lonely Romeo*. After several weeks of rehearsal, however, he was wise enough to see that there was no appropriate role for him in the show he envisioned. The focal point of *Poor Little Ritz Girl* had to be the earnest and misunderstood chorus girl.

If he had learned anything from *A Lonely Romeo*, it was that thinking young paid dividends at the box office. That show's weakest elements—the plot and the score—had been the products of established Broadway hacks. Young unknowns like Rodgers and Hart, and his son Herbert cost less; with Lew's guidance, they could get the job done just as well.

By the time rehearsals began in early April, the promising young trio had impressed Fields with their work on two more amateur shows. In his freshman year at Columbia University, Rodgers was selected to write the music for the Varsity production. Hart wrote the lyrics, Phil Leavitt collaborated on the book, and Herbert choreographed it. The result was *Fly with Me*, a satire on undergraduate life set in a Manhattan of the future ruled by the Soviets. Its limited run at the Astor Grand Ballroom from March 24 to the twenty-seventh attracted an unusual amount of critical praise. Of Rodger's music, S. Jay Kaufman of the *Globe* wrote: "Several of the tunes were capital. We have not heard of Richard Rodgers before. We have a suspicion we will hear of him again."

Two weeks later, the Akron Club presented another Rodgers & Hart score, *You'd Be Surprised*, at the Cort Theatre as a fund-raiser for a summer camp for poor children. It was truly a Fields family affair: Lew provided "professional assistance" (scenery, costumes, and advice on staging), Dorothy played one of the leads, and Herbert choreographed and provided the lyric to a show-stopping number about "poor bisected, disconnected Mary, Queen of Scots."[15]

Meanwhile, Fields was desperately looking for interpolations to replace the unsatisfactory score by Bryan and Meyer. He was already going over budget in his pre-production expenses, and the Boston tryout (in the Shuberts' new Wilbur Theatre) was booked for the end of May, only five weeks away. The quality of the songs in *Fly with Me* and *You'd Be Surprised* persuaded him to hire Rodgers & Hart to write the songs for *Poor Little Ritz Girl*. He knew the team would be inexpensive and fast. For five or six of the numbers, all he needed was for Hart to rewrite his lyrics to fit the new libretto.

News that Fields was entrusting his score to a pair of college kids was greeted with skepticism. *Variety* pointed out that Rodgers, at age seventeen, was even younger than George Gershwin when he wrote *La, La, Lucille*. In an interview, Fields publicly expressed his confidence in Rodgers: "[He] has real talent. I think that in a few years he will be in a class by himself."[16]

In another show of confidence, he hired Herbert as stage manager. Though his contributions are impossible to determine for certain, it makes sense to consider Herbert's influence on his father's production. Take the story itself, an unusual combination of the "intimate" Princess Theatre musical comedy and a door-slamming bedroom farce: the opening curtain reveals the stage of the Frivolity Theatre, where a grueling late-night rehearsal of a revue called "Poor Little Ritz Girl" is under way. The stage manager is berating several exhausted chorines. They answer him with wisecracks. Barbara, an innocent Southerner who has come to New York City to seek her fortune on the stage, invites fellow chorines Madge, Lillian, and Sweetie to her apartment for a late meal. Barbara lives in a well-furnished Riverside Drive apartment, rented to her for the unbelievably low rate of twenty-five dollars a month. Her colleagues wonder at the fine accommodations and speculate that either she comes from a wealthy Carolina family or "our little ingenue must have made a hit" (i.e., she has a "sugar daddy.") Actually, an unprincipled janitor has rented her the apartment of William Pembroke for a nominal amount without mentioning that the rightful lessee is only away temporarily.

Late that night, the handsome Mr. Pembroke returns to his apartment to find Barbara preparing for bed. For the wealthy young gentleman, it is love at first sight. Barbara finds that it is not hard to persuade him to let her stay in his apartment. Torn between emotion and propriety, he conspires on the phone with a bachelor friend, Dr. Russell Stevens. The doctor comes to the apartment and tells Barbara that Pembroke is too sick to go out in the rain, and offers to stay to avoid a compromising situation. When the doctor goes out to get some medicine, Pembroke expresses his love for Barbara. Flustered, Barbara retreats to her bedroom, and Act One ends with Pembroke restlessly waiting in the drawing room for the doctor to return.

Act Two's plot complications turn the simple romantic comedy into a bedroom farce. The next morning, Barbara's chorus-girl friends stop by to get her on their way to rehearsal. Recalling their suspicions, she hides Pembroke, but they find a telling piece of clothing that clinches their verdict. Barbara feigns a headache and does not go to rehearsal, for she wants to tend to the ailing Pembroke. At the theater, Madge and Lillian are fired for being late, along with Barbara.

Barbara's sister Dorothy shows up, and the doctor falls in love with her. Pembroke's rich and prudish Aunt Jane arrives unexpectedly, and the chorines return to bemoan their fate. The conflicting explanations about the relationships between Barbara, Pembroke, Dorothy, and Dr. Stevens suggest rampant immorality. Barbara and Pembroke sneak off to get married. With the help of Dorothy and Dr. Stevens, they clear up the misunderstandings and restore their good reputations by the final curtain. Surrounded by the entire cast, Pembroke celebrates his marriage to the "pure little, poor little Ritz girl." Thus, the plot of *Poor Little Ritz Girl* played with the stereotype of the gold-digging chorus girl (*The Gold Diggers* was still playing when it opened) but rejected its moral assumptions. Barbara Arden was not a gold digger looking for a sugar daddy; she was Cinderella looking for her Prince Charming.

The evocation of Cinderella may not have been an accident. The runaway hit of the 1919–1920 season had been *Irene*, the story of a poor shopgirl from the tenements who wins the heart of a young and wealthy Long Islander, and eventually wins over his snobbish family as well. Working in the spring of 1920, Fields and his co-authors were utilizing a still-fresh motif that quickly became a theatrical obsession. In the three seasons between 1921 and 1924, over a third of all the musical comedies on Broadway—twenty-one out of fifty-eight productions—used the Cinderella archetype.[17] "Cinderella" was by turns a shopgirl, a secretary, an orphan, a dishwasher, a waitress, a flower peddler, and, following the example of *Poor Little Ritz Girl*, a showgirl. The Cinderella musicals suggested an implicit solidarity between the plight of the actress—not the star, but the lowly chorus girl—and the struggles of other working women trying to succeed on their own in a harsh and corrupt urban environment. The stage, insisted Lew Fields, left no more "taint" than the office or the department store. To the chorus girl, Fields extended the social legitimacy that he had dreamed of for the rest of his profession.

If the message of *Poor Little Ritz Girl* was identifiably Lew Fields', some of the writing suggested more youthful, up-to-date influences, most notably, the Princess Theatre musicals. Rodgers, Hart, and Herbert Fields admired the way the Bolton-Wodehouse books relied on situation and character laughs instead of the usual Weberfieldsian crosstalk. Not surprisingly, the script for *Poor Little Ritz Girl* was at its best when it reproduced the slangy, cynical banter of the chorus girls, as when Barbara first brings her friends back to her Riverside Drive apartment:

> LILLIAN: *(All the girls enter)* Enter the mysterious palace of the enchanted princess.
>
> MADGE: Ah! Punk! Say if you want to act why don't you learn how. . . . Are we in the right flat?
>
> BARBARA: Don't you think it rather nice?
>
> MADGE: Nice, gee Lil, she's trying to lead us astray.
>
> SWEETIE: This is no place for a respectable chorus girl.
>
> MADGE: On the level, boys—is this the cheap little flat you told us about?

BARBARA: Yes—[. . .]

MADGE: Well, just grab your form over to our condensed flat, and we'll show you
the difference. But then we're only poor actorines at thirty-five per.[18]

Here was dialogue with the nervous, hyped-up rhythms of jazz, and the verve and
jaundiced wit that would characterize Herbert Fields' librettos for Rodgers &
Hart in the mid-1920's.

Side by side with these modern prefigurations were examples of the kind of
sidewalk crossfire dialogue that would not have been out of place in a minstrel
show or Weber & Fields' two-act. It would be unjust, and probably inaccurate, to
attribute all of the old shtick to the pen of Lew Fields, and everything young and
breezy to one of his four credited co-authors. After all, it was Fields who decided
what to keep of the efforts of Leitzback, Stillman, Campbell, and Jackson. But
was he perhaps guided by Herbert, whose recent experience as a choreographer
and stage manager gave him the opportunity for daily observation of the behavior
and speech patterns of chorus girls? Even in the tryouts, critics noticed a difference: "The dialogue is 'juvenile,' if anything, which may be a merit rather than a
defect, as the prevailing atmosphere of the play abounds in youth and buoy-
ancy."[19] The fact that the book for *Poor Little Ritz Girl* was actually the product
of at least two different generations of Broadway authors underscores its importance as a transitional work.

Conceived as an "intimate" musical comedy in the Princess Theatre tradition, *Poor Little Ritz Girl* used only two settings, the plush drawing room of
Pembroke's Riverside Drive apartment, and the stage of the Frivolity Theatre.
These parameters suited the Shuberts, who may have believed that "intimate"
meant "cheap" (at least it had at the Princess).

Evidently, the Shuberts did not take into account Fields' relentless pursuit
of novelty in stagecraft. As he had done in the past, he borrowed stage machinery
and techniques from the legit stage and adapted them for musical comedy. For
Poor Little Ritz Girl, the scene changes would be accomplished by putting the
apartment set on a pair of abutting "jackknife wagons." Each wagon was an-
chored by a big steel kingpin that served as a pivot at the extreme left and right
of the stage. To change the scene, the jackknife wagons split into two and swung
back on rollers, revealing the Frivolity Theatre stage. The arrangement allowed
for remarkably quick changes and seamless segues between dramatic and musical scenes. It also created a visual distinction between the revue numbers (on
the Frivolity's stage) and the character songs (in the apartment). The distinction
could be used realistically or whimsically, as when Barbara describes a revue
number to William. In less than ten seconds, the jackknife wagons split apart to
reveal Sweetie and the chorus performing "My Little Ming Toy." After the number, the scene goes back to the interior of the apartment, where Barbara and
Pembroke continue to get acquainted. The scene ends with the two confessing
their love in a tender ballad.

Artistically, the device was a success—a crowd pleaser and a formal innovation as well. For those worried about the production's bottom line, it was a
huge headache. The construction of the jackknife wagons cost around ten thou-

sand dollars even before the scenery was created. Despite the clever design of the stage machinery, the set changes still required more than the usual number of stagehands due to its weight: for the finale, during which the entire cast of thirty were in the apartment, with a bookcase full of real books, a real baby grand piano, tables, chairs, platforms, lighting, etc., the total *avoirdupois* was estimated at three tons. So taxing were the labors of the stagehands that on opening night Fields and Wayburn gave the first curtain call to the stagehands, who came on in their shirtsleeves and took their bows to enthusiastic applause.

In addition to the cost of its construction, the special stage machinery meant extra stagehands and rehearsals. Thanks to the recent contracts won by stagehands, musicians, and actors, rehearsal expenses had become a major consideration for producers. An article in the *New York Star* in mid-May reported that *Poor Little Ritz Girl* would rack up close to $75,000 in production expenses before the curtain went up on the first tryout on May 28. The large budget seemed particularly odd because there were no "noted names in the cast." To the consternation of the Shuberts, Fields had found a way to make even an "intimate" musical into an expensive undertaking.

Fields certainly did not squander any money on the new score by Rodgers & Hart. He bought their songs outright—no messy royalties to worry about—for a low but unspecified fee. Five of the tunes came from *Fly with Me:* "Don't Love Me Like Othello," "Dreaming Time," "Inspiration," and "Peekin' in Pekin" were refitted with new lyrics to become, respectively, "You Can't Fool Your Dreams," "Love Will Call," "All You Need to Be a Star," and "Love's Intense in Tents." (According to Rodgers, "You Can't Fool Your Dreams" was the first Broadway show tune to indicate a passing knowledge of the works of Dr. Sigmund Freud, a source Herbert Fields, Rodgers, and Hart would return to for their 1926 musical, *Peggy-Ann*). The fifth Rodgers tune, "Mary, Queen of Scots" kept its lyrics by Herbert Fields, and was used as a specialty number for Lulu McConnell, the talented comedienne who played the boisterous Madge. To round out the score, the eager songwriting team came up with ten new songs as well.

With less than a month before the May 28 tryout in Boston, directors William O'Neill and David Bennett faced a herculean task. The book was changing almost daily, and there were fifteen new numbers to choreograph and rehearse, with scene transitions unlike any tried before. Unlike the scores for most musical comedies, Rodgers & Hart's songs were not interchangeable; they were "book" specific, written to reveal a character's emotions at a particular moment or to develop a motif or theme.

To some extent, even the revue numbers paralleled the development of the romantic plot (Barbara and Pembroke) and sub-plot (the Doctor and Dorothy). As he refined *Poor Little Ritz Girl* in rehearsals, Fields must have realized how close he was to achieving the goal he first articulated in 1904: a coherent musical with a plausible plot, characters who develop, and a score that was integrated into the book.

The premiere of *Poor Little Ritz Girl* took place on May 28 and inaugurated the Shuberts' new Wilbur Theatre in Boston. The program credited Henry Stillman as the book's sole author, and Rodgers & Hart for their first complete score.

The principals were Eleanor Griffith (Barbara), Victor Morley (Pembroke), Roy Atwell (Dr. Stevens), and Lulu McConnell (Madge)—all competent but uncelebrated performers. The local reviews were encouraging, including some particularly kind words for Rodgers' music.

Variety's critic, however, was not impressed and said that the show needed "a lot of trimming." He thought it unfortunate that Lew Fields was connected with the show only as a producer, and he detected places where Fields inserted "bits" of comedy action "bordering on burlesque" that were "the big noise of the opening." *Variety*'s reviewer reserved his bile for the fledgling team of Rodgers and Hart: "It is said that both [Rodgers and Hart] are close friends of Fields' son, Herbert, and whether 'Daddy' dug down and put on the show to give his son's friends an opportunity and to put Herbert into the producing business in this manner is a question."

Lew Fields' assessment of the show was, if anything, even harsher. Despite the fact that it was drawing well (and continued to do so throughout its Boston run), he started making wholesale changes. He was convinced that it would not go over in New York. Moreover, it did not come close to the show he envisioned. He did not want another musical comedy where the comedy "bits" seemed arbitrarily inserted. He brought in a new writer—George Campbell—and worked closely with him in revising the book, adding three new scenes. He was also dissatisfied with the chorus numbers, so he called upon his erstwhile collaborator, Ned Wayburn, for help. Wayburn, now Ziegfeld's house director–choreographer, was a master of scene transitions and transformations. Wayburn joined Fields' company at the end of the month, after the opening of *The Ziegfeld Follies of 1920*.

With the already high production costs continuing to mount, there was increasing pressure on Fields to ensure that the show would make an immediate hit in New York. This may explain why Fields suddenly lost confidence in Rodgers' and Hart's score. Perhaps, as some have suggested, Fields became nervous about entrusting an entire score to a team of inexperienced college boys. Or perhaps he was advised by his equally nervous partners to supplement the score with the work of an established composer, such as Sigmund Romberg. Romberg, it so happened, was the Shuberts' house composer, frequently misused to provide tunes for Al Jolson and the Winter Garden shows. His big hit had been *Maytime* (1917); his specialty was operetta—Old World–style waltzes and tender romances. One would have had to look hard to find a composer whose style was less compatible with that of the young Rodgers. Working for the first time with lyricist Alex Gerber, Romberg composed three or four "serious" love songs and several silly revue numbers during the Boston tryouts.

With every other aspect of the show undergoing massive changes, it came as no surprise that Fields chose to replace three out of the four principal cast members as well. Then as now, the conventional wisdom dictated that a musical production had to have a star to succeed on Broadway. The addition of stars' salaries gave the Shuberts some leverage in the selection of the performers. Charles Purcell stepped into the role of Billy Pembroke. Purcell, a handsome nonentity with a pleasing voice, had supporting roles in three previous Romberg (and J. J. Shubert) productions, including *Maytime*. To play the Cinderella role, Fields chose

Gertrude Vanderbilt, a former vaudevillian who specialized in ingenue roles and displays of temperament.

It is doubtful that Fields would have cast either of them under better circumstances. He was more fortunate in his choice for Dr. Stevens, casting Andrew Tombes, a talented comedian described as "a second edition Ed Wynn." Tombes would provide the laughs, in tandem with Fields' favorite new comedienne, Lulu McConnell ("a youthful edition of Marie Dressler," according to the *Boston Post*).

It was by now mid-July, and the warm weather was driving down attendance. Fields insisted on two more weeks of out-of-town tryouts to give the new cast members time to learn their parts. Almost immediately, Vanderbilt began complaining that her role was smaller than she was promised, and that Purcell had all the "fat" lines. Less than a week before its New York opening, Gertrude Vanderbilt quit the show and booked passage to Europe. Rather than replace her with another star, Fields brought back the young woman who originated the role, Eleanor Griffith. The New York opening was delayed another two days.

When *Poor Little Ritz Girl* finally opened at the Central Theatre on July 28, all of Fields' tinkering and fussing seemed to pay off. The audience insisted on five curtain calls (including the one for the stagehands); for the sixth, Fields was persuaded to join his cast on stage to take a bow. He awoke the next morning to reviews that were the most favorable of any of he had received as a producer since the heyday of his Broadway Theater productions. The usually demanding critic at the *New York Post* was full of praise: "There is an intelligent plot, well worked out, and the fun, action and music are never lugged in. The dialogue sparkles with amusing lines, most of which may be credited to Lew Fields. . . ." What impressed critics the most was Fields' ability to integrate the music into the comedy: "There is a unique and skillful blending of farce and musical comedy to be found in *Poor Little Ritz Girl.*"[20] The plot, humor, chorus, and score were "so dexterously blended that the farce did not interfere with the musical comedy and the musical numbers are never allowed to interfere with the progress of the plot," said the *New York World*. "Jokes at Last Have a Place in Musical Shows," was how Heywoud Broun entitled his review. The innovative use of the jackknife stage was noted in passing, but nobody seemed to recognize how this technique facilitated the blend of farce and music comedy that they found so exceptional.

Perhaps the only unhappy theatergoers that night were the two with the greatest expectations. Dick Rodgers and Larry Hart, accompanied by Herbert Fields, arrived at the Central Theatre in a state of nervous excitement. Their day-to-day contact with the production had stopped when it moved to Boston for its tryouts. In June, Rodgers and Herb had begun working as counsellors at Camp Paradox. When Rodgers opened his opening night program, he was chagrinned to discover that half of his score had been replaced with songs by Sigmund Romberg and Alex Gerber. Hart was downcast, and Herb was mightily embarrassed. Lew had neglected to inform Rodgers and Hart of the substitution, and apparently avoided telling his son as well. Rodgers & Hart took small comfort in the fact that several critics singled out their contributions for praise.

If there was any weakness in the show, it was in Charles Purcell's performance. On opening night, his diffidence and lack of enthusiasm were noticeable.

Purcell soon made Fields aware that he was unhappy with the size of his role, and he took it upon himself to modify and enlarge his role by ad libbing and inserting unrehearsed business. Fields warned him about it repeatedly, but he felt constrained because Purcell had been "farmed" to him by the Shuberts, whom he was under contract with. On September 18, after a vociferous row, Fields fired him. In his place, Fields hired Frederick Santley. Ticket sales leaped $400 a night.

Ticket sales at almost every other Broadway theater were almost as strong. During 1920, an all-time high of five million dollars was invested in theatrical ventures; there were 163 shows, almost fifty of them musicals.[21] Despite the competition, *Poor Little Ritz Girl* held its own, averaging thirteen to fifteen thousand dollars a week through the summer. According to *Variety*, it was still one of the leading Broadway hits in the first two weeks of October.

So it came as a rude shock when Fields learned that Lee Shubert was closing *Ritz Girl* after 119 performances to make the Central available for a more lucrative venture. Fox Studios was offering a sizable percentage to rent a Broadway theaters to screen its new feature film, *Over the Hill*. Despite Fields' outraged protests, Lee hastily arranged some road engagements for *Poor Little Ritz Girl*. A pared-down version of Fields' show—dropping the fancy machinery and a few chorus girls—could do decent box office on the road. Fox's film deal was a bird in the hand.

Poor Little Ritz Girl finished out the year shuffling between three different Shubert houses in Brooklyn. The tour ended in Pittsburgh in early January, when attachments from various unhappy creditors closed it down: $2,000 owed to the New York Calcium Light Company, $1,000 to Ned Wayburn, and $3,000 to the Alvin Theatre's box office. The last-named amount was most likely a loan to Fields to meet his company payroll or to cover production expenses for the new show he was rehearsing. In previous years, Lee Shubert had on occasion permitted out-of-town theater managers to advance money from the box office to Fields and other producers in a pinch. By now, Lee Shubert knew better than to accept Fields' promissory note. He insisted that the theater management collect on the loan immediately.

It was the second Fields production in a row to close in this ignominious fashion. The series of reversals now extended back several years: the actors' strike, the influenza epidemic, and the war had curtailed the longevity of previous productions (*A Lonely Romeo, Friendly Enemies, Bosom Friends*), and he was never paid his guaranteed salary from *Miss 1917*. Most damaging of all, perhaps, was that he had been without a business manager since the death of his brother Charley.

The demise of *Poor Little Ritz Girl* was upsetting for other reasons as well. It was the production on which Fields had lavished the most time, energy, and money. It was the one that came the closest so far to fulfilling his ambitions for the musical comedy form. He did not expect the Shuberts to care about such matters, but he was deeply hurt by their willingness to jeopardize his financial well-being at the first opportunity.

Anxious to arrange for a new production, Fields began negotiating with other producers and backers during the tour of *Ritz Girls*. First, however, he needed a paycheck. He took over the staging of the Gus Edwards revue for two weeks before its New Haven tryout. The show folded, and Fields was never paid.

In desperation, Fields announced that he was planning to produce three new shows in the next three months. The first would be a revue, *The Wild Women of 19 and 20*, with a book by Fields and Tommy Gray. Next, Fields would produce a musical comedy called *Love Mad*, with music by Harry Von Tilzer and book by Marie Nordstrom, starring film actress Mae Murray. Finally, he would begin rehearsals on another book musical, *Blue Eyes*, by December 1. Knowing of his dispute with the Shuberts, Broadway insiders marvelled at Fields' damn-the-torpedoes attitude. Where did he expect to get the money? Who was he going to get to be his "angel"?

The Broadway "angel"—private backer—was not a new phenomenon, but he became increasingly common in the boom economy of the 1920's. For newly rich businessmen, backing a Broadway musical was not only a mark of prestige, but it provided entrée into the exotic world of stars, chorus girls, and other demi-mondaines. In some cases, an angel bankrolled a show—or found other backers—to please an aspiring actress he adored.

From a purely economic standpoint, backing a musical was not such a bad risk, falling somewhere between the stock market and the racetrack. The average musical cost around $50,000 in up-front production costs; a popular musical at a Broadway theater could expect to gross anywhere between $15,000 and $20,000 a week. In the first half of 1920, 45 of 145 new plays passed the 100-performance mark; i.e., they lasted more than twelve weeks. *Irene*, for example, cost $41,000 to bring in; it paid off its entire "nut" and banked $20,000 more after just six weeks at the little Vanderbilt Theatre.[22] Even some of the shows that flopped on Broadway paid off handsomely on the road. Still, the origin of the term was revealing and sometimes painfully appropriate: in the prewar argot of the underworld, "angel" referred to an innocent, a "mark," a prospective victim of a swindle.

Lew Fields' angel was an insurance man named Morris Rose. To a Broadway outsider like Rose, Fields' name still had luster. Fields' quiet, earnest demeanor offstage and his way with an anecdote would have made him seem like the ideal partner for a cloak-and-suiter intent on dabbling in theater. To visit Fields for dinner at his spacious townhouse just off Riverside Drive, and to meet his chic wife and their witty, sophisticated children, no one would have guessed that here was a man who did not know how he was going to be able to make his next mortgage payment. Not that Fields was intentionally deceiving his angel—the big money, in Fields' mind, was only a bet (or a show) away, and he simply needed a generous partner to help put up the stakes. Details of the agreement between Morris Rose and Fields were never revealed, although they appear to have included $1,000 a week salary for Fields.

Once again, Fields chose to try unknowns rather than established Broadway writers. The writers of *Blue Eyes*, Leon Gordon and LeRoy Clemens, had adapted a farce called *Let Tommy Do It*. The lyrics and music were the work of two newcomers from San Francisco, identified only as Z. Myers and I. B. Kornblum. The story told of blue-eyed Dorothy Manners, who is driving in Greenwich Village when she knocks down a young man named Bobby with her car. Naturally, they fall in love. Both Bobby and Dorothy are under the misapprehension that the other is wealthy. Bobby is a struggling writer who shares a studio with two other penniless artists; Dorothy and her family live in a Long Island mansion that they can no longer afford because they have lost their fortune. Instead of confessing their deceptions, they try to keep up the pretenses throughout a big party at the Manners' home, where Bobby's roommates also get into the act. In the end, Bobby and Dorothy see each other as they really are, but strike it rich anyway.

Initially, Fields was only going to stage the show, but its tryouts in Atlantic City were not well received. Morris Rose was convinced that the only possibility of saving the show was to rewrite it around Lew Fields in the principal role. Whether Fields encouraged this delusion is not known, but in the absence of any other viable projects, he accepted. In early January, 1921, Fields and Rose recast the other principals, bringing in Mollie King, Ray Raymond (Bobby), Andrew Tombes (the third roommate), and a delightful songstress named Delyle Alda. They also added two interpolations by George Gershwin with lyrics by Irving Caesar.

Meanwhile, Fields reshaped the script, enlarging the role of Bobby's roommate, a sculptor named Peter Van Damm, to give himself a more prominent role. The new version provided Fields a slim pretext to indulge in his comic specialties, playing with props and impersonating various tradespeople (in this case, a butler, a cook, and a chambermaid). Fields must have known by now that reshaping a libretto around burlesque caricatures and vaudeville-style specialties was precisely the wrong way to go about making a well-integrated musical comedy. In *Blue Eyes*, and for the rest of his career, Fields was faced with a troubling paradox: the kind of performer audiences wanted him to be was not compatible with the kind of musical comedy that he wanted to make.

Despite its many flaws, *Blue Eyes* opened at the Casino Theatre on February 21 to enthusiastic crowds. "The takings first week," said *Variety*, "surprised wiseacres with well over $21,000 drawn," attributable to the names in the cast. One of the evening's big laughs came when Fields, as the sculptor, attempted to mold the head of a persistent bill collector. One of the guests is a Bolshevik carrying what appears to be a bomb, which Fields must defuse. Fields also surprised audiences when he showed off his youthful dancing skills in a comedy number, "When Gentlemen Disagree," with Tombes and Raymond. Critics also repeatedly praised Mollie King's "decorative" appearance and her impish manner, and the singing and dancing talents of Delyle Alda.

By the end of the third week, Broadway audiences had found new and better shows. Box office receipts for *Blue Eyes* dwindled to less than $11,400 for the week. Morris Rose closed it down at the end of March; his angelic behavior had reportedly cost him $88,000. A month after the closing, Rose initiated a suit against Fields to recover $8,000, the amount Fields was supposed to invest in *Blue Eyes* but apparently never did. Fields filed a countersuit claiming that Rose owed him $1,000 for the last week's salary. Over the next three months, at least three more unhappy creditors sued Fields to recover unpaid loans, royalties, or unfulfilled contracts.

The spring of 1921 was a bad time for an aging actor with a high-living family to be broke and out of work. The previous two years had been champagne years for Broadway, but the rise in the cost of living brought on by the postwar inflation began to affect theater attendance. At the same time, stage expenses soared: overhead was up 300 percent since 1919; actors' pay, up 200 percent; railroad charges were increasing, as were federal and state taxes. By the time *Blue Eyes* had closed, the box office slump in Chicago was already being called the worst in years, and New York was not far behind. Broadway theater managers began adding movies and lowering ticket prices to lure patrons. Touring companies were especially hard hit; many disbanded, and their bookings were filled by motion pictures.

In the midst of these unfavorable economic conditions, Lew Fields searched frantically for a surefire formula for a money-making show. Since 1919, Broadway had been deluged with revues—not just Ziegfeld's Follies and the Shuberts' Passing Shows, but White's Scandals, Anderson's Greenwich Village Follies, and Raymond Hitchcock's eponymous editions. For the past three seasons, Fields had been tempted to ride the cresting popularity of revues, but when faced with a choice, he always opted to do a book show. Now he could no longer afford to buck the trend.

Whenever he was strapped for cash—in 1912, in 1915, and again in 1918—he had been able to fall back on a reunion with Joe Weber and a revival of the Weberfieldsian burlesque. To this end, he proposed to build a summer revue around Joe Weber, Nora Bayes, De Wolf Hopper, and himself in travesties of the musical successes of the past season. Instead of one author, as in the old Music Hall productions, he would follow the modern revue practice of using several well-known sketch writers.

Weber, however, wanted no part of it. Basking in the success of his recent ventures as a musical producer *(Eileen, Honeydew)*, he explained that he had no desire to perform during the summer months. Bayes and Hopper were more enthusiastic, and Fields supplemented them with younger talent: Lulu McConnell and her husband, Grant Simpson; Delyle Alda, Ernest Lambert, shimmy dancer Gilda Gray, and Dorothy Dickson. The choreography he delegated to Leon Errol, better known as a comedian for Ziegfeld and a star of the hit *Sally.*

Starting in late April, Fields began patching together the material for his still untitled revue. The sketches and music came from a variety of sources, including a script Fields had mentioned several years earlier called *You Must Come Over* or *Come On Over.* Some of it also came from an ill-conceived show produced by E. Ray Goetz, the Broadway composer. Ultimately, Fields selected sketches by Frances Nordstrom, James Montgomery Flagg, H. I. Phillips, John Hastings Turner, Morris Ryskind, and old standby Glen MacDonough.

Backing for the revue was still problematic. The Shuberts were interested; this was the kind of show they had wanted Fields to be doing all along. Fields, however, was still smarting from their treatment of *Poor Little Ritz Girl.* He did not refuse the Shuberts' offer outright. Instead, he quietly found more congenial partners in another pair of brothers, Arch and Edgar Selwyn, who were coming into their own as producers and theater managers. To prove that they had arrived as Broadway producers, the Selwyns wanted to create their own series of annual revues, along the lines of Ziegfeld's Follies, the Passing Show, and George White's Scandals. They gave Fields' revue the jaunty but fitting name *Snapshots of 1921*, and, presumably, smiled bravely when they discovered that company salaries were going to exceed $10,000 a week. Nevertheless, the Selwyns set a top ticket price of $3, lower than the Follies or the other big name revues.

Snapshots of 1921 had its premiere, three days late, at the Selwyn Theatre on Thursday, June 2, playing to a capacity house. Like Fields' two previous productions, *Snapshots* contained a curious and sometimes incompatible mix of old and new, juxtaposing slapstick and sophisticated satire, comic opera and jazz. Any production that featured performers such as DeWolf Hopper *and* Gilda Gray, sketches by MacDonough *and* Flagg, and music by Malvin Franklin as well as George Gershwin, could not be otherwise. Robert Benchley, writing for *Life*, noticed this dichotomy: "There is nothing so funny as good burlesque and nothing so ghastly as a poor one. . . . Both good and ghastly are to be found in *Snapshots of 1921*."[23] Benchley equated the more sophisticated, contemporary material with good burlesque, and damned with faint praise the slapstick and vaudevillian elements. Many of the newspaper critics disagreed with Benchley, preferring the broader humor. As a performer and producer, Fields proved himself capable of both styles. Everybody—highbrow and lowbrow—found something to like or knock.

The pinnacle of Act One (or the pit, depending on one's taste) was H. I. Phillip's "Clara da Loon," a rather obvious spoof of *Clair de Lune* that was variously described as "racy," "spicy," or "vulgar." De Wolf Hopper and Nora Bayes took aim at the roles originated by John and Ethel Barrymore. Lulu McConnell, as Clara, the former-duchess of Worcestershire, got the thrill she craved only after an affectionate wrestling match with Hopper. The zinger was Fields: as the blind girl who (according to one critic) must have lost her sight after catching a glimpse of herself in the mirror, he brought down the house. The Act One finale was an elaborate chorus routine set to the melody "The Bamboula," in which the girls performed an Argentine dance in front of an iridescent patent-leather backdrop.

In Act Two, "Who Done It?" by Frances Nordstrom poked fun at murder mysteries using rhymed couplets ("newspaper syndicate verse," Benchley called it). Then Nora Bayes sang several of her love ditties to her man of the hour, Alan Edwards. A final sketch featured the robust Lulu McConnell trying to assemble a collapsible bungalow on the roof of a Manhattan building while George MacKay looked on, not lifting a finger, but full of sympathy and advice. A final chorus spectacle closed out the evening.

Once it was trimmed and polished, Fields' *Snapshots of 1921* was as strong as any of the new editions of the established revues. "Here for once," wrote the *Herald*'s critic, "is a revue that actually fulfills the purpose for which such productions were originally designed and instead of depending on bathing costumes and dimpled knees for its principle theme, 'reviews' or burlesques other theatrical productions." Unfortunately, it had everything else going against it: an early and intense heat wave, competition later in the month from Ziegfeld and White, and a deepening economic recession. In the same issue in which the *Clipper* reviewed

Snapshots, it announced: "Broadway Theaters Hit by Worst Business Slump in Years." Of the thirty shows playing in early June, only ten showed a profit. By July 15, there were only sixteen Broadway shows still running (the smallest number since the end of the war)—and *Snapshots* was not one of them.

Snapshots, with its star-studded payroll, had to bring in $12,000 a week to break even. Though it started with a rush, by the third week it was below the break-even point. Fields asked the cast to take a salary cut of twenty-five percent; everybody was agreeable except Nora Bayes. Bayes was receiving a whopping $2,300 a week with a run-of-the play contract. Fields asked her to tear up her contract and renegotiate, or to withdraw from the show. She refused. The Selwyns had no choice but to close down the show.

Fields' weekly paycheck was now all that stood between him and financial ruin. The Selwyns' planned to reopen the show without Bayes later in the summer when they hoped business conditions would be better. Fields could not afford to be so patient. *Snapshots* reopened without Bayes after only two weeks, the minimum layoff allowed for voiding a contract. The cast's eagerness to continue may be attributed to the fact that their salary arrangement included profit participation.

Fields worked desperately to salvage the show. He redistributed Bayes' comedy duties to Lulu McConnell and her singing chores to Delyle Alda, and inserted two big scenes in the second act. One of the scenes involved a series of five specialty dancing acts. The other featured Fields in the delicatessen scene from *The Summer Widowers*, which Fields had prepared to send out on the vaudeville circuit earlier in the summer. Inserting one of his tried-and-true routines had always worked before when a show was foundering.

The expense of the new scenery, costumes, and dancing acts ate up most of what was saved by Bayes' departure. The heat wave had abated, but the audience's enthusiasm had likewise cooled. Though the renovated *Snapshots of 1921* had virtually the same cast except for Bayes, it only lasted another two weeks. When news of the closing reached several of Fields' hungriest creditors, they moved in for the kill. One of them held the mortgage for the Fieldses' home on West Ninetieth Street. For the better part of six years, Fields had been stumbling from one financial crisis to the next, but the imminent threat of public embarrassment to his family may have finally forced him to accept the inevitable.

On August 20, 1921, Lew Fields filed a voluntary petition for bankruptcy, with liabilities of $82,126 and assets of $10,500. The assets were described as "debts due on open accounts," including a $7,500 cash loan to Jack Dalton (Marie Dressler's husband-manager) while rehearsing *Tillie's Nightmare*. Among the principal creditors were the Aetna Finance Company ($23,000), B. Altman & Company ($6,005), Marcus Loew ($2,000), and Henry Waterson ($5,000). (Waterson, a music publisher and Irving Berlin's ex-partner, was, like Fields, a heavy gambler, mostly at the race track.) Published accounts listed only $50,000 worth of debts. No mention was made of the Shuberts or Fields' in-laws, the Marcuses, but it is fair to assume that they were among the creditors.

Through his attorney, Fields stated that his recent ventures had been unsuccessful and that he hoped "to make a fresh start unhampered by creditors." He was not the only noted Broadway figure in financial straits; recent bankrupts included Jack Norworth, Raymond Hitchcock, and Oscar Hammerstein, Inc. Around this time, veteran producer William A. Brady admitted that he had been broke ten times in the previous twenty years: "The line between solvency and stringency among Broadway producers is proverbially thin at most times. Being Broadway broke is a condition that has no equivalent in any other business save that, perhaps, of the race course. The purseless producer of today may be the prospective bonanza king of tomorrow."[24]

It was definitely an attitude Fields subscribed to. He was merely "Broadway broke." But like Dickens' Mr. Micawber, he lived by the belief that "something will turn up."

Meanwhile, he moved his fretting family to less expensive—but still fashionable—quarters, renting at 562 West End Avenue. In the presence of his family, he was ever the eternal optimist. Only those he tried to borrow money from, or stall on a payment, ever caught a glimpse of the desperation he must have felt.

Still, his sense of his role in the human comedy was as acute as ever. Three years after his bankruptcy, there was a telling scene in a show co-written by his son Herbert. Lew Fields' character is a man who has just lost his job, and he and his beloved daughter are flat broke. A young lady from his former place of employment stops by to see his daughter. It is hot and she would like some ice cream. The guest offers to pay for it, but Fields refuses, saying, "No guest can pay." Fields then takes a few steps towards the door, and turning away from his guest and his daughter, opens his pocketbook and peers into its empty recesses. What he sees is disturbing. "How dark it is," he says, still fishing hopefully in his pocketbook.

What Fields saw in 1921 was undoubtedly disturbing; all that he could do was to continue fishing.

CHAPTER XVI

Good Hokum

Despite our ongoing development in these genres in the last 15 years, they are not really provocative enough to tease the appetite, to tempt the taste further into the theatre. They may someday. That is their logical development, but today they are oftener desserts—*tours de force* in french pastry, hasty pudding, mince pie, bittersweet bonbons, nuts!

Oliver M. Sayler, *Our American Theatre*, 1923

It was hokum, but good hokum. . . . Slapstick is all right if it is served properly, and we can make even the high-brows like it if we just put it up in a nice, artistic manner. Hokum is life, you know.

Lew Fields, 1925

WARREN Gamaliel Harding was the first President who looked like he could have been sent from Central Casting; a white-haired version of William Farnum, the beefy Hollywood matinee idol. Harding fulfilled the popular image of a president; his genial manner and resonant voice could really "put over" the lines that others wrote for him. Perhaps this explains why he was the candidate of choice for so many actors at the time. Shortly after his nomination, a group of Broadway's established stars formed the Harding-Coolidge Theatrical League. Al Jolson headed it, and took credit for the official Republican campaign song, "Harding, You're the Man for Us." Lillian Russell, a vocal supporter of women's suffrage and Actors' Equity, campaigned for the Republican ticket. When Harding visited New York shortly after the Republican national convention, the reception committee of the Harding-Coolidge Theatrical League included Blanche Ring, De Wolf Hopper, and Lew Fields.

Fields, like most first- and second-generation Jews, had always been a solid Democrat. For a man of his background to vote Republican was the mark of a dedicated assimilationist. As he was a member of the Broadway establishment, however, his position made more sense. Harding was the candidate of big business, campaigning for tax reduction, law and order, and "normalcy." Show business was big business; Wall Street was buying into Broadway as never before. "Normalcy"—a nonexistent word to describe an illusory past—was what the aging Broadway establishment wanted most of all. Beneath this desire for normalcy was considerable uncertainty and a fear of change. In this regard Lew Fields was emblematic of Broadway at large.

For three years following his bankruptcy, Fields was a stranger to Broadway and musical comedy. Between the summer of 1921 and the beginning of 1924, he performed in New York for a total of thirteen weeks, and then mostly in vaudeville with Weber. His career was at low ebb; his vaudeville appearances kept his name in the public eye, but they also seemed to obscure the memories of his achievements as a producer before the war. Indeed, his prolonged absence from Broadway as a producer and performer led some to wonder if he had already retired.

Fields' self-imposed exile coincided with a serious slump in the quality and profitability of the Broadway musical. A combination of factors—the financial downturn, rising production costs, the onset of Prohibition, the growth of motion pictures—explained Broadway's economic problems, but not the artistic poverty of the Broadway musical. This same period saw an explosion of inspired plays for the non-musical stage—the early satires of George Kaufman and Marc Connelly *(Dulcy, Merton of the Movies, Beggar on Horseback)*, George Kelly's *The Show Off*, Stallings' and Anderson's *What Price Glory?*, and Eugene O'Neill's first full-length dramas, *Beyond the Horizon, The Emperor Jones, Anna Christie*, and *Desire Under the Elms*.

Broadway's best young talents were writing straight and often serious plays; their work focused on—even celebrated—the collapse of traditional standards. They regarded the studied cuteness and naïveté of the musical, with its endless variations of the Cinderella fairy-tale, as a vehicle for Babbits and hucksters. Younger playwrights aspired to artistic higher ground, addressing the social issues that had formerly embarrassed or intimidated the popular stage.

Far from being offended, Broadway audiences were titillated, even enthralled. During the latter half of the decade, Broadway (musicals and non-musicals alike) would boom as never before, from fewer than 150 productions in 1920 to a high of 264 in the 1926–1927 season. While New York was emerging as the imperial capitol of American theater, road companies and vaudeville went into a gradual decline. The centralization of the theatrical business in New York, begun by the Syndicate and completed by the Shuberts, strangled once-thriving musical production centers such as Chicago and Philadelphia and reduced these cities to mere stops on the itinerary of Broadway touring companies. As box office conditions worsened, legit theaters began booking motion pictures alone or in combination with vaudeville.

Between 1920 and 1925, Broadway was home to sophisticated, intimate revues and straight comedies. Few of them travelled well. The only musical productions to prosper both in New York and on the road were throwbacks to an earlier era of musicals: operettas such as *Blossom Time* and *Rose Marie*, both of which topped five hundred New York performances and spawned so many road companies that they became the Flying Dutchmen of the American heartlands. But for most musical comedy producers, any place outside of New York was treacherous territory. In the hinterlands—essentially, everywhere west of Newark—vaudeville was still king.

Veteran showmen were bewildered. "Public Attitude Towards Theatre Hard

to Figure," was the headline of an article about Hugh A. Anderson, manager of
the company that produced the *Greenwich Village Follies* and *Jack and Jill*.
Alongside the inscrutability of audience tastes, Anderson pointed out that it now
cost $100,000 to raise the opening night curtain on a well-mounted musical, with
a payroll between $9,000 and $12,500 a week. Ten years earlier, a run of 150
performances had been enough to cover the cost of a musical production; now,
it took 250 nights of big business.[1]

For Lew Fields, the quintessential "in-and-outer," whose career was based
on a constantly shifting blend of popular stage formats, the fragmentation of
public tastes was especially troubling. "Giving the public what it wants" had become an infinitely more complex task than in the days when musical shows such
as *The Girl Behind the Counter* and *Weber & Fields' 1912 Jubilee* were embraced by a national public. Compared to previous eras, there was less crossover
in the performers, subject matter, techniques, and, consequently, the audience,
and the amount of crossover diminished further as the decade wore on. For the
first half of the decade, Fields was on the road performing with and without
Weber in vaudeville; for the latter half, he would be producing and acting in
Broadway musicals for New York audiences. To a great extent, the sharply divided nature of Fields' activities in the 1920's could be said to represent the
tensions and contradictions within popular-stage audiences at that time.

Lew Fields' uncertainty about the direction of musical theater typified that
of the Broadway establishment. Familiar institutions and faces were disappearing
from the scene. The musical comedy spectacles Fields had pioneered and Ziegfeld and George White had perfected were sagging under the weight of their own
extravagance and the audience's jaded expectations. The ragtime vogue was also
waning; Tin Pan Alley had not succeeded in domesticating jazz yet, and the up-
and-coming young Broadway composers were still mastering the new idiom.

When Fields replaced half of Rodgers & Hart's score for *Poor Little Ritz
Girl* at the last tryout, it revealed the extent of his ambivalence about his creative
collaborators as well. He had for some time expressed impatience with the established composers and librettists. By 1919, he was already turning to younger associates—his son Herb and Rodgers & Hart—to provide material to rejuvenate
his productions. Yet, at the same time, his failures (and the uncertain economic
conditions) made him more cautious and conservative than ever. He did not have
the resources to take on unproven newcomers who did not inspire the confidence
of backers. Whenever there was uncertainty about the prospects of a show—and
uncertainty was chronic—Broadway's aging musical producers would fall back
on the same old writers and composers: Harry B. Smith, A. Baldwin Sloane, Raymond Hubbell, E. Ray Goetz, Victor Herbert. Evidently, Fields was not satisfied
with this solution. His inability to find suitable collaborators may have contributed to his temporary retirement from the Broadway musical stage.

A changing of the guard seemed to be taking place. Fields noted sadly the
passing of former colleagues and collaborators, several of them close friends as
well: John T. Kelly (the first star signed by Weber & Fields for their music hall),
Fields' longtime press agent William Raymond Sill, and Lillian Russell (all in 1922);

composers Victor Herbert and Louis Hirsch (in 1924) and A. Baldwin Sloane (in 1925), and the great Dutch comic Sam Bernard (1926). Increasingly, oldtimers like Cohan and Fields were being looked upon as the last of a dying breed.

Among theater folk, bankruptcy was a regrettable fact of life—it happened to the best of them, from Oscar Hammerstein to Marie Dressler. In the business world (and in respectable society), bankruptcy could still seriously damage a reputation. When the hapless breadwinner was an actor, it reinforced the stereotype of the actor as an irresponsible, indulgent child unable to cope with the realities of everyday life.

Lew and Rose Fields were, as we have seen, acutely sensitive to the negative stereotype of the actor. They did not have to look far to encounter these prejudices—on Sundays, no farther than their dining room table, when Frances and her husband Charles Marcus usually joined them for dinner. Before the bankruptcy, Charles' brother Bernard, who lived two blocks down West End Avenue, sometimes came to these Sunday dinners as well. For Bernie Marcus, first vice-president of the Bank of the United States, Fields' bankruptcy confirmed what he had always said about the family. Bernie could afford to be smug; he was running one of the city's largest banks, and his early attempts at large-scale stock market speculation were already making a name for him as one of the new breed of bankers. Meanwhile, he chided his brother Charles for lending so much money to "drunks and gamblers" (it is unclear who were the "drunks," since Lew did not drink; perhaps he was referring to Herb and Herb's circle of friends). Charles disliked Bernie's arrogance, but Fields' frequent pleas for "loans" had become an irritation. Aside from Frances, the other three Fields children seemed to be following their father's wayward path: Joe had returned to France after the war determined to become a painter; Herb seemed determined to be an actor or a playwright; Dorothy spent too much time doing amateur theatricals and not enough on her schoolwork, and she kept flunking math.

To borrow a Yiddishism that Charles' father, Joseph (founder of the bank), might have used: the Fieldses were *luftmenshn*—"people of the air"—living without visible means of support. The Marcuses had, for a time, provided the invisible means. After Lew Fields' bankruptcy, Bernie's disdain became increasingly apparent, and Charles rarely accompanied Frances to her family's Sunday dinners.

Fortunately, Lew Fields' greatest asset was still intact. His recent stage appearances in *A Lonely Romeo* and *Snapshots of 1921* proved that as a comedian he was as popular as ever—still youthful, too, surprising audiences with handsprings, triple taps, and vigorous roughhousing. True to his trouper's heart, he vowed to continue performing for as long as he was physically able to provoke genuine laughter. Performing was still a matter of survival for Fields, as it had been since his Bowery childhood. He once told his daughter Dorothy that there was only one cure for an unsuccessful show: "When a show flops, write another one." Whether the show was labelled a musical or vaudeville mattered little, as long as the money was green.

Less than a month after declaring bankruptcy, Lew Fields announced that he was returning to vaudeville. This came as no surprise; whenever Broadway had proven inhospitable to Fields in the past, he had returned to his roots, to the format that had made him famous. Considering his finances and his uncertainty about the public's changing tastes, vaudeville made perfect sense. It was, after all, the place where aging legit stars went to make a bundle before retiring.

The only surprise was his choice of circuits. In the spring of 1920, the Shuberts announced that they were, in Lee's words, "returning to an earlier love"— the two-a-day format of big-time vaudeville. A dozen years after the Shuberts' ill-fated alliance with Klaw & Erlanger and William Morris, Lee Shubert was eager to challenge the vaudeville heavyweights one more time. J. J., who reportedly knew "more about vaudeville than Lee has ever found out," refused to have anything to do with the scheme.[2] To a *Variety* reporter, Lee vowed: "If I spend every dollar I have got, I am going through with this. . . . I'll show that bunch that there are others in the business. We're in the show business, and vaudeville is as much in the show business as anything else." Behind his braggadocio was a certain urgency: the Shuberts were not exempt from the business slump of 1920–1922, and they were desperately searching for cheaper alternatives to book into their out-of-town theaters. Except for movie houses, vaudeville houses were the only kind of theaters outside of New York making any money at the time. Lee Shubert wanted a piece of it, fast. To organize the return of "Advanced Vaudeville," Lee hired away Arthur Klein, one of Keith-Albee's booking agents. The circuit would consist of thirty-four theaters across the East and Midwest, two shows a days for six days a week, and a "concert" on Sundays to circumvent local blue laws. The scale of ticket prices was from twenty-five cents to one dollar. Klein immediately began trying to sign U.B.O. headliners—Will Rogers, Eddie Cantor, Fred and Adele Astaire, Fanny Brice, Nora Bayes, the Marx Brothers—provoking a bidding war with Albee that sent salaries skyrocketing. Rogers, who had received $3,500 a week in the last season's *Follies*, received a cool $5,000 a week with the Shuberts. Other performers were able to double their usual fees.

Lee Shuberts' uncharacteristically generous contracts astounded the industry. Many of the theaters booking the Shubert vaudeville bills were too small to pay the star's salaries. The only logic to Lee Shuberts' strategy was that he intended to threaten the U.B.O. with a costly war of attrition. He may have thought that Keith and Orpheum, rather than go head to head with his opposition circuit, would once again offer a settlement. It had worked once, so why not try it again?

Ned Albee prepared to do battle by setting aside twenty million dollars to combat Shubert Vaudeville. During the coming two seasons, the Keith circuit underwent the biggest expansion in the history of vaudeville—buying, leasing, or building an additional thirty-eight theaters. Not only would Albee match Shubert dollar for dollar on salaries, he could offer forty-week guarantees in two big-time circuits, lucrative return dates, and long-term New York–area engagements.

By early 1921, it was already clear that the Shubert circuit could not compete with the combined might of the Keith and Orpheum organizations by playing straight vaudeville. With the collapse of legit revenues, Lee Shubert was also faced with the problem of what to do with all of the musical comedy and revue performers he had under contract. He recalled the "tab" (tabloid) shows developed by Marcus Loew and Lew Fields for the 1912–1913 season. Based on sketches

or condensed versions from Fields' most successful shows, these miniature revues consisted of a small cast and chorus headed by a "name" performer. The
shows were booked as a unit on the vaudeville circuits—an upscale alternative
to vaudeville but less expensive than a Broadway road company or bill of vaudeville stars. Advanced Vaudeville would consist of "unit shows," Lee Shubert told
Variety; he intended to create a new audience for "class vaudeville."

The unit show consisted of two sections separated by an intermission: a
vaudeville bill consisting of five acts, and a miniature revue. Its format was strongly
reminiscent of Weber & Fields' programs in the first three seasons of their music
hall. To John Shubert, J. J.'s son, the Shubert Advanced Vaudeville format went
back even farther, to the old minstrel show: a series of individual turns followed
by an afterpiece that brought together most of the bill's principal entertainers.[3]

Not straight vaudeville, then, or revue, or musical comedy, but a combination
of all three. The aesthetic distinctions between the popular stage formats were
less rigid than the underlying financial considerations. The Shuberts seized on
the hybrid stage format to circumvent the contractual categories established by
the stage unions. The new contracts for most performers and backstage personnel stipulated a graduated salary scale, from musicals and straight plays at the
top, through revues, vaudeville (big-time, small-time, and several shades in between), with burlesque at the low end. (Actually, the scale of salaries for big-time
vaudeville stars was usually higher than that of their counterparts on the legit
stage, but the average rate for anything less than big-time was considerably lower).
By the end of the first season of Advanced Vaudeville, *Variety* and the *New York
Star* were reporting that the Shuberts had negotiated separate contracts for the
vaudeville and revue sections of the unit show. The Shuberts claimed that they
were not presenting a straight vaudeville bill; neither was it a musical comedy,
and the olio of vaudeville turns in the first half of the show was incompatible
with the structure of a revue. What else could it be, the Shuberts reasoned, but
burlesque? By defining their unit shows as burlesques, they could justify paying
the lowest salaries.

Impresarios had been after Fields for almost five years to sign him up for
vaudeville. Even without Weber, he had considerable drawing power. In August,
1921, the Shuberts needed Fields almost as much as he needed them. And it must
have occurred to the Shuberts that Fields' financial straits made a reunion with
Weber a strong likelihood.

Salvaging the best comedy and chorus bits from the Broadway version, Fields
shrank *Snapshots of 1921* to seven scenes with a total running time of one hour.
He interspersed some of his own familiar sketches ("The Hat Shop," "The Eternal
Triangle," and "A Barbershop") with songs and chorus numbers. Because a small
cast and chorus were essential to the unit's profitability, performers had to be
versatile enough to appear in the vaudeville olio and to play two or more roles
in the revue. Of his original cast, Fields retained only Lulu McConnell to support
him in the comedy duties. The olio featured McConnell with her husband, Grant
Simpson, and a scrawny young comic with great bags under his eyes and a devastating deadpan. Fred Allen—dubbed "the great sourpuss" by S. J. Perelman—
was one of several promising performers who broke into the big-time touring in

the unit shows. For his turn in *Snapshots*, Allen sat at the edge of the stage with his legs dangling into the orchestra pit. He delivered his monologue in a nasal voice, accompanying himself on a dilapidated banjo, playing and singing with deliberate wretchedness.

The season officially opened in New York, at the Shuberts' Forty-Fourth Street, the theater that they had originally built for Weber & Fields. The reviews were not favorable. After several weeks on the road, however, *Snapshots* was prospering, primarily on the strength of Fields' performances: "[His] artistry in comedy work is more impressive than ever."[4] By mid-November, the Fields unit was playing to packed houses.

Personnel in the unit shows changed frequently, particularly the vaudeville acts. Once the companies were out of the New York area, the Shuberts urged the managers to replace acts that did not draw raves with less expensive talent. With the exception of Fred Allen and McConnell & Simpson, the vaudeville olio for *Snapshots* was completely changed by the end of the first month. One of the substitutes in the revue was Herbert Fields. Although he had supposedly given up his ambitions to be a performer, Herbert appeared in "The Eternal Triangle" with his father and danced with Ruth Thomas in the "Iridescent Symphony" scene. It is not clear whether Herbert's return to the stage signalled a reawakening of his ambitions, or whether his father was simply desperate to trim the payroll in every way possible. When he was not performing, Herbert made himself useful backstage, as stage manager and makeup man.

At about the same time that Herbert returned to the stage as a performer, his buddy Richard Rodgers replaced the original conductor, Malvin Franklin, whose contract had expired. Since the disappointing experience of *Poor Little Ritz Girl*, Rodgers and Hart had returned to writing for amateur musicals, hoping to showcase their talents to attract the attention of a Broadway producer. Rodgers was also pursuing a classical music education at the Institute of Musical Art under the direction of Dr. Frank Damrosch. There he received the training that transformed him from a amateur with good instincts into a trained musician. As devoted as he was to his classical studies, he never lost sight of his goal to become a Broadway composer. In late November, 1921, he left the rarefied atmosphere of the Institute to immerse himself in the hurly-burly of a vaudeville tour.

The gig was more than just a conciliatory gesture by Fields; it was a vital step in Rodgers' education as a Broadway composer. Joining the Fields unit in Pittsburgh, Rodgers had a week to study the music for the vaudeville acts and the revue. In each city, Monday mornings were for orchestra rehearsals, and the show opened in the afternoon. The pit orchestras consisted of local musicians of varying ability, and it was up to the musical director-conductor to enforce a semblance of unity. The pit musicians were usually middle-aged men, and some of them resented being directed by a nineteen-year-old college boy. Rodgers' obvious competence soon won them over. He made his professional debut as an orchestra conductor at the Shubert-Detroit Opera House. By the time he finished touring with Fields in the spring, he had learned many tricks of the trade.[5]

The success of Fields' unit shows was atypical, for the Shuberts and for the industry as a whole. By taking no risks, nor trying anything new, by giving the

public Lew Fields at his most familiar, he had profitted in a season described by
the *New York Clipper* as "the worst season in years" for both the road and
Broadway. One and a half million dollars had been lost on Broadway, and for
once, none of it belonged to Fields. The Shubert losses in vaudeville were estimated to be half a million; Lee Shubert announced "a financial re-organization"
and vowed that Advanced Vaudeville would be back for the 1922–1923 season.

Behind the scenes, Lee was frantically trying to line up stars to tour with
unit shows in the fall. He watched with dismay as Charles Dillingham tried to
bring Fields back together with Weber in a musical comedy. Neither of the veteran producer-comedians would commit without first seeing the script for the
proposed show—another indication of the general lack of confidence in musicals.

The erstwhile partners likewise passed up an opportunity to be a part of one
of the most lucrative displays of sticky sentimentality ever to emerge on the
American stage. *Abie's Irish Rose*, a formula comedy by a former actress named
Anne Nichols, was one of the few exceptions to the Broadway box office drought
of 1922. Anne Nichols' play told the familiar story of a Jewish girl who married
an Irish boy, and the conflicts between their in-laws. The battling ethnics are
reconciled in the end by a typically saccharine expedient: the married couple
produce twins, one named Rebecca, and the other, Patrick. Panned by most of
the New York critics (except for the *Times*), *Abie's Irish Rose* played for four
straight years and sent out a half dozen touring companies. Though it appears to
be part of a tradition of ethnic humor that began with Harrigan & Hart and included Weber & Fields, none of these early purveyors was ever as insipid or as
inaccurate in their Jewish and Irish stereotypes as Nichols' play.

Though Dillingham, Lee Shubert, and the Keith booking office were competing for the services of Weber & Fields as a team, Joe and Lew had not met face
to face to discuss it. The wounds from their dispute four years earlier had not
completely healed. Fields must have realized how much he had to gain financially
by a reunion tour, and so did everybody else on Broadway; still, he did not want
to be seen as the supplicant. Fortunately, his colleagues in the Friars' Club conspired to break the impasse. The Annual Friars' Frolic on June 4, 1922, celebrated
reconciliation within the profession. Antagonists in the Equity strike came together and made peace; the entertainment was provided by Eddie Cantor, one of
Equity's most outspoken supporters, and George M. Cohan, who had resigned
from the Friars' Club at the height of hostilities in 1919. The toastmaster was
Willie Collier, who had joined Cohan's union, Actor's Fidelity. Ted Lewis and his
jazz orchestra and George Gershwin supplied the music. The feature of the bill
was the reunion of Weber & Fields as Mike and Meyer in their famous "Choking
Scene."

It was the first time the two had been backstage together since their ill-fated
production of *Back Again*. Weber, who had not appeared on stage since then,
nervously chain-smoked Turkish cigarettes while he and Fields talked through
their routines. Without his belly and chin-piece, Joe looked wizened and fragile.
He worried that he would not remember his lines, prompting Cohan to kid him
about his age. Cohan lifted his straw hat and teased, "Say, Joe, you're getting

almost as gray as I am." Cohan was nine years younger than Joe and Lew, and his hair had gone gray when he was in his twenties.

Fourteen years before, the Friars' Club had been the scene of another Weber & Fields benefit performance that led to a personal reconciliation. After that performance, the Friars had insisted that the duo kiss and make up. Now, as "Noah Webster's worst enemies" resumed their violent friendship, the roughhousing was milder, the physical business a bit stiffer, but the malapropisms and crossfire banter were dizzying as ever. The old chemistry was still there.

Rumors of a reunion tour began circulating immediately and the bidding intensified. Lee Shubert guaranteed the team $3,000 and an unspecified percentage of the gross for thirty-five weeks. (By way of comparison, Rudolph Valentino's contract with Famous Players–Lasky paid him $1,250 a week). Weber stated that the offer was acceptable to him, but that he was waiting to hear from Fields; who pretended to be thinking over the proposition for several weeks.

Insiders regarded the signing of Weber & Fields as the salvation of the Shubert vaudeville enterprise; it was "a coup, with the comedians not only a sure fire for the particular show in which they will appear, but to impart strength to the entire franchise field."[6] In reorganizing the circuit, Lee Shubert had sold "franchises" in each unit show to interested backers, each of whom then became an officer in the Affiliated Theatres Corporation, the Shuberts' holding company for their vaudeville interests. It also meant that Lee had found a way to shift the burden of risk onto outside investors—the producers who held franchises. The franchise for Weber & Fields' *Reunited* was owned by one I. H. Herk, who assumed day-to-day responsibilities for its management. For the first time ever, Weber & Fields would be performing under a third party's management. It turned out to be a very wise decision.

I. H. "Izzy" Herk, along with Sam Scribner, headed the Columbia Wheel, the largest of the burlesque circuits. The Columbia was known for "clean" burlesque—no bare legs or breasts, no swearing, no smoking, no Irish dialects or references to women's suffrage or Prohibition. But when cabarets and revues began presenting spicier fare, independent burlesque managers rushed to provide the blue entertainment that the Columbia Wheel had discouraged. Scribner and Herk responded by organizing another circuit, the American Wheel, for the raunchier stuff. By 1922, both Wheels were being dogged by financial problems caused by labor disputes, the general box office decline, and disagreements between Scribner and Herk. When the American Wheel collapsed, Herk and a few other Columbia managers began negotiating with Lee Shubert, offering their theaters for the Shubert unit shows.

It was not without some trepidation that Weber & Fields put themselves under the managerial wing of a well-known burlesque producer. Weber, whose nephew Larry produced shows for small-time vaudeville and the burlesque wheels, checked into Herk's financial solvency. Fields, whose brother Sol had become a stage director in New York burlesque houses, worried that the association would tarnish their wholesome image. He was reassured when he learned that Herk had been behind the recent attempts to clean up burlesque.

For the 1922–1923 season, Lew Fields also had the franchise for a separate unit show, *Ritz Girls of 19 and 22*, which he directed but did not appear in. The revue portion of the show consisted of the soda fountain scene from *The Girl Behind the Counter* and the spiked candy routine from *A Lonely Romeo*. At the same time that Lew was recycling his old hits, his brother Nat was producing tabloid editions of old musical comedies for Loew and Pantages, the popularly priced (small-time) vaudeville circuits. This time, Nat, who had not always bothered to ask for his brother's permission in the past, secured the rights to *The Girl Behind the Counter, Hanky Panky, All Aboard, Hokey Pokey,* "Barbara Fidgety," and Cohan's *Forty-Five Minutes from Broadway.* For material that was originally concocted and served up as quickly as an ice cream sundae, it certainly seemed to have a durable shelf life. Was the material that good, or was the budget of available material so slim? Or were the names "Weber & Fields" and "Lew Fields" on a show still enough to sell tickets, no matter how shopworn the material?

The New York–area critics liked the visual production and polish of *Ritz Girls*, but they lamented Lew Fields' absence from the cast. Mostly, they felt that the humor was stale, but their opinions and attitudes seemed to have less and less to do with the tastes of theater patrons outside of New York. The cast of *Ritz Girls* who carried the Fields canon to a more or less eager populace included the veteran Dutch comedian Harry Cooper, the team of Shadow & McNeil, the Empire City Quartet, Norwood's Melody Charmers, Baby Josephine, and a charismatic young hoofer named James Cagney. In his memoirs, Cagney's only recollection of Fields indicates that Fields now had a reputation for overextending himself; he was "a gent who almost made a profession out of owing people money."[7]

Fields hoped that *Reunited* would change this. The Shuberts' press agents ballyhooed Weber & Fields' return to vaudeville "for the first time in ten years," conveniently forgetting their engagement at the Palace and their season on the Keith circuit in 1915. Rather than opening cold in New York, Weber & Fields brought their show to Hartford for a week of tryouts. The performances were ragged but profitable; several of the acts were clearly inferior and did not fit into the program. Of greater concern was the fact that Weber was having trouble with his throat (perhaps he was no longer accustomed to being choked twice a day, six days a week).

On September 18, 1922, *Reunited* officially opened its season in New York by selling out the Central (Forty-seventh and Broadway). The olio began with the acrobatic dances of the Ladellas, ditties sung by sweet-voiced, statuesque Lynn Canter, and a quick-change artist named Charles T. Aldrich. Two elaborate production numbers followed, "The Tick of Time" and "Tulip Land."

The second half consisted of old favorites from the Weber & Fields vaults—some of them now over a quarter of a century old—strung together with musical interludes and chorus routines: "The Pool Table," "The Hypnotist," "The Choking Scene," and "The Dying Gladiators." Their German dialect was not as fractured as of yore, and their physical assaults were fewer. Fields gave a typically energetic performance, "bobbing all over the stage until he seemed like a squad of actors."[8] Weber seemed less mobile and quieter, and therefore even more like a clueless victim. For an encore, instead of a curtain speech, Weber & Fields did a burlesque of quick-change artist Charles T. Aldrich, recalling that distant turning point in their careers when they had spoofed Fregoli's quick changes at Hammerstein's Olympia and thereby discovered the commercial power of theatrical travesties.

Alone among the critics, Alexander Woollcott was sufficiently clearheaded to look beyond the nostalgia and glad tidings. In his column "Second Thoughts on First Nights," he hinted that there might be something else behind the outpourings of sentiment: "Do not the reunions as such, begin to lack a little of their pristine eventfulness? Are they not a little too much like those clamors of young parents who announce breathless that it is the baby's birthday, and, when you ask for the exact date, you find they mean he is 17 weeks old this very evening?"[9] Most of the audience in the 1920's could not remember a time when Weber & Fields were not coming together again for a reunion. At a Friars' Club dinner in 1925, Cohan would tease Weber & Fields about it: "I'll stop retiring if you two would stop having reunions."

One New York reviewer, who praised *Reunited* lavishly, commented that the show was "an encouraging sign of the times in that it had their ever reliable, genuine humor and not even a faint whiff of jazz"—as if jazz was a kind of toxic gas poisoning those who were unfortunate enough to be exposed to it. In the context of popular entertainments of 1922, Weber & Fields were the antithesis of jazz. To the staid patron of the popular stage in the early 1920's, jazz represented all that was threatening and corrupt in modern urban life—dizzying change and guilty pleasures such as drinking, illicit relations, lewd dancing, decadent glitz— while Weber & Fields evoked fond memories of the innocent pleasures of old New York, with "reliable, genuine humor" from the turn of the century, when immigrants were buffoons rather than bootleggers or Bolsheviks. At a time when the cult of youth had begun to dominate popular culture, Weber & Fields were fifteen to twenty-five years older than any of the other current vaudeville headliners. Some of their routines were older than the performers they were now working with. Clearly, novelty was the last thing Weber & Fields' audience wanted; they wanted the reassuringly old-fashioned antics of Mike and Meyer—what passed for normalcy on the popular stage.

The farther the *Reunited* tour went from New York, the more enthusiastic the audiences became. Lee Shubert's hastily patched-together vaudeville circuit not only covered week-long gigs in the big cities, but split weeks in Altoona, Zanesville, and Wheeling. While Fields seemed to derive renewed energy from the daily ovations, Weber was suffering. Joe developed a bad cold to go with his chronic hoarseness, and there were persistent rumors that he was too fatigued to continue the tour. Weber repeatedly denied it, but the Shubert advance men found that repeating the rumor just ahead of Weber & Fields' next engagement helped boost ticket sales.

By December, 1922, *Reunited* was the only unit show making money. The rest of the Shuberts' circuit was in a state of disarray: every week, more theaters were withdrawing from the circuit and more franchise holders were forced to close down their units. Out of thirty unit shows at the start of the season, only ten had survived. One of the survivors—but barely—was Fields' *Ritz Girls*. His co-franchisees, I. H. Herk and Lee Shubert, viewed the collapse of the circuit as inevitable. Though *Ritz Girls* had started slowly, by the time it played in Cleveland over Thanksgiving, it drew $12,000 for the week, twice its weekly expenses. Nevertheless, Shubert ordered the unit disbanded in early December in St. Louis. Fields protested bitterly by wire:

> I HAVE RITZ GIRLS DOWN TO WHERE IT DOES NOT NEED TO DEPEND ON HOUSE FOR HELP AND WITH SAME CAST AND PERFORMANCE NOW HAS CHANCE TO GET YOU SOME OF THE MONEY BACK IT OWES YOU STOP [. . .] HOW CAN RITZ GIRLS GET YOU BACK SOME MONEY IF IT DOES NOT PLAY IT AINT FAIR AFTER PLAYING DEATH.[10]

"Playing death" had become a fair description of the Shubert vaudeville circuit. To make sure he had enough road theaters, Shubert had booked the unit shows onto the American and Columbia burlesque circuits in return for weekly guarantees from the theaters—the result of his deal with Herk. Though the unit shows were certainly a cut above any offered on the burlesque circuit, many vaudeville patrons (especially in the Midwest) were reluctant to be seen in a venue known for burlesque shows. Lew Fields had long insisted on the importance of this distinction; the association with something tawdry or vulgar was "death" to his brand of entertainment.

With growing indignation, the trade papers published weekly updates of Shubert theaters withdrawing and units going belly-up. In several cities, creditors enlisted police to attach the unit's scenery to pay overdue bills. Company members found themselves stranded out of town without their salaries or even return tickets to New York. With the Shuberts' vaudeville circuit crumbling around them, Weber & Fields continued playing to capacity theaters until early January, when they ran out of theaters to play (the rest of the theaters had dropped out of the circuit). *Reunited* closed in Worcester, Massachusetts, its banner tour stopped after nineteen weeks, eleven weeks short of its guaranteed season. The closing of Weber & Fields' show presaged the end of the Shubert unit shows. Within a week, Lee Shubert announced that he was abandoning the idea of an opposition vaudeville circuit. To save face, the Shuberts sued the Keith and Orpheum organizations for the "unlawful combination in restraint of trade" and demanded $10,000,000 in damages. *Variety* estimated that the losses in Shubert Vaudeville amounted to one and a half million dollars, most of it borne by the producer-franchisees.

The experience of I. H. Herk, producer of Weber & Fields' *Reunited* and co-producer with Lew Fields of *Ritz Girls*, was typical of those who bought franchises in the Shubert unit shows. Along with the collapse of the burlesque wheels, the early closing of *Reunited* spelled financial ruin for Herk, for the last ten weeks of the tour were calculated to be the "profit weeks" for the producers. In March, Herk declared bankruptcy, citing liabilities of over $1,300,000, with $30,000 owed to Weber & Fields under the terms of their pay-or-play contract.[11]

Like most of the other performers in Shubert vaudeville, Weber & Fields never recovered the money they had been guaranteed for the cancelled weeks. Headliners such as Jolson, Cantor, and Weber & Fields did not suffer the same consequences as the rank-and-file vaudevillians who had no choice but to return to booking through Keith and Orpheum. Some were blackballed for a year or more or re-employed at a greatly reduced salary. When the Keith office deigned to bless them with work, refugees from the unit shows had to publicly apologize for their former sins by taking out ads in *Variety* that specifically mentioned their unhappy experiences with Shubert vaudeville.[12]

For Fields, the important thing was to keep getting that weekly paycheck. Novelty and risk-taking—once the characteristics of a Fields production—were yesterday's follies. While his less-robust partner recovered from their arduous two-a-day schedule, Fields embarked on another eight weeks on the road. Combining elements from *Snapshots of 1921* and *Ritz Girls*, Fields opened *Snapshots of 1923* in the New York area in February, 1923. Once again, his troupe included Norwood's Melody Charmers, the Saxophone Sextet, Baby Josephine (who must have been an adolescent by now), the Leightons, James Cagney, and ten chorus girls. Instead of a vaudeville olio in the first half, the entire program consisted of revue sketches. Fields featured himself in five sketches, but he provided valuable opportunities for the versatile young Cagney, who came into his own as a performer during the *Snapshots* tour. Cagney played no fewer than eight parts, ranging from juvenile to old man. His comic timing and dancing drew raves. "Jimmy . . . is a dapper, smiling young chap," observed the *New York Star*, "full of ambition to rise in his adopted profession. He will. Just watch his smoke."

Except for a few talented unknowns such as Cagney and Fred Allen, Weber & Fields may have been the only performers for whom Shubert Vaudeville was a boost rather than a bust. *Reunited* proved that their names were still big box office, though it was impossible to determine whether this was out of nostalgia, curiosity, or the appreciation of a new generation of fans.

At the same time that Weber & Fields were trying to recapture a retreating past, they were not afraid to try something new. One of their other efforts in spring of 1923 was decidedly ahead of its time. A few months earlier, Dr. Lee De Forest returned from Europe to announce a new invention: he had developed a system for recording sound directly on film and reproducing it without the use of a phonograph. In 1908, Dr. De Forest had established himself as a radio pioneer by inventing the Audion tube and broadcasting records over the radio from a primitive studio in New York. Now, the De Forest Phonofilm would revolutionize motion pictures. To demonstrate it, he made several short films with vaudeville stars doing their most famous routines: Eddie Cantor, comedian Phil Baker (later a radio star), the songwriting and singing team of Noble Sissle and Eubie Blake (authors of the 1921 hit musical *Shuffle Along*), the husband and wife song-and-dance duo of Eva Puck and Sammy White, and Weber & Fields. De Forest deliberately picked performers for whom sound—spoken, sung, or instrumental—was an essential part of their act. The possibilities afforded by the sound film would finally show Weber & Fields to their full comic advantage.

Instead, the quality of the filmmaking was mediocre, technically and aesthetically, and Weber & Fields' performances look haphazard and mechanical. The

De Forest Phonofilms were simply filmed stage performances, with the camera static and frontal, and few cuts or close-ups, hardly more sophisticated in their visual design than the first silent films of twenty years before. In the surviving print of Weber & Fields, the lip synchronization was so poor and the sound levels so uneven that it was often difficult to follow the performers' crossfire banter or judge the timing of their stage business.

De Forest's program of Phonofilms premiered at the Rivoli Theater in New York on April 15, 1923, on the bill with *Bella Donna,* starring Pola Negri. There was surprisingly little fanfare: brief mention was made of three classical music and dance reels, but no mention of any vaudeville or jazz demos. Hollywood studios and film exhibitors greeted De Forest's new invention with stony silence. The studios and movie houses were thriving; they feared that the new technology would ruin their industry, necessitating vast outlays to rebuild the silent-film studios and to wire theaters for sound. It would be another three years before anybody in Hollywood was willing to gamble on the talkies.

With the collapse of Shubert vaudeville and the unsuccessful foray into talking films, Fields concluded that a long-term reunion with Weber was not the answer. He needed constant employment, and he found it as a comedian-for-hire, brought in by producer Hugh Anderson to rescue a sinking musical comedy.

Or was it a revue? Critics and the show's creators seemed uncertain. *Jack and Jill* had opened in New York in late March at the Globe Theater to negative reviews. Its loosely structured libretto, an adaptation by Otto Harbach, told the story of a chair that forces anybody who sits in it to tell the truth because it is made from the cherry tree that George Washington supposedly cut down. The premise was clever enough, according to the critics, and the show was beautiful to look at, thanks to director John Murray Anderson's way with chorus numbers, costumes, and lighting effects. The rest of show, however, was called "deplorable"; the libretto itself was slow and lacking in comedy, the performances were indifferent, while the music (by Augustus Barrett) and lyrics (by Barrett, Harbach, and John Murray Anderson) were so-so at best.[13] The one bright spot of the evening was the dancing of petite, sultry Ann Pennington, late of Ziegfeld's Follies and George White's Scandals.

Fields set to work immediately, charged with the task of injecting more humor and snap into the production. With him came two veterans of previous Fields productions, Charles Judels and Lulu McConnell. From the start, it was clear that Fields was to be more than a replacement actor. He rewrote his character, transforming him from Daniel Malone into Daniel Mandell, presumably to facilitate his familiar German characterization—the perpetually perplexed husband and father who stumbles from mishap to mishap with an air of deadly earnestness. A mere ten days after its opening, *Variety* noted that Fields' revised production was a considerable improvement. He continued to rehearse daily, even after the second opening. With the help of Charles Judels, he averted a walk-out by the tired and discouraged chorus girls.

By May, *Jack and Jill* was making money and drawing well, but not enough to cover its initial losses. Its backers refused to put up more money; Hugh Anderson announced that the show would have to close unless the cast including

Lew Fields and Joe Weber in their late teens, as the "Skull Crackers," circa 1885. It was around this time that Meyer asked, "Who vas dot lady I saw you wit last night?" and Mike gave his famous answer. *(Billy Rose Theater Collection, New York Public Library)*

Weber & Fields as the German Senators, in the early 1890's, when they first introduced their poolroom routine. *(Marc Wanamaker)*

"The Dying Gladiators" (a.k.a. the "Statue Scene") from *Hokey Pokey* (1912), the first Weber & Fields reunion. *(Special Collections Library, University of Southern California)*

Fifty years after their first appearance together in a Bowery amateur show, Meyer still manhandled Mike with the same old affection. From a 1927 Vitaphone short. *(Variety Arts Theater Library)*

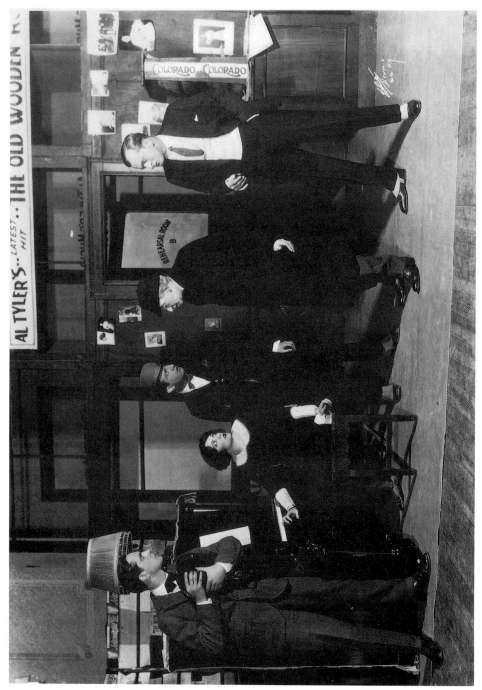

From *The Melody Man* (1924), by Herbert Richard Lorenz (Herbert Fields, Richard Rodgers, and Lorenz Hart). Fields starred as an Old World composer forced to work for a Tin Pan Alley hustler. From left, Fredric March, Eva Puck, Sammy White, and Lew Fields. *(Billy Rose Theater Collection, New York Public Library)*

"Pop" Fields rehearsing a scene from *A Connecticut Yankee* with William Gaxton and Constance Carpenter, at the Vanderbilt Theater (1927). "The entire production," according to the program, "is under the supervision of Lew Fields." *(Museum of the City of New York)*

Peggy-Ann (1926), with a score by Rodgers and Hart, was Herbert Fields' reworking of *Tillie's Nightmare* by way of Freud and the Algonquin Round Table. In this scene, a co-operative fish tows Peggy-Ann and her wedding party back to Havana after they are shipwrecked. *(Billy Rose Theater Collection, New York Public Library)*

Broadway meets Hollywood. From left, Lew Fields, Mack Sennett, Sam Bernard, and in front, Joe Weber. In 1915, Triangle Films spent lavishly on Broadway comedy stars, but the results were disappointing. *(Marc Wanamaker)*

The creative team behind *A Connecticut Yankee*. Behind Lew Fields and directly to his left is his son Herbert; Richard Rodgers, Larry Hart, and Busby Berkeley are all at his right. Fields produced five Rodgers & Hart shows, and Herbert wrote the books for seven. *(Courtesy of Dorothy Hart)*

In 1915, Lew Fields starred in the film version of *Old Dutch*, for World Film Corporation. The setting was changed from Austria to a Miami hotel. From left, top—Charles Judels, George Hassell, Vivian Martin. From right, top—Chester Barnett, Marie Empress, Lew Fields. *(Special Collections Library, University of Southern California)*

As the title character in *The Barker* (Selig, 1917), Fields had a rare opportunity to play a serio-comic role instead of the broad physical clowning he was known for. No print of the film survives. *(Special Collections Library, University of Southern California)*

Fred Astaire, Ginger Rogers, and Lew Fields in *The Story of Vernon and Irene Castle* (RKO, 1938). Fields performed a caricature of himself, thirty years younger. *(Turner Entertainment Company)*

Weber & Fields and Eddie Foy, Jr., in Zanuck's biopic *Lillian Russell* (1940), with Alice Faye, Don Ameche, and Henry Fonda. Zanuck liked their cameo so much that he asked them to "work it up" into a bigger scene and he reshot it. It was their last public performance. *(Twentieth Century-Fox)*

"From the Bowery to Broadway to Beverly Hills." In retirement, Lew Fields was supported in high style by his children, who had contracts with the movie studios. Behind Lew and Rose Fields, from left, Herbert, Dorothy, Joseph, Germaine (Joseph's first wife), and Ray Marcus (Frances' son). *(Courtesy of Ray Marcus)*

Lew, Dorothy, and Helen Hayes, in 1938. Dorothy had just won an Oscar with Jerome Kern for "The Way You Look Tonight," from *Swing Time*. Hayes recalled, "It was so strange to see Lew Fields with his children about him, for as I remembered him, the theater was his only world. . . ." *(Billy Rose Theater Collection, New York Public Library)*

the chorus agreed to a twenty-five percent salary reduction. When Fields heard that the chorus girls were approached first about the reduction, he protested: "It is always the poor chorus girl that is asked first to take a cut from her small salary. Now as a principal I wish to say that it is our business to first accept the concessions asked by the manager and if possible to see that the girls will not be subjected to having their wages reduced, as they need every cent they get." [14]

Salary cuts for the principals kept the show open until the end of June. It closed with the announcement that it would tour in the fall with Fields not only as star but as co-owner.

The possibility of working with Hugh's brother John on musical productions appealed to Fields. John Murray Anderson was the kind of innovative young collaborator Fields had been seeking. A former ballroom dancer and nightclub host, Anderson developed the "intimate" revue, emulating Ziegfeld's glamour but eschewing the Follies' overwhelming scale. When Anderson's *Greenwich Village Follies* first opened in July 1919, his imaginative and resourceful way with decor and musical routines attracted widespread critical praise. He mixed veteran performers—Bessie McCoy Davis and Blossom Seeley (both of whom got their start in Fields' productions)—with promising new talent such as Ted Lewis, Savoy & Brennan, and Joe E. Brown. Despite the presence of genuine stars, the emphasis in these revues was on what Anderson called the "colorful set pieces" and "ballet ballads." The artsy, sophisticated tone of his revue reflected the bohemian chic of the neighborhood in which the original production was located. So popular were Anderson's revues that after the first two editions, the Shuberts saw to it that the next six Greenwich Village Follies went directly to Broadway, where they lost much of their intimacy and insouciant charm.

In Anderson's command of choreography and design, Fields saw a stage director in the tradition of Julian Mitchell and Ned Wayburn. Consciously or not, he may have also recognized his own refracted image. Alexander Woollcott said that Anderson's 1920 revue, *What's in a Name*, contained "the most beautiful staging . . . New York has known"; the show is still considered a landmark in the development of the revue. Much of the acclaim was for the work of designer James Reynolds, who provided tasteful costumes, beautifully painted drapes and draw curtains, and clever sets. Its performers, sketches, and music were unremarkable, however, which may have accounted for its short run.

On the face of it, the collaboration of Lew Fields with Hugh and John Murray Anderson seemed ideal. Fields' strengths—casting, developing and performing comedy sketches, pacing—complemented the Andersons'—sophisticated staging and choreography on a shoestring budget. During the summer, Fields and Hugh Anderson read scripts for future productions together. Their inability to agree on a script was revealing: apparently, they could not agree on the genre, much less on an individual script. Even at the height of the revue's popularity, Fields' preference for book shows was stronger than ever. He still wanted a coherent story with room for character development, a consistent musical score, and some semblance of a plot. These concerns were of decidedly secondary importance to John Murray Anderson. Given a choice, he would rather have the patrons talking about the wardrobe than the plot. According to his brother Hugh, John Murray believed that "color schemes and dress designs constitute the best kind of small talk around tea tables to advertise a show." [15] Revues provided the best opportunity to emphasize these visual elements.

In the end, Anderson and Fields found themselves on opposite sides of the line dividing revue and musical comedy. The differences in their approaches were evident when *Jack and Jill* reopened in Chicago in mid-September. It was now subtitled "a musical comedy revue in three acts (nine scenes)," and the compromise did not appear to satisfy patrons, or most critics. Sheppard Butler of the *Chicago Tribune* characterized the show as "beautiful but dumb," noting that there was "much languid loveliness in evidence . . . but some how it seems meaningless and gets nowhere." Instead of praising the attempt to carry through a story line, the plot was dismissed as "rather a nuisance." Nevertheless, Fields' performance received unstinting praise: "His is not the casual method—he acts a role for all there is in it, and when there is not much in it he fools you with his adeptness at embroidering it round with nonsense. A comedian with brains beneath his buffoonery, I maintain, now as much as in the ancient days." [16]

Jack and Jill eked out its appointed four-week run in Chicago and then headed to Cincinnati for what turned out to be its final two weeks. Following the Saturday night performance, Fields and company learned that Anderson had closed the show—no advance notice, no salaries, only a party ticket back to New York. A lawyer for the costumer attached the costumes. Anderson had ignored warnings that his fall tour was under-capitalized, and by the time he closed the show, his losses topped $130,000. Many of the players were stranded without funds, so Fields and Lulu McConnell advanced them whatever money they needed.

A late casting change provided Fields with some unexpected consolation for the tour's premature demise. When Ann Pennington and Brooke Johns left the show, Anderson replaced them (presumably at Fields' suggestion) with the popular vaudeville song-and-dance team of Eva Puck and Sammy White. Puck and White were the kind of performers Fields most liked to work with: seasoned vaudevillians, energetic, charming, and versatile, equally adept at broad comedy and subtler farce, eccentric dancing, and love songs. On the vaudeville stage, Puck and White were known for their routine "Opera versus Jazz" in which White portrayed a dancing teacher trying to instruct the dimwitted Miss Puck, followed by burlesques of opera and ballet. [17] The opposition of classical music to jazz anticipated the theme of Fields' next venture, in which Puck and White were not only featured players but investors.

The "classical versus jazz" theme held an innate fascination for the rising new generation of Broadway writers and composers as well: the Gershwins, Rodgers, Hart, Herb Fields, and Oscar Hammerstein II. Unlike their elders, they saw nothing irreconcilable about the two styles. Their training and personal tastes combined popular and classical idioms, and their knowledge of the latter led to innovations in the former. The most deliberate in trying to reconcile the two styles was George Gershwin; as early as 1922 he wrote a one-act opera, *Blue Monday Blues*, for George White's Scandals. At the same time, Rodgers was studying at the Institute of Musical Art, though Broadway was his avowed goal; he split his time between classes in theory and music history and working on amateur musicals. While at the Institute, he and Hart wrote *Say It with Jazz*, a spoof of Rimsky-Korsakov's *Le Coq d'or*, which featured a battle between jazz and classical music, with dance numbers staged by Herb Fields. Herb's pluralistic background would not become apparent until he began writing Broadway librettos, but when he did, the models he chose to emulate were Lorenzo da Ponte, W. S. Gilbert, and Guy Bolton.

From a strictly musical standpoint, the issue was not "jazz" at all. In the early 1920's, few of the fledgling Broadway talents—with the exception of George Gershwin—were conversant with real jazz as developed by African-American performers in New Orleans and Chicago. To contemporary critics, such as Gilbert Seldes and Alexander Woollcott, "jazz" referred to the ragtime songs of Irving Berlin and other Tin Pan Alley (i.e., popular) composers, and to the syncopated dance music played by white bands like those of Paul Whiteman and Ben Selvin.[18] "Jazz is ragtime gone daffy," wrote Woollcott in his biography of Irving Berlin. While Woollcott's words betrayed his musical naïveté, for a time his enthusiasm made him part of a distinct minority. Most Broadway critics dismissed jazz as a passing fad foisted on audiences by Tin Pan Alley. Respected composers—Cohan, Sousa, even Kern (Gershwin's idol)—reinforced the attacks.

The vehemence of the attacks suggests that something more was at stake. As we have seen, jazz was already a social phenomenon—almost a bogeyman— before most Americans had ever heard a real note of it. Some of the epithets revealed the underlying moral prejudices: "unbuttoned music," "youth set to music," "symphonic rickets of musical malnutrition."[19] In the early 1920's, to attack jazz was to indict all of the other forbidden activities it was inevitably associated with: drinking, lewd dancing, promiscuity, fraternizing with criminals—in short, big-city life. Jazz, observed F. Scott Fitzgerald, "is associated with a state of nervous stimulation, not unlike that of the big cities. . . . The word 'jazz' in its progress toward respectability has meant first sex, then dancing, then music."

The first two meanings were what interested Tin Pan Alley's streetwise promoters. As so often happens in the history of show business, moral condemnation begets commercial appeal. Scrambling to devise a gimmick to replace ragtime, the song pluggers relabeled their familiar wares with the exotic allure of "jazz." (A few years later, when "blues" became the novelty item, it was slapped haphazardly onto the titles and lyrics of Tin Pan Alley tunes.) Before 1925, when records by James P. Johnson and Fletcher Henderson became national hits, jazz was a fashion statement rather than a musical form. As it appeared in the titles of Rodgers' and Hart's amateur shows—*Say It with Jazz, Jazz à la Carte*—it promised a certain style or attitude: youthful, irreverent, fast, hip.

Fields' *A Lonely Romeo* and *Poor Little Ritz Girl* celebrated the same characteristics the critics of jazz had derided—"unbuttoned music" and "youth set to music." If, as Fields said back in 1916, the function of musical comedy was restorative, "a tonic for the jaded intellect of age . . . [putting] new blood into infirm limbs," then the jazz style was ideally suited to musical comedy. Thus, Fields embraced, somewhat reluctantly, the jazz style for some of the same reasons as Tin Pan Alley. It was not out of any appreciation for the music itself, but as a commercial expedient.

To his credit, Fields recognized that applying the jazz style to musical comedies meant changing the content and tone of the comedy, and not just the music. In a 1924 interview, he described it in terms of the evolution of stage humor:

> Humor has changed as much in the last fifty years as the appearance of Broadway or the illustrations in the fashion magazines. Humor today has to work as fast as the saxophone or the drumsticks in a jazz orchestra. . . . Every joke has to be jazzed as successfully as the modern song writer transforms the bars of the operatic air. . . .
>
> Now humor on the stage is just like the music. It must shake and shimmy and make a lot of noise as the jazz bands do. . . . Everything must be obvious.[20]

Not long before, Fields had been praised as a performer with Weber for presenting a show that had "not a whiff of jazz." Now, as a producer, he was searching for a show that would positively reek of it.

Fields spent the summer of 1923 restlessly reading scripts, looking for a vehicle that would facilitate his return to Broadway as a producer. As the summer wore on, it became increasingly apparent that his new partnership with Hugh and John Murray Anderson was going nowhere. Meanwhile, nobody was trying harder to come up with a script for Fields than the struggling team of Rodgers, Hart, and Herb Fields. A year earlier, they had offered him their first joint effort, entitled *Winkle Town*, about an inventor who builds a new kind of "electronic" system that obviates the use of wires for communication and electric power, and then must convince the town fathers that the idea is practical. Fields did not recognize the prescient nature of the plot or the strength of the score, which included "Manhattan" and nine other songs that eventually found their way into later Rodgers and Hart shows. When Herbert, Rodgers, and Hart tried to peddle their work, other producers would inevitably ask, "If you guys are as good as you think you are, how come Mr. Fields isn't interested in producing your show?"[21] Lew Fields' blindness was also Broadway's blindness.

Upstairs, in the Fieldses' flat on West End Avenue (their elegant townhouse on Ninetieth Street had been sold off to repay creditors), the team would be working away, while Lew sat downstairs, ignoring them completely, perhaps even complaining to Rose about the lack of good material for musicals. In this atmosphere of benign neglect, Herbert, Rodgers, and Hart collaborated on seven amateur shows between *Poor Little Ritz Girl* and their next Broadway breakthrough. For most of them, Herbert was the choreographer, and, occasionally, stage director. Dorothy, a popular student and then a teacher at the Benjamin School for Girls, was sometimes involved as well, either as an interested observer or as a performer. She appeared in their Akron Club shows of 1920 and 1921, and when her school's drama department put on its annual benefit for the New York Child Labor Committee in 1922, she suggested adding several Rodgers & Hart tunes to the score. For her school's next annual benefit production, Herbert, Rodgers, and Hart adapted *If I Were King*, a romance about the beggar-poet François Villon who saved Paris by becoming king for a day. Herbert directed the all-girl cast, with Dorothy in goatee, doublet, and thigh boots starring as Villon. They presented *If I Were King* at the Maxine Elliott Theater on March 25, three days after the opening of *Jack and Jill*. Lew, who was preparing to take over the lead in *Jack and Jill*, did not see his children's Broadway debut.

Two months later, Herbert and Rodgers (with four lyrics by Hart) presented another adaptation, this time at Rodgers' school, the Institute of Musical Art. *A Danish Yankee in King Tut's Court* borrowed the premise and basic plot outline of the Mark Twain novel (and a 1921 silent film) and placed it in a setting that spoofed the current fashion craze, the Egyptian fad sparked by the discovery of the tomb of Tutankhamen. Writing of this in his memoirs, Rodgers provided an important insight into the trio's aesthetic goals. What attracted them to the novel was its "irresistible combination of fantasy and social commentary."[22] Like so much of the work that they did during this period, the material eventually found its way into their Broadway productions.

Despite the experience and exposure that their amateur efforts brought them, they could not win the confidence of a Broadway producer. Frustrated, they conceived a desperate plan. Knowing that Lew Fields was looking for a play, they decided to tailor one to his tastes and abilities. Indeed, it would be a shameless appeal to Pop Fields' vanity. Instead of a musical (which was by definition a more expensive, and therefore riskier, undertaking), they decided to write a straight comedy. Not just any comedy, but one based on one of Lew's favorite roles—the old composer in *The Music Master*, the Charles Klein–David Belasco melodrama that had featured David Warfield. It was, of course, Warfield's crossover from burlesque clowning to serious drama that Fields had long considered the paradigm of professional achievement. As Rodgers later described it, it was "a rather simple-minded sentimental tale," which he admitted "had the aroma of *The Music Master*."[23] The decision to do it, however, was anything but simple or sentimental. The clever young hopefuls were capitalizing on Herb's intimate knowledge of his father's psychology. Their early decision to use a pseudonym underscores their sheepish attitude towards the enterprise.

"Herbert Richard Lorenz," as they called themselves, probably began writing *The Jazz King* in the late summer and had a draft of it ready for Lew Fields in late October when he returned home following the early demise of the *Jack and Jill* tour. The elder Fields was apparently so enthusiastic about the script's potential that he refused several projects from established producers, including two from Lee Shubert. For Fields, *The Jazz King* had all the necessary ingredients: a seriocomic character in the lead, up-to-date references, lots of room for comic bits from supporting characters, maybe even some music. Its themes were familiar from *A Lonely Romeo* and *Poor Little Ritz Girl*: traditional versus modern values, the generational conflict, the temptations of urban life, the misunderstood morality of show people.

The problem was finding financial backing. No matter what Herbert, Richard, and Lorenz called themselves, they were still unknowns. Lew Fields in the lead was a plus, but his track record in nonmusicals was not impressive. It would take over four months before Fields could afford to begin out-of-town tryouts. Nevertheless, when the Shuberts tried to rush the show into one of their New York houses on the strength of its initial tryouts, Fields refused. He had seen too many of his own productions ruined by an overly hasty New York opening, and he was understandably wary of bringing in the Shuberts as partners. During the tryouts, the only backer ever mentioned by name was Fields, though it is doubtful that he could have bankrolled the show alone.

Although the nature of the project must have felt constraining to its otherwise more ambitious authors, *The Jazz King* did allow them to indulge their penchant for social commentary. This was in fact the common denominator between the young authors and their producer-mentor. In the original melodrama, an impoverished Austrian émigré composer loses his job and family at the hands of the Chairman of the Auto Oil Trust, an eccentric multimillionaire who bears a strong resemblance to John D. Rockefeller. For *The Jazz King*, the authors retained the émigré composer of classical music, but transformed the Rockefeller figure into Al Tyler, a slick hustler who heads a large Tin Pan Alley music publishing firm. The composer, Franz Henkel, was known in the Old Country for his lovely "Dresden Symphony," but the misdeeds of his wife forced him to flee to America. Hard times compel him and his beautiful daughter Elsa to work for the unscrupulous Tyler, who has made a fortune stealing classical melodies and reworking them as jazz tunes for cabarets and vaudeville. "Henky" (as Tyler insists on calling the composer) spends his days in the cacophony of the music factory devising jazz orchestrations for stolen melodies. Elsa, working as a stenographer, spurns Tyler's romantic entreaties. By chance, Henky discovers that his employer has turned the "Dresden Symphony" into a ditty called "Moonlight Mama." Outraged, he quits his job. When "Moonlight Mama" becomes an instant hit, he sues Tyler. The wily music publisher knows of Henky's clouded past in Austria and threatens exposure. Elsa smoothes things over, and for her father's sake, agrees to marry the man who stole her father's melody. Henky is heartbroken, especially when he sees his daughter becoming hard and cynical like her husband. Tyler, however, is not as ruthless as he tries to make everyone believe. Travelling in Europe, he and Elsa find evidence that exonerates Henkel. Supported by his son-in-law, Henkel returns to the old country to compose classical music.

Set mostly in Tyler's music factory, *The Jazz King* was at first glance an obvious satire of Tin Pan Alley. (At one point in its previews, Lew Fields secured permission to use the title "Tin Pan Alley".) Beyond the obvious contrasts between the ruthless hustler Tyler and the long-suffering, bewildered old composer, the cast of characters represented a cross-section of the milieu: the worldly female office manager, the smart-alec vaudevillian and his dumb but pretty wife, the Jewish lawyer, the innocent stenographer, the zealous young musician "lifting" classic melodies, and other assorted jazz musicians. Then there was the music itself, which Herbert Richard Lorenz shared the credit for. We hear the graceful melody of Henkel's "Dresden Symphony" turned into "Moonlight Mama," a typical Tin Pan Alley tune with its inane, slightly vulgar refrain: "My pretty moonlight mama / Wants her way / And she gets it all right. / All through the day she keeps forgetting / How my heart pines; / But ev'ry night I get my petting / She makes hay while the moon shines . . ."[24] They also wrote a song burlesquing the Tin Pan Alley novelty tunes, "I'd Like to Poison Ivy." Parodies of other forms of entertainment were common in the old Weber & Fields Music Hall, where minstrelsy, grand opera, melodramas, and early movies were all targets. Herbert, Rodgers, and Hart continued this tradition in their later shows, incorporating parodies of many show biz formats and institutions—Tin Pan Alley, minstrelsy, vaudeville, nightclubs, operetta, and, eventually, Hollywood.[25]

The long, circuitous road to Broadway began with tryouts in Bethlehem, Pennsylvania, on March 24, 1924, followed by one-or two-night stands in Harrisburg, Johnstown, Wheeling, and Toledo, and a week each in Detroit and Cleveland. Besides Lew Fields, the cast was primarily composed of talented unknowns—Betty Weston as Henkel's daughter Elsa, Donald Gallaher as the ruthless Al Tyler, and a handsome young newcomer named Frederic March as the enthusiastic young musician, Donald Clemens. The ensemble was galvanized by the addition of the vaudevillians Eva Puck and Sammy White to play the music office manager, Stella Mallory, and the small-time hoofer, Bert Hackett. Fields hired White to add verisimilitude to the role, but White's skill and energy turned it into a brilliant burlesque of the hammy, self-assured song-and-dance man. Eva Puck's abilities as a comedienne were limited by her rather superfluous role, but together, Puck and White performed both songs, "Moonlight Mama" and "I'd Like to Poison Ivy." Rodgers, Hart, and Herbert were so impressed by the duo that they promised to write a musical comedy for them—a promise that they redeemed two years later in *The Girl Friend*.

By mid-April, when *The Jazz King* arrived at Chicago's Lasalle Theater, the good word had filtered back to New York. Broadway theater managers were pressing Fields to bypass Chicago and bring the show directly to New York. In Chicago, Fields concluded that the title *The Jazz King* was suggestive of a musical comedy and therefore misleading. The new name, *Henky*, was so unprepossessing that it may have contributed to the show's disappointing attendance. Fields frantically tried to line up the money to bring the show to New York. Eva Puck and Sammy White invested, as did the songwriter Billy Rose. Fields was still $1,000 short to cover the costs of opening in New York; a friend of Hart's father came up with the money.

Instead of the scheduled one-month engagement, the show closed in Chicago after two weeks and moved to Fields' brother-in-law's theater, the Teller-Shubert in Brooklyn, for a week. Fields called in stage director Alexander Leftwich to help streamline the play and pull together its rather scattered third act. Renamed *The Melody Man*, it finally opened on Broadway at the Shuberts' Ritz Theater on May 13. Audiences and critics were caught off guard; late-season arrivals were usually revues or "summer shows," particularly when they featured Lew Fields. There was general agreement that the first act was a superior example of farce comedy, while the demands of the plot dragged down the second and third act in the effort to arrive at a happy ending. Several reviewers praised the snappy dialogue for being full of "the latest Broadway nifties and wisecracks." (Fields had been right about the importance of "jazzing" the comedy as well as the score.) Naturally, the critics approved of the choice of Tin Pan Alley as a target for satire.

Even those who criticized the play lauded Fields' performance. It was "a rich characterization," by turns "light and rollicking, and then again tender and faithful." Woollcott found Fields to be "quite his incomparable best. . . . There is no more likable comedian roaming our stage." Yet, one reviewer observed in Fields' performance the effects of age and, implicitly, the changing theatrical styles:

> [*The Melody Man* is] Lew Fields as we used to know him, Lew Fields a little older, a little less vigorous, a little less sure of himself, but unmistakably the same Lew Fields with the same bag of tricks.
>
> Instead of a fat, stupid Joe Weber for his foil, he uses an entire company of rather clever people. . . .[26]

The "we knew him when" lament may have echoed the sentiments of large numbers of the audience, old and young, who were unable to consider a Lew Fields performance except in the context of Mike and Meyer.

Considered on its own merits, there was a fundamental incongruity in Fields' role in *The Melody Man*. *Variety*'s reviewer, who saw it in Chicago when it was still being called *Henky*, identified the uneasy duality within the production: "The piece has modern comedy, flashes of solid fun, a fair sprinkling of hokum and good sentimental values. Behind it all there is a rather hard and sophisticated view of life and this reacts to the disadvantage of the sentimental character played by Fields." It was another indication of the growing gap between audience expectations of Fields the actor and Fields the producer.

While the social commentary provided a common ground for the elder Fields and his young collaborators, the differences between his Victorian morality and the Jazz Age sensibilities of "Herbert Richard Lorenz" were not so easily reconciled. The underlying assumption of *The Jazz King*—that jazz was merely a reworking of stolen classical melodies—was a canard that could be heard in the early 'twenties in any Broadway lobby at the premiere of any new musical comedy. Rodgers himself had been accused of this in reviews of *Poor Little Ritz Girl*. No less an exponent of jazz than band leader Paul Whiteman reinforced this notion: "Do you not know that half the art of composing a popular song comes in knowing what to steal and how to adapt it—also, that at least nine tenths of modern jazz music turned out by Tin Pan Alley is frankly stolen from the masters?"

According to the conventional wisdom, as expressed in *The Melody Man*, the terms of the equation were simple: classical music equals Art, "jazz" (popular music) equals commercialism. For Rodgers, Hart, and Herb Fields to parrot this seems disingenuous given their own backgrounds and ambitions. Perhaps they thought it was a sincere expression of the convictions of the man for whom they wrote the show. But what of the fact that it was Lew Fields, the popular entertainer from yesteryear, who embodied the cause of classical music? The unspoken but nagging question that Herbert Richard Lorenz (and Gershwin, Hammerstein, Porter, *et al.*) could not yet answer was: where did the Broadway musical fit into this equation?

Despite generally favorable notices and a large outlay for advertising, *The Melody Man* never caught on in New York. The cast willingly took pay cuts, and there was hope that the show would pick up trade from the Democratic convention, which began at Madison Square Garden on June 24. But Fields' efforts to save the show were as futile as the northern Democrats' efforts to save the convention. *The Melody Man* packed up for good on June 28 after only seven weeks. *Variety* was at a loss to explain the failure, finally attributing it to its late arrival and the summer heat. The team of Rodgers, Hart, and Herb Fields rejoined the amateur ranks, and Lew Fields was broke again. The failure of *The Melody Man* made Fields realize that the time was approaching when his familiar stage persona would not fit into the kind of jazzy, thoroughly modern shows that he wanted to produce.

The same month that Fields' flopped in his attempt to return as the star of a Broadway musical, the *Saturday Evening Post* began a series on Weber & Fields written by their old colleague Felix Isman and journalist Wesley W. Stout. The series detailed in a colorful, anecdotal fashion the rise of Joe Weber and Lew Fields from their Bowery childhood to their 1912 Jubilee. The Music Hall was treated as the pinnacle of their careers—only fitting, since the Weberfields were described as the nation's finest theatrical organization, comparable to Gilbert & Sullivan's Savoyards. By totally excluding any discussion of Fields' career apart from Weber, the series reinforced the misperception among younger (and future) audiences that Fields was only an aging Dutch comic. While the *Post* series stimulated public interest that resulted in a lucrative reunion tour with Weber (and restored Fields to financial solvency after *The Melody Man*), it all but ensured that Fields' solo career as one of the most prolific and influential producers of Broadway musicals would be forgotten.

Ironically, there were few people who were better placed than Felix Isman to know the intimate details of Fields' solo career. Isman had managed several prominent actors of the pre-war era: Dan Daly, William Faversham, and Louis Mann, and in 1906, Lew Fields. Originally from Philadelphia, where he made his fortune in real estate, Isman began buying business and theatrical property in New York at the turn of the century, and eventually added twenty-five motion picture houses to his holdings. As the owner of the Broadway Theater, he became the business partner of Fields and Lee Shubert in 1909 when Fields was installed there as the resident producer. Isman was among the fashionable first-nighters at the old Weber & Fields Music Hall; after the show, he invariably hosted a large table at Rector's, and in later years, at the Claridge. At one time, he was reportedly worth $16 million, much of which he lost backing unsuccessful shows. Among his three wives was the actress Irene Fenwick, who had starred in Fields' ill-fated venture in legit drama, *Bosom Friends.*

Though Isman's decision to focus on the beloved partnership of Weber & Fields can be justified in terms of what was most commercial or most easily shaped into a simple narrative, it was nonetheless a deliberate choice with several significant implications. If *The Melody Man* first hinted that the Fields' dual careers as an actor and producer were becoming increasingly difficult to reconcile, then the *Post* series confirmed it.

To understand why, consider the medium itself. George Horace Lorimer's *Saturday Evening Post* was the most widely read American magazine during the 'twenties, with a peak circulation of over two and a half million copies a week.

Though he published slick short fiction by such writers as Fitzgerald, Faulkner, Marquand, and Cather, Lorimer's primary goal was to mold a self-image for Americans by promoting traditional values. In almost any given issue of the magazine, one can see that these "traditional" values included racism, xenophobia, anti-unionism, and consumerism. Nostalgia was a common authorial stance, typified by celebrations of childhood, small-town life, and pre-war pleasures.

By 1924, vaudeville had become a nostalgia item. In the issues between Weber & Fields installments, the *Post* published articles by Marian Spitzer on vaudeville. Her article "The People of Vaudeville" included an explanation of vaudeville slang, as if it were an exotic or dead language. In September, the *American Mercury* published Spitzer's article, "Morals in the Two-a-day," in which she described the high moral standards (priggishness, some would say) of the vaudeville stage, the very characteristic Fields had labored so long to promote. Showgirls bared their breasts in Broadway revues (the Shuberts' *Artists and Models of 1924*), but vaude at the Palace banned bare legs. At a time when concerned Americans saw moral turpitude everywhere, from the corruption of the Harding administration down to the local bootlegger, vaudeville remained wholesome and respectable.[27] In contrast to the morally suspect nature of most other forms of popular entertainment—musical comedies, revues, cabarets, even movies tainted with jazz and licentiousness—vaudeville provided safe memories of a simpler time when earnest, unpretentious performers and morally minded entrepreneurs provided good clean fun for the entire family.

So it was as vaudeville stars—or proto-vaudevillians—that Weber & Fields were cast in the *Post* series. Of course, Isman's rags-to-riches narrative of the rise of two Bowery waifs to Broadway stardom was written with the active cooperation of its subjects. Joe and Lew had told variations of many of the anecdotes before—among them, the first performance at Turn Hall, Bunnell and the Chinese cyclops, Miner's poolroom, the Fregoli burlesque, the hiring of Lillian Russell—but Isman's versions added dashes of high color that were suggestive of the imaginative press agent. Nevertheless, his accounts of their early companies and the Music Hall contained fascinating new material, and his description of the world of popular stage entertainments in the late nineteenth century was unique at the time and remains a valuable source.

The omissions were equally revealing. The myth of Fields' national origins, first published in the early 1890's when the pair were promoting their "Thoroughly American Company," was intact: little Lew Schanfield, "like his future partner . . . had been born after his parents had crossed the Atlantic." Papa Schanfield's early disapproval was not mentioned, and their poverty and Jewishness were downplayed. Dates before the Music Hall were vague or inaccurate. Isman's portrait of their Bowery environs was reminiscent of the account of a "sport" on a slumming expedition. Missing as well was any mention of Weber & Fields' involvement with the White Rats, and the duo's conflicts with the Syndicate were reduced to a booking dispute over their final Western tour. There was next to nothing about their personal lives or tastes, probably because Weber's cantankerousness and Fields' gambling and spendthrift ways were character flaws that undercut the salubrious moral intent of the author. At the same time, Isman and Stout's omission of Fields' "other" career revealed something more about the growing polarization of American popular stage audiences. Overall, it was a lively, heartwarming, and ultimately superficial story—the prose equivalent of the illustrations by the *Post*'s house artist, Norman Rockwell.

The serialization proved so popular that it was published in book form by Boni and Liveright in December, 1924. It was among the first of a new genre: the show biz memoir. That same year, George M. Cohan and Francis Wilson (the comic-opera star and first president of Actors' Equity) published autobiographies. Two years earlier, *Cosmopolitan* had serialized Lillian Russell's memoirs. The public's renewed interest in these idols of the pre-war stage went beyond simple nostalgia. It signalled a new phenomenon: the elevation of popular stage and screen stars to the celebrity status of political figures and the social elite.

Weber & Fields: Their Tribulations, Triumphs, and Their Associates—the subtitle promised all that an adoring public needed to know about its idols. The introduction, added for the book, made it clear why the story of Weber & Fields had fitted so neatly into the pages of *The Saturday Evening Post:* "Messrs. Weber and Fields are but the mediums to tell the story of two young American boys born in the ghetto, raised in the slums, with all the disadvantages of foreign parentage of that particular period, who by their lives and living became shining examples of true American manhood. Through all the pitfalls and snares of life, Messrs. Weber and Fields came through untarnished and unstained, to rise to the greatest height of their profession. . . ."[28]

"Shining examples of American manhood"? One hopes Weber & Fields blushed—or at least shaded their eyes when they looked at each other. The reviewers at the major dailies and magazines went for it, hook, line, and sinker. Comments by the *New York World*'s critic hinted at the underlying tensions in the theater world when he lauded Isman for trying "to make permanent the fame of an entertainment that delighted playgoers of every class and was entirely free from any taint of vulgarity or unclean suggestion." Unsentimental, hard-drinking Herman Mankiewicz—assistant drama editor to George S. Kaufman at the *New York Times* and the future screenwriter of *Citizen Kane*—lavished praise on the book and its subjects and accepted without question its underlying moral "lessons." Mankiewicz, who was too young to have seen the Weberfields in their heyday but admitted to seeing them in their 1912 Jubilee tour, repeated the once-common suggestion that the Weberfields' were America's Savoyards.

No doubt Weber & Fields took pleasure in seeing their lives woven so neatly into the fabric of mainstream American life. Privately, the assumption that their careers were over and relegated to the past bothered Fields. But for the moment, it looked like there was a possible solution to his latest financial crisis. Response to the *Post* series suggested that there was still money to be made in the old partnership.

With a new installment every two weeks, the series ran throughout the summer and into mid-October. By early July, the series had already become so popular that it prompted agent Alf Wilton to sign Weber & Fields to a twenty-five-week tour of the Orpheum circuit at a salary of $3,000 a week. Although it was officially

billed as "Reminiscences," some press agents in the West also began calling it
"Weber & Fields' Farewell Tour." Weber & Fields' return to the San Francisco
Orpheum would mark their thirty-fifth "anniversary" at the circuit's flagship the-
ater, though the original edifice had been destroyed in the 1906 earthquake.

For a tour of this magnitude, Joe and Lew agreed that they needed a third
party to rehearse them and help select the routines. They turned to a trusted
colleague, Sam Bernard, whom they had known since childhood, beginning with
his appearances at the Grand Duke Theater in the Bowery over forty years before. Bernard, who had been the Music Hall's first stage manager, was still occasionally performing in musical comedies. He drilled the duo and helped put together a twenty-four-minute program consisting of six of their most popular
routines, including the poker game, the statue scene, and, inevitably, the pool
table and choking scenes. The supporting cast for Weber & Fields' sketches consisted of Armand Kalisz and Nanette Flack. The rest of the bill would vary, depending on the locale and the availability of less expensive talent among the
Orpheum minions.

An added inducement sweetening the Orpheum deal for the old stars was a
six-week layover in Hollywood to do a feature film. Weber & Fields signed with
Edward Belasco Productions to star in the film adaptation of *Friendly Enemies*
by Aaron Hoffman and Sam Shipman. The seriocomic play had been a nationwide
hit immediately after the war when Fields had headed one touring company and
Louis Mann the other. It would be the only time that Weber and Fields would
appear together in a movie in roles other than Mike and Meyer.

In late October, 1924, with the full force of the Keith-Orpheum publicity machine behind them, Weber & Fields embarked on their tour. Isman's book was
scheduled to go on sale in January, when Weber & Fields would resume their
Western tour after finishing their motion picture obligations. Keith's Boys Band
gave them a musical send-off at the train platform while the newsreel crews
cranked away. Their first stop was Springfield, Illinois, which they intended to
use as their "dog" (out-of-town tryout) for three days prior to the official start of
the tour in Milwaukee. Milwaukee at that time had the largest German immigrant
population in the country. In Milwaukee, the pattern for the tour was set: hoopla
at the train station, the mayor or councilman presenting a key to the city, capacity crowds for the entire week, curtain speeches, floral tributes at the final curtain, fond editorials in the local newspapers. The next stop was the Palace in
Chicago, the town where Weber & Fields received their first big city newspaper
write-up in 1893. Chicagoans had always been their most appreciative fans, and
the nostalgic nature of the enterprise was apparent to all:

> All Joe and Lew really had to do was go through the motions; the crowd knew the
> patter by heart and laughed before the words were spoken as well as after. . . .

> When they were bowing at the close everyone had a throatal lump. Here were two
> of the country's greatest comedians standing there on the stage as if they had stepped
> out of the pages of their own recently printed history, and it was the intimacy of the
> audience with their history which seemed to make the situation unreal. . . .

. . . The real kick is that Weber & Fields in the flesh and reunited stand before you as a living reminder of one of the most glorious and picturesque chapters of the American stage.[29]

Production on *Friendly Enemies* began after Christmas. Fields re-created his stage role of the comic-pathetic Karl Pfeiffer, the German émigré who discovers his Americanness too late, and Weber assumed the role of Henry Block, the Americanized German émigré originally played by Charles Winninger. Fields' wife was played by the veteran character actress Eugenie Besserer, and his son was played by Jack Mulhall, a romantic lead in contemporary farces during the silent era. The film was a curious blend of stage and screen, old and new; the captions were in the mangled English of the old Weber & Fields, with documentary footage of marching troops and cruising ships inserted at appropriate moments. No print of the film survives, but from the reviews after its New York opening in May, 1925, it would appear that the pathos was overdrawn—"an overdose of heart interest" as *Variety*'s Sime Silverman called it in his extremely indulgent review. Fields, in his David Warfield mode, apparently went in for some heavy emoting, leading several critics to once again point out what a great actor he was apart from his comedy achievements. Weber's role allowed for considerably less range, but there were enough comic moments between the "friendly enemies" to satisfy most critics. Block teases Pfeiffer throughout by calling him "Charlie" though Pfeiffer insists on being called "Carl." In the end, after he has seen the error of his ways, Pfeiffer rejects the German moniker in favor of his American nickname: his assimilation and his rehabilitation are simultaneous.

Reminiscences resumed its tear-jerking tour on February 1, when Weber & Fields returned to the San Francisco Orpheum, where they were visited backstage by their foremost imitators, Kolb and Dill. In Oakland, Weber & Fields inaugurated the new $1.5 million Orpheum and wowed a generation of theatergoers who for the most part knew the duo only by reputation. At the conclusion of their act in Los Angeles, tumultuous cheering continued through the presentation of the key to the city until Fields started to talk. Energized by their show of appreciation, the fifty-eight-year-old trouper made his exit by turning half a dozen handsprings.

As they worked their way east with stops in Denver, Minneapolis, a return engagement in Chicago, and Detroit, audiences were similarly effusive. The one unforeseen event was the arrival of a Dr. and Mrs. Jack Weiner at the hotel in Denver where Lew and Rose were staying. Mrs. Weiner, the former Dorothy Fields, had come west to explain her sudden marriage and to reassure her bewildered parents. Lew and Rose had proudly announced Dorothy's engagement to a prominent physician, Dr. Jack J. Weiner, in late October, 1924. Though no date for the wedding was stated, they had agreed privately that it would not take place until Lew had finished touring in May. To Lew and Rose, it seemed like an ideal match: even though Weiner was at least ten years older than Dorothy, he was a surgeon on the staff at Montefiore Hospital and from a respected Long Island Jewish family.

Before her engagement, Dorothy had been appearing in the amateur shows written by Herbert, Rodgers, and Hart. She had also taken to writing song lyrics. It had started innocently enough with a few "smarty verses" for magazines, including Franklin Pierce Adams' chic column, "Conning Tower." J. Fred Coots, a gifted Tin Pan Alley composer and song plugger ("For All We Know," "Santa Claus Is Coming to Town," "You Go to My Head") heard her play a medley of early Rodgers & Hart tunes at the Woodmere Country Club. Afterwards, they discussed the intricacies of how the songs were constructed and he asked her if she had ever considered writing her own lyrics. He urged her to try it and even volunteered two of his own melodies. Though the lyrics were terrible, according to Dorothy, Coots took her to see several music publishers. Their responses to Dorothy were much the same as the responses of Broadway producers to Herbert, Rodgers, and Hart: "If she's so damned talented why doesn't her father do something?" And he did: when he found out she was making the rounds of the Tin Pan Alley offices, he called the music publishers and told them to throw her out.[30] Perhaps Lew was having difficulty separating his stage role in *The Melody Man* from reality: during the time when his daughter was offering her talents on Tin Pan Alley, he was playing an old-fashioned composer who works for a music publisher and loses his daughter to a Tin Pan Alley hustler.

Dorothy's quite proper engagement seemed to suggest an end—or so her parents hoped—to her theatrical ambitions. The wedding would be in late winter. Naturally, it would be a big and splashy affair; Lew would not dream of letting his baby daughter go with anything less than what he had provided for Frances. Dorothy, however, knew that reality was less heartwarming. Although she may have had inklings of it earlier, the bankruptcy had made her realize how tenuous were her family's pretensions to affluence. Her sensitivity to their financial ups and downs would eventually color her lyrics, as would her acting experience and her fascination with street argot. Her ability to convey the have-not's point of view with wit and compassion (and without being maudlin or condescending) was unique among popular lyricists writing before the Great Depression, and it was evident from the opening verse of her first hit, written when she was twenty-four:

> Gee, but it's tough to be broke, kid,
> It's not a joke kid, it's a curse;
> My luck is changing, it's gotten
> From simply rotten to something worse . . .
> ("I Can't Give You Anything But Love," 1928)

Many of her best efforts, from "I Can't Give You Anything But Love" to "If My Friends Could See Me Now" forty years later, use economic hardship as the backdrop for the extravagant yearnings of dreams and romances.

The promise of a big wedding was typical of her father's Micawber-like attitude towards money; as ever, he was confident that something would turn up. So Dorothy turned up in Denver, having been married in a small, impromptu ceremony at the home of an Upper West Side rabbi. The fact that Dorothy felt it necessary to visit them first before going on her honeymoon suggests the kind of reaction she was anticipating. Apparently, she hoped to spare her father the expense of a big wedding and the awkwardness such an expenditure would undoubtedly cause for him. The sudden change in nuptial plans became the subject of a gossipy article in a New York Sunday magazine. Lew probably found Dorothy's intentions touching and a bit humbling, but the untoward publicity played upon his social insecurities. And Dorothy did nothing to lessen those insecurities. Upon her return to New York, she continued to spend more time with the men of Tin Pan Alley than with her new husband.

The publicity and strong box office receipts generated by Weber & Fields' Orpheum tour made it natural to cap it off with a stand at New York's Palace. To play the Palace, however, one could not merely repeat the same billing that had gone over in the sticks. Edward Darling, chief booker for the Keith circuit, brought together an all-time all-star bill consisting of Blossom Seeley, Marie Cahill, Cissy Loftus, songbird Emma Trentini, and Dr. Rockwell, whose quack routine featured a lecture on human anatomy using a banana stalk for a skeleton. In her book on the Palace, Marian Spitzer described it as a bill of "true vaudeville," which, significantly enough, was translated as "Old-Timers' Week" in the publicity.[31] The week of all-star old-timers began April 20 and brought in the largest vaudeville audience of the season. For the first time in Palace history, six of the eight acts on the bill were held over for a second week. Darling added old-time legit star Laurette Taylor, and the torrid pace at the box office did not slacken.

Weber & Fields came up with a plan to wring the nostalgia hanky for all it was worth—the ultimate old-timers' bill, a reunion of Weberfields stars. Peter Dailey and John Stromberg were long gone; their queen Lillian—"Nellie" they called her—more recently. But Willie Collier, DeWolf Hopper, and Frankie Bailey (whom they had visited when they were in L.A., where she had her own candy store) were still healthy. Their other diva, Fay Templeton, had retired from the stage in 1913 to marry millionaire contractor William Patterson of Pittsburgh. Recovering from a tonsillectomy, she had read the Weber & Fields biography and had been overwhelmed by a flood of fond memories. Ed Darling's offer could not have been better timed.

In the end, economics limited the scope of the reunion to Templeton and once-only cameos by Collier and Hopper, but this was enough. The Palace line-up for the week of June 8 was a repeat of the April 20 bill, with the notable addition of "the Dark Cloud of Joy," Bill "Bojangles" Robinson. A clever press agent pointed out that 1925 was the twenty-fifth anniversary of the Weberfields' production of *Fiddle-dee-dee*, the show in which Templeton had introduced her signature tune, "Ma Blushin' Rose." The display in the lobby reached back even farther, with a forty-year-old playbill for the Gus Hill Company listing Lottie Gilson as the soubrette and Weber & Fields as paper-tearers.

"Great stuff being sold over the footlights this week," was how *Billboard* described the show, adding, "it would be sacrilegious and untruthful to say it was all sentiment." The hot and humid evening began with a trio of contortionists, followed by Bill Robinson, with stories, songs, jokes, and, of course, virtuoso tap dancing. He ended with his version of the latest dance craze, the Charleston, performed in triple time. After a "dance revue"—a chorus of five women and a man in a lavishly produced routine—came the first of the old-timers to appear, Marie Cahill. Weber & Fields and Fay Templeton closed the first half of the show, entering with a typically irreverent bit of stage business that seemed to mock their own status as old-timers. A creaking roller chair appeared, bearing Templeton and Weber and pushed by Fields. Plump even in her prime, Templeton had grown stouter in retirement, and the sight of her ample figure wedged in with Weber's rotundity brought an immediate roar from the audience. Only a supremely confident and talented performer would dare to return to the stage in such a self-effacing manner after more than a decade. She got up with surprising nimbleness when Mike tried to kiss her, and she swatted Meyer for getting fresh. The "boys" then walked off singing "So Long, Mary," the Cohan song she had popularized in his *Forty-Five Minutes from Broadway*, leaving her to sing "How I Love My Lu," "Dinah," and "Ma Blushin' Rose." Weber & Fields returned during that last number and worked in at either end of the chorus. Then, in a tribute to "the American beauty," Lillian Russell, Templeton sang "My Evenin' Star." When she began singing, *Variety* reported, "there was many a dim eye in the audience that lighted with a new fire at the thoughts that came crowding back again." Adding fuel to the fire, Weber & Fields launched into their poolroom scene, with a few adjustments to allow for contributions from Templeton. In the matinee, they played poker with her instead of pool. Suave Armand Kalisz, taking the Collier role, then tried to train Mike and Meyer for high society; sizing up his partner, Meyer said, "He's too low for high society."

Weber & Fields' happiness and pride at sharing the stage with Templeton was evident to all; they played up to her and put her center stage for the thunderous ovations that followed their turn. In no time the trio were knee-deep in bouquets. Templeton tried to make a speech, and she was so overcome with emotion that she began to weep. Weber & Fields tried to soothe her but she eventually had to leave the stage. At every performance she tried to give her curtain speech, but she never got more than a few lines into it before the tears started to flow. Fortunately, Weber & Fields persuaded her to stay for a second week, and at the first matinee she finally managed to give her speech. The second week's bill held over Weber, Fields, and Templeton, but replaced the other stars with younger, more contemporary performers.

Watching the old-timers' reunion, many of the reviewers and performers seemed to agree that something had been lost. Since its humble beginnings, vaudeville had been sanitized, commercialized, institutionalized, analyzed (by artists and intellectuals), idealized; and now it was being eulogized. At the very least, vaudeville purveyors should have recognized a warning sign when the most popular bills of the season were old-timers' shows. Within the next three years, the crisis would become painfully apparent.

With the tide of nostalgia still going strong, Weber & Fields decided to ride it through the summer and, if possible, into the fall season. They played for a week in summer resorts in Long Island and Atlantic City while they entertained fabulous offers from vaudeville promoters, especially those who ran the motion picture combination houses.

Fields' other activities during the late spring and summer of 1925 reveal the extent of his ambivalence. He was not prepared to take to heart the nostalgia-mongers who were promoting the Orpheum tour, Isman's book, and their Palace engagement. Yet, he was too savvy a showman to do anything that might hurt their box office revenues. Twice a day, Fields provided heart-warming reminders of the good old days with his Music Hall colleagues, but at the same time he was also quietly searching for new and modern musical comedy vehicles to produce.

A little revue whose opening in May fell between Weber & Fields' Palace engagements gave him hope. On May 17, the Theatre Guild presented a light entertainment on a shoestring budget to raise money for its unfinished theater, the Garrick. *The Garrick Gaieties* was so well received that it was scheduled for an open-ended run beginning June 8. Without the money for lavish sets, big production numbers, and stars, they modelled their production along the lines of the small-scale, sophisticated *Charlot's Revue* (1924), which had relied on wit, melody, and engaging individual performances. The *Gaieties'* young talents supplied all of the above: Philip Loeb, Richard Rodgers, Larry Hart, Herb Fields (choreographer), sketches by Morrie Ryskind, Sam Jaffe, Edith Meiser, and a cast that included Sterling Holloway, Romney Brent, Betty Starbuck, June Cochran, Edith Meiser, Lee Strasberg, Libby Holman, and Sanford Meisner. Rodgers & Hart's score was full of infectious melodies and brilliant rhymes; "Manhattan" (salvaged from *Winkle Town*) and "Sentimental Me" emerged as standards. The latter was a replacement for a jazz opera, "The Joy Spreader," intended as a first-act finale but quickly dropped. "The Joy Spreader" told the story of a clerk and salesgirl who get locked in the department store overnight and are fired the next morning by their puritanical employer, who wrongly suspects hanky-panky. The situation and its outcome bore a strong resemblance to an early scene in Fields' *A Lonely Romeo*.

Most of the sketches and songs satirized the Broadway hits of their elders—operettas as well as the Guild's own pompous dramas. *They Knew What They Wanted* became "They Didn't Know What They Were Getting"; other sketches ridiculed *The Three Musketeers* and *Rose-Marie*. The burlesque of Broadway hits provided the framework for topical barbs directed at the Coolidges and their idea of a fun evening, and the Scopes Monkey Trial, featuring a jury in monkey suits and William Jennings Bryan singing: "The Congo's greatest menace is / A monkey who will not believe in Genesis." Their inspired lunacy proved that the spirit of the Weber & Fields Music Hall lived on, even as Weber & Fields themselves were leading soggy paeans for the dear departed days.

Meanwhile, Weber & Fields were determined to milk the last dollar out of the nostalgia craze that signalled the beginning of the end of vaudeville. Edward Darling of the Palace announced another old-timers' bill for the week of October 19, featuring Weber & Fields, Cissie Loftus, Emma Trentini, and, in her return to vaudeville, Marie Dressler. On the Monday morning before their engagement was to begin, Weber & Fields arrived as usual for a run-through with their supporting cast and the orchestra. Walking through the lobby, they were startled to discover that they had second billing to Marie Dressler. Was this a mistake? Vaudeville protocol had been violated: they were making a return engagement; what's more,

Dressler had been their employee. But it was no mistake: Dressler had insisted on top billing or she would not go on. Darling knew that Weber & Fields were reasonable guys, and he was sure a compromise could be worked out. He would probably have been right if it had been anyone but Marie Dressler. It is not known which of the partners was more indignant, for Weber had had his differences with Dressler over the years as well. They were both convinced that she was deliberately trying to embarrass her old employers. Shortly before noon, they expressed their sincerest regrets to the management and withdrew from the bill. In the Monday matinee, Armand Kalisz announced that Weber & Fields would not appear because the former was ill. Insiders already knew better, and the story made the front page of the next issue of *Variety:*

WEBER & FIELDS 'WALK-OUT,' MISS FIRST SHOW IN HISTORY

. . . Behind the alleged indisposition, is a story as old as show business, but which few would have anticipated in connection with such names as Weber and Fields—a disagreement over billing. . . .

An extraordinary feature of the incident is that throughout the entire career of this classic team, despite all vicissitudes of travel, disagreement, physical condition or any other cause, Weber and Fields had never missed a billed performance [they had on rare occasions due to injuries] until the Monday matinee of this week at the Palace. . . .[32]

It was a petty display of temperament uncharacteristic of Weber & Fields, but it was entirely in keeping with the behavior of aging stars who know that their greatness is behind them. Perhaps it was another sign of vaudeville's dotage that its classiest act was a no-show at its showcase theater.

Weber & Fields picked up far more lucrative engagements playing at the big new motion picture houses—$5,000 for a week in Buffalo, $3,000 plus a percentage of the gross for a week in Johnstown, Pa.—where they shared the bill with flickering shadows instead of live vaudevillians. Straight vaudeville was in fact on its last legs, squeezed out by the big new motion picture palaces and the popular-priced neighborhood theaters. The one hundred or so independent theaters still booking straight vaudeville acts paid such low salaries that they were known as the "C. and C."—the Coffee and Cake—circuit. Marcus Loew now paid more for the acts in his movie houses than the big-time vaudeville houses could afford. His formula of popular-priced movies plus a stage show was a better entertainment value; the film was the draw, and the vaudeville was the filler. The once mighty Keith and Orpheum circuits were crumbling, held together by mergers and banking syndicates. In April, 1926, came another symbolic blow: *Variety* moved film news to the front of the paper, replacing vaudeville news, which was curtailed and banished to the back pages. Within the coming year, radio and then talkies arrived to deliver the *coup de grâce* to big-time vaudeville.

At the end of Weber & Fields' last engagement at the Palace, Fay Templeton was asked if she would continue to perform. "It's been great fun," Templeton said, "but it's a new Broadway and a new theatre, and hereafter I'll be content to look on from out front."[33]

Joe Weber concurred. But not Lew Fields.

In late 1924, the team of Herbert, Rodgers, and Hart had tried to interest Lew Fields in another of their efforts, a musical comedy set during the American Revolution, entitled *Sweet Rebel.* Fields was at the start of a season's worth of vaudeville bookings with Weber on the Orpheum circuit, and he may have deferred a decision until after the tour was over. Not long before the May 1925 opening of *The Garrick Gaieties*, the young hopefuls submitted a revised script and score for Fields' consideration. Their new title, *Dearest Enemy*, had the disadvantage of sounding confusingly similar to the just-released Weber & Fields movie, *Friendly Enemies*, and the plot also involved consorting with a wartime enemy, though the similarities ended there.

Herbert, Rodgers, and Hart had received their inspiration for *Dearest Enemy* from an historical plaque they had found by chance on Thirty-seventh Street: "[General] Howe, with Clinton, Tryon, and a few others, went to the house of Robert Murray, on Murray Hill, for rest and refreshment. With pleasant conversation and a profusion of cake and wine, the good Whig lady detained the gallant Britons almost two hours. Quite long enough for the bulk of Putnam's division of four thousand men to leave the city and escape to the heights of Harlem. . . ." Lew rejected the script, saying that the public would not buy a musical based on American history. One can hardly blame him: strong historical references or settings characterized two of his costliest failures, *Jack and Jill* and *Back Again.* Moreover, Herbert's libretto rendered an important historical event through flip dialogue and sexually provocative situations, a juxtaposition that may have made Pop Fields uncomfortable. The old showman's overwhelming fear of yet another flop and his lack of confidence in its young authors blinded him to the show's obvious merits.

Lew Fields' rejection of the project once again had the effect of discouraging other producers as well—clearly, his opinion still carried weight with the Broadway establishment. Not even the commitments of Helen Ford, a talented newcomer, and Charles Purcell, a popular leading man, along with John Murray Anderson as director, could reassure the potential backers. George Ford (Helen's husband) volunteered to help raise the $50,000 production budget. Helen Ford's recollection of this has a Runyonesque ring to it: "We auditioned for every Tom, Dick, and Harry, for every cloak-and-suiter. Finally, after getting only half the money for the show—$25,000—we were doing it for gangsters, who were beginning to put money in the theater. We got the money."[34] The other half reportedly came from George Ford's brother, though he was said to be the show's sole backer.[35]

Despite the period sets and costumes, *Dearest Enemy* emulated the stylistic simplicity of the Princess Theatre musicals—one set for each act and a reduced chorus. Director John Murray Anderson had already demonstrated in his *Greenwich Village Follies* series that he could deliver elegant stage effects at minimal expense. Like the Princess musicals, the real emphasis would be on the script and the score.

Herbert Fields' libretto was his first to show that he could apply the lessons of his idols W. S. Gilbert and Guy Bolton to the contemporary needs of a Jazz Age musical comedy. Though the settings and syntax were eighteenth-century, the sexual and social attitudes were entirely up to date. The opening curtain discovers the women of Murray Hill singing "Heigh-ho, lackaday" because all their men have gone off to war. Mrs. Murray warns them (none too convincingly) about the dangers of fraternizing with British soldiers. Her warning provokes the comments of another woman, who sings "War Is War": ". . . A uniform can make the palest frail young fellow / Feel he's male! Male! Male!" To which the girls reply, "Hooray, we're going to be compromised!"

The love interest is Mrs. Murray's niece, Betsy Burke, who, in keeping with the Broadway vogue of the time, is a spunky Irish lass.[36] Betsy's lover is a British officer who first spots her while she is bathing in Kips Bay. The British soldiers steal her clothes to keep her from warning the garrison, so she makes her first entrance wearing only a barrel—a witty send-up of the kind of pseudo-artsy stage nudity that Broadway audiences had lately come to expect. Sexual attraction of a more mature variety is evident after Mrs. Murray plies the British commanders with sparkling conversation and a sumptuous meal. General Tryon succumbs to her charms, singing:

> . . . A soldier knows.
> You're like Venus and between us
> I prefer the riper charms
> That the autumn years disclose.
> Your equator may be greater,
> But I like to fill my arms
> With the most substantial foes.

The romantic cynicism of Fields and Hart were so perfectly matched that they were able to integrate songs with plot to an extent unprecedented in a musical comedy. "I'd like to hide it," sing the American girls, "I'd like to smother down the flame inside, / But though I've tried it, / I can't abide it. . . ." There is more than patriotic self-sacrifice behind their scheming. Hart's lyrics consistently give voice to the randy subtext of Fields' book, even in a novelty number. "Sweet Peter" tells the story of an earlier New Yorker, the autocrat Peter Stuyvesant, who "had a wife and couldn't cheat her" because the "boom-boom-boom" of his wooden leg made it impossible for him to sneak around. Meanwhile, the dallying British soldiers are being betrayed by their own desires.

Echoes of Bolton's scripts for the Princess musicals could be heard in the urbane banter of *Dearest Enemy*. General Tryon clumsily compliments Mrs. Murray on her delicious dinner: "The pig was worthy of you." "It takes a gentleman of breeding to appreciate a real pig," replies Mrs. Murray. When Tryon tries to warn his son Harry, a captain, not to get romantically involved, their exchange reflects a very modern attitude:

TRYON: I'm talking to you like a father.
HARRY: But you're not saying anything.
TRYON: *(confused)* Well—that's the way fathers talk.

Richard Rodgers' score sweetened and softened the underlying archness of the book and the cynicism of the lyrics. Rather than resorting to the predictable melodic expedients of Tin Pan Alley, Rodgers' tunes recalled the period setting with several charming ballads and a gavotte to open the second act. Even when using the conventional A-A-B-A structure, as he did in "Here in My Arms," he found ways to incorporate surprising effects with subtlety, and the song became the hit of the show.

Dearest Enemy opened on September 18, 1925, to overwhelming enthusiasm from critics and public alike. By most accounts, it was more than just another musical comedy. "By reason of the full-toned qualities of the music and the richly colored design of the plot," wrote the *Times*' critic, "*Dearest Enemy* is operetta, with more than a chance flavor of Gilbert and Sullivan." Frank Vreeland of the *Telegram* also discerned the influence of the Princess musicals: "We have a glimmering notion that someday they [Fields, Rodgers, Hart] will form the American counterpart of the once great triumvirate of Bolton, Wodehouse, and Kern." Percy Hammond *(Herald Tribune)* and Arthur Hornblow (*Theatre* magazine) astutely likened it to comic opera.

Almost ten years earlier, in the August 1916 issue of *Theatre* magazine, Lew Fields had predicted "the renaissance of true comic opera." At the time, he admitted that he had been looking for over two years for such a piece to produce. In 1925, when somebody finally offered him a new comic opera, he rejected it and elected to play it safe with the same old slapstick hokum and chorus girls. Perhaps it was a measure of how commercial exigencies had beaten him down. Or, as he put it in 1911: "Sometimes these big ambitions have to be put up in alcohol and preserved on the shelf. They won't always do for the box office." But to his surprise, *Garrick Gaieties* and *Dearest Enemy* did fine for the box office. Maybe it was time to take those big ambitions off the shelf. He knew that Herbert, Rodgers, and Hart were building a new musical comedy around the talents of Sammy White and Eva Puck. Two weeks after *Dearest Enemy*'s successful New York premiere, Lew Fields announced that he would produce their next show.

Marking time before his return to musical comedy, Fields decided to indulge his other hobbyhorse. "Having just performed his periodic routine of leaving Joe Weber after a tour in vaudeville," commented critic Frank Vreeland, "Fields naturally took the next step in the regular system, that of plunging into the legitimate. . . ."[37] The vehicle was a straight comedy called *Money Business;* its author, Oscar Carter, was a Yiddish playwright best known for *Three Little Business Men* starring Rudolph Schildkraut. *Money Business* was his first English-language effort, and it would provide his wife, Pola Carter, with her first English-language role.

Carter's story was essentially a folktale of Jewish-Americans in New York City, missing few of the clichés of the Yiddish or American stage. The mechanics of its plot dated at least as far back as Harrigan's farces. Jacob Berman is a Hester Street deli owner who wants to invest his family's $3,000 nest egg in Sam Madorsky's chain of laundries. His obstreperous wife, Sara, is seduced by the fast-buck promises of a young Wall Street hustler named George Braun, and she gives him the $3,000 to play the market. Braun's successful manipulations make them overnight millionaires, so they trade the idyllic poverty of the East Side for the venal luxury of Central Park West. The Bermans' daughter, Dora, is being wooed by the scheming Braun, though it is the plodding but trustworthy Madorsky who really loves her. Meanwhile, old Jacob resists efforts to make him into a gentleman, while Sara takes up "society" with a rush. When Braun is revealed to be a crook, he drags the Bermans into court, where they stand accused as accomplices. In the end, the Bermans are acquitted, Braun goes to jail, Madorsky gets Dora, and Jacob Berman leads his sadder but wiser family back to the idyllic poverty of the Lower East Side.

Lew Fields' portrayal of Jacob Berman represented the first and only time that he played an explicitly Jewish character. From the days of the first "Hebe" comics on the variety stage to the Jewish stereotypes in the long-running hit *Abie's Irish Rose*, Fields had resisted the temptation of self-parody and refused to play Jewish roles. Why the sudden change of heart? One reason may have been purely commercial: it was Lee Shubert who brought the play to his attention shortly after the opening of *Abie's Irish Rose*. Shubert saw an opportunity to capitalize on the hit with heartwarming ethnic hokum in a similar vein. By the time Fields had finished his vaudeville commitments, Shubert was no longer associated with the project. Fields may have also been aware that respected theater critics such as Gilbert Seldes and Stark Young were treating Yiddish theater as a worthy artistic enterprise. Popular stage audiences no longer distinguished between Yiddish and Dutch dialect humor, and the number of Dutch roles on the legitimate stage had been steadily shrinking since the war. And perhaps Fields sympathized with the circumstances of the character of Jacob Berman.

If he felt any misgivings in the part, he did not let it affect his performance. He gave the role of Jacob Berman his signature treatment—the flinging hands, the mangled English, the comical aggravation, the sardonic retorts, the sudden flurry of dance steps (this time, a Jewish Charleston). There were plenty of opportunities for characteristic comic bits: a clogged salt shaker, a pompous butler, reducing exercises, an argument about what to wear to jail.

After three weeks of out of town previews, *Money Business* opened in New York on January 20, 1926, at the National Theater. In addition to Pola Carter, who according to one reviewer tended to boom her lines "as if she were singing in the Moscow Art Theatre," the supporting cast included Luther Adler (as Sam Madorsky) and Harry Lyons (as the son). The director was Lawrence Marston, who had staged *The Melody Man*. Reviewers remarked on the play's heavily Jewish atmosphere, sometimes disparagingly: "If you don't understand the Yid shadings you are out of luck."[38] Brooks Atkinson and Frank Vreeland panned the play while heaping praise on Fields' performance:

> At the age of 59 . . . Mr. Fields has lost none of his comic bravura . . . [He] makes pantomime enrich burlesque; he seldom strikes twice in the same place. We have too few of his school on the stage.

> His still amazingly exuberant vitality continues to cast a spell, because he manages to stay almost miraculously fresh, despite all the musical comedy books through which he has had to gibber in his time. His zest, his sharp interest in his work, his desire to land a comedy line or a situation without ramming it down, all form a lesson to many a younger, languid actor. . . .

Their comments make it clear that Fields was not just an old-timer lingering on the stage for one more curtain call. His performance could not save *Money Business*, however, and it closed after only fourteen performances.

Had it not closed, Fields would have been obliged to leave the cast. In early February, his mother became seriously ill. Sarah was eighty-eight years old and had been living with her daughter and son-in-law, Annie and Morris Warschauer, ever since her husband's death in 1911. Lew felt bound to her by a special debt of gratitude: it was she who had indulged his early interest in the stage. She had applauded his first performance at Turn Hall (and many more since then); she had stood up for little Lew when his disapproving father found out about his theatrical aspirations.

Sarah's illness was mercifully short, and she expired in the company of her children on the evening of February 20. According to her wishes, her funeral was an Orthodox Jewish ceremony. It was the last Jewish ritual that Lew Fields ever observed.

CHAPTER XVII

The Evergreen Fields

It is a great pleasure to live at a time when light amusement in this country is at last losing its brutally cretin aspect. . . .

Lorenz Hart, in a letter to Ira Gershwin, 1926

The restlessness approached hysteria. The parties were bigger. The shows were bigger. The pace was faster . . . the buildings higher, the morals looser.

F. Scott Fitzgerald

A FTER four years of hokum, Lew Fields' comeback as a Broadway producer was in itself a surprise. The surprise was not simply that he could still produce hit musicals, or that he could do it without the Shuberts, or that he could have a hit he did not also appear in. What nobody would have dared to predict was that this beloved has-been would return as one of the foremost innovators of the musical stage.

As the gap between vaudeville and musical comedy widened, the contradictions in Fields' Janus-faced career in the 1920's likewise seemed to grow. Yet, it was the same Lew Fields who was a purveyor of vaudeville hokum and producer of innovative Broadway musicals. During this period his closest friend was once again Joe Weber, whom he would lunch frequently with, always occupying the same table in the Hunting Room of the Hotel Astor, their professional jealousies forgotten now that Weber was retired. At the same time, Fields' closest collaborators were his son Herbert—"a revolutionary without ideology" to borrow Ethan Mordden's apt description—and surrogate sons Rodgers and Hart, and a handful of others who were twenty to thirty years younger. Thus we must resist the temptation to pigeonhole and categorize Lew Fields merely for the sake of consistency or simplicity. Think of him instead as a man who, because of his unique experience on the popular stage, was in a position to look to the future and the past with equal ease.

As a performer, however, Fields could only look backward. Straitjacketed by audience expectations, he either had to be Meyer on the vaudeville stage, or he had to play the kind of comic characters who belonged in revues and vaude-inflected shows with weak books. He was a stage relic, like George M. Cohan or his old friend Sam Bernard.

As a producer, Fields had been considerably more forward-looking, at least until financial pressures forced him to seek refuge in vaudeville. In *A Lonely Romeo* (1919) and *Poor Little Ritz Girl* (1920), Fields had grappled with the basic questions that would trouble the rest of Broadway for the next five years: what was the role of jazz to be in the Broadway musical? Would popular stage audiences buy into the youth cult and accept what jazz symbolized? The answers began to emerge during the four-year period of Fields' absence from Broadway musicals.

One of the first and most potent symbols of the Jazz Age—the Charleston—arrived on Broadway at the start of the 1923–1924 season. Originating in the Southern city it was named for, the Charleston made its way north in the cabarets and speakeasies, but received its biggest boost when it was introduced on Broadway as a dance number in *Runnin' Wild,* one of several black musicals patterned after the successful *Shuffle Along* (1921). Within days, the trendy white patrons of the Silver Slipper and Texas Guinan's El Fey Club were flapping elbows and bumping knees. The Charleston sparked a national craze like no dance before it. Previous "jazz" dances such as the shimmy were exhibition dances, while the less athletic members of the public danced to fox trots cheek-to-cheek or, for the more daring, body-to-body. The Charleston bridged the gap between exhibition and public dancing, quickly becoming the favorite of flappers and performers alike.[1] With its successor, the Black Bottom, the Charleston announced that jazz was indispensable for truly chic and up-to-date Broadway entertainments.

The following season brought some more provocative developments. On December 1, 1924, the forces of jazz launched a victorious assault on Broadway with the opening of *Lady, Be Good!* at the Liberty Theatre. "Musical comedy," wrote Gerald Bordman, "was never quite the same again."[2] Most of the production elements had been thoroughly "jazzed"—not just the snappy humor of the book by Guy Bolton and Fred Thompson and the sleek art deco sets of Norman Bel Geddes, but the breezy, understated style of Fred and Adele Astaire and, most especially, the songs of George and Ira Gershwin. The plot was relatively simple and old-fashioned in its reliance on coincidence and disguise, but its fashionable trappings and references—bootleg booze, luxury cars, the latest slang—made it seem up-to-date.

Increasingly, Broadway musicals reflected the tastes of its chic New York patrons; and the provinces be damned. The emergence of jazz music and more explicit sexual and social issues on the popular stage polarized audiences along regional and class lines, and accentuated the differences between the audience for vaudeville (wholesome entertainment) and Broadway musicals/revues (titillation for affluent urban sophisticates). Producers could no longer assume that plays that were hits in New York would prosper on tour. When a smart new show by the Gershwins or Fields, Rodgers, and Hart would open in New York, it was not uncommon for theater critics to express doubt about its prospects on the road.

In a telling exception to the trend, operettas—usually by Rudolph Friml or Sigmund Romberg—were among the only musicals to prosper both in New York and on the road. Operetta was Broadway's antidote to jazz, in its own way as nostalgic an enterprise as vaudeville. After going into hibernation in the years immediately following the war, operetta enjoyed a new vogue with the appearance in the fall of 1924 of Friml's *Rose-Marie* and Romberg's *The Student Prince in Heidelberg*, followed in subsequent seasons by *The Vagabond King, The Desert Song, My Maryland, Rosalie, The New Moon,* and *The Three Musketeers,* all with Broadway runs of over three hundred performances. *Rose-Marie* went on to become the biggest-grossing musical of the decade, helped by four American road companies and productions in London, Paris, and other European capitals.

Unlike their godfather Victor Herbert, Friml and Romberg steadfastly refused to bow to musical fashion. From the standpoint of musical style, Romberg's score for *The Desert Song*, for instance, could have been written anytime since Herbert composed *Naughty Marietta* in 1910. The romantic sweep of their music defined the form, and the best of their librettists (Otto Harbach, Oscar Hammerstein II, William McGuire, and Dorothy Donnelly) created books that seemed to be extensions of the songs rather than the other way around. The earnest romanticism of the music dictated a rigid set of narrative conventions: overripe dialogue, dastardly villains, impulsive heroines, outlaw heroes, predictable plot turns, and, often, a flower in the title. On the other hand, it allowed for an integration of music and plot to an extent unprecedented on the American popular stage. Thus, a rather pretentious program note for *Rose-Marie* announced: "The musical numbers of this play are such an integral part of the action that we do not think we should list them as separate episodes." This was, in fact no more true for *Rose-Marie* than for several other musicals of the era.[3] Hammerstein's ambitions for *Rose-Marie* may have outstripped its achievements, but many of his bright young Broadway colleagues shared the same ambitions.

This did not prevent some of them—specifically, Herbert Fields, Rodgers, and Hart—from mocking *Rose-Marie* mercilessly in the 1926 *Garrick Gaieties*. Their understanding of the form was evident in their mini-operetta, *Rose of Arizona*, in which they burlesqued the operetta's romantic conventions, even down to the brawny male chorus and the marching song. In so doing, they reminded the creators and audiences of operetta that a well-integrated score and comedy could co-exist in the same show. Jazz babies like Rodgers, Hart, and Herbert Fields realized that the inherent properties of operetta and musical comedy were not really mutually exclusive; the distinction had been exaggerated by the symbolic significance attached to Old World music versus jazz. Why, the young talents were asking, couldn't a narrative of modern (jazz) sensibilities possess the structural integrity of an operetta? With *Dearest Enemy*, they had made a conscious attempt to fuse the tradition of operetta with that of musical comedy.

"The renaissance of true comic opera" that Lew Fields had predicted in 1916 was finally within his grasp. Though the young triumvirate of Rodgers, Hart, and Herb Fields were apparently unaware of Pop Fields' long-standing ambitions, they had chosen a mentor who had spent most of his career breaking down the boundaries between popular stage formats. Their collaboration would be a final attempt to hybridize the various popular theatrical genres—musical comedy, burlesque, vaudeville, and operetta—Fields had participated in throughout his career.

From the outside, the building that housed the Fieldses' suite of apartments at 562 West End looked more sober and thrifty than their beloved old townhouse on Ninetieth Street. Inside, despite the spacious rooms with high ceilings, there was a teeming, hive-like quality to the premises, and their extravagant lifestyle continued with increasing financial support from the children. Rose presided serenely over the tumultuous household, and it was the devotion that she inspired that held the family together under one roof. Dorothy had moved back in with her family shortly after her marriage to Jack Weiner, their relationship apparently already on the rocks. When the two had finally gone on their honeymoon, they had rented a cottage in the Adirondacks, and Dorothy spent most of the first night pacing back and forth on the porch. Why they bothered marrying in the first place remains a mystery. Though they stayed legally married for ten years, they led separate lives almost from the start. It was an odd arrangement for someone who made such a name for herself writing lyrics about love.

Visitors came and went from late afternoon till early morning. Herb loved to be able to get up from his work desk and find a few visitors to try a new scene on. He showed no interest in relinquishing bachelorhood, and it was only a matter of time before rumors about his sexual preferences began to circulate among Broadwayites. He grew particularly close to Larry Hart, whose bohemian lifestyle he tried to emulate.

Joe was also living with the family again. Joe's relationship with his natural brother had grown increasingly distant over the years as their contrasting personalities became more pronounced. Where Joe was burly and reserved, with a quiet wit and a stubborn streak, Herb was slight and excitable, and quick with a quip to defuse a conflict. Unlike Herb, Joe had tried to fulfill—rather reluctantly, it seems—his parents' social aspirations: college football, law school, active duty in the Navy during the war, marriage to the daughter of a wealthy French textile merchant. In Paris after the Armistice, with the help of foster brother Herb Harris and brother-in-law Charles Marcus, Joe had set up a perfume-exporting business that reportedly grossed $800,000 in its first year. But when Joe returned to New York in 1923, he apparently did so with little sense of satisfaction. Having separated from his wife, he pursued his business halfheartedly and finally surrendered himself to the family demon. For the next five years, he wrote revue sketches and plays, none of which was ever produced, though one, *The Night Club*, did elicit some passing interest from his father. Meanwhile, he watched the meteoric rise of his younger siblings in the profession that his parents had proscribed.

Returning with Joe to live with the family was his confidante and business partner, Herbert Harris. Growing up in the Fields household, Harris was no more immune to the theatrical bug than his foster siblings. At age thirteen, he became the envy of New York boydom when, thanks to a few strings pulled by Lew, he was appointed bat boy for John McGraw's New York Giants baseball team. During the war, he had helped produce benefit shows for enlisted men, and after being shipped off to France was commissioned in the field as a first lieutenant. Eventually, Harris took over Joe's interest in their joint perfume business. With the addition of the rising actor William Gaxton as a partner, the company became an extremely lucrative enterprise known as Parfums Charbert. By 1926, the twenty-nine-year-old Harris had accumulated enough spare capital to indulge his taste for Broadway shows in the manner of other successful businessmen in the 'twenties—as an "angel." Instead of backing shows for the sake of a wife or mistress, as did many a butter-and-egg man, Harris did it for his foster father.

Lew Fields' comeback was a family affair, an ironic payback for his sometimes vehement attempts to keep his children out of show biz. Herb's contributions as a librettist were only the most obvious. Without the financial backing of Herbert Harris, it is unlikely that Fields would have had the freedom to pursue the new directions in the Broadway musical suggested by Herbert, Rodgers, and Hart. And by the end of the decade, Dorothy was also writing songs for her father's shows.

As if to meet Pop Fields halfway, Herbert, Rodgers, and Hart temporarily retreated from the aesthetic ambitions of *Dearest Enemy*. They would break in the old horse gently. *The Girl Friend* picked up where *Poor Little Ritz Girl* had left off: an intimate, Princess Theatre–style musical comedy based on a youthful fad—this time, bicycle racing. Herbert wrote the book to showcase the talents of the husband-and-wife team of Sammy White and Eva Puck. White played the "hick" role of Leonard Silver, an aspiring cyclist who trains for a six-day race by means of an ingenious device: he peddles as he churns butter for his family's Long Island dairy farm. His sweetheart, Mollie Farrell (Puck), is both his coach and the daughter of a cycling champ. Mollie persuades a well-known race promoter named Arthur Spencer to sponsor Lenny by forging letters from several prominent sportsmen. Spencer's snobbish sister Wynn develops an inexplicable crush on Lenny. Wynn's boyfriend finds out and sets up a plan to keep Lenny out of the race: one of the trainers "accidentally" knocks Lenny off his bike, injuring his ankle, while another trainer tells him that his ankle is broken. Meanwhile, Spencer learns about the false letters of recommendation. Wynn strikes a deal with Mollie: Wynn will persuade her brother to keep Lenny, but only if Mollie lets Wynn marry Lenny. To save Lenny's racing career, she agrees. Lenny wins the race, of course, and at a celebration party, the romantic entanglements are set right.

The plot was typical musical comedy frippery, full of the kind of collegiate high jinks and trendy nonsense perfected the following year in the DeSylva-Brown-Henderson hit, *Good News,* (which also embroidered a love story around an athletic competition). Herbert Fields' book for *The Girl Friend* was hardly among his best, but it utilized some characteristic elements—countrified innocence (Lenny) pitted against big-city guile, social snobbery, and corruption. Here, as in most of Fields' plots, the catalyst was the female lead; Mollie was the second in a long line of spunky Fields heroines. In an exact reversal of their vaudeville roles, White played a dimwitted, slow-talking hick, while Puck was the street-smart, slangy operator. Though a country girl, she is not such an innocent:

> MOLLIE: . . . Love's like that.
>   ANN: Where did you learn so much about love?
> MOLLIE: *(impatiently giving her a dirty look)* Hiding under sofas, you pin-head.[4]

The humor ranged from the slapstick to the sophisticated, and in certain jokes and stage business the burlesque tendencies of the elder Fields overran the dramatic logic preferred by Herbert, Rodgers, and Hart. According to Dorothy, her father's solution for dead spots in the libretto or a joke that fell flat was to bring out his old black ledger-book full of tried-and-true jokes. The ledger contained almost half a century's worth of the best crossfire dialogues, sketches, and gags of Weber & Fields and their contemporaries, a veritable Dead Sea Scroll of American comedy. The worldly youths, however, rejected the patriarch's writ. Herbert's resistance usually crumbled in the face of his father's towering anger, for it was difficult for him to stand up to the man he had idolized for so long. Hart, with Rodgers' strong support, would then join the fray and battle vociferously. The young authors won out, Dorothy recalled, "and Dad's old chestnuts went back into the files to wait for the next show."[5] Despite these spirited confrontations, Rodgers could still write in his memoirs that in the seven Lew Fields productions he worked in, "there was never a single harsh word between us."[6]

(As for the black ledger, it became a rueful joke among Fields's show biz progeny; Herb cringed at the sight of it for as long as he worked with his father. Dorothy and Joe, in an interview almost twenty years after their father's death, and shortly after Herbert's, talked about "Pop's ledger." All of the children had contributed jokes to the ledger. Over the years, Lew also had numerous agents gathering jokes for him, including his brothers Nat and Sol and Rose's brothers Bobby and Jack, who covered the burlesque houses. By the time of the interview, the ledger no longer existed: Dorothy mentioned in passing that they had burned it, a symbolic gesture that was no doubt as liberating for her and her brothers as it is painful to stage historians.)[7]

With the Broadway premiere of *The Girl Friend* fast approaching, there were the usual frenetic last-minute changes. Between Saturday and its Broadway opening on Wednesday, March 17, Herbert trimmed the musical's three acts down to two by adding two more scenes to Act One. At the same time, the scenery itself was being cut down and refitted because it was discovered to be too large for the Vanderbilt's diminutive stage. The stage measured only nineteen and a half feet deep with a proscenium opening of thirty-four feet; the house sat 655 people, making it the same size as the old Weber & Fields Music Hall on Twenty-ninth Street. Though John Harwood was credited with staging the book and Jack Haskell with the musical numbers, Lew Fields was *The Girl Friend*'s hands-on producer throughout the rehearsals and tryouts. He supervised every detail, staying up all night Tuesday night with the crew to finish refitting the scenery.[8]

The Broadway first-nighters applauded enthusiastically, and the New York critics were favorable, if not ecstatic. Puck and White drew praise for their song-and-dance expertise, as did the comely, spry-legged June Cochrane (from *The Garrick Gaieties of 1925*). The *New Yorker*'s Gilbert W. Gabriel, who liked the show, nevertheless lamented the fact that Fields was not acting in it as well as producing it.

All agreed that the real strength of the production was its Rodgers & Hart score. Fields correctly predicted that the title number (a Charleston) and "The Blue Room" (a foxtrot ballad) would be the hits of the show. Indeed, "The Blue Room" was Rodgers & Hart at their best: a deceptively simple, uncluttered melody married to an effervescent lyric whose surges and pauses expressed the newlyweds' hopeful, playful fantasy—"A Love Nest" for sophisticates. A third number, a comic song for Eva Puck called "The Damsel Who Done All the Dirt," also caught the fancy of Broadway listeners.

Despite the positive reviews, attendance fell off unaccountably after the first month. It began to look as though the show would suffer the early curtain of other promising but ill-fated Lew Fields productions. This time, however, Lew Fields had more control over the show's fate; he was no longer dependent on the Shuberts for backing or a theater, and he had collaborators who were as desperate as he to keep it open. Herbert, Rodgers, and Hart agreed to suspend their royalties, the principals took salary cuts, and Fields negotiated a "summer arrangement" with Lyle Andrews, the Vanderbilt's manager. There was one more important difference: for the first time since his collaboration with Victor Herbert, Lew Fields had the luxury of a strong score. The popularity of "The Blue Room" and "The Girl Friend" helped attract larger audiences, as did word of mouth about the performances of Puck and White. By midsummer *The Girl Friend* had settled in for what ended up being a forty-week run.

Upon its closing in December, its three authors gratefully acknowledged the contributions of their mentor with a full-page announcement in *Variety:*

> To Mr. Lew Fields whose wisdom, experience and thoughtfulness has made possible a most auspicious opportunity to star on Broadway, we appreciatively acknowledge a most pleasant association.

> More than a personal manager, Mr. Fields, through the length of our professional and personal association, has been an inspiration and a guide.

It concluded by echoing (unintentionally) a sentiment from the heyday of the Weberfields: "To *The Girl Friend*'s cast we need say little beyond the query, 'Was there ever a happier backstage family on Broadway?'"[9]

When *The Girl Friend* finally caught on with Broadway audiences in the summer of 1926, Lew Fields began making plans to send it on tour. Once again, he tried to steer clear of the Shuberts; it was not just that he wanted to maintain control, but he still owed them an undisclosed—but apparently substantial—amount of money, and they were insisting on immediate repayment. Fortunately, Sammy White and Eva Puck were again willing to risk their own money, but even with Fields' share the road company was five thousand dollars short of its up-front costs. Producer Arthur Hammerstein made up the shortfall in the form of a loan to Fields, with the stipulation that Fields should play the comic lead in the new Oscar Hammerstein–Harbach–Friml operetta slated for the fall. The two Hammersteins, Harbach, and Friml were the team responsible for the fantastically popular *Rose-Marie.* With a cast and chorus of one hundred, *The Wild Rose* was to be even more lavish than its predecessor, and the initial involvement of Sam Harris (Cohan's former partner) added credibility to the enterprise.

From the start of rehearsals in late August, however, *The Wild Rose* showed signs of canker. Oscar Hammerstein II was dividing his time tending two roses, eventually spending more time on *The Desert Rose* with Sigmund Romberg. In concept, the two stories were quite similar, involving the intrusion of contemporary political events into traditional operetta landscapes. But Hammerstein's absence left the libretto in the hands of the more staid Otto Harbach. *The Wild Rose* unfolded as a series of plots and counterplots by capitalist manipulators and bolsheviks in the mythical kingdom of Borovina. Fields' role was that of an American oilman looking for new well sites.

Dissatisfaction with the book plagued the tryouts in Wilmington and Philadelphia. Although William Wilson was credited as the stage director, Fields apparently functioned as the director during the latter stages of the tryouts. When Wilson's choreography did not impress the Philly audiences, it was Fields who suggested an ambitious chorus dancer with the unlikely name of Busby Berkeley to restage the musical numbers. The scope and frequency of the changes overwhelmed even the usually unflappable Fields. Every night, sometimes less than fifteen minutes before curtain time, the stage manager would hand the cast a piece of script specifying certain changes. Rather than polishing their performances, cast members spent their rehearsal time trying to incorporate the new lines and blockings. Under these circumstances, Fields complained, "a capable performance was absolutely impossible." [10] Reviewers found little beyond Friml's music and Urban's sets to praise. Fields' performance was only satisfactory; the fact that the old trouper (three months away from his sixtieth birthday) had to resort to handsprings to generate any sustained applause is some indication of how desperately he was trying to "put over" the show.

Fields' desperation was not simply professional pride. Not only was he obligated to Arthur Hammerstein for providing the financing for the tour of *The Girl Friend*, but he was being dunned by the Shuberts for old debts. Some years earlier, probably during the *Snapshots of 1921* tour on the Shubert vaudeville circuit, the manager of a Shubert theater in Philadelphia, Leonard Blumberg, loaned Fields an unspecified sum of money drawn from the theater box office. In September, 1926, while Fields was suffering through the tryouts of *The Wild Rose* in Philadelphia, Blumberg received instructions from the Shuberts to collect the money. A few weeks later, they repeated the request more forcefully and revealed the unusual circumstances of the loan: "You loaned Mr. Lew Fields a certain amount of money. He is now in Philadelphia and we insist on your collecting the amount due. At the time he threatened to commit suicide unless the money was loaned him. . . . He is now earning money and must pay this." [11] It is not difficult to envision a scenario in late 1921 or 1922 in which a desperate Fields might have threatened suicide: recently bankrupt and mired in a floundering show, struggling to maintain a vestige of his dignity as breadwinner, he begs his old friend Lee Shubert for a loan to spare his family (and himself) further financial humiliation. Maybe Fields promised a Weber & Fields reunion tour for the Shubert circuit. The suicide threat itself may have been sincere, or just an extreme example of Fields' persuasive powers with his close colleagues (like the sad brown eyes and imploring manner that always won Weber over). A sincere threat or a calculated one would in this context be equally pathetic. Lee Shubert had no doubts that Fields genuinely needed the money; besides, hadn't Fields' debts made him one of the Shuberts' most loyal employees?

Blumberg's attempts at collecting the debt were unavailing, as evidenced by his next correspondence with Lee Shubert:

I had a talk with Mr. Lew Fields about paying something on the money he owes. I threatened him with attachments, etc. but he claims that he is deeply indebted to Hammerstein and if it were not for that fact he might not remain in the show *[The Wild Rose]*, that they are only advancing him sufficient money to live on as he owes them so much. He did promise, however, that if the show got over in New York that he would start paying me something each week.[12]

In other words, Fields' financial condition was as precarious as ever. Shubert, however, remained adamant:

[To Leonard Blumberg] . . . I hold you responsible to get this money. What difference does it make who loaned him the money? He has been working for a long time. He took the money from you and if he does not pay it back, he is just stealing. He has no right to give you any excuse whatsoever.[13]

Meanwhile, the prospects of making *The Wild Rose* a success continued to dim. A week before its scheduled New York opening, producer Sam Harris, despairing of the book problems and the lavish staging costs, withdrew from his partnership with Arthur Hammerstein, absorbing $19,000 (twenty-five percent) of the losses so far. The frenetic changes intensified, as Hammerstein tried to trim costs in preparation for its move to Broadway. Two days before the New York opening, Fields collapsed in the theater, clutching his abdomen. He was rushed to Fifth Avenue Hospital. Arthur Hammerstein called another old Music Hall alumnus, William Collier, to fill Fields' role. Collier appeared on opening night with only twenty-four hours of preparation, ad libbing about his unpreparedness but never faltering in his lines.

The diagnosis was reported in the *Times* as appendicitis but was quickly revised to "an abdominal inflammatory condition" requiring immediate surgery. Fields' new son-in-law, Dr. Jack Weiner, was one of the attending physicians. *Variety*, however, had a more dramatic explanation of the illness: "Lew Fields' Flip-Flops Land Him in Hospital. [. . .] Overwork in directing the new Hammerstein show and his performance in it are blamed for Fields' collapse. Despite being over 60, the comedian star was called on to turn flip-flops."

Oddly enough, Fields apparently preferred *Variety*'s explanation. In an interview several months later, he claimed that *The Wild Rose* had "thrown me into a nervous breakdown by the numerous changes ordered. . . . I stood it for three weeks and had to give it up when the New York opening was scheduled."[14] Fields' self-diagnosis made it sound similar to his breakdown in November, 1910, but it does not account for the surgery reported to have occurred on October 20.

For the next three weeks, while Fields remained hospitalized, his son-in-law issued periodic progress reports to the daily papers. As for *The Wild Rose*, it eked out sixty-one performances, which was still almost four weeks longer than Fields' convalescence. In the past, when injury or illness forced him out of a role, Fields always came back and stepped in as soon as he was capable. He showed no inclination to return to *The Wild Rose*.

The nature and timing of Fields' mysterious ailment resolved two of his most pressing problems—his impatient creditors and his contractual commitment to a show he knew would fail. These pressures, and the contradictions in the accounts, raise some troubling questions about whether the illness was a desperate ploy, a possible bout with neurasthenia, or a genuine case of appendicitis.

Was he taking advantage of some stress-induced symptoms to extricate himself from an intractable situation? Not according to producer Lyle Andrews, his partner in the Vanderbilt Theatre shows: "I saw him that morning [of his collapse]. He was grimly confident. I saw him two days later. He was a shadow, a wasted old man."[15] Whatever the cause of Fields' hospitalization, it appeared to Andrews as something more life-threatening than the "nervous exhaustion" Fields claimed.

Lew Fields finally emerged from his mysterious convalescence on November 15 to participate in a gala affair in the Grand Ballroom of the Waldorf. At 8:00 p.m. sharp, David Sarnoff's Radio Corporation of America (RCA) presented the inaugural broadcast of the National Broadcasting Company, the first national radio network. For the next four hours the disembodied voices and music of an all-star variety show crackled through the night air to twenty-three stations in twenty cities. The program was composed of the standard-bearers of high and low entertainment: Will Rogers, Mary Garden, Walter Damrosch and the New York Philharmonic, Eddie Cantor, the Ben Bernie and Vincent Lopez orchestras, the Gilbert & Sullivan Light Opera Company, baritone Tito Ruffo of the Metropolitan Opera, and—representing the salad days of vaudeville—Weber & Fields. In full Mike-and-Meyer regalia, Weber & Fields played to the audience of one thousand celebrities and newspapermen assembled at the Waldorf. Radio posed many of the same physical limitations as recording on the overall effectiveness of their act, but the laughter of a studio audience was usually enough to put a charge in the duo's delivery. Their routine lasted eight minutes, for which they were paid one thousand dollars (Cantor received $1,500, and Will Rogers, broadcasting from Kansas City, $2,500). An estimated two million people tuned in to the show; in their eight-minute stint, Weber & Fields reached as many people as they had in the eight years of their old Music Hall (if you include the tours). The feuding Dutchmen peppered each other with crossfire banter and insults, bringing to the Radio Age a tradition extending back over fifty years to the minstrel show end men, Tambo and Bones.

As national advertisers began to realize the power of the airwaves, they rushed to sponsor weekly radio shows with big-name entertainers. NBC paid Eddie Cantor one hundred dollars a minute for the "Eveready Hour," which, as far as Cantor was concerned, was only fifteen minutes long. Prizefighter Gene Tunney did a five-minute turn on the "Palmolive Hour" for $500 a minute. General Motors shelled out $624,000 to sponsor fifty-two weeks of entertainment on a twenty-eight-station hookup; their roster included William Collier, Leo Carillo, and Weber & Fields (in June and July of 1927).

After the NBC broadcast, Fields continued his recovery at home for another week or so. The forced inactivity made him restless and irritable. Every night he questioned Herbert on the new show's progress. In another month Lew would be sixty years old; a few more months and he could claim a half century since his first stage appearance. Taking stock of his career as a producer, he saw nothing but disappointments since his Broadway Theater productions before the war, at least until *The Girl Friend.* His efforts as a legit performer seemed "hoodoo'd," mocked by the continued success of his Dutch clown persona. Of all his musicals, the show he took the most pride in was still *It Happened in Nordland.* But now, over twenty years later, he had finally found some new collaborators as talented as Julian Mitchell and Victor Herbert. He would stake his future—or what remained of it—on them. In any case, he could not afford to retire.

"I believe he almost died during that stay in the Fifth Avenue Hospital," Lyle Andrews recalled. "Then he seemed, in some miraculous fashion, to be born again." [16] Perhaps what revived him was the prospect of producing the new musical comedies that his son Herbert was writing. It was Herbert who conceived of the idea of updating his father's old production of *Tillie's Nightmare* with a new book and score and a more attractive leading lady. *Tillie's Nightmare* had been a hit in 1910 for the rough-and-ready comedienne Marie Dressler. Lucky for Fields that her financial ineptitude was even greater than his own, for he had acquired her share of the rights to the show shortly after it had opened.

Rodgers & Hart loved Herb's idea, but they had committed themselves for the latter part of the summer to writing a show in London with Guy Bolton called *Lido Lady.* The script and score for *Peggy-Ann* were not completed until late October, about the same time as Lew's collapse and mysterious illness. Herbert stood in for his ailing father for the casting, and rehearsals began under the direction of Robert Milton, who had directed the Kern-Bolton-Wodehouse shows at the Princess Theatre. When rehearsals began in mid-November, the lead role of Peggy-Ann had not yet been cast; Herbert, Rodgers, and Hart had created the role for Helen Ford, but she was on tour with *Dearest Enemy.* After one particularly disheartening afternoon of auditions, Herb decided to give Ford one more try. He reached her on the phone in Cincinnati, and discovered that *Dearest Enemy* would be closing the following week. Overjoyed, Herb took a train the next day with the manuscript and a contract.

The production of *Peggy-Ann* was, in Rodgers' words, "a family affair." The presence in the cast of Helen Ford, Betty Starbuck, Edith Meiser, and other *Garrick* graduates added to the family atmosphere; veterans Lulu McConnell and her husband Grant Simpson (favorites of Lew Fields' from *Poor Little Ritz Girl* and *Snapshots*) took the "kids" in the cast under their wing. Reunited with Herb and Lew Fields, Rodgers later described the entire production as "a joy."

In addition to Rodgers & Hart, Fields was also playing mentor to another promising young Broadway composer. Former stockbroker and rehearsal pianist Vincent Youmans had already composed the scores for two of the decade's biggest hits, *Wildflower* and *No, No, Nanette,* including the songs "Bambalina," "Tea for Two," and "I Want to Be Happy." Shy and sickly, Youmans was not happy being at the mercy of producers and managers, and he was frequently dissatisfied with his lyricists and the way his songs were performed. At age twenty-eight, he decided to become his own producer, and approached the veteran Lew Fields about a partnership. Barely recovered from his illness, Fields announced that he and his young partner would produce musical versions of four straight plays that had appeared at the Belasco Theatre, including one that would star Sammy White and Eva Puck. The first one, for spring, 1927, would be based on the comedy *Shore Leave* by Hubert Osborne. Not surprisingly, Fields asked Herbert to write the libretto.

In no small measure, then, Lew Fields owed his renaissance as a musical producer to the emergence of his son Herbert as a first-class librettist. The elder Fields took over as supervising producer of *Peggy-Ann* in late November, 1926, shortly before the start of its Philadelphia tryouts. Herbert rechristened Tillie with the Cinderella musical–style name of *Peggy* (later lengthened to *Peggy-Ann* for a more down-home ring). In adapting *Tillie's Nightmare*, he seemed to take a perverse pleasure in keeping the plot intact while changing every other aspect—except for one gag line that remained from the original. In the original libretto, Edgar Smith had built his story around a comic character created by the show's star, Marie Dressler. As conceived by Smith and Dressler, Tillie Blobbs was the small-town slavey toiling in her mother's boardinghouse and dreaming of the pleasures and adventures she has been denied.

Herbert's transformation of *Tillie* into *Peggy-Ann* was in fact a radical reworking of the Cinderella musical by way of Freud's couch and the Algonquin Round Table. In 1920, shortly after the American publication of Freud's *A General Introduction to Psychoanalysis*, Rodgers & Hart had written a song called "You Can't Fool Your Dreams" for Lew Fields' show *Poor Little Ritz Girl*. During the next half decade, the terms "Freudian slip," "repression," and "fixation" entered common usage at the same time as "jazz," "pep," "Trojans" (as in the contraceptives), and "profiteer," creating a basic lexicon for urban sophisticates.[17] By 1926, Freud's theories had become grist for the popular press and a kind of litmus test for young intellectuals and hipsters. Herbert, Rodgers, and Hart saw that for all the discussion, Freud's theories had not found expression in the popular theater. As Rodgers put it in his memoirs, "the time seemed ripe for a musical comedy to make the breakthrough by dealing with subconscious fears and fantasies. That's exactly what we did with *Peggy-Ann*."[18]

Herbert divided the original Dressler character into two roles, a sweet young heroine (Peggy-Ann) and a coarse, middle-aged vaude actress in the Dressler mode (Mrs. Frost). Peggy-Ann still has the wishful dream, but the boisterous boarder Mrs. Frost accompanies Peggy-Ann in her dreamtime wanderings and provides the broad comedy bits. Herbert used the dream the same way that he used history in *Dearest Enemies*—as a way of keeping contemporary social foibles at arm's length, the better to mock them. Combining his understanding of stage forms such as vaudeville and operetta with his knowledge of hip culture, the son fashioned a libretto that made it possible for his father to realize his long-standing ambition to blend musical comedy with burlesque.

The first fifteen minutes of Herbert's book for *Peggy-Ann* were so crammed with exposition that there was no room for the traditional chorus number that usually opened a musical. Like his father's 1911 show, *The Hen Pecks, Peggy-Ann* begins as a rural farce in which the absence of music underscores the drudgery of country living. The opening curtain reveals Mrs. Barnes' boardinghouse in Glen Falls, New York, where the guests—a husband-and-wife vaudeville team (the Frosts) and their daughter Alice—are lingering over dessert before heading to the local

Loew's theater. The unseen Mrs. Barnes orders Peggy-Ann about in a harsh voice, while Peggy-Ann's nasty half-sister, Dolores, ridicules Peggy-Ann's three-year engagement to Guy Pendleton, an A&P clerk too poor to marry. Dolores is engaged to Arnold Small, wealthy owner of the local department store; her father, now deceased, was a rich Cuban whose property was seized by the Cuban government. The Frosts invite Peggy to see their show, and a group of friends arrive to ask Peggy and Guy to join them on a hayride. Among the group are Patricia and Freddy, a couple who introduce the show's first tune, "Hello," a self-deprecatingly comic love song ("I guess I must have done something awful / So God gave me you!"). The imperious voice of Mrs. Barnes reminds Peggy that she cannot go out because she must help can peaches. Guy begs Peggy to disobey her mother and go out with him; he is leaving for the city the next morning to make his fortune so that they can marry. He sings to her about their "little tree in the park," but she cannot defy her mother, and Guy leaves in a huff. The prologue concludes with a forlorn Peggy falling asleep in an armchair while reading the newspaper. She begins to dream. . . .

In a marvel of narrative ingenuity, the transition from country to city and consciousness to the dream state unfold simultaneously. A female chorus clad in gingham frocks changes into flapper togs while dancing and singing "Howdy to Broadway": "We're gonna go down where / Ladies' backs are bare / And the farm girls all go astray. . . ." This song of innocents eager for corrupting experiences sets the tone for the dream. Peggy-Ann is plunged into a surreal world of outlandishly exaggerated art deco settings, where a talking fish rescues shipwrecks, wedding vows are never completed, and people converse in Lewis Carroll–style double talk. At the corner of Forty-second Street and Fifth Avenue, Peggy-Ann is stopped by a policeman wearing a pink uniform who engages her in a bizarre conversation that keeps her from crossing the street with the signal. Mrs. Frost appears and takes Peggy-Ann in hand, eager to show her a good time. Peggy-Ann responds coyly, savoring her mother's warnings in the song "A Little Birdie Told Me So":

> Of very pure young girls I wouldn't say there's none that's left—
> The well-known statue called Miss Liberty's the one that's left!
> But purest driven snow
> Will sometimes drift, you know,
> A little birdie told me so.[19]

Peggy-Ann's dream world is an inversion of her waking one: her fiancé Guy is now the owner of the department store, Dolores and Arnold work for him, and Fred is an intellectual studying female psychology. Even the shopgirls are happy ("Store Opening") because the customers are so easy to please, and wealthy shoppers such as the Mmes. Astor, Biddle, and Gould shoot craps on the floor and give the girls big tips. Guy offers to marry Peggy-Ann in five minutes and closes the store to do so. In the Act One finale ("The Wedding Procession"), the mean-spirited Dolores sabotages the ceremony by sprinkling poppy seeds on the participants, who fall asleep one by one, leaving only Peggy-Ann awake to sing the last few measures of the song.

Act Two finds Peggy-Ann and company aboard the steam yacht "Peggy" en route to Havana. The unsavory-looking crew turns out to be a gang of pirates whose rallying cry is a mock Gilbert & Sullivan patter song: "We sea-hawks are sea-hawkin' / All we hawks from Weehawken. . . . Robbing boats around / Cutting throats around. . . ." The news that Peggy-Ann is on her honeymoon placates them until they learn that she has not been officially married yet. Their mood turns ugly; "they'd better have a ceremony soon, or the sailors'll start talking," warns Arnold Small. "You know how mid-Victorian sailors are." Adding to the sailors' moral outrage is the fact that Peggy-Ann has shown up in her scanties.

With the sailors on the verge of mutiny, Mrs. Frost finally agrees to act as the minister and begins the service reading from a telephone book as a Bible. Dolores again disrupts the proceedings by giving Mrs. Frost tainted wafers that make her seasick. Peggy-Ann's antidote. champagne, makes the hefty Mrs. Frost uncontrollably drunk—a parallel to the "souse act" that highlighted Marie Dressler's version—and causes the ship to founder. The next scene takes place in a lifeboat carrying Mrs. Frost, Guy, Peggy-Ann, and Alice on the open sea. Their dialogue becomes increasingly surreal:

> MRS. FROST: Peggy, my dear, I've attended lots of wrecks, but I must say that yours was just the last word.
>
> PEGGY: I thought it was kinda nice. . . . There were a few things that I didn't like. . . . The life preservers were served cold.
>
> ALICE: Mine were delicious!
>
> GUY: Did you forget to bring the Mah Jong tiles, dear?
>
> PEGGY: Oh, brother! I knew there was something.
>
> MRS. FROST: This is the loveliest lifeboat. . . . What period is it?
>
> GUY: It's early Queen Anne. Of course, it's very plain, but that's us. . . .[20]

Then the rudder breaks, and a loquacious fish tows them to Havana. Scene Three unfolds in Havana, where Peggy-Ann discovers that a racetrack has been built on her mother's property. Peggy-Ann makes a few bets and wins, and then bets on a talking horse named Peggy who bears a curious resemblance to her.

Mrs. Frost entertains in the clubhouse, where she performs a parody of Texas Guinan, the breezy blonde speakeasy hostess who embodied smart New Yorkers' resistance to Prohibition. Guinan had two catch phrases, "Hello, Sucker!" and "Give the little girl a hand," and Rodgers & Hart made the latter into a rambunctious Charleston. "A nightclub hostess is one of those dames / Whose natural father was old Jesse James," was how Mrs. Frost introduced herself. Like "Howdy to Broadway" and "A Little Birdie," the Guinan parody delights in naughtiness and the loss of innocence:

> Give this little girl a hand!
> Ain't she pretty, ain't she sweet?
> Biggest eyes in the land.
> Ain't she got the cutest feet?
> She reads her Bible every night at curfew's knell,
> A brand-new Bible at a different hotel,

Ain't her modesty just grand?
Come on girlie, shake that thing.
She's a girl who loves the outdoor life,
She walks up and down between the Astor and the Strand,
Won't you give this little girl a hand![21]

Of course, the nightclub is raided. During the tumult, the final horse race begins, and the fleeing customers become spectators at a futuristic paddock where they cheer for the horse named Peggy. With Peggy about to cross the finish line, the dream ends as Peggy-Ann awakes in the gloom of her mother's boardinghouse. Only ten minutes have passed since she dozed off. "I dreamed I had everything. Now, I haven't got anything," she says sadly.

Story logic dictated a quiet, bittersweet scene. Stage logic required a big, rousing finale. In a show of faith in his young collaborators, Lew Fields allowed the story logic to carry the day. Guy sneaks back and tries once more to get Peggy-Ann to accompany him to the Halloween dance. Peggy-Ann's dream has changed her, and she decides to defy her mother and marry Guy despite their poverty. The scene is dark—visually and emotionally—and dark scenes violated all the rules of musical comedy. A dark scene for a finale was unheard of, but Fields was willing to risk it.

The freewheeling visual style and the erratic rhythms of the story (increasingly frenzied activity bookended by quiet, pathos-ridden scenes) created some unique challenges in the staging and choreography. Herbert, Rodgers, and Hart had deliberately emulated the "intimate" (small-scale) musicals of Bolton, Wodehouse, and Kern for the Princess Theatre. So it made sense that a Princess veteran, Robert Milton, be hired to direct *Peggy-Ann*.

To fill the position of dance director, Fields turned to another veteran, an old vaude hoofer turned choreographer named Seymour Felix. Felix's first Broadway exposure came in 1908 in Fields' *The Mimic World* as part of a kid dance pair called Felix and Claire. Herbert Fields, who was an astute judge of production numbers and had staged the dances for most of Rodgers & Hart's amateur shows, had been impressed by Felix's efforts in various Shubert productions in 1924 and 1925. One of these, *Top Hole*, featured what the *Times* critic applauded as "a real Weber & Fields dancing chorus."

More impressive still was Felix's ambition, for his vision of theatrically integral show dances coincided perfectly with the aesthetics of his younger colleagues. Novelty dances were no longer enough; the bag of tricks had been emptied. Like his new collaborators, Felix believed that every number should have a dramatic and logical setting: "The best high kicker can kick no higher than the length of her legs. The daintiest, most graceful of young women can only dance a Charleston or a Black Bottom when she is supposed to dance a Charleston or a Black Bottom. In many instances the chorus interlude became a colorful but negative interruption to the action or comedy of the musical comedy book. It seldom aided development."[22]

In Felix, Fields found an innovative dance director cut from the same cloth as Julian Mitchell and Ned Wayburn. Felix later said that Fields was the first producer to allow him to collaborate with the show's authors "to build up the most unified show we could." [23] The intimate scale and atmospheric extremes of *Peggy-Ann* seriously challenged the dance director's resourcefulness. With only eighteen chorus men and women and a tiny, cluttered stage, he could not simply rely on group formations, novelty dances, and speedy stepping.

For the introduction to the second act, Felix had to forgo dancing altogether; Felix had half his chorus enter in a comic manner through the rather awkward device of the department store's revolving door. "Imagine," commented Felix to an interviewer, "a dance director who could overlook an opportunity for 'flash' in the old days." [24] Fields intended the scene to be a travesty of the ways of the rich while shopping, and he was willing to sacrifice flash to set up the bizarre humor of the scene in Guy's department store. Felix reworked the scene with Herbert, Rodgers, and Hart: the ensemble of shopgirls and customers entered singing "Charming, Charming," their dancing shading into comic business that re-established the principal characters in their new roles.

Later in the second act, in the clubhouse of the Havana race track, Felix had his opportunity for "flash." During the Philadelphia tryouts, Felix noticed that Rodgers' tune for the song "Havana" lent itself to interpretation in two dance rhythms—a tango and a Black Bottom (blues). By having Rodgers introduce a motif from W. C. Handy's "St. Louis Blues" into the song, Felix was able to set up a dance competition between the Cuban girls and the American visitors. The concept was in fact rather old-fashioned, like the "pick-out" (or "cutting") contests that used to occur late in the last act of a burlesque, when individual chorus members tried to impress the audience with their agility and fancy footwork.

Changes to the script, staging, scenery, and score continued up through the start of its Philadelphia tryout on December 13. At the time of her first public performance as Peggy-Ann, Helen Ford (who was onstage virtually every minute of the show) had been rehearsing for only two weeks, and she admitted to being petrified. After the show, she staggered to her dressing room, where she was congratulated by Lew Fields, Lyle Andrews, and the rest of the creative team. A few days later, Fields and Andrews signed the cast to run-of-the-play contracts. Nevertheless, Andrews remembered the opening night in Philly as "sadly deficient." Philadelphia's critics were not nearly so harsh, though *Variety* did note that " 'Peggy' [was] rapidly being whipped into shape. Much work was necessary, but there was enough real material to make fixing worthwhile." [25]

For Lew Fields, the real work was just beginning. Ever since the Music Hall, he had maintained that one could not really begin to fix a show until it had been performed before an audience. So in the two weeks of tryouts in Philly, Fields (in Andrews' words) "re-created the production." For once, the book was left relatively intact. Fields thought that some of his son's lines for Helen Ford were too long-winded, and asked that they be "punched up." Otherwise, Herbert's script underwent few changes except for the last scene, from which he dropped many lines to allow time for a finale that was still not satisfactorily worked out. Under Fields' prodding, Milton and Felix reworked and polished the staging and musical numbers. Fields also fired a chorus boy who could not resist some impromptu clowning during the performances. (Hadn't Weber & Fields committed the same crime when they were youngsters with Adah Richmond?) The miscreant in *Peggy-*

Ann was named Jack Oakie; having found his calling as a comedian, he later became one of the most popular screen clowns of the 'thirties.

In an effort to provide Felix with a snappier transition from country to city and consciousness to dream state, Rodgers & Hart replaced "Trampin' Along" with "Howdy to Broadway." Needing another romantic number for Peggy-Ann and Guy, Rodgers & Hart inserted "Maybe It's Me" ("I've learned what the taste of wine meant / To a lady of refinement"), which they had originally written for an amateur show *(Fifth Avenue Follies)* earlier in the year. Two other numbers were dropped, "Come and Tell Me," and "Paris Is Divine." Rodgers also reworked "Havana," as mentioned above, to facilitate Felix's competition between tangoers and Black Bottomers. But the major problem was still the big finale at the Havana racetrack and the transition back to the dreary boardinghouse.

The final tryout performance was on Christmas Day. The show had gone smoothly: Peggy-Ann awakes from her dream as the haywagon pulls up outside the boardinghouse porch, carrying the friends (the chorus) who implore Peggy-Ann to go on the hayride. After a brief reconciliation between Peggy-Ann and Guy (a reprise of "A Tree in the Park"), she decides to go on the hayride. Her mother's grating voice interrupts them, summoning her daughter from offstage. "Louder, Ma . . . and funnier!" is Peggy-Ann's wise reply as she exits with Guy. The Christmas audience responded enthusiastically, but Fields was still not satisfied. The tag line parodied the kind of thing a stage director or producer might say; it was an inside joke that called attention to the fact that the ending was in fact neither loud (big) enough nor funny enough. The company headed back to New York without knowing the details of the show's last fifteen minutes. The Broadway opening was forty-eight hours away.

The next morning, Fields arrived at the Vanderbilt, expecting to see the usual pre-opening hurly-burly of rigging and set construction. He was unprepared for the turmoil that greeted him. Milton and the crew foreman delivered the bad news: the scenery had been built too large to fit the Vanderbilt's narrow stage. They had already started to cut it down to size, but there were several scene changes that simply could not work, including the one mechanical effect agreed on for the finale—the haywagon. Valuable time had already been lost, time needed for establishing blocking and the cues for dozens of drops and lights. And there was still the little matter of working out the new finale.

The day unfolded in a series of technical mishaps—lights, rigging, scenery. Somehow, in the midst of this mayhem, Milton, Felix, and Fields were able to work out a version of the finale. Blocking continued late into the evening; the actors were allowed to retire for the evening, but the stage crew worked through the night. When the cast returned on Monday morning for the run-throughs, the crew was still working feverishly. By late afternoon, the carpenters were dead on their feet, and the electrician, prop man, and stagehands were in a daze. With all the resizing of scenery, reblocking, and the new finale, there was still a multitude of technical cues to rehearse. Observing the crew's extreme fatigue, Fields wondered aloud whether it would be a mistake to open. Milton sent the crew to a nearby tavern and paid for their steaks and coffee, hoping to stimulate their weary bodies. Fields paced nervously backstage while Herbert and Hart looked on helplessly. Peeking out at the house, Fields noted with grim satisfaction that the show was sold out, despite an increase in the top ticket price to $4.40.

At 8:30—ten minutes to curtain—the crew began straggling back to their posts. There they found their bosses and the show's creators ready to go to work. Union rules forbade non-union personnel to handle scenery or lights, but the Vanderbilt's crew would not refuse some helping hands. Milton perched himself in the fly loft, ready to guide the curtains, drops, and flying props. Hart went to the lighting operator's booth in the balcony to dictate the lighting cues. Felix and Fields remained on the stage to prompt the performers and help with the scene changes. The curtain went up on time, at 8:40.

While the chorus performed "Howdy to Broadway" in front of the drop curtain, Fields and Felix helped move the table and chairs. (The last time Fields had worked on a stage crew was with Gus Hill's outfit, thirty years earlier.) The premiere of *Peggy-Ann* proceeded smoothly, except for a wayward pink calcium spotlight, which flickered and frequently missed its mark, the result perhaps of some disagreements between Hart and the operator. Fortunately, opening-night audiences did not expect technical perfection.

From the climax of the show (the horse race) to the final scene, cast and crew were venturing into uncharted territory. Though there had been run-throughs for the performers to establish blocking, crosses, and dance routines, there apparently had not been time for technical run-throughs, and the movement of scenery, drops, and lighting was quite complex. Still, Fields insisted on trying the new finale. He approved Felix's daring solution: rather than imposing the big number where it was thematically inappropriate, they would exaggerate the solitude, the quietness, and the darkness.

At the height of the crucial horse race, Peggy-Ann and the other principal characters are rooting for "Peggy" (their horse) from the railing of the paddock. The musical number narrates the progress of the race. The chorus grouping was a spoof of an old-fashioned "watch the ponies run" number from before the war. As the ensemble joins in, the number builds with chant-like intensity towards the finish. The crowd surges forward to the front of the stage and the "traveler" curtain closes behind them. As the singing spectators follow the imaginary horses over the heads of the orchestra, they crowd to the center and Peggy-Ann slips between the gap in the traveler. While the race is finishing, Peggy-Ann is backstage making a complete costume change.

Fields and Felix, sensing success, eagerly helped the exhausted stagehands set up the boardinghouse interior. Onstage, the chorus of spectators faded into the wings as the cheering died down, and the curtains parted on the slumbering Peggy-Ann. She is awakened by Guy, who reconciles with her and asks her to come with him to New York City. They exit as a solo violin picks up their love theme, "A Tree in the Park." Slowly, pairs of the chorus tiptoe in and join in singing softly. The ensemble advances to the front of the stage and at the end of the song, in a gesture redolent of a fairy tale, they lean over and blow out the footlights. The fact that everyone (except for Peggy-Ann) was still in their Havana racetrack costumes did not seem to bother the audience in the least.

The New York critics responded with fulsome praise. "At last," Robert Cole-

man announced in the *Mirror*, "I have found a musical comedy that's different.
. . . I hereby go on record as placing this talented triumvirate [Herbert, Rodgers,
and Hart] in the foremost ranks of our youthful and talented show builders." The
Times echoed this judgement of the show's authors: "It is a bright and ambitious
musical comedy that came forth at the Vanderbilt Theatre last night. . . . From
the beginning they have brought freshness and ideas to the musical comedy field,
and in their new piece . . . they travel a little further along the road." Reviewers
singled out several Rodgers & Hart tunes as possible hits for the song-pluggers:
"Where's That Rainbow," "A Tree in the Park," "A Little Birdie Told Me So,"
"Maybe It's Me," and the comedic "Give This Little Girl a Hand." Thomas Van
Dyke (the *Morning Telegraph*) said that Hart's lyrics were as good as Ira Gershwin's—high praise indeed. Oddly enough, none of Rodgers & Hart's songs broke
through, and this fact alone may account for why *Peggy-Ann* is not remembered
among the 'twenties' most significant musicals along with *Lady, Be Good! No,
No, Nanette!* and *Showboat*. In the end, it is always the hit songs in the score
that determine the fate of a musical comedy for posterity.

Critics were equally enthusiastic about the cast, especially "little" Helen Ford
and her foil, the "robust" Lulu McConnell. In Helen Ford, they found a musical
comedienne who could not only put over a song, but who could act as well. But
it was McConnell who was said to embody "the free and easy tone of the production." Two *Garrick Gaieties* graduates also fared well: Betty Starbuck, as the
fresh "yaw-yaw" child Alice Frost, was "a delight"; Edith Meiser was "haunting"
as the villainess.

Veteran Alan Dale, who had been reviewing Lew Fields' productions since
the halcyon days of the original Music Hall, was able to discern Fields' distinctive
hand in the shaping of *Peggy-Ann:* "It is as though Lewis Carroll himself had
written the book and some musical Carroll had achieved the music, and they had
both been 'edited' by Lew Fields, filled to the brim with the liveliest brand of
humor. . . . Here we have pep, vim, life and fantasy." George Goldsmith also
attributed the show's rhythm and its "quick, titillating pace" to Fields' veteran
guidance.

On the eve of *Peggy-Ann*'s New York premiere and his own sixtieth birthday,
Fields observed, "Styles in musical comedy change slowly," as he cited *Peggy-
Ann*'s antecedents. The stylistic landmarks he referred to included the Weberfields travesties, "the big shows" (his Broadway Theater productions), and Ziegfeld's revues. He acknowledged the importance of the princess shows, but he
credited the intimate and trendy revues—*Charlot's* and *The Garrick Gaieties*—
with showing the way to *Peggy-Ann*. It was, according to Fields, in the small,
sophisticated revues that the spirit of burlesque (or "travesty" as he now preferred to call it) had survived. With the assistance of his son Herbert and his
young collaborators, Lew Fields had left behind the more archaic forms of the
musical comedy; in *Peggy-Ann*, he proved that he could master the idioms of the
Jazz Age musical.

Beyond his savvy as a musical stager, what Lew Fields contributed to *Peggy-
Ann* was a unifying sensibility. For all its modernist trappings, *Peggy-Ann* had

the spirit and tone of a Weberfields burlesque. Burlesque, Fields once observed, always has a specific target. In the case of *Peggy-Ann,* the target was the Cinderella musical. But in the hands of Herbert-Rodgers-Hart, the dream play grew into something more: in the words of one critic, it "delves to the very essence of burlesque, thus becoming to an extent creative instead of merely imitative."[26] The use of the dream provided a narrative justification for the screwball impulses of burlesque. Peggy-Ann's dream world turned waking reality inside out, just as the most successful of the Music Hall travesties inverted the morality and attitudes of the original plays. The breezy, flippant style of Herbert's dialogue— sometimes nonsensical, sometimes surreal—recalled the best of Edgar Smith's work for the Music Hall. There, current plays, actors, and celebrities were the favorite targets; where the Weberfields chose *Sappho,* Olga Nethersole, Teddy Roosevelt, and Abe Hummel, Herbert Fields chose vaudevillians, Mrs. Astor, and Texas Guinan. During one of the wedding scenes, in a parody of O'Neill's *The Hairy Ape,* Herbert's script called for the actors to don masks and move like automatons.

Herbert, like Smith, realized that the burlesque method demands that nothing in the show can be exempt from mockery. In *Peggy-Ann, Variety*'s critic noted, "even the love story is kidded throughout. . . ." The same applied to the score: Hart's sardonic lyrics for "Where's That Rainbow" and "Give That Little Girl a Hand" referred to other song hits of the day, such as "Look for the Silver Lining," "The Love Nest," "Ain't She Sweet," and Rodgers & Hart's own "Blue Room." The stylistic range of Rodgers' compositions was playful if not satiric—a love ballad, a patter song, a Charleston, a tango, and an *opéra-comique* finale for Act One that interwove snatches of "Where's That Rainbow," "A Little Birdie," "A Tree in the Park," and the Gettysburg Address.

Sime Silverman of Variety used the success of *Peggy-Ann* to needle an old adversary: "Lew Fields has produced two musical hits in a row. . . . These two hits may represent more in money profit as a producer to Fields than he secured for himself during all his eighteen years [*sic*] of association with the Shuberts as a producer. Broadwayites have noted this somewhat odd condition—that Fields should have accomplished more for himself substantially within a year when producing as an independent than he did during his eighteen years of Shuberts servitude."[27] The numbers were slightly exaggerated; Fields had been with the Shuberts for seventeen years, the Weber & Fields 1912 Jubilee (a Shubert co-production) had been hugely profitable, and *The Girl Friend* had been a critical success but had not made much money in the end. Sime's conclusions, however, were essentially correct. For years, Broadwayites *had* wondered about Lew Fields' continued association with the Shuberts: why had he stayed with them for so long? Fields' indebtedness to the brothers would probably have been less puzzling to them than his friendship (now cooled) with Lee.

A year later, in his annual assessment of the legit stage, Sime once again used the example of Fields' relationship with the Shuberts. By now, Fields had two more hit musicals to his credit; Sime now touted him as an example of the new breed of independent producer:

> These new producers appear to be the ones who are giving the new writers their chance. . . . They are fair-minded in selection and probably also in business, both in contrast to the legit methods of producing or operating in other days.
>
> Perhaps Lew Fields won't object if he's made an example of the new legit business. For 17 years Lew Fields was an adherent of the Shuberts. He produced with them and for them.
>
> No one thought it strange when the most popular Lew had to go into bankruptcy.

Old Pop Fields, exemplar of the new legit business? It seemed odd, to say the least, especially when Fields' name kept showing up in the filler columns under the headings "Twenty Years Ago" and "Forty Years Ago." Sime's suggestion that the Shuberts caused Fields' bankruptcy was another exaggeration. Still, the negative effects of the Shuberts on Fields' career were undeniable. Neither family nor colleagues knew the extent to which his career between the years 1914 and 1923 had been governed by one looming consideration: how to repay the Shuberts and other creditors.

With the money from his Keith-Orpheum vaudeville tour, Fields was able to put in his share as an investor in his new co-production with Vincent Youmans. *Hit the Deck* began rehearsing early in March; Fields did not join the company until ten days before the show's Philadelphia opening. Several of his hirees were already hard at work: veteran director Alexander Leftwich, the hot young choreographer Seymour Felix, *Peggy-Ann*'s costumer Mark Mooring, and the ageless comedienne Stella Mayhew. Unlike his partnership with Lyle Andrews, Fields had to share creative supervision with Youmans. Youmans selected the principals: perky, curvaceous Louise Groody (Youman's original Nanette) and the darkly handsome Charles King.

Ten days was not enough for Fields to work his staging magic in pulling together the production. Youmans, who had had several unhappy experiences with previous interpreters of his work, did not always defer to Fields' superior production know-how. *Hit the Deck* opened in Philadelphia at the Chestnut Theatre on March 28 with shabby scenery, sloppy chorus work, and pacing problems. Nevertheless, the first week of tryouts caught the public fancy on the strength of its leads (the dynamic trio of Groody, King, and Mayhew) and—most unexpected in a musical comedy—its book.

Herbert Fields' adaptation of Hubert Osborne's *Shore Leave* was unusually strong for a 'twenties libretto. Once again, Herbert seemed to be realizing one of his father's enduring ambitions, stated almost a quarter century earlier, for a musical with "a consistent plot, capably worked out." The story was once again built around a headstrong heroine. Herbert urbanized her, changing her from a spinster dressmaker named Connie Martin to a coffee shop proprietor called Loulou (named for a close friend of Dorothy's and Herbert's from the Benjamin School). Loulou's coffee shop is located dockside at Newport, Rhode Island, and she runs it with the assistance of her mammy, Lavinia (Stella Mayhew in blackface). The coffee shop is a favorite with Navy gobs on shore leave. Into it swaggers a handsome, hardboiled sailor named Bilge Smith. An inveterate womanizer, Bilge charms Loulou, promising to return for her after his six-month tour of duty. Loulou falls madly in love with Bilge, but he has disappeared. She believes his promise until she realizes that he does not know her name. She arranges to throw a party on the deck of the USS *Nevada* for all the sailors in port named Smith. She finds Bilge, and is on the verge of persuading him to marry her when she missteps: she offers to use her newfound wealth to buy him the freighter of his dreams. Bilge, who did not recognize her at first in her elegant party clothes, insists that he cannot be kept by a rich wife because a man has to be boss. He goes to sea, still the feckless sailor.

The Act Two curtain opens to reveal a seaport town in China—a major departure from the original play and indicative of Herbert's extravagant tendencies. Having Loulou wander through China searching for her beloved sailor may have been another example of Herbert's "kidding the love interest" (mocking the romantic conventions of the musical) as he did in *Peggy-Ann*. Like Evangeline and Gabriel, Loulou just misses Bilge in the Chinese seaport and then in a mandarin's mansion, but she learns that he truly loves her. She goes home to Newport, reopens her coffee shop, and waits. Bilge returns and, thinking that Loulou has exhausted her capital, proposes to her. Later, she explains that she put it in a trust fund for her baby if his or her last name is Smith.

Returning to see *Hit the Deck* two weeks into its Philadelphia tryout, *Variety*'s critic noted that the show had undergone "considerable fixing," including cast and scenery changes. The original scenery was junked, and the production budget was soaring. Youmans added or substituted at least four new tunes, though two of the "new" songs were actually salvaged from Youmans' previous scores. "Hallelujah!" a syncopated strut sung by Stella Mayhew, was actually Youmans' first composition, written in 1918 when he was in the Navy. "Sometimes I'm Happy," a langorous love ballad sung by the romantic leads, had been in two flop shows (with different lyrics). Both songs inspired repeated calls for encores, sometimes as many as seven or eight. Yet, it was on the strength of the book, according to the *Variety* reviewer, that the show would succeed or fail: "Some theatregoers may say 'too much plot'; others will be pleased at the logical, legitimate and believable yarn which is worked out to its plausible conclusion, and which is never thrown overboard to make way for specialities. . . . This may be and should be a big asset for the show, but it will be something of an innovation, and there's no telling how it will strike the public."[28]

Hit the Deck hit the Belasco on April 25, the first musical ever to play on its staid old stage. In the words of critic Brooks Atkinson, it landed "with snap, ginger and a cocky, hat-on-one-ear self-confidence." As predicted, Herbert's book, Youman's score, and the performances of the three leads inspired glowing reviews. The big surprise was that the rest of the production achieved the same high standard. For Loulou's shipboard party, John Wenger designed a spectacular scene depicting the forward deck of the USS *Nebraska* complete with three twelve-inch rolling gun turrets and web masts. This setting and others not so elaborate provided splendid showcases for Seymour Felix's chorus routines. Reviewers singled out the precision chorus work, the soft-shoe and acrobatic efforts of Edward Allen, the "knee-twisting" ballet of Madeline Cameron atop the gun turret. Most of all, they praised the male chorus: "For once," wrote Atkinson, "a male chorus on the stage fairly reeks with masculinity." Instead of "a lot of nancy juveniles posing around in navy blue and gold braid and a chorus of male cuties . . . every man on the stage looks as though he might have served a hitch with the fleet." Reviewers predicted that *Hit the Deck* would sail through the summer, possibly even beyond Christmas. The producers were assured of a big payday.

Then Lew Fields, as he had done several other times in his long career, walked away from a sure thing. Within two days of the opening of his third hit musical in a row, he withdrew from the production. Youmans bought Fields' share of *Hit the Deck* for the sum of $25,000. Whether this figure simply represented Fields' total investment or included some profits was never made clear. If it was the former, it was arguably the dumbest deal he ever made. True, the production had gone over budget in its tryouts, and its overhead at the Belasco was much higher than predicted. Youmans, now the sole owner, stuck by his guns, and *Hit the Deck* ultimately ran for 352 performances (more than *No, No, Nanette*) to become one of the most memorable musical comedies of the decade.

Was the old gambler Lew Fields losing his stomach for the high stakes of Broadway producing? Not necessarily. But he *was* tired—exhausted, in fact, from five months of nonstop work: the frenzy of producing *Peggy-Ann*, then the tour with Weber (two performances a day, six days a week for seven weeks), followed by the equally intense production of *Hit the Deck*. Shortly after the opening, he and Rose headed for Atlantic City for a two-week vacation at the beach.

Ever since the Florida land boom began a few years earlier, it had become fashionable for the movers and shakers of Broadway and Wall Street to sport year-round tans. A sallow complexion was too reminiscent of the sweatshop and the tenement. Lee Shubert prided himself on his deep tan; by the mid-'twenties, he was known as "the Broadway Indian," and rumor had it that he had concocted a secret face lotion that he used to keep his coppery hue. Lew Fields developed a similar predilection for lying in the sun. While he was sunbathing in Atlantic City, he explained his withdrawal from *Hit the Deck.* He objected to the script changes proposed by Youmans. Herbert's book had been lavishly praised, so why tamper with it? Oddly enough, Herbert agreed to make the changes even after his father left the show.

Fields had never relished sharing creative control, but there were other reasons for his sudden move. New opportunities beckoned: the movies and a London engagement for *Peggy-Ann.* The same day that Fields left *Hit the Deck, Variety* announced that the Vitaphone Talking Picture Company had signed Weber & Fields to make a nine-minute sound film of "one of their famous arguments" culminating in the choking scene. For this familiar bit of by-play, they were reportedly paid $10,000.

The Vitaphone sound-on-disc process was actually a technological step backwards from Lee De Forest's sound-on-film system. The difference was that the Vitaphone experiment had the backing of a movie studio—albeit a struggling one, Warner Brothers. In 1926, Sam Warner persuaded his three brothers to enter into a licensing agreement with Western Electric. On August 6, 1926, Warner Brothers presented the first Vitaphone program with the premiere of *Don Juan* with John

Barrymore (synchronized music but no lip-synchronization) and short films, including a speech from Will Hays and performances by the New York Philharmonic and Metropolitan Opera stars. The public excitement about Warner's "invention" sent shock waves through the show business. Installation of the Vitaphone system cost $16,000 to $25,000 per theater, but Warner's helped foot the bill in key cities to encourage popular demand. In January, 1927, Fox debuted their Movietone process, and RCA rushed to market the Photophone, an improved sound-on-film system.

Initially, it was the Vitaphone short subjects that attracted all the attention. Warner's promoted Vitaphone as the magic medium that would bring vaudeville headliners such as Jolson and Will Rogers, opera, and Broadway stars to every provincial theater.[29] Within months, theaters across the country were presenting programs of Vitaphone shorts at popular prices—in some places, as low as forty cents top. The wizened warlords of big-time vaudeville recognized another serious threat to their besieged kingdom. In February, 1927, in the middle of Weber & Fields' tour, the Keith-Albee, Proctor, and Moss circuits extended their sanctions forbidding "artistes" to appear in radio broadcasts; they added Vitaphone "or any other synchronizing device" to the dreaded "opposition" list. Booking agents began rubber-stamping performers' contracts with a clause threatening immediate cancellation as the penalty for violation. It was a desperate and ultimately empty threat.

Thus, Weber & Fields, the ambassadors of old-time show biz, gave their blessing to another innovation in popular entertainment, just as they had with De Forest's Phonofilms and NBC's inaugural broadcast. Their Vitaphone offering survives only as a listing in the Vitaphone catalogue: "Joe Weber and Lew Fields, Broadway's Favorite Comedians, in Mike and Meyer."

When Fields returned to New York City in late May, following his vacation and his Vitaphone junket, he was tanned and well rested and brimming with enthusiasm. The "wasted old man" of the previous November had, in Lyle Andrews' words, grown stouter with work and been miraculously transformed. Fields was about to fulfill one of his longtime ambitions: to direct and produce a musical in London. Since the early 'twenties, the jazz-inflected Broadway musicals had become all the rage in London; Rodgers & Hart, in between their productions with Fields, had already worked on two successful shows there. West Enders eagerly awaited the arrival of the next Rodgers & Hart entertainment, *Peggy-Ann.* Herbert anglicized the script (Glen Falls, New York, became Little Nest, Hampshire; Forty-Second Street became Piccadilly Circus, etc.) and Hart anglicized the lyrics ("Howdy to London" instead of "Broadway," "A Country Mouse" instead of "A Little Birdie," etc.). Nevertheless, the show remained distinctly American in tone. Fields embarked for England on June 17, rehearsed the British cast (with Dorothy Dickson as Peggy-Ann) for a month, and stayed through the London opening on July 27. The London version of *Peggy-Ann* opened to mixed reviews but lasted a respectable 135 performances. The relatively casual attitude of the actors towards the rehearsal process frustrated Fields, and he was not satisfied with the quality of the chorus dancers. He had on occasion expressed the greatest admiration for certain British musical performers; he once said that the three

stars of *Charlot's Revue*—Gertrude Lawrence, Jack Buchanan, and Beatrice Lillie—were the only contemporary performers who could have shared the stage
with the original Weber & Fields Music Hall company. But his experience directing *Peggy-Ann* in London reinforced his convictions that the modern musical
comedy needed American jazz, American slang, and, for the most part, American
talent. The experience may have also revealed to him the possibilities in the new
Herbert-Rodgers-Hart project, an adaptation of Mark Twain's *A Connecticut Yankee in King Arthur's Court.*

The 1927–1928 season was a boom year for Lew Fields and Broadway. Over
seventy theaters were open for business. According to *Variety*'s count, 264 plays
reached New York, fifty-three of them musicals—a record still unequalled. But it
was the quality of so many of the offerings, as well as the quantity, that made it
a memorable time on the Main Stem: musicals such as *Good News*, *A Connecticut
Yankee*, *Funny Face*, *My Maryland*, *The Three Musketeers*, *Blackbirds of 1928*,
and the epochal *Show Boat;* straight dramas that included *Strange Interlude*,
Paris Bound, *Porgy*, *Marco Millions*, *The Royal Family*, *Burlesque*, and *The
Trial of Mary Dugan.*[30]

Author Edna Ferber compared the years immediately preceding the Great
Crash to Little Red Riding Hood, "tripping through the buttercups and daisies,
knowing nothing of the Big Bad Wolf." These were giddy times, never more so
than on Wall Street. The mania for buying and selling Florida real estate, damp-
ened by the 1926 hurricane, turned its speculative frenzy to the stock market. By
the end of 1927, the *New York Times* index of industrial averages stood at 245, a
gain of sixty-nine points on the year. Three months later, in March, the great bull
market on Wall Street began, with the average rising nearly twenty-five points by
the end of the month. Playing the stock market became a pastime, then an obsession. *Variety* reported that stock issues were being sold over the radio. Well-
to-do women with time on their hands would meet at their broker's office for an
hour or two of margin roulette. When the *Variety* reporter went to the Palace
building looking for show biz gossip, everybody from the elevator boy to the
booker was asking about the market or giving tips. Show people who were big
plungers at the gaming tables or the track shifted their attention to the market,
still hoping for that big payday.

Giddy times, indeed. Women's skirts were the shortest of the decade, and
fashionable young men cultivated the collegiate look (saggy Oxford pants, saddle
shoes, sack coats). The Charleston and Black Bottom were superseded by new
dances such as the Varsity Drag and the New Low Down. Speakeasies and the
better nighteries—those with a minimum four-dollar *couvert*—were thriving as
investments for racketeers and legitimate businessmen alike. Joints like the Casa
Lopez, the Club Richman, and the Silver Slipper offered many of the same performers as the best Broadway shows, but provided booze and an intimate atmosphere as well.

Presiding over the city's nonstop festivities was none other than "Hizzoner,"
Jimmy Walker. Jimmy, as everyone called him, was the ideal Jazz Age mayor, a
wire-thin, cocky ex–Tin Pan Alley song-plugger and lyricist with the looks of an

ageing Broadway juvenile. He had written the lyrics for a minor hit of 1905, "Will You Love Me in December as You Do in May," and the prophetically titled "After They Gather the Hay." His election in 1925 came with the help of an old Alley colleague, Irving Berlin, who wrote the campaign song, "It's a Walk-in with Walker." Like one of George M. Cohan's streetwise strivers—only ten times more jaded— he had a gift for fast comebacks and wisecracks that disarmed his critics and endeared him to his constituents. He rarely arrived at City Hall before noon, and he was seen most often in evening clothes, escorting a pretty chorus girl or his regular companion, actress Betty Compton, to a Broadway opening (he always arrived late) or to one of the fashionable nightspots. Mrs. Walker stayed home, and Jimmy stayed at the Mayfair Hotel. Jimmy preferred the company of show people; Lew Fields sometimes bumped into him backstage and at benefits and meetings of the Friars' Club. The Friars honored "our Jimmy" in a testimonial dinner on November 27, 1927, with the speeches and entertainment broadcast over WMSG. According to Friar Abbot George M. Cohan, Jimmy and his fellow Friars had "always spoken the same language and kept the same hours. We understand each other perfectly." Toastmaster William Collier summed up the general attitude: "Whose business is it if the Mayor wants to go to the theatre or to his club or to dinners or a supper club as long as he has done more good and beneficial work for this city than any other mayor has ever done?"[31] Loud applause from the enthusiastic Friars, Lew Fields included.

Newspapermen loved Jimmy; they made jokes about his "nocturnal cabinet" but never called him to account, either for his personal life or his backroom politics. So what if there were widespread rumors of corruption in his administration? He knew how to have a good time, and he was always good for a round at Billy La Hiff's tavern. To quote Lloyd Morris, "Americans of the festive era found Jimmy a symbol of the kind of life to which they aspired."[32] But behind the symbol was a web of corruption that ran deeper than Tammany in the heyday of Boss Croker.

There was some of Jimmy Walker in the character of Martin, the brassy, caddish hero created by Herbert Fields for *A Connecticut Yankee*. Years before Walker arrived on the scene, Herbert, Rodgers, and Hart had wanted to adapt *A Connecticut Yankee in King Arthur's Court*. Back in 1921, the trio had seen a silent film based on Twain's satiric novel. With its combination of fantasy and social commentary, they were certain that it had the makings of a first-class musical comedy. To their surprise, they were able to secure a six-month option on the rights from the Twain estate without paying a cent. Not surprisingly—given their untried reputations and the cynical tone of the novel—they were unable to interest a producer. Two years later, they adapted the premise for an amateur show at the Institute of Musical Art, with Herbert writing the book and most of the lyrics. *A Danish Yankee in King Tut's Court* displayed in crude form the principal devices that they would employ in *A Connecticut Yankee*—anachronistic language, topical references, and an inter-epoch romance.

In London during the summer of 1927, Rodgers & Hart met with Lew Fields to discuss their next project. They gave him the Twain novel to read. Back in New York, they received a cable from Fields in which he said that he could see nothing in the book that would make a good musical—there was no strong romance, and he preferred a contemporary setting for musical comedy. Fields urged them to turn their attention to a 1921 Belasco production called *Kiki* as a vehicle for Sammy White and Eva Puck.

It was a measure of the trio's growing confidence that they went ahead and started their adaptation anyway, certain that another producer would want it even if their first choice did not. When Fields returned to New York in early August, they asked him to read Herbert's script. Perhaps remembering the mistake he made rejecting *Dearest Enemy*, he agreed. To his surprise, he found that once again his young collaborators were right. "It's my sort of show," he admitted. Despite its medieval setting, it was an unmistakably contemporary story. Fields had no trouble persuading Lyle Andrews, his co-producer for *The Girl Friend* and *Peggy-Ann*, to finance the production. Fields' foster son, Herb Harris, also agreed to back the new show.

Like *Peggy-Ann*, *A Connecticut Yankee* was a dream play. As a starting point, Twain's novel made Herbert's job easier: the framing device of a prologue and epilogue in the present, the humorous juxtaposition of "olde English" and modern slang, the parodies of chivalry and medieval macho, and the author's sugar-coated misanthropy all survived the adaptation more or less intact.

Herbert did change the settings for the framing device, and these changes reveal his early mastery of the librettist's craft. In the prologue, he established a romantic triangle involving the protagonist, who must choose between social expediency and true love. The setting is now the grand ballroom of a hotel in Hartford, Connecticut, where Martin's tony friends are throwing a bachelor party to celebrate his impending marriage to the socialite Fay Morgan. Martin is a socially ambitious, impertinent young businessman who sees it as a great opportunity, but he secretly agrees with the thrust of one of the congratulatory speeches: "There are three great events in our lives. . . . We are born, we get married, and we die. . . . You, my boy, have been born. . . . Tomorrow you will be married, now there's nothing left for you to do but to die!"[33]

Martin's hobby happens to be medieval England, so his friends give him a suit of armor. Fay and her bitchy girlfriends arrive, and their song "A Ladies' Home Companion" reveals her intention of turning Martin into "a sweet domestic animal." Martin is distracted by another girl who has sneaked into the party. Poor, unassuming Alice is the "most wonderful girl in the world" to Martin, and she has to see him one last time, prompting their mutual declaration of love ("My Heart Stood Still"). Fay discovers Martin with Alice on his lap and flies into a jealous rage. She breaks an empty champagne bottle over Martin's head, knocking him unconscious.

Martin dreams that he is in Camelot in A.D. 528, and that his friends are all members of King Arthur's court. He awakes beside the road to Camelot, where he meets Sir Kay in full battle dress. Martin is not at all intimidated. He has a slangy quip or a put-down for every situation. He looks the knight up and down and asks, "How long can you stay fresh in that can?" Upon first seeing Camelot, he comments, "Say, I bet the inside looks like the Paramount Theatre." On his way, he spies his lady love, Demoiselle Alisande (called Sandy). The pretty maiden is shy but naturally takes to Martin. She is, like most of Herbert's heroines, eager for experience:

> SANDY: Wouldst kiss my lips, m'lord?
>
> MARTIN: *(eagerly)* And how I wouldst, milady. *(Takes her face in his hands)* Turn up thy pan. *(They kiss)* [. . .]
>
> SANDY: What is love?
>
> MARTIN: Nobody knows, but it's getting found out.

Which cues the song "Thou Swell:"

> Thou swell!
> Thou witty!
> Thou sweet!
> Thou grand!
> Wouldst kiss me pretty?
> Wouldst hold my hand?
> Both thine eyes are cute, too—
> What they do to me.
> Hear me holler
> I choose a
> Sweet lolla
> Palooza
> In thee.

And in the second verse:

> Thine arms are martial
> Thou hast grace.
> My cheek is partial
> To thy face. [. . .]

More than ever before, the syntax of Hart's lyrics formed a seamless continuum with Herbert's dialogue. In text and lyrics, the highly idiosyncratic mix of archaic and modern English underscored the clash between the cynical urbanite and provincial sensibilities. As in *The Girl Friend* and *Peggy-Ann*, the country mouse does not mind that the city rat is leading her astray.

The use of verbal and visual anachronisms as a basis for stage humor was hardly new. Like malapropisms, it was a staple of minstrel show sketches that the Weberfields had incorporated into their turn-of-the-century burlesques. Their burlesques of *DuBarry* ("DuHurry" from *Hoity-Toity*, 1902) and *Quo Vadis* ("Quo Vass Is?" from *Fiddle-Dee-Dee*, 1900) used these devices extensively. Herbert's version was less crude than Edgar Smith's, but the frequent "thees" and "thous" were tedious to modern ears.

Back in Camelot, Sir Kay brings Martin in chains into the courtyard of King Arthur's castle. Martin is not worried: a feast is underway ("At the Round Table"), and he sees that the fabled figures of Camelot are quite an eccentric lot indeed. The Arthurian triangle is played as bedroom farce: King Arthur is an equivocating old cuckold, henpecked by the worldly Queen Guinevere, and Lancelot is vain and easily distracted. Sir Galahad is innocent and dumb, much to the frustration of his hot-to-trot lady, Evelyn. The Galahad-Evelyn romance becomes the libretto's comic subplot ("On a Desert Island with Thee").[34]

The magician Merlin (played by the same actor who predicted Martin's grim future at the bachelor party) is suspicious and urges the King to burn Martin at the stake. Just as he is about to be torched, Martin conveniently remembers his medieval history. There will be a total eclipse of the sun at three minutes past noon, the time of his execution. In Act One's operatic finale, Martin threatens to blot out the sun forever, but Alisande pleads for her people and he graciously spares them. Once released, Martin makes a deal with Arthur that guarantees him one percent of the gross profits on any money he (Martin) earns for the kingdom. The grateful knights proclaim Martin "Sir Boss."

The Act Two curtain reveals a Camelot transformed by the entrepreneurial genius of Sir Boss. Martin has Americanized Camelot according to the latest in industrial efficiency, featuring a factory with an assembly line, time clock, switchboard, and lunch break. A full-sized Ford is assembled from a workbench. Martin's nemesis, Morgan Le Fay, indulges in the joys of room service; she has three slaves, whom Martin has dubbed DeMille, Goldwyn, and Lubitsch. Merlin does weather forecasts while he and Morgan plot Martin's downfall. Morgan throws a party with entertainment provided by a medieval jazz band. They play off-key, but Morgan defends them: "They are really finished musicians." "They will be if they don't quit that," cracks Martin, and he has them dragged away to be hanged. "Now that's a system that should never have been abolished," he says smugly. Out for a good time, the wiseacre businessman shows his ugly side.

Martin soon discovers that the progress he has fostered has its disadvantages. The Knights of the Round Table are grumbling; they are being trained as travelling salesmen and must wear sandwich boards advertising Lux soap, Coca Cola, Camel cigarettes ("I would fain walk a furlong for a Camel"), and Broadway shows ("Ye Hibernian Rose of Abie"). Worse still, his beloved Sandy becomes a suffragette and rallies the ladies of the court to her cause ("Nothing's Wrong"). Meanwhile, the simple bonehead romance of Sir Galahad and Evelyn is thriving, as expressed in the song "I Feel at Home with You:"

> . . . I feel at home with you,
> Your brain is dumber
> Than that of a plumber,
> That's why I feel at home with you. . . .
> Our minds are featherweight—
> Their together weight
> Can't amount to much . . .

When it comes to love, ignorance is bliss. Martin gradually loses control of his idyll: Morgan kidnaps Sandy and slips Martin a love potion. He can extricate himself only by regaining consciousness. In a rather weak epilogue, Martin awakes in the hotel garden. Naturally, he decides that he must marry Alice, the girl he loves.

If Herbert's book was not the equal of *Peggy-Ann* in its inventiveness or characterization, Rodgers' & Hart's score more than made up for it. For *A Connecticut Yankee*, they wrote two songs that became standards ("My Heart Stood Still" and "Thou Swell") and two others (a patter song called "On a Desert Island with Thee" and the dance tune "I Feel at Home with You") that enjoyed a brief vogue. Ironically, the two future standards almost did not make it into the show. "My Heart Stood Still" had not been in the score in the first tryouts in Stamford. The song was already a hit in England, where it had been featured in Charles Cochrane's revue, *One Dam Thing After Another.* In September, 1927, the American producer Charles Dillingham spoke with Rodgers & Hart about writing a score for a show starring Beatrice Lillie. The score would include the American debut of "My Heart Stood Still." The songwriting team had the greatest respect for Lillie as a comedienne, but they believed that her voice was not strong enough to put over their song. They lied to Dillingham, telling him that the song was already slated for *Yankee.* Then they negotiated with Cochrane to buy the song back. Cochrane knew he had them in a corner, and he insisted that they take a substantial cut in show royalties. The word on Broadway was that it cost Rodgers & Hart $10,000 to put "Heart" in *A Connecticut Yankee.* Herbert found an excellent place for it in his libretto—in the second slot, within the first scene. Lew Fields plugged the surefire hit for all it was worth, reprising it at least four more times during the program.

It was Lew Fields himself who almost kept "Thou Swell" from a Broadway hearing. Not that he disliked the song, but in the Philadelphia tryouts, the audience had been consistently cold to it. For half a century, Fields had been living by the adage "Give the public what it wants," and the public—at least in Philadelphia—clearly did not want "Thou Swell." Herbert, Rodgers, and Hart disagreed, but Pop Fields was adamant. Rodgers acquiesced in the other song changes, but "Thou Swell," he insisted, deserved to stay in, at least until the Broadway premiere. This sounded reasonable to Fields: if the New York first-night audience did not warm to the song, he would cut it.

On opening night, Rodgers conducted the orchestra for *A Connecticut Yankee.* Not eight bars into the refrain of "Thou Swell," he could feel the people getting excited over the song. The applause at the end was deafening, and performers had to do several encores.[35] The enthusiastic response vindicated Rodgers and his young collaborators in a way that made it easy for Lew Fields to admit his mistake.

Alexander Leftwich was once again the director, but once again the entire production was "under the personal supervision of Lew Fields." Fields entrusted the choreography to a newcomer he had met on *The Wild Rose*, a lanky thirty-two-year-old dancer with steely blue eyes named William B. Enos, better known as Busby Berkeley. Berkeley, though inexperienced, enforced the same high standards of precision and physical appearance as Seymour Felix. Moreover, he faced the challenge of designing dances for a chorus of twenty-four for the Vanderbilt's small stage, in a production that relied more on complex scenic effects more than any previous Vanderbilt show. Fields had originally intended to bring in Seymour Felix to put the finishing touches on the dance routines, but Berkeley's work was so good that it was not necessary.

As in most of the Herbert-Rodgers-Hart shows produced by Lew Fields, it was difficult to tell whether they were mocking or emulating the conventions of operetta. Like the best of Lew Fields' productions, *A Connecticut Yankee* was a hybrid, defying the critic's (and theater historian's) rigid categories. "We were invading a new field of musical comedy," Fields said. "It is easy enough to put on stodgy costume operetta"—a dig at the Shuberts—"that is done more than once a season. But *A Connecticut Yankee* is Mark Twain plus modern pep together with a great amount of original satire of modern institutions." [36]

While certain aspects of the story, score, and production bordered on operetta, the casting and performance style leaned more towards vaudeville and revues. Fields first spotted Jack Thompson high-kicking in vaudeville and had cast him in *Peggy-Ann* before giving him the role of Sir Galahad in *Yankee*. Mistress Evelyn, his love interest, was played by June Cochrane; Fields saw her in the first *Garrick Gaieties* and then gave her a supporting role in *The Girl Friend*. Constance Carpenter (Alice/Alisande) came over with *Charlot's Revue* and was Gertrude Lawrence's understudy in *Oh, Kay*.

For the lead role of Martin, Fields recruited another Broadway newcomer. Like Lester Cole *(Peggy-Ann)* and Sammy White *(The Girl Friend)*, William Gaxton was a robust young hoofer with a two-a-day background. The character of Martin bore a passing resemblance to the vaudeville persona Gaxton created for a sketch called "A Regular Businessman," the routine that made him a headliner. In real life, he was more than "regular"; born Don Arturo Antonio Gaxiola, he attended a military academy and the University of California in the early 'twenties, and later went into business as a partner with Herb Harris in Parfums Charberts. His first love, however, was performing. *A Connecticut Yankee* launched his career, and his performances in *Fifty Million Frenchmen, Anything Goes, Of Thee I Sing, Let 'Em Eat Cake, Louisiana Purchase,* and many others proved him to be one of the great leading men of the Broadway musical. By the mid-'thirties, between his business interests and his hit shows, Gaxton was reputed to be one of the richest actors on Broadway.

The eagerly awaited arrival of *A Connecticut Yankee* on Broadway finally occurred on November 3—a Thursday evening, in accordance with Fields' superstition. The high ticket prices ($5.50 tops) did not prevent a sell-out crowd. Before the end of the prologue, by the time Gaxton and Carpenter finished singing "My Heart Stood Still," Fields and company knew that they had another hit. The entertainment did not let up even for the intermission: on the drop curtain was a parody of a medieval tapestry designed by Robert Benchley, depicting a rather cockeyed map of Camelot.

A few critics nattered over the small voice of Constance Carpenter. Herbert's book was variously criticized for the overuse of Arthurian language, prehistoric gags, and modern wisecracks. "They [the gags] are almost all good," one critic admitted, "but there are so many that the audience is apt to tire. . . ." Mostly, reviewers extolled the Rodgers & Hart score and the overall production. Frank Vreeland *(Telegram)* was among the most enthusiastic: "Boyishly spontaneous and merry, this piece was an ideally captivating transcription of Mark Twain's grand old fantasy," and he composed his own sandwich-board advertisement for it: "GO, THOU SLUGGARD, AND ENJOY 'A CONNECTICUT YANKEE' AND TELL YE COCK-EYED WORLDE THOU HAST HAD YE HELLUVA TIME." The usually reserved Brooks Atkinson praised the "intelligent book" and proclaimed: "'My Heart Stood Still' is one of the loveliest musical compositions of the season. . . . Mr. Rodgers has now graduated from the class of beginners. In his unhackneyed score for the current piece he composes with genuine feeling and versatility. There are many fine passages in his score. . . . Mr. Hart continues to write intelligent, witty rhyme-schemes. . . ."

Unlike the relatively intimate Vanderbilt productions of *The Girl Friend* and *Peggy-Ann*, Fields mounted *Yankee* with more of the elaborate trappings of his pre-war shows. Somehow, Fields and his colleagues were able to squeeze a cast of forty-two, an orchestra of nineteen, and thirty-two stagehands into the tiny confines of the Vanderbilt. Most of the budget, as *Variety* rightly surmised, went into John F. Hawkins' ingeniously designed sets and costumes. For Martin's dream of Camelot, Hawkins created startlingly colorful expressionistic scenery with topless, tottering towers that reminded one reviewer of "stained glass windows gone cuckoo." With little available space backstage, Herbert Ward (who engineered the sets) arranged for the "flying" (lifting by cables) of practically every piece, including sofas, tapestries, the electrical switchboard, the throne, the hotel garden, and the entire factory set. The trick Ford car collapsed into a rectangle and was stored in front of the switchboard. A roadside hedge was kept in the basement, then marched upstairs and positioned onstage between scenes with a stagehand hiding in its concave interior. Backstage was so crowded that Sir Kay in his spiky armor had to stay in a special corner to avoid possible injury to the dancers rushing by. Ward suggested flying him as well. Having learned from the near-disaster of *Peggy-Ann*'s opening night, Fields double-checked every detail of the scenic effects himself.

Lew Fields' merry burlesque of Mark Twain and modern institutions became the longest-running show of his career, lasting at the Vanderbilt for over a year— a total of 418 performances. During that period—a landmark year in Broadway history—it prospered despite some of the stiffest opposition any musical ever faced: *Rio Rita, Good News, My Maryland, Show Boat, Rain or Shine, The Three Musketeers, Blackbirds of 1928, The New Moon.* Significantly, *A Connecticut Yankee* resembled none of the above; it was a distinctly Fieldsian entertainment: elaborate, flashy, funny, part old-fashioned hokum and part newfangled musical, impossible to pigeonhole. Despite doubts about whether its smart, insider tone would play outside of New York, it toured for almost two years.

Anticipating a long run for *Yankee* at the Vanderbilt, Fields leased a theater from the Chanin brothers for his spring production. Irwin and Henry Chanin were theater-smitten contractors responsible for constructing five beautiful theaters in the Times Square area. With these holdings, they were among the most influential of the independent theater owners, and Fields preferred to deal with them rather than the Shuberts. The Chanins' Mansfield Theatre, on West Forty-seventh Street, was just a year old; Fields took over the lease beginning January 1, 1928, and renamed it Lew Fields' Mansfield Theater. It would be the sixth and last Broadway theater to bear his name.

Flush with the success of his revived Broadway career, Lew Fields should have been more favorably inclined to allow another of his children to enter the family business. About a week after *A Connecticut Yankee* opened, Dorothy announced to her parents that she and composer Jimmy McHugh were working on the songs for a revue to be presented at the Cotton Club in Harlem. "The *what* club?" bellowed Lew. Rose shook her head sadly and shot an I-told-you-so look at her husband. Everybody knew that the Cotton Club was run by gangsters and bootleggers. The clientele was all white, the entertainers were black, and what Dorothy was doing was in essence entertaining.

"Ladies don't write lyrics!" Lew proclaimed. Dorothy's supposedly responded by paraphrasing her father's most famous line: "I'm not a lady, I'm your daughter." (The response seems too cute not to be apocryphal, but then, clever lines were her business.) She went on to say that she would write a show for the Westchester Kennel Club if they asked her.

Women did not, in fact, write lyrics in those days, at least not for Tin Pan Alley and all-black revues. Operettas were the occasional exception; Rida Johnson Young and Dorothy Donnelly had written lyrics (and books) for Victor Herbert, Friml, and Romberg. Apparently, the elevated tone and sentimentality of the form made it more appropriate for "a woman's touch." Tin Pan Alley, even more than Broadway, was a male reserve built on hard sell and mass production. The big music publishers hired scores of "pluggers" to perform the songs in their catalogues. Song-pluggers were essentially musical hustlers, men of great personal charm and contacts, who sold songs by demonstrating them in music stores and department stores during the day, and then making the rounds of theaters, beer halls, vaudeville houses, and other less-reputable night spots.[37] Many of the composers and lyricists broke into the business as song-pluggers or in-house demonstrators.

Lew knew the scene well. He pictured his pretty and proper twenty-three-year-old daughter in a dingy cubicle of a music publisher's "professional department"—like the setting for *The Melody Man*—seated next to the battered upright piano. There she would be working cheek-by-jowl with a cigar-chomping pianist-composer, trying to come up with coy and slangy rhymes until called upon by the firm's Professional Manager. Then they would demonstrate their latest songs for all the two-bit vaudevillians who stopped in for new material before going out on tour. It was not the kind of place for a well-brought-up girl from a family striving for respectability. To Fields' way of thinking, the truth about life in Tin Pan Alley was bad enough; to make matters worse, sensationalized tales of Tin Pan Alley shenanigans—corrupt managers, lecherous performers, dissolute composers—had become the stuff of stage and screen.

In 1925, Lew had used his influence to persuade music publishers to refuse to see Dorothy. She was not so easily discouraged. The man who had encouraged her initial writing efforts, composer-plugger J. Fred Coots, continued to shepherd her around to other publishers. Finally, he introduced her to the professional manager at Jack Mills, Inc., a streetwise, gregarious Bostonian named Jimmy McHugh. McHugh had gotten his start as a "bicycle plugger" for Waterston, Berlin & Snyder in Boston, riding around town playing and selling the firm's songs. He came to New York in 1921 and was hired by Jack Mills as a staff pianist, eventually becoming a partner. Taught by his mother (who used to rap his knuckles if the melodies he improvised sounded too familiar), McHugh became a gifted pianist who could instantly transpose a song into any key to suit the needs of a customer. He had an equally keen ear for new talent or a catchy melodic idea, and he liked to frequent the jazz clubs uptown for inspiration. He composed for several Cotton Club revues throughout the decade, and it was for them that he wrote his first hit, "When My Sugar Walks Down the Street." His work in the 'twenties was an important and overlooked early link between the worlds of black jazz, white Tin Pan Alley, and Broadway theater. Alec Wilder, in his book *American Popular Song*, described McHugh as one of the great craftsmen and innovators.

In temperament and background, Jimmy McHugh and Dorothy Fields were an unlikely team. He was from a lower-middle-class Catholic background, with more charm than polish, rather like one of the relentlessly upbeat urban smartalecks in a Cohan script. In addition to being an excellent pianist, he was a terrific salesman, never hesitant about hyping a song or himself. Dorothy, by contrast, seemed ill-suited to the Alley. She was shy, even timid, and she could not "plug" herself, much less a song. She would never be "one of the boys," and her chic clothes suggested expensive tastes. The wily McHugh may have figured that, if nothing else, Dorothy could eventually give him access to her father. Or perhaps McHugh valued Coots' recommendation and thought that her fledgling efforts showed genuine talent (maybe it ran in the family). Dorothy's intellectual sophistication impressed McHugh, too—as long as it was not too obvious in her lyrics.

Their first published effort showed Dorothy's early predilection for "smarty" rhymes mixed with slang in the manner of her idols, Ira Gershwin and Larry Hart. For the dance tune "Collegiana," Dorothy wasted no time showing her influences, beginning the lead-in with a pair of internal rhymes: "On the campus they try to vamp us / With anything new, anything blue. . . ." McHugh's melodic line for the verse consisted of a boogie-woogie-like arpeggio ending in the kind of tricky full stops preferred by Charleston dancers. Dorothy even built a few surprises into the song's bridge:

> Honor students and every pedagogue
> All go to bed agog at night.
> Two step, new step, you'll get along with me,
> You'll get a new degree
> Dancing . . .

As the title suggests, "Collegiana" was written to capitalize on the varsity craze, with its suggestions of youthful hedonism running wild ("Miss Pollyanna was never glad / Until she grabbed an undergrad . . ."). Dorothy's lyrics reinforced the bouncing, cascading rhythm of McHugh's melody; indeed, her ability to use a conversational syntax to put over clever rhymes gives the song's only real surprises. "Collegiana" was a silly song, but it was a harbinger of greater things to come. On the promise of this and one or two more collaborations, McHugh became Dorothy's mentor. For the next eight years—through Tin Pan Alley, cabarets, Broadway musicals and revues, and Hollywood—she had no other partner.

The Mills shop in the mid-'twenties was known for its novelty numbers, and to a lesser extent, blues and jazz. When Enrico Caruso died, Mills offered mourners a lyrical condolence called "They Needed a Songbird in Heaven So God Took Caruso Away." One of Dorothy's first assignments was to write a lyric honoring Ruth Elder, the aviatrix who was preparing to fly across the Atlantic. Jack Mills gave Dorothy a title—"The American Girl"—and the first two lines of the chorus— "You took a notion / To fly 'cross the ocean." Fifty dollars for fifty words was the deal. As it turned out, Ruth Elder did not make it, and neither did the song, but Dorothy was established as the $50-a-night girl.[38]

Charles Lindbergh, of course, did make it across the Atlantic, and his heroic feat sparked a barrage of Lindbergh songs, not to mention a dance (the Lindy Hop), 3,500,000 letters, and hundreds of thousands of dollars of contracts in vaudeville and films. Mills wanted to join the parade and assigned the task to McHugh and his $50-a-night girl. They quickly obliged with "I Can't Give You Anything But Love, Lindy," but once again, their topical tune failed to catch on. Later that year, a hoofer-turned-producer named Harry Delmar asked McHugh if he had a song for his upcoming revue, and McHugh recalled the Lindy song. Delmar wanted the number for a sketch involving two poor kids, played by Patsy Kelly and Broadway newcomer Bert Lahr, sitting on the steps of a tenement.

Drawing on her ability to see the world through the eyes of a character (a product of her acting experience and her familiarity with theater songwriting) and her feel for vernacular conversation, Dorothy came up with lyrics that seemed to be a perfect fit. Delmar axed the number and the sketch before its New York opening in late November because they had been a flop in tryouts. The song was consigned to McHugh's trunk.

By 1927, the Cotton Club was the most fashionable of the Harlem "black and tan" nighteries, with a clientele consisting of theatrical folk, trendy professionals, and socialites. The producer was Dan Healy, who had created floor shows for the Palais Royale, the Follies, and the Silver Slipper. The fact that the management hired Healy and two white Tin Pan Alley writers to create the songs was indicative of the kind of audience the management hoped to attract. Harlem now represented the apotheosis of "slumming," just as the Bowery had in the 1880's and 'nineties. Like the Bowery, it employed the talent and energies of its local citizens to provide entertainment for more affluent New Yorkers; unlike the Bowery, the majority of its local citizenry—those who were black—were not welcome as guests, no matter how much money they had. In effect, it was another form of minstrelsy, in which the entertainers played to white fantasies about blacks as guileless "naturals" or "primitives." Instead of the minstrel show's emphasis on buffoonery, the Harlem joy spots put the accent on animal sensuality.[39] Several of the McHugh-

Fields song titles made this apparent: "Hottentot Tot," "Harlem River Quiver," "Freeze and Melt," "I'm a Broken-Hearted Blackbird," "Doin' the Frog," and "Red Hot Band." In the vernacular of white promoters, it was known as "jungle music." The McHugh-Fields numbers were arranged and performed by Duke Ellington and his Orchestra in their Cotton Club debut. The big attraction, however, was the chorus of "tall, tan and terrific" women, many of whom could pass for white, though, as one white critic was quick to point out, "their hotsy-totsy performance when working sans wraps could never be parred by a white gal."

Adding to the thrill of the illicit was the fact that the entertainment took place in a "mob joint"; i.e., a club known to be run by a gangster. Usually, the gangster had a partner who actually managed the club: rum-runner Larry Fay was partners with Texas Guinan in the chic El Fey Club and partners with Frankie Marlow in the Ambassadeurs; Dutch Schultz was the proprietor of the Embassy Club where Helen Morgan sang. The Cotton Club was one of several joints owned in part by the notorious Owney "the Killer" Madden.

After his angry response to Dorothy's news, Lew showed his true colors: he said that the entire family would be there opening night. He may have recalled how it felt when his own father had refused to come see him perform. Late in the evening on December 4, 1927, the Fields family—Lew, Rose, Frances, Joseph, Herbert, and Dorothy—bundled into their finery, boarded a taxi and journeyed out from civilization through the wilds of Central Park to 142nd Street and Lenox, the heart of "the Black Belt." Freezing rain had been falling all afternoon and the roads were clogged with slush.

Lew had invited a young up-and-coming journalist by the name of Walter Winchell to accompany them. At the time, Winchell was writing theater reviews and a regular column called "Your Broadway and Mine" for the *New York Graphic*, the city's tackiest tabloid. Winchell was a tenement kid (raised in Harlem) and a failed vaudevillian who, in his own words, longed "to become a figure in the world." He had fond memories of Weber & Fields' 1912 Jubilee. His show-biz background gave him an edge in gathering the gossipy tidbits, rumors, and anecdotes that went into his columns. Their slangy, insider tone had the rhythm and patchwork quality of a vaudeville turn: the latest *bon mots*, put-downs, sentimental or satiric doggerel, and sly innuendoes. Using Broadway as a taking-off point, Winchell's columns were really a forum for his knee-jerk populism in all matters cultural and political. Although Winchell was not yet the journalistic demogogue he would eventually become, a favorable review and mention in his column already had box office impact. Why Lew Fields would make it a point to invite him for his daughter's professional debut is an interesting question. Other Broadway celebrities were also present, including Benny Rubin, George Beban, and the vaudeville team of Van and Schenck.

The revue was a racier entertainment than either Lew or Rose Fields was used to. At the Cotton Club, according to *Variety* reviewer Abel Green, "the undressed thing goes double. The almost caucasian-hued high yaller gals look swell and uncork the meanest kind of cooching ever exhibited to a conglomerate mixed audience."[40] As Dorothy's parents listened to the woman singer (Aida Ward) perform Dorothy's lyrics, it soon became apparent that the words were even more salacious than what they were seeing. Looks of worry and shock crossed the Fieldses' table. Lew had always been sensitive to matters of propriety in mixed company, particularly when his wife was present. He double-checked the credits listed in the program, and then he asked Dorothy if she was responsible for those lyrics. Dorothy, equally surprised, denied authorship; those were not the lyrics that she had heard in rehearsals. The next two McHugh-Fields numbers had been similarly "blued" without Dorothy's prior knowledge. Lew was now enraged, and springing from his chair, he strode over to confront Harry Block, the manager and partner to Owney "the Killer" Madden. "If you don't make an announcement that my daughter Dorothy didn't write those lyrics," Fields threatened, "I'll punch you right on the floor."

In later years, Dorothy told the story of her father's confrontation with Owney Madden's partner as an example of Lew's violent temper. Unfortunately, no account mentions the manager's response, but he may have found Fields' moral indignation amusing. The manager instructed his emcee to announce at intermission that contrary to the credits in the program, McHugh and Fields did not write all of the songs that were performed. The experience prompted Lew to reiterate his earlier advice to Dorothy in the form of a command: get out of show business.

With four consecutive Broadway hits to his credit, a Vitaphone film with Weber, and a new theater bearing his name, Lew Fields qualified as a celebrity. The "Amusements" column of the *New York Telegraph* provided a rather quirky thumbnail sketch of Fields at the crest of his rediscovered popularity: "He started the fashion of black bicycle shirts, he tells stories better than any other actor, he always looks mad except when he smiles, he rarely smiles, his favorite playwright is Herbert Fields, he can still turn handstands, he has never failed to spot the song hits in his shows [he missed "Thou Swell"], his passion in life is sitting in the sun."[41] The description was ambiguous: was he a man in touch with fashion and audience tastes, physically vigorous, and proud of his son? Or a rather vain and self-centered curmudgeon?

Now that he had a string of successes to maintain, Fields became especially cautious about the production that would inaugurate his new theater. For the first time in his entire career, he would have the sole producing credit. His primary backer was a businessman named Lew Leavitt, who agreed not to intrude on any aspect of production. Fields announced his intention to make the Mansfield into an American Savoy. He now believed the critics who, show after show, compared Herbert, Rodgers, and Hart to Gilbert and Sullivan. He tried to assemble a regular company of actors and technicians around his writing team.

Oddly enough, it was Herbert's idea to play it safe with *Present Arms*, though he probably would not have seen it that way at the time. Herbert's first attempt at a musical comedy about men in uniform, *Hit the Deck*, had been written in collaboration with Vincent Youmans, Clifford Grey, and Leo Robin, and had been a rousing success. Still, Herbert was intrigued by the musical and comic potential of the military setting, and he wanted to develop it with Rodgers & Hart. His collaborators were concerned about its resemblance to *Hit the Deck*, but Herbert persuaded them by pointing out all of the differences: instead of being sailors, the men were U.S. Marines; instead of going to China, they went to Hawaii. This time, the hero would chase the heroine, instead of the other way around. Rather than making her the boss of a lowly coffee shop, the heroine would be a member of the English aristocracy.[42] If, as Ethan Mordden suggests, Herbert deserves credit for devising the conventional mode for the Broadway libretto, then *Present Arms* was the crucible for testing his new formula. As a starting point, only the most threadbare of Broadway clichés would do. *Present Arms* was a Cinderella tale written by and for those who no longer believed in such things. Underneath the familiar structure were the glimmers of mockery that characterized all of the Fields-Rodgers-Hart musicals.

Lew Fields, looking for the safe bet, presumably encouraged them in the project. Perhaps he wanted to see if he could top *Hit the Deck*. He had no fear of formula; he had perfected a few himself, including the musical spectacles at the Broadway Theater, which he then repeated mercilessly until audiences grew bored with them. But the derivative nature of *Present Arms* worked against Fields' plan to create an American Savoy. In the role of Chick, the tough but lovesick Marine, he cast Charles King, the same actor who had played Bilge in *Hit the Deck*. For Chick's sidekick, he once again cast Franker Woods. In so doing, Fields effectively undercut any hopes the authors had for discouraging comparisons between the two shows. The only casting distinction of note was to be the Broadway return of the venerable Fay Templeton, but this plan fell through. The rest of the creative team were Fields' regulars: director Alexander Leftwich, stage manager Teddy Hammerstein, set designer Herbert Ward, and dance director Busby Berkeley.

Like Fields' Broadway Theater spectacles, *Present Arms* was intended as a "summer show"—light on the plot, heavy on the chorus numbers and stage effects. Herbert's story began at the Marine base at Pearl Harbor, and the rest unfolds like an inverted Cinderella tale. Private Chick Evans (King), son of a Brooklyn plumber and a graduate of the "dese, dem, and doze" school of hard knocks, has pretensions to high society and the attentions of Lady Delphine (Flora Le Breton), daughter of Lord Witherspoon. To court her, Chick borrows his captain's uniform and tells her that he is the son of the president of Yale. Lord Witherspoon, a pineapple magnate, prefers a rich German named Ludwig Von Richter (Anthony Knilling) for his daughter's hand. Delphine's friend, Edna (Joyce Barbour) serves as the go-between, and in delivering a party invitation she encounters her ex, Douglas (Busby Berkeley), a buddy of Chick's. The party breaks up early, but before Chick can retire, the grounds are invaded by a group of his drunken Marine buddies and their "frails," who turn the place into a nightclub. Dancing and making "whoopee," they wake up the Witherspoons. Delphine discovers that Chick is not a captain, and, outraged at his deception and his buddies' rowdy behavior, she tells him that she never wants to see him again.

Act Two begins on Edna's spacious yacht, where she is throwing a party and trying to arrange a "chance" meeting between Delphine and Chick. Delphine spurns him, but a sudden storm wrecks the yacht and the two of them, plus Frank, end up on a raft. Chick takes command and guides them to a desert island, that second-act haven of so many turn-of-the-century musical comedies. Despite Chick's heroism, she decides to marry von Richter for propriety's sake. Delphine's sister Maria hires an island fortuneteller to describe Delphine's future with Von Richter. It is a bleak picture, and Delphine decides to forgive Chick. She goes to the docks at Kohala to meet him as he arrives on a huge troop transport. There the English lady proposes to the Marine.

In comparison with the sparkling wit and repartee that filled Herbert's three previous scripts, the comedy in *Present Arms* was less frequent and less original. Herbert once again succeeded in reproducing the idioms of his chosen milieu, which in the case of the Marines' vernacular tended to be profane. Walter Winchell, who only a few months before had seen Lew Fields risk personal injury over "dirty" lyrics credited to his daughter, complained about the "vulgar brand" of humor that Lew permitted his son: "dialogue dealing with skunks, castor oil and 'Your name came up' is not particularly in the very best taste, although it's quite true that some of the best people are talking that way these whoopee-making mornings."[43] The opening night audience found the rough argot quite delightful.

A summer show, as Lew Fields was well aware, did not depend on the book. What mattered was the spectacle. To this end, the entire second act seemed to be written to provide excuses for stunning stage effects, snappy chorus routines, and a few catchy songs. The yacht breaks apart in full view of the audience, and Chick, Delphine, and Frank are cast adrift on a raft in choppy seas. As they squabble, palm trees gradually become discernible on the horizon, getting nearer and larger until the shoreline comes into view and broadens into a wooded waterfront with a small native hut. The bobbing raft runs ashore and its passengers are tumbled headlong onto the island.

In the final scene, at the dock at Kohala, the massive bow of the troop transport *St. Mihiel* is shown moving into its berth. Its steam whistles emit an ear-splitting roar that vibrates the theater. Soldiers line the decks and wave from the portholes—a more elaborate version of the stage effect that had been a favorite of Lew Fields' since the Music Hall burlesque, "The Stickiness of Gelatine" (1902).

Marines—rather than chorines—were the featured performers in Berkeley's dance routines, with boys outnumbering girls thirty to twenty-four. Rugged, rowdy, and breathtakingly energetic, the Marines were drilled in the kind of tricky formations that Berkeley later perfected in Hollywood, breaking the unison effect with character bits and multiple rhythms. Berkeley did not neglect the girls, either. When Chick's drunken buddies and their "frails" show up after the Witherspoons' party, they carry on with feverish jazz antics to Rodgers' and Hart's "Crazy Elbows." ("Crazy motion / Like a pendulum to my brain / Crazy ocean / Moving forward and back again!")

No summer show was complete without one or two catchy tunes. Rodgers & Hart came up with at least three. The best two were unexpected: "You Took Advantage of Me," a wryly unremorseful rhythm number that became a pop standard, and "Tell It to the Marines," bellowed at march-tempo by a rowdy all-male ensemble. The former was not sung by the principals, but by the comic couple (played by Busby Berkeley and Joyce Barbour). Rodgers and Hart had the highest expectations for the love ballad "Do I Hear You Saying, 'I Love You,'" and Fields had spotted it throughout the show, but it never caught on. Dance bands picked up on "Crazy Elbows," but most civilians would not attempt the dance itself.

Out-of-town previews for *Present Arms* began in Wilmington in March, 1928. The tryout period was uneventful except for some problems with the Marine chorus: Fields and Berkeley had insisted on recruiting tough-looking, virile men rather than the usual effeminate juveniles. According to Rodgers, their Marines not only looked the part onstage, but acted the part offstage. During the tryouts, they spent most of the time barhopping and engaging in acts of petty vandalism—living up to the popular prejudices about actors that Fields had struggled to overcome. In Wilmington, Fields fired the actor playing Chick's buddy, Douglas. Busby Berkeley, whose previous acting experience included three years in the road company of *Irene*, volunteered to step into the role.

A year and a day after the opening of *Hit the Deck* (on April 26, 1928), *Present Arms* arrived to a hero's welcome at Lew Fields' Mansfield Theatre. Two of the orchestra seats in the sold-out house were occupied by Joe Weber and Mayor Jimmy Walker, and the breezy, exuberant proceedings entertained them mightily. The complex scene changes and stage effects worked flawlessly. "Rough, loud, compact, and feverish," was how Brooks Atkinson described it, calling it a cross between *Hit the Deck* and *Good News*, the jazzy college musical.[44] Beyond the inevitable comparisons to *Hit the Deck*, reviewers marvelled at the pacing and the staging. Burns Mantle commented that it was a "hard and trying pace" to maintain through an evening, "but Lew Fields . . . is an old and wise showman, and he skilfully placed his contrasts of sentiment and pleasing balladry." Though *Billboard* complained that there was too much ensemble dancing, another critic praised it as "the chorus's show" and attributed its "whirlwind pace" to the acrobatic chorus. Rodgers' score was called the most beautiful element in the production. The scenic effects (especially the voyage to the desert isle and the arrival of the troop transport) elicited applause from an audience jaded by years of Follies and operettas. Most dismissed the book and admitted that the cast was stronger on dramatic ability than singing voices.

Although *Present Arms* broke no new ground artistically, it reaffirmed Lew Fields as a master chef of the Broadway musical. Alan Dale, who probably reviewed more Lew Fields shows than any other contemporary critic, put it like this: "As in all the Fields shows . . . there were features last night that cannot be duplicated in any current attractions. Mr. Fields seems to ferret out the unusual, pepper it with his own imagination, and serve [it] up hot."[45] As another critic observed, "The glad paternal eye of Sahib Lew Fields [was] evident everywhere."[46]

Despite generally enthusiastic reviews, *Present Arms* did not match the runs of the four previous Fields offerings. Still, it managed a respectable run of 155 performances. Perhaps, as Rodgers had feared from the start, *Present Arms* was hurt by its similarity to *Hit the Deck*. Or perhaps it just could not hold its own in a season with so many long-running musicals: *Good News, My Maryland, A Connecticut Yankee, Show Boat, Funny Face, Rosalie*, and the low-budget revue that outlasted all of these and catapulted Dorothy Fields to fame.

Lew Leslie's *Blackbirds of 1928* opened inauspiciously at the Liberty Theatre on May 9, about two weeks after *Present Arms*. Though its producer intended it to be in the tradition of black musicals such as *Shuffle Along* and *Runnin' Wild*, the creative team behind *Blackbirds* was all white: Leslie, McHugh, and Dorothy Fields (who also reportedly contributed sketches); except for the orchestrator Will Vodery. The cast was all black, including Bill Robinson, singers Adelaide Hall and Aida Ward, and comedian Tim Moore. In a jolting reminder that the theater site was Broadway and not Harlem, the producer resorted to the old-fashioned expedient of having his comedians wear blackface. Lew Leslie had no interest in social experiments; he was trying to recoup a substantial loss from his association with Larry Fay and Frankie Marlow in the Club Ambassadeurs.

The score by McHugh and Fields consisted of eleven songs, four of which became popular hits. "Doin' the New Low Down" provided a showcase for Bill Robinson's tap-dancing magic; Adelaide Hall sang "I Must Have That Man" and "Diga Diga Do," the latter in a typical "jungle" setting. "Diga Diga Do" had the kind of lyrics that would have probably had Lew Fields up and threatening to punch the manager, but for the fact that Dorothy had actually written them. The smash hit of the evening came out of McHugh's trunk, where it had lain for half a year since Harry Delmar had cut it from his revue.

Even with "I Can't Give You Anything But Love," *Blackbirds of 1928* was not an immediate success. The reviews were almost uniformly negative (unjustly so), and one critic complained of "a sickeningly puerile song called 'I Can't Get You Anything But Love, Baby.'" Their real ire was reserved for the sketches, and though it is easy to believe that the comedy writing was simply bad, it is also possible that the nature of the comedy touched a nerve. Several of the sketches had sexual overtones (almost *de rigeur* for white revues): "What a Night," "Getting Married in Harlem," and a black version of Elinor Glyn's "It." With two exceptions, critics blasted the material, calling it "jaded," "suggestive," and "unsuited to the negro." One of the exceptions, Tom Van Dyck (the *Morning Telegraph*), questioned this harsh treatment in a follow-up article a few days later, in which he laid bare the underlying prejudice: "One mustn't forget that the colored performers must do nothing but hoke. . . . The sex stuff is out for Afro-Americans."

With the indulgence of the theater's owner (Abe Erlanger) and a low payroll to meet, Leslie kept the show open through the summer and continued to rework it. Meanwhile, the jazz bands in the clubs picked up on "I Can't Give You Anything But Love," and by midsummer it was being heard everywhere. When cooler weather arrived in September, *Blackbirds* was among the most profitable shows on Broadway, doing $18,000 a week with very low overhead. The *Times* deemed it worthy of reconsideration and concluded, "To this song ["Anything But Love"] goes most of the credit for putting over the show." The song not only became one of the year's biggest hits, but it has since become one of the most recorded songs of the century.

Blackbirds of 1928 flew until 1930, lasting 518 performances on Broadway—longer than any other revue for a decade, and longer than anything Lew Fields ever did, including *A Connecticut Yankee*. "I Can't Give You Anything But Love" gave Dorothy the opportunity to live—in her words—"in the style to which I was unaccustomed."[47]

Success was all it took to change her father's mind.

Summer, 1928: theatergoers braved four weeks of unrelentingly oppressive heat to keep two Lew Fields productions in the black. *Present Arms* and *A Connecticut Yankee* were averaging just under $15,000 per week (the latter still going strong after forty weeks); *Blackbirds of 1928*, with smaller expenses, was doing even better. It was also the summer that Flo Ziegfeld could boast three smash hits running simultaneously: *Rosalie, The Three Musketeers*, and *Showboat*.

Meanwhile, Herbert, Rodgers, and Hart were already well along on their next project. *Violet Town*, as it was tentatively called, was an adaptation of a 1927 novel by Charles Pettit, *The Son of the Grand Eunuch*. This was not your typical musical comedy material: it told the Candide-like story of a thirty-nine-year-old Chinese man who does not want to follow in his father's footsteps and become the next Grand Eunuch in the Emperor's court. And Herbert, Rodgers and Hart did not intend to give it the typical musical comedy treatment. In its form as well as its subject matter, their new musical would be as daring and ambitious as *Present Arms* was tame.

Back in 1911, a rueful Lew Fields had observed, "Sometimes these big ambitions have to be put up in alcohol and preserved on the shelf." Now, thanks to his young collaborators, it was time to take them down and dust them off.

CHAPTER XVIII

Rough Stuff

> Eventually musical comedy will develop away from the standardized form. Finally, I should not be surprised to see [musical comedy] develop into the true American opera, something quite distinct from the European opera grafted upon us by European writers and producers. Our more youthful nation with its superior vitality may express itself musically through this gayer medium and thus create a form as new as the "Rhapsody in Blue" was in music.
>
> Lew Fields, 1928

> It's a great business. If you stay in it long enough it will break you. But it will go on forever.
>
> Joe Weber, 1930

ENTERTAINMENT that you would not be ashamed to bring your mother to—that was the avowed goal of the purveyors of big-time vaudeville. By enforcing a Victorian code of gentility that discouraged sexual references and coarse language, they took variety out of the Bowery saloon and put it in palatial theaters in fashionable neighborhoods, thereby making it into a respectable middle-class entertainment suitable for the entire family. From the time of the first Weber & Fields company, Lew Fields believed in the importance of maintaining these standards of decency and moral propriety. For Fields, as we have seen, it was not simply a sound business strategy; his ability to appeal to a "respectable" audience was his ticket to social acceptance and the redemption of his stigmatized profession. He always spoke with pride of the clean, wholesome character of the Music Hall burlesques, Frankie Bailey's legs and the Weberfields' chorus notwithstanding. Had he not condemned the nudity and bawdiness he had seen in the European music halls? Had he not defended the virtue of the chorus girl against the stereotype of the loose-living gold digger? In some ways, he had always seemed more prudish than his audience. The controversy about Lotta Faust's provocative Salome dance and her low-backed gowns, for example, made him uncomfortable. But audiences loved it, so he left it in until local censors forced him to remove it.

Indeed, he had always regretted the vulgar associations of the word "burlesque," preferring to call what he did "travesties," instead. As the Weberfields' presentations developed into the prototypes of revue and musical comedy, the term "burlesque" became the label for the branch of the show business that featured the sexual display of women, blue humor, and less and less emphasis on any kind of narrative. From the turn of the century, "burly-cue," as *Variety* called it, was at least a marginally permissible diversion for working-class men. It stood for everything that vaudeville and musical comedy—and Lew Fields—were trying to shun.

According to show biz legend, striptease originated in 1917, at the National Winter Garden Theater (on the Lower East Side), when the Minsky brothers built a runway from the stage into the auditorium so that patrons could get a better look at their cooch dancers.[1] In the 'twenties, as the established burlesque circuits (the Columbia and Mutual Wheels) were "out-stripped," so to speak, by the increasingly daring Broadway revues, cabarets, and nightclubs, only the cheapest and coarsest kind of burley-cue shows could survive. Entrepreneurs like the Minsky brothers took over theaters in run-down neighborhoods and installed "stock" companies. In the stock companies, the flashes of female flesh were featured and the comedy and production numbers became the fillers and chasers for the program. By the mid-'twenties, burlesque commentators began referring to stock burlesque as "dirt shows."

No wonder Lew Fields was so anxious to avoid confusion over the kind of burlesque he presented. No wonder he was concerned when the Shuberts brought in Izzy Herk, head of the Columbia and Mutual Burlesque Wheels, as a partner in Shubert Advanced Vaudeville and co-franchisee of the Weber & Fields unit show. And it may also explain why he had become increasingly distant from his brothers Solly and Nat. Before the war, Solly had worked closely with Lew as a stage manager at the Broadway Theater, the Lew Fields Roof Garden, and the American Music Hall in Chicago. After the war, however, Solly became the stage manager for the Union Square Theatre, a once prestigious legit house that went burlesque. The Minskys hired him to stage the dance numbers at their National Winter Garden and Park Music Hall, and he freelanced on the Columbia Wheel.

Nat "Duke" Fields had been a source of embarrassment to his famous brother since before the war, when he started producing unauthorized versions of Weber & Fields and Lew Fields sketches in the South and Midwest, sometimes with Lew's brother-in-law Bobby Harris, sometimes alone. For a time, Nat (he preferred being called "Duke" but was also known as "Fashion Flash") worked with Solly at the National Winter Garden, appearing as a Dutch and blackface comedian and writing some of the gags for the shows. Most likely, Nat's material consisted of blue versions of Weber & Fields' travesties and Lew Fields' sketches or other material filched from vaudeville and musical comedy. (This was not unusual: Nat's former employer, Abe Minsky, said in 1933 that not one new burlesque sketch had been written and performed in the past twenty years.)[2] In September, 1922, Nat severed his relations with the National Winter Garden and moved uptown to Harlem to work as a producer for a "colored" stock troupe that was being installed at the Lafayette.

As stock burlesque began to take hold, Solly also got in on the action. In the fall of 1924, he became the managing producer of the stock burlesque company at the Strand Theatre in Newark, New Jersey. His big break came early in 1926, when he learned that the old Miner's Eighth Avenue Theatre was up for sale. Miner's Eighth Avenue, along with Miner's Bowery, was a regular stop on the Weber & Fields itinerary in their pre–Music Hall days. Like many vaudeville houses, Miner's Eighth Avenue had fallen on hard times, trying motion pictures and, finally, as the Chelsea Theatre, burlesque. After considerable negotiating, Solly took over the Chelsea and installed a stock burlesque company performing six days a week, year-round. Not three months later, police detectives raided the Chelsea and arrested the entire company after witnessing the first two scenes of the matinee. All of the Chelsea burlesquers—except for Solly Fields, who could not be found—were herded into paddy wagons and booked at the West Thirtieth Street Station. The charge: violation of Section 1140a of the New York Penal Code; i.e., presenting a manifestly indecent performance likely to be a corrupting influence on minors and others. Later, the twenty-six chorus girls were discharged, but the nine principals and the lone captive administrator were held for trial in special sessions.

The trial was typical of the proceedings directed against "indecent" stage presentations. Each of the defendants was required to take the stand and perform his or her lines and stage business. The effect was often wonderfully ludicrous. A comedian named Harry Seymour, with the aid of another comedian named Beasly, re-enacted "the identification of nationalities" scene. A blindfold was placed over Seymour's eyes, and a series of young women (played in court by Beasly) would sit on his lap; using his hands, he would feel her face and then tell where she originated. According to the arresting officers, Seymour's actions and ad libs in the theater were much more "pronounced," as were those of the female lap-sitters. When asked who hired them and paid their salaries, each defendant identified the absent Solly Fields. The court found them guilty, Solly Fields included, and fined them $100 each or thirty days in jail. Taking advantage of the new city ordinances, the License Department refused to renew the Chelsea as long as Solly Fields was manager. Solly re-opened the Chelsea anyway, and defiantly announced that he would have two stock companies in the coming season. The following year, he also set up his own burlesque and vaudeville booking office while continuing to produce numbers for the Minskys.

Variety covered the Chelsea case in detail; the New York dailies, in passing; with occasional reminders about who Solly's brother was. One can imagine the distaste with which Lew Fields regarded the affair. Under these circumstances, he would have probably preferred that his brothers had not changed their names. At that moment, Lew was desperately trying to re-establish his credibility as a Broadway producer. *The Girl Friend* opened a month after Solly took over the Chelsea, and the publicity surrounding the trial continued through the summer during the time Lew was trying to fend off impatient creditors and raise money to send *The Girl Friend* on tour.

In this context, it is interesting to consider what Lew Fields had to say in July, 1926, about the differences between current musical comedies and those of twenty years earlier:

> The modern musical comedy has to compete against opposition quite different from that met by its ancestor twenty years ago. The modern musical is clean . . . yet,

they [musical producers] are vying for customers with revues in which risqué sketches and scantily draped women are often the features. . . .

Audiences have become accustomed to more daring material, however. Just as the French farce, the bedroom play and others of its ilk have more or less passed away from our stage, so will the present sex play and nude revue eventually go their ways. The musical comedy will never tamper with that sort of material.[3]

But it already was, and his son Herbert was among those doing the tampering. By the mid-'twenties, Pop Fields' concept of musical comedy as clean, wholesome entertainment was at odds with another of his most cherished suppositions: a musical comedy, like a newspaper, had to be (in his words) "up to date and in the fashion of the day." And the fashion of the day could not be called wholesome: not when the most popular newspaper was the tabloid *New York Graphic* (a.k.a. the "porno-*Graphic*"), and the year's bestsellers included Nan Britton's *The President's Daughter*, which told of her backstairs love affair with President Harding and the illegitimate daughter they produced. Not when Mayor Jimmy Walker was hailed as "a model for our youth" by the businessmen of New York.

Burly-cue was far from being the only format that threatened the "wholesomeness" of the popular stage. Writing about the proliferation of "rough stuff" in the American theater of the 'twenties, Abel Green observed: "Very little was *verboten* on the wide-open stages of the decade." Sights and language formerly available only in the tawdriest gin mills and burlesque houses were being incorporated into mainstream theater.[4] The patrons of Broadway revues in 1919 and 1920 began seeing chorus girls bare their legs, and within five years, everything else, in the Ziegfeld Follies, the Shuberts' Artists and Models, and the Earl Carroll Vanities. (Even the publicity became more explicit: in 1905, Ziegfeld created a furor merely by inventing a story about Anna Held's milk baths; twenty-odd years later, Earl Carroll made headlines when he paid $17,000 to seventeen-year-old Joyce Hawley to sit naked in a bathtub of champagne for a party he was hosting.) The floor shows in the fashionable cabarets and night clubs were usually even more daring, or seemed to be because of their greater intimacy, and columnists debated which club's "torso tossers" (jazz dancers) were hottest. On the legit stage, authors pushed aside long-standing taboos regarding subject matter and strong language; Avery Hopwood in coy bedroom farces such as *The Demi-Virgin* (1921); John Colton in *The Shanghai Gesture* (1926), a melodrama about Mother Goddam, proprietor of a Chinese brothel; Eugene O'Neill in *Desire Under the Elms* (1924). Critics occasionally chastised both Herb Fields and Larry Hart for "blue" jokes and lyrics, but their witty innuendos were seen as mild compared to the outright lewdness of *Broadway Brevities* or *Cat's Meow.* And for a new note in illicit thrills, there was miscegenation: *Lulu Belle* by Edward Sheldon and Charles MacArthur and the musical *Deep River* raised the issue on Broadway a year or so before *Show Boat.* It was entertainment you would not be ashamed to bring your mother to—if she happened to be a jaded, gin-guzzling flapper with progressive pretensions.

By the mid-'twenties, bluenoses across the country were calling for legislation to censor stage entertainment. Hollywood had already accepted prior censorship under the watchful eyes of "czar" Will Hays. The Hays Office (i.e., the

Motion Picture Producers and Distributors of America, which Hays was president of) prohibited films depicting "any licentious nudity," "inference of sexual perversion," miscegenation, disrespect for clergy, casual references to "the sale of women," and cracks about Will Hays and Prohibition—some of the favorite subjects of 'twenties' stage entertainment, legit or otherwise. Big-time vaudeville (i.e., Keith-Albee) was already policing itself; dubbed "the Sunday-school circuit" by harassed performers, its ever-growing list of taboos drove more patrons and performers to burlesque and the small-time.

Broadway producers were less willing to clean up their acts. After producer Al Woods successfully fought an attempt by the New York License Commissioner to close down one of his shows, District Attorney Joab Banton created a panel of voluntary jurors known as the "Citizens' Jury" to judge the moral content of stage shows. When the Citizen's Jury tried to shut down an inept revue called *Bunk of 1926*, the producers got an injunction and used the publicity to turn a sure flop into a modest money-maker. In 1926, Mayor Jimmy Walker warned a group of Broadway producers that they had better clean up their shows or face punitive action. Not surprisingly, his finger-wagging on matters of morality had little effect. Public outcry in the press prompted District Attorney Banton to give the Citizen's Jury a list of unacceptable shows; among them *Lulu Belle*, the dramatization of Dreiser's *An American Tragedy;* a serious drama about lesbianism called *The Captive*, by Edouard Bourdet; and *Sex*, an utterly facetious play by Mae West. Police raids closed *The Captive*, *Sex*, and one other play. Newspaper scares and rumors about impending raids were successful in scaring off the carriage trade and the cut-rate ticket buyers from several other "objectionable" shows, causing them to close.

In 1927, the New York legislature institutionalized censorship with the passing of the Wales Padlock Law. Police now had the right to arrest the producers, authors, and actors of objectionable plays, and to padlock the theater for one year if they were convicted. D. A. Banton spared O'Neill's *Strange Interlude* but intimidated the producers of *Maya* (about a French prostitute) into shutting down. The following year, Mae West returned with a milder affront to decency, *Diamond Lil*, about an 1890's underworld queen who performs in saloons, trains thieves, dispenses cocaine, and recruits whores. The moral outrage was just enough to help the show to a profitable summer at the Royale.

So it was not without trepidation that Lew Fields agreed to produce Herbert's adaption of *The Son of the Grand Eunuch*. Still, the triumvirate of Herbert-Rodgers-Hart had proven themselves to be excellent judges of audience tastes, whether it was unconventional subject matter *(Dearest Enemy, A Connecticut Yankee)* or innovative formal devices *(Peggy-Ann)*. Seen in context, their work was very hip and stylish. Together, they had brought Pop Fields out of the Gilded Age and into the Roaring Twenties. He had good reasons to trust them.

Herbert discovered Pettit's novel shortly after the opening of *Present Arms*. It is not difficult to see why the material appealed to him: set in the Chinese imperial court in the late nineteenth century, the novel's wry, off-handed treatment of horrific material gave it a satiric bite not unlike Twain's *A Connecticut Yankee*. The love of the son, Li Pi Tchou, and his wife, Chti, recalled the musings of another great satirist, Voltaire, and his tale of the relationship between Candide and his beloved Cunegonde "in the best of all possible worlds." To protect the rather bumbling Tchou, Chti must bestow her favors on several antagonists, but she always returns to swear her eternal love for her husband. Chti prospers while Tchou is reduced to abject poverty. In the end, Tchou is installed in the Violet City as the new Grand Eunuch, and father and son are reconciled, agreeing that after age forty, material prosperity is more important than romantic love.

With Gilbert & Sullivan's *The Mikado* as his model (it had recently been given a handsome production by Winthrop Ames), Herbert would use the Oriental milieu as an attractively exotic backdrop for satirizing contemporary American attitudes about morality. The relationship between Tchou and Chti echoed a recurrent theme in Herbert's librettos: the strong and resourceful woman willing to go to any lengths—even sexual infidelity—to protect her man. In *Dearest Enemy*, the Yankee women's seduction of the British soldiers was a kind of patriotism; in *The Girl Friend*, Mollie renounces her claim to Lenny so that he can ride in the big race.

True love, in a Herbert Fields scenario, required moral compromises. Here he was in direct opposition to his colleague Oscar Hammerstein II, whose scripts *(Desert Song, Show Boat)* spoke reassuringly of the ultimate triumph of love and justice. Not surprisingly, Broadway audiences preferred (and continue to prefer) the sappier alternative. Despite Herbert's appreciation for operetta's formal structures, his cynicism about romantic love made it impossible for him to avoid burlesquing operetta's passionately earnest characters and plots. So while Hammerstein's fusion of musical comedy and operetta produced the American operetta, Herbert perfected what his father had wanted all along—comic opera.

Something else about *The Son of the Grand Eunuch* may have hooked Herbert as well, worth mentioning only in light of the fact that he was, after all, the first to try to apply Freud to the Broadway libretto. Herbert was by now thirty years old. For the past ten years, all of his professional work in the theater had been for his father, whom he worshipped and, in private, derided for his old-fashioned ways. Petit's novel told the story of a son (about to turn forty) who wants to succeed to his father's privileged position but does not want to be castrated in the process. Herbert, as we have seen, was fond of inside jokes.

He immediately showed the novel to Larry Hart, his soul-mate, who agreed that it had the makings of a sensational musical. Together, they persuaded Pop Fields. If he expressed any misgivings about the subject matter, they overcame them by pointing to the formal possibilities. Here was Lew Fields' chance to produce a real comic opera; serious art, but funny. Herbert and Larry then called Dick Rodgers in Colorado Springs, where he was vacationing, and told him about the book. He read it and concluded that they had gone crazy in his absence. They told him that Lew Fields had agreed to produce it, which he found surprising. When Rodgers returned to New York, the three were swept up in the excitement of trying to put their most ambitious ideas about the unity of story and song to the test. The challenge was to make the music an integral part of the story rather than a diversion or digression. The solution, as Rodgers explained it, was "to use a number of short pieces of from four to sixteen bars each, with no more than six songs of traditional form and length in the entire score."[5] Herbert, Rodgers, and Hart interwove score and text throughout, using vocal and instrumental miniatures, verses without choruses, leitmotifs, finalettos, even recitative, in addition to the more traditional reprises and incidental music. They ended up with approximately thirty-eight musical passages, compared to twelve for *Present Arms.*[6] This violated several "rules" regarding the structure of songs and their layout in the program. The conventional length for Broadway show tunes and Tin Pan Alley songs was thirty-two bars. The musical comedy score was supposed to contain a more or less standard list of song types: theme song, rhythm number, comedy or novelty number, the eleven o'clock number (for the star), and so on. To depart too wildly from these conventions, Lew Fields knew, would jeopardize the possibilities for the kind of hit songs that could be "plugged" to carry a Broadway show. Still, he supported the experiment.

Libretto and score took less than three months to complete; remarkable, given their complex interrelationship, indicating a collaboration of unusual closeness. Herbert's original title was *Violet Town,* from the name of the Emperor's palace where the imperial concubines and eunuchs live. (Violets as a symbol of homosexuality had also been much publicized as a consequence of the *The Captive*'s notorious run in 1927.)

Herbert's adaptation emphasized Li Pi Tchou's passivity as he stumbles from one misadventure to the next. Instead of being a paragon of masculine bravery, Tchou is a rather abject creature. The real catalyst is his resourceful wife Chti, who is anything but the pure and innocent Cinderella. Chti became another in Herbert's long line of willful, dynamic heroines. During the tryouts, Tchi became "Chee-Chee," and her name became the show's title. (*Chee-Chee*— intended perhaps to echo mock-Oriental names like Ko-Ko and Yum-Yum of *The Mikado*— also sounded like it could be the name of a cooch dancer in stock burlesque.) Tchou's father, the Grand Eunuch Li Pi Siao (or "the G.E." as he is otherwise known in the libretto), remains the crafty, farcical glutton of the novel. Before he had risen to his position at court, he had a wife and two children, and he sees himself as the progenitor of a dynasty of Grand Eunuchs. For the comic-romantic subplot, Herbert built up the relationship between Li-Li Wee, the G.E.'s sixteen-year-old daughter, and Prince Tao-Tee, the Emperor's son.

A detailed summary of the first scene gives ample indication of the tone— playful to the point of archness—and the interplay of text and music. Curtain's rise establishes the sacred precincts of Violet Town (accompanied by the instrumental "Prelude"), where the Emperor's eighty-one concubines live, attended by eunuchs supervised by the much-feared G.E. A chorus of eight eunuchs introduce themselves, singing: "We're men of brains, endowed with tact! / We're muscular and neat / And yet our lives, to be exact, / Are rather incomplete." The eunuchs tell the Prince, who has sneaked in, that the G.E. will be arriving any minute, carrying jade tablets with concubines' names on them for the Emperor's nightly selections. The G.E.'s daughter, Li-Li Wee, has just turned sixteen and wants to add her jade tablet to the lot. She whines like a spoiled teenager: "Anyone who is anyone around here is a concubine!" The eunuchs herald the entrance of the G.E. with "The Most Majestic of Domestic Officials." During the G.E.'s prayer for guidance in choosing the right concubine, his daughter asks to have her name added to the list. The G.E. exits with his list, and the Prince comes out of his hiding place. Li-Li Wee is smitten, and she vows to be his only concubine. The Prince demurs, worried about what the neighbors would say: "Living with a single mate / Is an impropriety / Such things would arouse the hate / Of polite society."

When the G.E. returns to bring the chosen concubine, he brings momentous news for his benighted son, Li-Pi Tchou: the Emperor has ordered that Tchou succeed his father to the post of Grand Eunuch. Tchou will be castrated on his next birthday, and will henceforth be allowed to see his wife Chee-Chee only once a month. Tchou is distraught, and declares his love for his wife in "I Wake at Morning." When the couple refuse to appreciate the honor of the appointment, the G.E. is enraged and banishes them both. And that is just Scene One.

Scene Two puts Tchou and Chee "on the road to the future," riding in a rickety cart drawn by a footsore donkey. Out of pity for the animal, Chee asks Tchou to switch places with it. They meet an all-seeing owl; sounding like a New England schoolmarm, the owl chastises them for their rash actions: "Your evil doom can be foretold in three words." Chee-Chee wants to know the three words. "Sex! Sex! Sex!" replies the owl, who was a descendant perhaps of the cynical owl who spied on lovers in Lew Fields' *The Midnight Sons*.

The owl, of course, is right. Tchou suffers an escalating series of humiliations and abuse: he is robbed, placed in the stocks, whipped, dressed in rags, used as menial laborer, and offered as a human sacrifice to Buddha. Whenever Tchou's ineffectual actions put him at risk, Chee-Chee saves Tchou from the ultimate penalty by giving herself to their tormentors. Chee-Chee is the ultimate pragmatist. In song, she explains: "It was my fate to save your life. / I was a true and faithful wife." Each time she "saves" him, she insists on an expensive piece of jewelry (a bracelet) from her ravisher. When she saves him from being burned at the stake and returns wearing a new bracelet, it is too much for him. Thoroughly emasculated in spirit, he decides to comply with his father's wishes. The G.E. condemns Chee-Chee to the Gallery of Torments, where she is confined with wax figures representing Theft, Lust, Avarice, Drunkenness, Murder—all male figures—and Infidelity, which resembles her. In Herbert's early drafts, she smashes the statue of Infidelity and the play ends. In a concession to convention, Herbert added a scene in which Chee-Chee is released from the Gallery of Torments to see Tchou one more time. She has a few moments alone with the Prince of Medicine and persuades him not to castrate her husband but to pretend that he has. She returns wearing a new bracelet, but Tchou is left intact and their ruse succeeds. It was the formula happy ending, albeit with a disturbing twist.

Rehearsals for *Chee-Chee* began in August. Despite the obviously daring subject matter, Lew Fields did not attempt to dilute it or clean it up, even though the censorship hysteria was at its peak. There were no interpolated jokes from the infamous black ledger, no spectacular scenic effects or dance numbers, none of Fields's usual musical comedy hoke. Yet he was intimately involved in the supervision of every detail. He assembled his familiar staff: Alexander Leftwich to direct, John F. Hawkins to design the sets, and Herbert Ward to execute them. For the choreography, Fields wanted Seymour Felix because he was especially good with small ensembles and "book" numbers, but he was now the hottest dance director on Broadway and was unavailable.

Fields' cast showed the strength of the Gilbert & Sullivan model. In the thankless role of Tchou, Fields cast a handsome singer named William Williams, who had appeared in Winthrop Ames' recent Gilbert & Sullivan revivals. George Hassell, the August Grand Eunuch, was a Gilbert & Sullivan veteran of elephantine proportions, from the same tradition of broad burlesque comedy as Fields. They had shared the stage in Fields' *The High Cost of Loving* (1914) and in the film version of *Old Dutch*, 1916. Hassell's flamboyant buffoonery was right in keeping with Pettit's and Herbert's conception of the G.E. The menacing Tartar Chief was played by George Houston, a baritone who had toured with the American Opera Company. To no one's surprise, Fields agreed to Helen Ford in the pivotal role of Chee-Chee. Ford had misgivings about the show's commercial prospects as well as the cynical, possibly immoral aspects of her character, but Herbert Fields persuaded her otherwise.

Chee-Chee was supposed to begin its Philadelphia run on August 27, but Fields delayed it by a week to get the first-string critics. He had no illusions about his new show's mass appeal; he needed a sophisticated audience, and for that he needed critical approval. When *Chee-Chee* opened at the Forrest on September 4, *Variety*'s reviewer confirmed this, calling the show "too sophisticated for rank and file, and its real clientele not in town." The first night audience was perhaps the coldest and most unappreciative of any in Fields' experience, and box office receipts were quite disappointing. "Half the house didn't know what the word 'eunuch' meant," grumbled one unidentified Fields employee, "and the half that knew were afraid to believe that a play actually joked about such a subject." Still, most of the critics responded favorably, praising almost every aspect of the production. It quickly became the most hotly debated musical in years. *Chee-Chee* was hailed as "heralding a new era in musical shows," and denounced as "repellent" and "wholly unsatisfactory." Never had an audience of a Fields show been so polarized. In the midst of the controversy, Fields and his young collaborators gave the production its pre-Broadway shake-out, dropping several musical passages and adding one full-fledged, pluggable song number.

On September 25, Broadway first-nighters whose last trips to Lew Fields' Theatre had been to see *Present Arms* were perhaps more shocked than anyone at what replaced it. From the same producing team that had created a noisy but conventional musical comedy about burly Marines and cute socialites, came a quietly innovative comic opera that dared to make light of castration and female promiscuity. The program notes warned of an evening with artistic ambitions. *Chee-Chee* was subtitled "a musical narrative," and a notice declared: "The musical numbers, some of them very short, are so interwoven with the story that it would be confusing for the audience to peruse a complete list." Four years earlier, Oscar Hammerstein had put a similarly pretentious note in the program for *Rose Marie*. Perhaps it was morbid curiosity about its alleged indecency, but the theater was filled to capacity on opening night, and its first week's gross was over twice as much as *Present Arms'*.

From outside the theater, the marquee for *Chee-Chee* on West Forty-seventh

Street may have seemed like just another sign advertising the moral decay of a once-proud neighborhood. On the corner with Broadway was the Columbia, a burlesque house offering such fare as the "Powder Puff Frolics" or "Isabelle Van and Her 12 Pretty Runway Girls." "Dirt" houses seemed to be closing in on the legit theater district from all sides; a portent of things to come. Across the street at the Biltmore, Mae West opened her latest assault on moral propriety, *Pleasure Man*. (Three blocks away, *Diamond Lil* was still going strong.) *Pleasure Man* featured a party of drag queens and a rakish main character, an unrepentant seducer of ingenues, who gets his come-uppance in the form of—what else?— castration. West's play survived only two performances before the New York Police Department backed up their paddy wagons to the stage door. The coincidence of such sensational subject matter, however, did not help *Chee-Chee*'s claims to artistic legitimacy. *Variety* could not resist the comparison:

> Between *Chee-Chee* and Mae West's newest opera, *Pleasure Man*, West 47th Street becomes the theatrical red light district and the great American neuter gender is in its element. . . .

> Between [these two], the explosiveness of *The Front Page* and the utterly vicious expletives of *Jarnegan*, careful indeed must the layman be where he escorts any feminine companion.[7]

In this censorious atmosphere, the critics could not decide whether to hurl rotten fruit or bouquets, often doing both in the same review. *Billboard*'s reviewer, Wifred J. Riley, gave it the most bouquets:

> At last a sophisticated musical show! . . . It is a sincere attempt to overthrow the old order of things—a step forward.

> Make no mistake, *Chee-Chee* is a song and dance show for intelligent people only. . . . What a relief to realize that American musical comedy has progressed to the point where its heroines are not sweet, simple virgins, its heroes brave, upright mama's boy nor its humor aimed at the minds of morons.

> . . . Herbert Fields deserves a host of praise for his daring, his foresight and his initiative.

Jay Kaufman (the *Morning Telegraph*) also praised the courage of Herbert-Rodgers-Hart, and Lew Fields, for producing it. He thought that Rodgers & Hart did "a grand and glorious job" with the score, which in itself was enough to recommend the show. The book, however, became tedious after the novelty of the subject matter wore off. Brooks Atkinson had similar complaints about the libretto, adding that it was uncharacteristically humorless for long stretches.

Rodgers' score was universally praised, with several calling it the best of his career. Though there were only six full-length songs, four were singled out: "I Must Love You," "Dear, Oh Dear," "Moon of My Delight," and "Better Be Good to Me." According to *The Stage*, expressing a commonly held opinion, the pity of the whole affair was that Rodgers' score and Lew Fields' production were wasted on this objectionable material.

The worst of the brickbats came from St. John Ervine, the British critic and ever-so-serious playwright on loan to the *Morning World*. It came with the head-line "NASTY! NASTY!":

> This dull and, in most respects, nasty piece contains two jokes which are incessantly repeated: the first, a reference to enforced sterility, and the second, a reference to the heroine's seduction. The humor, in short, is of the kind that causes small boys to run into corners and titter. . . .

> There can rarely be a play so ornately produced to so little effect. All the mind there is in *Chee-Chee* seems to have been put into the decorations—a little of it might have been put into some disinfectant. . . .

The tone of this and several other reviews was the most negative of Lew Fields' career. What may have disturbed him most was that he had misjudged so drastically his audience's tastes. Also disturbing were the moral pronouncements: how could a respected producer with Fields' reputation for clean, wholesome entertainment allow such indecency to be presented in his name? Was he really responsible for it, or had he relinquished control to his three young collabora-tors? Rumors began to circulate that the District Attorney's office had put *Chee-Chee* on its list; *Variety* said that the police were "rubbering" (monitoring) the show, a prelude to the padlock. Ironically, box office grosses were averaging $24,000 a week, well above the best weeks of *Present Arms*, placing *Chee-Chee* solidly among the more profitable shows in town. Then, in its fourth week, the cut-rate ticket agencies suddenly announced that they would not renew their "buy" (commitment to purchase blocks of unsold tickets). The well-publicized threat of padlocking may have persuaded the agencies that *Chee-Chee* was a poor gamble. This alone would not necessarily have forced Fields to close the show, but close it he did after only thirty-one performances, the quickest hook for any Rodgers & Hart show. That same week, *A Connecticut Yankee*, the longest run-ning Fields-Rodgers-Hart show, closed after fifty-two weeks to go on tour.

Chee-Chee represented the culmination of Fields' ambitions to create an American comic opera, a synthesis of burlesque, vaudeville, musical comedy, and operetta. And it was making money to boot. We can only speculate about why he did not give it a longer run. Perhaps he was uncomfortable with the moral oppro-brium heaped upon it and, by extension, upon him as producer. The fact that he could be charged with an offense to public decency—the same charge that had tarred his brother Solly, the "burly-cue" producer—was a possibility too humili-ating to risk.

For its creators, the failure of *Chee-Chee* had several unhappy consequences. It was the last time Lew Fields would work with Rodgers & Hart, a parting that contained no bitterness or permanent intent. Helen Ford, however, felt that all her worst misgivings about the show had been borne out, and she blamed Her-bert for conning her into going along with it. The experience also persuaded Lew Fields to put those big ambitions back on the shelf—permanently. It shook his confidence in his own ability to understand what the public wanted. What Fields did not realize was that the public had rejected the subject matter of *Chee-Chee* but not the form.[8]

Within a week of *Chee-Chee*'s demise, Fields was reported to be at work on a new production. Everything about it seemed calculated to reassure the public that he still believed in clean, wholesome stage entertainment—wholesome, at least, by 'twenties' standards. The vehicle was *The High Cost of Loving*, the straight farce written by Frank Mandel, about three respectable middle-aged men black-mailed into paying a wily old flame to support the same illegitimate son. When Lew Fields had starred in it in 1914, it was considered to be in questionable taste; in 1928, it had just the right red-blood-cell count to amuse mainstream Broadway audiences. One may wonder, too, if it was simply coincidence that Fields had suddenly recalled this story of a decent man being persecuted by the local Purity League.

An old, familiar play and an old, familiar comedian dressed up in the latest fashions, with a book by his son and lyrics by his daughter. Jimmy McHugh could do the music—after *Blackbirds* he was almost like family, too. It would be a family affair—great publicity angle—and they would call it *Hello, Daddy*.

If Herbert's adaptation was not already in the works before *Chee-Chee*, then he wrote it in record time. He compressed Mandel's three-act farce into the conventional two-act musical structure, and opened up the one-set interior into four different scenes: in front of the Cedarhurst School for Girls, on the club car of a commuter train, in the Blocks' reception room, and in the Block's sun parlor. The characters and locale were anglicized and gentrified: Ludwig Klinke became Henry Block, his friend Anthony Tiedsmeyer was renamed Bennett, Block's daughter Cora became Connie, and her friend Rose became Betty, and the action was moved from Milwaukee to a generic upper-middle-class suburb. As the thoroughly assimilated Henry Block, Lew Fields had no need for his German dialect. Herbert also added several characters, mostly school chums of Connie Block, for help in the musical numbers, and he expanded the romantic sub-plot.

To play the other two old friends with the guilty secret, Lew Fields returned to the actors who had originated the roles: George Hassell (the Grand Eunuch in *Chee-Chee*) as Edward Hauser and Wilfred Clark as Anthony Bennett. Also retained from *Chee-Chee* was the vivacious Betty Starbuck to play Betty Hauser. The director was once again Alexander Leftwich, with dances staged by Busby Berkeley. But instead of supervising the production himself, Fields tapped a younger man whose work he respected, John Murray Anderson. Fields' name appeared in the credits as the show's presenter. The time was past when Fields would be able to handle the acting and producing chores simultaneously.

Hello, Daddy opened in New York at Daddy's theater on December 26 despite numerous cast changes and an unusually short tryout period. Not surprisingly, it had the look of a production that had been assembled in a great hurry. Three years had passed since Broadwayites had seen Fields in a legitimate role. Now they saw a venerable comedian who had become somewhat quieter in his methods, but whose physical clowning could still bring gasps of laughter to delighted viewers. For the first-act finale, when Fields first spied the young man who was supposed to be his illegitimate son, he turned quickly on his heels and then fell, timber-like, on his back. Joe Weber, watching this from an orchestra seat, almost leapt from his chair in concern. Fields matched his "benign irascibilities" against the undersized Wilfred Clark, who evoked memories of Meyer's old partner, and the oversized George Hassell, who wriggled and roared to great effect. Audiences did not seem to mind that Fields had returned in a thoroughly conventional musical-comedy vehicle, including such threadbare jokes as "a wolf in cheap clothing." The important thing was that it was good, clean hokum. Brooks Atkinson called his review "Restoring Lew Fields," and that was what *Hello, Daddy* was really about: restoring Fields' reputation as a respectable purveyor of popular entertainment.

Fields' return to musical comedy helped draw a capacity house, but what gave the show its staying power was the McHugh-Fields score, the dance numbers, and the performances of the juvenile and ingenue, Billy Taylor and Betty Starbuck. "Futuristic Rhythm" provided Berkeley with an excuse to create a flash finish for the first scene. "I Want Plenty of You" gave the two romantic leads a torchy number that according to one critic "would be a hot portion in the hands of impolite singers given to suggestive grimaces." Dorothy's rhymes were sometimes too intricate for Tin Pan Alley tastes, but two of the songs became popular enough to help sustain the show: "Let's Sit and Talk About You" (a ballad for Mary Lawler and Allen Kearns) and "In a Great Big Way" (an offbeat courtship scene between Billy Taylor and Betty Starbuck).

Despite only lukewarm reviews, *Hello, Daddy* became one of the few musicals of the winter to prosper. But it was not easy. The latter half of the 1928–1929 season was proving to be (in *Variety*'s words) "plenty tough." Business at the legit houses was down by fifty percent. The number of new Broadway musicals had decreased significantly, and there were fewer profitable musicals. The presidential elections, the flood of movie musicals, and the wild gyrations of the stock market were all offered as explanations.

In his struggle to put over *Hello, Daddy*, Fields showed the kind of persistence and energy that he had failed to show for *Chee-Chee.* When trade at Fields' Mansfield was disappointing, he decided that the theater's location was no help— too many undesirable neighbors, and too far off Forty-second Street. Over his partner's objections, Fields moved *Hello, Daddy* to George M. Cohan's Theater, on Broadway and Forty-third, and returned the lease on the Mansfield to the Chanins. Box office receipts showed immediate improvement. At the same time, Fields continued to revise and hone the production itself: several slack passages in Act Two were deleted and the order of three numbers reversed. Finally, he brought in a new choreographer to help stage the new numbers and put some consistency into the dance program.[9]

By April, the show was running in the black, but the rigors of performing were taking their toll on Fields. Offstage, he looked positively exhausted—"a little tired," he admitted. There was a certain desperation to Fields' efforts to keep this slight entertainment from fading away. In early May, when the Cohan switched over to its summer schedule of motion pictures, Fields moved *Hello, Daddy* again, this time to the Erlanger. With a shrinking number of musicals on the boards, Fields was hopeful of playing through July. But on a Saturday evening late in May, during one of the more strenuous moments of clowning in the first act, Fields did a flip over a couch. As he landed, he felt a something snap in his right ankle, followed by a searing pain. He doubled over on the couch to hide the pain that contorted his face, then straightened up with what looked like a wry smile as the audience laughed at the stunt. He limped through the scene; to the audience, he appeared even more comical, while his fellow actors thought he was ad-libbing some new stage business.

It was not until he got offstage that anybody in the company knew what had happened. Without taking off his shoe, Fields iced his ankle. He insisted on playing the second act, concealing his injury by keeping all his weight on his good leg. The audience did not notice any lessening of his customary vigor. After the show, his doctor told him that he needed surgery, bed rest for at least a week, then gradual rehabilitation. Evidently, the show meant too much to Fields. Like the over-the-hill boxer who risks permanent injury to return to the ring for one more big payday, Fields refused to consider closing the show. He wanted the doctor to perform the surgery right away—Saturday night—so that he could have a day and a half to recover before going on Monday evening. The doctor argued, and Fields replied: "Those little kids in the chorus must live—and all those others—they've worked with me for six months now, I can't quit on them. . . ." The minor surgery occurred late Saturday night. Fields limped through his performance Monday night and for the next two weeks—twelve evening shows and four matinees—in constant pain. The public never knew. But when attendance began to slacken in the summer heat, no amount of stoicism could keep the show open. *Hello, Daddy* finally said good-bye in mid-June, after a surprising 198 performances. Fields denied to *Variety* that it was his injury that forced it to close; he did not want people to think that he no longer had the stamina to perform. Still, it must have occurred to him that this could be his last appearance in a Broadway musical.

Fields spent the summer recuperating, watching with a mixture of pride and distress as others vied for the services of his young collaborators. In May, Dorothy and Jimmy McHugh joined the exodus of songwriters heading west to Los Angeles to work in radio and movies for unheard-of weekly salaries. Hollywood was buying out Tin Pan Alley: Warner Brothers acquired Harms, Remick, and Witmark; MGM made a deal for Robbins. The Gershwins' producers, Alex Aarons and Vinton Freedley, approached Rodgers & Hart about composing the score for *Spring Is Here* (March, 1929) and then retained them for the show that eventually became *Heads Up!* (November, 1929). Herbert began meeting with another young Broadway composer who was just coming into his own, Cole Porter. Tired and uncertain, Lew would not commit to any of the story ideas Herbert offered him. For the first time in a decade, Lew Fields had no scripts in the works, no productions in rehearsal, not even any plans for a reunion with Weber. Having severed his ties with Lew Leavitt over the Mansfield lease, Fields was without an angel as well.

During that summer, two landmarks of Fields' childhood went up in smoke. As Broadway theater-building reached its peak, the most famous of the old Bowery resorts were reduced to rubble. Miner's Bowery Theatre (165 Bowery) burned twice in three months, razing the auditorium where as young boys Weber & Fields braved the rattan whip of the Post to express their delight for the stars of the variety stage. Between the two fires at Miner's, a spectacular blaze consumed the stately Thalia at 46 Bowery. Originally called the Bowery Theatre, the Thalia once played host to *Mazeppa*, Forest and Booth, George L. Fox in *Humpty-Dumpty*, and Lillian Russell. Its entertainment reflected the successive waves of immigration to settle in the neighborhood: German plays, Italian light opera, Yiddish drama, and, finally, Chinese plays. The Bowery had become a mile and half of ramshackle wreckage, from which the ruins of the Thalia stood out impressively: the massive pillars in the front reaching up to the nonexistent roof, the dark, cavernous interior, the spiral staircases leading nowhere, now overrun with stray cats.

Joe Weber had good business instincts; he must have sensed the Great Crash coming. In June, 1929, after years of pleas and demands from his impecunious partner, Weber finally agreed to sell the West End Theatre. It was on the eve of another stock market crash—in 1903—that Weber & Fields had purchased the West End, paying half its value because the owners feared that the crash would wipe them out. Weber & Fields spent $20,000 to renovate it, but soon after they split, Weber leased it out for motion pictures. A new uptown stop on the Eighth Avenue subway made the site of the decaying theater attractive to developers. The selling price was reportedly $400,000.

Few others on Broadway—or anywhere else, for that matter—were as perspicacious as Joe Weber. By the summer of 1929, the stock market not only dominated the news, it dominated the culture. One and a half million Americans had accounts with brokerage firms, and one third of them were buying on margin. Speakeasy chatter was as likely to be about hot tips as hot jazz. Throughout the 'twenties, *Variety* commented periodically on the growing intimacy of Wall Street and Broadway. Spurred by the success of motion pictures and radio, amusement stocks such as RCA and Paramount became the pride of the bull market. RCA climbed to 500 and split five to one. Then, on October 24, 1929, RCA opened at $83\frac{3}{4}$ and dropped steadily; the rest of the market followed suit. And Broadway, as *Variety* noted, felt the impact almost instantaneously:

NO JOY ON SALE; MISERY—HOW!

> Broadway, kicked, heeled, punched and gouged by Wall Street, came within an inch of its night-life last week, shattering all records for gloom in the country. . . .
>
> As a business center—with joy on sale—no other locale or community suffered a greater depression. Main Stem had no buyers. The bottom dropped out of hilarity. . . .
>
> Yet Broadway laughed and sang through a World War; wise-cracked through all kinds of trouble and catastrophe, but in the present misfortune of unfortunate quotations, hadn't a come-back![10]

Although he probably would not have admitted it at the time, Lew Fields was fortunate not to have been tied up in a Broadway production. When Wall Street laid its famous egg, the legit theater was the first to suffer. Anxious producers reasoned that people would be in no mood for high-priced entertainment, and they were right. The number of new musicals in the 1929–1930 season dropped to its lowest level in eleven seasons. The era of extravagant annual revues was over, and the frivolities of the Jazz Age musical comedy soon palled. Five thousand actors were out of work on Broadway alone. Fields' producing colleagues— Ziegfeld, Dillingham, Arthur Hammerstein, Al Woods—teetered on the edge of bankruptcy. The only reason the Crash did not have the same immediate impact on Fields was that he was not wealthy enough to venture anything in the stock market. All of his money was tied up in his shows and in supporting his family's comfortable lifestyle. Only recently had he acquired any capital to speak of, from the tour of *A Connecticut Yankee* and the sale of the West End Theater.

Family members, led by his son-in-law Charles Marcus, encouraged Lew to put the money in the bank. What better place than his in-laws' bank, the Bank of the United States? In a letter to shareholders, bank president Bernard Marcus said that 1929 earnings and profits for the bank and its "real estate investment affiliate" Bankus Corporation were "in excess of $8,600,000." Despite the effects of the Crash, their stock was still valued at over sixty dollars a share. "From its modest beginnings," Bernard wrote with obvious pride, "the Bank of the United States has, within a period of sixteen years, grown to a position of prominence." Among the 27,000 banks in the country, the Bank of the United States was ranked twenty-eighth, with the third-largest branch banking system in the state of New York. Lew Fields could sleep soundly knowing that in these volatile times, his money was being shepherded by this reputable institution whose president was, after all, family.

Black Tuesday ended any hopes Fields had for producing a musical that season. Offers from several vaudeville bookers for another Weber & Fields reunion tour did not excite the erstwhile partners; the two- and three-a-day performance schedule was too demanding, and the vaude circuits seemed to be dying by degrees. By the summer of 1929, when Hollywood's hunger for movie musicals had consumed all of the current stage stars and their hits, the studios turned their attention to old-time favorites. A week after Black Thursday, MGM announced a musical revue "based on incidents connected with the Weber & Fields Music Hall" at the turn of the century. The studio would bring together the surviving Weberfields—Marie Dressler, William Collier, Louis Mann, De Wolf Hopper, Fay Templeton, and Weber & Fields—in a film with a younger set of principals, with Harry Rapf directing; Gus Edwards, Howard Johnson, and Lou Alter providing words and music; and Sammy Lee staging the dances. Tentatively entitled *Then and Now*, it had a big budget ($750,000) to cover the costs for eighteen dance numbers involving four hundred chorines and what was being touted as one of the largest sets ever constructed for a talking film. It sounded like a worthy showcase for Weber & Fields' first talking feature.

Perhaps Fields thought (as so many did) that by the time he returned East, business on Broadway would be back to normal. Two weeks after the stock market crash, on the day before the market hit bottom, Mr. and Mrs. Lew Fields and Mr. and Mrs. Joe Weber boarded the Santa Fe "Chief" for Los Angeles. In their contract negotiations, they had specified that their wives must accompany them at the studio's expense and that the wives be entitled to read the script.

They were greeted at Union Station by a group of transplanted stage folk (now sporting deep tans), including their old Music Hall writer Edgar Smith, Gus Edwards, director Harry Rapf, and an old-fashioned German band. The following morning, a limo sent by the studio met Weber & Fields at their hotels and took them to the MGM lot, where they signed their contracts. Shooting for *The March of Time*, as it was now being called, was scheduled to begin on December 1.

Shortly before filming was to commence, Herbert Fields joined his parents and Dorothy in Hollywood. Herbert had stayed in New York just long enough to see the Broadway opening of *Fifty Million Frenchmen*, his first musical with Cole Porter and his first production for somebody other than his father. In a troubled Broadway season, *Fifty Million Frenchmen* became one of the few certifiable hits. It was the start of a collaboration between Herb Fields and Porter that would last through six more shows, including some of the biggest hits of the late 'thirties and early 'forties.

Warner Brothers brought Herbert to Hollywood with a two-year contract to write two musicals. Thanks to Jack Warner, who also signed Rodgers & Hart to a multi-picture deal, Herbert was reunited with his old team. The trio were delighted to be working together again, even if the story they were given—*The Hot Heiress*—was rather puerile. The pleasures of the collaboration ended up being the only satisfying part of their first sojourn in the film colony, though Hart adapted quickly to the social scene.

During pre-production for *The March of Time*, Weber & Fields met for several days with the director, production supervisor, additional writers, and endless executives to discuss the comedy routines and anecdotes to include in the script. Listing their best comedy bits, Weber & Fields named the broker's office and the poolroom scenes—surefire material to lead up to the Fallen Gladiators (living statues) as the wow finish. They ran through the routines once to demonstrate them, and the "picture people," as Fields called them, smiled politely and agreed to use them. Weber & Fields were certain that the Fallen Gladiators, which had sent two generations of theater audiences into hysterics, would be a panic. But they obviously did not understand the ways of Hollywood:

> The picture people wanted the gag done with every elaboration. Six plaster statues of the gladiators, costing $500 each, were ordered—and broken, in six different shots of the gag. By that time, we thought, it would be perfect. We went to see the rush prints. But nobody was in the projection room to show the rushes. There were no rushes to be shown.
>
> And when, fearful and trembling, we inquired, we were told that executives had seen the gag screened and promptly decreed: "Out. Nobody will laugh at that."
>
> Heartbreaking? No. You've got to get used to this sort of thing in Hollywood.[11]

Having spent almost four weeks rehearsing and shooting their familiar gags only to be told that they would be cut, they learned at the last minute that their big finale was to be something completely different. They were brought to a formerly empty lot in Culver City where they were dazzled to see a full-scale reproduction of the Weber & Fields Music Hall, complete with lampposts, hansom cabs, and trolley cars, show girls with trains, and top-hatted mashers. William Collier and Louis Mann were there in costume as well. Collier, suave and smiling, led them inside. Instead of the bandbox auditorium with the shallow stage, there was a spacious hall dominated by a horseshoe banquet table. The scene was to be a fantasy production number, staged by Broadway choreographer Sammy Lee: the old-timers sit at the table and watch misty-eyed while the parade of years—in the form of costumed chorus girls—passes before them. In the parade, amongst the girls, they would see themselves as well. It was not long before Collier announced that it was Weber & Fields' turn to join the March of Time. With their other scenes already cut from the script or left on the cutting-room floor, this was their biggest remaining moment. They did as they were asked, but they were understandably ambivalent, as an article they wrote for *Collier's* some months later revealed:

> Now you can understand what Hollywood can do to anybody when, in terms of 1930, a comedy team that panicked two generations can be persuaded to step out into routines with jazz show girls. . . .

> . . . On our last evening we strolled through a garden of glitter transformed from the dunes and flats of Culver City and we tried to find words to fit this scene of stupendous showmanship where money was water, and youth and beauty and talent were lavishly spent. It was almost painful to recall days when a brilliant performer like Elsie Janis would gladly accept a $5 for a concert appearance in our theater on Sunday afternoons and a great entertainer like George Cohan would work for $35 a week.

> . . . And that, ladies and gentlemen, is show business as we know it. We don't quite understand what it is now.[12]

The truth of their final statement would become painfully apparent to Fields in the year following his return to New York.

In April, Fields arrived in New York to find his beloved Broadway transformed by the aftereffects of the stock market crash. The gloom was pervasive. Of the eighteen theaters on Broadway between Forty-second and Fifty-third Streets, all but one were playing movies instead of legit theater; the one exception was the Palace, which scraped by with vaudeville. Travelling shows had practically vanished. A legit show was considered a hit if it lasted twelve weeks. Broadway hotels reported a seventy percent vacancy rate. By the end of the year, Actors' Equity announced that half its membership were unemployed. Where there had once been a handful of apple sellers in the entire city, *Variety* estimated that there were now over 4,500 of them. Quips and anecdotes took a decidedly darker turn: "Have you heard the one about the two men who jumped hand in hand, because they had a joint account?" Pawning was said to have become the national sport.

For Lew Fields, there were few offers. *March of Time* was supposed to be released later in the spring; perhaps it would spark some interest. Although he had some capital of his own, he knew that to try a legit production now was suicidal. Instead, he appeared as a solo performer in three Vitaphone shorts. At least one of them, *23 . . . Skidoo*, was obviously scripted by him, or by somebody who knew his work very well. In *23 . . . Skidoo*, Fields played Otto, manager of an 1890's beer garden, whose nagging *frau* fires all of his waiters. In their place, he is forced to hire and train a freakish assortment of new waiters. If the premise sounds familiar, it is because Fields was once again recycling familiar material, some of it over twenty years old: the waiter bits from *The Girl Behind the Counter*, lines from *The Hen Pecks* and *The Summer Widowers*. In between, Otto flirts with the waitress and tells her about the show he saw at Weber & Fields' Music Hall. In another short, *The Duel*, Fields gets mixed up with a jealous French husband and his wife, and is forced to fight on the field of honor with boxing gloves, pistols, and swords. Neither of these undistinguished efforts attracted much attention. At about the same time, he apparently made a third Vitaphone short called *Lew Fields' Road to Paradise*, of which nothing is known beyond the intriguing title.

Any hopes he had for a new career in Hollywood were dealt a serious blow when he learned that MGM was putting off the release of *The March of Time* indefinitely. Studio executives had decided that musical films—their major attractions during the previous year—were suddenly a glut on the market. The Depression had begun to affect Hollywood as well; production was shut down for days, sometimes weeks at a time. By the end of the summer, Warner's, MGM, and Paramount were frantically buying out the services of the show writers, composers, and performers they had seduced away from Broadway a year or two earlier. Herbert, Rodgers, and Hart found themselves back in New York in the fall of 1930 without an assignment. For the first time in five years, their phones were not ringing with new offers.

As for *The March of Time*, it remained unreleased; musical numbers were cannibalized for use in several short subjects and features. In 1933, MGM produced a movie revue called *Broadway to Hollywood*, featuring appearances by Jackie Cooper, Mickey Rooney, Frank Morgan, and Jimmy Durante. It included a few scenes from *The March of Time*, but no trace of Weber & Fields, except for a shot in which their names were visible on their dressing room door. According to the film's production book, Weber & Fields appeared incognito with William Collier and Barney Fagan as horses pulling a hansom cab.

Humbled and disappointed, Fields retreated to the family's summer home in Chappaqua to contemplate his future. Herbert had been the driving force behind the purchase of this rambling country estate, and it was his success (and Dorothy's, of late) that made it possible for the family to afford it. Now that the Fields children were coming into their own in the family business, Lew and Rose could live in the high style that had slipped away after the bankruptcy. The Chappaqua spread featured a manor house set off from the main road by gates, large gardens, livestock loose in the yard, horses in the stable, and a patio where Lew could lie in the sun. Herbert named the four horses after characters from his favorite Wagnerian operas. He had become a serious horseman, winning ribbons in several horse shows. With his sixteen-cylinder Cadillac parked in the circular driveway, the manor was the picture of gracious country living. The inside of the house was filled with English period furniture and knickknacks. It was a rare weekend when the Fields children did not bring a few of their show biz friends out from the city. In short, it was the perfect retirement home for a Bowery kid who had made good.

As the summer dragged on, Lew Fields became increasingly restless. The new Broadway season was rapidly approaching; like a migratory bird reacting to its seasonal imperative, Fields could not resist the urge to plan new productions. He talked with radio advertisers who were looking for stars to front weekly broadcasts. He met with Lyle Andrews, the owner of the Vanderbilt, who admitted that business at his house had slumped since *A Connecticut Yankee* ended its year-long run. Andrews was anxious to work with Fields again, but like most producers at the time, was strapped for cash. Why not make a virtue of necessity and stage an intimate revue at the Vanderbilt? The catch was finding the backing: the Shuberts would guarantee the Equity bond (which required no cash outlay) in return for a piece of the show. Though Fields probably had misgivings about the Shuberts' involvement, he knew that there were few other solvent backers left. The principal backer for *The Vanderbilt Revue* was, ironically enough, Abe Erlanger, the Shuberts' arch-enemy. Prior to the Crash, the Shuberts had insisted on producing their own shows, but extreme conditions called for extreme measures, and they saw the advantages of investing in other producer's shows and thereby limiting their own financial exposure. The arrangement may also have been part of short-lived scheme by the Shuberts and Erlanger to get a piece of the ticket brokers' action. They organized the Theater League, a group of New York theater owners who agreed to sell tickets only through a new agency, to be administered by the once-mighty Postal Telegraph Company.

Rehearsals for *The Vanderbilt Revue* did not begin until late September. Fields assembled a grab-bag of bright young sketch writers: Kenyon Nicholson, Sig Herzig, Ellis Jones, and Fields' other son, Joseph. Topping the long list of performers were several familiar names from previous Fields productions: Lulu McConnell, Franker Woods, Paul Everton, and Evelyn Hoey. For art's sake, he hired a Russian choir. As was typical of a Fields show, there was also the best new talent vaudeville had to offer: this time, a nut comedian named Joe Penner, whose catchphrase—"Wanna buy a duck?"—would soon make him a leading radio star of the 'thirties. Fields regulars Jack Haskell and Herbert Ward handled, respectively, the dance numbers and set design. The music was by Jacques Fray and Mario Braggiotti, with lyrics by E. Y. "Yip" Harburg, but Fields quickly saw a need for interpolations. Naturally, he turned to Dorothy and Jimmy McHugh, just back from Hollywood, where they had written ten songs for MGM. The dependable duo bolstered the score with a hit, "Blue Again," and a near-miss, "You're the Better Half of Me."

The original program consisted of twenty-two scenes, including a dozen or more sketches and a chorus of seventy-five—not by any means an "intimate" revue. Shaping and polishing an entertainment of this scale and diversity was a daunting task, and it would appear that Fields was simply not up to it. By the time *The Vanderbilt Revue* arrived at Lyle Andrews' theater on the evening of November 5, it had ballooned into thirty-six scenes. Quantity, however, could not make up for the uneven quality. The best that could be said about the program overall was that it was well-paced. The comedy-sketches—the glue that binds together an intimate revue, and usually Fields' forte—were disappointing, despite McConnell's and Penner's best efforts. The funniest ones were borrowed from other sources: McConnell and Penner played "A Quiet Game of Bridge," the same skit that McConnell had played in vaudeville with her husband Grant Simpson; another sketch borrowed shamelessly from a recent *Music Box Revue.* So many other performers walked on for brief bits and then departed, never to reappear, that one reviewer compared the show to a subway turnstile. Another critic pointed to the odd deployment of the Russian choir—sixteen harmonious men in a fina-letto singing gay madrigals of sunny Spain, while several costumed señoritas dance. In a sign of the times, several critics complained about a risqué song sketch about a gigolo, while *Variety*'s reviewer cited the fact that there was "no nudity and little spice" as a liability. Unjustly overlooked was a sketch called "Mickey the Mouse," a burlesque of the Disney cartoon with performers pantomiming to arti-ficial sound effects.

The show was a hodge-podge—a collection of oddments and remainders, Atkinson called it—lacking a consistent tone or idea. Once Lew Fields had been able to find ingenious ways to tie together a disparate collection of acts into a unified whole. But now, without the luxury of a strong book like the ones Herbert provided, the sheer variety of it overwhelmed him.

Whitney Bolton (the *Morning Telegraph*) was probably correct when he wrote, "I can't believe that either Mr. Fields or Mr. Andrews are satisfied with their show as it is." The problems in the front office, however, were even worse than those onstage. The Theater League ticket agency scheme had provoked a discounting war with the established ticket brokers. When Andrews tried to get the League to agree to reduced prices, they refused; he resigned, but after a meeting the Shuberts, he had to rejoin. Andrews told *Variety* that he would have been better off doing business with the regular brokers. Calling *The Vanderbilt Revue* "an-other victim of the League," he sadly informed Fields that he would have to close the show. It had lasted only fifteen performances, making it the biggest flop of Fields' career.

On November 18, 1930, when Lew Fields left the theater after the final per-formance of *The Vanderbilt Revue*, his career as a Broadway producer was effec-tively at an end. He had to face it: he no longer knew what the public wanted, and the business itself had changed in ways he could not understand. So when Herbert and Rodgers & Hart approached Fields with a promising new musical satire, *America's Sweetheart*, based on their experiences in Hollywood, he de-clined. What's more, according to Rodgers, Fields vowed never to do another Broadway musical. There would be no more comebacks.

If the likely end of his career was not upsetting enough, events in the month that followed struck at the very heart of his personal life. The final blow came, not from Broadway, but from Fifth Avenue by way of Wall Street. On the night of December 10, 1930, Bernard Marcus and nervous executives of the Bank of the United States met with the State Superintendent of Banks, working through the night at their main office on Fifth Avenue and Forty-fourth Street. At 4:00 a.m. the following morning, faced with the strong likelihood of a bank run as soon as doors opened for business, they agreed to place the bank's affairs in the hands of the State Banking Department. The Bank of the United States had gone bust.

Disturbing rumors about disappearing assets had been circulating for several days. By the dawn of December 11, throngs of worried depositors were already gathered at bank branches all over New York, milling about in the intermittent rain, reading and rereading the terse notice pasted on the front doors: "Bank Closed by Order of the New York State Banking Department." Many simply stood there in a state of shock, some cried, others pounded their fists in frustration on the cold wet walls. Police sent reinforcements for the guards who had been posted at the bank branches all night. Depositors from the more prosperous neighborhoods seemed to take the news philosophically. But in "the less favored parts of the city," as journalists called them, large crowds of bewildered depositors, many of them foreign-born and speaking little English, stood determinedly in the rain, disregarding the police requests to go home, hoping that they could find some way to get to their money.

When Joseph Marcus had founded the Bank of the United States in 1913, the hard-working immigrants of the Lower East Side had flocked to it on the strength of his reputation for integrity and prudence. The majority of its depositors were those who saved out a dollar or two a week from their wages, building savings at a painfully slow rate. For many of them, the collapse of the Bank of the United States meant the shattering of a lifelong dream after years of diligent scrimping.

They had trusted Joseph Marcus because he was one of their own. Like many of them, he had sacrificed so that his children could be properly educated, and then he had brought his sons into the family business he had started. Charles, the husband of Frances Fields, already had his law degree when his father made him first vice-president of the newly formed bank. His younger brother Bernard left Columbia Law School to work in the bank as a cashier, but he quickly rose through the ranks. Where Charles was steady and unimaginative, Bernie's aggressive, daring style was ideally suited to the unbounded optimism of the era. In the late 'teens, Bernie, in the words of a relative, "edged" his brother out; Charles started his own perfume-importing firm, which prospered throughout the decade. Bernie's success, however, made Charles look like a piker. When Bernie Marcus and family left for Europe each summer, he needed a specially built van to haul his thirty trunks and suitcases down to the pier. There they would board a luxury liner and stay in the most expensive cabins. Though he lived only a block away from the Fieldses, he had nothing but scorn for that family of "actors and drunks" that his brother had married into.

It was no coincidence that Bernie's fortune grew with the expansion of the Bank of the United States. In 1926, when he supplanted his aging father as the effective leader, the bank had six branches. Over the next three years, he engineered a series of whirlwind mergers with other banks, bringing the number of branches to fifty-nine and the total value of deposits to over $302 million. In July, 1927, Bernie officially took over as president of the bank, thereby becoming one of the youngest bank presidents in the country. Shortly after the second merger, he set up a securities and real estate subsidiary called the Bankus Corporation.

Using the bank deposits for speculation, Marcus and two of his partners entered the bull market in a big way. Instead of returning the profits to the depositors, they kept the profits—entirely legal in those days. Once they netted a cool million overnight by stock transfers.

State investigators knew as early as July of 1929 that the bank was being mismanaged, but they still gave the bank a clean bill of health. But when the stock market crash in October, 1929, wiped out the bank's paper gains, the shell game began in earnest. In a series of transactions that made Mike and Meyer's "Starting a Bank" routine seem straightforward, Bernie Marcus took eight million dollars' worth of deposits from his bank and replaced it with stock from subsidiary companies, to which he arbitrarily assigned the equivalent value. When the state authorities forced him to ante up, Marcus was negotiating yet another merger. Bank examiners soon discovered that in the three months prior to its closing, net deposits had shrunk by $42 million, with roughly half of it disappearing in the last four days. On the day before the bank closed, Marcus authorized a buying order for 20,000 units of Bank of the United States by the Bankus Corporation using certified checks signed by one of his vice-presidents.

It was the largest bank collapse on record. For the legit theater, it was a double whammy: Broadwayites and the garment industry were particularly well represented among its creditors. Wealthy "cloak-and-suiters" had played angel to many a Broadway show. William Klein, the Shuberts' attorney, acted on behalf of the garment manufacturers in their proceedings against the bank.

For Charles Marcus, the failure of his brother's bank was devastating, financially and emotionally. In the years immediately after his marriage to Frances ("the merger," her witty siblings had mockingly called it), he had helped his new father-in-law out of one financial scrape after another. By the time Lew Fields had declared bankruptcy in 1921, Charles had run out of sympathy, probably concluding that the actor had brought it on himself. For years after that, Charles had criticized his father-in-law for his gambling and the entire family for their spendthrift ways. When the Fieldses' various stage successes in the late 'twenties helped restore the family's financial stability, Charles browbeat them into doing something sensible with their money, like putting it into the Bank of the United States. He demonstrated his faith by investing heavily in the bank's securities and real estate activities. One by one, the Fieldses followed his lead, starting with Herbert.

Now Charles Lionel Marcus would pay for his hubris. He lost his business and brought ruin upon his wife and the kin whom he had patronized. Although there is no evidence that he had specific prior knowledge of Bernie's misdeeds, he blamed himself, and so did they. After the trauma of the bank failure came the public humiliation of a criminal trial that lasted for months. Bernard Marcus and three of his partners went to prison for seven years. Charles, according to his son, was irrevocably changed. He was not ennobled by his come-uppance but withdrew instead into bitterness and guilt. Frances, whose sheltered upbringing left her unprepared for a life without servants and ready cash, struggled to adjust. They moved from their luxurious apartment on the corner of Broadway and Eighty-ninth to a dreary suburb where, in their son's words, they had to learn to live like everybody else.

With the failure of *The Vanderbilt Revue* and the Bank of the United States, Lew Fields had come full circle in the 'twenties. Ten years earlier, he had begun the long, slow climb back from bankruptcy and professional oblivion by returning to vaudeville. Too old now for the rigors of a tour, he turned to radio. Every Monday night from October 1930 through May 1931, he reunited with Joe Weber on station WOR, "brought to you by the Webster Cigar Company, makers of the cigar for champagne tastes and beer pocketbooks."

When all else failed, there was always Mike and Meyer. For the first time in over fifteen years, Weber & Fields worked up some new routines, interweaving their old familiar gags with topical material. Sometimes the topics were painfully close to home. Within a month or so of the collapse of the Bank of the United States, Mike and Meyer were discussing Wall Street on the air:

> MEYER: . . . Don't you remember the machine made a noise like Tsk! Tsk! and pushed out paper with numbers on it? Well, *that* was a stock.
>
> MIKE: Oh, you mean a stock tickler. . . . I thought they was just to get paper from to throw out the window when there's a parade.
>
> MEYER: Now suppose I'm a broker—
>
> MIKE: You ain't no broker than I am.
>
> MEYER: Did I say I was? I'm a Wall Street broker.
>
> MIKE: In Wall Street are they more broker than on other streets?
>
> MEYER: You should only know!

What use was the pain if you could not wring a good laugh from it?

The weekly performances provided him with some measure of financial and psychological relief. But this time what saved his family from financial ruin was the success of his children in the business he had discouraged them from entering. The year 1930 had been a good year for Dorothy: in addition to her contract with MGM, she and Jimmy McHugh had written two more huge hits, "On the Sunny Side of the Street" and "Exactly Like You," whose residuals soon took the sting out of the bank failure. And three nights before the Bank of the United States collapsed, Lew and Rose had attended the opening of Herbert's new musical with Cole Porter, *The New Yorkers.* Subtitled "a sociological musical satire," the Fields-Porter vision of giddy, gilded Gotham distracted care-worn theatergoers through five long months of the Depression. Hard times kept the show from getting the long run it deserved. But *The New Yorkers* and other exceptional shows in the coming year—*The Band Wagon* and *Of Thee I Sing*—should have reassured Lew Fields that all his efforts to develop the Broadway musical had not been in vain.

From the Bowery, to Broadway, to Beverly Hills

> . . . If I never have a cent,
> I'll be rich as Rockefeller.
> Gold dust at my feet
> On the sunny side of the street. . . .
> Dorothy Fields, 1930

FEW of those most directly responsible for the growth of vaudeville in the 1890's were still active in the business when it went bust forty years later. Along with Joe Weber and Lew Fields, Ed Albee had the dubious honor of becoming obsolete with the institution he helped create.

Edward F. Albee, overlord of vaudeville, was a rich and bitter man when he died in March, 1930. Rich, in part, because he had sold 200,000 shares of stock in the newly formed Keith-Albee-Orpheum Circuit (K-A-O) at above-market price to Joseph P. Kennedy. Bitter, because he had been outfoxed by his intended "mark": Kennedy, who already owned the Film Booking Office (FBO) and had the backing of RCA, used his stake in K-A-O to oust Albee ignominiously from the empire he had created.

Kennedy had little interest in vaudeville. In one shrewd move, he had acquired enough theaters to guarantee the dominance of the RCA Photophone sound-on-film system and an outlet for FBO movies. He quickly unloaded his stock in K-A-O to RCA. In front of the Palace in New York, workmen lowered the old Keith-Albee marquee and replaced it with one bearing the initials "RKO," for Radio Keith Orpheum. In forced retirement in Palm Beach, Florida, Albee lingered just long enough to see his name returned to obscurity and his step-child, vaudeville, in decline.

Lew Fields' acquaintance with Albee reached back almost half a century to the days when vaudeville was still called variety and Weber & Fields were happy to be earning forty dollars a week. Lean, steel-eyed "Ned" Albee had been the ballyhooer at Keith & Batchelder's Dime Museum in Boston when Weber & Fields first appeared there in the early 1880's. There was no love lost between Fields and Albee, but Albee's passing and the crumbling of the once-mighty Keith-Orpheum Circuit were potent symbols, nonetheless.

Vaudeville's demise followed closely on Albee's heels. By November, 1929, there were only four straight vaudeville houses left in the country: the Palace and the Riverside in New York, the Palace in Chicago, and the Orpheum in Los Angeles. Straight vaude could not compete with the combination houses, which offered one hour of live entertainment in addition to a feature film—all for half the price of a ticket to the Palace. At the same time, vaudeville's biggest headliners—Will Rogers, Eddie Cantor, Lou Holtz, Fanny Brice—were being lured away by musical comedy, talkies, and radio.

As the Great Depression took hold and left almost one quarter of the country's workers unemployed, many theaters resorted to a straight film policy of double features. Among vaudevillians, the unemployment rate was more like seventy-five percent and climbing. For Lew Fields, it was clear that the big-time two-a-day was no longer the meal ticket it once had been when times were lean on Broadway.

It was on Friday the thirteenth, a gloomy May evening in 1932, that the Palace Theatre in New York played its last two-a-day, reserved-seat program. Novelist Sarah Addington likened it to a wake, and a poorly attended one at that: "The corpse is vaudeville . . . and another ghost walks the American scene."[1] The following day, the Palace went to a continuous schedule that included movies. Business picked up.

Weber & Fields had been so instrumental in vaudeville's rise that it was only fitting that they should take their farewell bows just before the curtain finally came down. To prepare for their final appearance at the Palace, Weber & Fields played a series of week-long engagements in selected Eastern cities. By the time they reached the Palace in mid March, they had perfected their nostalgia-inducing patter. Headlining with Paul Whiteman and his twenty-five-piece orchestra, singer Russ Columbo, and emcee Jay C. Flippen, Weber & Fields were greeted with a long salvo of applause. They did their poolroom skit and—reaching back still farther—the song and dance they used to do in the Bowery museums. And in a good-natured demonstration that there was nothing new beneath the sun, they showed how the Eddie Cantor–George Jessel "Pal" act (a recent hit at the Palace) fit neatly in the Mike and Meyer tradition, using it as a build-up for their announcement that they had been together for fifty years. Then, as they finished their turn, the sixty-five-year-old Fields did a pair of handsprings.

In addition to the master of ceremonies, the bill also included a troupe of midgets, and the following week, a pair of foot-balancers—more echoes of the old dime-museum variety shows. The Palace held over Weber & Fields for a second week, and the duo substituted their poker act for the poolroom skit. For the first time, however, reviewers committed to print what many had been saying in private for years:

> To many the appearance of Weber & Fields on the Palace Stage during the current week was a pitiful sight. Weber & Fields' comedy is long outmoded. . . .

> It would have been better for the younger generation to have heard tales about Weber & Fields as great comedians than to have had the opportunity of seeing them as they are today. Sir Herbert Beerbohm Tree expressed it perfectly when he said, on retiring from the stage, "Better an hour too soon than a minute too late."[2]

Three months after the Palace went to a continuous schedule, the dailies and trades were full of announcements for Weber & Fields' Golden Jubilee Dinner, to be held at the Hotel Astor on September 25. The Jubilee was to be a public celebration of Weber & Fields' fiftieth anniversary as a team. Lew Fields was finally ready to submit to the rites and ceremonies that would signal his retirement to all.

No intimate send-off or sedate little soirée would do. As it had been so often in their Music Hall, an evening with Weber & Fields was once again the pretext for bringing together an unusually broad cross-section of New York society. The Honorary Committee hosting the festivities included Governor Franklin Roosevelt, Irving Berlin, William Morris, Colonel Jacob Ruppert, Will Rogers, Lee Shubert, Douglas Fairbanks, Rabbi Stephen S. Wise, and Adolph Zukor. Invitations in their names went out to twelve hundred people prominent in show business, sports, commerce, and politics.

The publicity intensified in the month before the big event: several of the New York dailies ran interviews and profiles of the duo's joint careers, with Fields' solo career as an actor and producer getting short shrift. Ace reporter A. J. Liebling, not yet in his prime, wrote a long retrospective, "Fifty Years of Fun-Making," for the *New York World-Telegram*. Liebling called his five-part series "a picaresque" and made no effort to distinguish between historical fact and the yarns recounted by Isman in the *Saturday Evening Post* article in 1924. Interviewing the sparrowlike, pugnacious Joe Weber, who could still deliver volleys of streetwise quips while gesticulating in his shirt-sleeves and chain-smoking Turkish cigarettes, Liebling found a spiritual granddaddy for the "characters" he later specialized in depicting, the kind of New York entrepreneur "who knows how to get a dollar and the rest haven't got what to eat." Fields was perhaps less interesting in this regard; more reserved and polished in his speech, tastefully attired in a double-breasted suit, he may have seemed too respectable. Together, the two old comedians were a fascinatingly odd couple; Liebling enshrined them in the Astor's Hunting Room, "where they have met for luncheon almost every day for twenty-five years"—a gross but endearing exaggeration. Through the Hunting Room's windows, wrote Liebling, Weber & Fields could look down upon the new Broadway, where crowds hurried to moviehouses instead of plays, "lapping up cocoanut milk and near beer, buying pirated songs, dashing between the wheels of taxicabs."

Ironically, the "new" Broadway, having been mugged by the Great Depression, looked like the old Bowery of Weber & Fields' youth, especially at night. Hard times made the posters gaudier, the lights more glaring, and the burley-cue barkers more insistent in their pitches. By 1932, there were three burlesque shows on Forty-second Street and several more on Broadway. A genuine freak show—Huber's Museum—had also made Forty-second Street its new home. Penny-a-dance ballrooms opened, and Chinese restaurants proliferated. Despite Prohibition, liquor was available for the asking, for regulars at tony restaurants or from the corner newsstand or candy store. Prostitutes cruised the sidewalks of the Main Stem, jauntily swinging their handbags. Child panhandlers pestered customers, while their older brothers charged a fee to watch your car, or stuck an ice-pick in the tire if you rejected their services.[3] Neighborhood property owners joined with city officials in a cleanup of the theater district, arresting unlicensed street hawkers and targeting burlesque houses for vice squad raids. In the same *New York Times* editorial that mentioned Weber & Fields' Golden Jubilee, the editors wrote of the need "to rescue the Broadway and Forty-second Street region from the frowsy and noisome cohorts that threatened to submerge it." For ex–Bowery boys like Weber & Fields, the view from the Hunter's Room at the Astor must have seemed eerily similar to the old panorama from the poolroom of Miner's saloon.

Other ceremonies in advance of the Jubilee emphasized the extent to which Weber & Fields had achieved the social legitimacy that they had craved. In a ceremony at the Hotel Astor, they presented eleven albums of theatrical photographs (mostly from their Music Hall productions) to the New York Public Library. On September 16, representatives of the Jewish, Episcopalian, and Catholic Actors' Guilds gathered at an uptown synagogue to honor the old partners. The eulogies praised their exemplary family relations and "the beauty of the home life of stage folk." On behalf of the Catholic Actors' Guild, Gerald Griffen said that the accusation "that theatrical people are without morals is a libel upon the profession." Rabbi Tintner used the occasion to point out that there was "no kind of endeavor in which the Jew has not excelled," and he reminded his listeners that "the men of the stage are just as important as other walks of life."[4] Fields, for one, found this very gratifying to hear.

On the evening of September 25, 1932, Joe Weber and Lew Fields mounted the dais of the Hotel Astor's grand ballroom to the applause of the 1,200 well-connected well-wishers who had assembled to celebrate the Golden Jubilee. For weeks, Fields had been dreading the symbolic finality of the event. Now, as he somewhat sheepishly acknowledged his peers' unqualified approval, the dread turned to delight. Mayor McKee, making his first official appearance since Jimmy Walker had resigned in disgrace, offered his congratulations to Joe and Lew in a brief whispered conversation and then took his seat at an inconspicuous table far from the dais. Toastmaster William Collier ad-libbed his way through a slate of illustrious speakers that included Daniel Frohman, Gene Buck, William Brady, Representative Sol Bloom, Harry Herschfield, and S. L. "Roxy" Rothafel. In glowing words and humorous anecdotes, the speakers recalled the happy family of the Weberfields. Roxy mentioned that he intended to dedicate a reception lounge in his new Radio City Music Hall in honor of Weber & Fields. Collier read congratulatory telegrams from Governor Roosevelt, Fay Templeton, and President Hoover.

Two burly waiters carried in a huge birthday cake ornamented with fifty candles and placed it in front of Weber & Fields. Collier presented each of the guests of honor with a large gold loving cup. When it came time for Joe and Lew to say a few words, they were too overwhelmed to speak as themselves. They took refuge behind their comic masks and once more gave the audience what it wanted, thanking them in the manner of Mike and Meyer. Fields began, "Not that we was together fifty years yet, it was fifty-six. But we never had it a golden jubilee. Und whatever it is coming to us, we want it." Eddie Dowling emcee'd the evening's entertainment, which was broadcast on WOR Radio. Gus Edwards' juvenile actors impersonated the old Music Hall stars, followed by adult entertainers such as Sophie Tucker, Cissie Loftus, Blanche Ring, and Lou Holtz.

Fields' pensive demeanor on the way home from the Jubilee was in marked contrast to his animated performance at the Hotel Astor. As he slumped in the back seat of his car with Rose beside him, the dread came creeping back. After fifty-six years as an entertainer, it could not have been easy to accept that he had taken his final bow.

Roxy's Radio City Music Hall was variously described as "vast," "mammoth," and "sybaritic," a showcase for superlatives rather than talent: the world's largest and costliest playhouse, the tallest chandelier, the biggest mural, the widest and tallest and deepest stage. The stage alone was 144 feet wide and 80 feet deep, big enough to hold an S.R.O. audience at the old Weber & Fields Music Hall with room to spare. The shimmering contour curtain elevated in flexible folds powered by thirteen motors. The interior design was inspired by Roxy's vision: dawn at sea, as seen from the prow of a ship. The semicircular proscenium arch reinforced the rising-sun motif, with steadily enlarging semicircles repeated along the walls and ceiling, intersected by "rays" formed by fluted bands emanating from the proscenium. Although Roxy conceived of it as the ultimate vaudeville palace, its overwhelming scale and dazzling decor upstaged most human entertainments, except for the most garish extravaganzas.

By 6:30 in the evening on December 27, the sidewalks outside the Radio City box office were a mob scene. All 6,200 of the tickets had long since been accounted for by VIP's and celebrities. Only a cold and steady rain, and 700 extra policemen, kept the crowds from getting out of hand. Ushers held umbrellas for the parties of arriving notables—John D. Rockefeller, Jr.; his dashing son, Nelson; Alfred Smith; Gene Tunney; Leopold Stokowski; David Sarnoff; Irving and Ellin Berlin; Amelia Earhart—while a radio reporter pestered them to say a few words into the mike. To give them time to admire their surroundings, Roxy delayed the curtain for half an hour.

Recalling the days when variety was played in the gas-lit basements of Bowery dime museums, Lew Fields never believed he would see the day when a Rockefeller would build a music hall, or when its opening was national news. But then Radio City Music Hall was as far removed from Weber & Fields' Broadway Music Hall as the latter was from the Bowery dime museums. Awed by the edifice and honored to be a part of the event, Fields was still too much the old-time showman not to be dubious about Roxy's approach to programming. The opening-night program was Roxy's first not to include a motion picture, and his lack of understanding of the composition and rhythms of a variety show became painfully obvious. "Variety" to Roxy meant, not only acrobats, hoofers, ethnic comedians, jazz bands, and comic sketches, but also classical ballet, modern dance, symphonic music, choirs, *son et lumière* scenes, and opera. The Radio City bill ran the gamut, from dancing comedian Ray Bolger, to excerpts from *Carmen;* the Flying Wallendas, to Martha Graham; Dr. Rockwell, to a Berlin opera diva; minstrelsy, to the Tuskegee Choir—"something for everybody," *Variety*'s reviewer complained, "and therefore nothing much for anybody." Roxy's attempt to elevate vaudeville to the status of other high-brow art forms may well have been the final nail in its coffin as a vital cultural expression.

Weber & Fields were to be part of the minstrel show afterpiece that Roxy intended as the heartwarming finale to the evening. Fields waited backstage as the program crept on, increasingly nervous—not for himself, but for another performer on the bill. His daughter Dorothy and her songwriting partner Jimmy McHugh contributed two numbers to the program, "With a Feather in Your Cap" and "Hey! Young Fella" ("better close your old umbrella"). The former was a production number featuring the Roxyettes (forty-eight of 'em), choreographed by Russell Markert. The latter was a nightclub sketch that included Ray Bolger, the Berry Brothers, Jimmy McHugh at the piano, and Dorothy Fields singing her own lyrics. The last time she had performed publicly was in an amateur production at the Benjamin School nine years earlier. With remarkable poise, she stepped up to the mike on the world's largest stage to sing her own lyrics to 6,200 bigwigs. According to *Variety*, Fields and McHugh "managed a lot better than others on this bill who do nothing else but appear on stages." Why she did at Radio City Music Hall, nobody knows; perhaps it was to prove something to her parents, who had discouraged her from becoming a performer. Henceforth, she and McHugh confined their performances to occasional radio broadcasts.

After waiting backstage for almost five hours, Weber & Fields finally had a chance to do their turn. It was half past midnight, and almost half of the crowd (and all of the newspaper critics) had already left. Those who remained did so to see Weber & Fields and De Wolf Hopper, but the old-timers' appearance seemed like an afterthought. One last time, the beloved duo of Weber & Fields were the designated ambassadors of good times past, the show biz patriarchs giving their blessings to the new enterprise. Hopper, spry and stately, introduced Weber & Fields, who took their seats in the minstrel show as the end men Tambo & Bones. With Hopper as the interlocuter and the entire cast assembled in tiers around them, Weber & Fields traded crossfire banter, did some light choking, and reminisced. From most seats except the very front rows, the audience had a distant view of two frail and wizened old clowns, lost in the vastness of what their music hall had become. They ended with an awkward salute to the modern music hall. Roxy entered from the wings and hugged them heartily, then began his speech. Joe Weber and Lew Fields stepped aside and were lost from view in the mass of robust young performers.

Fields appeared on stage once more, solo, in a straight drama. It was a lark: a summer theater in Pelham Manor, not far from his Chappaqua home, was staging *Broomsticks, Amen*, about the rather unlikely topic of witchcraft in Pennsylvania Dutch country. Playing Emil Hofnagel, the hex doctor, was an opportunity for Fields to show off his legit abilities one last time, even if it was in a dialect role. (He probably did not recall his comments about summer stock, many years earlier, when his son Herbert had asked about pursuing an acting career: "Stock is a place where a great many bad actors go before they die.") According to one reviewer, Fields' performance was one of the "discoveries" of the summer. To the very end, he still managed to surprise with how good a serious actor he was.

Lew Fields' waning years were spent as far away from the Bowery—socially and geographically—as one could go and still be in the continental United States. Beverly Hills in the mid-1930's was the fastest-growing community in the country, a creation of real estate speculators and the motion picture industry. With 25,000 residents (most in the top one percent of incomes) and a new house being completed almost every day, Beverly Hills had a boomtown sensibility. Living in this oasis of mansions and palm-shaded swimming pools, it was easy to forget about the grim realities of the Depression that gripped the rest of the country. Cemeteries were outlawed within city limits, and police routinely stopped outsiders, fingerprinting salesmen and any others who looked as if they did not belong.

By the mid-'thirties, Dorothy and Herbert Fields most definitely belonged. With their big studio contracts, extravagant spending habits, and youthful self-confidence, they fit right in with the rest of the chic New York and European-born talent who came west to grow fat at the Hollywood teat: Jerome Kern, Rodgers & Hart, the Gershwins, Fanny Brice, Ernst Lubitsch, Rouben Mamoulian, the Marx Brothers, and many others. In 1932, while Dorothy was working with McHugh at MGM and Herbert was under contract to Warner's, they rented the first of four lavish Beverly Hills mansions. Their older brother Joe moved in with them; Joe had come to Hollywood as a $300-a-week writer of "B" pictures for Republic, his fortune from the perfume business lost in the crash of the Bank of the United States. For a time, he was jokingly referred to as "the family failure," a cruel reminder that a few years earlier he had been the family's most conspicuous financial success.

Dorothy, Herbert, and Joe continued their New York custom of round-the-clock "open house" for their show-biz colleagues. The rented splendor always included a piano or two, a swimming pool, and spacious veranda with a wet bar. Herb mixed generous drinks at the bar, while Dorothy played gracious hostess, attired in the latest swimwear. Joe, despite his sorrowful countenance, could make the dullest gin game hilarious. He had inherited his father's gift for telling stories, and he could sketch a cutting caricature. Their lively intermixing of their professional and personal lives was the exact opposite of their famous father's, who had felt compelled to protect the sanctity of his family from the profane influences of the stage profession. So much about show biz had changed: now, when Pop Fields visited his children in Beverly Hills, he could preside serenely over their social gatherings from his favorite deck chair, sunning himself and enjoying the endless parade of talent and beauty.

With the Fields children spending an increasing amount of time in California, Lew and Rose found their Chappaqua estate too big and lonely. The enforced idleness seemed to accelerate Lew's aging: he now had a persistent cough—not surprising, since he was still smoking two packs a day—and he complained of being tired. He caught colds frequently, and in early 1934 one of these developed into pneumonia. Recovery took months; though Fields insisted that he was healthy, he had to postpone an audition at NBC Radio and the offer was ultimately dropped. Those closest to him noticed that he seemed to be moving a little slower and that he had acquired a slight stoop.

More out of habit than necessity, Fields maintained an office on Broadway with a secretary, hoping to keep open the possibilities of new offers to perform or produce. The office became just a stopping point on his way to lunch with Weber at the Hotel Astor. Lew and Rose went to see the new musicals, usually refusing the "comp" tickets, because Lew believed it was impossible to judge a show fairly when you got in for free. He consoled Herbert over the failure of *Pardon My English* (1993), which flopped resoundingly despite the Gershwins' fine score. The flop was all that was needed to send the sensitive and undisciplined Herbert back to the easy lifestyle and relatively undemanding chores of a Hollywood contract writer. Herbert tried to persuade his parents to join the rest of the family in Beverly Hills. The cost of supporting the Fieldses' bicoastal residences had become staggering. Besides, Herb reasoned, Pop would have no trouble landing a few movie assignments once he relocated. After all, look at what had happened to old-timers like Marie Dressler, Fred Stone, and George Arliss.

In the end, it was this lingering hope for work, as much as the need to be with family, that lured Fields away from his beloved New York. When Lew and Rose finally left Chappaqua for California in the spring of 1936, they arranged to auction off nonessential furniture and decades' worth of "objets d'art" rather than pay to have them moved. Many of the artifacts had sentimental value: the keys to the cities of St. Louis and Milwaukee, and the trophy cup for the winners of the weekly tennis matches between Fields, Marcus Loew, Adolph Zukor, and Sam Bernard before the war. Statuettes of Don Quixote and Mephistopheles and a quarter slot machine—badly dented, apparently by an angry loser—also went under the hammer.

Lew and Rose Fields moved into the mansion on Rodeo Drive that Herb and Dorothy had rented, bringing with them the imposing English dark-wood dining room furniture, with its long table and scrolled legs and the straight-backed overstuffed chairs. The perpetual open house continued, but Rose reinstituted the family ritual of Sunday dinners. It was the one time in the week when the whole family could count on being together to catch up on their latest activities. In Beverly Hills, the Sunday gatherings took on increasing importance for Lew. Now that his own career was clearly over, he lived vicariously through the professional success of his children. And, not coincidentally, the child who thrilled him the most was the one he had done the most to discourage.

Dorothy's star at MGM had been steadily rising since her arrival in Hollywood in 1930. With Jimmy McHugh, she continued to craft hit songs: "Cuban Love Song" (from the film of the same name), "Don't Blame Me" (from *Dinner at Eight*), "I'm in the Mood for Love" and "I Feel a Song Comin' On" (from *Every Night at Eight*). On loan to RKO, in 1935 she worked for the first time with a partner other than McHugh—the veteran Broadway composer Jerome Kern, in Hollywood to adapt his stage hit *Roberta* for Fred Astaire and Ginger Rogers. Her deft lyrics for "Lovely to Look At"—a tricky sixteen-bar melody—convinced Kern that she should be the lyricist for his next RKO assignment, an original musical for Astaire and Rogers. The Kern-Fields score for *Swingtime* (1936) not only yielded six hit songs, but was arguably the most thoroughly integrated score for any Hollywood musical to date. One of the songs came together in the Fields' home; Kern was struggling at the piano with the syncopated melody for "Bojangles of Harlem" (an *hommage* to Bill Robinson), and Astaire came over and danced around the room—on the hardwood and red tile floors, up and down the staircase—providing inspiration until Kern had a breakthrough. While Dorothy polished her lyrics, her father dozed by the pool in his favorite lounge chair, oblivious to the commotion of geniuses at work nearby. Pop Fields was wide awake and beaming, however, when "The Way You Look Tonight" received an Oscar for best song. "Your lyrics are great, funny stuff," he wrote in a letter to Dorothy a few months later. "I'm just coo-coo about them. . . ." Eleven years earlier, Lew had ordered a music publisher to throw Dorothy out of his office waiting room.

In the film collaboration of Kern and Dorothy Fields, Lew Fields saw the culmination of three generations of musical theater (Lew was eighteen years older than Kern, who was nineteen years older than Dorothy). It was Fields who had bought one of Kern's earliest efforts for the Weber & Fields production of *An English Daisy* (1904). The Kern-Bolton-Wodehouse musicals for the Princess Theatre had been a reaction against Fields' oversized Broadway Theater musical spectacles; the Princess musicals then became the aesthetic model for the next generation of writers and composers, including the Gershwins, Rodgers & Hart, and Dorothy and Herbert Fields. Working with Herbert, Rodgers, and Hart in the 1920's, Fields openly acknowledged the influence of the Princess musicals and augmented it with his own flair for social burlesque and dynamic staging. Now, with their collaboration on *Swing Time*, Kern and Dorothy had created an original Hollywood score that was as well integrated with the plot as those of the best Broadway musicals. The "coherency" that Fields had prescribed for the Broadway musical in 1904 had found its way into a new medium.

In addition to paying the rent, buying the cars (there were always at least four), and hiring the servants, the younger Fieldses also provided their parents with a modest allowance. There was rarely any food in the house; they called the market on a meal-to-meal basis and had whatever they needed delivered. They indulged their father's expensive tastes in clothes, and on occasion, his yen for betting on the horses. During the week, old friends like Willie Collier and Adolph Zukor (who griped about the state of the movie business compared to the early days) came over for cards; the men played poker and pinochle while the women played bridge.

Although Lew and Rose rarely went anywhere together in public, Lew felt the need to keep up appearances. His grandson Ray Marcus recalls going to lunch with Fields at the Brown Derby and the customers applauding as the old man was shown to his usual table. At boxing matches, Fields' presence was announced along with the names of other celebrities in attendance. The guests who came to the house—even notables like Jerry Kern, Fred Astaire, and Cole Porter—always showed the utmost respect for Lew, addressing him as "Mr. Fields." Within show business circles, he still inspired the respect accorded a legend. "I never conquered my awe of him," Helen Hayes remarked. It was not until she visited him in Beverly Hills in the mid-1930's and saw him with his children around him that he became "a real person" for her. "As I remembered him, the theatre was his only world and I couldn't believe that he ate, slept, and had a family."[5]

Retired from the stage, the father who had always been larger than life and remote had become stooped and cozy, a family man cared for by Rose and supported by Dorothy and Herbert.

Six months after Lew and Rose Fields moved to Los Angeles, Joe and Lillian
Weber followed. The reason given was to make it easier for Weber & Fields to
take advantage of film offers; few of these "offers" ever materialized. The more
convincing reason was a lifelong friendship renewed by the emotional needs of
retirement and advancing age. The show business they had helped build, together
and separately, had passed them by; what else was there to do but to bask in the
shared memories? Once a month, the old partners attended the Friars' Club and
Masquers' Club meetings, spending an evening trading speeches, quips, and anecdotes with many of the other old-time theater folk and performers who had
retired to Southern California. Every few weeks, a small group consisting of Fields,
Weber, ex-vaudevillian Charlie Evans, and ex-legit actor George Arliss would meet
at Evans' home to reminisce, sing the old songs, try out the old comedy and
dance routines. Evans' cousin, a young girl then, would sometimes be allowed to
eavesdrop on the group; she later remarked how happy—and somehow younger—
they seemed to be when together.

In the fall of 1936, Weber & Fields were asked to participate in a Federal
Theater project reviving popular stage shows from the late nineteenth century.
They were joined by old colleagues such as Marie Dressler, Willie Collier, and
Frankie Bailey (now working in a candy store). The show lasted two weeks,
during which Weber & Fields re-enacted several of their classic routines, including the poolroom and poker game. Fields later admitted that rehearsing with
Weber was more fun than the show itself. So it was that at the end of their
careers, as at the very beginning, the deepest satisfaction was in the unscripted
give-and-take of their friendship rather than in the thrill of performing.

Still, Fields would not let go of the notion that there was a place for him and
his partner in the movies. Since their first short films for Kinemacolor in 1914,
Weber & Fields' film appearances were the most conspicuous disappointment of
their long careers. (George M. Cohan's films were similarly disappointing.) Partly,
it was a matter of bad timing: the synchronous sound film—so essential for cap-
turing the pair's knockabout-dialect style—came into being after Weber & Fields
were past their prime physically and during a period when Fields' primary interest was producing Broadway musicals. Their high hopes for *The March of Time*,
their feature debut for MGM in 1930, had been dashed when the film was held up
and not released until 1933, as *From Broadway to Hollywood*, and Weber & Fields'
scenes were left on the cutting-room floor.

The much-anticipated repeal of Prohibition in 1933 proved to be a good pretext for comedy, as thirsty patrons and eager purveyors tried to get a head start.
With the return of beer came all its former associations—beer gardens, brewer-
ies, and cranky German *biermeisters*. MGM teamed motormouth Jimmy Durante
with the fading Buster Keaton for *What! No Beer?* about two would-be beer barons. Almost simultaneously, an obscure company called Standard Motion Pictures sought to revive the Weber & Fields Dutch dialect act. Originally called *Beer
Wins, Beer Is Here* was the first release from Standard, a forty-minute short with

a script by Harold McCracken and Sig Herzig and directed by H. H. Rogers. Weber and Fields played feuding ex-partners in a brewery–beer garden, fallen on hard times due to Prohibition. Repeal meant a return to a prosperous partnership, except that their children had just eloped. It was basically the same plot as their 1915 film for Lewis Selznick, changing the grocery to a brewery. In *Beer Is Here*, Weber looked so frail that the mere threat of knockabout mayhem seemed painful, and Fields seemed to be sleepwalking, lacking his customary energy (he was reportedly in poor health during the filming). The performances were so uncharacteristically poor that at least one film historian concluded that the leading roles were actually played by a team of Weber & Fields imitators.

Late in 1935, shortly after his daughter began working with Jerome Kern at RKO, Fields was offered the featured role in an RKO comedy short. "A Wedtime Story" was the fourth in RKO's Headliner series of "theater add-ons." Fields played Herman Schmidt, complete with German accent, who wins $5,000 when he writes the best entry about how to be happy and married. Shortly before the check is delivered, the Schmidts' know-it-all lawyer son discovers an arcane statute that invalidates his parents' marriage and therefore makes Herman ineligible for the cash prize. Complications develop around a persistent salesman, reporters, and police, until another lawyer straightens out young Schmidt's misreading of the law. "A Wedtime Story" opened at the Palace in New York, once the crowning jewel of big-time vaudeville. Reviews complimented the gentle humor of Fields' characterization. *Variety*'s reviewer speculated about the short's prime audience, saying that it was good for any program, "but particularly strong for Jewish neighborhoods." The distinctions between the "Dutch" and Jewish brands of ethnic humor had long since been blurred.

The sad fact was that the comedy style of Weber & Fields had become so dated that finding a place for them in a contemporary film plot was next to impossible. B. P. Schulberg at Paramount thought he had a vehicle, a musical using Broadway, Park Avenue, and other New York locales. Initially called *Park Avenue Follies*, it starred Edward Arnold as a confidence man who lures a young farm girl to New York City with promises of a stage career. Frank Loesser, Leo Robin, and Ralph Freed wrote the songs. Weber & Fields donned their old music hall garb for some feeble and familiar routines, then assumed the guises of two opera impresarios for the finale, an opera performance gone ragtime, with the actors and audience swinging the music and truckin' on stage. In this sequence, Weber & Fields were seen to their best advantage yet in a film. Nevertheless, the film—released as *Blossoms on Broadway*—was a flop, dismissed as "definitely grade B quality."

The only screen roles that could fit Weber & Fields were Weber & Fields, so the films had to be period pieces or film biographies. The latter seemed the best bet: in the late 1930's, Hollywood turned to a subcategory of the "biopic" genre—the show-biz biography—as the latest gimmick for presenting musical entertainments on film. Following the success of *The Great Ziegfeld* (1936), the studios frantically began developing biopics about the stage stars of yore: Cohan, Lillian Russell, Vernon and Irene Castle, Will Rogers, Nora Bayes and Jack Norworth, Al Jolson, minstrel man Dan Emmet, Oscar Hammerstein I, Marilyn Miller, songwriter Paul Dresser, Texas Guinan, even *Variety* founder Sime Silverman. Some were not so bygone: Jerome Kern, Rodgers & Hart, Eddie Cantor, Gus Kahn. Why not a biopic about Weber & Fields?

Early in 1937, Weber met with executives at RKO, who were cool to the idea. At MGM, Weber reportedly met with a warmer reception; according to *Variety*, Russell Crouse wrote the script, entitled *Music Hall Days*. Research has turned up no evidence of the script or any deal at MGM. Joe Fields' widow, Marion, recalled that Joe had done a script on Weber & Fields and that Sigmund Romberg had composed a score, but this has not been substantiated, either. With so many of his show biz colleagues becoming enshrined in celluloid, Lew Fields was hurt and disappointed that nobody wanted to make the Weber & Fields story.

Instead, he had to be satisfied doing cameo roles in biopics about colleagues, or in the case of his next film, a performer he had discovered and mentored. Near the end of 1938, RKO was looking for new stories that would feature the talents of Fred Astaire and Ginger Rogers. To this end, they purchased the rights to *Castles in the Air*, Irene Castle's memoir of her life with Vernon. As with the previous Astaire-Rogers vehicles, Hermes Pan choreographed the dances. Richard Sherman, Oscar Hammerstein, and Dorothy Yost shared screenplay credits. In *The Story of Vernon and Irene Castle*, Lew Fields was cast as himself, thirty years younger. The illusion was not helped by the makeup department, who planted a brunette wig on his head that made him look like an aging *roué*.

The adaptation begins with Vernon Castle's days as a supporting comedian in Lew Fields' *The Hen Pecks*. Castle is content to play second banana until he meets Irene Foote of New Rochelle. She is an aspiring performer, too, but she recognizes his true talent as a dancer and rescues him from vaudeville buffoonery. Perhaps because Hammerstein was a friend of the Fields children and regarded their father with genuine respect, the Lew Fields character was not depicted as the usual Hollywood stereotype of a musical producer, the tyrannical, penny-pinching Broadway vulgarian. Fields' paternal affection for Castle is evident in their first encounter outside the backstage entrance, when he loans the young comic ten dollars to pay for flowers to court the fickle leading lady. Dispensing wry advice in a slightly accented voice, Fields is a self-effacing presence. Despite all the factual inaccuracies and distortions, the script allowed for Fields' Old World gentility. When, in the next scene, Castle asks for another advance, Fields' reputation as a notorious "soft touch" was confirmed.

A most unfortunate casualty was Fields' and Castle's famous barbershop scene, which was deliberately made to look crude and antiquated. In the movie, Irene has brought some friends to a performance to show off her new boyfriend. She is humiliated and infuriated to see him doing low comedy. What had been an elaborate and well-constructed slapstick revenge scene in its original form was condensed into a series of sadistic assaults punctuated by vaudeville sound effects. Though Fields' performance retained surprising vigor, Astaire's attempt at slapstick was too cautious and studied to be funny. Later, after watching an audition of Vernon and Irene as a dancing team, Fields comments, "Who's gonna pay money to see a man dance with his wife?" and then tries to demonstrate the new slapstick routine he has in mind for Vernon. One comes away sympathizing with Irene's outrage and wondering what all those people in the old days were laughing about.

Not long before shooting began, Fields wrote in a letter to Dorothy about his upcoming role: "Soon I'll be in front of a hot camera, I'm to play myself. . . . A few weeks ago they wanted me for a screen test. I was scared stiff, maybe I wouldn't look like Lew Fields, so I said to myself, so what?" As it happened, in *The Story of Vernon and Irene Castle,* he did *not* look like himself. Nor was he playing himself; perhaps what scared him was playing the caricature of himself that Hollywood had created.

Fields' work on the Castle picture lasted for two weeks, for which he received $2,000. Even with the Astaire-Rogers magic and almost forty old songs, box office receipts were a disappointment. Reviewers mentioned Fields' appearance only in passing, if at all. Fields said that he was glad to play in the movie because it dispelled rumors that he had died years ago.

One afternoon about two months after the release of the Castle movie, Fields' sunbathing was interrupted by a breathless phone call from Joe Weber. His voice aquiver with excitement, Weber asked, "How'd you like to do a picture for Zanuck?" "About us?" Fields felt his pulse begin to race. "No," Weber replied quickly, "it's about Nellie"—their pet name for Lillian Russell.

The next day, Joe and Lew chain-smoked their way through a meeting with Darryl Zanuck. Naturally, Weber & Fields were to play themselves, with fellow old-timer Joseph Cawthorn as Leopold Damrosch, and Eddie Foy, Jr., as Foy senior. Zanuck planned to build a detailed replica of the Music Hall auditorium and backstage area. But there all similarities between real life and reel life ended. As was true with most biopics, Zanuck's bowdlerized and sentimentalized the life of its subject (previous victims included Stephen Foster and Alexander Graham Bell). Screenwriter William A. McGuire excused the distortions by claiming that he portrayed Lillian Russell "as she is remembered rather than as she was." In the leading role, Zanuck cast Alice Faye, who had neither the curves nor the charisma of the real Lillian Russell, but her singing voice was pleasant enough to revive such period favorites as "Ma Blushin' Rosie" and "After the Ball." Two of Russell's four marriages were conveniently omitted; her sordid divorce from Edward Solomon (Don Ameche) was turned into a tragic death watch; her strange friendship with Diamond Jim Brady (Edward Arnold) and her long affair with Jesse Lewisohn were glossed over. Accordingly, Alice Faye does not age between her debut at Pastors' at age nineteen and her final marriage to industrialist Alexander Moore at age fifty-one. Moore (Henry Fonda) is portrayed as having pined for her for thirty years or more. For her audition at Pastor's in 1880, Russell sings "Come Down My Evening Star," which she first performed with Weber & Fields in 1902.

The presence of the real (old) Weber & Fields in this fairy tale seems a first glance like a colossal miscalculation. Shooting for Weber & Fields' scene began early in January, 1940, a few days after Lew's seventy-third birthday. Their five-minute scene in the final shooting script was set in their dressing room, where they were waiting for Russell to finish. They argue about whose idea it was to hire her, then Fields pokes Weber in the eye. Evidently, it was assumed that their behavior offstage was a continuation of their Mike and Meyer stage routines. To pass the time until their turn, Fields suggests that they play cards—casino, instead of pinochle, since Weber does not know how to play. Fields' explanation of the rules was his characteristic con job; Weber's frustration led to the inevitable physical confrontation. The choking was interrupted by the call of the stage manager. Fields, pumped up with excitement, encouraged his partner with rather hard slaps on the cheek, saying, "Come on, Joe! I'm in a wonderful mood for our scene. . . ." Their performance was letter-perfect on the first take.

When Zanuck saw it, he decided it was so good that he wanted the duo to do a longer scene. He suggested that they "work it up" just like in the Music Hall. Weber & Fields were delighted at the opportunity. Their revised version was three times as long and at least three times as funny. Three days were set aside to shoot the expanded scene, but once again Weber & Fields managed to execute flawlessly on the first take. The other actors and extras on the set served as their audience, giving them a standing ovation after the take. Weber & Fields repeated the routine four more times for over-the-shoulder shots and close-ups, and wrapped their scene in six hours. It was their last public performance. When the picture opened in May, 1940, several critics thought that the scenes with Weber & Fields were the liveliest and most entertaining in the entire movie.

After his turn for Zanuck, Fields returned to his deck chair in Beverly Hills. Family members noticed that he was lethargic and frequently short of breath. At times, he seemed preoccupied or lost in his musings. He no longer talked about acting in movies. Broadway, however, was very much on Fields' mind. Not the old Broadway, for he knew it no longer existed—"it was that close human touch of its people that made Broadway what it was," Fields concluded. "All the intimate oldtime friendships are gone, and with them the favorite meeting places."

It was the news from the new Broadway that gave him a vicarious thrill. The Fields name was once again in lights. In 1939, Herbert had returned to Broadway after two difficult years recovering from a heart attack and depression brought on by the death of George Gershwin. *Du Barry Was a Lady* reunited Herbert with Cole Porter and brought him together with Buddy DeSylva as co-librettist and Ethel Merman as star and unlikely muse. The combination clicked, and clicked again the following season in *Panama Hattie*. That same year, Herbert's late-blooming brother Joseph, fed up with Hollywood, penned an adaptation of a Ruth McKenney story with his B-movie partner Jerry Chodorov. *My Sister Eileen* ran for 865 performances, but before it had finished its run, the team had a follow-up hit, *Junior Miss* (710 performances), and Joseph, solo, had yet another, *The Doughgirls* (671 shows). Pop Fields savored the success at a distance, vowing to come to New York to see if it was all true, but knowing all the while that he was too sick to travel.

In mid-July, 1941, while Herbert and Joseph were still in New York working on their next shows, Lew contracted pneumonia. His physician did not expect him to recover, and acceded to Fields' request to spend what time he had left at home. An oxygen tent was delivered to the house. Rose, Frances, and Dorothy kept the bedside vigil, along with Joe Weber. An audience of familiar faces gathered around Lew; seeing this sustained his sense of humor. When the oxygen tent was brought into his room, he quipped, "Well, I've been in almost everything else, so I suppose it's only natural to put me back in a circus."

Lew Fields died quietly on the afternoon of July 21, 1941. It was a Sunday, the trouper's travel day. As was true with almost everything else about his off-stage life, his funeral was an intensely private affair. The hour and place of the service were kept secret. Only Rose, the children, and Joe Weber were present for the simple rites. Cremation followed. The Fieldses took the ashes east and placed them in the family vault in the Union Field Cemetery in Westchester, New York.

A grief-stricken Joe Weber told reporters, "We've been together so long. . . . It's like losing my right arm." Weber died the following year.

The obituaries emphasized the glory days of the Weber & Fields Music Hall. "With the passing of Lew Fields last Sunday," wrote Charles Darnton, "went the gayest spirit of Broadway's Gay '90s." Burns Mantle lamented that Joe Weber and Lew Fields represented "the joy of my youth." A *New York Times* editorial eulogized the Music Hall rather than the man: "In the town of their [Weber & Fields'] time their theatre—was it our first little theatre?—was an institution, a temple of drollery, a place where it was "right" to go. . . . 'Weberfields' was a landmark." The *New York Tribune* acknowledged that Fields "made for himself a secure place in the bespangled annals of our theater"; he "had a hand in many successful musical comedies," and he was "a shrewd showman, although at times given to grandiose ideas." But most of the notices were like the one in *Time* magazine: they seem to have forgotten Fields' extensive career as a producer and solo performer. Eulogists referred wistfully to Weber & Fields' humor as "simpler and heartier than ours," belonging to "the generation before the last one." No one else recalled that Lew Fields had been a shaping force behind some of the most sophisticated musical comedies of the late 'twenties. It was as if Lew Fields had been absent from the popular stage for three decades rather than for one.

Of all the tributes and obituaries, only one seemed to understand the scope and context of Lew Fields' entire career. "Fields a Master of Social Burlesque," was the apt title of Ralph Warner's summation. Warner saw the connections between Fields' immigrant origins, his Bowery childhood, and his unique brand of comedy. According to Warner, the burlesques at the Music Hall "were a link between the immigrant and the native born American, blending every one in the crucible of laughter." Fields' long career linked "the distant past of free enterprise" to the era of the Syndicate and the Shuberts; his work as a producer of musical comedies and occasional actor in Hollywood forging the final link with the age of technological mass entertainment. Of Lew Fields the man, Warner concluded: "[Fields] had a great genius for understanding what makes masses of people laugh. His sense of comedy values was keen, his eye for beauty, especially in the musical stage was unchallenged. He was the predecessor of Flo Ziegfeld as the master of the New York musical. . . ."

But this broad perspective on Lew Fields was the exception. In their rush to attach easy labels and elicit cheap pathos, journalists reduced the breadth and diversity of Lew Fields' achievements on the popular stage to a quaint and sporadic vaudeville act. Fields had always feared that his ethnic comic mask would determine posterity's view of his worth as a person and as a professional, and in the end, he was right. At least *Variety*'s obituary for Lew Fields appeared in its legit section, a fact that undoubtedly would have pleased him.

Five months after Fields' death, a musical opened on Broadway that was the first of many to refute the idea that Lew Fields' influence died with twenty-three skidoo and vaudeville. *Let's Face It* had a book by Herbert and Dorothy Fields, a score by Cole Porter, and a cast consisting of Danny Kaye, Eve Arden, and Vivian Vance. Herbert and Dorothy freely admitted that it was really Pop's idea. For years, he had been after them to do an adaptation of the 1925 hit *The Cradle Snatchers*, about three wives who try to make their philandering husbands jealous by hiring three "escorts." Following Pop's dictum that a musical has to be up-to-date, Herbert and Dorothy replaced the gigolos with three young Army draftees. The show's biggest laughs, however, came in a scene filched from the old Music Hall—the Roman Gladiator sketch, the one in which Weber & Fields had whitened their bodies and faces and assumed increasingly ludicrous poses to impersonate a priceless statue. Broadway audiences found *Let's Face It* sufficiently contemporary and amusing to make it the longest-running musical of the season (547 performances).

Within two years of their father's death, Joseph, Herbert, and Dorothy Fields had a string of six Broadway hits—four of them running at one time. As writers, they dominated Broadway during the 1940's the way their father had as a producer and performer thirty years earlier. Through shows such as *Annie Get Your Gun, Wonderful Town, A Tree Grows in Brooklyn, Gentlemen Prefer Blondes,* and *Sweet Charity,* Joseph, Herbert, and Dorothy continued the traditions of musical comedy that their father had established.

What survives of the popular stage pioneered by Lew Fields? It has been almost one hundred years since Lew Fields began to define the entertainments that made Broadway the epitome of American show business, and Broadway itself has been dying by degrees for the past twenty years or so. Despite the remoteness of Lew Fields' heyday, it is fascinating to see what has not changed. English imports once again dominate the boards, challenged only by revivals from Broadway's Golden Age. Established stars (now from film or television instead of opera or vaudeville) are required before backers will bankroll a production. Audiences still resist (and occasionally resent) the funnymen who attempt to be serious or to infuse their comedy with pathos: Woody Allen and Neil Simon are but the most recent examples. Bloated spectacles such as *Miss Saigon, Phantom of the Opera,* and *Starlight Express* rely on elaborate stage machinery and dazzling scenic effects to compensate for weak scores and weaker librettos, grim-faced descendents of Fields' big Broadway Theater productions. (Even at their most gigantic, however, Fields' shows never took themselves too seriously.) As a producer, Lew Fields developed standards of showmanship that were representative of Broadway's limitations as well as its aspirations.

Of the six Broadway theaters that bore Fields' name between 1896 and 1927, only two of the structures are still standing. One of them, the theater that Oscar Hammerstein built on Forty-second Street in 1904, was for many years a grind house, and then in 1988 was gutted for retail space—specifically, peep shows and X-rated videos. Lew Fields' Mansfield Theater is now named for the critic Brooks Atkinson and still occasionally hosts a show. Looking for traces of Lew Fields in today's Broadway shows is like searching for the old theaters themselves: most of them are long since razed or renamed and remade so many times that they are almost unrecognizable. One must look beyond Broadway. Fieldsian gags, characterizations, and staging techniques continue to surface in many forms of mass entertainment, like found architectural fragments whose origins do not matter as long they function efficiently in their new context.

Shortly before his death, Fields expressed curiosity in a new medium. Television, he speculated, would be the perfect vehicle for the return of Weberfieldsian burlesque. In this, he was once again the astute judge of popular tastes. The legacy of the Weber & Fields Music Hall has survived in the irreverent topical humor of *Saturday Night Live*, the brilliant ensemble comedy in *Your Show of Shows*, the surreal genre parodies of Monty Python. If the old Weber & Fields Music Hall was unique in its day as a place where one encountered "a cross-section of all New York," then the best of the television variety shows similarly bring together a cross-section of Americans to laugh at the foibles of today.

Though he lacked the charisma of Ziegfeld and Cohan, and he did not benefit from the same kind of Hollywood hype that followed their immortalization on film, Fields' influence has been subtler and more pervasive. His stock-in-trade was comedy rather than personality. The styles and techniques he popularized—broad physical comedy laced with pathos, social satire softened with silliness, exaggerations observed from everyday life—have become commercial mainstays of American mass entertainment. The popular stage formats he helped develop—musical comedy and the revue—freely mixed low-brow and high-brow material, the techniques of the grand opera and the minstrel show, naturalism and ethnic comedy, Strauss and W. C. Handy, to produce an uniquely American art form.

As an immigrant growing up in the Bowery, Lew Fields recognized in his downtrodden neighbors a desperate need for diversion. By giving them what they wanted, he was able to move uptown. But there he discovered that the need was no less desperate. Nor is it today. Lew Fields was among the first to understand that making people laugh was a serious business, whether the product was called vaudeville, musical comedy, revue, farce, or whatever. Comedy styles may change, as Fields pointed out, as often as ladies' fashions and the newspapers, but the comedic impulse—the deep-seated need to indulge the corrosive and redemptive powers of laughter—is a constant.

In a 1911 interview, at the height of his success as a producer, Fields observed: "We are the most frivolous nation on earth in some respects. We can get a laugh out of the most gruesome subjects. We are a laughing nation. We refuse to take anybody or anything seriously."

In this fundamental regard, we differ little from the patrons of Broadway—or the Bowery—Lew Fields entertained.

The Works of Lew Fields

Stage performances, stage production and management, phonograph records, radio, and movies

Stage

1889–90	**Weber & Fields Own Company,** toured 23 cities in 27 weeks.
1890–91	**Weber & Fields Own Company,** toured 40 cities in 44 weeks.
1891–92	**Weber & Fields Own Company,** toured 26 cities in 26 weeks.
1892–93	**Weber & Fields Own Company,** toured 40 cities in 36 weeks.
1893–94	**Weber & Fields Own Company,** toured 29 cities in 28 weeks.

Russell Brothers Company, toured 33 cities in 32 weeks.

1895–96   **Weber & Fields Own Company,** toured 24 cities in 24 weeks.

Russell Brothers Company, toured 24 cities in 24 weeks.

Vaudeville Club, toured 30 cities in 30 weeks.

Weber & Fields Own Company, "German Senators," New York area, five weeks.

Weber & Fields, Hammerstein's Olympia (Fregoli burlesque), New York, five weeks.

1896–97   **Weber & Fields Own Company,** toured 17 cities in 22 weeks.

Russell Brothers Company, toured 16 cities in 18 weeks.

Vaudeville Club, toured 19 cities in 20 weeks.

Weber & Fields Music Hall, opened Sept. 5, 1896.
First part was olio, closing with "The Pool Room" skit
Second part was burlesque: **"The Art of Maryland,"** five weeks, **"The Geezer,"** 19 weeks, **"Under the Red Globe,"** nine weeks, **"Mr. New York Esquire,"** seven weeks.

1897–98   **Vaudeville Club,** toured 31 cities in 31 weeks.

Russell Brothers Company, toured 19 cities in 22 weeks.

Vesta Tilley Vaudeville Company, toured nine cities in 13 weeks.

Sam Bernard, one city in one week.

Weber & Fields Music Hall, opened Sept. 2, 1897.
"The Glad Hand" and "The Worst Born" (replaced "The Glad Hand" and "Secret Servants"), four weeks; **"The Wayhighman"** (replaced "The

Worst Born"), 17 weeks; **"The Concurers"** (replaced "The Wayhigh-man"), four weeks.

"Pousse Café" with **"The Concurers"** and **"Tess of the Weber-fields,"** Grand Opera House, Chicago, eight weeks.

1898–99 **Vaudeville Club**

Joe Hart Specialty Company

The Concurers Company

The Glad Hand Company

Pousse Café Company
(All of these companies had erratic and infrequent bookings the entire year.)

Weber & Fields Music Hall, opened Sept. 8, 1898.
Hurly Burly, 30 weeks, with **"Cyranose-de-Bric-a-Brac"** and **"The Heathens,"** ten weeks; **"Catherine"** (replaced "Cyranose" and "The Heathens"), 20 weeks.

Helter Skelter (replaced *Hurly Burly*), eight weeks, with **"Catherine"** and **"Zaza," "The Great Ruby," "Lord and Lady Algy," "Trelawny of the Wells,"** and **"The Three Musketeers,"** eight weeks.

Weber's Parisian Widows Company, Sept. 1898–June 1899.

Weber's Dainty Dutchess Company, Oct. 1898–June 1899 (directed by Weber & Fields; operated by L. Lawrence Weber).

1899–1900 **Weber & Fields Company,** *Hurly Burly* and **"Cleopatra,"** New York area, four weeks.

Weber & Fields Music Hall, opened Sept. 21, 1899.
Whirl-I-Gig, 33 weeks, with **"The Girl from Martins,"** four weeks; **"The Other Way"** (replaced "The Girl from Martins"), seven weeks; **"Barbara Fidgety"** (replaced "The Other Way"), 13 weeks; **"Sapolio"** (replaced "Barbara Fidgety"), nine weeks.

Hurly Burly Extravaganza and Vaudeville Company, touring early 1900, six cities.

1900–01 **Weber & Fields Music Hall,** opened Sept. 6, 1900.
Fiddle-Dee-Dee, 32 weeks, with **"Quo Vas Is?"** seven weeks; **"Arizona"** (replaced "Quo Vas Is?"), eight weeks; **"The Gay Lord Quex"** and **"The Royal Family"** (replaced "Arizona"), 14 weeks; **"Captain Jinks of the Horse Marines"** (replaced "The Gay Lord Quex" and "The Royal Family"), three weeks.

1901–02 **Weber & Fields Music Hall,** opened Sept. 5, 1901.
Hoity-Toity, 33 weeks, with **"Depleurisy,"** 11 weeks; **"A Message from Mars"** (replaced "Depleurisy"), 17 weeks, **"The Curl and the Judge,"** five weeks.

Hoity-Toity, with Weber & Fields, toured five cities in three weeks at the end of the season.

Weber & Fields Orpheum Stock Company, Chicago, 54 weeks, featuring Sol and Nat Fields.

1902–03 **Weber & Fields Music Hall,** opened Sept. 11, 1902.
Twirly-Whirly, 31 weeks, with **"I, Mary McPain,"** six weeks; **"Hummingbirds and Onions"** (replaced "I, Mary McPain"), seven weeks; **"The Stickiness of Gelatine"** (replaced "Hummingbirds and On-

ions"), 11 weeks, **"The Big Little Princess"** (replaced "The Stickiness of Gelatine"), seven weeks.

Twirly-Whirly, with Weber & Fields, toured seven cities in four weeks at the end of the season.

1903–04   **Weber & Fields Music Hall,** opened Sept. 24, 1903.
Whoop-Dee-Doo, 19 weeks, with **"Looney Park,"** ten weeks; **"Waffles"** (replaced "Looney Park"), seven weeks; **"Catherine"** (replaced "Waffles"), two weeks.

Whoop-Dee-Doo and **"Catherine,"** with Weber & Fields, New Amsterdam Theater, New York, two weeks ending May 16, 1904, their last performance together.

"An English Daisy," opened Jan. 18, 1904 (41 performances).

1904–05   *It Happened in Nordland,* opened Dec. 5, 1904; Fields produced and starred, 22 weeks, with Marie Cahill and Joseph Herbert; in Chicago, ten weeks.

1905–06   *It Happened in Nordland* and **"The Music Master,"** opened Sept. 21, 1905; Fields produced and starred, twelve weeks in New York, with Blanche Ring and Harry Fisher, 20 weeks on tour.

1906–07   *About Town* and **"The Great Decide,"** opened Aug. 30, 1906; Fields managed and starred, 15 weeks, with Blanche Ring, Peter Dailey, Louise Dresser, Edna Wallace Hopper, Louise Allen Collier, Jack Norworth, Vernon Castle.

The Orchid, Fields owned American rights, April 8, 1907; Eddie Foy, Trixie Friganza, Irene Franklin.

Lew Fields' All Stars, *About Town,* 18 cities in 18 weeks.

1907–08   *The Girl Behind the Counter,* opened Oct. 1, 1907, Fields managed and starred, 38 weeks, with Connie Ediss, Louise Dresser, Vernon Castle.

Lew Fields' All Stars, vaudeville, 33 cities in 21 weeks.

On May 14, 1908, Weber & Fields played "The German Senators" for the Friars Club.

1908–09   *The Girl Behind the Counter,* on tour from Sept. 1908 to April 1909.

The Mimic World, opening July 9, 1908, Fields and Shubert produced, 16 weeks; Irene Bentley, Josie Sadler, George Monroe, Lotta Faust starred.

The Midnight Sons, opened May 22, 1909, Fields produced and starred, 33 weeks; with Lotta Faust, Vernon Castle, George A. Schiller, Blanche Ring, Fritz Williams, extensive tour.

1909–10   *The Rose of Algeria,* opened Sept. 22, 1909, Fields managed six weeks in New York; Lillian Herlein, Eugene Cowles, Anna Wheaton; on tour for eight weeks.

Old Dutch, opened Nov. 22, 1909, Fields managed and starred, 11 weeks, with Ada Lewis, Alice Dovey, John Bunny, Vernon Castle, Helen Hayes; on tour for ten weeks.

The Jolly Bachelors, opened Jan. 6, 1910; Fields produced, 22 weeks, with Nora Bayes, Jack Norworth, extensive tour.

The Prince of Bohemia, opened Jan. 13, 1910; Fields managed, 2½ weeks, with Andrew Mack.

The Yankee Girl, opened Feb. 10, 1910; Fields managed, 13 weeks, with Blanche Ring, extensive tour.

Tillie's Nightmare, opened May 5, 1910; Fields produced, 26 weeks, with Marie Dressler, extensive tour.

The Girl Behind the Counter, road show, 16 weeks.

The Midnight Sons, two road companies, irregular schedule.

The Summer Widowers, opened June 4, 1910; Fields produced and starred, 18 weeks, with Fritz Williams, Jack Henderson; on tour for nine weeks.

1910–11   *Up and Down Broadway,* opened July 18, 1910; Fields half-owner, 14 weeks, with Eddy Foy and Irving Berlin.

I'll Be Hanged If I Do, opened Nov. 1910; Fields produced, 13 weeks, with William Collier.

The Henpecks, opened Feb. 4, 1911; Fields produced and starred, 26 weeks, with Vernon Castle, Blossom Seeley.

1911–12   *When Sweet Sixteen,* Lew Fields produced for five weeks and dropped in rehearsal, opened Sept. 14, 1911.

Hanky-Panky, opened Oct. 31, 1911; Fields produced, 30 weeks, starting in Chicago; Carter DeHaven, Max Rogers, Bobby North; played eight weeks in New York the following season.

The Never Homes, opened Oct. 5, 1911; Fields produced, 11 weeks, with Jack Santley, Ray Cox, Helen Hayes.

Take My Advice, opened Nov. 11, 1911; Fields produced, six weeks, with William Collier, Helen Garrick Collier.

The Wife Hunters, opened Oct. 30, 1911; Fields produced, five weeks, with Emma Carus, Fanchon Thompson, Fred Santley.

Weber & Fields 1912 Jubilee Company, Hokey Pokey and **"Bunty Pulls the Strings,"** opened Feb. 15, 1912; 14 weeks in New York, with Lillian Russell, Fay Templeton, Bessie Clayton, William Collier, John T. Kelly; toured 32 cities in one month.

1912–13   **Tabloids:** Fields produced and backed, along with Marcus Loew, Aug. 1912 to April 1913.
"Fun in a Delicatessen"
"Fun in a Barber Shop"
"Fun in a Restaurant"
"Fun in a Cabaret"
"The Girl Haters"
"Seashore Frolics" (or **"Fun at the Seashore"**)
"Fun in a Turkish Bath"
"Fun Aboard Ship"
"Fun in a Drug Store"
"Fun in the Court House"

A Scrape o' the Pen, opened Sept. 26, 1912; Weber & Fields produced, 11 weeks.

The June Bride, opened Sept. 23, 1912; Fields produced, played in Boston and Pittsburgh only, with Arthur Aylesworth, Amelia Stone.

Never Say Die, opened Nov. 12, 1912; Fields produced, with William Collier.

Roly Poly and *Without the Law,* opened Nov. 21, 1912, Weber & Fields produced and starred, eight weeks, with Arthur Aylesworth, Helen Collier Garrick, Marie Dressler, Frank Daniels, Bessie Clayton.

The Sun Dodgers, opened Nov. 30, 1912, Fields produced, four weeks, with George Monroe, Bessie Wynn.

Roly Poly Company, opened Jan. 27, 1913, with Weber & Fields, toured 31 cities in 48 days.

"Marie Dressler's All Star Gambol," opened March 10, 1913, Fields produced, one week.

Tid-Bits, opened March 24, 1913, with Weber & Fields, toured three cities in four weeks.

All Aboard, opened June 5, 1913; Fields starred, 15 weeks, with Carter DeHaven, Lawrence D'Orsay; toured 16 weeks.

1913–14   **A Glimpse of the Great White Way,** opened Oct. 27, 1913; Fields produced, one week; Sam Bernard, Frances Demarest.

The Pleasure Seekers, opened Nov. 3, 1913; Fields produced, eight weeks, with Harry Cooper, Bobby North, Max Rogers, George White, Dorothy Jardon; toured 12 weeks.

Weber & Fields All Star Company, opened Feb. 22, 1914, with Nora Bayes, George Monroe; toured two cities in three weeks.

Weber & Fields Jubilee Company, opened March 2, 1914; toured 36 cities in 38 days.

1914–15   **The High Cost of Loving,** opened Aug. 25, 1914; Fields starred, 12 weeks; with Alice Fisher, George Hassell, Vivian Martin, toured 15 weeks.

Suzi, opened Nov. 3, 1915; Fields produced, seven weeks, with Jose Collins, Connie Ediss, Tom MacNaughton; toured six weeks.

1915–16   **Hands Up,** opened July 22, 1915; Fields produced and starred, rehearsed but quit show before it opened; with Elizabeth Brice, Charles King; ten weeks.

Weber & Fields Vaudeville, opened Jan. 1, 1916; toured 12 cities in 16 weeks.

Step This Way, opened May 29, 1916; Fields produced and starred, 12 weeks, with Blanche Ring, Louise Clark; toured for ten weeks.

1916–17   **Bosom Friends,** opened April 9, 1917; Fields starred (produced by Belasco), nine weeks, with John Mason, Irene Fenwick, Helen Ware.

1917–18   **Miss 1917,** opened Nov. 5, 1917; Fields featured (produced by Dillingham and Ziegfeld), nine weeks, with Elsie Janis, Irene Castle, Bessie McCoy, Bert Savoy.

1918–19   **Friendly Enemies,** opened Aug. 18, 1918; Fields starred, three weeks; (A. H. Wood, produced) reopened Dec. 30, 1918; with Charles Winninger; nine weeks, on tour seven weeks.

Back Again, opened April 24, 1919; with Weber & Fields and The Dolly Sisters, nine weeks; on tour seven weeks.

A Lonely Romeo, opened June 10, 1919; Fields produced and starred, 14 weeks (Equity strike closed show), with Harry Clarke, Frances Cameron, and Alan Hale; on tour 12 weeks.

1919–20   **Wild Women of 19 and 20,** Fields staged and rehearsed; but never opened.

1920–21   **Poor Little Ritz Girl,** opened July 28, 1920; Fields produced, ten weeks, with Charles Purcell, Luke McConnell, Eleanor Griffith; on tour 12 weeks.

Blue Eyes, opened Feb. 21, 1921; Fields produced, with Mollie King and Andrew Tombes; took over as star on the road prior to New York run; four weeks on road, five weeks in New York.

Snapshots of 1921, opened June 2, 1921; Fields produced and starred, eight weeks, with Nora Bayes, DeWolf Hopper.

1921–22   *Snapshots of 1921,* opened Sept. 16, 1921; Fields produced and starred, six weeks, with Lulu McConnell.

Lew Fields' Merry-Go-Rounders, Feb. 1922 (vaudeville); Fields produced and starred.

1922–23   **Weber & Fields "Reunited,"** opened Sept. 17, 1922 (Shubert vaudeville); Weber & Fields starred, with Charles Aldrich, Lynn Cantor; toured 11 cities in 17 weeks.

Ritz Girls of 19 and 22, opened Sept. 11, 1922 (Shubert vaudeville); Fields produced, 17 weeks.

Snapshots of 23 (combination of "Ritz Girls" and "Snapshots"), opened Feb. 12, 1923 (vaudeville); Fields produced and starred, with Lulu McConnell, Harold Thompson, James Cagney; toured three cities in six weeks.

Jack and Jill, opened April 22, 1923; Fields starred, nine weeks, with Ann Pennington, Clifton Webb.

Jack and Jill reopened Sept. 1923, Fields produced and starred, with Sonny White, Eva Puck, Frederic March, 3 weeks.

1923–24   *Greenwich Village Follies,* opened Sept. 27, 1923; Fields directed sketches, with Joe E. Brown, Martha Graham, Eva Puck, and Sammy White.

The Melody Man, opened May 13, 1924; Fields produced and starred, six weeks, with Sammy White, Eva Puck, Frederic March.

Lew Fields and Company, opened Aug. 20, 1924 (vaudeville); Fields produced and starred, four weeks, with Evelyn and Charles Blanchard.

1924–25   **Weber & Fields Vaudeville,** opened Oct. 24, 1924, Orpheum circuit; toured five cities in five weeks.

Weber & Fields Vaudeville, opened Feb. 1, 1925, Orpheum circuit; toured eight cities in 12 weeks.

Weber & Fields Vaudeville, opened April 20, 1925, Palace Theater, with Emma Trentini, Dr. Rockwell, Cissie Loftus, Marie Cahill, three weeks. Return engagement June 8, with Fay Templeton, for two weeks.

1925–26   **Weber & Fields Vaudeville,** opened Nov. 9, 1925; toured two cities in two weeks.

Money Business, opened Jan. 20, 1926; Fields starred with Pola Carter, Harry Lyons, Luther Adler, five weeks.

The Girl Friend, opened March 17, 1926; Fields produced, with Eva Puck, Sammy White; 39 weeks, toured for ten weeks.

1926–27   *The Wild Rose,* Fields starred (but injured one week before opening; replaced by William Collier), opened Oct. 20, 1926; ten weeks, with Joseph Santley, Desiree Ellinger.

Peggy Ann, opened Dec. 27, 1926; Fields produced, with Lulu McConnell, Helen Ford Lester Cole, Edith Meiser; 42 weeks, toured for 50 weeks; London, England, company, 20 weeks.

Weber and Fields Vaudeville, opening Jan. 23, 1927; ten weeks, eight cities.

Hit the Deck, opened April 25, 1927; Fields produced (but sold out his portion of the show three days after opening), with Louise Groody, Charles King, 44 weeks.

1927–28   *A Connecticut Yankee,* opened Nov. 3, 1927; Fields and Lyle Andrews produced, 50 weeks, with William Gaxton, Constance Carpenter; road company toured 22 weeks; New York company toured 30 weeks.

Present Arms, opened April 26, 1928; Fields produced, with Charles King, Franker Woods, Joyce Barbour, Busby Berkeley; 20 weeks. Toured Chicago and Philadelphia, two weeks.

1928–29   *Chee-Chee,* opened Sept. 25, 1928; Fields produced with Helen Ford, William Williams, George Hassell, four weeks.

Hello Daddy, opened Dec. 26, 1928; Fields produced and starred with Wilfred Clark, George Hassell, Alice Fischer; 26 weeks.

1930–31   *The Vanderbuilt Revue,* opening Nov. 5, 1930; Fields and Lyle Andrews produced with Lulu McConnell, Joe Penner, Evelyn Huey; two weeks.

1932–33   **Weber & Fields Vaudeville,** March, 1932, Palace Theater, New York, two weeks.

Weber & Fields, opening of the Radio City Music Hall, Dec. 27, 1932, one week.

Broomsticks, Amen, opened July, 1933; Fields starred, Pelham Manor, two weeks.

Phonograph Records

(All records were performed by Weber & Fields.)

Etiquette Scene—Col A - 1203, New York, March 7, 1912.

Mike and Meyer—Hypnotist Scene—Col A - 1159, New York, March 14, 1912.

Mike and Meyer—Drinking Scene—Col A-1159, New York, March 14, 1912.

Mike and Meyer—Race Horse Scene—Col A-1203, New York, March 14, 1912.

Mike and Meyer—Mosquito Trust—Col A- - 1168, New York, March 22, 1912.

Mike and Meyer—Hymie at College—Col A - 1168, New York, March 22, 1912.

Contract Scene—Col A - 1219, New York, July 9, 1912.

Stock Exchange Scene—Col A - 1219, New York, July 9, 1912.

Insurance Scene—Col A - 1220, New York, July 16, 1912.

Singing Scene—Col A - 1220, New York, July 16, 1912.

The Pool Game—Col (rejected), New York, Aug. 26, 1915.

Mike and Meyer—Going to War—Col (rejected), New York, Aug. 26, 1915.

Restaurant Scene—Col A - 1855, New York, Aug. 28, 1915.

Trust Scene—Col A - 1855, New York, Aug. 28, 1915.

The Marriage Market Scene—Col A - 2092, New York, June 14, 1916.

Baseball Game—Col A - 2092, New York, June 27, 1916.

Mike and Meyer at the Firehouse, Part 1—Vic (rejected), New York, Oct. 3, 1933.

Mike and Meyer at the Firehouse, Part 2—Vic (rejected), New York, Oct. 3, 1933.

Mike and Meyer at the Football Game, Part 1—Vic 24430, LPV-580, LSA-3086, New York, Oct. 3, 1933.

Mike and Meyer at the Football Game, Part 2—Vic 24430, LPV-580, LSA-3086, New York, Oct. 3, 1933.

Radio

1926:   Weber & Fields, NBC Inaugural Radio Program, Nov. 15, 1926.

1927:   Weber & Fields, NBC Radio, advertising for General Motors, June and July.

1930:   Weber & Fields Comedy, WOR, Webster Cigars, from Oct. 1930 to May 1931, weekly.

1931:   Weber & Fields Comedy, NBC Radio, Lucky Strikes, from Sept. 1931 to Nov. 1931, three times a week.

1933:   Edwin C. Hill, Ace Reporter of the Air, "The Inside Story of Weber & Fields," Socony-Vacuum Corp., April 7, 1933.

1937–38   "30 Minutes in Hollywood," George Jessel as star/emcee, Weber & Fields performing routines, Oct. 10, 1937; April 3, 1938.

Movies

1914:   Weber & Fields, "Mike and Meyer" (or "Children of Mike and Meyer Elope"), Kinemacolor Co., Whitestone, Long Island, two reels, purchased and distributed by Marcus Loew.

1915:   Lew Fields, "Old Dutch," World Films, Lewis Selznick Co. Five reels, with Vivian Martin, George Hassell, Charles Judell.

1915:   Weber & Fields, "Two of the Finest" and "Two of the Bravest" (never released?), World Films, Lewis Selznick Co., two reels.

1916:   Lew Fields, *The Man Who Stood Still,* World Films, W. A. Brady, full-length feature.

1916:   Weber & Fields, "The Best of Enemies," "The Worst of Friends," "Fatty and the Broadway Stars," Triangle Film Corp., Mack Sennett, two reels, Keystone Studios.

1917:   Lew Fields, *The Corner Grocer,* World Pictures, full-length feature.

1917:   Lew Fields, *The Barker,* Selig Studios, five reels.

1923:   Weber & Fields, "Pool Room Skit," presentation sound film for Lee De-Forest, one reel.

1925:   Weber & Fields, *Friendly Enemies,* E. Belasco Productions, Producers' Distributing Co., full-length feature, seven reels.

1927:   Weber & Fields, "Broadway's Favorite Comedians: Mike and Meyer," Vitaphone short.

1927–30(?): Lew Fields, "The Duel," Vitaphone short; Arthur Henley, director; one reel.

1927–30(?): "Lew Fields' Road to Paradise," Vitaphone short.

1930:   Lew Fields, "23 Skidoo," Vitaphone short.

1930: Weber & Fields, *The March of Time*, MGM, never released.

1933: Weber & Fields, "Beer Is Here," Vitaphone short.

1933: *From Broadway to Hollywood*, MGM, using some footage from *The March of Time*, but Weber & Fields' scenes eliminated (production book indicates that Weber & Fields appeared in a horse costume, a routine included in the new film).

1936: Lew Fields, "A Wedtime Story," RKO short.

1937: Weber & Fields, *Blossoms on Broadway*, Paramount Pictures, starring Edward Arnold, full-length feature.

1939: Lew Fields, *The Story of Vernon and Irene Castle*, RKO Pictures, starring Fred Astaire and Ginger Rogers, full-length feature.

1940: Weber & Fields, *Lillian Russell*, 20th Century Fox, Darryl Zanuck, starring Alice Faye, Don Ameche, Henry Fonda, full-length feature.

Notes

I From the Bowery to Broadway

1. John D. McCabe, *New York by Gaslight* New York: (Greenwich House, 1984), p. 191.
2. Brooks McNamara, "A Congress of Wonders: The Rise and Fall of the Dime Museum," *Emerson Society Quarterly,* vol. 20 (3rd quarter, 1974), pp. 224–25.
3. *Ibid.*
4. D. Hart and R. Kimball, editors, *The Complete Lyrics of Lorenz Hart* (New York: Alfred A. Knopf, 1986), p. 87.
5. *Ibid.,* p. 88.

II Adventures in Human Nature

1. Ronald Sanders, *The Lower East Side* (New York: Dover Publications, 1979), pp. 4–5.
2. Irving Howe, *World of Our Fathers* (New York: Simon & Schuster, 1983), p. 563.
3. "A Duel Interview with Weber & Fields,," *Theatre* (April 1912).
4. "Adventures in Human Nature," *The Associated Sunday Magazine* (June 23, 1912).
5. Dick Poston, *Burlesque Humor Revisited* (New York: Samuel French, 1977), pp. 22–24.
6. *New York Times,* Nov. 8, 1868.
7. Douglas Gilbert, *American Vaudeville* (New York: McGraw-Hill, 1940), p. 113.
8. McCabe, 1984, pp. 579–80.
9. Herbert Asbury, *The Gangs of New York: An Informal History of the Underworld* (New York: Paragon House, 1990), p. 244.
10. Joe Laurie, Jr., *Vaudeville: From Honky-Tonks to the Palace* (New York: Henry Holt & Co., 1953), p. 81.

III The Emigrant Train

1. *Motion Picture World* (August, 26, 1916).
2. G. Odell, *Annals of the New York Stage, 1883–1889* (New York: Columbia University Press, 1949), reprint of 1890 edition, p. 351.
3. Lloyd Morris, *Incredible New York* (New York: Random House, 1951), p. 33.
4. Buster Keaton, *My Wonderful World of Slapstick* (New York: DaCapo, 1960), p. 33.
5. E. J. Kahn, *The Merry Partner: The Age and Stage of Harrigan & Hart* (New York: Random House, 1955), p. 72.
6. "The Actor in the Street," *Theatre* (July 1908), p. 178.

IV Tambo and Bones in Whiteface

1. "Weber & Fields' Partnership," *Billboard* (Nov. 5, 1904).

2. Joe Weber, "My Beginning," *Theater* (Feb. 1907).

3. *Ibid.*

4. F. Isman, *Weber & Fields* (New York: Boni & Liveright, 1924), p. 72.

5. C. Samuels and L. Samuels, *Once Upon a Stage* (New York: Dodd, Mead, 1974), p. 35.

6. *Ibid.*, p. 89.

7. R. C. Toll, "Show Biz in Blackface: The Evolution of the Minstrel Show as a Theatrical Form," from M. Matlaw, *American Popular Entertainments* (Westport: Greenwood Press, 1979), p. 23.

8. *Ibid.*, p. 29.

9. *Ibid.*

10. D. Paskman, *Gentlemen Be Seated! A Parade of the American Minstrels* (New York: C. N. Potter, 1976) revised edition, p. 87.

11. *Ibid.*

12. "Weber & Fields' Partnership," *Billboard* (Nov. 5, 1904).

13. "How Joe Weber and Lew Fields Began Their Stage Life Together," *Cleveland Plain Dealer*, May 10, 1914.

14. Isman, 1924, p. 51.

15. "Weber & Fields' Partnership," *Billboard* (Nov. 5, 1904).

16. Gilbert, 1940, p. 77.

V A Company of Their Own

1. Gus Hill, unidentified newspaper article, no date, clipping file, New York Public Library (NYPL), Billy Rose Theater Collection.

2. Isman, 1924, p. 180.

3. C. Bode, *P. T. Barnum Struggles and Triumphs* (New York: Penguin, 1981), p. 22.

4. G. Bordman, *American Musical Theater* (New York: Oxford University Press, 1978), p. 83.

5. Odell, 1949, p. 523.

6. Bordman, 1978, p. 72.

7. J. A. Kouvenhoven, *The Columbia Historical Portrait of New York* (New York: Harper & Row, 1972, p. 381.

8. Isman, 1924, pp. 83–85.

9. Gilbert, 1940, p. 115.

10. Isman, 1924, pp. 125–26.

11. Isman, 1924, p. 131.

12. Arthur Meier Schlesinger, *The Rise of the City* (Chicago: Quadrangle Books, 1971), p.292.

VI In-and-Outers

1. A. L. Bernheim, *The Business of Theater* (New York: Actors' Equity Assn., 1932), p. 34.

2. Isman, 1924, p. 179.

3. G. Barth, *City People: The Rise of Modern City Culture in Nineteenth-Century America* (New York: Oxford University Press, 1987, p. 219.

4. Schlesinger, 1971, p. 289.

5. Isman, 1924, p. 164.

6. Isman, 1924, pp. 166–70.

7. Gilbert, 1940, p. 78.

8. F. F. Proctor, "A Prehistoric Continuous Performance," *Dramatic Mirror* (Dec. 24, 1898).

9. W. C. Young, *Famous Actors and Actresses on the American Stage*, vol. 1 (New York: Bowker, 1975), pp. 1,154–55.

10. *Ibid.*

11. *Ibid.*

VII Music Hall Days: "Such a Muchness"

1. Bordman, 1978, p. 128.

2. Morris, 1951, p. 185.

3. C. Hamm, *Yesterdays: Popular Song in America* (New York: W. W. Norton, 1983), p. 188.

4. Isman, 1924, p. 205.

VIII Music Hall Days: Part Two

1. James Metcalfe, *Life Magazine* (1903).

2. *Dramatic Mirror*, Dec. 29, 1900.

3. *New York Sun*, Feb. 23, 1901.

4. *Dramatic Mirror*, Sept. 5, 1901.

5. *Cosmopolitan* (July 1922).

6. Unidentified newspaper, 1904, clipping file, NYPL, Billy Rose Theater Collection.

7. Bernheim, 1932, p. 52.

8. Bernheim, 1932, p. 56.

9. Norman Hapgood, *International Monthly* (1900).

10. *New York Herald*, June 17, 1902.

IX Business Suicide

1. *Dramatic Mirror*, Sept. 20, 1902.

2. *Cosmopolitan* (July 1922).

3. *New York Evening Sun*, Sept. 12, 1902.

4. Dorothy Fields interview, ASCAP newsletter (January 1974).

5. *New York World*, Sept. 25, 1903.

6. Bordman, 1978, p. 196.

7. *Dramatic Mirror*, Jan. 9, 1904.

8. J. and J. B. Csida, *American Entertainment: A Unique History of Popular Show Business* (New York: Billboard Publications, 1978), p. 75.

9. Bernheim, 1932, p. 54.

10. *Dramatic Mirror*, April 16, 1904.

11. Unidentified newspaper, May 1904, clipping file, NYPL, Billy Rose Theater Collection.

12. *New York Herald*, May 29, 1904.

13. *Call Board Magazine* (June 1942).

X The King of Musical Comedy

1. Lew Fields interview, June, 1904. Unidentified newspaper clipping, Robinson Locke scrapbook, vol. 198.

2. *Dramatic Mirror,* April 15, 1908.

3. *Dramatic Mirror,* Sept. 28, 1910.

4. *Dramatic Mirror,* Jan. 7, 1914.

5. G. Bordman, *American Musical Comedy* (New York: Oxford University Press, 1982), p. 85.

6. *Stage Magazine* (May 20, 1905).

7. *New York Herald* (Dec. 6, 1904).

8. Unidentified newspaper clipping, Dec. 10, 1904, R. L. Scrapbook, vol. 198, NYPL, Billy Rose Theater Collection.

9. *Dramatic Mirror,* March 29, 1904.

10. "It Happened in Nordland," unidentified newspaper, no date, R. L. scrapbook, vol. 198, NYPL, Billy Rose Theater Collection.

11. John McCabe, *George M. Cohan: The Man Who Owned Broadway* (Garden City: Doubleday & Co., 1973), p. 56.

12. *New York Sunday Telegraph,* Aug. 27, 1905.

13. *New York Herald,* Oct. 8, 1905.

14. Unidentified newspaper clipping, Oct. 13, 1905, Robinson Locke scrapbook, vol. 198, NYPL, Billy Rose Theater Collection.

15. Bernheim, 1932, p. 66.

16. Correspondence File, March 8, 1906, Shubert Archive.

17. *Loc. cit.*

18. Lew Fields interview, *New York Herald,* Feb. 26, 1911.

19. Bordman, p. 222.

20. Correspondence File, Nov. 26, 1906, Shubert Archive.

21. Correspondence File, June 10, 1911, Shubert Archive.

22. Edgar Smith, "The Girl Behind the Counter" script, NYPL, Billy Rose Theater Collection.

23. *New York Tribune,* Oct. 5, 1907.

24. *New York Globe,* March 16, 1908.

25. E. B. Marks, *They All Sang: From Tony Pastor to Rudy Vallee* (New York: Viking Press, 1934), p. 115.

26. *New York Telegram,* Oct. 3, 1907.

27. *Dramatic Mirror,* quoted by Bordman, 1978, p. 236.

28. *New York Times,* July 5, 1908.

29. Shubert Archive, correspondence file, July 1, 1908.

30. Shubert Archive, Correspondence, Oct. 13, 1908.

31. *Theater Magazine* (July 1904).

32. *Blue Book Magazine* (September 1910).

33. B. N. Cohen, The Dance Direction of Ned Wayburn: Selected Topics in Musical Staging 1901–1923" (Ph.D. dissertation, New York University, 1980), p. 112.

34. Cohen, 1980, p. 86.

35. Unidentified newspaper article by Charles Darnton, September 1910, Robinson Locke scrapbook, vol. 199.

36. *Billboard Magazine* (Dec. 11, 1909).

37. See note 35.

38. "European Music Halls," *Dramatic Mirror* (Jan. 31, 1912).

XI The King of Musical Comedy: Part Two

1. *New York Herald,* June 1, 1909.

2. *Green Book* (Sept. 1909).

3. *Pittsburgh Leader,* Dec. 6, 1909.

4. *Dramatic Mirror,* Oct. 2, 1909.

5. *New York World*, Sept. 22, 1909.

6. *Detroit News*, Oct. 9, 1910.

7. Reconstruction based on several 1910 newspaper accounts.

8. *New York Review*, Oct. 10, 1909.

9. C. H. Brown, *Letter to Mary* (New York: Random House), p. 14.

10. *Stage* (January 1937).

11. J. Robbins, *Front Page Marriage* (New York: G. P. Putnam's Sons, 1982), p. 47.

12. H. Hayes with Sanford Dody, *On Reflection* (New York: M. Evans, 1968), p. 51.

13. *Ibid.*, p. 61.

14. Bordman, 1978, p. 252.

15. Unidentified newspaper, March 20, 1910, clipping file, NYPL, Billy Rose Theater Collection.

16. *Ibid.*

17. Shubert Archive, Correspondence file, March 7, 1910.

18. Bordman, 1982, p. 87.

19. *Variety* (April 2, 1910).

20. A. Slide, *The Vaudevillians* (Westport, Conn.: Arlington House, 1981), p. 58.

21. *Boston Transcript*, Nov. 3, 1910.

22. *New York Evening Telegram*, June 6, 1910.

23. *New York Clipper*, June 11, 1910.

24. *Boston Transcript*, Nov. 1, 1910.

25. *New York Herald*, May 20, 1910.

26. Shubert Archive, Shubert press release (no date, probably 1910).

27. *New York Times*, July 15, 1910.

XII Tailor's Tricks

1. Bordman, 1978, p. 258.

2. Mordden, 1983, p. 21.

3. Shubert Archive, Sept. 29, 1910.

4. Shubert Archive, Sept. 6, 1910.

5. Shubert Archive, Sept. 8, 1910.

6. *New York Telegraph*, Nov. 21, 1910.

7. *New York Clipper*, Feb. 20, 1911.

8. Vernon Castle scrapbook, Robinson Locke Collection, NYPL, Billy Rose Theater Collection.

9. *New York Times*, Feb. 5, 1911.

10. *Dramatic Mirror*, April 5, 1911.

11. *Ibid.*

12. McCabe, 1973, p. 99.

13. *New York Telegraph*, May 30, 1911.

14. Unidentified newspaper, 1910, clipping file, NYPL, Billy Rose Theater Collection.

15. *New York Clipper*, Aug. 12, 1911.

16. Bordman, 1978, p. 267.

17. H. Faulkner, *The Quest for Social Justice* (Chicago: Quadrangle Books, 1971), p. 153.

18. *New York Times*, Oct. 6, 1911.

19. *New York Evening Sun*, Oct. 6, 1911.

20. *Chicago Tribune*, Nov. 5, 1911.

21. *Ibid.*

22. *Evening Sun*, Nov. 3, 1911.

23. *Green Book* (May 1912).

24. *New York Morning Telegraph*, Feb. 11, 1912.

25. *New York Sun*, Jan. 24, 1912.

26. *New York Tribune*, Feb. 9, 1912.

27. Isman, 1924, p. 313.

XIII Spendthrifty

1. *New York Times*, Feb. 11, 1912.

2. *Christian Science Monitor*, June 24, 1924.

3. *New York Tribune*, Aug. 6, 1912.

4. *New York World*, Aug. 6, 1912.

5. *Dramatic Mirror*, May 29, 1912.

6. A. Green and J. Laurie, Jr., *Show Biz from Vaude to Video* (New York: Henry Holt, 1959), p. 70.

7. Stein, 1984, pp. 283–84.

8. Slide, 1981, pp. 147–48.

9. *Variety*, Aug. 16, 1912.

10. *New York Herald*, Dec. 1, 1912.

11. *Dramatic Mirror*, Dec. 4, 1912.

12. *New York Sun*, Dec. 1, 1912.

13. Shubert Archive, letter, Nov. 14, 1912.

14. *New York Clipper*, Nov. 30, 1912.

15. Unidentified newspaper clipping, clipping file, NYPL, Billy Rose Theater Collection (no date).

16. *Green Book* (May 1912).

17. Shubert Archive, letter, Nov. 14, 1913.

18. *Equity Magazine* (Sept. 1923).

19. *Variety*, Aug. 19, 1913.

20. *Variety*, Aug. 31, 1913.

21. Shubert Archive, letter, Nov. 8, 1913.

22. Shubert Archive, letter, Nov. 10, 1913.

23. Shubert Archive, letter, May 1, 1914.

24. *New York Herald*, June 17, 1914.

25. Shubert Archive, letter, April 5, 1914.

26. A. Green & Laurie, 1951, p. 113.

27. Bordman, 1978, p. 301.

28. Bordman, 1978, p. 305.

29. Wodehouse and Bolton, quoted by Stanley Green, *The World of Musical Comedy* (South Brunswick, N.J.: A. S. Barnes & Co., 1968), p. 56.

30. G. Bordman, *American Musical Comedy* (New York: Oxford University Press, 1982), p. 104.

31. Shubert Archive, contract, May 22, 1914.

32. *Variety*, Oct. [?], 1914.

33. *New York Times*, Aug. 26, 1914.

34. *Dramatic Mirror*, Nov. 11, 1914.

35. Shubert Archive, letter, Oct. 8, 1915.

XIV The Man Who Stood Still

1. T. Ramsaye, *A Million and One Nights: A History of the Motion Pictures Through 1925* (New York: Simon & Schuster, 1986), p. 472.

2. Blum, D., *A Pictorial History of the Silent Screen* (New York: G. P. Putnam's, 1953), p. 17.

3. C. Musser, "The Changing Status of the Film Actor," *Before Hollywood: Turn of the Century American Film* (New York: Hudson Hills Press, 1987), p. 61.

4. R. Sklar, *Movie-Made America: A Cultural History of American Movies* (New York: Random House, 1975), p. 46.

5. Ramsaye (1986), p. 569.

6. *Dramatic Mirror*, Sept. 17, 1913.

7. *Chicago News*, Feb. 12, 1915.

8. *Chicago Herald*, April 4, 1915.

9. Used by permission, estate of Cole Porter.

10. *New York Telegraph*, July 1, 1915.

11. *Ibid.*

12. *New York Telegraph*, Aug. 10, 1915.

13. Sklar (1975), p. 114.

14. *Dramatic Mirror*, Oct. 29, 1915.

15. Shubert Archive, correspondence, Sept. 29, 1915.

16. Shubert Archive, correspondence, Oct. 3, 1915.

17. Shubert Archive, correspondence, Nov. 28, 1915.

18. Shubert Archive, correspondence, Dec. 14, 1915.

19. Shubert Archive, correspondence, Jan. 3, 1916.

20. *New York Telegraph*, May 11, 1916.

21. Unidentified newspaper clipping, clipping file, NYPL, Billy Rose Theater Collection, Nov. 12, 1915.

22. *Theater* (August, 1916).

23. *Chicago Herald*, Aug. 13, 1916.

24. *Variety*, March 30, 1917.

25. *New York Review*, June 3, 1916.

26. Museum of the City of New York, Herbert Fields correspondence files.

27. *Green Book* (June, 1917).

28. *Chicago News*, Feb. 12, 1917.

29. *New York Review*, April 14, 1917.

30. *New York Times*, Nov. 6, 1917; *New York Herald*, Nov. 6, 1917; *New York Sun*, Nov. 6, 1917.

31. Museum of the City of New York , Harry B. Smith, unpublished manuscript.

32. *New York Telegraph*, Feb. 22, 1918.

33. *Boston Post*, Aug. 27, 1918.

34. *Boston Herald*, Sept. 15, 1918.

XV Broadway Broke

1. A. Erenberg, *Steppin' Out: New York Nightlife and the Transformation of American Culture, 1890–1930* (Westport, Conn.: Greenwood Press, 1981), p. 241.

2. Museum of City of New York, Harry B. Smith, script for *A Lonely Romeo*.

3. *New York Herald*, June 11, 1919; *Variety*, June 13, 1919.

4. S. Marx and J. Clayton, *Rodgers & Hart: Bewitched, Bothered & Bedeviled* (New York: G. P. Putnam & Sons, New York, 1976), p. 41.

5. R. Rodgers, *Musical Stages* (New York: Random House, 1975), p. 29.

6. *Ibid*, p. 30.

7. *New York Review*, June 3, 1916.

8. Lorenz Hart, "Any Old Place with You," *Thou Swell, Thou Witty*, edited by Dorothy Hart (New York: Harper & Row, 1976), p. 22, used by permission.

9. *Variety*, Aug. 16, 1919.

10. *New York Times*, June 1, 1919.

11. McCabe, 1973, p. 152.

12. Erenberg, 1981, p. 221.

13. *New York Sun,* July 8, 1916.

14. Unidentified clipping in Lew Fields File 2, Free Library of Philadelphia.

15. Rodgers, p. 35.

16. D. Ewen, *The Story of America's Musical Theater* (Philadelphia: Chilton Book Co., 1961), p. 75.

17. Bordman, *American Musical Comedy,* 1982, p. 107.

18. Script, "Poor Little Ritz Girl," Act 1, p. 3, Ned Wayburn Collection, University of Southern California Library.

19. *New York Clipper,* June 2, 1920.

20. *New York Clipper,* Aug. 4, 1920.

21. *New York Clipper,* Jan. 5, 1921.

22. Bordman, 1978, p. 347.

23. *New York Star,* July 6, 1921.

24. A. Green & J. Laurie, 1951, p. 207.

XVI Good Hokum

1. *New York Herald,* March 22, 1923.

2. A. Green and J. Laurie, 1951, p. 273.

3. Brooks McNamara, *The Shuberts of Broadway* (New York: Oxford University Press, 1990), p. 117.

4. *Variety,* Nov. 11, 1921.

5. Rodgers, 1975, p. 48.

6. *Variety,* July 14, 1992.

7. J. Cagney, *Cagney by Cagney* (New York: Doubleday, 1976), p. 30.

8. *New York Herald,* Sept. 19, 1922.

9. *New York Times,* Sept. 24, 1922.

10. Shubert Archive, correspondence file, Dec. 11, 1922.

11. *New York Clipper,* April 4, 1923.

12. Bernheim, "The Facts of Vaudeville," *Equity* (Nov., 1923).

13. *New York Herald,* March 23, 1923.

14. *New York Clipper,* June 6, 1923.

15. *New York Herald,* April 22, 1923.

16. *Chicago Tribune,* Sept. 18, 1923.

17. Slide, 1981, p. 118.

18. C. Hamm, *Yesterdays: Popular Song in America* (New York: W. W. Norton, 1979), p. 351.

19. A. Green & J. Laurie, 1951, p. 320.

20. *New York Telegraph,* June 22, 1924.

21. M. Wilk, *They're Playing Our Song* (New York: Atheneum, 1973) p. 55.

22. Rodgers, 1975, p. 106.

23. Rodgers, 1975, p. 52.

24. D. Hart, and R. Kimball, *The Complete Lyrics of Lorenz Hart* (New York: Alfred A. Knopf, 1986), p. 25.

25. J. Rubin, "Lew Fields and the Development of the Broadway Musical" (Ph.D. dissertation, New York University, 1990), p. 373.

26. *New York Post,* May 14, 1924.

27. Stein, 1984, p. 325.

28. Isman, 1924, p. xi.

29. *Variety,* Nov. 5, 1924.

30. H. Kraft, "Lyrics by Dorothy Fields," *Ascap Today* (January 1974); interview with David Lahm.

31. Spitzer, 1969, p. 119.

32. *Variety*, Oct. 21, 1925.

33. *Morning Telegraph*, June 20, 1925.

34. D. Hart, *Thou Swell, Thou Witty: The Life and Lyrics of Lorenz Hart* (New York: Harper & Row, 1976), p. 50.

35. S. Marx and J. Clayton, *Rodgers and Hart: Bewitched, Bothered, and Bedeviled* (New York: G. P. Putnam & Sons, 1976), p. 80.

36. Bordman, 1978, p. 404.

37. *Telegram*, Jan. 21, 1926.

38. *Morning Telegraph*, Jan. 21, 1926.

XVII The Evergreen Fields

1. A. Green & J. Laurie, 1951, p. 228.

2. Bordman, *American Musical Comedy*, 1982, p. 121.

3. Bordman, *American Musical Theater*, 1978, p. 392.

4. Script, *The Girl Friend*, Act I, p. 33, NYPL, Billy Rose Theater Collection.

5. Marx and Clayton, 1976, p. 99.

6. Rodgers, 1975, p. 81.

7. *New York Herald Tribune*, June 7, 1959.

8. Rubin, 1990, p. 389.

9. *Variety*, Dec. 15, 1926.

10. *Philadelphia Inquirer*, no date.

11. Shubert Archive, correspondence, Oct. 4, 1926.

12. Shubert Archive, correspondence, Oct. 9, 1926.

13. Shubert Archive, correspondence, Oct. 11, 1926.

14. *Philadelphia Inquirer*, no date.

15. *New York Times*, Oct. 30, 1927.

16. *Ibid.*

17. L. Gordon and A. Gordon, *American Chronicle: Six Decades in American Life, 1920–1980* (New York: Atheneum, 1987), p. 14.

18. Rodgers, 1975, p. 91.

19. D. Hart and R. Kimball, editors, *The Complete Lyrics of Lorenz Hart*, (New York: Alfred A. Knopf, 1986), p. 88.

20. Script, *Peggy Ann*, Act 2, p. 2, NYPL, Billy Rose Theater Collection.

21. Hart and Kimball, 1986, p. 91.

22. *New York Tribune*, Jan. 16, 1927.

23. "Seymour Felix," *Dance Magazine* (October 1927).

24. *New York Herald Tribune*, Jan. 16, 1927.

25. *Variety*, Dec. 22, 1926.

26. *Morning Telegraph*, Jan. 8, 1927.

27. *Variety*, Jan. 26, 1927.

28. *Variety*, April 13, 1927.

29. S. MacQueen, "Vitaphone," *American Cinematographer* (Sept. 1990).

30. Bordman, 1978, p. 425.

31. *Variety*, Nov. 30, 1927.

32. *Ibid*, p. 340.

33. Script, *Connecticut Yankee*, Act I, NYPL, Billy Rose Theater Collection.

34. Rubin, 1990, pp. 448, 460.

35. Rodgers, 1975, p. 108.

36. *Boston Sun Globe*, Nov. 14, 1928.

37. D. A. Jasen, *Tin Pan Alley* (New York: Donald I. Fine, 1988), p. xvii.

38. Hy Kraft, "Lyrics by Dorothy Fields," *ASCAP Today* (Jan. 1974).

39. Erenberg, 1981, p. 256.

40. *Variety,* Dec. 7, 1927.

41. *New York Telegraph,* May 9, 1928.

42. Rodgers, 1975, p. 114.

43. *New York Evening Graphic,* April 27, 1928.

44. *New York Times,* April 27, 1928.

45. *New York American,* April 27, 1928.

46. Clipping, Theater Collection, Museum of the City of New York.

47. Kraft (Jan. 1974), p. 8.

XVIII Rough Stuff

1. R. A. Allen, *Horrible Prettiness: Burlesque and American Culture* (Chapel Hill: University of North Carolina Press, 1991), p. 248.

2. *New York Times,* Nov. 29, 1933.

3. *New York Times,* July 4, 1926.

4. A. Green & J. Laurie, 1951, p. 347.

5. Rodgers, 1975, p. 118.

6. Rubin, 1990, p. 482.

7. *Variety,* Oct. 3, 1928.

8. Rubin, 1990, p. 502.

9. Rubin, 1990, p. 505.

10. *Variety,* Oct. 22, 1930.

11. *Collier's* (June 19, 1930).

12. *Ibid.*

Notes to the Epilogue

1. Stein, 1984, p. 364.

2. *New York Telegraph,* March 25, 1932.

3. A. Green & J. Laurie, 1951, p. 352.

4. *New York Times,* Sept. 17, 1932.

5. Helen Hayes, "The Things I Learned From Lew Fields," *Stage* (Jan. 1937).

Selected Bibliography and Source Materials

Archives, Collections, Libraries

New York Public Library at Lincoln Center–Billy Rose Theater Collection
Shubert Archive
University of Southern California Special Collections Library
Institute of the American Musical
University of California at Los Angeles Cinema Collections
University of Texas–Harry Ransom Humanities Research Center
Library of Congress
RKO Pictures, Inc., Corporate Archives
Academy of Motion Pictures Arts and Sciences
American Film Institute
New York Public Library, Mid-Manhattan Branch, Genealogy Division
The Mormon Library, Salt Lake City
Museum of the City of New York
Variety Arts Theater Collection
Culver Pictures, Inc.
Turner Entertainment Co.
Princeton University, Firestone Library

Periodicals, Newspapers

New York Clipper, Jan. 1875 to July 1923.
New York *Dramatic Mirror*, Jan. 1880 to Dec. 1922.
Variety, Dec. 1905 to Dec. 1941.
Theater magazine, May 1902 to May 1931.
Selected issues of *Billboard* magazine, *Stage* magazine, *Cosmopolitan*, *Saturday Evening Post*, *Life* magazine, *Scribner's*, *Green Book*, *McClure's*, *Motion Picture* magazine, *Liberty*, *ASCAP Today*, *New York Times*, New York *Herald-Tribune*, New York *World*, New York *Sun*, New York *Morning Telegraph*, *New York Post*, New York *Star*, *Chicago Tribune*—selected newspaper articles from 1890 to 1941.

Books: Historical and Social Background

Asbury, H. *The Gangs of New York: An Informal History of the Underworld.* New York: Paragon House, 1990.

Baedeker, K. *Baedeker's New York.* New York: Hippocrene Books, Inc., 1985. (Reprint of 1899 edition.)

Barth, G. *City People: The Rise of Modern City Culture in Nineteenth-Century America.* New York: Oxford University Press, 1980.

Cashman, S. D. *America in the Twenties and Thirties.* New York: New York University Press, 1989.

Cook, A., M. Gittell, H. Mack, editors. *City Life, 1865–1900.* New York: Praeger Publishers, 1973.

Crouse, R. *It Seems Like Yesterday.* Garden City, New York: Doubleday, Doran & Co., 1931.

Harlow, A. F. *Old Bowery Days: The Chronicle of a Famous Street.* New York: D. Appleton & Co., 1931.

Howe, I. *World of Our Fathers.* New York: Simon & Schuster, 1976.

Kouwenhoven, J. A. *The Columbia Historical Portrait of New York.* New York: Harper & Row, 1972.

McCabe, Jr., J. D. *New York by Gaslight.* New York: Arlington House, 1984. (Reprint of 1882 edition.)

Morris, L. *Incredible New York.* New York: Random House, 1951.

Riis, J. A. *How the Other Half Lives.* New York: Dover Publications, 1971. (Reprint of 1901 edition.)

Sanders, R. *The Lower East Side.* New York: Dover Publications, 1979.

Schlesinger, A. M. *The Rise of the City.* Chicago: Quadrangle Books, 1971.

Schoener, A., editor. *Portal to America: The Lower East Side, 1870–1925.* New York: Holt, Reinhart & Winston, 1967.

Veblen, T. *The Theory of the Leisure Class.* New York: Random House, 1931.

Wolfe, G. R. *New York: A Guide to the Metropolis.* New York: McGraw-Hill, 1983.

Books: Theater, Vaudeville, Popular Song, and Film

Allen, R. A. *Horrible Prettiness: Burlesque and American Culture.* Chapel Hill: University of North Carolina Press, 1991.

Atkinson, B. *Broadway.* New York: MacMillan Co., 1970.

Bernheim, A. L. *The Business of Theater.* New York: Actor's Equity Assn., 1932.

Blum, D. *A Pictorial History of the Silent Screen.* New York: Putnam's, 1953.

Bordman, G. *American Musical Theater.* New York: Oxford University Press, 1978.

———. *American Musical Comedy.* New York: Oxford University Press, 1982.

———. *American Musical Revue.* New York: Oxford University Press, 1985.

Brown, T. A. *A History of the New York Stage,* 3 vol. New York: Blom, 1963. (Reprint of 1903 edition.)

Coffin, C. *Vaudeville.* New York: Mitchell Kennerlly, 1914.

Csida, J., and J. B. Csida. *American Entertainment: A Unique History of Popular Show Business.* New York: Billboard Publications, 1978.

Engel, L. *The American Musical Theater.* New York: Macmillan, 1975.

———. *Words with Music: The Broadway Musical Libretto.* New York: Schirmer Books, 1972.

Erenberg, A. *Steppin' Out: New York Nightlife and the Transformation of American Culture, 1890–1930.* Westport, Conn.: Greenwood Press, 1981.

Ewen, D. *The Story of America's Musical Theater.* Philadelphia: Chilton Book Co., 1961.

Gilbert, D. *American Vaudeville.* New York: McGraw-Hill, 1940.

Green, A., and J. Laurie, Jr. *Show Biz from Vaude to Video.* New York: Henry Holt Co., 1959.

Green, S. *The World of Musical Comedy.* South Brunswick, N.J.: A. S. Barnes & Co., 1968.

Hamm, C. *Yesterdays: Popular Song in America.* New York: W. W. Norton & Co., 1983.

Hapgood, N. *The Stage in America, 1897–1900.* New York: Macmillan, 1901.

Hart, D., and R. Kimball, eds. *The Complete Lyrics of Lorenz Hart.* New York: Alfred A. Knopf, 1986.

Jasen, D. A. *Tin Pan Alley.* New York: Donald I. Fine, 1988.

Kislan, R. *Hoofing on Broadway: A History of Show Dancing.* New York: Prentice Hall, 1987.

Lahue, K. C. *Kops and Custards: The Legend of Keystone Films.* University of Oklahoma Press, Norman, Okla., 1968.

J. Laurie, Jr. *Vaudeville: From the Honky Tonks to the Palace.* New York: Henry Holt & Co., 1953.

Matlaw, M. *American Popular Entertainment.* Westport, Conn.: Greenwood Press, 1979.

McLean, A. F. *American Vaudeville as Ritual.* University of Kentucky Press, Lexington, 1965.

McNamara, B. ed. *American Popular Entertainments.* New York City Performing Arts Journal Publication. New York, 1983.

Mordden, E. *Better Foot Forward: The History of American Musical Theater.* New York: Grossman Publishers, 1976.

———. *Broadway Babies: The People Who Made the American Musical.* New York: Oxford University Press, 1983.

Musser, C. *Before Hollywood: Turn of the Century American Film.* New York: Hudson Hills Press, 1987.

Odell, G. *Annals of the New York Stage 1883–1889.* New York: Columbia University Press, 1949. (Reprint of 1890 edition.)

Page, B. *Writing for Vaudeville.* Springfield, Mass.: Home Correspondence School, 1915.

Paskman, D. *Gentlemen Be Seated! A Parade of the American Minstrels.* New York: C. N. Potter, 1976. (Revised edition.)

Poston, D. *Burlesque Humor Revisited.* New York: Samuel French, 1977.

Ramsaye, T. *A Million and One Nights: A History of the Motion Pictures Through 1925.* New York: Simon & Schuster, 1986.

Rubin, J. *Lew Fields and the Development of the Broadway Musical.* Ph.D. dissertation. New York University, 1990.

Sklar, R. *Movie-Made America: A Cultural History of American Movies.* New York: Random House, 1975.

Slide, A. *The Vaudevillians: A Dictionary of Vaudeville Performers.* Westport, Conn.: Arlington House, 1981.

Smith, C., and G. Litton. *Musical Comedy in America.* New York: Theatre Arts Books, 1981.

Spitzer, M. *The Palace.* New York: Atheneum, 1969. (Revised edition.)

Stein, C. W. *American Vaudeville, As Seen by Its Contemporaries.* New York: Alfred A. Knopf, 1984.

Toll, R. C. *Blacking Up: The Minstrel Show in Nineteenth-Century America.* New York: Oxford University Press, 1974.

———. *On with the Show: The First Century of Show Business in America.* New York: Oxford University Press, 1976.

Wilk, M. *They're Playing Our Song.* New York: Atheneum, 1973.

Witmark, I., and I. Goldberg. *The Story of the House of Witmark: From Ragtime to Swingtime.* New York: L. Furman, 1939.

Wittke, C. *Tambo and Bones: A History of the American Minstrel Stage.* New York: Greenwood, 1968.

Books: Biographies, Autobiographies

Allen, F. *Much Ado About Me.* Boston: Little, Brown, 1956.

Bergreen, L. *As Thousands Cheer: The Life of Irving Berlin.* New York: Viking, 1990.

Blumenthal, G. (as told to A. H. Menkin). *My Sixty Years in Show Business.* New York: Frederick C. Ofberg, 1936.

Bordman, G. *Jerome Kern: His Life and Music.* New York: Oxford University Press, 1980.

Carter, R. *The World of Flo Ziegfeld.* New York: Praeger Publishers, 1974.

Castle, I. *Castles in the Air.* New York: Doubleday, 1958.

Cohan, G. M. *Twenty Years on Broadway and the Years It Took to Get There.* New York: Harper, 1925.

Cohen, B. N. *The Dance Direction of Ned Wayburn: Selected Topics in Musical Staging, 1901–1923.* Ph.D. dissertation, New York University, 1980.

Dressler, M. (as told to Mildred Harrington). *My Own Story.* Boston: Little, Brown, 1934.

Hart, D. *Thou Swell, Thou Witty.* New York: Harper & Row, 1976.

Hayes, H., with Sanford Dody. *On Reflection.* New York: M. Evans & Co., 1968.

———, with Katherine Hatch. *My Life in Three Acts.* Orlando, Fla.: Harcourt, Brace, Jovanovich, 1990.

Hopper, D. W. *Once a Clown, Always a Clown.* Garden City, New York: Garden City Publishing Co., 1927.

Isman, F. *Weber & Fields.* New York: Boni & Liveright, 1924.

Kahn, E. J. *The Merry Partners: The Age and Stage of Harrigan & Hart.* New York: Random House, 1955.

Keaton, B. *My Wonderful World of Slapstick.* New York: Da Capo, 1960.

Leavitt, M. B. *Fifty Years in Theatrical Management.* New York: Broadway Publishing Co., 1912.

Marx, S., and J. Clayton. *Rodgers & Hart: Bewitched, Bothered & Bedeviled.* New York: G. P. Putnam & Sons, 1976.

McCabe, J. *George M. Cohan: The Man Who Owned Broadway.* Garden City, New York: Doubleday & Co., 1973.

McNamara, B. *The Shuberts of Broadway.* New York: Oxford University Press, 1990.

Morell, P. *Lillian Russell, The Era of Plush.* New York: Random House, 1940.

Rodgers, R. *Musical Stages.* New York: Random House, 1975.

Sheean, V. *Oscar Hammerstein I: The Life and Exploits of an Impresario.* New York: Simon & Schuster, 1956.

Stagg, J. *The Brothers Shubert.* New York: Random House, 1968.

Index